AN OXFORD ANTHOLOGY OF
CONTEMPORARY CHINESE DRAMA

AN OXFORD ANTHOLOGY OF

Contemporary Chinese Drama

Edited by
Martha P. Y. Cheung and Jane C. C. Lai

HONG KONG
OXFORD UNIVERSITY PRESS
OXFORD NEW YORK
1997

Oxford University Press

Oxford New York
Athens Auckland Bangkok Bogota Bombay
Buenos Aires Calcutta Cape Town Dar es Salaam
Delhi Florence Hong Kong Istanbul Karachi
Kuala Lumpur Madras Madrid Melbourne
Mexico City Nairobi Paris Singapore
Taipei Tokyo Toronto

and associated companies in
Berlin Ibadan

Oxford is a trade mark of Oxford University Press

First published 1997
This impression (lowest digit)
1 3 5 7 9 10 8 6 4 2

Published in the United States
by Oxford University Press, New York

© Oxford University Press 1997

British Library Cataloguing in Publication Data
available

Library of Congress Cataloging-in-Publication Data
An Oxford anthology of contemporary Chinese drama / edited by Martha
Cheung and Jane Lai.
p. cm.
ISBN 0–19–586880–3 (alk. paper)
1. Chinese drama—20th century—Translations into English.
I. Cheung, Martha. II. Lai, Jane, date.
PL2658.E5094 1997
895.1'25208—dc21
                                                    97–5298
                                                    CIP

Printed in China
Published by Oxford University Press (China) Ltd
18/F Warwick House, Taikoo Place, 979 King's Road,
Quarry Bay, Hong Kong

— ACKNOWLEDGEMENTS —

The genesis of this work can be traced to a project initiated by Dr Vicki Ooi of the Department of English, University of Hong Kong, in 1991. She was then planning a research project on drama in South-East Asia and we were invited to help select some plays from mainland China and Hong Kong for detailed study. In the process, we discovered that a lot of fascinating works of drama had been produced in these two areas in the last few decades. When we expanded the scope of our research to include Taiwan, the discoveries were equally exciting. We believed there was sufficient material to compile a collection of plays from the Greater China region and have them translated so that English-speaking readers and the international theatre community would have access to the plays across the language barrier. Dr Ooi was very supportive of this idea. We are grateful for her encouragement all these years.

To the playwrights who participated in this project we offer our thanks. Our playwrights have been most generous in granting us the right to translate their works into English. Many of them—Liang Bingkun, Jin Yun, Guo Shixing, Ma Zhongjun, Xu Pinli, Ma Sên, Hwang Mei-shu, Lai Shêng-ch'uan, Lee Kuo-hsiu, and Raymond To—have also kindly provided us with photos for use in this anthology. For permission to use the photos on the title pages of *The Other Side, Before the Dawn-wind Rises,* and *American House*, we are grateful to the Hong Kong Academy for Performing Arts, the Hong Kong Repertory Theatre, and the Shatin Theatre Company. Zuni Icosahedron provided us with the slides for use in *Chronicle of Women—Liu Sola in Concert*, while Liu Ching-min gave us permission to take photos of the U Theatre's rehearsals of *Mother's Water Mirror* and to use those photos in this anthology.

This project would not have been possible without the contributions of our translators, to whom we are very grateful. Apart from doing a professional job, they have also been most cooperative in giving us permission to publish their translations. In addition, we would like to thank Lau Ming Pui, our research assistant, for her patience and dedicated assistance in bringing this project to fruition in publication.

The Hong Kong Baptist University and the Chinese University of Hong Kong have given each of us a research grant to carry out this project. The Centre for Translation of the Hong Kong Baptist University has helped us with the preparation of the manuscript.

In addition, we acknowledge with gratitude the support provided by the David C. Lam Institute for East–West Studies of the Hong Kong Baptist University; the Council for Cultural Planning and Development, Taiwan; and the Hong Kong Arts Development Council—towards permission fees, translation fees, and publication costs of this anthology.

This project is supported by the Arts Development Council.

── TRANSLITERATION OF PROPER NOUNS ──

Several different systems of romanization are in use in the different Chinese-speaking regions. Mandarin Chinese is spoken in both mainland China and Taiwan so words are pronounced in the same way, although Mandarin is known as *Guo yu* in Taiwan and *Putonghua* on the Mainland. In transliterating the names, however, different systems are used in the two regions: the Wade Giles system in Taiwan and the Pinyin system in China. In Hong Kong, names are mostly transliterated according to Cantonese dialect pronunciation using the English alphabet.

The following guidelines have been adopted:

- Names of individuals and dramatis personae are transliterated according to the systems in prevalent use in their particular region.

- Where a person is known to have lived and worked in different regions, the transliteration is done in accordance to the person's own choice or usage, or in accordance to his regional affinity: Yao Ke, from northern China, worked for a while in Hong Kong, but was not Cantonese. His name is not transliterated from Cantonese pronunciation, but according to Pinyin.

- Titles of books and articles and names of literary and mythical figures transliterated from Chinese are in Pinyin.

- Names of well-known people are transliterated according to common practice.

CONTENTS

PLAYS FROM HONG KONG

ABOUT **THE EDITORS**

Martha P. Y. Cheung received her Ph.D. in English and American Literature from the University of Kent at Canterbury. She has taught English Literature and Translation at the University of Hong Kong, and Translation at the Chinese University of Hong Kong. She is now Associate Professor of Translation and Associate Director of the Centre for Translation at the Hong Kong Baptist University. She has translated many works of Chinese literature into English, including those of Han Shaogong (*Homecoming? and Other Stories*, 1992), Liu Sola (*Blue Sky Green Sea and Other Stories*, 1993), Zhu Tainxian, and of Hong Kong poets such as Leung Ping Kwan (*Foodscape*, 1997), Tsai Yim Pui, and Choi Ka Ping.

Jane C. C. Lai studied at the University of Hong Kong and the University of Bristol. She taught English Literature and Translation at the University of Hong Kong for many years, and is now Chair Professor of Translation, Director of the Centre for Translation, and Dean of the Arts Faculty at the Hong Kong Baptist University. She has a long association with the Hong Kong theatre scene, mainly in the area of translation of playscripts for performance. Plays translated include those by Shakespeare, Harold Pinter, Tom Stoppard, Eugene O'Neill, Arthur Miller, Edward Albee, Samuel Beckett, Bertolt Brecht, and Jean Genet.

– ABOUT **THE TRANSLATORS** –

Shun CHENG graduated from the Arts Educational School in England and worked in England for many years before becoming a freelance translator. She now lives in Malaysia.

Y. P. CHENG, formerly Chief Conference Interpreter of the Hong Kong government, has, since his retirement, taught Translation and Interpretation at the Monterey Institute of International Studies at Monterey, California, and at the Graduate Institute of Translation and Interpretation Studies at the Fu Jen University in Taiwan. He is now a part-time lecturer at Lingnan College, Hong Kong, and a freelance interpreter and translator.

Martha P. Y. CHEUNG (See 'About the Editors')

HWANG Mei-shu (See 'About the Playwright')

Eva HUNG received her BA (1st Hons.) and M.Phil. in translation studies from the University of Hong Kong, and her Ph.D. from the University of London. She has been Director of the Research Centre for Translation and Editor of *Renditions* since late 1986. Her literary translations include the fiction of contemporary women writers such as Wang Anyi (*Love in a Small Town*, 1988; *Love on a Barren Mountain*, 1991), Xi Xi (*My City: a hongkong story*, 1993; *Marvels of a Floating City*, 1997), Eileen Chang, Zhu Tianwen, and the poetry of Shu Ting, Gu Cheng, and the younger generation of Hong Kong poets.

KWOK Hong Lok received his education in Hong Kong and Canada, and teaches translation at the Hong Kong Baptist University.

Jane C. C. LAI (See 'About the Editors')

David E. POLLARD received his MA in Chinese from the University of Cambridge and his Ph.D. from the University of London. He was Professor of Chinese at the University of London from 1979 to 1989, when he joined the Chinese University of Hong Kong as Professor of Translation and co-editor of *Renditions*. He has written extensively on modern Chinese language and literature, and more recently on various aspects of translation. He is a major translator of Chinese classical modern prose into English.

Jo RILEY graduated in English Literature from the University of Cambridge. She has conducted extensive research work in mainland China on traditional Chinese theatre, performed in the United Kingdom with the Beijing Opera 2nd Company, and led practical workshops on Peking Opera for theatre students in Cardiff and London. For the last seven years she has been working as theatre researcher at the German universities of Bayreuth and

Mainz. Her latest work, published by Cambridge University Press in 1996, is *The Articulate Figure: A Study of Presence on the Chinese Stage*.

Janice WICKERI studied Chinese at Middlebury College and Princeton University and has lived in Taiwan, Hong Kong, and the People's Republic of China. She is Editor of *The Chinese Theological Review*—an annual volume of translations—and Managing Editor of *Renditions*. She has also edited *Explosions and Other Stories* by Mo Yan (1991), and is co-editor of *May Fourth Women Writers: Memoirs* (1996).

YING Ruocheng, celebrated actor and director of the Beijing People's Art Theatre, has translated Lao She's *Teahouse* and various other modern and contemporary Chinese plays into English, mostly for the purpose of stage performance. He has also translated many English and American plays into Chinese. His translation of *Death of a Salesman* has been endorsed by Arthur Miller as the authorized translation.

INTRODUCTION

In Chinese drama, the word 'drama' embraces two broad categories: traditional drama[1] and spoken drama (*huaju*). Spoken drama, the concern of this anthology, was imported into China from the West at the beginning of the twentieth century.[2] It followed closely the realistic forms and conventions of nineteenth-century drama in the West, and relied primarily on dialogue, individualized characters, naturalistic sets, and acting. Chinese intellectuals of the time believed that dialogue and the conventions of realism and naturalism were particularly effective in dealing with topical social issues and urgent national problems. Despite heated debates amongst intellectuals at the time on how best to make use of Western learning, spoken drama was soon accepted as a potentially powerful educational tool. It could serve as 'the vehicle of the way' (*wen yi zai dao*), regarded by Chinese literati since ancient times as the central preoccupation of literary writing. Spoken drama therefore began to take root in China as a literary form capable of answering an immediate political purpose—rallying the people to the national cause, whether it be the need for China to fight off the aggression of Western imperialism (as in the first two decades of the twentieth century), or to defend the country against Japanese expansionism (as in the years before and during the War of Resistance against Japan, 1937–45), or to enhance ideological awareness (as in the years after the establishment of the People's Republic of China until the present day).

The history of the growth and development of spoken drama in China in the twentieth century has been admirably charted by Edward Gunn in the introduction he wrote for his fine collection of plays, *Twentieth Century Chinese Drama, An Anthology*.[3] Published in 1983, Gunn's anthology of

---

[1] Traditional Chinese drama includes Peking Opera and other regional operas. It relies for its appeal on music, singing, stylized acting associated with well-established character roles (bearded men, elderly matrons, young scholars, virtuous beauties, warriors, clowns, etc), and the spectacle provided by acrobatics, costumes, painted face masks and heavy stage make-up. The characters are seen more as types than as individuals, and the pleasure for the audience comes from the recognition of a well-known story drawn from history, legends, myths, or literary works, and their familiarity with the acting style and/or a particular way of singing and delivering the notes.

[2] In December 1906, a group of Chinese students studying in Japan formed the drama group Spring Willow Society, and performed a scene from *Camille* (*La Dame aux Camélias*). Done largely in accordance with Western dramatic conventions, it was, and still is, generally regarded to be the prototype of Chinese spoken drama. Then in June 1907, Spring Willow Society performed *Heinu Hen* (The Agonies of the Black Slaves), a stage adaptation in five acts, of a Chinese translation of Harriet Beecher Stowe's novel, *Uncle Tom's Cabin*. Adapted mainly for the political purpose of alerting the Chinese to the fate of becoming slaves to the Western powers if China failed to resist their hegemony, *Heinu Hen* is considered by critics in both mainland China and Taiwan now to be the first Chinese play, albeit in adaptation. See Chen Baichen and Dong Jian (eds.), *Zhongguo Xiandai Xiju Shigao* (Archival Material on Modern Chinese Drama), Beijing: Zhongguo Xiju Chubanshe, 1989, p. 41.

[3] Edward M. Gunn (ed.), 'Introduction', *Twentieth Century Chinese Drama, An Anthology*, Bloomington: Indiana University Press, 1983, pp. vii–xxiii. Page references for further citations are included in parenthesis in the text.

sixteen plays (fifteen from mainland China and one from Taiwan) spans the sixty years between 1919 and 1979. The works included, according to Gunn, were selected not so much for their intrinsic merit as works of literature, but as examples of the 'bold experiments' of young Chinese writers using a Western form to convey views for social reform and revolution (p. vii). The plays have important 'historical significance' and are intended to 'fill the basic need for an anthology of twentieth-century Chinese drama based on a systematic appreciation of its development and representative concerns.' (p. xx).

Much has happened in Chinese drama since the appearance of Gunn's landmark work. Spoken drama has flourished not only in mainland China, but also in Taiwan and Hong Kong. In less than two decades, the Greater China region has produced dramatic works which, although interesting as reflections of social and political situations in China and for the ideological controversies they excited in their homeland, are essentially noted for one or more of the following qualities: their theatricality, their innovative blending of elements of traditional Chinese culture (Peking Opera, for example, or Chinese martial arts such as tai chi chuan) with a Western dramatic form, their performability, or simply the poignancy of the stories themselves.

In view of this, and in view of the fact that few Chinese plays written or produced in the 1980s and 1990s have been translated, the editors of this anthology decided that it was now time to select some of these exciting dramatic works for translation in order to introduce them to Western readers. The result is the present anthology, which includes six plays from mainland China, five from Taiwan, and four from Hong Kong. We hope that by presenting these plays in their entirety rather than in a condensed form, this anthology—the first of its kind—will give the reader a full impression of each individual work, as well as a broad view of the range of dramatic works from these three areas.

The anthology covers the years 1981 to 1995. This period witnessed the gradual coming of age of Chinese spoken drama in mainland China, Taiwan, and Hong Kong. For nearly sixty years, the process of cultural exchange between Western and Chinese dramatists has largely been one way—from West to East. But Chinese spoken drama in the 1980s and 1990s has produced works that deserve a place on the international stage, and the many interesting examples of fruitful cross-cultural fertilization may well serve as a source of inspiration for Western dramatists. Drama schools in many English-speaking universities in the West, as well as directors and playwrights of the West, have often expressed an interest in staging Chinese plays in translation. This anthology will, we hope, be a first step in making that possible.

*   *   *

Spoken drama developed differently and yielded different results in mainland China, Taiwan, and Hong Kong in these last two decades of the twentieth century. On the Mainland, spoken drama, which had come to a virtual standstill during the Cultural Revolution,[4] began to show signs of rebirth after the fall of the Gang of Four in 1976.[5] Theatres were reopened, drama journals re-appeared, and between 1976 and 1979 over two hundred plays were performed.[6] But, like most of the literary works that appeared in this period, spoken drama in the late 1970s and early 1980s often fell into the category of so-called 'wound literature' (literature which bitterly denounced the Cultural Revolution). Others were written primarily to re-establish people's faith in the Communist Party—by blaming problems on the Gang of Four, or by portraying members of the Communist Party as models of virtue and strength. Even award-winning plays such as Zong Fuxian's *In a Land of Silence* (*Yu Wusheng Chu*, 1978), Cui Dezhi's *Flowers Announcing the Arrival of Spring* (*Bao Chun Hua*, 1979), and Xing Yixun's *Power and Law* (*Quan Yu Fa*, 1979) are heavily dominated by these themes. The playwrights remained guided by the theory of socialist realism imported from the Soviet Union in the 1950s.

To this day, socialist realism, which calls for the 'portrayal of the "essence" (*benzhi*) of an era through ideal types of characters as determined by Party doctrine'[7] still characterizes a considerable portion of mainstream spoken drama on the Mainland. It would not be too much of an exaggeration to say that over half of the plays published or produced are socialist realist plays. Or, to be more exact, they are socialist realist plays with Chinese characteristics—a qualification much insisted on after China's split with the Soviet Union. After the Cultural Revolution, drama critics would describe them in less dogmatic terms such as 'social problem plays' (*shehui wenti ju*), 'plays about reform and opening up' (*gaige kaifang ju*), or quite simply, 'realistic plays'. But in the hands of more sophisticated playwrights, socialist realist works are not simply predictable 'directional plays' (*dingxiang ju*)—a label used by the more outspoken critics for plays that serve merely

[4] For a detailed account of the ferocious political struggle which led to the suppression of stage productions and the publications of all plays on the Mainland during the Cultural Revolution, and the unique situation of allowing only a total of eight 'model revolutionary works' (*geming yangbanxi*) to dominate the entire Chinese stage all through those years, see Zhao Xun, 'Jianchi "Baihua qifang, Baijia zhengming" de fangzhen fanrong shehuizhuyi xiju shiye—Zhongguo xijujia xiehui gongzuo baogao' (Upholding the policy of 'letting a hundred flowers blossom and a hundred schools of thoughts contend' to enable socialist theatre art to flourish. Report of the work of the Chinese Dramatist Association), *Juben*, 12 (1979): 5–25.
[5] They were Jiang Qing, Yao Wenyuan, Zhang Chunqiao, and Wang Hongwen. Jiang Qing, wife of Mao Zedong, wielded enormous influence during the Cultural Revolution. She exercised absolute control over the performing arts from 1966 to 1976, and was responsible for launching the 'model revolutionary works'.
[6] For a useful summary of the development of spoken drama on the Mainland between 1976 and 1979, see Wang Zheng and Li Yin, 'Huaju chuangzuo zonghengtan' (The length and breadth of drama creation), *Juben*, 11 (1979): 43–6.
[7] Gunn, *Twentieth Century Chinese Drama*, p. x.

as the Party's mouthpiece. Some socialist realist plays can be warm, funny, gripping, and moving, especially those produced as 'well-made plays'.[8] While they portray ideal characters bearing out Party doctrines, the characters nevertheless come to life as full-blooded individuals who can voice the grievances as well as aspirations of the people. Shui Yunxian's *Let's drink to Happiness!* (*Weile Xingfu, Ganbei!*, 1980), Su Liqun's *Quiet is the Night* (*Shenye Jingqiaoqiao*, 1980), and Liang Bingkun's *Who's the Strongest of Us All?* (*Shuishi Qiangzhe*, 1981, included here) are some illustrative examples.

Also in the mainstream is 'slice-of-life drama'.[9] Based on Zola's theory of realism and Belinsky's emphasis on art as a reflection of life, this genre was introduced to the Mainland in the 1930s by leftist writers such as Xia Xian, and subsequently ennobled by Lao She's *Teahouse* (*Chaguan*, 1957).[10] 'Slice-of-life drama' saw a major revival after the Cultural Revolution. Many acclaimed and popular productions were of plays written in this form, but often invested with a strong element of explicit or implicit social criticism, and a strong sense of historical depth. Li Longyun's *Xiaojing Alley* (*Xiaojing Hutong*, 1981), Li Jie's *Old Pagoda Street* (*Guta Jie*, 1987), He Jiping's *Number One Restaurant in the World* (*Tianxia Diyi Lou*, 1988), and Guo Shixing's *Birdmen* (*Niaoren*, 1993, included here) are amongst the most representative.

With the open-door policy and economic reform movements adopted by China after 1976, exchanges between the Mainland and the outside world increased, and the flow of ideas and information became more vigorous. With the reaffirmation of the policy—set forth by Mao Zedong in 1956—of letting 'a hundred flowers blossom and a hundred schools of thought contend' (*Baihua qifang, baijia zhengming*), the Party's ideological control over the people began to loosen. Writers took the opportunity to explore in their works the influence of the West. Even spoken drama, which has always been subject to harder scrutiny by the Party because of its inherently public nature, benefited from this 'large climate' (*da qihou*). Western plays were once again translated and put on stage, the most famous of these productions being *Death of a Salesman*. Many dramatists put aside the creation of model revolutionary figures. Instead, they concentrated on depicting characters as individuals with psychological depth and complexity, strengths as well as weaknesses. Truly memorable characters appeared, the most notable being Uncle Doggie in Jin Yun's *Uncle Doggie's Nirvana* (*Gouerye de Niepan*, 1986, included here).

The exploration of new techniques continued in other aspects of

[8] The 'well-made play' is a type of realistic drama that emphasizes intricate thematic development through the twists and turns of a plot structured upon the notion of cause and effect.

[9] This is a type of naturalistic drama that seeks to mirror life, often by portraying a cross-section of society, and with a sustained effort to capture everyday speech.

[10] *Teahouse* is still the most popular of all drama productions on the Mainland. The Beijing People's Art Theatre has toured with it to many parts of the Western world, receiving rave reviews.

production. A large number of what the Chinese critics call 'exploration plays' (*tansuo ju*) appeared. Rather than relying on the conventions of realism and naturalism, these plays experimented with the techniques of symbolism, expressionism, stream-of-consciousness, and collage. Other 'exploration plays' sought to introduce the alienation effect of Brecht, or to explore the implications of the absurd theatre. The conventional narrative plot was often replaced with a non-linear plot governed by psychological logic or the logic of association. At the same time, playwrights attempted to incorporate into spoken drama some of the characteristic features of traditional drama, such as masks, martial arts skills, acrobatics, and bold or stylized representations (using actors to represent moving or static background objects, for example). Lighting, sound effects, and sets were all designed with a spirit of adventure unknown since the time of Hong Shen's *Yama Zhao* (*Zhao Yanwang*) in the 1920s and Cao Yu's *Wilderness* (*Yuanye*) in the 1940s, when Chinese dramatists attempted, but failed, to win their audience's support for plays written in the modernist experimental mode.

It is significant that the Mainland critics have chosen the slightly more tentative term 'exploration plays' to describe the more adventurous works of the 1980s rather than 'experimental plays' (*shiyan ju*) or 'avant-garde plays' (*qianwei ju*) current in Western critical vocabulary. The term 'exploration' is more neutral in its ideological connotations and therefore less provocative to the authorities. Besides, the Mainland critics are probably also aware that the kinds of exploration carried out in these works are, by the standard of Western theatres, no longer experimental or avant-garde due to the developmental time-lag—a result of the political situation which had isolated China for over a decade.

An offshoot from the general fascination with 'exploration plays' was the rise of the 'little theatre movement' (*xiaojuchang yundong*), a phenomenon brought about by Lin Zhaohua's 1982 production of Gao Xingjian's *Absolute Signal* (*Juedui Xinhao*). The production took place in a rehearsal room in the Beijing People's Theatre and was staged on a raised platform with no backdrop and just a simple metal frame to suggest the setting—breaking the illusion of four walls created by the proscenium stage and naturalistic setting. With the audience seated around the stage and on the floor, the production also broke the barrier that exists between the actors and the audience in traditional theatre. Powerful lighting and innovative sound effects were used, and a style of acting was created that was completely different from the Stanislavsky method that the Chinese audience were used to. Discussion sessions arranged after the performances contributed to the production's enormous success—with the audiences, the critics, and other theatre practitioners. As a result enthusiasm grew for staging similar productions in small or makeshift venues. Interest also developed in studying the theoretical questions that came with such a move, specifically questions about the dynamics of theatre space, the relationship between a stage performance and its audience, and, most importantly, about the significance of the little theatre movement in the context of theatre development in various countries in the West and in China.[11] Moreover, the 'little theatre movement' was seen as a solution to the problem faced by the Chinese theatre in the early 1980s, that 'stage productions resulted in loss of money, fewer productions resulted in less loss of money, and no productions resulted in no loss of money', to quote a popular saying of the time.

China's 'little theatre movement' in the 1980s was therefore quite different from the anti-commercial drive of the 'little theatre movement' in the West. It was more akin in spirit to the experimental drama that flourished in Europe and America in the early decades of the twentieth century and later on in the 1960s and 1970s.

Of course, the quality of these Mainland productions varied. Many were exercises in naturalism, or socialist realist productions done in a small theatre. But the movement itself was enormously significant in the history of spoken drama in the Mainland for its liberating effect on the dramatists and audience alike. In the little theatre, audience participation was lively, the exchange of views direct, and the sharing of experience between actors and audience full and exciting. As a result, there was a serious reconsideration of fundamental assumptions about the function and purpose of spoken drama. For over seventy years, the major, if not the sole function of spoken drama had been the education of the masses, and the rationale for its existence had been to serve the needs of the country. The conventional theatre with its proscenium stage, large auditorium, and fixed seating—so conducive to the 'teachings carried out on a high platform' (*gaotai jiaohua xiaoguo*)—was regarded by many pioneers of the 'little theatre movement' as restricting the creative imagination of the playwright. They turned instead to the 'little theatre', which they believed was a place where the imagination could be liberated and where a vital alternative theatre could be established.

The 'exploration plays' and the plays of the 'little theatre' therefore marked a major development in contemporary Chinese spoken drama. Many of these plays, including popular successes like Gao Xingjian's *Bus Stop* (*Chezhan*, 1982), *Absolute Signals* (*Juedui Xinhao*, 1982), and *Wild Man* (*Yeren*, 1985), Wang Peigong's *WM* (*Women*, 1985), Zhu Xiaoping's *A Chronicle of Mulberry Plain* (*Sangshuping Jishi*, 1988), Zhang Xian's *The Owl in the House* (*Wulide Maotouying*, 1989), Su Lei's *The Fire God and the Autumn Girl* (*Huoshen Yu Qiunü*, 1989), Sha Yexin's *Jesus, Confucius and John Lennon* (*Yesu, Kongzi Yu Liannong*, 1988) might not strike an audience familiar with recent Western theatre as particularly avant-garde, or even experimental. These works may even appear to some as rough or clumsy, or still entrenched in the idea of drama as a vehicle for teaching or preaching. Nevertheless,

---

[11] Discussions and views on these issues are collected in *Xiaojuchang xiju yanjiu* (A Study of Little Theatre Productions), Nanjing: Nanjing University Press, 1991. These views were expressed by theatre practitioners on the Mainland at the 'First Chinese little theatre drama festival' which took place in Nanjing in 1989.

they have laid the foundation for more mature and innovative experiments like Gao Xingjian's *The Other Side* (*Bi An*, 1986, included here), Xu Pinli's *Ye Zi* (1989) and *Old Forest* (*Laolin*, 1991, included here), Ma Zhongjun's *The Legend of Old Bawdy Town* (*Lao Fengliu Zhen*, 1988, included here), and The Central Experimental Theatre's collective work *The Tale of the Nun and the Monk* (1993). Future development along this line is likely to be fraught with difficulties, given the Party's insistence on adherence to the Four Cardinal Principles and the efficiency of its ideological apparatus.[12] But, as many drama critics have stressed, exploration and experimentation will represent an important, albeit marginal and marginalized, trend of development in mainland drama in the years to come.

*   *   *

In Taiwan, spoken drama developed in a very different manner. Although it was also introduced there in the first decade of the twentieth century, Taiwan's status then as a colony of Japan[13] meant that the Japanese new school of theatre (*shimpa*)[14] rather than the Western realistic tradition exerted a stronger influence on this new art form. Productions in Japanese, however, were not popular among the people of Taiwan. The majority of them were Chinese who rejected their colonial ruler and continued to speak their own dialects (Fujianese or Hakka, both dialects of southern China) despite the colonists' attempts to establish Japanese as the language of the island. Plays from the Chinese Mainland were no more successful, either when performed in Mandarin, the national language, or adapted for production in one of the Taiwan dialects. There were plays written in the local dialects, but, lacking the rallying subject matter of the Mainland dramatists (national salvation, for example), spoken drama was not as readily embraced as it was in China. The Japanese also practised heavy

[12] The Four Cardinal (or Fundamental) Principles were laid down by Deng Xiaoping in 1979 and stress the need for the Chinese to 'uphold the socialist road; uphold the dictatorship of the proletariat; uphold the leadership of the Chinese Communist Party; and uphold Marxism–Leninism and Mao Zedong Thought'.

[13] Taiwan was ceded to Japan under the terms of the Treaty of Shimonoseki after the 1895 Sino-Japanese war.

[14] *Shimpa* drama developed in Japan in the 1880s under the influence of Western drama. It took the form of *kabuki* (meaning 'music, dance, skill') drama, but replaced singing and dancing with dialogue—then perceived to be the main feature of Western drama. By advocating political thoughts and reforms on liberty and civil rights, it also broke with the *kabuki* tradition of not reflecting contemporary life. For an analysis of the relationship between *shimpa* drama and Chinese spoken drama during the early years of its inception on the Mainland, see Chen Baichen and Dong Jian (eds.), *Archival Material on Modern Chinese Drama*, pp. 51–3. As for *shimpa* drama's much stronger influence on spoken drama in Taiwan, see Ma Sên, *Zhongguo Xiandai Xiju de Liangdu Xichao* (The Two Waves of Western Influence on Modern Chinese Drama), Taipei: Wenhua Shenghuo Xinzhi Chubenshe, 1991, pp. 197–204. Its chapters on Taiwan carry a particularly illuminating analysis of the development of spoken drama in Taiwan over the years. For a detailed and comprehensive treatment of the evolution of Taiwan drama from its earliest history until the 1950s, see Lü Su-shang, *Taiwan Dianying Xiju Shi* (A History of Taiwan Cinema and Drama), Taipei: Huaying Chubenbu, 1961.

censorship in Taiwan. Throughout the fifty years of Japanese colonial rule (1895–1945), it was traditional drama—Peking Opera and traditional glove puppet shows—that enjoyed mass support.

Spoken drama did not thrive much after Taiwan's return to China as a province in 1945, or even after the Nationalist government of Chiang Kai-shek retreated to Taiwan in 1949. With constant threats of Communist invasion resulting in political upheavals, the Nationalist government declared martial law and banned all exchanges with the Mainland. Spoken drama was used mainly for propaganda, and only plays with anti-Communist or anti-Soviet messages could be performed, mostly in Mandarin.

It was only in the 1960s, with the active promotion of drama activities in schools and universities by Professor Li Man-kui, Professor Yao Yi-wei, and other theatre enthusiasts, that spoken drama began to develop in a more diversified manner. Even then, language remained a stumbling block. Spoken drama remained firmly in the hands of the non-natives, and the plays they wrote, though not exclusively anti-Communist in tone, dealt mostly with politically safe subjects. They included historical plays, period drama, plays of nostalgia and reminiscence about living in and emigrating from China, plays dealing with romance and sentiments, or plays with a mildly didactic or moralistic purpose—serving the time-honoured tradition of literature as 'vehicles of the Way'. These works, one drama critic in Taiwan has observed, largely represented a continuation of the early spoken drama developed on the Mainland and cannot be said to reflect Taiwan society at that time, whether in terms of the language used or in subject matter.[15]

Between 1966 and 1976, while mainland China was preoccupied with the political turmoil of the Cultural Revolution, rapid and major changes were taking place in Taiwan. The land reforms implemented since 1949 (enabling peasants to buy their own land), the vast improvements in educational facilities in the 1950s and 1960s, and the massive economic construction programme undertaken by the government (with economic aids from the United States) began to bear fruit, and Taiwan was transformed from a provincial, agricultural island into a society with a vibrant economy and strong cultural and intellectual ties with America and Europe. In the 1970s, however, Taiwan suffered a series of diplomatic setbacks in the international community, and this forced its people to experience, in a new and intense manner, the alienation and isolation introduced by the processes of modernization, industrialization, and urbanization.[16] The

---

[15] Ma Sên, *The Two Waves of Western Influence on Modern Chinese Drama*, p. 215.

[16] In October 1971, Taiwan lost its United Nations and Security Council seats to the People's Republic of China. In the next few years, Taiwan's international position continued to weaken as the US adopted a new policy of *détente* towards China. In January 1979, this culminated in the full normalization of Sino-US relations, which necessitated the cutting of US defense ties with Taiwan, although in the same year the US also passed the Taiwan Relations Act, which allowed for the sale of defensive arms to Taiwan. Other Western nations, and Japan, followed suit and ended diplomatic relations with Taiwan. In 1980, Taiwan was also expelled from the International Monetary Fund and the World Bank in favour of the People's Republic.

country experienced a deep identity crisis, as it struggled to rethink its relations with China and the United States in its attempt to define itself in the international world, and as it sought to find a balance between traditional Chinese culture and twentieth-century American and European culture.

Dramatists of this period, stimulated by the influx of new ideas and the personal experience of studying in the West, found in the symbolist, expressionist, and absurdist schools appropriate forms for expressing the psychology of the people. At the same time, these playwrights had a strong sense of ambivalence towards the cultural influence of the Western powers. Many were unwilling to follow wholeheartedly their Western models, and sought to experiment with ways to blend their traditional culture with their adopted culture. Some representative examples are Yao Yi-wei's *A Suitcase* (*Yikou Xiangzi*, 1973), Ma Sên's one-act play, *Flower and Sword* (*Hua yu Jian*, 1977, included in this anthology), Hwang Mei-shu's *The Fool who Wins an Ass* (*Sha Nüxu*, 1973) and *Cathay Visions* (*Konglong Gushi*, 1986, also included here), and Chang Hsiao-fêng's *Seats* (*Weizi*, 1977). These plays are more than an extension of the tradition of realistic drama established on the Mainland during the 1930s and 1940s, they have a distinctly modernistic feel of their own.

The play that really set the direction for the development of spoken drama in Taiwan in the 1980s and 1990s was Chin Shih-chieh's *Hê Chu's Parentage—a New Version* (*Hezhu Xinpei*), produced in Mandarin in 1980. The policy of promoting Mandarin had been in place for over thirty years and language was thus no longer a stumbling block for the audience. The play, a satirical farce about people's obsession with money, was an enormous success. The audience loved this modern adaptation of the well-known Peking Opera, *Hê Chu's Parentage*. Its setting in contemporary society rendered its satiric impact much more immediate. Elements of Peking Opera—stylized acting, typical character roles, and music—were subtly integrated into the performance, thus giving the audience at once the pleasures of familiarity and novelty. The critics praised its innovative adaptation. Moreover, after two years of training by Wu Ching-chi, who had spent some time with the La Mama Experimental Theatre Club in New York, the actors showed great control, not only of the notoriously difficult body movements required of a Peking Opera actor, but also of those appropriate for the modern stage.

While path-breaking for its time, by today's standards the play seems dated (which is why it has not been included in this anthology). But its influence cannot be overemphasized. It made the general public realize that spoken drama could be amusing, entertaining, exciting, and relevant to their everyday life. It convinced many dramatists that experimental drama was a viable path of development for spoken drama in Taiwan. Most important of all, it reinforced the belief of Taiwanese playwrights that to be experimental, they must not simply model themselves on the experimental theatres of the West: they had to strike out on their own.

There followed a growth of experimental theatre workshops in Taiwan, the most dynamic of which were the Lan Ling Theatre Workshop, the Performance Workshop, and the Ping-Fong Acting Troupe. Their productions helped experimental drama—until then seen as an élitist or campus culture—to put down roots in the most fertile soil available for any form of art: the hearts and souls of the people. One good example of such productions is *Pining . . . In Peach Blossom Land (Anlian Taohuayuan*, 1986), included in this anthology. With an initial conceptual framework provided by Lai Shêng-ch'uan, co-founder of the Performance Workshop, and brought into existence by the method of collective improvisation, this play shows the influence of Western dramatists such as Chekhov, Pirandello, Tom Stoppard, and Dario Fo. But it deals with a subject that is the primary concern of most Taiwanese people—the relations between Taiwan and mainland China: in particular, the question of whether reunion with the motherland would be a success, or a bitterly disappointing experience. Another example of experimental drama, albeit in a different vein, is *National Salvation Corporation Ltd. (Jiuguo Zhushi Huishe*, 1991, also included here) by Lee Kuo-hsiu, founder of the Ping-Fong Acting Troupe. This play relies heavily on stylized acting, and moves freely in and out of the realm of farce and the absurd, blurring, deliberately, the line between fact and fiction. It deals with another subject that touches a raw nerve with the Taiwan populace—police incompetence and the law and order situation in Taiwan.

As the first generation experimental theatre groups became established, new theatre workshops such as Left Side of the River Theatre, Huan Xu Theatre, U Theatre, Viewpoint Theatre, Critical Point Theatre Phenomenon, and 425 Environmental Theatre, were set up, maintaining the anti-establishment, anti-tradition, rebellious, uncompromising spirit which is the definitive feature of experimental and avant-garde theatres everywhere in the world.[17] With the lifting of the martial law in 1987, and the introduction of democratic reforms, drama in Taiwan entered an era of unprecedented freedom. Dramatists were able to draw freely from, and to explore with, the theories and practice of European and American avant-garde theatre groups such as Jerzy Grotowski's Polish Laboratory Theatre, Judith Malina and Julian Beck's Living Theatre, Joseph Chaikin's Open Theatre, Ellen Stewart's La Mama Experimental Theatre Club, Peter

---

[17] For a comprehensive overview of the growth of experimental drama (sometimes also called the 'little theatre movement' by the Taiwan critics) in Taiwan in the 1980s, and some pertinent remarks about the prospects of its development, see Chung Ming-tê, 'Xiaojuchang fazhan zhi pinggu: juchang shinian de huigu yu zhanwang' (Ten years of little theatre: a review and a look at the future), in *Zhonghuaminguo wenhua fazhan zhi pinggu yu zhanwang* (Cultural Developments of the Republic of China: a Review and a Look at the Future), Taipei: Wenhua jianshe jijin guanli weiyuanhui, 1992, pp. 209–29. For some useful information on theatre groups in Taiwan, their founders, their aims, a list of their productions, their contact addresses, etc., see *Biaoyan yishu tuanti huibian: xiju tuanti* (A Directory of Performing Arts Companies: Theatre Companies), Taipei: Wenhua jianshe jijin guanli weiyuanhui, 1992.

Schumann's Bread and Puppet Theatre, Richard Schechner's The Performance Group, and Robert Wilson's The Byrd Hoffmann School of Byrds. As a result the Taiwanese dramatists became more daring in their handling of different topics, more political, more radical, more critical of the establishment and establishment culture, and wholly committed to performance aspects (as opposed as to spoken aspects) of stage drama. The works of Liu Ching-min, a student of Grotowski and founder of the U Theatre, are some of the most innovative explorations of the notion of drama as performance to have appeared in Taiwan. Her *Mother's Water Mirror* (*Muqin de Shuijing*, 1995) is included in this anthology.

There is now in Taiwan a strong tradition of experimental and avant-garde drama. Dramatists of this tradition constantly look towards what Europe and America have to offer, but maintain a distinct sense of Taiwan identity in their works, and always focus on issues that concern the people of Taiwan. They also draw inspiration from their local culture as well as from traditional Chinese culture, and apply both to training stage performers and to aspects of performance ranging from music, sound effects, gestures and body movements, to the use of rituals, folk art, masks, and costumes. Perhaps the most amazing feature of the development of spoken drama in Taiwan and its main difference with that of mainland China is that experimental and avant-garde drama should have supplanted realistic drama and become the major trend.

*   *   *

The earliest performances of spoken drama in Hong Kong date back to the 1920s,[18] but they made little impact on audiences more attuned to traditional Chinese opera as entertainment. In the 1930s, as social and national issues in mainland China became more urgent, they found expression in the works of Mainland dramatists, and the influence of spoken drama began to spread to southern China and to the British colony of Hong Kong. The Japanese invasion of China in 1937 caused refugees to pour into Hong Kong from the Mainland. With them came drama groups which staged propaganda plays in the Territory to alert the Hong Kong population to the plight of the nation and to raise funds for the war effort against the Japanese. Local schools and other concerned groups joined in, but all these activities came to a stop during the three years and eight months of the Japanese Occupation of Hong Kong.

When the war ended, the Colony rebuilt itself, and soon received another influx of refugees from the Mainland when the People's Republic

---

[18] Recorded by veteran Hong Kong dramatist Li Woon Wah in his article 'Drama in Hong Kong— Reminiscences and Reflections', *Studies on Hong Kong Drama*, Gilbert C. F. Fong and Hardy S. C. Tsoi (eds.), Hong Kong: High Noon Productions Co. Ltd., 1992, pp. 51–68. This article, and L. Y. Chan's 'Original Plays in Hong Kong, 1950–74', pp. 29–49, in the same anthology provide much interesting material on the subject.

of China established itself in 1949. This political turmoil brought to Hong Kong many writers and dramatists, such as Hsiung Shih-yi and Yao Ke, who had started their writing careers in mainland China. By the 1950s and 1960s, their work, together with the efforts of local dramatists in teachers' colleges and schools, had gradually stirred the Hong Kong drama scene to life. Drama performances in the local Cantonese dialect were widespread. Of the major works of this period, most were period costume plays adapted from historical romances, traditional operas and literary masterpieces. Yao Ke's *The Sorrows of the Ching Palace* (*Qing Gong Yuan*, 1957) and *Xi Shi* (1957), and Lai Kok Bun's *Dream of the Red Chamber* (1962) were some notable examples of these period costume plays. The themes tended towards the celebration of the traditional values of love, loyalty, moral rectitude and fortitude. A few plays written in the realistic mode reflected the social problems of poverty and drug abuse, the most successful being Yao Ke's *The Dark Alley* (*Lou Xiang*, 1962). But already a trend was developing towards the performance of Western plays in translation such as Shaw's *Arms and the Man*, and Ibsen's *Pillar of Society*.

The channelling of creative efforts to subjects in the past, and the generating of performance effort towards Western plays in translation was probably a consequence of the political tensions in the 1950s. The Hong Kong government was anxious to avoid any open confrontation between the Communist and the Nationalist elements which co-existed in the Territory in a delicate balance. A censorship system was in place in the 1950s and drama scripts were vetted for politically sensitive material before approval was granted for performances. This censorship practice, together with self-censorship as a result of public opinion, made it safer for playwrights and directors to work with more innocuous topics in the Chinese past or with problems in other times or in other climes.

The impact of new developments in post-war Western drama reached Hong Kong in the early 1960s and inspired students, amateurs, and professional theatre groups alike. The plays of Ionesco, Pinter, Brecht, Beckett, Edward Albee, Thornton Wilder, Tennessee Williams, Arthur Miller, Pirandello, Durrenmatt, and others, translated into Cantonese, were widely performed. From this point, plays in translation became mainstream on the Hong Kong drama scene, and this trend continued well into the 1980s. In the ten years between 1980 and 1990, about 130 Western plays were translated and performed in Hong Kong.[19]

The exposure to post-war Western drama since the 1960s proved an enriching experience for people involved in the theatre in Hong Kong, especially for university and college students. Encouraged by inter-school and inter-college drama festivals, first organized in 1966, new drama— modest efforts in the form of short, mostly one-act plays—began to emerge for performance. Somewhat derivative in theme and style, many of these

[19] Fong and Tsoi, *Studies on Hong Kong Drama*, pp. 179–92.

plays attempted to explore the universal questions of life and death, and the value and meaning of human existence, but were seen more as exercises than statements of conviction. By the mid-1970s, playwrights were exploring contemporary social issues, such as housing and education or the problems related to public examinations and shortage of university places,[20] through the use of the realistic mode.

The cataclysmic Cultural Revolution in China, which began in 1966, deeply influenced the political and cultural awareness of Hong Kong people. Ten years later, when the turmoil was over and Deng Xiaoping introduced his open-door modernization policies, new alignments—economic, political, and cultural—became crucial questions. These questions gained urgency after the signing of the Sino-British Joint Declaration in 1984 which determined Hong Kong's return to China in 1997. Hongkongers were forced to rethink the fundamental questions of who they were, their affinities with and differences from their estranged countrymen whom they would soon have to join, of how to preserve their way of life, and how to come to terms with an unknown destiny—with pride at freedom from colonialism, or with trepidation at the nightmare of history they had tried to forget? Many wanted an alternative choice, and began the painful process of uprooting themselves in search of a new life.

These life issues gave Hong Kong dramatists ample subjects to explore. Hong Kong drama gradually came of age as dramatists used their experience of working and studying in the Western theatre to express the current turmoil in their lives. Tsang Chui Chiu's *Marking the Boundaries* (1985) uses an episodic structure to present Hong Kong's history during the cessation of the Territory to the British in the late Qing Dynasty. Yuen Lap Fun collaborated with Lam Tai Hing and Tsang Chui Chiu on a series of plays about the historical and cultural life of Hong Kong to explore the question of identity. Raymond To's episodic *Where Love Abides* (1986) looks back with nostalgia at old world values and the warm relationships among members of a family business in its hundred-year history. Joanna Chan uses the 'well-made play' form in *Before The Dawn-wind Rises* (1985) to focus the symbolic reunion of a family. Anthony Chan's play *American House* (1990) uses the same structure for his examination of the mixed feelings and anxieties of young Hongkongers abroad, living in a house on which the lease is about to expire. The American setting provides a distancing perspective for a poignant observation of the plight of Hong Kong people living in a 'borrowed place' on 'borrowed time'. These three plays, included here, are by three of the major playwrights of their generation.

There were other plays and musicals, staged in a variety of forms, which made performances interesting, not only because of their topical

---

[20] *One in Six* (1974) and *School Certificate Exam 1974* (1975) are two examples. These were joint student efforts under the leadership of Lam Tai Hing.

concern but as theatrical experiences.[21] Other playwrights attempted to blend Chinese myths with theatrical spectacle (Anthony Chan's *Nüwa*, 1992), or to incorporate into spoken drama elements of traditional Cantonese Opera (Raymond To's *P-side*, 1989, made into a film in 1995). A younger generation of playwrights continued to write on topical issues with a distinctly local flavour in short plays for performances in studios, schools, or in the street.

More experimental in approach were the efforts of the performance group, the Zuni Icosahedron, established in 1982, which its founder Danny Yung calls 'an art collective'. Many of the Zuni performances were overtly political in their response to the events of the time.[22] In addition to politics, Zuni performances questioned and explored orthodox positions in issues of culture, gender, and power—as in *Chronicle of Women—Liu Sola in Concert* (1993) included here—as well as the very definition of drama and theatre experience. Influenced perhaps by the Russian director Meyerhold,[23] by Pina Bausch, Robert Wilson, and early 1970s Japanese avant-garde groups, Zuni plays follow a non-narrative structure, but are filled with evocative motifs—gestures, sounds, and visuals—suggestive of themes and implications. This attempt to break free of the concept of 'spoken drama' created controversy on the local drama scene and resentment for its opacity of meaning. But it is exactly this refusal to rely on words which has made Zuni productions more accessible to non-Cantonese audiences in Hong Kong and elsewhere in the world.[24]

This brief summary of the development of drama in mainland China, Taiwan, and Hong Kong provides a context in which to place the plays in this anthology. Although drama in each of the three regions originated from the same scion of a Western form, it has grown through different cultural and political climates on different types of soil, gaining nourishment from their different affiliations. The rich fruits garnered from the three lands should be interesting in themselves, and significant for their revelations.

*　　*　　*

[21] Anthony Chan's *1841* (1985), Raymond To and Hardy Tsoi's *I am a Hongkonger* (1985), Seals Theatre Company's production of *Hong Kong Trilogy: Jasmine, Bazaar and General Guidelines* (1986) by Vicki Ooi are some examples.

[22] *The Book of Mountain and Ocean* (1996) deals with the suicide of the Chinese writer Lao She during the Cultural Revolution, and quotations from the Basic Law, Hong Kong's post-1997 constitution, were used in the installation display as part of the performance. *The Opium War* (1994) was another overtly political production.

[23] See Michael Waugh's review of Zuni's *Decameron*, 'The Great Plague of 1997', *South China Morning Post*, 23 June 1988.

[24] The use of regional dialect in drama is likely to become an important issue in the post-1997 era, since Cantonese speakers form a minority in the population of China.

With the exception of *Uncle Doggie's Nirvana*, *The Other Side*, and *Cathay Visions* (which have been carefully revised for this anthology) all other plays have been translated into English specifically for the purpose of this anthology, and all fifteen are published here in English for the first time. The translation and editing work was undertaken in Hong Kong. Two of the plays, *Mother's Water Mirror* and *Chronicle of Women — Liu Sola in Concert*, did not have complete playscripts when this anthology was first planned, and both artistic directors were sceptical about the medium of words as an effective means of capturing the performance quality of their work. Liu Ching-min yielded to persuasion and produced a script for translation, while Danny Yung provided video tapes of the performances of *Chronicle of Women — Liu Sola in Concert*, upon which the present translation is based. The productions of *Pining . . . In Peach Blossom Land* and *National Salvation Corporation Ltd.* preceded the Chinese playscripts. Lai Shêng-ch'uan went over the translation in detail, restoring lines which had appeared in the stage productions but not in the published Chinese playscript, while Lee Kuo-hsiu provided extra information also absent from the published script.

In translating and editing the plays in this anthology, the translators and editors have kept close to the source texts, and have been guided by the consideration that these translations are meant not only for reading, but should also be able to function as texts for performance.

PLAYS FROM

MAINLAND CHINA

WHO'S THE
STRONGEST OF US ALL?

A PLAY IN SIX ACTS

1981

By
LIANG BINGKUN

Translated by
SHUN CHENG

— ABOUT **THE PLAYWRIGHT** —

LIANG BINGKUN (1936–) has been working in the Beijing People's Art Theatre since the age of eighteen, first in the Lighting Division, then as a secretary in the Performance Division, and occasionally as an actor. He started writing plays in 1964. He is a representative example of those playwrights in the Mainland who believe that plays should tackle issues which are of immediate relevance to the people and, in so doing, contribute to the task of spiritual rehabilitation which the country so desperately needs after the Cultural Revolution. He has written seven full-length plays. *Who's the Strongest of Us All?* was awarded the 'Outstanding Play of the Year' in 1981 by the Chinese Theatre Association and was first performed by the Beijing People's Art Theatre in 1981.

Liang Bingkun is now a National Grade 1 playwright of the Beijing People's Art Theatre.

ABOUT **THE PLAY**

This play deals with a social phenomenon all too familiar in mainland China in the post-Mao era: corruption. It belongs to the category of 'socialist-realism' which has been, since the founding of the People's Republic of China in 1949, the mainstream approach to drama and other arts on the Mainland. This genre includes works which are produced, not for art's sake alone, but to further political ends and promote socialism. Plays in this anti-élitist, 'art-for-the-people' mode are officially endorsed by the Communist Party, and support government policy—in this case, the anti-bribery and anti-corruption campaigns of the day.

The play departs significantly from the usual drama in this mould in that there is no high-handed or empty denunciation of corruption, and there are no larger-than-life heroes and villains. The protagonist's attempt to fight corruption, in fact, is shown to be something of a quixotic venture. This drama not only gives the audience a full and uneasy awareness of the immense scale of the problem, but also forces them to consider how they, themselves, would act at various key stages of the drawn-out battle.

DRAMATIS PERSONAE

YUAN ZHICHENG, male, about 50, factory director at the New China Cotton Mills

FANG JING, 50 years old, wife of YUAN ZHICHENG. Deputy Secretary of the Discipline Review Commission (DRC) of the Municipal Light Industries Office

YUAN XIAOLAN, 26 years old, daughter of YUAN ZHICHENG and a worker in the New China Cotton Mills

WU YIQIAN, female, nearly 60 years old, and Chief Engineer at the New China Cotton Mills

SUPERVISOR LI, about 40, male, supervisor of the Director's Office at the New China Cotton Mills

ALARM CLOCK, nickname of ZHONG, 26-year-old daughter of the director of the Northern Cotton Mills, YUAN XIAOLAN's friend and a sales assistant in a grocery store

ZHENG, 50-something, male, Chief of the Municipal Light Industries Office and Deputy Secretary of the Communist Party cell

NI, male, 40 years old, a section head at the Electric Company

ZHAO, 40 something, male, head of the Marketing & Supply Section of the Jiangnan Textile Machinery Factory

LIN TONG, 28 years old, fiancé of YUAN XIAOLAN and Office Secretary at a construction company

LIU, about 50, male, Manager of the Electric Company as well as Communist Party Committee Secretary

MA YUXIU, about 30, female and a worker at the Electric Company

NI'S WIFE, about 30, peasant woman from the city's outskirts

This play is respectfully dedicated to the present-day pioneers of the 'Four Modernizations' who spared no effort in their life-and-death struggle to bring China into the contemporary world.

ACT *1*

[New Year's Eve, 31 December 1979. The scene is set inside YUAN's home, a two-room unit on the second storey of an unprepossessing dormitory block in the staff quarters of the New China Cotton Mills situated in a large city in northern China. The set shows the outer room with four doors. One door leads to the outside corridor, one to the kitchen, another to the inner room while a fourth leads to the balcony. The family use this outer room to receive visitors, eat their meals, and, at night, as XIAOLAN's bedroom, which is why there is a bed against the wall in the corner. The furnishings are exceedingly simple, the YUANs do not even own a sofa—an essential status symbol. The window opens to show the impressive newly erected workshop with its 9,000 spindles.

The curtain rises. FANG bustles in and out, preparing the New Year dinner. XIAOLAN has just finished decorating the flat and is trying to decide where to hang the red lantern in her hand. The occasional but deafening sound of firecrackers can be heard through the window. Festive music is playing on XIAOLAN's small radio, which sits on her bedside table. FANG enters, wearing an apron and carrying a dish of cooked food.]

FANG *[reproachfully]* My goodness, Xiaolan, you're not going to hang up that lantern!

XIAOLAN Well, it's New Year. Time for celebration. I'm just trying to decide where it'll make the room look most festive.

FANG All right, just do it quickly. *[Listening]* Someone's at the door.

XIAOLAN Really? Maybe it's Papa coming home. Eh, why isn't he singing his couple of lines from the Hebei opera? *[Imitates her father's singing]*

'The wilful nobles like wild jackdaws,
Come before Judge Bao to thwart the law'*

FANG *[laughing]* Don't be cheeky. Go and open the door.

XIAOLAN Okay! *[Hangs up the lantern on the ceiling lamp and goes to open the door]*

[Before she gets there, the front door opens with a bang. ALARM CLOCK shouts, 'I'm here!' and enters.]

ALARM CLOCK *[holding a plastic doll in her left hand, a bottle of Luzhou wine is cradled in her right arm]* I'm here! What are we having for New Year dinner?

XIAOLAN *[going up to her]* Oh! It's only you! Come in. We're so busy! You won't get anything for dinner!

ALARM CLOCK Huh! What a warm welcome! *[Takes out a long list]* Here! Take this. Your furniture list.

* Judge Bao was well-known as an incorruptible judge in the Song Dynasty.

XIAOLAN *[taking it]* Why is it so long?

ALARM CLOCK It isn't. It's the same list I had when I got married.

XIAOLAN I don't want people to think I'm greedy.

ALARM CLOCK Make the most of it. You only get married once.

XIAOLAN *[hesitantly]* I think I'll speak to Lin about it again.

ALARM CLOCK Can't you make even this small decision for yourself? I know, we'll speak to Uncle Yuan later. It's not fair he never has time for you. Will he be home soon? *[Takes back the list]*

XIAOLAN I called him just before you arrived. He'll be back any minute.

ALARM CLOCK *[suddenly remembering]* Oh, I keep forgetting everything! *[Takes out a letter from her coat pocket]* Here's a letter for your father.

XIAOLAN *[takes the letter and reads]* 'With respects to Director Yuan.'

ALARM CLOCK Must be a prank or something, I found it taped to the corridor wall.

XIAOLAN *[opens the letter and reads]*

> 'Our leader is a fool,
> Who knows nought about the rule.
> Graft and corruption he holds in spite,
> And plays righteous Judge Bao with delight.
> Stubborn to the core, old-fashioned at the best,
> He feathers not his drab little nest.
> Against the trend, he leads his team,
> Bonus, housing—oh, forget the dream!
> He can't even ensure a stable output;
> Another six months, he's sure to get the boot!'

ALARM CLOCK So that's what it is. Look! There's even a caricature. What an unlucky thing to get at New Year!

XIAOLAN *[displeased]* Why can't people say what they mean out in the open?

[The sound of someone singing some lines from a Hebei opera can be heard coming from the corridor.]

ALARM CLOCK Your father's here! Put the letter away!

[XIAOLAN hurriedly puts away the letter. YUAN enters, singing in a jubilant mood.]

YUAN *[singing]*

> 'The wilful nobles like wild jackdaws,
> Come before Judge Bao to thwart the law.
> They think I will the Empress's pleading hear,
> I will be just e'en if the Emperor is here.'

[WU follows carrying a rug for YUAN.]

WU [*smiling*] Where's Fang?

[FANG *enters from the kitchen.*]

Here's Yuan, bound and delivered. Look after him well.

[FANG *smiles and takes the rug from her.*]

YUAN Wu, can't we talk about this some more?

WU No! You haven't had a reunion dinner with your family in at least six months. You must celebrate New Year with them today.

[FANG *looks expectantly at* YUAN.]

XIAOLAN I'll second that.

ALARM CLOCK Me too.

WU [*to Yuan*] See? You've been out-voted. The construction of the new workshop is already complete, let me take care of the installation.

YUAN [*light-heartedly*] All right! I'll bow to the wishes of the majority. But on one condition. You have to come back later, and we'll celebrate New Year together.

FANG Yes, you must! I've brought you some wine.

XIAOLAN Yes, Auntie Wu, you must come.

WU [*seriously*] I'll see. It all depends on how the installation work goes. If all goes well, I'll be here with or without an invitation. If not, you won't be seeing me. Bye now! [*Exits*]

YUAN Well, Alarm Clock, I hear that they finished fitting out the new workshop at the Northern Mills last week. How did your father manage to get it done so soon? He moves faster than a plane!

ALARM CLOCK Was it last week? I really don't remember. Anyway he's been going round in his car carrying large and small gifts with him—to make sure he gets the equipment and raw materials the workshop needs.

XIAOLAN Why else would they call him a 'Buddhist monk' director?

YUAN What nonsense is this? What's a 'Buddhist monk' director?

XIAOLAN Well, he knows how to make offerings and plenty of them. Right, Alarm Clock?

ALARM CLOCK Yes. Nowadays you find yourself very unpopular if you don't play the 'Buddhist monk' director. [*Notices* FANG *nearby and cries out suddenly*] Oh no!

FANG [*holding back her laughter and looking at her*] What's the matter?

ALARM CLOCK Well, here I am, opening my big mouth in front of the Deputy Secretary of the Discipline Review Commission at the Municipal Light Industries Office. Auntie Fang, you've heard nothing, all right?

FANG Pleading for your father? Too late! Silly child! *[Gives ALARM CLOCK a gentle slap on the cheek and exits]*

ALARM CLOCK *[smiles nonchalantly]* Come, here are some New Year presents! *[Picks up the plastic doll from the table and gives it to XIAOLAN]* This is for you, old friend. *[Picks up the bottle of Luzhou wine and gives it to YUAN]* Uncle Yuan, this is for you.

XIAOLAN *[looking at the doll]* Oh, she's adorable. I suppose it wasn't easy to get?

ALARM CLOCK Well, they do sell like hot cakes. I had to ask my mates in the department store to keep it especially for me. See what connections can do for you?

YUAN And how did you manage to get this bottle? Not over the counter, I suppose?

ALARM CLOCK There's a saying about getting things these days:

> 'The best take offerings through the front door;
> Second class people try the back.
> Third class people via contacts,
> Those without contacts hope no more.'

It's like that these days.

YUAN You sure know all about it!

ALARM CLOCK Of course, I sell things.

YUAN Let me tell you, your Uncle Yuan has put on a show to rival yours. The construction of our new workshop is completely above board—no offerings made, no strings pulled. You're smiling. You don't believe me, do you?

ALARM CLOCK *[laughing]* Oh, of course I believe you. But, as my father says, the construction is just half the work. The fun and games come later.

YUAN Well, we'll see!

ALARM CLOCK Uncle Yuan, shall we have a little bet?

YUAN What? You want to have a bet with me?

ALARM CLOCK Yes. To see if you can get everything done without making a single offering to anyone. If you do I'll buy you another bottle of Luzhou wine.

YUAN Done.

ALARM CLOCK But what if you can't?

YUAN *[thinks]* Mmm, then I'll buy you a doll. How about that?

ALARM CLOCK That's fine. *[Holds out her hand]* Here!

YUAN What?

ALARM CLOCK We'll seal our pact.

YUAN All right. *[Hooks his little finger with* ALARM CLOCK's]

ALARM CLOCK Say, 'May one hundred years pass before we break our pact!'

YUAN What does that mean?

ALARM CLOCK That means we'll never break our promise. Anyway, all the kids in our yard say the same. Come on, let's say it together . . . one . . . two . . .

YUAN, ALARM CLOCK *[together]* May one hundred years pass before we break our pact.

FANG *[bringing in a dish of food]* Look at you. Behaving like children.

YUAN *[laughing]* Come on, let's all go to the kitchen and give your Auntie a hand. *[Turns to Fang]* What shall I do?

FANG You're useless in the kitchen. Go and wash and tidy up your hair. You look like you haven't had a bath for over a month.

YUAN *[feeling his hair and beard]* What about a compromise? I'll wash and brush up later.

FANG What am I to do with you? *[Goes into the kitchen]*

XIAOLAN My father's middle name is 'Lazy'.

YUAN *[suddenly takes out a bundle of firecrackers from his pocket]* I was passing the late-night store just now and I couldn't resist buying a bundle of these firecrackers. I'll go out to the balcony to let off one or two first.

XIAOLAN Papa!

ALARM CLOCK *[snatching the firecrackers away]* Please sit down! There's something we have to talk over with you.

YUAN That sounds serious. *[Sits down]*

ALARM CLOCK Your daughter is getting married on July 1st. Just this once, don't you think you ought to show some interest? *[Exchanges glances with* XIAOLAN]

YUAN Of course. Lately, I've been rushed off my feet by the new workshop, but the end is in sight now. Tell me what you need, Xiaolan. I'll take care of it.

ALARM CLOCK *[giving the list to* XIAOLAN] Here, read it!

XIAOLAN *[not taking it]* No, you read it.

ALARM CLOCK All right. Listen carefully.

YUAN Is it very long?

ALARM CLOCK Don't worry, it doesn't even include the 'Eight Key Appliances'!

YUAN [*baffled*] What are the 'Eight Key Appliances'?

ALARM CLOCK Television, tape-recorder, fridge, washing-machine, camera, sewing-machine—

YUAN Enough! Enough! Just tell me what's on your list.

ALARM CLOCK [*reads out*] One three-door wardrobe, one utility cupboard, one liqour cabinet, one metal clothes rack, one sofa suite, one coffee-table, one sprung mattress—

YUAN [*interrupting*] Why on earth would you want to sleep on a sprung mattress? It sags and is not comfortable at all!

ALARM CLOCK I bought one when I got married and it looks so stylish.

YUAN All right, I'll think about it.

ALARM CLOCK [*to* XIAOLAN] Good. Now that Uncle has said the word, I'll handle everything for you.

YUAN You?

XIAOLAN Papa, don't look down on Alarm Clock just because she's a sales assistant in a grocery store. She knows how to cut through the red tape and get things done!

[YUAN *shakes his head and is about to speak when* LIN *enters.*]

ALARM CLOCK Hello, Lin. We were just talking about you and Xiaolan. You take your time, don't you?

LIN [*honestly*] I would have come sooner but the work never seemed to end. [*Takes out a document*] Uncle Yuan, Wang the Building Supervisor asked me to give you this.

YUAN What is it?

LIN It's a job completion certificate. He wanted Chief Wu to sign it as soon as possible.

YUAN Mmm. She'll be here later. [*Takes the document*] Excellent! A new workshop successfully completed! Not a bad harvest for the year!

[FANG *calls out from the kitchen, 'Xiaolan, come and give me a hand!'*]

XIAOLAN Coming!

ALARM CLOCK I'll go with you.

[XIAOLAN *and* ALARM CLOCK *go into the kitchen.*]

LIN [*with a touch of embarrassment*] Uncle Yuan, I, mm, I hear that you gave a pep talk to some of the workers last week?

YUAN Yes. I spoke at the Workers' Representative Meeting.

LIN I hear, too, that you made a public appeal to them to try everything possible to boost the mill's earnings?

YUAN That's right. I want the factory to contribute more to our country's finances. Why do you ask?

LIN Someone raised the question of whether it was possible to grub for money and still follow the red banner.

YUAN I can do both. Where would the red banner be without money to support it?

LIN *[smiling]* You do have guts.

YUAN I don't think I said enough. 'Money' is not a dirty word! When the new workshop is up and running, I can make an extra eighteen million yuan for the country. What's wrong with that? If I have an opportunity to make money but let it go, if I fritter away the money like a spendthrift, then I'm wrong. But I don't do that. I believe in two theories: the theory about the unique importance of productive forces and the theory about the importance of human nature. And that's how I'll run the factory. These theories are open to criticism, of course, but I don't care.

[FANG enters with bowls and chopsticks. XIAOLAN and ALARM CLOCK follow.]

FANG Come on, set the table.

[Everyone helps to set the table and arrange the chairs.]

[SUPERVISOR LI enters with SECTION HEAD NI.]

LI Director, let me introduce you to Section Head Ni of the Electric Company.

NI *[warmly]* Let's not stand on ceremony, just call me Ni.

YUAN *[shakes hands with NI]* Welcome. Please take a seat.

[XIAOLAN, ALARM CLOCK and LIN go into the inner room.]

NI *[not standing on ceremony]* Are you about to eat? Well, I just want a few words with you.

FANG Take your time. Please sit down. *[Goes into the kitchen]*

YUAN *[warmly]* Have a seat. Li, please pour a cup of tea for Section Head Ni.

[LI pours out tea for YUAN and NI.]

NI *[sits down]* Li, please sit down as well.

YUAN Ni, I'm a blunt man and I'll come straight to the point. I'm counting on you to make sure there's sufficient power for our new workshop.

NI Please don't worry: that's my job. The green light is now on for the light textiles industry to move ahead at full speed. Isn't that right, Yuan?

YUAN Yes, we're two separate divisions of the same army. We're fighting the front and you're at the rear. Without your support, we'll lose the battle.

NI We understand. But things aren't easy for us these days. What could be done in a day before the Cultural Revolution now takes more than two weeks. To begin with, power supply is insufficient, and the voltage is too low. What with so many people wrangling and bickering over trifles, it's really not easy for us to see through this project.

YUAN *[a little anxious]* Ni, We are—

NI My dear director, don't misunderstand me. Mr Liu, our manager, has instructed us to make sure that your factory will get the power it needs, no matter what difficulties there may be.

YUAN *[excitedly]* That's excellent!

NI Mr Liu has gone so far as to say that everyone in our building would work by candlelight if it would help the new workshop to start production on time.

YUAN *[much moved]* Ni, you've just eased our biggest worry! *[Pours out some wine]* Come! It's nearly New Year! Let's drink a toast to you!

NI There's really no need, Director Yuan. We're all pleased to be of service to you.

YUAN No, no! You must accept this toast to you. *[Hands a glass of wine to* NI*]*

LI Ni, our director is indeed grateful to you. Please don't refuse.

NI With pleasure then.

YUAN Cheers!

*[*YUAN *and* NI *down the wine in one.]*

YUAN Ni, when will you switch on the supply? We have to wait until the electricity is on before we can install the machinery.

NI *[looks at his watch]* You'll be connected at 7pm sharp.

YUAN *[delighted]* Quick, Li, call Wu and give her the good news.

*[*LI *goes to telephone. The lights in the new workshop suddenly go up.]*

NI *[sees the lights]* Wait. *[Points towards the window]*

LI Director, the lights are on!

*[*YUAN *goes to the balcony to have a look and hurries back excitedly.]*

NI *[looks at his watch]* 6.50pm. It came through early. Well, Director, I have to go now.

YUAN *[shaking NI's hand firmly]* What more can I say? Please extend my sincerest thanks to Mr Liu. Li, please show Comrade Ni out.

NI No, please. Don't stand on ceremony. I'm sure there'll be further co-operation between us.

[NI and LI exit. YUAN looks with elation at the lights shining from the new workshop. He picks up his hat and goes towards the front door.]

YUAN *[singing in a self-satisfied manner]*

'The wilful nobles like wild jackdaws,
Come before Judge Bao to thwart the law.
They think I will the Empress's pleading hear,
I will be just e'en if the Emperor is here.'

[FANG enters.]

FANG Stop right there! Where do you think you're going?

YUAN I'm going to wash and tidy up my hair—

FANG Don't try to fool me! Now that the lights are on, you're itching to go back to the workshop, aren't you?

YUAN *[pointing outside the window]* Come! Have a look! Isn't it beautiful? Gives me more joy than cuddling a big, fat baby. I tell you, I shall see to it that this project remains absolutely above board, from start to finish. You can take it as a show-case project to the Discipline Review Commission. Please, let me go! *[He picks up his hat.]* I'll be back very quickly.

FANG *[snatches back his hat]* You're not going anywhere today, not even for a minute. *[Towards the inner room]* Xiaolan, finish laying the table. Dinner is ready.

[XIAOLAN, ALARM CLOCK, and LIN enter.]

YUAN *[smiles and picks up the telephone]* Please put me through to the new workshop. Hello . . . this is Yuan, please find Wu for me.

[With his back towards FANG, he lights a cigarette.]

FANG *[noticing immediately]* Yuan! You know our rules!

YUAN *[not giving in]* Please, just one!

FANG *[seriously]* Where did you get that cigarette? Did you buy it?

YUAN No, I asked Li for one of his.

FANG *[resolutely]* Give it to me! You're not allowed to have even one.

YUAN Okay, Okay! You win! *[Gives the cigarette to* FANG*]*

> *[*FANG *stubs out the cigarette and goes into the kitchen. With a flourish* YUAN *pulls out another cigarette from his pocket and lights it. They all laugh.]*

YUAN *[stopping the laughter]* Shush! I must obey my dear wife but I must satisfy my craving too. That's what they call 'balancing everyone's needs and striving for all-round development'! *[Speaking on the telephone again]* Hello, is that Wu?

> *[*WU *enters.]*

WU Speaking of the devil?

YUAN There's no need to look for her anymore. *[Hangs up the telephone]* Wu, how's everything in the workshop?

WU *[excitedly]* Everything's fine. The lights are shining gloriously! The motors are humming and the installation work has begun.

YUAN *[in high spirits]* Excellent! Let's have dinner. *[Softly]* When we've finished eating, let's both go and have a look.

WU *[nods and puts a paper-wrapped parcel and a box of food on the table]* Xiaolan, guess what I've brought you. It's something you've loved ever since you were a child.

XIAOLAN *[picks up the parcel and feels it]* Oh, I know! It's red crumble candy, isn't it?

WU *[laughing]* You're right. And I bought two take-away dishes from the canteen too.

> *[*FANG *enters.]*

FANG Wu, you needn't have bought anything!

YUAN *[hurriedly putting out his cigarette]* Xiaolan, thank Auntie Wu.

XIAOLAN Thank you Auntie Wu.

YUAN Come on, sit down everyone.

ALARM CLOCK I'll pour out the wine.

> *[Everyone sits down at the table.]*

FANG Let Wu have the first glass.

ALARM CLOCK Okay. *[Pours out the wine]*

WU Yuan, this uncompromising, surly old woman will say something to please you today.

YUAN *[jokingly]* That will be rare indeed!

WU Do you remember, in the early days of the Great Leap Forward in the 1950s, you were the supervisor at the looms in a weaving factory and I was your deputy. At the time, we were ordered to speed up the looms, speed them up like crazy, until they were working at a rate of 250 turns.

YUAN Yes, I was worried to death about it and I remember I took you aside and asked for your opinion.

WU And I said the looms would start breaking up at 220 turns. Afterwards, you told me to keep quiet about what I'd said and you surreptitiously turned down the looms, leaving only a few dozen working at high speed for the inspectors.

YUAN With the result that all 2,000 looms in the factory were saved.

WU [sighing with feeling] Yuan, I'll remember that incident all my life. You made me see that members of the Communist Party do have integrity, vision, and selflessness. Goodness knows I never flatter anyone but I'll certainly give you credit for the way you've stood up to the corruption around you during the construction of this workshop. I don't know how you pulled it off, and I could never do it. But I know it wasn't easy! [To FANG] Right?

FANG We're going to prepare a report on the lessons to be drawn from your experiences. The provincial papers and the municipal TV station will be sending their reporters to the workshop to do some interviews and a write-up.

YUAN No, don't do that. If you ask them to come, they'll create a stir before the workshop is ready for operation. And if we so much as slipped, we'd end up looking like fools. No, we'd better tread carefully.

[ALARM CLOCK laughs. XIAOLAN stops her.]

Alarm Clock, what are you laughing at?

FANG Take no notice of them.

YUAN To tell you the truth, Wu, at first, I was very nervous, especially on the day we were going to sign the contract with your construction company, Lin. There's a popular saying these days. How does it go again?

LIN 'For the cutting edge use the best steel,
Pay respects to Buddha when you do a deal.
Light him some incense,
Or he'll show you his heels.'

YUAN That's right. But I thought I'd just grit my teeth and see if I could stand firm. Ha! I made it! As the folks in my village say: 'The idiot who sleeps on a cold, bare bed has to have a lot of fire in him'. Looks as if I could rely on my fire, not the incense.

[XIAOLAN *and* ALARM CLOCK *are still whispering on one side.*]

Xiaolan, what are you whispering about?

FANG Yuan, let's have dinner now. Help Wu to some food.

YUAN Yes, let's eat.

ALARM CLOCK Lin, you've done the least work today, you should serve us now.

LIN That's fine by me. [*Helps them to food*]

ALARM CLOCK Oh, Uncle Yuan, you haven't opened the bottle of Luzhou wine I gave you, don't you like it? [*Opening the bottle and pouring out the wine*]

XIAOLAN Come on! Cheers!

YUAN [*earnestly*] Are you hiding something from me? Tell me now, or I won't be able to enjoy the food or the wine.

ALARM CLOCK If you insist. Xiaolan!

XIAOLAN Papa, someone in the factory has written a silly poem about you and drawn a caricature of you.

YUAN Oh yes?

XIAOLAN [*takes out the poem and caricature and passes them over to* YUAN] It was found taped to the corridor wall just now.

ALARM CLOCK It's outrageous!

YUAN [*looks at it and laughs out loud*] Wu, take a look at this.

[WU *looks at it.*]

[*pointing to the drawing*] Why these funny strands on the top of my head? They look like curly noodles.

ALARM CLOCK That means you're a fool.

YUAN I won't deny that!

XIAOLAN [*protesting*] Papa!

YUAN Well, look at it this way. It shows that my relation with the masses must be pretty good or no one would dare to make such an exhibition of me. Give it to me. I'll keep it as a memento. [*Puts the poem and drawing into his pocket*] Nowadays, harsh words from the workers are all part of the job.

WU As long as they're not the majority, it's all right.

YUAN Agreed. Now, let's eat.

FANG Help yourself!

YUAN What nice dishes have you made today? No meatballs?

XIAOLAN Of course there are! We made those first.

FANG Blabber-mouth! *[Goes to get the meatballs]*

YUAN Wu, she's only just learnt how to cook meatballs, and they rival those of the greatest chefs in Yangzhou!

WU Really? Then, I must try them.

[LI enters.]

YUAN Li, come and join us.

LI No, you go ahead and eat your dinner, I just have a few things to report to you.

YUAN All right, I'll eat as we talk. Sit down. *[Hands a glass of wine to LI]*

LI *[takes the wine]* Has Wu signed the job completion certificate for the construction company yet?

YUAN Lin brought it over but it hasn't been signed yet.

WU *[conscientiously]* I still have to check the air-conditioning plant before I sign it.

LI Sure. Well, we've contacted the Synthetic Fibres Factory and they've agreed to supply us with their top-quality synthetic fibres.

YUAN Mmm.

LI All the machinery has been delivered, with the exception of two fly-frames*. I made a long-distance call to Jiangnan Textile Machinery Factory this afternoon and they said someone was on his way here.

YUAN *[jubilant]* Good! This calls for a real celebration. Fang Jing, bring us a couple more dishes. Whatever you have in the kitchen. Li, help me drink some of this wine! These others aren't up to it!

[The telephone rings.]

LI *[glances at YUAN and then picks up the phone]* Hello, Li speaking. Yes, you can speak to me. Hm . . . hm . . . really . . . Okay. . . . I'll tell the Director at once. *[Puts down the telephone]*

YUAN What's the matter?

LI That was the workshop site-office. They've just discovered that at least a quarter of the work in the air-conditioning plant hasn't been finished yet.

YUAN *[surprised]* Is that true?

WU Goodness, it's lucky I haven't signed the certificate yet.

YUAN Lin, do you know what the matter is?

* High-speed frames for cotton spinning.

LIN Wang, the Building Supervisor, only told me to bring
the certificate over and ask Wu to sign it as soon as
possible.

LI *[hesitantly]* They . . . they . . .

YUAN Speak up!

LI Could it be that they've deliberately left part of the job
unfinished so they could come back and demand some
favours from you?

ALARM CLOCK I think that's exactly it. Here's another saying for you:
'Offer two bowls of beancurd first, then you'll get two
bowls in return'. That's the way things are!

WU Hm, would they be so blatant about it?

LI Perhaps not.

YUAN *[shaking his head]* Hard to say. Wu, Li, let me be frank
with you. I'm no fool, and I'm no idiot either. I know
very well the dangers of being tough in a job like this.
It's no joke. If I take one wrong step, I'll be thrown to
the dogs.

FANG *[trying to calm him down]* Yuan—

YUAN *[having difficulty controlling his feelings]* But what really
worries me is: to bring order out of chaos is like
bringing the dead back to life, if we don't do it
properly and do it soon, then—*[Doesn't want to say
more]* Come, let's eat. When the Tripitaka went to India
to fetch the scriptures, he had to overcome eighty-one
obstacles. What we have is just a small hiccup. Come,
fill the glasses.

[All pour wine or orange juice.]

YUAN This first glass is in celebration of the new workshop,
and in anticipation of an early completion of the
installation work. Come, let's drink to a timely start to
production and the making of good profits for our
country!

WU And a toast to you too, our fool of a Director!

YUAN And to our uncompromising, surly Chief Engineer.
Cheers!

ALL *[raising glasses]* Cheers!

*[As they are about to drink, the lights in the new workshop
suddenly go out.]*

YUAN *[putting down his glass]* What's up? Li, call the
workshop and find out.

[LI is about to pick up the telephone when it rings.]

LI *[picking up the telephone]* Hello. Yes, it's Li. *[To* YUAN*]* It's the workshop. *[Continues to talk]* What? *[Hangs up the phone]* They've cut the power!

WU *[gets up abruptly]* Yuan, we must deal with this at once. I can't work if there's no light. *[Exits]*

YUAN Li, we must have the equipment up and running by midnight of April 1st. Go and talk to Ni now. I'm going to the capital construction department to find some gas lights. Whatever happens, we have to continue with the installation work. Let's go!

*[*YUAN *and* LI *exit together.]*

FANG I never thought we'd have to break up this New Year Dinner!

ALARM CLOCK *[smiling]* Auntie Fang, do you know why the power has been cut?

XIAOLAN You're making wild guesses again.

ALARM CLOCK Wild guesses? I know I'm right!

FANG So why did they cut the power?

ALARM CLOCK I don't want to say anything just yet. *[Laughs out loud]*

FANG *[shaking her head]* You mad child. You think you're so smart!

[Quick curtain down]

ACT 2

[Sunday afternoon, a week later. YUAN's *home.*

When the curtain rises, the stage is empty of people. A moment later, YUAN *walks in, utterly exhausted. He paces up and down in agitation. Finally, he pulls out a packet of cigarettes from his pocket.*

FANG *enters from the inner room, wearing a pair of spectacles, a pile of documents in her hand.]*

FANG *[stopping him]* Yuan! *[Snatches the cigarettes]* Haven't you found Ni yet? *[Pours out a cup of tea for* YUAN*]*

YUAN *[thinking]* Do you think he's avoiding me?

FANG *[sidestepping the question]* Don't get upset just yet. See what he has to say for himself when you find him.

YUAN We've been without power for a whole week now. So much for efficiency, urgency, and manufacturing at full speed!

FANG Why don't you speak to Zheng? After all, he's head of the Municipal Light Industries Office.

YUAN That's no use.

FANG *[puts down her spectacles and documents]* You must be hungry, I'll make you some noodles. *[Exits into the kitchen]*

*[*YUAN *finishes off the tea in one gulp.* LI *and* ALARM CLOCK *enter.]*

LI Director, we have something important to tell you. Alarm Clock, go on.

ALARM CLOCK You tell him!

LI No, it's better coming from you.

YUAN Hey, it doesn't matter who tells me.

ALARM CLOCK Li asked how my father handled the Electric Company before they began installing the machinery in their new workshop.

YUAN *[showing interest]* How did they do it?

ALARM CLOCK *[sighing]* He simply asked his office to send Ni two bolts of patterned woollen fabric and a stack of rugs at eighty yuan each.

YUAN *[not knowing whether to believe it or not]* Are you sure?

LI I happened to be listening when Zhong, their Director, was talking about it just now.

ALARM CLOCK It's fairly common.

LI Zhong also advised us to—

YUAN What?

LI He said we'd better not be so stubborn. If we offend the people at the Electric Company, things could get rough.

[FANG *enters carrying a bowl and chopsticks.*]

ALARM CLOCK Does it matter if you help them buy a few black-market goods? Where can you get your power supply if you don't pay them off? You really have no choice.

FANG [*with a shade of embarrassment*] Why don't you all sit down and have some tea. I've just made some, fresh in the pot.

YUAN [*understanding her situation*] Fang Jing, why don't you go inside and read your documents? I'll make some noodles myself in a minute.

[FANG *takes her spectacles and the documents into the inner room.*]

ALARM CLOCK [*cheekily*] Uncle Yuan, will Auntie Fang investigate you, too?

YUAN She'll investigate whoever is next on her list. Well, it looks like we won't be able to bulldoze through this mountain that the Electric Company have put in our way. Hmm? [*Takes out another cigarette from his pocket and lights it*]

LI [*speaking to himself*] We can manage with the installation, but when it comes to testing out the machinery, it won't be too good if there's no power.

YUAN It will be a disaster! We'll be done for!

ALARM CLOCK Uncle Yuan, you should lay in a supply of gifts. I'm sure it's not illegal. If my father is allowed to do it, then so are you!

LI [*waiting anxiously*] Director . . . shall I . . .

YUAN [*suddenly*] We'll talk about this after I've seen Ni.

ALARM CLOCK Are you really afraid of Auntie Fang?

YUAN You don't understand.

ALARM CLOCK [*anxiously*] If you wait until you get to see Ni, it'll be too late. He's been keeping out of your way these last few days to allow you some time to get the goods together. [*Urging* LI *to speak with a glance*]

LI [*with misgivings*] Hm, just now I went to the supply and marketing section at the wool mill and an old school friend of mine was on duty.

YUAN What do you mean?

LI [*softly*] I managed to obtain some woollen material and some rugs.

YUAN *[surprised]* What? You've already got the goods together?

LI Well, I've left them in the office.

YUAN *[pacing up and down in anger. Suddenly stops and stands still]* How could you make such an important decision without consulting me first? *[Resolutely]* No, it's not right! I won't budge. I won't be carried along by this flood. This is our bottom line. We can't stoop so low!

[LI keeps silent.]

ALARM CLOCK Uncle Yuan, I've said all I wanted to say. No one knows yet which of the two of you is right in this case. Goodbye now! *[Exits]*

YUAN *[pacing twice around the room]* Li, do you really think you're right and I'm wrong?

LI *[diverting him]* Oh, I almost forgot, Wu wants to speak to you.

YUAN I know—about when power supply will be resumed. Of course she wants to speak to me. Who else could she speak to? We just want to work for the 'Four Modernizations'*, but how can we when we don't even have the bare necessities? And what sort of performance is that from me, as Factory Director?

[A knock on the door. LI goes to open it.]

LI Director, Chief Zheng from the Light Industries Office is here.

[ZHENG enters.]

YUAN *[standing up to welcome him]* Hello Zheng.

ZHENG Is Comrade Fang at home?

[FANG enters from the inner room.]

FANG Looking for me?

ZHENG I hear that you've asked for the report on them *[Pointing to YUAN]* to be delayed. Is that true? I think it reads well and would make a good impact when it's published in the papers. I do think it's time you let your findings be known. You should expose all the problems encountered in applying the 'Code of Practice' and you should publicize the good models. Well, Yuan must have influenced you. I know him better than you do.

FANG He doesn't know about this. The comrades on the DRC asked for the report to be delayed.

---

* The modernization of agriculture, industry, national defence, and science and technology.

ZHENG Why was that?

FANG *[glances at* YUAN*]* I don't think he can stick it out anymore.

YUAN I think it's better to put the report aside for the time being.

ZHENG *[to* YUAN*]* Have you run into difficulties? What's the problem? Power supply?

YUAN Yes. Power has become an obstructive force.

ZHENG Have things become that serious?

YUAN Installation has ground to a halt. Li, show the Chief our progress in the last two days.

*[*LI *opens a diary and shows it to* ZHENG.*]*

FANG Well, I'll leave you to it. I'll see you, Zheng. And we hope you'll take our decision about the report seriously.

ZHENG Of course, I'll see you later.

*[*FANG *exits.]*

[indicating the diary] You can't go on like this. If installation is delayed, you can't start production; if production doesn't start on time, you'll have difficulty reaching your 1.8 million earnings target. Don't forget you promised this to the Light Industries Office.

YUAN I know. The trouble is, I've no idea what the Electric Company is up to. Zheng, do you know what the Northern Mills have been doing?

ZHENG *[laughing]* The Party Cell are in the middle of conducting a big investigation into malpractices, so you'd better watch out. Don't let me down!

YUAN *[bluntly]* You and your high-sounding words. But if things go wrong, I'll have to take the rap. We've just started to set up the machinery, and the Electric Company has decided to halt all progress. I've got to fight them off somehow or I'll be done for!

ZHENG *[avoiding the issue]* Well, things have never been easy for us! The two of us have been through hell and fire in the past, but didn't we manage to take them all in our stride? Didn't we manage to force our way through? Hmm? *[Laughs]*

YUAN Have you finished? *[Seriously]* Look, Zheng, don't bluff with me! Why can't you give me a straight answer?

ZHENG Come on! You're quick and sharp. You don't need any instructions from me. *[Looks at his watch]* Let's leave it here. I have to pop over to the cotton factory for a brief visit. *[Stands up]*

YUAN [*unable to hold himself back anymore*] Zheng, tell me
     straight. What do you want me to do? Should I go and
     get things done under the table or should I go into
     hiding and let this investigation business blow over?
     Or do you want me to stick to my guns come what
     may?

ZHENG [*stops for a minute*] Listen, then. There are two
     principles you should uphold. First, you should firmly
     resist all evil influences: I want you to remain
     uncorrupted from start to finish. Second, I will not take
     one fen less than the 1.8 million yuan profit you have
     projected for this year. [*Lightly*] I'm sure you can take
     care of this. Where there's a will, there's a way.
     [*Laughing*] I have to go now. Goodbye! [*Walks towards
     the front door*]

     [YUAN *and* LI *rise to their feet.*]

ZHENG [*to* LI] No need to show me out. You've still got lots
     to discuss. I'm sure you won't allow the Electric
     Company to hold things up for too long. [*Laughs again
     and exits*]

LI [*positively*] Director, did you hear that? He's given you
     the go-ahead!

YUAN [*has got the point too, but remains firm*] I didn't hear
     anything! To adhere strictly to 'The Code' is the
     direction the Party are going in, and what the masses
     want too. We shouldn't just pay lip-service to it. Yes,
     we've got to. stand firm! Return those goods to your
     friend at the wool mill!

LI But—

YUAN No more buts. I'm not criticising the way you've
     handled this, but you must return those things to your
     friend, at once.

LI [*pauses*] All right. [*About to go*]

     [WU *hurries in.*]

YUAN Are you looking for me?

WU [*plumps herself down on a chair*] So, Comrade Director,
     how much longer will it take before we can have our
     electricity?

YUAN Soon, very soon.

WU I don't need a vague answer like that. Tell me when
     exactly! What day? What time?

YUAN Calm down, Wu! Be patient!

WU Patient! The machinery has been installed but I can't start testing it until we have power. Don't you understand?

LI *[explaining]* Wu, the Director has been looking for Mr Ni all day, but—

WU You can keep quiet! I know nothing about pulling strings and buying influence and I don't want to. I only know that if the opening of the workshop is delayed, the country will lose 20,000 yuan per day, or 836 yuan 66 fen per hour! I thought you wanted to make money for the country. Well, it's trickling through your fingers right in front of your eyes!

YUAN I know! I know!

WU *[earnestly]* Good. Then, when will this problem be solved? Today? Tomorrow? I'm responsible for the technical side of things, and I rely on you for the power supply. I know that you have difficulties, great difficulties, but I can't help you! That's your responsibility.

YUAN I know, I know.

WU I'll tell you one more time: if I don't get the power by tomorrow, I can't guarantee that the workshop can go into operation on April 1st. If that happens, you'll be blamed first. Then the Light Industries Office will withhold your salary! Every last yuan of it! *[Stands up]*

YUAN Wu, Wu—

[WU hurries out.]

LI That uncompromising, surly old lady! There's no reasoning with her!

YUAN If everybody behaved like her, there'd be hope for the 'Four Modernizations'. *[To LI]* What are you staring at? Go and return those things at once!

LI Director, don't you think we should—

YUAN Should what?

[LI doesn't move or speak.]

If you have something to say, say it. I can't stand your silence! *[Sits down and lights another cigarette]*

LI *[sincerely]* Our country's economy is in the red now and this can't be a good thing. If we can start production sooner, at least we can help to fill in some of the holes. *[YUAN doesn't speak.]*

I'll be honest with you. I know that Ni is crooked but we can't afford to offend people like him these days.

YUAN So we have to lick his arse?

LI It doesn't matter if we do. The wool mills have the right to sell off part of their production to whomever they wish. If the employees at the Electric Company want those goods, then we're only acting as a channel between the two sides. Anyway, lots of factories do this.

YUAN *[silent for a while]* Forget it! Let's leave it for now!

[The telephone rings.]

LI *[answering the telephone]* Hello, this is Director Yuan's home. Who's speaking? . . . Oh, Ni, it's you! I'm so glad to have found you at last! . . . What?

YUAN Ask him where he is! I'll go there at once!

LI *[nodding]* You'll be here at 6 o'clock? . . . Good . . . Okay . . . The Director will be here. We'll wait for you! *[Hangs up]* Ni said that he'd be here at six, he has something important to tell you.

YUAN There can't be anything more important than connecting us to the electricity supply!

LI Don't talk like that. Just listen to what he has to say.

YUAN Sure, sure. I'll listen to anything!

LI Director, don't you think we should hold on to those goods a while longer?

YUAN I know what you're up to, Li. You're dragging your heels because your mind is set. No, don't wait! Go now!

LI *[looking at his watch]* Why don't we wait until after we've spoken to Ni? After all, he'll be here in less than an hour.

YUAN *[shaking his head]* You—! *[Goes into the inner room]*

LI Well, I'm going back to the office. *[Exits]*

[A knock on the front door. FANG comes out from the inner room to answer the door offstage.]

ZHAO *[offstage]* Sorry to trouble you, Comrade. Is this Director Yuan's home?

FANG *[offstage]* Yes, it is. Please come in.

[A travel-stained ZHAO enters, carrying a bulging synthetic leather bag. FANG follows.]

ZHAO *[wiping his brow]* I'm so glad to have found you at last! The staff quarters here all look alike. It's so easy to get lost!

FANG This must be your first time here, Comrade. What should I call you?

ZHAO Oh, yes. *[Takes out a letter of introduction]* I'm Zhao
Rongquan from the supply and marketing section of
the Jiangnan Textile Machinery Factory.

FANG *[reading the letter]* I see, have a seat. Please sit down.

ZHAO Comrade. You're——?

FANG I'm Yuan's wife.

ZHAO Oh. That's good. *[Puts his bag on the table and opens the
zipper]* Do you also work in the New China Cotton
Mills?

FANG No. I work at the Discipline Review Commission of
the Light Industries Office.

ZHAO *[freezes at once and zips up his bag again. Pauses]* Oh,
that's good.

FANG *[pours out some tea]* Comrade Zhao, have some tea.

ZHAO Thank you. It's very kind of you. *[Takes the opportunity
to put his bag down on the floor]* I understand that
vegetables here aren't easy to come by?

FANG It's winter so vegetables are scarce, but what there is
isn't too bad.

ZHAO You won't have much to choose from then.

FANG No, not really.

ZHAO Oh. Good. Good.

FANG Do have some tea. It'll keep you warm.

ZHAO *[sipping the tea]* Thank you, thank you.

　　　[YUAN enters from the inner room. ZHAO rises.]

FANG Yuan, Comrade Zhao here is looking for you. *[Gives
YUAN the introduction letter]*

YUAN *[looks at the letter]* Good. Welcome. *[Shakes hands with
ZHAO]* We're just waiting for your fly frames.

FANG Comrade Zhao, please excuse me.

ZHAO Oh, yes, of course.

　　　[FANG goes into the inner room.]

YUAN Please sit down.

ZHAO *[puts his bag on the table again, opens the zipper and takes
out a plastic bag of bamboo shoots, fresh lotus roots, wild rice
stems]* Director Yuan, I know you don't care for gifts
from visitors and it's not my usual practice to give gifts
either. But, I heard that you don't get a lot of fresh
vegetables here so I took the opportunity to bring you
some. There's not much, but I thought you could do
with them . . .

YUAN Zhao, are you——

ZHAO *[interrupting him]* Director Yuan, I don't want to make things difficult for you, so you can pay me back if you like. The bamboo shoots are 30 fen, lotus roots 25 fen and 40 fen for the wild rice stems, the lot add up to just under one yuan. Fair and square. All above board.

YUAN *[smiling]* Let's talk about this later. Tell me, what's happened to the fly frames we ordered?

ZHAO *[putting his bag on the floor]* That's exactly why I'm here. Quite frankly, Director, we need your help.

YUAN Tell me what it is. I'll certainly help you if I can.

ZHAO I'm sure you can. It's a shame really, but last year, we didn't meet our output quota and funds became tight. So, my director wondered if you could purchase some spare parts for your fly frames to help us out.

YUAN What kind of spare parts?

ZHAO The dividing wall panels on either side of the fly frames.

YUAN *[laughing]* You must be joking, Zhao! Those wall panels are made of steel and the workers call them 'prison walls that last for ever'. They wear well. Why bother to stock up on them?

ZHAO Let me explain a little. Our funds are all tied up and, to help us out, we would like you to buy five of these panels for 10,000 yuan.

YUAN If I agree to buy these panels, then what about the fly frames?

ZHAO The fly frames will be delivered at once and your installation can continue smoothly.

YUAN *[nodding]* I understand now. So, we have to buy a basketful of withered eggplants before we can get five catties of good tomatoes. Well, Zhao, this is only the first time we've met but I like your frankness. Let's be honest, it won't hurt a large factory like ours to keep 10,000 yuan of spare parts lying around.

ZHAO Oh, good.

YUAN But still . . . why don't you let me think about this? *[As he speaks, he puts the bag back on the table and stuffs the vegetables back in.]*

ZHAO Oh, sure, of course. But—

YUAN *[when the vegetables are all in, zips up the bag]* I appreciate your kindness but we really have enough vegetables. Forgive me for being so blunt, but, frankly, whether or not I accept your suggestion has nothing to do with these vegetables.

ZHAO No, of course not.

YUAN *[with concern]* Have you got somewhere to stay?

ZHAO Yes, I'm staying on the first floor of the hostel. It's very good. Director Yuan, would you let me know your decision as soon as possible? Everyone back home is waiting to hear from me.

YUAN Please don't worry. I'm more anxious than you are. The machines still have to be installed!

ZHAO That's good. Well, goodbye then.

YUAN Goodbye.

[YUAN shows ZHAO out. FANG enters from the inner room. YUAN looks at his watch and picks up the telephone.]

FANG Yuan, I'd like a few words with you.

YUAN *[puts down the telephone and sits down]* Did you hear my conversation with Zhao?

[FANG nods her head.]

YUAN And you know all about the goods that Li has obtained?

[FANG nods again.]

Then tell me what you have to say!

FANG *[after a pause]* I've just read a document. It left a bad taste in my mouth.

YUAN What document?

FANG An old shepherd from Xinjiang has written us a letter. It says: 'Do not speak to me of poverty; we were much poorer before the Liberation. In those days, society was unstable, bandits were everywhere and disturbances were common. We lived in terror everyday. Why then did I turn my face from Allah and look to the Communist Party? Because the Communist Party was a party of clean and upright officials, and they cared about the common people. Now, everything has changed. Many party members and cadres are concerned only with feathering their own nests. They don't care about the masses. Gradually my heart grew cold and I've turned again to Allah.'

[Pause.]

YUAN *[with deep feeling]* He's right. When I learn how the masses are cursing and swearing at the corruption within the Party, I get so angry I am ready to burst. But what can I say to them?

FANG *[movingly]* Yuan, that's why we shouldn't—

YUAN Become involved in anything unethical, right?

FANG For one thing, I don't want to be stabbed in the back because of what you may do.

YUAN That's why I asked you to go into the other room earlier on, so you can be in the clear.

FANG But I can't just pretend I didn't hear what you were talking about.

YUAN Frankly, I'm fed up with fighting.

FANG I know. But, as soon as you let your principles slide, even for one moment, you'll find that it's just the start of a long, downhill descent.

YUAN *[suddenly]* Well, you're the one who works on the DRC. You and the comrades there should do something! All those crooked and corrupt officials, they should be exposed and reported to the proper authorities for disciplinary action. But you've done nothing!

FANG Nothing? You should come to my office and take a look at my desk. It's piled high with letters of complaint and denunciation. But it's just not possible to conduct a thorough investigation when the evidence is so thin.

YUAN I don't believe that none of your cases can be substantiated.

FANG *[candidly]* In some cases, we know exactly what's been going on but it's impossible to take any action. What happens now is, as soon as we start investigating a case, someone will come to hush it up.

YUAN That's just it! The problem is that none of you have the guts to prod the bee hive in case you get stung!

FANG You know I don't need to lie to you. The fact of the matter is, the realities are more complicated than you can imagine. Frankly, there's only so much we can do. There are just too many 'no-go' areas.

YUAN What about your superiors? Can't they do something? What about the Party Cell at the Light Industries Office? Can't you personally bring the cases to their attention? Can't you put up a fight?

FANG What if we did? Many of our big investigations have already become mere trifles all of a sudden and the small cases have just slipped through our fingers.

YUAN Well then, take down the DRC plaque and be done with it. Xiaolan and I both need you at home!

FANG You don't have to take it out on me, though I know you're only doing it to provoke me. Well, it's not that we can't do anything, but we may end up making things much worse than if we had done nothing at all.

[Pause.]

YUAN [agitated and dejected] So either way we're stuck? What a pretty state of affairs!

FANG It's the after-effect of the Cultural Revolution—ten years of calamity. People have forgotten their principles and ideals. It can't be put right overnight!

YUAN There's no way out then?

FANG Yes, there is. There is one thing you can do. Even if you can't beat them, make sure you don't join them.

YUAN [disgruntled] Oh come on! You've worked on the shop floor too. Say something practical, will you? Can't you see what's wrong? The Party is ashamed of the graft and string-pulling among its members; at the same time, it's afraid that the 'Four Modernizations' won't work. But if the Central Government can't stand firm, what are we to do?

FANG But, it's not that we don't want to do something, it's just that we don't know how to.

YUAN So, you're going to give up? Go to work just to drink your tea and read your reports? I don't care for such an easy life!

FANG [hesitates a moment] The Light Industries Office is going to run an industrial management training course for cadres in industry. If you wish, I can get you enrolled. You only have to leave work for six months. It'll help you in your job.

YUAN [laughing sarcastically] Ha! How clever! This way I can fly the banner of the 'Four Modernizations' and at the same time stay out of the hotbed of dissension at the workshop, right?

FANG [also getting heated] I can't say anything right, can I? I ask you to stand firm and you say you can't. I ask you to take a training course and you won't. I have no more suggestions! All I can say is that this family won't tolerate crooks!

[YUAN, greatly upset, takes out a cigarette and is about to light it.]

You're not allowed to smoke! [Blows out the match]

YUAN Leave me alone! [Lights the cigarette and paces up and down] Why don't you leave me alone just this once? I really must do something this time! [Stands still] Fang

Jing, let's pretend that this conversation never took place, that you never heard anything and that I never said anything. We'll both turn a blind eye just this once. It's my neck on the line, and I've got to get the power supply any way I can!

[FANG *takes no notice and walks towards the inner room.*]

That's settled then. I'll swallow my convictions and bend my principles just this once. If I ever do it again, you can call me a contemptible dog!

FANG [*reaches the door to the inner room and stops*] Even if you're really set on doing this, you should first convene a Party Committee meeting or else call a Director's work meeting.

YUAN What for?

FANG If you discuss this together, then you can make a collective decision.

YUAN [*opens his eyes wide*] Fang Jing, you—

[ALARM CLOCK *runs in.*]

ALARM CLOCK [*excitedly*] Uncle Yuan, Auntie Fang, I've got good news!

FANG What good news?

ALARM CLOCK [*taking out a pile of furniture coupons*] Look, furniture coupons! I've managed to get them all! Aren't I clever?

YUAN [*glumly*] Yes, you have more pull than I do.

ALARM CLOCK I shouldn't boast, but I really do know my way around!

FANG Where's Xiaolan?

ALARM CLOCK She's on her way. Uncle Yuan, have a look at these coupons. They're for the mill's domestic inventory. You can just walk in and choose your furniture from stock. You don't even have to queue up!

YUAN [*takes the coupons and looks at them*] This system of back-door influence is getting more and more high tech all the time!

ALARM CLOCK But, first, I must ask you a question.

YUAN What is it?

ALARM CLOCK Tell me, do you love Xiaolan?

FANG What tricks are you up to now?

ALARM CLOCK Auntie Fang, please keep out of this. Uncle Yuan, please answer me.

YUAN What shall I say? During the ten years of the Cultural Revolution, she went through hell because of me. She lost the best years of her youth because of me. How could I not care about her? How could I not love her?

ALARM CLOCK Really?

YUAN Of course.

ALARM CLOCK Good, then the next move is up to you!

> [XIAOLAN *enters. She is holding five sticks of candied haws behind her back.*]

XIAOLAN [*in high spirits*] Papa, I've bought your favourite snack. Guess what it is.

YUAN [*thinking*] Candied haws, right?

XIAOLAN Right! Here, two for you. The rest of us have one each! [*Shares out the sticks*]

FANG You always put your father first!

XIAOLAN Well, he likes it!

ALARM CLOCK Xiaolan, I've already told them about your furniture.

XIAOLAN [*a little embarrassed*] Papa, I hesitated a long while before deciding that I would like to have a sprung mattress. Please don't be angry with me.

YUAN As long as you feel comfortable sleeping on such a flimsy thing, that's all right by me.

XIAOLAN You really are good to me!

FANG And your mother isn't?

XIAOLAN My mother's even better!

ALARM CLOCK All right! Let's get back to the point. Uncle Yuan, I've already collected all the furniture coupons. But the boss at the timber mill wants your help.

YUAN [*to* FANG] Here we go again! [*To* ALARM CLOCK] What help?

ALARM CLOCK No, you must promise to help first!

YUAN But what if I can't help him?

ALARM CLOCK No, you can, I know. Just say yes!

XIAOLAN Come on, Papa!

YUAN [*not without reluctance*] All right, I promise.

XIAOLAN Tell him, Alarm Clock.

ALARM CLOCK He isn't asking for the moon. He just wants you to help him get a ton of steel.

FANG Oh, that's not right!

ALARM CLOCK What's wrong with that? Everyone barters like this. Uncle Yuan, all you have to do is sign your name and it's done!

> [*Pause.*]

YUAN [*resolutely*] I can't do it. [*Puts down the furniture coupons on the table*]

FANG That's right, he can't do a thing like that.

ALARM CLOCK Uncle Yuan, he's only asking for one ton of steel!

YUAN I don't care if it's only a catty of scrap iron!

XIAOLAN But just now you promised you'd help.

YUAN Child, if you had asked for anything else, I would have been happy to give it to you but I really can't agree to this.

ALARM CLOCK Is that it, then, Uncle Yuan?

YUAN *[firmly]* My mind is made up.

ALARM CLOCK All right. Xiaolan, don't say I didn't try and help you. I'll leave the coupons here. See what you want to do with them. *[Hurries out]*

XIAOLAN Papa, won't you think about this a little more?

FANG Xiaolan!

YUAN *[patiently]* Xiaolan, your father is an old guard of the Communist Party and a long-time cadre. Don't you think I should stick to my principles and follow the Party's directives?

FANG Xiaolan, don't make things difficult for your father. He cannot agree to this. Steel is a controlled material. How can he deploy it any old how? If you've set your heart on the furniture, then we'll buy it the proper way, even if it costs more. All right?

[XIAOLAN doesn't speak.]

Let's go into the other room. Papa has a visitor coming here in a moment.

YUAN *[gently]* Xiaolan, go inside and talk it over with your mother. I'm willing to do anything except this.

FANG Xiaolan, come on! I know you'll understand.

[XIAOLAN stands still for a while and is about to go into the inner room when LI enters carrying some woollen cloth and some rugs.]

XIAOLAN *[catches sight of him and hurries back at once]* Oh? Uncle Li, did you get those for the Electric Company?

LI Yes.

XIAOLAN *[exasperated]* Papa, you . . . you . . .

FANG Xiaolan, please go inside, now!

XIAOLAN *[shouting]* Papa! So you call yourself an old guard of the Communist Party and a long-time cadre? Is this what you call the 'Code of Practice'? Is this how you stick to your principles? Tell me!

YUAN *[at a loss for words]* I . . . Ai! I don't know how to explain this!

LI *[baffled]* Director, what's going on?

XIAOLAN You're showing your true colours now. At home, you rant and rave about being upright and honest but, outside, you're as corrupt as the others! Shame on you, Judge Bao! You're no 'fool'! You're just like the rest, you're a . . . a . . . 'Buddhist monk' factory director!

FANG *[annoyed]* Xiaolan! Don't talk to your father like that!

[YUAN is furious, his face has turned deathly pale. He goes to the table and tears up the furniture coupons.]

[XIAOLAN bursts into tears and rushes into the inner room, followed by FANG.]

LI Director, what—

YUAN *[shaking his head]* It's a long story, I won't go into it now. Ni will be here soon. I'll speak first and you fill in the rest, all right?

LI All right. But it'd be better if you brought up the subject first.

YUAN *[thinks]* I think it would be better if you spoke to him.

LI All right then.

YUAN And if he really accepts these things, there's no need for you to report to the Secretary or the other factory directors. I'll take full responsibility if there's any trouble in the future.

LI *[full of admiration]* Director . . . You . . .

YUAN Let's leave it at that!

[NI hurries in carrying his dinner in a box.]

NI Director, I'm sorry to have kept you waiting!

YUAN I've been looking for you for days! Come and sit down!

NI I hurried over as soon as I heard. Oh, I wish I could be more organized! Things keep cropping up and I just seem to be rushing about without getting anything done!

YUAN Did you come from the office?

NI If only! I've been out with the emergency repair team all day. I haven't even had time to think about my dinner!

LI *[taking the initiative]* Oh Ni, let me talk to you about a small matter first.

NI Sure.

LI Through our connections with the wool mill we've managed to get hold of some coarse-knit textiles which are in short supply elsewhere.

NI Is that right? What are they?

LI Nothing special, just some patterned woollen fabric and some eighty-yuan rugs. They're normally sold to the workers at the factory.

NI And if some of our people need to buy some?

LI Well, we can probably spare some. Anyway, these are part of the quota that the factory has authority to sell off. Besides, it's not as if we're pulling strings to obtain them.

NI [sternly] What else do you call it but pulling strings? If you hadn't used your influence, could you have got any? Are they available to the common people? The directive on the 'Code of Practice' has only just been circulated these last few days and you're taking part in this nonsense? Director Yuan, I don't think this is proper.

LI Ni, it was my idea.

NI It doesn't matter whose idea it was. This is precisely the type of corrupt practice that's being investigated now. You know, lots of people have asked me for help. Just this morning, a young man asked me to help buy a rug for his wedding. I told him to go to the department store to get one and not involve me in his devious practice.

LI Actually, I was only asking in passing. It doesn't matter if you don't want any.

NI Li, I appreciate your offer. But this sort of thing is not on. I hope you don't mind my being blunt.

YUAN Never mind! Let's talk about more important things.

NI I'm actually here for an important reason. The power supply to your workshop was interrupted a few days ago because there was a blow-out in one of the underground cables. We've had a team working flat-out, twenty-four hours a day, doing emergency repairs. [Looks at his watch] You'll be reconnected very shortly.

YUAN [overjoyed] Really?

NI Well, they do say that seeing is believing!

[The lights go on in the new workshop.]

NI There, see for yourself. You have a supply you can depend on now. As for me, it's a load off my mind. See you!

YUAN [firmly shaking Ni's hand] Ni, I thank you from the bottom of my heart!

NI Don't mention it! Bye now! *[Exits]*

YUAN *[laughing]* Well, Li, I would be wronging you to call you an idiot, but you weren't quick enough to realize that you were on the wrong track after all! We didn't have to make any offerings to anyone and we still got our electricity. See?

LI I must say it's a surprise!

YUAN Come, let's go to the workshop! Wu will be overjoyed.

[Starts to sing]

'The wilful nobles like jackdaws,
Come before Judge Bao to thwart the law.'

[Suddenly remembering] Wait! I have to tell Fang Jing what happened. No, never mind. She'll have heard it all in the other room. Let's go!

[YUAN and LI exit together. FANG hurries out from the inner room and looks out of the window. Curtain falls.]

ACT 3

[Eve of the 1980 Spring Festival—Lunar New Year. Inside YUAN's *home.*

The curtain rises. The festive red lantern is still hanging up in the room, and the loud and cheerful sound of firecrackers can be heard through the window. Because FANG *is busy at work,* XIAOLAN *has prepared the Spring Dinner, assisted by* LIN. *The food is all ready and waiting on the table for* YUAN's *and* FANG's *return.*

XIAOLAN *is practising how to tie knots from a spool of yarn slung across her shoulders.* LIN *is standing to one side looking unhappy.]*

LIN *[pleadingly]* Will you please listen to me!

XIAOLAN *[blocking her ears]* No, I won't. I won't!

LIN Come on, just a few words.

*[*XIAOLAN *doesn't reply.]*

You're really not going to listen, are you?

*[*XIAOLAN *still ignores him.]*

[deliberately] Okay, then, I'll go and join the queue now. *[Picks up his book and makes to go]*

XIAOLAN *[looks up]* Come back!

LIN On my way here, I noticed they were issuing queue numbers at the furniture store. It's New Year's Day tomorrow and there won't be many people, we should be able to buy our furniture then.

XIAOLAN Even if you manage to buy anything, I don't want it.

LIN Why not?

XIAOLAN It's none of your business!

LIN *[returns and sits down]* I know you've been depressed lately.

XIAOLAN Who told you that?

LIN Is it because you failed to make the grade as an advanced artisan?

XIAOLAN Well, it's all my fault. I can't even tie a knot properly.

LIN *[sympathetically]* You really are unlucky. Your early days in the factory were a complete waste of time, what with those theory sessions and propaganda classes. Not only that, most of you were sent to carry out special case investigations and organize self-criticism mass meetings and what not. There was just no time for you to improve your technical skills. But—

XIAOLAN *[greatly distressed]* Oh, stop it!

LIN *[stops a while]* But a lavish wedding won't make up for your loss.

XIAOLAN Do you really think I'm like Alarm Clock? Let me tell you, in my heart I know exactly what I need!

LIN *[delighted]* Good!

[XIAOLAN unintentionally looks at the plaster on the forefinger of her right hand.]

[noticing it] Xiaolan, what's happened to your finger? *[Takes hold of it]* It's bleeding. Did you hurt it practising your knots?

XIAOLAN *[snatching her hand away]* The Cultural Revolution cost me ten years of my life. I've lost so much it's high time I planned for myself. Getting married is an important event in my life.

LIN Eh . . .? Then you—

XIAOLAN I've asked Alarm Clock to get me some more furniture coupons. We picked up the furniture already, this afternoon.

LIN *[surprised]* Really?

XIAOLAN They wanted us to help them get 20 metres of woollen cloth. My father can't turn them down this time.

LIN Well, after all that's been said—

XIAOLAN I don't need much furniture, but I won't go without it either. And when I've set my mind on something, I'll see to it that it is done. That's me through and through.

LIN *[worried]* Do you really think your father will agree to this?

XIAOLAN He's got no choice because I've already bought the furniture.

[A knock at the front door. LIN goes to open it and LI enters.]

LI Xiaolan, hasn't your father come back yet?

XIAOLAN No. Is something wrong?

LI *[pointing to LIN]* Let me speak to him first. Lin, have you spoken to Wang, your Building Supervisor, these last two days?

LIN I talked to him today.

LI What about?

LIN He asked me to give you a message. *[Not happy with the message]* Something about taking over some of your factory's housing units.

LI He must be up to something! Yesterday, he called to ask us if the dormitory block had been completed yet. Yes, I think there's something fishy here. You really should speak to the Director about it.

LIN Yes! I think I will.

[YUAN *and* WU *enter.*]

YUAN [*singing*]

> 'The wilful nobles like wild jackdaws,
> Come before Judge Bao to thwart the law.
> They think I will the Empress's pleading hear,
> I will be just e'en if the Emperor is here.'

Xiaolan, is your mother home?

XIAOLAN No.

YUAN In that case, we can relax a bit. [*Lights a cigarette and takes a deep draw*] Mmm. This is paradise!

[*All laugh.*]

YUAN [*extremely excited*] Wu, you were saying, except for the two fly frames, we've completed all the installation?

WU Yes. If we had had power this last week, at least 30 per cent of the testing would have been finished by now.

YUAN We haven't done too badly then these last few weeks. If we can keep at it, we'll be doing our bit for the 'Four Modernizations', don't you think?

WU I'm keeping my fingers crossed.

YUAN Li, come and sit down. Xiaolan, is our Spring Dinner all ready? Are we having meatballs?

XIAOLAN Dinner's all ready. But no meatballs, I'm afraid. I don't know how to make them.

YUAN Well, it's enough that you prepared the dinner. We'll wait for your mother to come home and then we can eat. We didn't manage to finish our New Year's Dinner, so tonight we shall enjoy every bit of this Spring Dinner. Or, as Wu calls it, [*Imitating her Shanghai accent*] 'Lunar New Year's Eve dinner'.

WU Well done, well done. [*Takes out a packet of candies and two lunch boxes*] Here, I've brought the same things again: a catty of red crumble candy and two dishes from the canteen.

YUAN Xiaolan, would you please take them from Auntie Wu?

[XIAOLAN *takes both candies and food from* WU.]

What do you think, Wu? Can we manage to squeeze some extra time and start production earlier? As you keep reminding me, we lose 836 yuan, 66 fen for each hour of delay.

WU Don't I know it! You're getting restless again, aren't you?

YUAN Well, I was at a meeting in the city yesterday and
several heads of the Finance Committee were pulling
long faces and making worried noises about profits.
How can we not push ourselves harder?

WU *[thinks]* The air-conditioning plant is going to be our
next problem.

LI *[taking the initiative]* Lin, you should tell the Director
what happened.

YUAN What's up?

LIN *[hesitantly]* I talked to Wang, our Building Supervisor,
this morning and he told me to ask you—

YUAN *[attentively]* Yes?

LIN He wanted to know if he could have two of our
factory's housing units.

YUAN *[quiet for a while]* They must be up to something! The
DRC have only just finished their investigations!

LI One more thing. Since Zhao's return to Jiangnan, we've
sent him three telegrams urging him to speed things
up. All we got were telegrams asking us how many
wall panels we would be ordering. There was no
mention at all about our fly frames.

YUAN Hear that, Wu? When the power supply was
reconnected I thought all would be well but now it
looks like that's not the case. Lin, tell me exactly what
Wang said.

LIN This morning he suddenly turned up. And as soon as
he opened his mouth, I knew what he was up to.
Although he said he only wanted use of the housing
units temporarily, it's obvious he has no intention of
returning them to us. But knowing that he's about to
be promoted to Assistant Manager, I didn't want to
offend him and make things difficult for us in the
future, so I promised to pass the word to you.

WU In that case, he must have been plotting this for a long
time. Remember how he urged me to sign the job
completion certificate?

LI Well, what can I say, Wu? There are just too many
clever people around these days!

[XIAOLAN goes into the kitchen.]

WU *[dismayed]* Oh Yuan, I don't understand! I don't
understand!

YUAN I think I do. And I guess it'll be quite some time
before this problem can be resolved.

wu Don't Comrade Fang and her colleagues know about this? Can't they do anything?

YUAN *[shaking his head]* I think they do know what's going on. But, maybe the more they know, the harder it is for them to do anything. *[Bursting out in anger]* Wu, I'll be honest with you. I'm fed up, I just want to say 'no' to every request. If the workshop isn't finished, so be it. If there's nothing to do at work, so be it. I could relax and play card games or even take a long nap! But, the minute I think about the 18-million yuan profit we could be making, or our country's 170-billion yuan deficit—

LIN Well, I'll just go and tell Wang he can't have the rooms. *[Makes to go]*

YUAN Lin! Wait!

LI Wait, wait!

YUAN *[painfully]* I see it all too clearly now. The wine is sour, but I must drink it. Nothing is more important than finishing the workshop to start production on time. Wu, don't you think we should give way just a little?

wu *[angrily]* That's ridiculous! This Wang is a bully and a good-for-nothing. Are you going to kowtow to him? Are you going to renounce all your principles? What about the rights and wrongs of the matter?

LI But the air-conditioning plant will never be finished unless he gets our housing units!

wu *[indignantly]* All right. Then our Director will have to make this decision. *[Exits suddenly]*

LI *[shouting]* Wu! Wu!

YUAN Xiaolan, can you go quickly and ask Auntie Wu to come back!

[XIAOLAN comes out of the kitchen.]

Make sure you bring her back!

XIAOLAN Okay. *[Hurrying out]*

LI Director—

[YUAN paces back and forth uneasily.]

YUAN *[stands still]* Well, I'll just have to put it down to my rotten luck! Lin, tell Wang . . . he can have the rooms.

LIN Right! *[About to leave]*

YUAN But tell him it's disgusting the way he rushed Wu into signing the certificate when the air-conditioning plant hadn't even been finished. And then, to blackmail us like this!

LIN Okay. [About to leave]

YUAN There's more! Tell him that some of our workers have been married for three years and have children, and still they haven't got any housing! And there are other families who still live three generations to a room that's no bigger than twelve square metres!

LIN Right. I'll tell him. I'll tell him all you said. [About to leave again]

YUAN [suddenly] Oh, forget it! What's the use? Just tell him that he'll have the rooms once the dormitory block has been built. I'll make sure of that. And tell him that the air-conditioning plant must be finished first, not because I'm waiting to move in, but because we're waiting to start production.

LIN All right. I'll go and tell him now. [Exits]

YUAN Li, the wine is sour indeed!

LI Indeed it is!

YUAN Li, get out your diary and put this down, now: 'Lunar New Year's Eve, 1980: Yuan Zhicheng and Li Danian together drank a large bowl of sour wine.'

LI [pausing] Director, about Zhao from Jiangnan—

YUAN I'm not in the mood to talk about that now. Let's leave it until tomorrow. Okay?

LI All right . . . But it's only those two fly frames that are holding up the installation.

YUAN I know. I know all that.

LI Okay. There's nothing else then. [Exits]

[YUAN sits down and is about to close his eyes when LI ushers in a travel-stained ZHAO.]

ZHAO [deeply apologetic] I'm really sorry. It's me again!

YUAN [rises to his feet] Good, good. Welcome. Have a seat!

LI Zhao, why are you here on Lunar New Year's Eve?

ZHAO I can't enjoy the Spring Festival anyway if I'm still worried about things. Director Yuan, I'm afraid I've come with my begging bowl again.

YUAN Don't be upset. Relax and let me know what the problem is.

[LI pours some tea for ZHAO.]

ZHAO The leaders of our factory have been meeting night after night but they still can't think of another way round our problem. We're not trying to force you into buying any spare parts. It's just that our factory is small and we are running into all sorts of difficulties.

In fact, we even have trouble paying our workers next
month! Please, help us! Take some of our wall panels
and we'll be indebted to you for life.

YUAN So, what you really mean is, like it or not, we have to
stock some of your spare parts.

ZHAO Frankly, Director Yuan, we're just a small factory with
low-ranking cadres. We have neither power nor
position. If we didn't use our connections, we wouldn't
be able to stay in business.

YUAN And you've set your sights on us, right?

ZHAO We're desperate! We have to use what resources we
have. If we can't rely on a big client like you for help
who can we turn to? Director Yuan, on behalf of the
four hundred workers in our factory, and their families,
let me thank you in advance for your kindness!

LI Calm down, Zhao! Calm down!

YUAN [sighing] Ai! He's left nothing unsaid. But, to ask me
to—

ZHAO Director Yuan, our director has told me that this
problem must be solved. He told me not to go back to
the factory if I can't secure your help.

LI Director, do you think—

YUAN [pauses] All right, we'll do it your way.

LI Did you hear that, Zhao? We'll have the fly frames and
the wall panels together. Just deliver our order at once!

ZHAO Yes, of course. I'll deliver the order as soon as I'm back
at the factory. Director Yuan, thank you, thank you,
thank you so much!

YUAN Go! Go!

ZHAO Goodbye, Li.

LI Bye! I won't see you out!

ZHAO No, there's no need. [Exits]

[Pause.]

YUAN How many bowls of sour wine have we drunk now?

LI Two.

YUAN H'm. This second one isn't too bad. It won't kill us.
All right, you might as well tell me the rest! What
about the raw materials?

LI I was at the lab in the spinning mill yesterday. The
yarn that the chemical-fibre factory sent us was not bad
at all. It had little static and its composition matched
our requirements. It'll make our lives much easier.

YUAN *[with a grimace]* It goes without saying that they want something in return, right?

LI No, they don't. They just wrote us a letter. *[Takes out a letter]*

YUAN I'm listening.

LI *[reads the letter]* 'To facilitate the opening of your factory and to contribute to the "Four Modernizations", we have sent you our best-grade materials in the hope that our two factories may, in future, forge stronger ties, enjoy closer co-operation, learn from each other, and support each other.'

YUAN Would you mind translating that for me? What does he really mean?

LI He's saying—

YUAN Speak up. When the place is full of lice, you don't feel their bites. And when you're hopelessly in debt, you stop worrying about it!

LI In the latest jargon, it's known as 'payment in advance'. You see, we now owe them a favour. When the chemical company gets into trouble in future, even if they don't ask us to return their favour, we'll have to keep their well-being in mind, won't we?

YUAN *[shaking his head]* I get it. They want something for next to nothing. Well, one is never too old to learn. All right, does this count as half a bowl of sour wine?

YUAN, LI *[together]* Two and a half bowls!

[WU and XIAOLAN enter.]

WU *[rudely]* Xiaolan, go into the other room. And you too, Li. Sorry but I need to speak to the Director alone.

[XIAOLAN goes into the inner room. LI exits.]

[in a huff] Comrade Yuan, I want you to transfer me back to Shanghai! At once!

YUAN Relax, Wu, relax.

WU My children wrote to me a month ago asking me to go back to Shanghai. They've made arrangements for me to work as a researcher in the Textiles Research Institute. It'll be satisfying work! Please, Director, let me go.

YUAN *[taken aback]* I can let you go, but I don't think you really want to.

WU No, this time I've made up my mind.

YUAN Deep down, I don't think you mean it. *[Gently]* Wu, tell me what's bothering you. Don't bottle it up. Let's have a heart-to-heart talk, just like in the old days.

WU Well, the way things are going—it makes me feel
   awful. Really terrible!

YUAN I know it was considered revolutionary a few years ago
   to be honest, and even now, it's not easy to tell the
   truth. But forget all that and tell me what's troubling
   you.

WU You know that in the fifties, I took part in the
   'Movement Against the Three Evils' and also in the
   'Movement Against the Five Evils'*. I suddenly feel that
   some of our cadres are now no different from the
   corrupt capitalists and greedy bribe-takers of that
   period. In fact, they're just the same!

YUAN *[reflects a while]* You're quite right. Some of those who
   hunted tigers have now turned into the tigers
   themselves.

WU *[much agitated]* Yuan, you know I'm fast approaching
   the evening of my life. I'm nearly sixty and there aren't
   many days left to me.

YUAN *[nodding]* I know, I know.

WU *[heavily]* The construction of this new workshop will
   probably be the last project I'll ever be involved in.
   In the interests of our factory and our country, I've
   decided to stay here all by myself, and I've forced these
   old bones of mine to work. I'm not asking for too
   much, am I? So, why is it that I'm frustrated again and
   again? Why? *[With tears in her eyes]* I've thought long
   and hard about this, but I just don't understand.

YUAN Calm down, Wu! Calm down!

WU *[rubbing away her tears and taking out a letter]* When I
   got home just now, I thought about this question again
   and I got so upset that I wrote a letter to the
   municipal Party Committee leaders. I asked them
   whether the likes of Supervisor Wang are bound by the
   directives of the Party, especially the one that says, 'All
   Party members, especially senior cadres, should comply
   with the codes of state discipline, labour discipline, and
   work discipline, and should observe the high moral
   standards of the Communist Party'.

   [YUAN takes the letter from her and reads it.]

* The 'Movement Against the Three Evils' took place in mainland China between 1951 and 1952. It was
an initiative to stamp out corruption, waste, and bureaucracy. The 'Movement Against the Five Evils' took
place at the same time to fight against capitalist bribery of government workers, tax evasion, theft of state
property, cheating on government contracts, and stealing economic information for private industrial and
commercial enterprises.

Oh yes, the letter also complains about you. It says you don't have any backbone and are compromising your principles.

YUAN *[finishes reading the letter]* I agree with you totally, Wu.

WU It's my way of showing my loyalty to the Party.

YUAN *[also getting emotional]* Frankly, I'd like to add my signature to this letter. I'd like to join forces with you and raise hell. I want to expose Wang, and to expose myself, too. Yes, I want nothing so much as to set this whole damn thing alight and burn out all the corruption.

WU *[sympathetically]* Yuan—

YUAN But, for now, I can't. I can't!

WU Why not?

YUAN What's more, I must beg you to suppress this letter for now.

WU No, you can't talk me out of it!

YUAN Don't say no just yet. Listen to what I have to say first.

WU *[shaking her head]* No, I won't. I know what you're going to say—that you have no other recourse but to resort to bribery and power politics. I'm sick and tired of these excuses!

YUAN All right, then we won't talk about that today. But Wu, you're a pragmatic person, so let's be pragmatic and talk about your letter.

WU What else is there to be said? I'll send it off whether or not you approve.

YUAN Let's suppose that your letter cuts some ice with the authorities. Even then, judging from the way these cases are handled these days, it will still take months to have our problem resolved.

WU Do you really think so?

YUAN And I'm looking at it from the bright side. It's now the beginning of February. Even if they managed to get everything sorted out by the middle of March, the air-conditioning plant would still have to be finished. Who knows when that will be? There's no way we could meet our April 1st deadline.

WU *[surprised]* I never thought of that!

YUAN Well, it bears thinking about. That's the situation as it stands. No one is happy with it and yet it's so complicated that no one can change it overnight.

[WU doesn't speak.]

Frankly, it was only lately that I managed to force myself to take a hard look at the situation and I've slowly come to a difficult decision. The power supply is our main problem. Since we've already solved that problem, I think we should give way on these minor matters. What can we do otherwise?

WU [*shaking her head*] I don't understand, I really don't understand!

YUAN Do you remember a film made in the fifties called *The Tempering of Aleusha's Character*? Well, today, we have to start tempering our own character.

WU I know what you mean! We have to temper ourselves until all our fighting spirit is gone!

YUAN Wu, I'm trying to be patient. Impatience will ruin everything. If you send out the letter, you'll make things even more difficult. I still believe that we cannot survive without economic success. Shouting and screaming won't help production a bit. For now, the important thing is to ensure that the new workshop unfurls its banner and begins operating.

WU [*after a short pause*] Some of what you said I can accept. But, I still feel so defeated.

YUAN Wu, we have to learn a new skill: to work as normal while feeling defeated. Remember the saying? 'Serious work makes you mad; taking it easy ain't so bad.' Do you drink?

WU I sometimes have a little wine.

YUAN [*laughing*] I'm talking about the sour wine that we drink as we hold back our tears. All right, let's not talk about it any more. [*Gives the letter back to* WU] Keep this as a memento. You can tell this story to your grandchildren. Believe me, they'll take it as a joke!

WU Yuan, you really know how to make light of the hardest situation. I can never hope to rival you.

[FANG *and* LIN *enter.*]

YUAN It's New Year's Eve, how come you're so late?

FANG [*fuming*] When I think about it, I get so angry.

YUAN See? Serious work makes you angry. [*To* FANG] Sit down and have a rest, Fang Jing. Let me tell you something that will cheer you up. If we keep on at the rate we're working now, we'll be able to meet our April 1st deadline. Isn't that right, Wu?

WU Yes.

YUAN The road ahead may be crooked but the future is bright. Lin, tell Xiaolan to come and have dinner.

[LIN goes into the other room and comes out again. XIAOLAN follows.]

YUAN *[takes out a bunch of firecrackers from his pocket]* Lin, take these to the balcony and let them off. Let's frighten away one or two evil spirits.

[LIN takes the firecrackers and goes to let them off.]

Wu, let's have a drink first!

[WU and FANG pour out some wine and raise their cups.]

[raising his cup] What do we care if the wine is sour? Life has got to go on! The road to success is full of obstacles anyway. So, what shall we drink to? H'm, we'll still drink to the prompt opening of the new workshop on the first of April!

ALL Cheers!

[All about to drink when the lights in the workshop go out suddenly.]

XIAOLAN Papa, something's wrong! The power to the workshop has been cut again!

[All rush to the window and look. LI rushes in.]

YUAN Give them an inch and they'll take a mile! They're doing this on purpose! *[Bangs on the table]* I'm going to report them! Fang Jing, this time, there's no need to withdraw into the other room. We'll give you all the details in writing and you go and conduct a thorough investigation for us!

WU The nerve! Yuan, I'm going back to the workshop. Getting us reconnected is more important than dinner. *[Rushes out]*

YUAN Fang Jing, just tell us what evidence you need. Li, write down every last detail for her. Leave nothing out!

FANG *[thinks for a moment]* Calm down a bit, Yuan. It's not that we don't want to do anything, but are you quite sure you want to take them on? If you're ready to make an enemy of these people, we'll start an investigation at once.

YUAN Yes, start the investigation at once. I'm resolved!

LI *[hesitantly]* Director, there's something I don't know if I should tell you.

YUAN Tell me!

LI To report them now. Isn't that a little, hm . . . a little premature? Like mobilizing your army without a good cause?

YUAN This is the second time they've cut our power. Don't you think that's reason enough?

LI But if Ni just grins and says it was an accident, wouldn't that make us look ridiculous?

YUAN *[impatiently]* They are evil! You feel their vile presence, but there's just no way you can pin the blame on them.

LI I don't think now's the time to report them.

YUAN Why not?

LI The Northern Mill started construction of a new workshop at the same time as we did, but they were able to start production yesterday. And today, the Construction Bank notified us formally that if we can't start production on April 1st, our penalty for late repayment is 300 yuan per day. And . . .

YUAN And?

LI The workers have been talking on the trams and in the locker rooms. They're worried that they'll only get small bonuses this year. They're also saying that you . . .

YUAN Yes? Go on.

LI Well, nothing important really. There's no need for you to know.

YUAN No, I want to know.

LI They're saying that you're a stupid, good-for-nothing idiot! They're calling you all sorts of names. *[Pauses]* Let's not mince words. Since you were reinstated, you've managed to keep up good relations with everyone, but the minute you make a wrong move, you'll lose their support. How could you lead them then?

[Pause.]

YUAN *[with a forced smile]* If that happens, I don't think I could still be the Director! I probably couldn't even remain an ordinary party member!

LI Director, rather than going on the offensive, isn't it better to use your guile and tact instead?

YUAN *[pauses a moment]* Fang Jing, what do you say?

FANG If you have no real proof, we can't do very much.

YUAN *[vexed]* Heavens! What the hell is going on? All right, Fang Jing! I have to inconvenience you again and ask you to make yourself scarce. I have to have a good talk with Li.

XIAOLAN Mother, I'll go with you.

[FANG, XIAOLAN, and LIN go into the other room.]

YUAN Li, what do you think should be done?

LI Don't you think we should first find out exactly what Ni wants? If we don't make the right offerings, the gods won't listen to our prayers.

YUAN But what would appease this particular god?

LI Well, he doesn't care for woollen cloth and rugs! Nor do they need housing as they've just constructed a new dormitory building.

YUAN So, what do they want?

LI Director, I think we should ask him to his face. And the quicker the better.

YUAN Mmm. That will at least save us from this damned uncertainty. Well, I guess I'll just have to put it down to my rotten luck again. That's what you get for sweating for the 'Four Modernizations'! Okay, it's decided then. Find Ni as soon as possible.

LI All right.

[ALARM CLOCK hurries in.]

ALARM CLOCK Uncle Yuan, where's Xiaolan?

YUAN She's inside.

ALARM CLOCK [shouting] Xiaolan. Xiaolan. Come here quickly!

[XIAOLAN comes out from the inner room. LIN follows.]

XIAOLAN [delighted] It's you! Have you brought the furniture?

ALARM CLOCK It's all been taken to my house. But this time you must speak to Uncle Yuan about the arrangements.

XIAOLAN Papa, Alarm Clock managed to get me some more coupons and the furniture's already been bought. This time, they asked us to help them get twenty metres of woollen cloth.

[YUAN doesn't speak.]

Papa, woollen fabric isn't controlled material, surely you can agree to that?

[YUAN glances at XIAOLAN and paces up and down.]

LI Director, that's easy. Just nod your head and I'll make the phone call.

[YUAN still doesn't speak.]

ALARM CLOCK Xiaolan, listen to me. This is their final offer. If you can't meet even this requirement, then there's nothing more I can do.

XIAOLAN Papa! Just say the word!

YUAN *[with difficulty]* Child, I . . . I can't!

XIAOLAN What? You won't even do this for me?

ALARM CLOCK Uncle Yuan, you're so inflexible!

XIAOLAN *[anxiously]* You've yielded to so many demands already, why not twenty metres of fabric?

YUAN Okay, I'll let you know my position. When it comes to anything personal, I won't yield at all, I cannot promise even one single skein of yarn.

XIAOLAN Papa, don't you think you're being unreasonable?

LIN Xiaolan, don't talk nonsense!

ALARM CLOCK Xiaolan, let's go to my house. I'll ask my father to help. I can't believe we can't handle this.

XIAOLAN No, I must find out if my father cares about my welfare. Besides, the furniture has already been bought.

YUAN *[resolutely]* I won't budge.

XIAOLAN *[furious]* In that case, I'm leaving this house! *[About to run out]*

LIN *[stopping her]* Xiaolan, don't be foolish!

LI Xiaolan, don't make things difficult for the Director. How about this? I'll take care of everything and we'll forget that the Director ever knew about this. All right?

YUAN *[losing his temper]* I'm not going to do this and no one else will do this either!

XIAOLAN *[shouting]* What? In that case, I'm leaving! *[Picks up her coat and her bag and rushes out of the door]*

[ALARM CLOCK and LIN run after her. FANG hurries in from the other room.]

FANG *[baffled]* Is it Xiaolan? What's happened?

YUAN She wanted to leave so let her leave!

FANG *[shouting]* Xiaolan! Xiaolan! *[Runs after her]*

YUAN See that? You can't even keep your own personal life undefiled!

[LI nods understandingly.]

How many bowls does that make?

LI *[thinking]* Three and a half.

[FANG enters.]

FANG Three and a half bowls of what?

YUAN *[spits out the word angrily]* Poison!

[Curtain comes down quickly.]

ACT 4

[*Morning, a few days after the last act. The scene is* NI's *home in a village on the outskirts of town. He has a new brick house with a tiled roof. One door leads to the courtyard, another to the inner room. The furnishings are a mixture of old village-style furniture and the most up-to-date. There is a large wardrobe, a utility cupboard, wine cabinet, sofa, television, tape-recorder, refrigerator; everything that one could possibly need is there.*

The curtain rises. NI *is sitting on the sofa with his legs crossed, reading his fortune with a pack of playing cards. Pop music is coming from the tape-recorder. A moment later,* NI'S WIFE *comes in with a cup of milk.*]

NI'S WIFE [*puts the milk on the table and switches off the tape recorder*] Hey! When are you going to take me to the city to see *Madame Yang Goes to Court?*

[NI *takes no notice and continues to tell his fortune with the cards.*]

Hey. Lost your tongue? Speak to me!

[NI *still takes no notice.* NI'S WIFE *snatches away the cards.*]

When are you going to take me to the opera?

NI [*lighting a cigarette*] The tickets are sold out.

NI'S WIFE What do you mean, sold out? Can't you nip us a couple of tickets? Does the theatre manager dare to refuse you knowing that you can cut off his power anytime? Come on, when are we going?

NI [*sitting in repose with his eyes closed*] Even if we get the tickets, you know we have no car. Can you stand crowding on to the bus?

NI'S WIFE What about the company car?

NI Who do you think you are? The car is for our Manager, Liu.

NI'S WIFE Cut that crap! Would the drivers dare refuse a request from Nipper Ni?

NI [*snatching back the cards*] Go away! Leave me alone!

[*The telephone rings.*]

[*picking it up*] Hello. Yes, speaking. What's happening with that thing I asked you to help me with? . . . I tell you, I'm doing it for a close relative. . . . The wedding is near, there's no time to waste. . . . Well, I'll be brief. You'll have to do this for me whether you like it or not, and that's the end of it! [*Hangs up*]

NI'S WIFE That was Supervisor Wang at the construction company, wasn't it? That fellow really doesn't know how to get things done. What's the big deal? It's just two housing units.

NI Shut up!

[The sound of LI's voice from the courtyard.]

LI [offstage] Does Section Head Ni live here?

NI [hurriedly picks up the cards and goes into the inner room] Go and answer the door. Tell him I'm not back yet. Do you hear me?

NI'S WIFE I'll see. If he's brought something with him, I'm going to ask him in. [Exits]

NI Her bloody greed will be the death of us! [Goes into the inner room]

[A moment later, NI'S WIFE leads YUAN and LI in. LI has a red rug in his hand.]

LI We're from the New China Cotton Mills. This is our Director, Yuan.

NI'S WIFE Please sit down. Here, on the sofa. It's more comfortable.

[YUAN looks around and sits on a chair. He lights a cigarette.]

LI Is Section Head Ni in?

NI'S WIFE [staring at the rug] Yes, he is.

LI I hear he's not feeling too well.

NI'S WIFE Oh, it is nothing serious. That rug you have looks nice. It's got quite a deep pile, hasn't it? I don't suppose you can get it on the open market?

LI Not really. Coarse-knit goods are in short supply at the moment!

YUAN [impatiently] Li, can we see him or not? We haven't got all day!

LI Yes. Is he—

NI'S WIFE I'll go and get him for you. Now that rug! Wouldn't it be great to warm your feet in, in winter? I've been talking about having a rug for a long time now but Ni keeps putting me off.

LI We brought it along for Ni.

NI'S WIFE [grinning widely] Really? That's excellent. How can I thank you enough? [Hurriedly takes the rug] It's not bad at all! Not bad! How much does one of these cost?

LI It's something the mills sell at exhibitions. Let's see if Ni likes it first. We'll talk about money later.

NI'S WIFE [claps her hands once, her face beaming] That's excellent! Why don't the two of you have some tea and help yourselves to some cigarettes? [Pointing to the table]

There are plenty of filter-tipped cigarettes over there!
Help yourself!

YUAN *[holding back his anger]* Li, if we can't see him, let's go.

NI'S WIFE *[oblivious to* YUAN's *feelings]* Wait. I'll go and get him
now. Oh, isn't this rug just lovely. Ni! Ni!

[NI comes out to welcome them. They stand.]

NI *[pretending to have only just woken up]* Oh, so it's you
two? I was feeling a bit dizzy just now and was just
going to lie down for a while, but ended up falling
asleep! Have a seat!

LI Our Director has been looking for you for a few days
now. Then we heard from someone in your company
that you were ill and that's why we—

NI I'm so sorry that Director Yuan has had to come all
this way! Oh, Li, you should have telephoned me. I
could have popped over to discuss things with you.

[The telephone rings.]

[to his wife] Aren't you going to make some tea and
offer our guests some cigarettes?

NI'S WIFE *[puts the rug down reluctantly, offers* YUAN *a cigarette]*
Director, try these. Here, have one!

YUAN *[putting out his cigarette]* No, thank you. I don't often
smoke.

NI *[picking up the phone]* Hello, speaking. . . . Listen, go and
ask the hostel to prepare a single room at once. This
afternoon, send a nice car to the bus stop to pick up
the guest. What? . . . Yes, that's right. It's Zhao from
the Jiangnan Textile Machinery Factory. . . . Yes, he's
Boss Liu's guest so make sure he's well looked after.
[Hangs up] Director Yuan, have a cigarette. Have some
tea. Make yourself at home.

[YUAN and LI *look at each other in amazement. The phone
rings again.]*

Oh, it's such a bother! I told them I didn't want a
telephone but the company made me install one. They
said it would be more convenient for my job! *[To his
wife]* Tell them I'm not in.

[NI'S WIFE picks up the phone and says that NI *is out.]*

YUAN Li, let's get down to business now.

NI Yes, we will. *[To his wife]* Isn't it time you went to the
market?

NI'S WIFE Don't get up. I have to get some food from the market! *[Puts the rug on top of the chest]*

NI Director Yuan, I really must apologise again. Our distribution plant malfunctioned and we haven't yet been able to locate the fault. Isn't it enough to drive anyone crazy!

YUAN Are you saying you still can't reconnect us?

NI I'm afraid so. It must make things extremely hard for you. I know you're quite desperate but there's really nothing I can do.

LI *[winking at* YUAN*]* Director, didn't you have something else you wanted to say to Ni?

YUAN *[doing his utmost to calm himself down and speaking uneasily]* Ni, tell us exactly what you want and don't beat about the bush! *[As he finishes speaking, he looks down at once.]*

LI *[chipping in immediately]* Yes, feel free to tell us! After all, it's not as if we're total strangers. If you need something and if it lies within our means, we'll be only too glad to help you.

NI *[smiling]* It's good of you to say so. *[Writes something on a matchbox with a ball-point pen]* Although we're not in the same organization, we're really one big family. As Director Yuan said, we make up the front and the rear guard. You can't do without me and I can't do without you. Isn't that right? Well, I'll certainly let you know if there's anything I need.

LI You're sure you need nothing right now? Quite sure? Have another think!

NI Really, there's nothing! All we have to do is fix the malfunction and you'll be reconnected at once! Excuse me a moment. I'll just go and put the kettle on.

LI Oh, don't go to any trouble.

NI You two have come a long way. I can't send you back without at least a drink of hot water. Li, *[Gives the box of matches to* LI*]* light a cigarette for Director Yuan. I won't be long. *[Softly]* We use an electric stove! It's very quick. *[Picks up the water flask and exits]*

YUAN *[overcome with impatience]* Li, how can you bear to sit here like an idiot? *[Standing up]*

LI Patience! Patience! I think we've got a break.

YUAN What break?

LI I think he was trying to tell us something in his last sentence.

YUAN Which one?

LI Didn't he say, 'All we have to do is fix the malfunction and you'll be reconnected at once'? He meant that the 'malfunction' lies with us and that we should fix it quickly.

YUAN [impatiently] What nonsense! [Sits down again]

LI He's trying to find out how far we'll go. Keep your temper a while longer. Here, have a cigarette first.

YUAN I'm not having one of his! [Takes out a cigarette from his pocket]

LI [picks up the matchbox and strikes a match, discovers something, and blows it out] Director. Here's our break! It's on the matchbox!

YUAN What's on the matchbox?

LI What he wrote down just now—'The Workers' University'.

YUAN And what does that mean?

LI Have you forgotten? The textile factories all across the country are going to pool their resources together to set up a Workers' University. I bet he wants us to offer one of our factory's university places to someone he knows!

YUAN [incredulous] You're being too clever again! Be careful you don't make a fool of yourself.

LI [reflecting cautiously] I'm sure I'm right. It's easier to get into the Workers' University than the regular universities. What's more, you still get your salary, and after graduation, your status is the same as other graduates. It's such a great opportunity, it must be what he's after!

YUAN Do you really think so?

LI If not, then why did he write those three words? And why did he make a point of handing me the matchbox! [Imitating NI] 'Light a cigarette for Director Yuan.'

YUAN [standing up] The man is vile! A large factory like ours with a few thousand employees is only assigned a few places, and he's trying to snatch one! Let's go. I'm leaving.

LI [grabbing his arm] I think we should give it a try. In any case, we have more to lose than he does.

YUAN [with great reluctance] How?

LI It's no good being direct so we'll have to talk around it. [Hears Ni coming back] Listen, he's coming back!

YUAN *[grudgingly]* If that's what you want, then you do it!
[NI *enters.*]

NI Here, have some hot water. *[Pours out the water]* Oh, are
my cigarettes not good enough for you, Director Yuan?

LI No, the Director's heart isn't too good and he has to
cut down.

NI Yes, you should look after your health.

LI Ni, we wonder if you could help us.

NI Tell me. If there's anything I can do—

LI Our factory is helping to set up a Workers' University.
We haven't filled all the places yet. If you know of
anyone suitable, would you let us know?

NI Oh. So that's it. All right. I'll ask around for you.

LI *[not letting up]* You know so many people. Don't you
have someone suitable in mind? The Workers'
University wants the places to be filled before teaching
starts.

NI Let me see. . . . Let me see. . . . Ah! I've got such a
rotten memory! *[As if someone suddenly springs to mind]*
Well, it just so happens there's someone who could fill
the place, but he may not be suitable.

LI Who is it?

NI I was at the company the other day and heard that the
son of one of our comrades wanted to get into the
Workers' University. His age and qualifications are
about right.

LI Perhaps you could arrange an introduction?

NI But he's just an unemployed youth waiting for a job.
He's not from your organization. No, it wouldn't be
right.

LI *[egging him on]* Don't worry, he could work in our
factory for a while first.

NI Is that so? Wouldn't it violate our labour policy?
Director Yuan, it wouldn't be right, would it?

YUAN *[candidly]* If I fix it for you, then what about our
power supply?

NI Well then, I'll fix it for you, too. I'm not boasting, but
all it would take is a word from me.

YUAN *[holding back his temper]* So whose son is it?

NI Well, I don't suppose there's any need to insist on
anonymity. You see, he's our manager's son, Manager
Liu.

YUAN *[nodding his head]* I get it now.

NI *[complacent]* Good. I never lie to my friends and I'll
come to the point. Earlier on, when they kicked up
that big fuss about those who violated the 'Code of
Practice', we had to lie low to avoid the blitz. But now
that it's all over, it's time to stock up on our winter
stores! After all, the economic principles of socialism
are based on barter and exchange!

YUAN *[rising abruptly to his feet]* Let me tell you, I will never
exchange anything with you, even if the sky were to
fall down!

NI Li, eh . . . look . . .

YUAN No, look at you! What you're proposing is extortion,
corruption, the subversion of justice and the sabotage of
the 'Four Modernizations'!

NI Director Yuan, it's your man Li who brought it up, not
me. We should stay on good terms. If you can't do it,
then you can't do it, and we'll forget about it. There's
no need to upset our good relations.

YUAN Upset what good relations? Whose good relations?
When I see how you have blackened the name of the
Communist Party, I feel terrible! I can't stand it!

LI Director—

NI *[sincerely]* All right, let's all speak from the heart. I've
been meaning to offer you a word of advice: your way
of doing things may have worked before 1957, but it's
completely out of date now! Unless you become more
flexible, you won't be able to move an inch! When you
understand this, then you'll understand everything!

LI *[trying to stop him]* Ni—

YUAN Let him finish!

NI You may have heard that everybody calls me 'Nipper
Ni'. But how did I earn that name? Do you think I
wanted it? No! *[Hits the rug]* It all happened because
people have been sucking up to me all these years. Let
me tell you, after ten years of suffering, everyone has to
learn to be smart, to take, to pinch, to nip. Even you,
Director, you will become a nipper sooner or later!

YUAN *[enraged]* Nonsense! Do you think our great country is
just a school for people like you? Let me tell you, no
honest person would ever become like you, not in a
lifetime! People like you exploit your position for
personal gain, bleed your organization dry just to line
your own pockets. You're worse than nippers. You're
rats that gnaw away at the foundations of socialism.

Tell me, what level cadre are you? How much money do you make in a month? Do you dare tell me where you got all these things? Do you dare? *[Points to all the furnishings around the place]*

NI *[somewhat intimidated]* Where did I get them? Why, where do you think? I worked hard for them, of course! All right, I can see you don't care for my advice. Anyway, what's the use of talking to someone who has his eyes fixed on the past, you can only see if you look ahead. If you won't listen to me, so be it. We'll see who's right! I must excuse myself now, I have to go to the clinic for an injection. *[Hurries out]*

LI *[shouting]* Ni! Ni!

YUAN Let him go! *[Pacing up and down in anger]*

LI Director, do you think—

YUAN *[stops pacing]* I've been trying very hard to keep my temper all along! *[Goes to the wine cabinet and pulls aside a cloth to show all kinds of wine]* Do you know what this is? This is someone's blood, sweat, and tears. No true member of the Communist Party could come in here and not fly into a rage!

LI But this matter . . . our electricity . . .

YUAN Electricity can go to hell! I'd rather go without it than to be like him! He abuses his office just so he can live comfortably! He makes a mockery of the law and has nothing but contempt for our Party discipline! Come, let's go!

[As YUAN and LI are about to leave, MA YUXIU rushes in.]

MA Is this Section Chief Ni's house?

LI *[surprised]* Ma, why are you here?

MA I wanted to talk to Ni. It's urgent!

LI He's gone to the clinic for an injection.

MA *[after some hesitation]* I'll go and look for him there. I must talk to him today!

LI *[to YUAN]* We used to be neighbours. She works at the Electric Company.

MA Uncle Li, why are you here?

LI Why? Because of the electricity supply, of course!

MA Yeah, I know. No wonder people compare us to the district court in the feudal days, the 'yamen'. We're indeed a court of sorts, nobody can do without us and nobody can afford to offend us. And Ni is one of the tyrants in our 'Electric Court'!

LI *[noticing from* MA's *expression that something is wrong]* Why
are you looking for Ni?

*[*MA *bursts out crying with a 'Wah!'.]*

Hey, what is it? This is our Director, Yuan. Tell us
what's wrong!

MA Uncle Li, I . . . I've been cheated!

LI Easy, easy! Tell me slowly.

MA Last year, I asked Ni to help my husband to get
transferred here. He said he knew the person who
stamped all the documents at the labour office and
asked me for 300 yuan—

LI And?

MA Not only has he done nothing up till now, I can't even
get to see him! Uncle Li, Director Yuan, this 300 yuan
wasn't easy money for us. The two of us together don't
make 100 a month, and we have a child and an ageing
mother! Uncle Li, I've scrimped and saved to get the
money! *[Cries even harder]*

LI And what are you going to do now?

MA When I find Ni I'm going to make a stink until I get
a satisfactory answer from him! *[Rubbing away her tears]*
I can't allow my hard-earned money to be devoured by
a wolf! *[Hurries out]*

YUAN *[beside himself with anger]* Let's go, Li. We'll gather all
the evidence and file a complaint against Ni.
Tomorrow, we'll hand it to Fang and her colleagues!
Let's go! *[About to leave]*

LI *[not moving and with some anxiety]* Do you think we're
doing the right thing? Director, don't you think you
should think about it more carefully?

YUAN *[returning]* Li, why . . . Why do you try so hard to be
like them? Why do you waste your time racking your
brains to decode their sleazy, circuitous, miserable
tactics? And then nose your way after them like a dog?
Does that make you feel good? Gloried? Turn you on?
Uh?

LI *[aggrieved]* Director . . . I . . . I . . . If it wasn't for the
electricity . . .

YUAN Are you saying I've wronged you? Come on, you're too
old to be snivelling like that. *[Loudly]* Let's go! If I
don't get away soon, I'm going to start swearing!

*[*YUAN *hurries out.* LI *cradles the rug and follows him. A
moment later,* NI *and his wife enter.]*

NI'S WIFE *[carrying a bundle of chives in her hand]* Hey, are they really gone? *[Discovers that the rug has gone too]* Aiya! How could they do this? My rug! My rug!

NI Go away! Go! What do you know about anything! *[Picks up the telephone]* Is that the Electric Company? Get me Manager Liu. . . . What? Oh, it's you. . . . Ni here. Manager, I have to report an emergency—

[Curtain falls.]

ACT 5

[A month later, sometime in early March.

Inside YUAN's *office. For a Director's office, it is extremely plain. Because it's on the second floor, the new workshop can still be seen. One door leads to the corridor, another into the next room. The wall facing the audience is full of charts and diagrams setting out the factory's eight economic targets. Apart from a desk and a small sofa suite, there is also a single bed put up in the corner. Simple blankets cover the bed. This is where Yuan often sleeps at night.*

The curtain rises: YUAN *is pacing up and down excitedly.* FANG *is holding a small handbag and sitting in front of the desk. She has obviously only just arrived.]*

YUAN *[elated]* So you've finally finished investigating?

FANG Yes.

YUAN Did we win?

FANG You could say that.

YUAN *[goes to the calendar]* One month! A quick battle and a quick resolution. The DRC really did a good job this time! Fang Jing, *[Giving her the thumbs up]* everyone should marry a cadre from the DRC!

FANG What nonsense!

YUAN You really deserve a big thank-you! Oh dear, I have nothing here. Well, have a cup of tea at least! *[Pours out a cup of tea]*

FANG Oh, come on! Let's get down to business!

YUAN *[sits behind the desk]* Have the documents been released?

FANG Yes, I came here specially to deliver them to you!

YUAN Good. I'll get Wu and Li as well.

FANG *[nodding]* Sure.

YUAN *[talking on the phone]* Hello, I want the Chief Engineer's office. *[To* FANG*]* Can you go next door and get Li?

FANG Okay. *[Goes into the next room]*

YUAN Is that Wu? It's Yuan. The DRC has dealt with our complaint against the Electric Company! . . . Yes. Fang Jing has brought over the papers. Come here now and we'll listen to her report . . . Be careful you don't trip over in your haste! Ha ha! *[Hangs up]*

*[*FANG *enters.]*

YUAN Is Li in?

FANG He'll be here at once. Oh yes, Alarm Clock just called me.

YUAN *[with concern]* Was it about Xiaolan?

FANG She's managed to persuade Xiaolan to come back home today.

YUAN *[delighted]* Oh, good. I know I haven't been able to take care of things this last month and have had to rely on you to do all the work. Here's another cup of tea in appreciation. *[Pours out some tea]*

FANG When she comes home, you should have a good talk with her.

YUAN Of course. *[Starts to softly hum the song from the Hebei opera]*

[WU and LI enter. YUAN waves them to sit down. FANG takes out her papers.]

YUAN *[extremely excited]* Wait. Today is such a special occasion, may I smoke while we listen?

WU *[laughing]* Comrade Fang, look the other way just this once!

FANG All right. Just one cigarette and no more!

YUAN Yes, just one. *[Winks at LI]* Li, give me a cigarette!

LI *[surprised]* But, you . . . *[Understanding dawns.]* Oh, yes, of course. *[Gives him a cigarette]*

YUAN *[lighting it and smoking]* Okay, let's start!

FANG To be honest, the DRC has placed great importance on this case and we worked round the clock on it, which is why we managed to deal with it so quickly. *[Opening the documents]* Now, I'll read out the comments of the comrade in charge of the investigation. He wrote: 'Liu of the Electric Company has no respect for anything. He flouted the Party's discipline and the laws of the state and was corrupt in all his dealings—'

YUAN Read that again! Read that again! He says it so well!

FANG 'Liu of the Electric Company has no respect for anything. He flouted the Party's discipline and the laws of the state and was corrupt in all his dealings. His shady deeds are causing direct damage to the "Four Modernizations". If he is not dealt with severely and with due gravity, there can be no way of addressing the indignation of the people—'

WU Hear, hear!

FANG *[continuing to read]* 'This case has once again reinforced the words of Comrade Deng Xiaoping: "We should not allow even a day's delay in implementing the 'Four Modernizations'. At the same time, we should not allow even a day's delay in the work of the Discipline Review Commission."'

WU That's very proper. Exactly what I feel in my heart.

YUAN Let her finish.

FANG 'After a careful investigation by the Discipline Review Commission, a report was submitted to the Municipal Party Committee for approval. It was decided that Manager Liu would be publicly censured and disciplined with an internal warning from the Party.'

WU *[deeply moved, rises to her feet and shakes* FANG's *hand]* Comrade Fang, thank you so much! Truth has prevailed and righteousness has triumphed.

LI Director, it's a pity there are no firecrakers left over from the Spring Festival.

YUAN Why's that?

LI This is the perfect time to set them all off and celebrate!

WU You're right!

YUAN Hold on! Our country has been suffering these last few years from an economic imbalance. True, the total output of electricity has increased, but demand for power still far exceeds supply and that makes life very difficult for those working at the Electric Company. It would be wrong for us to flaunt our victory in their faces. And that's especially true of the two of us, Li.

LI *[nodding]* Yes.

YUAN But enough of this chat. Let's get back to business. Wu, tell us what's the next step.

WU As soon as we're reconnected, I'll set up three teams to run simultaneous tests on the machinery. If we run them in three non-stop shifts, we can start production on May 1st for sure.

YUAN *[decisively]* All right, let's do it! Li, you will help Wu in every way you can. Give her whatever she requires and put all our resources at her disposal. If we don't manage to start production by midnight on May 1st, the three of us might as well hang ourselves from the nearest tree! Wu, don't you agree?

WU Absolutely!

YUAN After all, the DRC have given us so much support, we've got to have something to show for ourselves. Fair's fair. Fang Jing, set aside May 1st to attend our opening ceremony. And I believe my observation is still valid: the road ahead may be crooked but the future is bright!

WU *[rises to her feet]* All three of you are Party members and you . . . you've made me feel deeply touched. Once again, I can see the Party's glorious tradition in the three of you. I feel as if I've come home. I . . . I want to give you something. It's been on my mind for many years.

YUAN What is it?

WU I'll go and get it now.

YUAN Why such a hurry?

WU I must give it to you at once. *[About to go]*

[The sound of a car pulling up can be heard through the window.]

LI *[looking out of the window]* Director, you've got visitors. It looks like the Electric Company's car.

YUAN Li, give the new workshop a call now and tell them they'll be reconnected very shortly. Tell them to assemble everyone so that Wu can explain to them the new testing schedule.

LI Right! *[Makes a telephone call]*

[LIU and NI enter.]

NI Director Yuan, this is our manager, Liu.

LIU *[moves forward and takes the initiative to shake hands with* YUAN*]* Comrade Yuan, I've come to offer you my apologies!

YUAN Let me introduce you. This is Wu, our Chief Engineer.

LIU *[shakes hands with* WU*]* Wu, I'm deeply ashamed!

YUAN This is Li, our Office Supervisor.

LIU *[shakes hands with* LI*]* I know I must have made things very unpleasant for you!

YUAN This is Comrade Fang, Deputy Secretary of the Discipline Review Commission at the Municipal Light Industries Office.

LIU I have long heard of your name. *[Shakes hands with* FANG*]* I appreciate your criticisms and your denunciation. You have shown us the error of our ways.

YUAN Come and sit down.

LIU *[sitting down]* Yuan, with one hard blow, you've shown us how we've strayed from the path of integrity and enabled us to retreat from misfortune's snare. Comrade Fang, I've just been to the Electric Company to declare my position. I'm now here to make it known to you, too. I've learnt my lesson well. I will accept any punishment you care to meter out and I promise you I'll never make the same mistake again.

NI Yes, I've learnt my lesson as well and will mend my ways.

LIU Ni's faults were certainly very serious. To have disconnected your supply twice without consulting his superiors! It was quite unforgivable!

NI I must accept most of the responsibility.

LIU Of course, as the commanding officer, I'm the one to be blamed. It does not befit the Manager and the Secretary of the Party Committee to have acted as I did. Comrade Yuan, I've already had a word with the Union Supervisor and he's going to organize a showing of the film *The Tribunals* for the staff in our company. This will give them a better example of the high moral standard of the Party.

YUAN Liu, you've really fallen flat on your face this time. But as the old peasants say: 'You grow wiser every time you fall'. If you can learn a lesson, then nothing is more precious than the prodigal's return! Now, let's talk about the future, shall we?

LIU We've already made some arrangements for you. *[To NI]* Correct?

NI Yes, yes.

LIU I wanted to discuss this with you personally, but I've still got two important meetings to attend. Perhaps you could talk to Comrade Ni about the details?

YUAN That's fine by me.

LIU I'm really sorry about this. But I'll be pleased to go over any questions you may have after you've talked with Ni. *[Rising to his feet]* Yuan, Comrade Fang, from now on, if you find out that any of my staff is doing something dishonest, please take any action you think is suitable, even if you have to bypass their supervisors. We would welcome it! Shall we make this a gentleman's agreement? Good! Goodbye! *[Shakes hands with everybody]* Thank you once again for granting me the opportunity to make my self-criticism. Oh, please get on with your discussion, there's no need to see me out. *[Exits]*

YUAN Ni, tell us your arrangements.

NI *[taking out some documents]* I have two documents here. Would you please take a look at them. This one is from the Tourist Office. They've brought forward the date when they will start receiving overseas visitors. The other concerns the early opening of the tourism building.

YUAN [*baffled*] What's the meaning of all this?

LI Why don't we discuss that after you've read them?

[YUAN *and* WU *look over the documents.*]

Briefly then. You'll understand that this means the Foreign Affairs Department, in other words the Politburo, will require electricity. I don't need to point out that if there's a power shortage, or if the supply so much as falters, I'll be severely disciplined.

YUAN What's that got to do with us?

NI It's got everything to do with you. You're on the same power grid as the new Tourism Building. They've been given top priority to be connected and, once we've done that, we can't really guarantee to keep up the supply to you.

LI Then, what are we to do?

NI We've already set up a special team to tackle the problem of voltage increase. As soon as that's done, you'll be the first to be connected.

YUAN [*patiently*] And how long will that take?

NI I can't say. It could take half a day, but if things go slowly, then it might well take three to six months. But external affairs do command our attention first, don't you agree? Well, Director Yuan, if there's nothing else, I'll take my leave now.

LI [*anxiously*] You—

NI [*looking resigned*] Li, we should look at the overall situation. Nobody would doubt that tourism is very important to us right now.

LI Director—

YUAN [*waving his hands*] Let him go.

NI Wait for the good news then, Director. [*Exits*]

[*Pause. It seems as if the looms in the workshop are becoming louder and louder, making the people in the room more and more annoyed. The telephone rings.*]

LI [*answering the phone*] Hello. Yes. Who is it? . . . Section Head Zhao! How are you? It's Li here. . . . What? You can't deliver the fly frames just yet? . . . Why not? . . . Hello. Hello. [*Hangs up*]

WU [*concerned*] So the fly frames won't be arriving?

LI Zhao only said he couldn't go into details on the phone.

YUAN It never rains but it pours!

[LIN *rushes in.*]

LIN Uncle Yuan. I don't know why, but Supervisor Wang came looking for me early this morning. He said he wouldn't turn over the finished air-conditioning plant until he got the housing units. He didn't even explain why he'd gone back on his word.

LI *[baffled]* What's happening today? Nothing has gone right!

[The telephone rings. LI picks it up.]

Hello. Speaking. . . . Please wait.

[To YUAN] Director, it's the new workshop. They say that everyone's already assembled. When is Wu going to address them.

YUAN Dismiss them!

LI Hello, can you dismiss them for now. *[Hangs up]*

YUAN *[banging the table and standing up]* Fang Jing, I'm going to report him again. *[Pacing up and down]* I can't believe there is nothing we can do!

FANG It did cross my mind that if we didn't manage to rein him in, it might make things worse for you, but I never thought the repercussions would be so serious! *[Hangs her head in shame]*

WU *[goes to her]* Comrade Fang—

FANG To think that the Deputy Secretary of the Discipline Review Commission, and a cadre to boot, would turn out to be merely a paper tiger! I feel so ashamed! *[Tears run down her face.]*

YUAN *[after a short pause]* I don't understand! This is blatantly wrong and yet he struts around and is able to get away with murder! In the twinkling of an eye, he overturns the DRC's findings and gives you a vengeful blow in passing. What do we have laws for? What for?

WU *[exceedingly agitated]* Oh, Yuan! I really want to go back to Shanghai now. I do!

YUAN Wu, why don't you tell me what's really bothering you?

WU *[after a while]* To be perfectly honest, I've lost all confidence. I don't know any more if the Party's decisions still carry weight or if its directives are still effective. The way the Party has been trying to curb all these unhealthy tendencies in our society, don't you think it just makes things worse?

FANG I take your point, Wu. But you mustn't lose your confidence.

WU Fang, Yuan, I've been with the Party for thirty years
now and, in all that time, I've rarely lost confidence in
the Party. Even now, it causes me great pain to say
what I've said, you should know that.

YUAN *[also getting more and more upset]* It's not right! I'm
going to call Manager Liu. *[Goes to the telephone]*

LI Director—

YUAN *[his hand on the telephone]* The Party has been paralysed
for over ten years and their traditions and policies have
been reduced to nothing. It doesn't surprise me that
some people should have forgotten what the Party
stands for, but he's an old guard, he should know
better. When the Party is corrupt, then society mirrors
that corruption. He should be able to see that, even if
others can't. That upstart Ni is able to wield power
simply because of the events of recent years. But are we
going to play deaf and blind then? If we cut our ties
with the Electric Company, does it mean we'll be left
high and dry? No. I'm going to ask him, without
pulling rank, as one Party member to another, whether
he still has any respect for the principles and ideals of
the Party.

FANG *[with agitation]* Yuan, you have my full support. Call
him and ask him.

LI Director, I don't think there's any use.

YUAN It's my duty to speak to him even if nothing comes of
it. I'm not going to lose my temper, and I don't care if
he accepts what I have to say or not. I just have to
speak my mind. If I keep it inside, it'll fester like a
cancer. *[Dials]* Give me the Electric Company.

[Lights fade.]

[Lights go up again. It's the morning of the next day.]

*[YUAN has a light overcoat draped over his shoulders. He's
fast asleep, sprawled over his desk. It's obvious he has worked
through the night again. A moment later, WU rushes in.]*

WU *[loudly]* Yuan! Director! Quick! Wake up! Wake up!

YUAN *[waking up with a start]* What is it, Wu? What's
wrong? *[Stands up and goes to the door]*

WU *[smiling and shaking her head]* No, nothing's wrong! It's
good news! Wonderful!

YUAN *[puzzled]* Good news?

WU Yes, news so good you'll sing your favourite song
again!

YUAN Oh come on, tell me quickly!

WU Come and see for yourself! *[Goes to the window and draws the curtains]*

YUAN *[sees at once that the lights are on in the new workshop]* Great! We've been reconnected! Come on, let's go and have a look!

WU All right! All right!

[LI rushes in.]

LI Director, I've got good news!

YUAN *[laughing]* Young man, you're too late! Wu beat you to it! *[Points to the window]* Right?

LI *[excitedly]* There's more! Zhao just called and said that the fly frames would definitely arrive today!

YUAN Good. This is double happiness indeed!

LI There's more!

YUAN More?

LI Lin also called. Apparently Supervisor Wang has agreed to finish the air-conditioning plant first!

YUAN Excellent! We've got a triple happiness now! *[Happily lights a cigarette]* Wu, Li, are you sure we're not dreaming? Pinch yourselves and see if it hurts!

WU You must be joking! How could we be dreaming?

LI I can't believe our luck either. I wonder if—

YUAN *[laughing]* Ha ha! All I did was to make a phone call. Mind you, it lasted for forty-five minutes, but I was all patience. There was no ranting and no raving. I just explained everything to him gently. And look at the result!

WU Oh, you're talking about Manager Liu—

YUAN Well, Wu, old comrades are still old comrades after all. All these years of being a Party member hasn't been for nothing! There's an unwritten rule in the Party: if you make a mistake, be sure you put it right. When you've put it right, then everything's all right! I really want to call him again. No, I should find time to go and have a real talk with him. No one is a saint anyway. It's all too human to make mistakes.

WU True, true!

YUAN *[suddenly remembers something and takes out a diary from his drawer]* Li, did you leave this on the desk yesterday?

LI *[taking the diary]* Yes, I've been looking for it.

YUAN Don't be angry but I've glanced through it.

LI That's all right, there's nothing secret in it.

YUAN *[apologetically]* Li, I've wronged you! I'm sorry I lost my
temper with you at Ni's house—

LI *[graciously]* It doesn't matter. You were angry and
worried at the time.

YUAN Wu, on the face of it, this fellow seems so keen on
using connections, going through the backdoor, you
name it. But in fact, he's been damning them to hell
in his diary! *[WU nods understandingly.]*
[pats LI on the shoulder with deep feeling] Li—

LI *[after a short pause]* There must be many people like me
nowadays.

YUAN *[thinking]* These days, it seems that everyone is shaking
their fists at corruption and yet they all seem to find it
impossible to stay honest!

WU And therein lies the root of the problem.

LI Or maybe the answer to it!

YUAN *[nodding]* Well said! You're becoming a skilled arguer.
Let's go to the workshop and arrange for the machinery
to be tested, the sooner the better!

WU Sure!

LI Let's go!

YUAN *[singing again]*

'The wilful nobles like wild jackdaws,
Come before Judge Bao to thwart the law.'

[ALARM CLOCK enters.]

Yes? Alarm Clock?

ALARM CLOCK *[pouting]* I wanted to sneak off from work to watch a
restricted film, but my dad told me to bring this letter
to you.

YUAN So that's why you're sulking? Where's the letter?

ALARM CLOCK *[taking it out]* Here it is. Oh yes, he said it was good
news.

YUAN Well, well, today's a day for good news! *[Reads the
letter]*

ALARM CLOCK Uncle Yuan, now that you've got the letter, I have to go!

YUAN *[becoming serious]* Wait! What time did your father give
this to you?

ALARM CLOCK Just now. He told me to bring it over straight away
and said you'd feel more relieved when you'd read it.

WU *[with foreboding]* Yuan, what's up?

YUAN *[shaking his head]* I never thought it'd turn out this
way! Never!

LI *[concerned]* Is it the electricity again?

YUAN *[angrily]* It's much worse than that. *[Gives the letter to LI]*

LI *[reading it]* What? Some bigwig has instructed him to give Liu's son one of our places at the Worker's University!

WU *[surprised]* Really?

LI So the phone call the Director made was a total waste of time!

YUAN *[suddenly]* Some bigwig assigned a place to Liu's son. Who was that? *[To ALARM CLOCK]* Did your father say?

ALARM CLOCK I really don't know. Well, I better go to see that film now. *[Looks at her watch]* Oh, it's going to start soon. *[Hurries out]*

[YUAN lights another cigarette and, from habit, paces up and down.]

WU *[frustrated and angry]* So that's it for our effort! That's it for the DRC's intervention! And that's it for your long talk over the phone! They've all come to nothing! And all because this bigwig has signed his name on some document. Isn't that so?

YUAN *[struggling to control himself]* Well, we've all learnt our lesson now. If you want to work for the 'Four Modernizations', it's not enough to put everything down to your rotten luck, you've got to be obsessed with your rotten luck, feel drawn to it, completely besotted with it, like someone head over heels in love. You don't let a day pass without thinking of it, missing it! Damn! Wu, no wonder people say that hard work is easy but frustration will kill you! *[With tears in his eyes]* I'm sorry to speak so ominously, but if the 'Four Modernizations' is just going to make people die from exasperation, we will soon need a mass memorial service!

LI Director—

YUAN *[grimacing with pain]* Sooner or later, I'm going to find out who assigned our university place to Liu's son. *[Wipes away his tears]* Let's go! We have to test the machinery.

[All three go outside.]

[Curtain comes down quickly.]

ACT 6

[July 1st, 1980. It's the day of the opening ceremony for the new workshop. Inside YUAN's home.

The curtain rises: YUAN has been ill the last few days and is resting in the inner room. It is XIAOLAN's wedding day and she is wearing a wedding dress. ALARM CLOCK is anxiously calling LIN on the telephone.]

ALARM CLOCK Hello. Lin? Guess who? It's Xiaolan. *[Mimics XIAOLAN's voice]* When are you coming over? Ha ha! . . . Hey, our bride is all ready and waiting. Can't you be any quicker with the car? You shouldn't keep us waiting like this. . . . Yes. Okay . . . If you're late, you won't get off lightly! *[Hanging up and speaking to XIAOLAN]* I've made all the arrangements. The car will be here in a quarter of an hour.

XIAOLAN *[glances over at the inner room]* Shh! Not so loud!

ALARM CLOCK *[also looks at the inner room]* Is your father—

XIAOLAN *[nods]*

ALARM CLOCK Come on! Let's get ready. *[Suddenly remembering something]* Oh, the red flower! You must remember to wear the red flower. *[Picks up a red flower from the table and pins it on the bosom of XIAOLAN's dress]* Isn't it nice? This is the bride's trademark!

[The phone rings, ALARM CLOCK answers it. WU enters.]

XIAOLAN Auntie Wu.

WU Well, how's the bride? Are you all ready?

XIAOLAN Nearly. Have a seat.

WU *[taking XIAOLAN's hand]* I've been thinking long and hard about your present. I didn't buy you anything fashionable, but I thought you might like this scroll to remember me by. *[Takes out a scroll]*

XIAOLAN Thank you, Auntie Wu.

[ALARM CLOCK hangs up.]

ALARM CLOCK What's this? Open it. Let's have a look.

XIAOLAN *[opening it and reading]*

> 'Holding firm to the mountain,
> My roots grip the rocks well.
> Undaunted by trials,
> I dare the winds that hurl.'

WU Do you like it?

XIAOLAN *[nodding]* It's a poem about bamboo, isn't it?

WU Yes.

ALARM CLOCK Oh, is it a poem? Auntie Wu, you're such a scholar, I'm afraid I don't have the slightest idea what it means.

WU I did the calligraphy, but the poem was written by Zheng Banqiao.

ALARM CLOCK *[remembering something]* Oh yes, Xiaolan, the Light Industries Office called to ask your father to wait here. Chief Zheng will be coming here to talk to him about something urgent.

XIAOLAN Okay. I'll go and tell him.

WU How's your father, Xiaolan?

XIAOLAN Not too good.

ALARM CLOCK I don't know why, but he wears a long face all day and loses his temper at the slightest thing. Oh yes, and he says he's not going to Xiaolan's wedding.

WU *[nodding her head understandingly]* Isn't your mother at home, Xiaolan?

XIAOLAN She's attending a DRC meeting. She hasn't been back for days.

[ZHAO enters.]

ZHAO Wu, how are you?

WU *[surprised]* Oh, Zhao! I thought you'd gone back to your factory.

ZHAO I'm leaving now. I've got the train ticket already.

WU Is anything the matter?

ZHAO I wanted to speak with Director Yuan. Xiaolan, do you think—

XIAOLAN *[to ZHAO]* My father isn't feeling well.

ZHAO I won't keep him long. Just a few words and then I'll be off.

XIAOLAN All right then. I'll go and get him. *[Goes into the inner room]*

WU Have a seat.

[ALARM CLOCK pours a cup of tea for ZHAO.]

ZHAO *[courteously]* Thank you.

[YUAN enters. XIAOLAN follows.]

YUAN Zhao, you wanted to see me?

ZHAO Oh, Director Yuan, I have to let you know what's on my mind, I can't rest easy until I tell you.

YUAN Here, sit down. Take your time.

[XIAOLAN and ALARM CLOCK go into the inner room.]

ZHAO *[suddenly]* Director Yuan, you're still being kept in the dark. Do you know who it was that got into the textile Workers' University through the backdoor?

YUAN Why? I thought it was the son of the Electric Company's manager, Liu.

ZHAO *[shaking his head vigorously]* No, it wasn't him at all!

YUAN Then who was it?

ZHAO It's our director's future son-in-law.

YUAN Your director's future son-in-law? Are you sure?

ZHAO Yes.

YUAN *[puzzled]* Does this mean that Manager Liu has some sort of connection with your director?

WU But they've got nothing to do with each other!

ZHAO It's a long story, you'll have to be patient with me. *[Takes a deep breath]* Manager Liu comes from the town where our factory is. See? Manager Liu has two nephews who live in the county and are earning their living in one of the rural communes. See? Manager Liu has long wanted to have his two nephews transferred to our factory as workers. See? Our Director had two vacancies in his recruitment quota but was reluctant to give them away for nothing. See? Our Director's future son-in-law is looking for work right here. See? So, they struck a deal. The two nephews joined our factory as workers, the son-in-law got into the Workers' University. Manager Liu and his two nephews are happy. Our director and his daughter's fiancé are happy. Everyone is satisfied!

WU Oh dear! It's too complicated, too complicated!

YUAN *[pouring out some tea]* Here, have a drink.

ZHAO *[taking a sip and speaking painfully]* Director Yuan, Wu, the goals you work towards, and your hopes and aspirations are so different from theirs! Before I made up my mind about coming here, I kept asking myself whether there was any point in letting you know the truth and whether any good would come of it. And I had a good mind not to get involved. But the more I thought about it, the more I knew that come what may, I am still a cadre and have been with the Party for a long time. . . . *[Suddenly]* Director Yuan, Wu, please don't tell anyone what I've just told you. You could get me into deep trouble. I have to go now. Goodbye!

YUAN [shaking ZHAO's hand warmly] Comrade Zhao, I thank you from the bottom of my heart.

WU Take care, Zhao!

ZHAO Goodbye. Goodbye! [Exits]

[Pause.]

YUAN [with deep feeling] Wu, you remember that legend about General Wu Zixu, how his hair turned all white overnight in a series of crises? I suppose that could well be true. What Zhao has told us—well, stories like that really hurt. They shorten a man's life.

[ZHENG enters. YUAN and WU greet him together.]

Hello, Zheng. Looking for me?

ZHENG Ah yes. [Changes the subject] Where's Xiaolan? She hasn't left yet, has she?

YUAN No, she's still here.

[XIAOLAN and ALARM CLOCK enter.]

ZHENG Oh good. I'm still in time. [Taking out a pair of fountain pens] Here. I bought these pens overseas. It's just a small present for you.

YUAN Xiaolan, say thank you to Uncle Zheng.

XIAOLAN [taking the fountain pens] Thank you, Uncle Zheng.

ZHENG [waving his hands] It's nothing. I didn't have time to buy anything. I only heard this morning that you were getting married! Congratulations.

YUAN Thank you! Sit down, Zheng. You have something urgent to talk to me about?

ZHENG There's no hurry. [Sits down]

ALARM CLOCK Uncle Zheng, didn't you also give me a pair of fountain pens like that for my wedding?

ZHENG Yes. I brought them back the first time I went overseas on a study tour.

ALARM CLOCK [teasing] Are you worried that we don't study hard enough?

ZHENG Cheeky! [Laughing] So Yuan, how are you?

YUAN I'm all right. What urgent business brought you here?

ZHENG There's no hurry. I haven't finished offering you my congratulations! I must congratulate you, too, on the opening of the new workshop. For all the setbacks, you've finally managed to start production. That's no mean achievement! Oh, by the way, I have some good news for you. Secretary Zhang from the Municipal Party Committee will be taking part in today's opening ceremony, it's going to be a grand event! *[Takes out a bulletin]* Here's the bulletin the Light Industries Office produced to help with your publicity.

YUAN There's something I really have to ask you, Zheng. Who was it that permitted Liu's son to jump the queue for the Workers' University?

ZHENG Do you really need to know? The whole thing is already over and done with.

YUAN You still don't understand me, do you? I was stubborn as a child and I'm stubborn as an adult.

ZHENG Aren't you worried you might create more trouble for yourself?

YUAN When I don't understand what's going on, that's when I feel troubled.

ZHENG So you want Fang Jing to investigate this further?

YUAN That would be letting him off lightly!

ZHENG Wu, look at your director. His temper hasn't improved at all! Well Yuan, if you really must know, then I'll tell you. It was me.

YUAN *[flabbergasted]* You?

WU Was it really you?

ZHENG That's correct. I authorized it.

YUAN *[unable to contain himself]* How could you, Zheng? Not only did you not support us, but you did your best to cut away the ground from under our feet!

ZHENG Come on, my old friend. I was helping you to shore up your ground. If I hadn't stepped in and made that decision, your workshop wouldn't have been able to start production, not even by the end of the year! And there wouldn't have been any opening ceremony today. I also had to put in a lot of good words for you before Manager Liu finally agreed, very grudgingly, that the Tourism Building and your workshop would be connected at the same time. You have no idea at all of what this all involved, do you?

YUAN *[a little stupified]* Today is supposed to be a happy occasion, but I just want to cry.

WU So do I!

ALARM CLOCK Come on, Uncle Yuan, cheer up! Today's Xiaolan's wedding day, a time for joy and happiness. Why are you still in such low spirits? You'll only upset Xiaolan. Is it worth it?

ZHENG See how the child is trying to cheer you up! You shouldn't take things so seriously. Look at the big picture. At the worst, you've overstocked on ten thousand yuan worth of spare parts, given out two housing units and, as for that boy who jumped the queue to get into university . . . that can't be worth more than twenty thousand, can it? But as soon as the new workshop starts production, you'll be able to recoup this sum with just a day's earnings. You haven't made a loss, old fellow, you've made a profit! Come on, let's go.

WU *[candidly]* I feel really old and useless. I can't move with the times!

YUAN *[suddenly]* Zheng, I too have done some calculations and counted the cost.

ZHENG *[surprised]* Oh? *[Looks at his watch]* All right, tell me, tell me.

YUAN I'm a foolish old man and I've done some foolish calculations. *[Trying his best to calm himself down]* The ten thousand yuan worth of spare parts, the two housing units, and that place at the university you've given away—none of these did I include in my calculations.

ZHENG *[amazed]* Why?

YUAN Because these things pale by comparison with what I did include.

ZHENG Oh?

YUAN *[getting more and more indignant]* Since we had to bribe our way through this, that, and the other network to get the workshop up and running, production was delayed by a whole quarter of a year. What does this work out to in terms of working time? Three threes are nine. That's ninety days. And time is money. So what are the financial implications of ninety wasted working days? Well, to begin with, three months of bank interest at 300 yuan a day—that's 27,000 yuan. Then there's three months' worth of production. By Wu's calculations, that's 20,000 yuan a day—so it's 1,800,000 yuan in all. If we add the two together, it's enough to build another new workshop!

[All are taken aback. ZHENG lights a cigarette and smokes it slowly.]

WU That's the correct way to calculate our losses. *[To ZHENG]* I agree with him!

YUAN The figures weren't just pulled from my head. I've checked them and gone over them many times. Yes, we have lost a new textiles workshop fitted with the latest machinery. Like a magician's trick, it has vanished into thin air. And who has conjured it away? Where has it gone? Has it been bombed by our enemies or burnt to the ground by the counter-revolutionaries? No! There's been no trace of any bomb or even the glimmer of a flame. It's disappeared into the hands of some of our dear comrades. It's been lost and wasted by those heartless, brainless good-for-nothings who idle away their time laughing, joking, swaggering around, and scratching each other's backs. Our country is poor enough as it is. Can she still survive such horrible devastation?

[Pause. YUAN gets even more indignant.]

These things at least can be calculated. But what about those that can't? *[Pointing to his brain]* Here, how much damage has it sustained? You just can't measure it. If we carry on like this, what is at stake is not the speed with which the 'Four Modernizations' can be completed, or even the success or failure of the 'Four Modernizations'. What is at stake is the very survival of the Communist Party. These aren't my words, they're the words of Comrade Chen Yun.

XIAOLAN *[agitated and worried]* Papa, please don't say any more.

YUAN *[kindly]* Xiaolan, and you too, Alarm Clock, I really don't want to see this terrible disease infecting your generation.

XIAOLAN *[wanting to say something]* Papa, I—

YUAN Zheng, I know you probably don't see eye to eye with me, but what I've said is really—

ZHENG *[nodding his head]* Mmm. Yours is certainly another way of looking at things.

WU *[deeply moved]* Yuan, what you said is true. Very profound.

YUAN Oh well, we won't talk about this anymore. *[Changing the subject]* Isn't the car here yet?

XIAOLAN *[with remorse]* Papa, I . . . I . . .

YUAN *[bemused]* What's the matter with you? You're leaving home today. Is there anything you want to tell me before you go?

[LIN enters.]

LIN The car's here.

ALARM CLOCK Xiaolan, let's go.

YUAN If you have nothing to tell me, then it's time for you to go.

ALARM CLOCK Come on. I'll get your things. *[Picks everything up]*

[XIAOLAN still hesitates.]

LIN Let's go now.

ZHENG Xiaolan, Lin, let me wish you both a long and happy life together! *[Shakes hands with XIAOLAN and LIN]*

LIN Thank you.

XIAOLAN Thank you. *[Holding back tears]* Papa—

YUAN My child—

XIAOLAN *[reaches the door and stops]* Papa, I can't go yet! I did something dreadful behind your back. I have to tell you before I leave.

YUAN All right, tell me.

ALARM CLOCK Aiya! Why don't you tell him after your wedding? There are guests waiting for you.

XIAOLAN *[resolutely]* No, I have to do it now. You don't know, Papa, but I used your name and pulled a few strings to buy my furniture.

LIN And I agreed to it.

ALARM CLOCK Uncle Yuan, it was all my doing. I'm the one you should punish.

XIAOLAN No, Papa. I deserve a scolding, a severe scolding! . . . And a good beating too. You've never given me a beating. *[Bursts into tears]*

YUAN *[holding back his tears]* How could I raise my hand against you? You're grown-up now, Xiaolan. I'm so happy for you! *[Pauses]* Off you go, all of you.

XIAOLAN All right. I'll go now, Papa. Don't forget to take your medicine.

YUAN No, child, I won't forget.

ZHENG Cheer up, Xiaolan! Don't cry on such a happy occasion!

[XIAOLAN, LIN, and ALARM CLOCK all exit.]

WU Yuan, I have something to say to you.

ZHENG Excuse me a moment! *[Goes to the desk to write something]*

WU *[takes out an application to join the Communist Party]* Comrade Yuan, today is the anniversary of the founding of the Party. I've thought about this for a long time and I've decided to hand you this application. I want to join the Communist Party.

YUAN *[taking it and looking at it]* Oh, Wu, that's marvellous!

WU *[passionately]* I was much moved by your speech just now, especially that part about Comrade Chen Yun's warning. It made me feel that when all's said and done, the Communist Party is still the Communist Party. . . . I know that the Party faces tremendous difficulties now and needs all the firepower it can muster. Well, they're welcome to what little I can contribute.

YUAN *[shaking hands with Wu]* Comrade Wu Yijian, the Party will be delighted to welcome you.

WU All right. I'm going to take a look at the new workshop. Goodbye, Zheng.

ZHENG Goodbye. Goodbye.

[WU exits.]

Yuan, there's something you should know.

YUAN What?

ZHENG The Light Industries Office has decided to promote you to Assistant Manager of the Cotton Textile Company.

YUAN *[stunned]* This is entirely unexpected!

ZHENG Age catches up with all of us, old man. Your health isn't too good, you can't fight on the front line for the rest of your life! Ever since the New China Mills were built twenty-five years ago, you've been sweating and toiling hard at this place, and there's no denying that you've made a valuable contribution to the factory's expansion. You can rest assured that you've earned your place in history.

YUAN Stop talking in circles and tell me straight. Are you doing this because I don't care a damn which way the wind blows? Have I become a liability?

ZHENG Come on, take the good news for what it is. Don't you worry, I've made all the arrangements for you. Now that you're in your sunset years, we'll make sure you enjoy a comfortable life. You can take my word for it!

YUAN I'm not in my dotage yet! I promise you, I'll step aside when I reach sixty. But, for the moment, I'll fight any evils to the death!

ZHENG *[brings over the note that he had been writing]* Do you know the famous saying of Zheng Banqiao?

YUAN No, I don't. I only know that he was good at painting bamboo. The paintings raise your spirits.

ZHENG *[pointing to the note]* 'It's not easy taking it easy.' You have to learn to take things easy sometimes.

Understanding is hard to come by, but taking it easy is even more difficult. And it's worse having to take it easy when you understand what it's all about!

YUAN *[putting the note on the coffee table]* Communist Party members aren't trained to appreciate this kind of philosophy. Did you ever stop to think about the consequences of your actions, Zheng? Fang and her colleagues reported the doings of the Electric Company to their superiors and managed to get the support of the Party Committee. You're the head of the Light Industries Office and yet you gave them no support at all. Why?

ZHENG *[shaking his head]* It's easy for you to criticize.

YUAN *[not letting him off]* You still don't realize what you've done, do you? With one stroke of your pen, you've allowed someone to jump the queue. Do you know how many dedicated comrades you've hurt? Do you know how you've inflated Ni's and Liu's corrupt egos? Let's be painfully honest. You're more of a headache than 'Nipper Ni' and you're even more difficult to deal with.

ZHENG *[displeased]* Are you saying that I'm the chief culprit?

YUAN As the saying goes, if the top beam is not straight, then the house will be crooked. Do you have the determination to clean up your own house and make it absolutely spotless? Do you have the courage to declare that we stand inviolate against all corrupt practices? Are you brave enough to do that? Are you?

ZHENG I sympathize with your feelings and I even agree with what you've said—

YUAN That's good. We've both dirtied our hands with this new workshop. Can we examine our mistakes and start again? Can we?

ZHENG But who will the Municipal Finance Committee chase after when it's time for the year-end dues? Me and nobody else! You're ready to defend your 1.8 million yuan profit to the death. Don't you think I should also defend to the death our revenue of 250 million?

YUAN Defend! What are you going to defend it with? Tell me, Zheng, in the history of the Communist Party, has anything ever been accomplished that wasn't directed by a top cadre?

ZHENG Don't give me the Party line!

YUAN I know it's not easy these days to stand by our principles but that doesn't mean we should just drift with the tide. If we do that, how can we ever bring the Party back on the right track? How can we revive society's conscience? The central authorities have stressed again and again the need to carry out the directive on the 'Code of Practice'—why is it that the Light Industries Office hasn't been able to enforce it?

ZHENG You tell me.

YUAN It's because you're too weak. Your backbone's not stiff enough.

ZHENG You . . . *[Looks at his watch]* Let's leave it at that. Come on, we have to go. It's nearly time. We can't cancel the opening ceremony!

YUAN *[explodes]* I'm not going to the opening ceremony. I'm going to lodge a complaint with the Municipal Party Committee.

ZHENG Against whom?

YUAN *[bluntly]* Against you! And against myself!

ZHENG *[after a slight pause]* All right. You have the right to do that. But, I hope you will think before you act.

YUAN I've been thinking about this for six months now. There's no point sitting there uttering fine words. The longest journey begins with a single step. My mind is made up. It's time for me to take action. If I get no joy from the Municipal Party Committee, then I'll go to the Provincial Party Committee, then to the Central Committee. If one year is not enough, I'll take two years, or even three. After all we were able to rout the eight million strong Kuomintang army in three years, I just don't believe that in three years, we can't put a stop to this evil.

[He is about to walk out when FANG *and* LI *hurry in.]*

FANG Zheng, I want a word with you.

ZHENG What's up?

FANG *[to* LI*]* All right Li, you tell them.

LI Yesterday, Fang asked me to go to the Electric Company to have a word with Ma and the technicians in the transformer plant. It was only then that we found out that the new Tourism Building and our factory are actually on two separate power grids. So the reason we didn't have any power was all because Liu and Ni were up to their old tricks again!

ZHENG *[astonished]* Can this really be true?

FANG Well, Zheng, a full report regarding the misfortunes at the new workshop has already been presented to a forum we convened for the DRC. *[To* YUAN*]* Li has given me his notebook and it has provided us with just what we needed.

YUAN Well! Li—

ZHENG *[taking notice]* Oh . . .?

LI Director, I really couldn't stand it anymore. Even the workers in our Power Section have put their names to a letter to the DRC denouncing the Electric Company's actions.

FANG Zheng, even if you kick me out of the Commission, I have to get to the bottom of this. That lot have broken our laws, made a mockery of Party discipline, and spent their time taking vindictive revenge on those who tried to fight them. If we give in to them or try to appease them, we'll be doing a grievous wrong to our people.

ZHENG All right, all right. Well, Yuan, we have to go and attend the opening ceremony now. Secretary Zhang will be arriving soon and it would be rude of us not to be there.

FANG Secretary Zhang has decided not to come.

ZHENG *[completely taken by surprise]* Really?

FANG *[taking out a note]* And he asks you and Yuan to go and see him at the Party Committee.

ZHENG *[looks at the note]* All right. *[To* YUAN*]* Let's forget about the opening ceremony then.

YUAN Li, tell Wu to make sure that the machinery starts operating on schedule.

LI I will. I'm going now. *[Exits]*

FANG Yuan, I have to go and see how Xiaolan is doing. There's hot water in the flask. Why don't you two have some tea before you go. *[Exits]*

ZHENG *[after a short pause]* Yuan, I don't need any tea. But I suppose I do need a whip.

YUAN What for?

ZHENG To save them the trouble of whacking me when I appear before the Committee. I can do it myself.

YUAN I think I should come with you.

ZHENG *[laughs]* Old fellow, why would they want to whack you?

YUAN I did go to someone's house with a rug under my arm. Well, let's go. We'll take your car.

ZHENG *[shaking his head]* No, you go first.

YUAN *[after a short pause]* All right. As you wish. *[Exits]*

[ZHENG sits down and lights a cigarette. He closes his eyes and rests his head on the back of the chair.]

[Curtain falls slowly.]

THE END

UNCLE DOGGIE'S NIRVANA

1986

By
JIN YUN

Translated by
YING RUOCHENG

— ABOUT **THE PLAYWRIGHT** —

JIN YUN (Liu Jinyun, 1938–) graduated from the Chinese Department of the Beijing University in 1963 and taught for a while in a middle school outside Beijing. He took part in the 'four clean-ups' movement (a nation-wide movement to clean things up in the fields of politics, economy, organization, and ideology, 1963–6), but was purged during the Cultural Revolution (1966–76) and spent many years living and working with the peasants, from whom he drew inspiration for most of his works. In 1979, he was transferred to the Propaganda Unit of the Beijing Municipal Party Committee, and he started writing fiction in his spare time. In 1982, he was transferred to the Playscript Division of the Beijing People's Art Theatre and became a full-time playwright. He is noted for his ability to portray the peasants with humour and compassionate detachment. He has written five full-length plays, the most successful of which is *Uncle Doggie's Nirvana*. First performed by the Beijing People's Art Theatre in 1986, the play has been translated into German and Japanese and has received high critical acclaim not only in mainland China but also in Hong Kong, Macau, Taiwan, Singapore, and the United States, where it featured as part of the programme for the 1988 International Arts Festival in New York. In 1992, it was performed in English at Virginia University in the United States, with Ying Ruocheng as the translator and the director.

Jin Yun is now Party Secretary, First Deputy Head, and a National Grade 1 playwright of the Beijing People's Art Theatre.

ABOUT THE PLAY

Uncle Doggie's Nirvana falls into the general category of 'socialist-realist drama'. However, the playwright also employs expressionist and symbolist techniques, weaving Time Present and Time Past into a seamless web. The play portrays a peasant's life, from the early years of Communist rule—when the landlords were purged and their land redistributed to the peasants—to the more liberal economic atmosphere of the post-Mao era, in which a 'get-rich-quick' mentality prevails amongst the Chinese people. The drama focuses upon the plight of the protagonist, nicknamed 'Uncle Doggie', as he struggles to adjust to the dramatic changes in his fortunes over the years.

Because Uncle Doggie's dilemma is presented with a fine sense of control—and devoid of sentimentality, hysteria, or rancour—his sufferings become a moving testimony of the irreparable damage done to the peasants by the policies of the extreme left. The play thereby conveys a powerful denunciation of such policies.

The playwright's sympathies for the peasants, however, do not prevent him from also exposing their weaknesses. Jin Yun, through his subtle delineation of Uncle Doggie's consciousness and humorous portrayal of his behaviour, produces a complex study of the psychology of the peasants, and an incisive critique of their conservatism, imperviousness to change, and inward-looking mentality.

── **DRAMATIS** PERSONAE ──

UNCLE DOGGIE (Chen Hexiang), a peasant
QI YONGNIAN, the landlord (and his apparition)
LI WANJIANG, a villager, at one time a Communist Party cadre, and later head of the village and leader of the production brigade
SU LIANYU, a villager who once owned a piece of land; he is also a travelling barber and has seen something of the world
FENG JINHUA, UNCLE DOGGIE's wife
CHEN DAHU, UNCLE DOGGIE's son
QI XIAOMENG, DAHU's wife and QI YONGNIAN's daughter

Time: The Present, with flashbacks.
Place: A small village by the side of the mountains, northern China.

THE **PLAY**

SCENE ONE

[Time: the present—one night in the 1980s.
Total darkness on the stage. Gradually, in the flickering light, the towering outline of an old grey brick arch can be seen.
The persistent sound of scratching. Then a match flashes, catching fire. In the flash which dies out immediately in the wind, UNCLE DOGGIE can be seen. 'Doggie'—the somewhat inelegant nickname has stuck with him all his life, all 70-odd years, a reminder of his own and his father's miserable lives. The men, young and old, seem to have forgotten his real name, Chen Hexiang. By now he is doddering, hoary, but seems like a beast at bay, watching, searching, and waiting for his chance. He strikes another match, which blows out again.]

UNCLE DOGGIE Shit! Just my damned luck. Even the damned matches don't work. Ain't that evil . . . just evil . . .

[He strikes another match and it catches. He lights a torch made of straw and branches. Behind him the apparition of QI YONGNIAN appears. QI blows at the torch and, with a whistling gust of wind, the torch in UNCLE DOGGIE's hand is blown out.]

[turns around in shock, then quietly] Oh, it's you?

QI YONGNIAN It's me.

UNCLE DOGGIE You're not alive.

QI YONGNIAN No . . . not alive.

UNCLE DOGGIE You're a ghost.

QI YONGNIAN Yes . . . a ghost.

UNCLE DOGGIE Why are you here?

QI YONGNIAN Because you miss me.

UNCLE DOGGIE Why would I miss you?

QI YONGNIAN Because . . . you're lonely. At your age, the people you miss are conjured up just by thinking of them.
[Pointing at the arch] You're going to burn it, just like that?

UNCLE DOGGIE Yes, I'm going to burn it.

QI YONGNIAN Arson's against the law.

UNCLE DOGGIE It's my son's property, I can burn it.

QI YONGNIAN My daughter has a half share.

UNCLE DOGGIE I'll finish that too!

QI YONGNIAN Burn it, finish it. You're finished too, aren't you? Ha ha ha!

UNCLE DOGGIE What are you laughing at?

QI YONGNIAN You.

UNCLE DOGGIE Why?

QI YONGNIAN Because you never had it as good as I did.

UNCLE DOGGIE Me? Never had it as good as you? *[With contempt]* Me? Never?

QI YONGNIAN Well, Doggie, you never measured up. I lived behind that arch; I was known as the big shot with a big fat purse. When I died—not exactly under happy circumstances, it's true—I was still the big shot who owned fifty acres of land, so I can lie in peace. And you? You got the arch, but you'll burn it now. You know what that's called? You can't make a wolf out of a wolf's hide!

UNCLE DOGGIE Get out of my sight, you stinking landlord!

QI YONGNIAN We are in-laws, remember?

UNCLE DOGGIE I never recognized the relationship, you foul my doorstep!

QI YONGNIAN Just look at the two of us, at loggerheads all our lives. Time to make peace. The young couple over there are planning for the good life. . . .

[The lights go up on CHEN DAHU, *in his late 30s, and* QI XIAOMENG, *in her early 30s, on the other side of the arch.]*

QI XIAOMENG That arch means the world to your dad. Do you dare touch it?

CHEN DAHU When a broken-down cart blocks the way, it has to be removed.

QI XIAOMENG He made such a scene this afternoon.

CHEN DAHU *[lowering his voice]* Old people are easy to bamboozle.

QI XIAOMENG Not your dad.

CHEN DAHU He's no different from anybody else. This afternoon I told him that we had to sell the arch to pay off old debts. *[Normal voice again]* He's been ill for twenty years; we have to sell the arch to pay for his medicine.

[UNCLE DOGGIE and QI YONGNIAN listen carefully.]

QI YONGNIAN Did you hear that? Sold!

CHEN DAHU We'll tell him tomorrow that it's been sold. Then we can tear it down.

UNCLE DOGGIE Tomorrow? I'm going to burn it down tonight! Oh, I'll feel so good, I'll be satisfied; I'll have settled the score . . . I'll . . .

QI YONGNIAN Burn it! Burn it! Make some real fireworks! Burn it!

UNCLE DOGGIE What are you so gleeful about? A miserable landlord with only fifty acres! Small timer! You've not seen anything grand. Now, let me tell you, I've been a big shot. I was . . .

QI XIAOMENG The old man seems to have gone to bed.

CHEN DAHU High time. He's made enough trouble.

QI XIAOMENG Old people can sometimes be such a pain. First they become sharper; then the older they are, the more obstinate they get; and then they become more and more difficult. Your dad is one of them.

CHEN DAHU All they think of is money.

QI XIAOMENG You think you're any better? Look at yourself! You run around like a headless chicken all day, and by the time you come to bed, you're a wreck!

CHEN DAHU Who am I doing all this for? My job is to earn the money, and you are the box I keep it in. My safe box!

QI XIAOMENG Enough of that. Better go and see what your dad is up to!

QI YONGNIAN Hee hee! You couldn't earn a rich man's fart! And you talk about being a rich man . . .

UNCLE DOGGIE I was a rich man! Your Uncle Doggie won a medal for his harvest.

QI YONGNIAN Come off it! We all know you made your fortune by stealing the sesame harvest from my land.

UNCLE DOGGIE Hah! What do you mean your land? When the cannons started blasting, you cowards ran off, and deserted the village. *[In rapt reminiscence]*

[The distant rumble of cannons is heard.]

All that was left was this endless expanse of a golden harvest, ripe with grain—it made my heart glad, my eyes open, and it was ready for my hands! Now, who was there to take it? I was! It belonged to Uncle Doggie! Oh that life was a life worth living! Ha Ha!

QI YONGNIAN Typical! These peasants! They'll hold on to the little they have even if it kills them! Ha! Ha! Ha ha ha!

[Voice of CHEN DAHU *calling his father urgently, 'Dad! Dad!' The laughter and the voices recede as the sound of gunfire grows louder.]*

BLACKOUT

SCENE TWO

[Time: flashback to the civil war between the Kuomintang and the Communist Party, 1946–9.

Sound of distant gunfire interspersed occasionally with near shots. Behind UNCLE DOGGIE, *a great expanse of ripe crops, ready for the autumn harvest.* UNCLE DOGGIE's *white hair is gone and he is in his robust prime.]*

UNCLE DOGGIE People make fun of me. They say that in bed I see only my wife, out of bed I see only my shoes, and out of doors I see only the good earth—that's not true! The good earth is not like a wife, it never throws tantrums, it doesn't go to the fairs and temple gatherings, and it's never cross. If your young wife is not happy with you, watch out! She puts on airs, won't let you touch her, pretends to be shocked at your perfectly natural demands, turns her face away and leaves you staring at her cold back. Now, the good earth is always so yielding, so soft, anyone could plant it, reap from it. When the big guns started firing, my wife took our child and ran off, as though her tail was on fire. The rich ran off, too, as well as the poor. But the good earth did not run off; it kept me company. Such a harvest! And there was only me left, and a little cricket that didn't fear death. . . .

[Two spotlights, one on either side of the stage, rise on the faces of CHEN DAHU *and* QI YONGNIAN's *apparition, still in the present.]*

QI YONGNIAN Fate deals out our life and death, hardship, and wealth. Don't be so smug. A wolf's hide never makes a wolf out of a dog!

CHEN DAHU That was probably the proudest moment of my father's life. I was told about it when I was in the cradle, and about it again when I was learning to walk. Now, if you have nothing else to do, go and listen to him. For me, once is enough. With banknotes rolling all over the place like fallen autumn leaves. I have better things to do!

[The lights fade on figures on left and right.]

UNCLE DOGGIE Well, shouldn't I have reaped the harvest? To let such a ripe and heavy crop go to waste is a sin that has to be answered for on the day of reckoning! Look at it! Such lovely cereal! And such good stock. *[Indicating the field]* 'Top-heavy Gold', 'Drumsticks,' 'Phoenix's Nest,'

'White-of-the-Eye,' and, ho ho, a shortie, but what
huge spikes—that's the 'Pig-lifting-her-Leg.' Put it in
my basket and it's my meal . . . Phew! You clodhopper,
sorghum ain't good grain, have too much of it and you
have trouble shitting. Now, this corn is different,
'Golden Queen!' Hey, what have we here? Sesame!
Fully ripe, ready to burst, long stalks, the 'Tyrant's
Whip'! This belongs to the Qis. What a stretch of
land. At least five hundred yards! When I worked for
him it took more than half a day to hoe one furrow.
And now all the Qis are gone, vamoosed. Who owns it
now? Uncle Doggie! What am I waiting for? *[Hacks
down the sesame]* Damn it, this is what I call life. After
the sesame we'll dig for the peanuts, and after that the
sweet millet—so when New Year comes, we'll have
plenty of sweet cakes . . . *[Sound of cannons]* 'You
miserable bastard, you don't give a damn about your
own wife and kid!' That's how my wife cursed me
when she ran off with my boy. But I figured if she was
not marked for death, she'd come back alive. If she
was, a bomb would get the two of them and not me.
But then if they got lucky and came back alive, what a
lot of fine oil they'd have! *[Hacking and muttering]*
Nothing ventured nothing gained. If you lock up the
kid, you can't trap the wolf; if you lock up the wife,
you can't trap the monk; if you lock up the . . .

*[He recedes into the depth of the stage. The cannonade dies
out.]*

SCENE THREE

[Time: after the civil war, in the immediate years after the Liberation. QI
YONGNIAN *is back from his life as a refugee and ready to settle accounts with*
UNCLE DOGGIE.*]*

QI YONGNIAN *[viciously]* A wolf's hide never makes a wolf out of a
dog! Doggie! Hey, Doggie—
*[*UNCLE DOGGIE *enters.]*

UNCLE DOGGIE *[complacent, even swaggering, humming a tune from some
local opera]* 'Took me eighteen years to secure the throne
in the capital . . .' Tell you the truth, being a landlord
ain't easy. It's hard work! I nearly broke my back
trying to move those thirty bushels of sesame around.

[*Correcting himself at once*] You clodhopper! You may not have tasted pork, but you've seen pigs, haven't you? You'll grow into the part. When the time comes you are going to be Mr Chen, Esquire! Just like Qi Yongnian. Look at him, all year round dressed in his silk gown and brocade jacket, clean shoes and socks, never lifting a finger to do any work, always riding a donkey when he goes out and feasting on salted turnips dipped in sesame oil every damned day . . . Now, there, who is it? Greet me properly by my full name—the name is Chen Hexiang!

QI YONGNIAN [*with contempt*] The cannons brought you luck, sonny boy, didn't they? You got quite a harvest, eh?

UNCLE DOGGIE You said it! [*Mysteriously*] I'll be honest with you, the pots and pans, basins and bowls, even the inside of shoes are filled with sesame oil. You know what I found out? You really can have too much of a good thing. It's not only that your stomach can't take it any more, but too much oil sets you running to the outhouse.

QI YONGNIAN [*expressionless*] Out with it, how much do you want for your wages?

UNCLE DOGGIE Wages? What wages?

QI YONGNIAN You harvested my crop of sesame, right? I should pay you wages.

UNCLE DOGGIE Oh, that. Three acres of sesame. I risked my life for that. You want the sesame? It costs a life.

QI YONGNIAN Let me tell you this: the landlords' militia will be back any day now.

UNCLE DOGGIE And let me tell you this: the People's Liberation Army is over there, just across the river.

QI YONGNIAN The sesame belongs to me, it was on my land.

UNCLE DOGGIE The sesame belongs to me, it's in my pocket.

QI YONGNIAN There is such a thing as the law.

UNCLE DOGGIE The law was blown away by the cannons.

QI YONGNIAN You born scoundrel, you son of a bitch!

UNCLE DOGGIE Don't you abuse me.

QI YONGNIAN I blame it on your ancestry—your father was a son of a bitch.

UNCLE DOGGIE *Your* father was a son of a bitch!

QI YONGNIAN Can you deny it? Don't we all know? Didn't your father make a bet and eat a puppy alive, just for a miserable bit of land? And didn't he lose his life and earn you the name Doggie?

UNCLE DOGGIE *[truculently]* That's because my dad had no land. He
　　　　　　loved land, but he had none. Your dad, was he no son
　　　　　　of a bitch? Was he born with an inscription on his
　　　　　　forehead saying 'Big Shot'? Phew! Fifty years ago when
　　　　　　Guangxu was the Emperor, and there was that great
　　　　　　flood, every inch of land was flooded, not a blade of
　　　　　　grass was above water, but somehow, on the roof of
　　　　　　your house, above the flood, there grew those beautiful,
　　　　　　two-foot high corianders. I don't understand it to this
　　　　　　day, how all those corianders could grow on your
　　　　　　bloody roof-top.

QI YONGNIAN You foolish boy, the roof-tops were all plastered with
　　　　　　mud, and it must have been the god of fortune who
　　　　　　made my father mistake a bag of coriander seeds for
　　　　　　the usual wheat husks.

UNCLE DOGGIE My dad heard the story. So the next year, when we
　　　　　　plastered our roof-top, he mixed the husks with seeds
　　　　　　of coriander, pumpkin, and squash and, of course, it
　　　　　　didn't rain for forty-nine days! We made offerings to
　　　　　　the god of fortune as usual, but it would have done
　　　　　　more good if we had fed the seeds to the dogs.

QI YONGNIAN There, it all comes down to your father's cheap
　　　　　　pedigree.

UNCLE DOGGIE Your father's pedigree was no better, but his corianders
　　　　　　weren't cheap. The big restaurants paid ten cents a
　　　　　　stem for the stuff! That's how your family got your
　　　　　　fifty acres of land.

QI YONGNIAN Sure that's how we got them, that's how we got rich!

UNCLE DOGGIE So you got rich! It's my turn now. And how!

QI YONGNIAN You are doing it the crooked way!

UNCLE DOGGIE I earned it with the sweat of my brow, what's crooked
　　　　　　about that?

QI YONGNIAN Oh, shut up and hand over the sesame!

UNCLE DOGGIE Like hell I will!

QI YONGNIAN A dog will always be a dog. You're behaving just like
　　　　　　you did when you let my prize mule fall into the well
　　　　　　that year—

UNCLE DOGGIE Was that my fault? I was hired to work on your land.
　　　　　　You never gave me any rest. You never gave the poor
　　　　　　beast any rest either, and it became so tortured with
　　　　　　thirst it threw itself into the well! For that, you
　　　　　　hoisted me up on the Qi family arch and had me
　　　　　　whipped with ropes, ropes soaked in water. My skin
　　　　　　and flesh healed and grew again. But I couldn't get

over the way you ruined my brand new jacket, of handwoven cloth, fresh from the loom. My beating paid for the mule, but you still owe me my jacket! Pay me back!

QI YONGNIAN Stop pestering me! Hand over the sesame and I'll call it quits.

UNCLE DOGGIE You can forget the sesame. There's no way I'll hand it over.

QI YONGNIAN I own the land! Don't you forget that.

UNCLE DOGGIE When the cannons started roaring, you fled. I own the land now!

QI YONGNIAN I own the land!

UNCLE DOGGIE I own the land!

[Deafening gunfire, LI WANJIANG appears, rifle in hand, running. He is in his late 20s and the leader of a militia unit in the People's Liberation Army.]

LI WANJIANG Who owns the land?

UNCLE DOGGIE [pointing at QI YONGNIAN] He does!

LI WANJIANG [admonishing] Listen carefully, you fugitive landlord Qi Yongnian! Go home now, make a complete list of your liquid assets, get the title-deeds of the land you own, and be ready for the struggle meeting* and the people's final verdict.

QI YONGNIAN [in panic] Yes—Comrade.

LI WANJIANG Behave yourself, no tricks!

QI YONGNIAN No, Comrade! [About to go]

UNCLE DOGGIE [arrogantly] Come back here!

QI YONGNIAN Yes.

UNCLE DOGGIE Behave yourself, no tricks! You may go.

QI YONGNIAN Yes, Comrade. [Exits]

UNCLE DOGGIE [with happy excitement] Brother Li Wanjiang, have our troops fought back?

LI WANJIANG Yeah, we fought back.

UNCLE DOGGIE Are we liberated?

LI WANJIANG Yeah, liberated!

UNCLE DOGGIE We won't be bullied by Qi Yongnian any more?

LI WANJIANG Never again!

UNCLE DOGGIE We'll have land to work on?

LI WANJIANG Land will be redistributed very soon.

---

* Public meetings at which the masses openly criticized and exposed the crimes and wrongdoings of the landlords, tyrants, and despots of the old society, or enemies of the Socialist revolution.

UNCLE DOGGIE Oh, what kindness! What bounty! Now, brother, Doggie here has suffered all his life at the hands of the Qis, so I don't want any other house. I got my eyes set on that arch of theirs, where they had me hoisted up and whipped. Give that to me, will you?

LI WANJIANG Sure, it's yours!

UNCLE DOGGIE Oh, what kindness! What bounty!

[SU LIANYU, *a neighbour, enters, running and breathless. He is a barber. Because of his profession, he is frequently at the fairs and travels a lot in the vicinity, hence, a well-informed person. He is the sort who, when he tries to do some good, nothing very good comes of it and when he tries something bad, nothing really bad comes of it either. He is always keen to help his neighbours.*]

SU LIANYU Brother Doggie . . . Sister Doggie is no more!

UNCLE DOGGIE *[frantic]* What—

SU LIANYU We were all hiding in the Willow Lane at East Sand Ridge when a cannon shot came down, blasted a huge hole in the ground, and Sister Doggie—

UNCLE DOGGIE What about my son? My Dahu?

SU LIANYU The kid is all right. He's fine. In my house now.

UNCLE DOGGIE *[wailing]* My wife . . . my son . . .

BLACKOUT

SCENE FOUR

[*Time: back to the present.* CHEN DAHU's *voice is heard: 'Dad, Dad!' A corner of the arch becomes visible.* UNCLE DOGGIE, *his hair once more white, is sitting on the ground, leaning against the arch.* CHEN DAHU *finds him.*]

CHEN DAHU Dad! What's wrong now?

UNCLE DOGGIE *[without moving]* I miss your mother.

CHEN DAHU *[calmly]* When Mother died you weren't even there. You stayed with your sesame crop.

UNCLE DOGGIE I miss your stepmother.

CHEN DAHU She left you. All because you were so damned stubborn, taking everything so hard—

UNCLE DOGGIE *[hugging the brick corner of the arch]* The arch! My arch!

CHEN DAHU That's all you've got now, the arch, and me. Which one do you want? Just say the word!

[QI XIAOMENG *appears.*]

QI XIAOMENG Dahu, they called long distance from the city. They want to know when we are going to start building our marble factory.

CHEN DAHU As we planned—tomorrow.

QI XIAOMENG Tomorrow? What about the arch?

CHEN DAHU We'll pull it down. How can the trucks pass through with that thing there? Dad, go back to your room.

QI XIAOMENG Don't torment yourself. You'll get ill and we'll have to take care of you.

UNCLE DOGGIE *[helplessly]* Oh, Dahu's mother, my dear wife—

BLACKOUT

SCENE FIVE

[Time: at the start of the implementation of the Land Reform Policy (1950–2).
  Offstage, the voice of SU LIANYU *saying 'Brother Doggie, time to go!' The*
lights come up. It is the dawn of a fine day in spring with a cool breeze. UNCLE
DOGGIE *and* SU LIANYU *appear, walking side by side.]*

SU LIANYU Come on, Brother, look at you, dragging your feet like that. This is supposed to be a happy event. You're going to get married, not executed!

UNCLE DOGGIE I know it's supposed to be happy, but, in such haste! I'll be a laughing stock in the eyes of the folk round here!

SU LIANYU No one's going to laugh at you. As the saying goes, women are like layers of mud on the wall, one layer falls off, there's another one waiting; the one with the red dress goes, sure enough, another one in green will appear. Haven't you suffered enough as a second-time bachelor? Working in the fields, running that oil mill, taking care of everything inside and outside the house, being a mother as well as a father? That's no way to live! I've always kept my eyes open for you as I went around with my barber's kit through the villages.

UNCLE DOGGIE With the war only just over, maybe we shouldn't be in such a hurry.

SU LIANYU Come off it, Brother Doggie! Stop playing shy. I've passed the word around to Peach Village. I told them that Mr Chen lost his wife in the prime of his life. An affluent man. He has two, maybe three huge vats of pure sesame oil. When the pretty young widow heard that, she beamed from ear to ear! And talk about pretty! I was trying to figure out which girl in our village could match her in looks, I couldn't! . . . You remember the New Year print of Diao Chan that was on your wall, the legendary beauty? Well, she is just like her!

UNCLE DOGGIE Really?

SU LIANYU Go and see for yourself. I'm not asking you to buy dud goods! It may sound heartless, but when I set eyes on her, I really wished the cannon shell that hit your wife in Willow Lane had hit mine instead—you know who I mean, the slop. She's getting to be more and more like a millstone!

UNCLE DOGGIE Stop that nonsense. How old is the girl?

SU LIANYU Nineteen.

UNCLE DOGGIE But I'm thirty-eight.

SU LIANYU So what? With your forty bushels of sesame seeds, you could marry a virgin, let alone a young widow. Listen, let's not waste time. We've got to be going. A bird in the hand is worth two in the bush. And the early bird gets the worm. We must—snatch her!

UNCLE DOGGIE Snatch her?

SU LIANYU That's right. Do as I tell you. It's still enemy held territory over there, and they don't go in for that 'Women's Liberation' business. Over there, if a widow wants to remarry, she's not respectable and therefore open game for any bachelor who can snatch her. Brides have even been kidnapped on their way to their weddings. Look, I've brought along a club. [Shows the club behind his back]

UNCLE DOGGIE [also prepared] I brought a rope, just in case—

SU LIANYU [sudden realization] You son of a bitch, you've been ready all this time! Why are we wasting time jabbering? Let's get moving before daybreak.

UNCLE DOGGIE It's only five miles, we can get there in no time.

SU LIANYU Remember, when you're there, don't let on that you're thirty-eight.

UNCLE DOGGIE All right.

[They disappear. The lights rise on a blooming peach tree. FENG JINHUA is standing under the tree with her back to the audience, UNCLE DOGGIE is pleading his case. SU LIANYU is hiding not far away, the club in his hand.]

So your name is Feng Jinhua?

[FENG JINHUA nods.]

You willing to hitch up with me?

[FENG JINHUA shakes her head.]

Come on, we don't have time. Don't put it off any longer. What about turning round and showing me your face?

FENG JINHUA *[turning round]* There now, have a good look.

[Pretending to smoke his pipe, UNCLE DOGGIE strikes a match to have a better look at her face. As he does so, she sees his face.]

UNCLE DOGGIE My! She's pretty!

FENG JINHUA My! How old are you?

UNCLE DOGGIE Thirty . . . Thirty-one.

FENG JINHUA Twelve years older than me!

UNCLE DOGGIE So you were also born in the year of the dog?

FENG JINHUA What are you talking about?

UNCLE DOGGIE *[calculating in confusion]* Rat, ox, tiger, rabbit . . . I, I mean snake . . . we are both snakes.

FENG JINHUA You are too old for me.

UNCLE DOGGIE Old? Don't forget, a young husband will beat you, but an old husband will feed you. An old husband will pamper you, you silly girl! I'm going to pamper you—

FENG JINHUA Pah!—How?

UNCLE DOGGIE Well . . . *[Suddenly he catches sight of SU LIANYU showing him three fingers.]* Oh, yes, I promise you three things.

FENG JINHUA Three things? And what are they?

UNCLE DOGGIE In a family, the man should be the plough and the woman the money box—not a bottomless box, of course. Once you cross the threshold of my house, I'll hand you the keys. How's that?

FENG JINHUA Sounds all right. The second?

UNCLE DOGGIE For harvesting, in summer or autumn, you won't have to work in the fields.

FENG JINHUA I do have sensitive skin, I get boils all over if I'm exposed to the sun.

UNCLE DOGGIE I have no problem there. We peasants may die of idleness, but never from too much work. I don't have much land now anyway, but when I do, what's to stop me from hiring some farm-hands?

FENG JINHUA Is that right? You mean we could really hire some farm-hands?

UNCLE DOGGIE Why not? Why should I always be the hired one? Listen to me, we have . . . we have money stashed away.

FENG JINHUA So I've been told. And the third?

UNCLE DOGGIE The third . . . *[Sees* SU LIANYU *showing him three fingers again]* Oh, yes, I promise to spare you from three chores. First, you don't have to fetch water from the well. South of the village there's a sweet water well and north of it there's a sparkling spring. I'll have all the tubs and vats in the house filled. Second, you won't have to grind our own wheat or corn, turning in circles behind the arse of a donkey. It's no work for a woman anyway. Third, you won't be tied to the kitchen. I can bake pancakes and make omelettes, shred salted turnips and toss them in sesame oil. That's the kind of food we're going to have, everyday. What else do you want? Say it, and it's yours. How's that?

FENG JINHUA You men are all the same. When you want something, you'll promise anything. Later, it's a different story.

UNCLE DOGGIE Your Uncle Doggie is not that type.

FENG JINHUA *[hiding her giggle]* Hee . . .

UNCLE DOGGIE I've got a proper name too, Chen Hexiang. Listen, mother of my children—

FENG JINHUA It's a bit early to call me that!

UNCLE DOGGIE Well, I've promised you all you want. There's something I want, too. You must take good care of Dahu. He is our son and heir, he will carry on the Chen lineage.

FENG JINHUA *[saddened]* I lost my husband, and recently, I lost my baby too. My milk is still flowing, *[Feeling her breasts]* I can feel the swelling. There is something lacking in my bosom, I need a baby.

UNCLE DOGGIE Isn't this a miracle? Everything fits! Brother Lianyu, we've made it!

FENG JINHUA Who says you've made it?

UNCLE DOGGIE Haven't I? That's all right. I'm a patient man. I've got all the time in the world. What else do you want?

FENG JINHUA We have a custom here. When a girl is married, her feet mustn't touch the ground when she leaves the village, even if it's a second marriage. I can't have the story going around that I came walking to you on my own.

UNCLE DOGGIE But right now, where can I find a horse and cart? I know . . . I'll carry you on my back. *[Assumes the pose]*

FENG JINHUA You'll never survive it!

UNCLE DOGGIE Tender feelings for me, eh?

SU LIANYU I can always help. *[Trying to frighten her]* Look! There's a gang coming on the road!

UNCLE DOGGIE Mother of my child, hurry—

FENG JINHUA *[climbing on his back, hitting him]* You big Doggie.

UNCLE DOGGIE Let's go home, my Mrs Doggie! *[Starts running]*

FENG JINHUA Hey! Be careful! *[Giggling, she is carried off by* UNCLE DOGGIE.*]*

SU LIANYU *[with envy]* That man has all the luck! Well, mustn't be late for the nuptial drinks!

SCENE SIX

[Time: a year or two after Scene 5.

The stage is fully lit, even a little dazzling. The grey arch has been repaired and looks brand new. Under the jujube tree, its branches heavily laden with claret-red fruits, there are a few stools and a low table. FENG JINHUA *is sitting on one of the stools, stitching the sole of a cloth shoe, casually humming a popular tune of the time. Offstage,* UNCLE DOGGIE *is shouting: 'Wait till I catch you!' A little later, he enters, holding a few red dates in his hand.]*

FENG JINHUA Who are you shouting at? Must you raise your voice like that?

UNCLE DOGGIE Having a good time, are you? I just turned my back for a moment, to mix some fodder for the mare, and those rascals might have uprooted an entire jujube tree for all you care! Never seen brats like them! Even before the fruits appeared, when the blossoms were hardly off the branches, they started pilfering. Plain stealing I can deal with, but what do you do with a thief who has his heart set on your property? *[Shouting again towards the wings]* Listen, you miserable brats, you want the good things in life? So do I!

FENG JINHUA Calm down, the house is not on fire, don't make a laughing stock of yourself. Just a few dates, that's the custom anyway. What if people eat a few? It's not the family inheritance. And they're all neighbours from the same village, you run into them every day. You can't put your front gate on your rooftop, can you?

UNCLE DOGGIE You lose three of them today, tomorrow you may lose five. *[Looking at the dates in his hand]* Where is our Dahu?

FENG JINHUA Auntie Lianyu next door has taken him over there to
play. Come and look at this.

UNCLE DOGGIE What is it?

FENG JINHUA The sole for Dahu's shoes. Nearly as big as yours!

UNCLE DOGGIE No! A young boy with feet as big as mine?

FENG JINHUA Hey, tomorrow I want to go to the fair!

UNCLE DOGGIE They weep, then they smile, go to the fair, then to the
temple in style. Women are all the same.

FENG JINHUA I want to see a doctor. I've been with you quite a few
years now, but I still haven't—

UNCLE DOGGIE So that's what's on your mind. Well, I had my fortune
told when I was young, and I know my destiny: one
son. What's wrong with that? One good son is worth
more than ten good-for-nothings.

FENG JINHUA But when I think about it, I always feel I have let you
down. *[Sobs]* If I had a child, boy or girl, I would have
someone to count on.

UNCLE DOGGIE The way you care for Dahu, you think he wouldn't care
for you? Look after you?

FENG JINHUA Who knows? He's not from my womb.

UNCLE DOGGIE Dahu is a good boy, and soon he'll grow up . . . and I'll
be an old man.

FENG JINHUA You are not old, and even if you are, I don't mind.

UNCLE DOGGIE What did I tell you, a young husband will beat you.

FENG JINHUA There you go again! I won't forget the way you talked
me into it, you with your honeyed words, singing them
like a song of love—your three, or was it five,
promises. And what happened once I came into this
family? You've used me like a donkey, I'm lucky to be
alive.

UNCLE DOGGIE You have to strain your muscles and work your fingers
to the bone to make a decent living. Look at us now,
we've made it! We've bought the mare, Chrysanthemum,
my Chrys. We have our cart with rubber tyres. We
don't have to worry about the next meal anymore. Now
that land is cheap, we must grab every little plot we
can lay our hands on. First of all we'll buy up Su
Lianyu's triangle, half an acre, and next year we'll buy
more. *[Looking up at the arch and talking to himself]* Ha!
The lights in the Qis' house have been snuffed out, the
Qis are finished! What an arch, such fine workmanship,
the pride of the community for miles around—it now
bears the name of Chen! I walk past it several times a

day and I feel so pleased even if I'm hungry! Now, you Qis—suppose one of these days I should hoist one of you up on this arch and let you swing a bit? Ha! Uncle Doggie has the power to do that? Oh yeah! Who gave me the power? Our government!

[SU LIANYU enters.]

SU LIANYU *[shouting]* Brother Doggie!

UNCLE DOGGIE Look who's here, the fatted pig offering itself—

FENG JINHUA Oh, Brother Lianyu, come and sit down.

SU LIANYU Sister, that Dahu of yours is brilliant. I remember him counting on his fingers when he was three, and guess what he went up to? Three hundred! I always say, you can tell what a kid will grow up into from the age of three. This kid is going places. *[Turning around, calls]* Come over. You should know this place well enough.

[QI YONGNIAN enters, looking wretched and dejected. He stops at the sight of the arch, the edifice which was his but now bears another name. His troubled thoughts seem unfathomable.]

UNCLE DOGGIE *[drawing SU LIANYU aside]* Why bring him here?

SU LIANYU For buying and selling land, you must have papers, documents. In our village, he's the only one who can read and write.

UNCLE DOGGIE Couldn't you just scribble something to get it over with?

SU LIANYU Me? I can't read or write to save my life. Last New Year, when everybody was pasting lucky sayings on the wall, you know what I stuck on my bedroom wall? 'May this sty abound with fat pigs!' Don't you worry. This won't hurt the spirit of our struggles. We just want the thing done properly; we're using his hands, so to speak. It's time he did us some service.

UNCLE DOGGIE Right, we'll make him serve us for a change. Qi Yongnian, come over and sit down.

QI YONGNIAN No, no, I'll stand.

SU LIANYU Do as you are told. How are you going to write standing?

QI YONGNIAN All right. *[Sits down, takes out pen and ink from their wrapper]*

UNCLE DOGGIE Mother of Dahu, where's that piece of tough paper?

FENG JINHUA In the leather box at the east end of the wall chest.

UNCLE DOGGIE Quick, give me the keys.

[FENG JINHUA hands him the keys with a little brass bell attached to it.]

FENG JINHUA *[behaving with propriety]* Would you like a drink of
water, Mister Qi?

QI YONGNIAN Oh, no, that would be presumptuous. I can see that life
is treating you well.

FENG JINHUA Thanks to the Party.

QI YONGNIAN Of course, of course. And now, ready to buy more
land?

*[UNCLE DOGGIE is back with the piece of paper and motions
to FENG JINHUA, who goes back to the room.]*

UNCLE DOGGIE *[picking up the conversation]* Just happened to have some
spare cash. Why leave it idle? Might as well buy some
land. To the farm-hand, land is everything, his roots,
his hope. Without land, the farm-hand is no better
than a travelling monk, at the mercy of anyone and
everyone. You should know this—you're a past master!

QI YONGNIAN Sure, sure.

UNCLE DOGGIE *[bragging]* You know that mare, Chrysanthemum? A
real bastard! For the past two days she wouldn't eat!
I've been adding handfuls of beans to the fodder, but
she wouldn't even sniff at them. Finally, I force-fed her
two spoonfuls of sesame oil. That cured her! Hey,
Brother Lianyu, these inflated rubber tyres are so much
better than the old-fashioned hard wheels. When you
have them properly pumped, the cart drives itself!
Ain't that strange? The other day, even Chrysanthemum
couldn't hold it down the slope; two of the leather
straps simply snapped!

SU LIANYU *[humouring him]* You're right. There's a dragon
somewhere in every horse.

UNCLE DOGGIE And the arch. After the repairs, it looks grander, eh?

SU LIANYU A lot grander.

UNCLE DOGGIE Qi, what do you say?

QI YONGNIAN It's grand.

SU LIANYU *[to QI YONGNIAN]* What are you waiting for? Start
writing.

QI YONGNIAN Su, you intend to sell—

SU LIANYU The triangular plot, east of the village, half an acre.

QI YONGNIAN *[full of memories]* The Great Triangle—

SU LIANYU You should know all about it. It used to belong to the
Qi family.

QI YONGNIAN *[reading aloud what he is writing down]* The document is
drawn up by the vendor, Su Lianyu, who, because of
personal difficulties—

SU LIANYU I sure have personal difficulties. My old woman is half an invalid, hardly ever able to work; bearing children seems all she's good at. So, more and more mouths to feed, without more hands to do the work. Me, all I'm good at is cutting people's hair, and you can't make a fortune out of that. The little land I have lies waste. Go on writing.

QI YONGNIAN . . . because of personal difficulties, is willing to sell the Great Triangle, half an acre in area—

SU LIANYU Don't forget the well.

QI YONGNIAN *[blurts out]* I won't!

SU LIANYU Of course you won't! Brother Doggie, remember? That mule years ago . . . Sister Jinhua, it was right here, on the arch, he had Doggie—

UNCLE DOGGIE *[not wanting to be reminded of that at this glorious moment]* Oh, stop it! Go on.

QI YONGNIAN . . . covering land bordered by the Willow Lane in the east and the Old Official Road in the west—

SU LIANYU The Willow Lane in the east and the Old Official Road in the west. Hell, you know it better than me, I've only been working on it for a short time!

QI YONGNIAN *[writing]* And the agreed price is . . . How much?

SU LIANYU Eight bushels of sesame seeds.

QI YONGNIAN Eight bushels? *[To* SU LIANYU*]* But that's cheap!

SU LIANYU So what? We're buddies.

QI YONGNIAN *[to* UNCLE DOGGIE*]* That's too cheap!

UNCLE DOGGIE What's it to you? If you think it's such a bargain, go ahead and buy it yourself! Just write down what you're told, and be done. Don't poke your nose into my business. Go on, write it down, eight bushels of sesame seeds.

QI YONGNIAN *[shaking his head with pity, writes]* Eight bushels of sesame seeds, sold to—

UNCLE DOGGIE Now, the full name, Chen Hexiang!

QI YONGNIAN All claims relinquished, now or in the future. An oral agreement being no legal guarantee, a written statement is hereby given. Signatories of the document: Su Lianyu, Chen Hexiang; Scribe: Qi Yongnian. Now, do you have your personal seals?

UNCLE DOGGIE Seals? *[Shakes his head]*

QI YONGNIAN In that case . . . your thumb prints will do.

[Solemnly he takes out the seal box he always carries with him. UNCLE DOGGIE *and* SU LIANYU *put their thumb*

prints on the document, QI YONGNIAN *uses his personal seal
to do the same.* UNCLE DOGGIE *gazes at the seal, fascinated
and feeling disconsolate for some reason.]*

QI YONGNIAN Here, we still need a witness.

UNCLE DOGGIE Witness?

QI YONGNIAN You need a witness for buying and selling property, for
loans and pawns.

UNCLE DOGGIE I know that.

SU LIANYU There's just the right man—Li Wanjiang, head of the
village.

UNCLE DOGGIE I'll get him now.

SU LIANYU *[with his own reasons]* There's no hurry. Ours is a case of
mutual agreement, no dispute—it is mutual, isn't it?

UNCLE DOGGIE Sure, it's mutual all right.

SU LIANYU There! One of these days, when we meet him, we'll tell
him about it and make him soil his thumb like we
did, there we are! Now, write down the name: Li
Wanjiang.

[QI YONGNIAN *writes it all down, then puts all his
paraphernalia back into the cloth wrapper, ceremoniously.]*

UNCLE DOGGIE Now, let's take a look around the land!

SU LIANYU You are more impatient than when you went to meet
your bride! Can't even hold back a fart, can you? Okay,
let's go!

UNCLE DOGGIE *[trying to get rid of him]* You go first, I'll be there in a
moment, I just . . . I just want a word with Qi here.

SU LIANYU The Great Triangle—I'll be there. *[Exits]*

UNCLE DOGGIE *[not sure of himself]* Well . . . Qi, Comrade Qi.

QI YONGNIAN *[alarmed at his politeness]* Oh . . . I . . . I'm at your
service!

UNCLE DOGGIE You think this land is worth it?

QI YONGNIAN *[on safe ground now, enthused]* Absolutely! The earth is
half sandy, half clay, it will stand up to drought or
flood, and it's so near the village. Why would he give
it up at such a price? Strange, if you ask me!

UNCLE DOGGIE That's what I feel too.

QI YONGNIAN *[musing, forgetting himself]* Well, Comrade Su gets
around with his barber's kit, from place to place, and
he keeps his eyes peeled and his ears open, he knows
what's going on. Could it be . . . could it be the third
world war is coming?

UNCLE DOGGIE What? So, you are dreaming of a comeback?

QI YONGNIAN No, no, I didn't say anything, I never said anything!
[*Anxious to leave*]

UNCLE DOGGIE Don't run away!

QI YONGNIAN I beg you, let me go.

UNCLE DOGGIE I didn't hear a word, is that all right? Let's talk about
something else. These days, you know how it is.
[*Indicating the arch, and the courtyard beyond*] You have
no use for them anymore, so why hang on to that little
box [*Pointing to the seal*], and the stone, the little cube,
why don't you sell them to me? Maybe I could use
them. How about it, Comrade?

QI YONGNIAN [*seems to get the point*] This seal? Well, you can't use it.

UNCLE DOGGIE Bloody nonsense! Why can't I? Only you can use it?

QI YONGNIAN It's got my name engraved on it—Qi Yongnian.

UNCLE DOGGIE We can always rub it off, rub you off and engrave me
there—Chen Hexiang.

QI YONGNIAN Well, let me put it this way: you people have
denounced me and taken away all you were supposed to
take. This is the only thing I still have. I'd like to
keep it, maybe I'll need it some day.

UNCLE DOGGIE Oh-ho, you rascal, you still have designs up your sleeve!

QI YONGNIAN No, no, what I mean is, neighbours might need me to
write an IOU or some such document, it'll come in
handy, like today. Now, you must excuse me—[*Slips
off*]

UNCLE DOGGIE Pah! Keep it, keep it till it rots! What's the big deal?
A tiny wooden box with a stone chop in it! Next time
I go to the fair I'll buy them by the bushel!
[*FENG JINHUA, hearing him shout, comes out of the room.*]

FENG JINHUA Who are you shouting at now?

UNCLE DOGGIE Qi Yongnian, the old fox.

FENG JINHUA How people change with the change of times!
Remember the airs he used to put on? And look at
him now, a dried-up shrimp! Give him a break, he's
really down and out.

UNCLE DOGGIE He still has his pipe-dreams, the bastard! Mother of
Dahu, [*With pride*] I'll just pop over and look at our
new land. [*A horse neighs offstage.*]
Don't you forget to feed Chrysanthemum, and mix the
fodder with black beans, Mrs Doggie!

FENG JINHUA Don't worry, I won't forget your true love!

UNCLE DOGGIE I must go look at that land. [*With a jingle, throws down
the keys with the brass bell*]

SCENE SEVEN

[Time: the mid-1950s, during the height of the movement, introduced in 1954, to collectivize agriculture.

UNCLE DOGGIE *staggers into view. He is in the ancestral burial ground of the Chen clan. Dim light comes from a crescent moon. A couple of crickets are chirping.]*

UNCLE DOGGIE I'll go and look at the land. Yeah, the land. I'll take a good look at the land, my land! But it's not mine anymore: it belongs to the collective. This could well be my last trip. . . . A jug of liquor, a full jug—he drank a shot, I another; I took a swig, he another. The little jug turned over, no more liquor, we were both drunk. No more Chrysanthemum. No more cart with the rubber wheels. And no more land.

[Two spotlights, one on either side of the stage, rise on the faces of QI YONGNIAN *and* CHEN DAHU.]

QI YONGNIAN Rivers change courses and the sun never stays at noon forever. Look, you had hardly three days of a good time, and there was trouble everywhere. Come, trouble, come! The messier the merrier!

CHEN DAHU Still the same old hackneyed, boring story! Dad, can't you say something new? All right, carry on if you must. Maybe by repeating yourself you'll finally realize why you didn't make it even after a lifetime of worship to the god of prosperity! Thank heavens I didn't follow your footsteps—I can see straight.

[Both figures, right and left, disappear.]

UNCLE DOGGIE Our land is gone, Dad! It wasn't my liquor, he brought it—Li Wanjiang, head of the village—brought the liquor. A full jug. He's a good man, Li, a benefactor. He gave me plenty of face, how could I say no? So he downed a swig, I another; I downed a shot, and he another; soon the jug toppled over: no more liquor. We both got pissed, and I lost everything! I'm not supposed to say 'lost' though. Village Head Li said, according to instructions from above, the whole village was to turn 'Red All Over.' When everyone else is 'Red,' how can Uncle Doggie remain the 'Black Spot!' Sure, I said, I've been in the vanguard, supporting the war against the Nationalists, I've been at the forefront during the land reform—I told him all that—but now, all of a sudden, everything, the land, the animals, the

men, are to be 'collectivized'? You think it'll work?
You think you are a god reincarnated? You going to
give orders to hundreds of farm-hands? Will it work?
Don't forget, even blood brothers have beaten each
other's brains out over a tiny strip of land! 'It will
work,' he said. 'Just wait, you silly clodhopper. In the
blink of an eye, we'll be living in modern buildings,
upstairs and downstairs, with electric lights and
telephones; we'll be drinking milk and eating biscuits.'
I said, 'But I don't want the damned stuff.' And he
said, 'You're a typical money-grabber, an earthworm,
the tough nut no one can crack!' I got really angry, and
I said I'd rather be a 'Black Spot'. I don't care what
happens to me. Then he said, 'In that case we'll have
to get rid of the "spot". I asked him how, and he said,
'Easy, we'll take over the land you bought—the Great
Triangle—and the land right here under our feet, the
"Neck of the Gourd", which happens to be the burial
ground of the Chen clan, and we'll give you some other
land, equivalent in area, but scattered and far away.
What can you expect? If you're a Black Spot, we'd
rather have you on our toes than on our chest, right?'
My reply was, 'Don't try to bamboozle me, everyone
knows the saying, "A distant daughter and land next
door are priceless treasures." Besides, I know what land
you're referring to, it's barren and alkaline. You get
barely half of what you put in. I'll never agree to such
a swap!' 'Well then, join the collective,' he said, 'Be
part of the "Red All Over." Our leaders are waiting for
the good news. Come on, drink up! Drink up!' And at
that moment, my wife, Jinhua, butted in, 'We farm-
hands, peasants, we've always gone with the trend. We
never try to be different, to be the odd bird, to stick
our necks out! Brother Wanjiang here is running back
and forth, day and night, isn't it all for us? Let me tell
you—and I don't care if you don't like it—if you refuse
to join the collective, we'll go our separate ways; Dahu
and me, we'll join in. We won't be the "Black Spot"
along with you'. Well, well, did you hear that? So the
women have had their meetings too. Then Li Wanjiang
said, 'She's right, she has it all worked out. Brother
Doggie, make up your mind now. Soon we'll be living
in modern buildings, upstairs and downstairs.' What
can a man do? With words drumming in your ears,
and liquor going to your head, with people pushing

you from within and without, you have to give in! And
so I allowed myself to be collectivized, collectivized!
Oh, Dad! Chrysanthemum, Chrys, she didn't want to
go, she couldn't leave the brand new manger I had just
made for her from real willow-wood boards! And the
land, it's all gone too. Dad, that puppy, you ate it for
nothing! I didn't live up to your—*[His voice cracks as he
throws himself to the ground. QI YONGNIAN comes up, stops
before him and pats him.]*

QI YONGNIAN It's past midnight, the cold air of autumn can kill you,
you'll catch your death of cold lying here.

UNCLE DOGGIE *[delirious]* Dad, Dad, this is Doggie here, I'm coming!

QI YONGNIAN Brother Doggie—

UNCLE DOGGIE *[bleary-eyed]* Who are you?

QI YONGNIAN Brother, what did I tell you? You'd hardly warmed up
the earth in your palms when you lost it all! As I said,
you can't make a wolf out of a wolf's hide. In those
days—

[A spotlight centres on them.]

UNCLE DOGGIE *[recognizes QI YONGNIAN]* It's you! You vicious
landlord! You thrive on other people's disasters, you
gloat at their funerals, rejoice when their houses catch
fire! The land is gone, and how you celebrate! Get out
of my sight! *[Soundly slaps QI YONGNIAN on the face]*

[LI WANJIANG appears.]

LI WANJIANG Well done, Brother Doggie! That's the way to deal
with scum like him. We're not going to let him laugh
at us, are we? Tomorrow we're going to hold a big
meeting, and the County Chief himself is going to pin
a huge red blossom on your chest! Qi Yongnian,
remember to behave yourself!

QI YONGNIAN Yes, Comrade.

LI WANJIANG Don't get ideas in your head. We've never relaxed our
vigilance over you. If anything funny should happen,
you know who we'll go after!

QI YONGNIAN Yes, Comrade.

UNCLE DOGGIE *[overjoyed]* Brother, you are the only person to put him
in his place. You really are the big hero, I'll follow you
till the end of my life.

LI WANJIANG My good brother, let's go home now, there's the
meeting tomorrow.

UNCLE DOGGIE *[brooding]* But, I don't want meetings, I don't want
glory, I want my land, my horse, my cart,—

LI WANJIANG Come, come, we can't turn back now, Brother.

UNCLE DOGGIE Can't turn back?

LI WANJIANG Right. It's getting late, and your pretty wife is waiting. Go home now!

UNCLE DOGGIE Home, home. *[Suddenly turning back]* I've lost my land . . . Dad!

> *[All this time,* QI YONGNIAN *is watching, crouched in a corner.* UNCLE DOGGIE *collapses to the ground.]*

LI WANJIANG Qi Yongnian!

QI YONGNIAN Here.

LI WANJIANG What the hell are you waiting for? Carry him on your back, and take him back to the village.

SCENE EIGHT

[Time: the late 1950s, during the Great Leap Forward, in the days of communes, famine, and natural disasters.

A kind of demented laughter rises from one of the tracks in the planted fields. Then UNCLE DOGGIE *enters. Grey-haired now, he is running wildly, followed by* FENG JINHUA. *She is trying to catch up with him, a bundle of medicinal herbs in her hand. They have just returned from a visit to the doctor.]*

FENG JINHUA Father of Dahu, stop running, be good—

UNCLE DOGGIE Be gone, you evil spirit, you bring misfortune to my house! You siren, stop laying your vile hands on me, I don't know you. *[Rushing off]*

FENG JINHUA *[grabbing him]* Don't go into the fields. With the rain last night, you'll get your feet all muddied up. Be good now. Let's go home.

UNCLE DOGGIE Woman, take your hands off me.

FENG JINHUA Come on, please. Don't run off. Let's go home and take the medicine.

UNCLE DOGGIE Go away.

FENG JINHUA But you're not well.

UNCLE DOGGIE I want to shit!

FENG JINHUA *[at her wits' end]* Well, do it here.

UNCLE DOGGIE Oh! That's nice—do it here! I call that a damn waste! When it comes to fertilizer, gold and silver aren't as good as human manure. One share of it is good for three seedlings. You think I'd waste it? That's why we say, 'Cats never defile heaven and dogs never stain the soil.' I'm going to my Great Triangle.

FENG JINHUA The Great Triangle is gone.

UNCLE DOGGIE To my 'Neck of the Gourd' then.

FENG JINHUA That's gone too.

UNCLE DOGGIE Have they run off? Flown away? Have they got wings? You silly woman. [*Laughing foolishly and talking to himself*] Such good land! Stretch after stretch, that's Heaven's bounty to you poor mortals, and is this the way you treat it? Shame on you! Just look at the weeds growing wild! Bales of it, smothering the crop. You scoundrels, how can you face your peasant ancestors? When the day of reckoning comes, you'll answer for it—

[SU LIANYU *enters, a basket on his back.*]

SU LIANYU Hi, Brother Doggie, feeling better these days?

UNCLE DOGGIE Sure. Strip the bloody fool and at least he feels cool! We've torn down our kitchens, cut down all the trees. Didn't you tell us we could only keep our wives and our smoking pipes, and everything else was to go to the collective?

SU LIANYU That's what our production brigade leader Li Wanjiang said.

UNCLE DOGGIE Who are you then?

SU LIANYU [*loudly*] Deputy production brigade leader Su Lianyu.

UNCLE DOGGIE [*laughing foolishly*] Ah. Do you want to sell more land? Eight bushels of sesame seeds—real cheap! The fatted pig offered itself, and what did I get for eight bushels of sesame seeds? A bucket of honour and glory! You got more land to sell? You'll have to wait—I've got some pressing business.

SU LIANYU Don't run off, Brother Doggie, listen to me—

UNCLE DOGGIE You're just as stupid as this woman. Listen to me— [*Whispering in his ear*]

SU LIANYU Oh! Go then!

[UNCLE DOGGIE *staggers off.*]

FENG JINHUA [*shaking her head in distress*] When he meets you people, he seems to have some sense left, I'm the one he never recognizes. In the day he is a lunatic, at night he drops off like a log. What a life it is for me—[*Sobs*]

SU LIANYU [*at a loss what to say*] Sister, here's a sack of peas, twenty-five kilos, take it. [*Hands her a sack of peas from his basket*]

FENG JINHUA We're lucky to have good leaders like you to take care of us.

SU LIANYU Well, mustn't let him learn about this, you know.

FENG JINHUA Who?

SU LIANYU Li Wanjiang.

FENG JINHUA Why?

SU LIANYU *[mysteriously]* This is private distribution, not in the books, you understand?

FENG JINHUA Oh! Then I can't take it.

SU LIANYU My, what a model member of the brigade led by Li Wanjiang! So, he won't budge an inch with his rules and you won't bend a bit of your principles! Where does that leave me? Come, take the food as my gift for a sick brother, all right?

FENG JINHUA The down and out can have no pride. But, we must be fair. Brother Wanjiang is a decent person. Always fair, never scheming for himself, never selfish where money is involved. If you leaders were all like him, there'd be hope for us.

SU LIANYU Like him? Making a virtue of suffering? And suffering more than everyone else? Pulling a long donkey face whenever he meets any of the brigade members? And look at the way he lives, his hut! All that he has—the roof, the mattress, even the curtain that serves as the door—are nothing but straw! Call that a home? He's well over thirty now, but still without a wife, and after a day of back-breaking labour, he has to kneel with his arse pointing to heaven, to light the fire and cook himself a meal! He's a model all right, but a model of miseries.

FENG JINHUA *[putting a hand over her mouth to hide a smile]* The way you put it, he's a real wretch! But the other day, when he came back from the meeting in the county, in his uniform with four pockets, he looked like a real leader! With his newly cut hair under the Lenin cap, his big eyes flashing, he looked so handsome. How is it . . . *[Forgetting herself]* No wonder people say, a good man never gets the good wife he deserves, but louts often get to marry the fairest maids!

SU LIANYU *[fascinated, and surprised by her reaction]* You don't say!

FENG JINHUA *[embarrassed, yet unconsoled]* Look at me, as if my own troubles aren't enough! *[Pointing at the bag]* Even with this, how are we going to last till the new crop is reaped? How will we manage?

SU LIANYU Sister, it's harvest time now. Why should we starve when food is beckoning at us all over the place. In a

day or two the millet will turn yellow, the skin of
corncobs will become crisp. Don't you know the saying,
'A little effort at harvest brings more than hard labour
in spring?' These days, all the members of the brigades
are scooping up the odd bucket of grain on the sly.
When it's harvest time, even the horses and mules are
allowed to take a bite or two from the roadside; so
what should stop you from getting a basket, making a
few rounds at night, and picking up something here
and there?

FENG JINHUA I've never stolen anything in my life. What if I get
caught?

SU LIANYU This ain't stealing! As the higher-ups say, this is at
most 'pilfering,' a minor offence. If you get caught, just
laugh it off. With what we are up against, everyone
will turn a blind eye, except perhaps our leader Li
Wanjiang, that pigheaded slave-driver!

FENG JINHUA There you go again.

SU LIANYU As I said before, if all leaders behaved like him,
everyone in the brigade would starve to death.

FENG JINHUA Suppose they all behaved like you?

SU LIANYU Like me? Then we'd all be so poor we'd have to sell
our trousers!

FENG JINHUA That'd make life easy.

SU LIANYU How?

FENG JINHUA No one could go to work in the fields then.

SU LIANYU Oh, you're funny!

[*At this moment, the sound of* UNCLE DOGGIE'*s silly
laughter rises from a field of crops.* SU LIANYU *runs over to
have a look.* FENG JINHUA *sighs with a frown.* SU LIANYU
runs back.]

You better take him home and wash his trousers!

SCENE NINE

[*Time: a few days after Scene 8, in the dark of night. The storm is almost over,
with the thunder receding into the distance and dim moonlight reappearing. There is
the sound of corn leaves flapping, then the sharp crack of a corncob being broken off
from the stalk.* LI WANJIANG *starts to shout. He is holding the wrist of someone
carrying a basket on her back and is now dragging the person from the shadows of
the maize into the light. The person turns out to be* FENG JINHUA.]

FENG JINHUA Brother Wanjiang, it's me.

LI WANJIANG I don't care who it is, all I know is, you're the seventh one I've caught tonight. Put that basket back on your shoulders and come with me to the brigade headquarters. We'll have a big meeting first thing tomorrow morning, and all of you will have to confess!

FENG JINHUA A struggle meeting?

LI WANJIANG Don't you deserve it?

FENG JINHUA Come on, Brother, turn a blind eye, and I'll get by.

LI WANJIANG If I let you get off once, you'll be just as shameless the next time.

FENG JINHUA Say that again. Who is shameless?

LI WANJIANG Whoever steals. Just because so many people are doing it, we have to call it by another name, do we? So, it's not stealing, but 'pilfering' now—well, it's the same thing! With all this 'pilfering', when harvest time is over, what am I supposed to deliver to the State, and what are the brigade members going to eat?

FENG JINHUA *[recklessly]* Eat me! Eat me up, eat up this shameless old hag!

LI WANJIANG Stop it! Don't you try acting the bully or the lunatic! Weren't the Japs bully enough? The landlords' militia were a real bunch of lunatics, weren't they? They didn't scare me. I've been in the people's militia since I was sixteen!

FENG JINHUA How glorious! Sure you're not scared by bullies and lunatics, but what about the starving? I married into your village at nineteen: did I ever do anything shameless for money? You wanted 'Red All Over'. Didn't I help you get rid of the 'Black Spot?' Yeah! The 'Black Spot' was gone all right. But in a few years, that old miser of mine went totally nuts, and apart from eating and drinking, he doesn't know a thing now! So what am I left with? Nothing, except to keep an eye on him, waiting for I don't know what, day and night. Let me tell you, I've had enough! You said I was shameless—I've been shameless for years! I've been taking grain, shameless grain from Su Lianyu—

LI WANJIANG You what?

FENG JINHUA You've got a dirty mind. There's nothing between us. It was just a gift: distribution on the sly, not in the books.

LI WANJIANG The scoundrel!

FENG JINHUA And you call me shameless. I've certainly got you wrong. You don't have to call a struggle meeting against me. I've had enough of this miserable, half-dead life anyway. I'll jump into the well this minute, and you can have your struggle meeting over my dead body. *[Wailing]* Oh, my mother—

LI WANJIANG Don't cry like this, Elder Sister. It's the dead of the night, it sounds terrible.

FENG JINHUA I'm shameless, shameless. I can't live to face people. *[Her wailing, at first a recitation, now turns into traditional keening—rhymed verses women recite to lament their misfortunes.]* Oh laundry stone, your face is smooth and shining; but the kidney beans are shrivelled and pining! Oh my mother—

LI WANJIANG All right, Elder Sister. I am shameless. Are you satisfied?

FENG JINHUA *[wiping off her tears and rising]* Of course you are! Because of you, the whole village has nothing to eat, no firewood to cook with. You should be ashamed of yourself, but you throw your weight around, treating everyone like dirt! No wonder people say you are not worth a cent!

LI WANJIANG *[carrying the bag for her]* Elder Sister—

FENG JINHUA Don't call me Elder Sister anymore, it gives me goose-pimples. You are older than me.

LI WANJIANG But Brother Doggie is my elder.

FENG JINHUA Don't mention him now!

LI WANJIANG Listen, you mustn't do this again.

FENG JINHUA Like hell I won't. I will do it again.

LI WANJIANG Again?

FENG JINHUA Yes. Just so that you will catch me. Just so that I can look at that handsome face of yours. You know, whenever I see you, you always have on that official, gloomy look, as though everyone present owed you a hundred yuan. Never seen you smile, not once.

LI WANJIANG *[lost for words]* Ha, ha.

FENG JINHUA I love those canine teeth when you laugh.

LI WANJIANG Now stop it. How can I be a leader if you behave like this?

FENG JINHUA I won't stop!

LI WANJIANG Now, now, Uncle Doggie is a sick man, we know. Don't tell me you are sick too.

FENG JINHUA I am, I am!

LI WANJIANG What? You're sick like him?

FENG JINHUA No! I'm sick because I'm hungry.

LI WANJIANG Hungry?

FENG JINHUA Yes, hungry! When you're hungry, you can't sleep, and
you start thinking. Thinking about everyone in the
village . . . about you. You're over thirty now, and still
without a woman in the house. Don't you miss
something?

[*A moment of silence. The patter of rain becomes audible.*]

It's raining again. Mustn't get soaked. I have a sack
here, let's make use of it.

[LI WANJIANG *does not reply.* FENG JINHUA *runs over,
trying to protect him and herself against the rain with the
sack.*]

I . . . I can't stand it anymore—[*Flings her arms around*
LI WANJIANG. *Their heads are securely protected by the
sack.*]

SCENE TEN

[*Time: evening; a few months after Scene 9, in the late 1950s.*
A street in the village. UNCLE DOGGIE *enters with a sack of fodder for his
imaginary horse.*]

UNCLE DOGGIE Beasts, people, they're all the same, they all love a taste
of something fresh. So first, you clean up the manger.
Mustn't let it smell stale. Next, the hay. The hay must
be chopped up fine. The animal will be plump and
sturdy so long as you chop the hay with care. Then
spread the grain feed in. The feed must be roasted, to
give it that delicious smell. Finally, sprinkle water over
it, clean fresh water. Not the kind you give the poor
beggars, not the dirty murky stuff. The hay will help
fatten up the animal, the grain is for energy and the
water for spirit. Mix them well, then, you can lie in
bed and listen to her chomping away—chomp, chomp.
Horses thrive on meals at night! Listen to my
Chrysanthemum, what beautiful molars she has! When
I crack my red-tasselled whip in the air, just look at
her galloping away, flipping her hoofs as if she were
striding the wind. . . . [*Examines the imaginary horse*] Lost
weight, lost a lot of weight, the mane is not combed,
the hair not brushed—[*Shouting into the distance*] Hey,

you! You mustn't tie the rein that tight, her neck is
straining, you hear? You work her too hard, not enough
feed, and you're not treating her right. How can she
not lose weight? No one cares. I care! Here's your feed,
all prepared. It's what I saved from my rations, roasted
over a gentle fire, *[Tasting a grain]* yum yum, delicious.
Wait, wait, here I come—

*[The front of a cottage appears, from where comes the sound
of laughter and talking. Someone is shouting: 'Husband and
wife now bow to each other. Time for the bridal chamber!' SU
LIANYU comes out of the cottage, somewhat tipsy.]*

SU LIANYU Oh, Brother Doggie! You shouldn't come here tonight!
You're not invited!

UNCLE DOGGIE No, let me go in, I miss her so much—

SU LIANYU It's too late to say that now!

UNCLE DOGGIE Let me just take a look.

SU LIANYU One look from you is enough for some real trouble.

UNCLE DOGGIE Just a look at my Chrysanthemum.

SU LIANYU Chrysanthemum? *[All is clear.]* You gave me a fright!
There's no Chrysanthemum here.

UNCLE DOGGIE Isn't this the stables?

SU LIANYU No, it's the bridal chamber. We're having a wedding
here. You better go.

UNCLE DOGGIE Who . . . who's getting married?

SU LIANYU *[hesitant]* Li Wanjiang.

UNCLE DOGGIE Brother Wanjiang, finally. It took him a long time, eh?
He is half way to his grave. How old is he?

SU LIANYU Thirty-eight.

UNCLE DOGGIE When I married Jinhua, I was thirty-eight, too,
remember?

SU LIANYU *[sounding him out]* Where's Sister Jinhua?

UNCLE DOGGIE *[trying hard to remember]* She? Hasn't she . . . gone to the
fair?

SU LIANYU Right. She's gone to the fair!

UNCLE DOGGIE Be back soon.

SU LIANYU Sure. On your way now!

UNCLE DOGGIE No! Wanjiang's getting married, I must drink his
health.

SU LIANYU Oh no, you won't. Didn't you want to look at
Chrysanthemum?

UNCLE DOGGIE *[confidentially]* Lost weight, the rounded rumps are all
angles and edges! I'm bringing her some grain,
delicious smell! Keep your paws off! It's not for you!

SU LIANYU Sure, not for me. *[Humouring him]* Hey, Brother, the stables are over there.

UNCLE DOGGIE *[trying to find his bearings]* Right you are, my arch is over there, my Great Triangle is over there, and my Chrysanthemum is over there. Now, how is that? And they call me muddle-headed! It's all clear in my head. My pet, I'm coming, coming—*[Exits]*

SU LIANYU Take it easy, Brother, watch your step, in this darkness, we don't want you to break a leg. *[Heaves a sigh of relief, then shouts to the cottage]* Hey, fellows, let's call it a day, shall we? It's getting late, they deserve a rest.

[Sound of people taking their leave dies down. FENG JINHUA comes out of the cottage. She is dressed as a bride and looks the part.]

FENG JINHUA You must be tired out, Brother Lianyu.

SU LIANYU Yes, you too. Go in now!

FENG JINHUA I'll never live this down! To remarry at this time of my life, was it right?

SU LIANYU No problem at all. If it wasn't the right thing to do, do you think the Commune authorities would have approved a divorce? There's not much we can do about Brother Doggie, so why should you suffer as well? Mind you, you've kept your feelings under wraps. I always prided myself on my sharpness, and I could kick myself for not spotting what you felt for Wanjiang!

FENG JINHUA There you go again. Be serious. What I can't get over is how long can the old man and the boy carry on? I said to him as much. *[Indicating the cottage]* I said to him: 'I've lived for almost ten years with the Chen family. I'm taking this step because I have nowhere to turn. Now I am married to the Li family, but I still have my duties to the Chens. As a beast of burden I am harnessed to both, cart and millstone, I have to do both. Now, you're supposed to be an official of some kind, so if they get into trouble or anything, I want you to make special allowances for them, both of them, the old and the young. And don't try to put on airs with me.'

SU LIANYU Oh, he wouldn't. Didn't you say Brother Wanjiang was such a nice person?

FENG JINHUA Don't interrupt me! After I'd said my piece, you know what he said? I nearly exploded!

SU LIANYU What did he say?

FENG JINHUA [*imitating Wanjiang*] 'Don't worry, I'll be even kinder to them than you think. The old man, I'll treat as my father-in-law, and the boy, my brother-in-law!' Bullshit!

[WANJIANG's *voice calling from the cottage: 'Jinhua, Jinhua'.*]

SU LIANYU There, he sounds frantic. He may be well over thirty, but it'll take you some time to break him in!

FENG JINHUA Shut up! You're supposed to be an elder brother!

SU LIANYU As they say, within three days of the wedding, no rules apply! Well, it's time I made myself scarce! [*With a chuckle, exits*]

[FENG JINHUA *goes towards the cottage and stops at the door, preoccupied with her thoughts. UNCLE DOGGIE comes back from the stables with the empty bushel in his hands.*]

UNCLE DOGGIE The brat, he's supposed to be in charge of all the beasts, but he doesn't feed them properly. Worse still, he won't let others do it. Thank God I slipped in. But as soon as I poured the beans into the trough, eight mouths dug in and in a jiffy, the beans were gone! Chrysanthemum hardly got a mouthful. This idea of eating from the same big pot, or the same big trough, it doesn't work—not for beasts and not for men. Skin and bones, that's how they all end up! Ho! I'm back to this place again. All quiet now. Guests all gone I guess. Well, I missed the nuptial drinks, might as well enjoy myself with some 'eavesdropping.' Let's get an earful of what they're saying!

[As UNCLE DOGGIE *approaches the cottage,* FENG JINHUA *turns around. They face each other, point blank.*]

FENG JINHUA [*suddenly on her knees*] I let you down. May I turn into a beast of burden in my next life to repay you.

UNCLE DOGGIE [*clearly not recognizing her and thinking it's a great joke*] My, no eavesdropping for me, but in time for the bride's ritual greeting! What shall I do? Haven't got a penny on me to give her any lucky money! Better hide my face. Wait here, I'll go home and find my keeper of the keys for your greeting money.

[FENG JINHUA *runs into the cottage, slamming the door behind her.*]

[*trying to remember*] Went to the fair, didn't she? Or to pray at the temple? Well, a nun might marry a monk any day!

SCENE ELEVEN

[Time: a few years later, at the start of the Cultural Revolution (1966–76). In the shade of the arch. UNCLE DOGGIE *is cleaning out an earthenware water pitcher with care.]*

UNCLE DOGGIE Wind and rain, the gods in heaven are having fun again. When they bring a yellow dust storm, it's gold from the skies. You can be sure of a bumper harvest. But when fish fall from the sky with the rain, big fish a foot long, and small fish like shrimps, that means trouble. Fish is wasteful. When you have fish, you eat up a lot of rice, and the god of the underworld—he's not pleased, he won't allow it. When he gets angry, the earth quakes and the mountains shake. There's leftover food that beggars won't take, and yet they all eat their fill. And when their bellies are full, they'll make trouble, too. Then what a world! Fools are scared of bullies, bullies are scared of the desperate who don't give a damn about life, yours or theirs. So they wanted to pull down my arch. They said it was 'reactionary'. I said, 'Just you dare! I don't give a damn about you!' What happened? They went away. But there are two things you have to give a damn about. One is the land. The other is your wife. I ignored them once, and they're both gone. No matter. I'll go and get it back again. Not the wife, but the land. When you have land, what you don't have you will have. But without land, what you have will go for sure. And where shall I find it? Not at the edge of heaven, not at the ends of the earth. Let me tell you, *[Mysteriously]* at Windy Slope. There's an oak tree on that slope, and under the tree there's a cool spring, and near the spring there's a little cave, just right for me. Plenty of land around, and what you take is yours. It's cool there and breezy too. And not a fly to pester you. You want to come with me, eh? Nothing doing. Li Wanjiang signed the permit for me alone, it's supposed to be special treatment. Isn't that strange? The way I see it, it's because I've got the strength and the know-how. No doubt about that. With this pitcher, and this pickaxe, I can go anywhere and start afresh! I'll spread my roots wherever there's land! I won't ever forget you, Li Wanjiang, my great benefactor. *[Looking up at the arch]* Old pal, I'll be away for a while, but I'll be back, so don't be sad, you'll be taken care of—by my son. Where is my son? Where is Dahu? Dahu? Dahu? Oh yes, he's running around with some girl, someone told me. I just hope he won't be fooled by a pretty face, and pick up a woman who can't run a house. Now, she should be someone like my Jinhua, nimble with her fingers and quick with her tongue. Can't find them any more these days. She has her faults, of course. Loves to go to the fair, and once there, she loses her head, still not back, not back . . . to the fair, to the temple, to burn incense, to pray . . . *[Leaning on the arch, he dozes off.]*

[QI YONGNIAN appears before him as an apparition.]

QI YONGNIAN Uncle Doggie, long time no see. Still in good health?

UNCLE DOGGIE Qi Yongnian? You have aged . . . Go away, you scum!

QI YONGNIAN I'll go if I'm not welcome.

UNCLE DOGGIE No, stay. Let's talk. I feel lonesome.

QI YONGNIAN Where's your son?

UNCLE DOGGIE Gone after a girl.

QI YONGNIAN What about your woman?

UNCLE DOGGIE Not yet back from the fair.

QI YONGNIAN And Chrysanthemum?

UNCLE DOGGIE Dead! There is a Chrysanthemum Junior, though, from her. Harnessed by this time.

QI YONGNIAN Belongs to you?

UNCLE DOGGIE Nah, belongs to the collective.

QI YONGNIAN How does the old saying go? Remember?

UNCLE DOGGIE Sure. What belongs to Mother is better than what belongs to Dad, what belongs to you is better than either, what you have in your pocket is better still, but what you hold in your hand is the best! O-ho, you are a reactionary! Li Wanjiang, he's spreading—

QI YONGNIAN Hush. Look at this—*[Opens up a cloth parcel to show him the seal box]*

UNCLE DOGGIE The seal box, hand it over!

QI YONGNIAN You have no use for it anymore.

UNCLE DOGGIE Oh yes I have. Listen, I'm going up to the Windy Slope!

QI YONGNIAN You can't have it anyway.

UNCLE DOGGIE I know, we clodhoppers are all the same. We never forget a good turn and we always remember an insult. You are still angry with me because I slapped you that time. Come, give me a slap, we'll call it quits.

QI YONGNIAN I can't, because I am dead.

UNCLE DOGGIE [*not surprised*] You dead? Yeah, I remember hearing about it.

QI YONGNIAN The young Red Guards bashed me with a club—and I died like a dog for all my crimes.

UNCLE DOGGIE Dog or man, it was a life. It wasn't easy to have the god of the underworld grant you a human skin! Pity, it's a pity!

QI YONGNIAN I never spent money on food or pleasure, I saved and scraped to buy land. Never even enjoyed a whole cucumber, and now, at the end of it all, I've got no one to offer incense in remembrance of me. I can't stand that lonely feeling, so I came to you.

UNCLE DOGGIE Didn't you have a daughter? What's her name?

QI YONGNIAN Xiaomeng. Same age as your Dahu. She has suffered too.

UNCLE DOGGIE She's your daughter. Serves her right.

QI YONGNIAN She is of age, should get married.

UNCLE DOGGIE Who'd dare touch her? No one with a clean family background would ask for such trouble. Hand it over now, that little box.

QI YONGNIAN Nothing doing.

UNCLE DOGGIE You're dead stubborn.

QI YONGNIAN That's what they all say.

[CHEN DAHU, *leading* QI XIAOMENG, *enters.*]

CHEN DAHU Come, he's so muddle-headed, he won't recognize you.

QI XIAOMENG What if he does?

CHEN DAHU So what? Sooner or later you are going to be a member of the family.

[*The apparition of* QI YONGNIAN *remains, but only visible to* UNCLE DOGGIE, *not to* CHEN DAHU *or* QI XIAOMENG.]

Dad! Dad!

UNCLE DOGGIE [*half awake*] Hmm. Dahu. Your Mother not back yet?

CHEN DAHU She's gone to the fair. Right?

UNCLE DOGGIE Pretty lively at the fair, eh?

CHEN DAHU Yeah, very.

UNCLE DOGGIE Who is this?

CHEN DAHU [*to* QI XIAOMENG] Come and greet him; call him 'Dad.'

QI XIAOMENG [*shy*] Uncle.

UNCLE DOGGIE [*pleased*] Oh, good, good, so this is the girl you've been after? [*Suddenly looking at* QI XIAOMENG *and pointing to* QI YONGNIAN] Why, how is it you look like him?

QI YONGNIAN My daughter should look like me.

UNCLE DOGGIE *[not believing, turns to* QI XIAOMENG*]* What's your family name?

*[*QI XIAOMENG *hesitates.]*

CHEN DAHU Say it.

QI XIAOMENG It's Meng. My full name is Meng Qi.

UNCLE DOGGIE You're not the daughter of this Qi Yongnian?

QI XIAOMENG *[painfully]* No.

QI YONGNIAN What if she is?

UNCLE DOGGIE I won't have her in my house.

QI YONGNIAN Maybe you won't, but he will—the honoured son-in-law of the Qi family.

UNCLE DOGGIE I'll kill him!

QI YONGNIAN Won't you give the poor girl shelter?

UNCLE DOGGIE Well, the Qis and the Chens, we did drink water from the same well, even if we weren't on the best of terms. Hmm, you've got a point. I could get the child out of your stinking shadow and give her some shelter—

QI YONGNIAN That's the way to talk! No reason for her to be burdened with the reactionary label they stuck on me.

UNCLE DOGGIE No! Not on your life! This girl may be pretty as a blossom, but if she's a Qi, and marries into the Chen family, then who's going to be the master of this arch here? Eh? Will it be the Chen arch or the Qi arch?

*[*CHEN DAHU *and* QI XIAOMENG *exchange glances, shaking their heads.]*

QI XIAOMENG *[timidly]* It wouldn't take the name of Qi.

UNCLE DOGGIE But the more I look at you, the more you resemble—

CHEN DAHU *[changing the subject]* Why are you fooling around with that old pitcher again?

UNCLE DOGGIE Old pitcher? With one pitcher of cold water in my hands, I'll outwork any farm-hand, be it reaping wheat or hoeing fields, I'll beat ninety-nine of them out of a hundred. That's why the Qi family was always glad to hire me, hire Uncle Doggie! Even if I did let their mule go down the well . . . Oh, I should be on my way.

CHEN DAHU Where to?

UNCLE DOGGIE *[rapt]* To Windy Slope. With the oak tree, the cold water spring—

QI XIAOMENG Don't you remember, Dahu? We went there when we were kids, there were sour dates, red fruits, and tiny little blue flowers, like stars.

UNCLE DOGGIE Have you been there, girl?

QI XIAOMENG Yes.

UNCLE DOGGIE That's where I'm going. But I'm still uneasy. Sure you are not Qi's daughter?

QI XIAOMENG No, I'm not.

UNCLE DOGGIE Did you know the old fool's dead! The god of heaven decided to call him in. No, I'm wrong, the god of heaven doesn't bother himself about human beings. He's in charge of the immortals. It was the god of the underworld. He sent the armies and generals, created havoc, and with one swish of his club, busted his brains.

CHEN DAHU Dad, you were saying you were going up the Windy Slope. Did Uncle Wanjiang agree to it?

UNCLE DOGGIE Whenever he sees me he's all smiles, as if he owes me something.

QI YONGNIAN Hee hee.

UNCLE DOGGIE What are you giggling about? I'm not done with you yet. *[To* CHEN DAHU*]* Kneel down!

CHEN DAHU Dad—

UNCLE DOGGIE Kneel in front of our arch. Go on! *[Helpless,* CHEN DAHU *kneels down.]* You too. Since you are going to be a Chen, you have to behave like a Chen too. *[*CHEN DAHU *pulls* QI XIAOMENG *down on her knees with him.]* Now, repeat after me. Right. *[To* QI YONGNIAN*]* You stay there. Listen and observe. We'll show you the kind of stock the Chens are made of. We, the Chens are blessed with progeny, not like you, cut off at the root! Now, the first vow: I'll never forget the benefits of our new society, never forget the bounties of our great saviour. Say it.

CHEN DAHU We have.

UNCLE DOGGIE I'll always hate the Qi family, and never meet with the Qis.

CHEN DAHU What crazy talk! Hey, Xiaomeng, this is not so bad, we may as well have our marriage ceremony right here!

QI XIAOMENG I'm supposed to be taking a vow about hating the Qis. How can you joke about it?

UNCLE DOGGIE Say it!

[A bell begins to toll.]

CHEN DAHU Dad, you'd better stop. Uncle Wanjiang is ringing the bell, everyone should start working.

UNCLE DOGGIE No hurry. Qi Yongnian, listen carefully—

QI YONGNIAN Yes.

UNCLE DOGGIE I'll always hate the Qi family, and never meet with a
Qi. Now, my daughter, say it!

QI XIAOMENG *[forcing herself]* Hate the Qi family, never meet with the
Qis—Dad.

UNCLE DOGGIE *[satisfied]* Good.

[The bell is heard again, with LI WANJIANG *shouting:
'Time to work!']*

S C E N E   T W E L V E

*[Time: three years after Scene 11, during the Cultural Revolution.
Windy Slope.* QI XIAOMENG *is bringing food to her father-in-law.]*

QI XIAOMENG *[calling]* Dad!

*[UNCLE DOGGIE enters. He looks like a mountain peasant
from the last century, the only item lacking is a pigtail at
the back of his head.]*

UNCLE DOGGIE A drink of cold spring water, three feet of shade under
a tree. That's a life fit for an emperor!

QI XIAOMENG Dad, I made you some pancakes with wheat and
cornflour. I call them gold and silver pancakes. Look at
the silver under the gold.

UNCLE DOGGIE With work, one must be thorough, but with food, one
shouldn't be choosy. That's the secret of a long life. The
god from the underworld told me I shouldn't eat up all
the oil in this jug, so I didn't. I fed the oil by the
spoonful to each and every root of corn. All living
things are greedy, take it from me. With the oil, the
young corn started stretching their muscles. I could
hear them at night, competing with each other in
growing tall. Crack! Crack! Look at them now, the
corncobs opening up like trumpets, the tassels peeping
out. . . . But there was a time when it looked like there
would be a serious drought. Never mind. I prayed to
the gods. Sure enough, the clouds came running over,
the rain came down, not a downpour, but a gentle
drizzle, every drop sucked into the earth. That's why
the stalks are so tough. You know what? I didn't use
up the half jugful of oil on the corn. No one can
blame me for being wasteful. But the rats got to it,
and finished it all! They'll answer for it to the god of
the underworld. Now, my good daughter, are you
exhausted from work?

QI XIAOMENG As you always told us, people may die from idleness, but never from exhaustion.

UNCLE DOGGIE Good answer, that. Have you repaired the arch?

QI XIAOMENG We have. It looks brand new now.

UNCLE DOGGIE Did you meet with anyone from the Qi clan?

QI XIAOMENG Never.

UNCLE DOGGIE Good. Let's eat.

[As they eat, SU LIANYU rushes in.]

SU LIANYU Brother Doggie!

QI XIAOMENG Uncle Lianyu.

UNCLE DOGGIE Why the rush? You got more land to sell?

SU LIANYU The only thing I might sell is that old woman of mine! People in the village are all going mad, brandishing knives!

UNCLE DOGGIE A little blood-letting is good for your health. Hey, master-barber, what about giving me a haircut? I look like a monk in exile!

SU LIANYU Haircut? They're out to cut . . . the tails!

UNCLE DOGGIE What tails? Pigs' tails?

SU LIANYU No, people's tails: their bad habits, corrupt ideology, and the like.

UNCLE DOGGIE [ignoring his explanation] People grow tails?

QI XIAOMENG When we were in school, the teachers told us that people came from monkeys.

UNCLE DOGGIE What about the god of the underworld? Did he come from tigers?

SU LIANYU Don't waste time. Harvest the corn.

UNCLE DOGGIE It's not ripe yet.

SU LIANYU That's all you're going to get. In a moment it'll all be gone.

UNCLE DOGGIE What are you talking about? Start from the beginning.

SU LIANYU The beginning? Well, it all began with her.

QI XIAOMENG Me?

SU LIANYU They are saying, Uncle Doggie has come to Windy Slope, but that wasn't his own idea, it was hers. It wasn't in his nature, but in hers. Well, not really in hers, but in her father's.

UNCLE DOGGIE It was in my nature all right.

SU LIANYU You fool!

QI XIAOMENG I see. Because of me, the old man here has to suffer. I should have died with my own father long ago.

UNCLE DOGGIE Die? With this beautiful crop on Windy Slope? No
way! Even if I could bring myself to leave it, it
wouldn't want to leave me. You know who I am? I'm
the hedgehog that never dies from a fall. You know
why, Daughter? Because when you throw a hedgehog
on to the ground, it rolls up and doesn't get hurt. But
then the weasel knows how to deal with it. That's
nature's law.

[LI WANJIANG, CHEN DAHU, *and some villagers enter.*]

LI WANJIANG Oh, Su, you are here already?

SU LIANYU Well, just to pass on the news. Oh, give him a break!

CHEN DAHU Dad, let's go home, forget the crop on Windy Slope.

UNCLE DOGGIE What's going on? Have the demons descended from
heaven? Give up a good crop? Never! Even when the
landlords' militia was shooting everybody on sight in
those days, I didn't give up a good crop! I'm
depending on it to get ahead of the Qis in the final
count. And more immediately, I have to make it up to
this wonderful girl here. She married into the Chen
family without getting any bridal gifts. I'm going to
put that right.

CHEN DAHU Dad, get this into your head—if you don't give up
Windy Slope, people will blame her and harass her.
And she's been pregnant now for more than three
months.

UNCLE DOGGIE Oh, thank heaven and earth! All the gods of wealth,
pay attention! We, the Chens are going to be blessed
with children! My old village headman, you are invited
to my grandson's birth celebrations.

LI WANJIANG Sure, sure. But we have to decide about the land.

UNCLE DOGGIE Well, my brother, tell them this is 'special treatment'.

LI WANJIANG *[embarrassed]* Well, circumstances change, you know.
Nowadays, it's all about cutting off tails. And you
happen to have no ordinary tail, no usual tail, no
everyday sort of tail. Your tail trails a long way.
Because your daughter-in-law, her father, your relative
by marriage, you know who I mean . . . the one that
died . . .

UNCLE DOGGIE What are you going on about? You took some wrong
medicine?

LI WANJIANG *[throwing discretion to the winds]* She is Qi Yongnian's
daughter, for God's sake!

UNCLE DOGGIE I won't tolerate such slander! Open your eyes and take a good look. Could that son-of-a-bitch produce such a wonderful daughter?

SU LIANYU That's the trouble, my brother. Because of your association with the Qis, your 'class origin' is no longer pure and clean, and you have been working independently on Windy Slope, away from the collective. Your tail is a mile long. They sure as hell will try to cut it off. No doubt about it. She is Qi Yongnian's daughter.

UNCLE DOGGIE *[unsure now]* Daughter, are you the girl Xiaomeng from the Qi family?

QI XIAOMENG I am Xiaomeng, Dad.

UNCLE DOGGIE And you, both of you, have been lying to me?

QI XIAOMENG Dad, I have no brothers and no sisters, I'm all alone in this world. With my clumsy hands I have served you for the past three years. Please accept me.

UNCLE DOGGIE You are taking advantage of me because my woman is away!

CHEN DAHU Dad, give up Windy Slope!

UNCLE DOGGIE Never!

CHEN DAHU Then they will take her away, to a big meeting—

UNCLE DOGGIE *[explodes]* Over my dead body! So what if she is Qi's daughter? Even puppies from the same litter aren't all the same. Go tell them, you have changed your name, you are called Chen now.

LI WANJIANG Whatever she calls herself, we still have to cut off this tail of yours, because—

UNCLE DOGGIE Stop it! You know what I'm thinking? Life today is worse than before the liberation!

LI WANJIANG *[stunned]* What are you saying? How dare you!

UNCLE DOGGIE In those days, when the landlords' militia got too tough, we could always run to the Communists. Who can I turn to now?

SU LIANYU It's no good talking like that. We must deal with this business of cutting off tails. And your tail is certainly no ordinary tail.

UNCLE DOGGIE Tails is it? Some real devil must have thought up that idea. All right, I'll show you—now my daughter-in-law, will you excuse us a moment and turn the other way? I'm going to let everybody see whether Uncle Doggie has a tail on his arse!

QI XIAOMENG [*slowly*] Uncle Wanjiang, the old man is not himself, let's not bother him any more. Whatever is illegal or criminal about Windy Slope, I will take full responsibility as a Qi family member. I'll come with you. Let's go.

UNCLE DOGGIE Oh no, you won't. Who will bring me my meals?

[FENG JINHUA *appears among the crowd.*]

FENG JINHUA Li Wanjiang, what was our agreement? What did you promise? What are you trying to do, flapping your wings like a headless chicken! The way you hang on to that miserable official hat of yours makes me sick! You can't eat it, you can't drink it, but you think it's the whole world. Drop it once and for all, and your conscience will be clear! I'll take care of this 'cutting tails' business. Let them come to me. Go away now! Let this family have a reunion, here on Windy Slope! [*Breaks down*]

UNCLE DOGGIE Listen to the lady here. She doesn't mince words, and how right she is. And she's only a woman. Shame on you officials!

[*Everyone on stage fades out, with only* UNCLE DOGGIE *remaining.*]

SCENE THIRTEEN

[*Time: back to present. Morning of the day in Scene 1.*
UNCLE DOGGIE, *aged* 72, *looks disconsolate.* QI YONGNIAN's *apparition appears.*]

QI YONGNIAN Recognize me?

UNCLE DOGGIE Yeah, I've seen you before.

QI YONGNIAN Look, they're here again, that couple.

[LI WANJIANG, *now in his 60s, and* FENG JINHUA, *in her 50s, appear in the distance, talking to each other.*]

UNCLE DOGGIE More tails to cut off?

QI YONGNIAN Nah, that's all over. This time it might be something nice for a change.

UNCLE DOGGIE Times change, like the weather.

QI YONGNIAN Sure, sunshine after a storm.

UNCLE DOGGIE Go away.

QI YONGNIAN Let's chat.

UNCLE DOGGIE I'm busy. [*Both of them disappear.*]

FENG JINHUA *[reminds him again]* Take young Chrysanthemum with
    you.

LI WANJIANG I will, I will. That's why I'm going there.

FENG JINHUA No wonder they say, when you buy a horse, take a
    good look at its mother first. She's the spitting image
    of her mother. And the liquor?

LI WANJIANG I've got it.

FENG JINHUA The salted eggs. He is very fond of them.

LI WANJIANG Here they are.

FENG JINHUA Don't look so distracted, like a lost soul. Cheer up.

LI WANJIANG How the hell can I cheer up? After more than twenty
    years, here I am taking the horse back to him. What
    have I been doing with my life?

FENG JINHUA Now, for heaven's sake, don't you go round the bend as
    well. I have enough on my hands as it is. You just take
    the horse to Windy Slope and have a nice time
    drinking with him. Who knows, it might cheer him
    up, relieve him of his grievances, and Buddha
    permitting, he might regain his senses.

LI WANJIANG That would be great. For me too! I could return both
    the horse and you to him.

FENG JINHUA I'll whip you! Do you think I'm just a horse? Is that
    what a woman is worth to you?

    [A horse neighs. Blackout. When the lights come up again,
    UNCLE DOGGIE *and* LI WANJIANG *are sitting together on*
    Windy Slope.]

LI WANJIANG Have another. I brought a full jug.

UNCLE DOGGIE A rare occasion. Say what's on your mind, my young
    brother. If you want the world 'Red All Over', Doggie
    here won't let you down by being a 'Black Spot'.

LI WANJIANG Let's forget that now. Have something to eat.

UNCLE DOGGIE Salted eggs? Hmm, nice. Yeah. The right flavour, too.
    Where did you get this?

LI WANJIANG Well, it's home-made.

UNCLE DOGGIE Who made it?

LI WANJIANG My wife.

UNCLE DOGGIE Yeah, wives are good at these things. Cheers!

LI WANJIANG Cheers! Are you clear-headed now?

UNCLE DOGGIE When was I ever muddled?

LI WANJIANG Then I'm the one who has been muddle-headed. What
    a world! Things stay the same for decades, and then,
    over night, all is changed. You wake up one morning
    and you don't know where you are. It's weird.

UNCLE DOGGIE Just like Monkey King in the stories. But, as the god of the underworld says, no matter how things change, the arch will belong to the Chens. That will never change.

[QI YONGNIAN's apparition enters.]

Talk of the devil, here he is.

QI YONGNIAN This wilderness makes me lonely. So here I am looking for a free drink.

UNCLE DOGGIE Go away!

QI YONGNIAN But we are family. My daughter married your son.

UNCLE DOGGIE True. Not only that, I have a grandson now. One thing though, the two sides of this family have nothing to do with each other.

LI WANJIANG *[troubled]* Brother Doggie, are you all right?

UNCLE DOGGIE Let's drink. Don't pay him any attention.

LI WANJIANG Who?

UNCLE DOGGIE Qi Yongnian.

LI WANJIANG I was just going to talk about him.

QI YONGNIAN You see?

UNCLE DOGGIE *[to QI YONGNIAN]* You stay out of this! *[To LI WANJIANG]* What were you going to say?

LI WANJIANG If you were . . . Well, put it this way, suppose he was here now, we'd have to treat him as an equal. It's fine to be a landlord now.

QI YONGNIAN There, you see. *[Sits down in comfort]*

UNCLE DOGGIE No, no. His presence would foul the place.

LI WANJIANG It won't do to say that now. The Cultural Revolution is over.

UNCLE DOGGIE Do we have to offer him a drink then?

LI WANJIANG By the rules of the game these days, I'd have to do that.

QI YONGNIAN You see. *[Holds out his hand for the cup]*

UNCLE DOGGIE *[grabs the cup from LI WANJIANG's hand, and throws the liquor in QI YONGNIAN's face]* There! You want a drink, do you? You are an equal now, are you? You want me to treat you as a relative? Never! *[The two of them begin to tussle.]*

LI WANJIANG Hey, what's the matter, Brother Doggie? *[Failing to stop UNCLE DOGGIE]* Chen Hexiang! I've come to return your horse!

UNCLE DOGGIE My horse? *[With a guffaw]* Ho, ho, trying to trick me again? Electric lights and telephones! Hah?

LI WANJIANG No! No tricks this time. I've got Chrysanthemum right
here!

UNCLE DOGGIE I don't want her. Some day you'll come along with a
jug of liquor, and you'll take her away again.

LI WANJIANG It won't happen again.

UNCLE DOGGIE Suppose it did?

LI WANJIANG I promise it won't.

UNCLE DOGGIE You and who else?

QI YONGNIAN Stubborn mule!

UNCLE DOGGIE You shut up!

LI WANJIANG If anyone ever tries to bully us again into doing those
crazy things, I'll spit in his face. I'll stop working on
the land, and let them starve! Oh yes, speaking of land,
you can work on your 'Neck of the Gourd' again. All
land has reverted to its former owners.

UNCLE DOGGIE Really?

LI WANJIANG If I lie, may I be struck dead by lightning!

[A horse neighs.]

UNCLE DOGGIE Chrysanthemum! My Chrysanthemum, my pet, where
are you?

LI WANJIANG By the cold spring, tied to the oak tree.

QI YONGNIAN By the cold spring, tied to the oak tree, tied to the oak
tree—

UNCLE DOGGIE Scram! I don't want to see you in a thousand years!

[QI YONGNIAN disappears.]

First I must water her, let her enjoy the sparkling
spring water, enjoy it to the full.

*[Exits in high spirits. Moments later, his cry of excitement
resounds in the valley: 'I have my horse'. LI WANJIANG runs
after him with mixed feelings.*

*   UNCLE DOGGIE re-enters, holding the water pitcher with
both hands, scrutinizing his own reflection in the water. LI
WANJIANG follows him.]*

[in a low voice] Uncle Doggie, Chen Hexiang, old
fellow, not a single black hair left! What did I get in
return for this hoary white head? *[Looks up at* LI
WANJIANG*]* Brother Wanjiang, can this be you? Your
face is wrinkled like a walnut. You must be what—
forty?

LI WANJIANG *[with a wry smile]* Sixty-four.

UNCLE DOGGIE You're sixty? I am eight years older, I must be seventy-
two. Good God.

LI WANJIANG The gods don't care.

UNCLE DOGGIE Oh then, god of the underworld—

LI WANJIANG Forget your god of the underworld. By the textbooks the kids use, this is the law, the law of nature.

UNCLE DOGGIE Well then, most honourable nature, please let me go back thirty years; no, twenty will do. I'll muster all the energy in me, I'll wear out ten pickaxe handles, but I'll get ahead of Qi Yongnian. I'll get hold of that box with his seal in it. I'll own all the land there is around here. If I fail, let me plunge into the cold spring here and end it all!

LI WANJIANG [to himself] Still not all there. [To UNCLE DOGGIE] Old brother, it's not too late yet!

UNCLE DOGGIE True. I still have my son and grandson! I'll teach them how to plough, till, hoe, loosen the soil, sieve, winnow, and gather it all in. Only when you have mastered all that can you call yourself a man of the soil. Yes, I'll teach them myself all the tricks of the trade. Why, even with animals, you have to train them before they can be harnessed.

LI WANJIANG Yes, it's the right time now. Before 'white dew', it's too early; and after 'cold dew', it's too late.

UNCLE DOGGIE For winter wheat the Autumn Equinox is the right time.

LI WANJIANG And sowing seeds timely in the field—

UNCLE DOGGIE Will give you tenfold in the yield.

LI WANJIANG What are you waiting for? Take Chrysanthemum, pack up your bedding, and home you go! Your son, daughter-in-law, and your grandson are anxious to have you back. Go home, my old brother.

UNCLE DOGGIE [elated for the moment] Let's go! My son, daughter-in-law, grandson, Chrysanthemum, my arch. . . . [Trying hard to remember] Mother of Dahu, where is Mother of Dahu? Gone to the fair? [Shakes his head] No, it doesn't make sense. . . . Brother Wanjiang!

LI WANJIANG What is it?

UNCLE DOGGIE We must get back to the village at once! I must find Jinhua, my Jinhua. Alive or dead, she laboured and suffered with me all these years, I must make it up to her!

LI WANJIANG You . . . remember her?

UNCLE DOGGIE How can I forget? She is my wife!

LI WANJIANG Come. When we're back at the village—I'll tell you something.

SCENE FOURTEEN

[Time: the same afternoon.

A horse neighs. The lights go up dimly on the arch which looks shabbier than ever.

The sound of a truck braking to a stop. CHEN DAHU *and* QI XIAOMENG *enter, looking happy and excited.]*

CHEN DAHU *[waving]* Thanks a lot for the lift!

QI XIAOMENG What a trip to the city, I'm exhausted!

CHEN DAHU My frail young lady from the house of Qi! Better go and see how our boy is.

QI XIAOMENG That's all you care about, your precious son.

[SU LIANYU enters, breathless.]

SU LIANYU When the truck arrived I knew the two of you had come back. I was counting every minute! Don't worry, wife of my nephew, your boy, Little Dragon, had a wonderful time in my house. What a brilliant child, counting on his fingers, he can count up to five hundred—

QI XIAOMENG I'm so grateful for Auntie's help.

CHEN DAHU What about the bulldozer, Uncle?

SU LIANYU It will be here tomorrow. And the contract?

CHEN DAHU It's all settled. Three thousand tons.

SU LIANYU My! These days, when people talk, it's in the thousands and tens of thousands! Three thousand tons, three times three is nine, and . . . Well, with this deal, there'll be quite a bit of money!

CHEN DAHU Peanuts really. We are way behind the marble factory in Dawang Village.

SU LIANYU I've always said, you are going places. Talk of ambition!

CHEN DAHU Uncle Wanjiang still seems doubtful.

SU LIANYU You know what the kids in the village say about him? 'Uncle Wanjiang sits on a stool, he loves to be poor, says the fool. Give him an ingot made of gold, he'd rather starve than have it sold'. That goes for your dad, too. Me? I'm different, I'm open to new ideas.

QI XIAOMENG That's why you never lose out!

SU LIANYU Now, don't tease me, my girl. I know I'm selfish. I've made up my mind now. I'll join forces with you, come what may let's sink or swim together. Who knows, we might end up with ten thousand yuan in the bank. Right, I'll be on my way to the township authorities, and come back with the business permit for our factory.

CHEN DAHU We'll have a drink when you come back, and work out the details about going into operation tomorrow.

SU LIANYU I won't be late. *[Exits]*

CHEN DAHU *[gently]* What about a little rest?

QI XIAOMENG *[giggling]* Hee hee.

CHEN DAHU What are you laughing at?

QI XIAOMENG Those girls in the city, with their scanty clothes, baring their arms and legs. Nice, though. Saves a lot of fabric and feels so cool.

CHEN DAHU It's progress. Why don't you get something like that too!

QI XIAOMENG In our village? My, people would be scandalized!

CHEN DAHU What do I care! As long as I like it.

QI XIAOMENG Go on.

CHEN DAHU Didn't you see the young people in the streets? They go around arm in arm, holding hands and all. *[Puts his arm round* QI XIAOMENG's *shoulders]*

QI XIAOMENG I'd never get used to being so intimate in public.

CHEN DAHU That's feudal—

[FENG JINHUA enters, unsure of herself.]

FENG JINHUA *[hesitant]* Dahu—

CHEN DAHU *[awkwardly]* Oh, Auntie—

QI XIAOMENG *[warmly]* Auntie! Come in and sit down.

FENG JINHUA No, I don't think I will. Just you two at home? The arch is so run down. Aren't you going to fix it up?

CHEN DAHU There's no need. We are pulling it down tomorrow.

FENG JINHUA Pulling it down?

CHEN DAHU The bricks have rotted through. Even if we don't pull it down, the arch will crumble by itself.

[QI XIAOMENG offers the rare guest a plate of red dates.]

QI XIAOMENG Auntie, have some dates.

FENG JINHUA Dates, everyone likes dates.

CHEN DAHU Auntie, you've come to—?

FENG JINHUA I've come to see your dad.

CHEN DAHU You know he is at Windy Slope. He hasn't been home for years.

FENG JINHUA Your Uncle Wanjiang took the horse to him today.

CHEN DAHU A lot of good that'll do.

QI XIAOMENG *[trying to stop him]* Dahu!

CHEN DAHU Well, isn't it true? Eye drops won't help a bellyache!

FENG JINHUA How can you talk that way? The horse was his prized property. He pinned all his hopes on that horse. Maybe when he sees the horse, he'll regain his senses.

CHEN DAHU Let's hope not. If he does and comes back, I'll be in trouble. And you too—

FENG JINHUA Don't say that, child. These years, it hasn't been easy for him, even surviving wasn't easy. I want to see him live a few more years, in his right senses, to see his family, this arch, you, and, in his right senses, to have another look at me . . . Dahu, I let you down, you and your dad!

CHEN DAHU Say no more . . .!

QI XIAOMENG *[bursting into tears]* And my dad . . . if he could have lived to see this day, how wonderful it would—

CHEN DAHU Oh, my precious lady, don't you join in!

[A horse neighs. UNCLE DOGGIE enters, moving with big healthy strides.]

UNCLE DOGGIE Here is the horse!

QI XIAOMENG *[rushing towards him happily]* Dad!

UNCLE DOGGIE Yes, my good daughter. Now, clear up the east room, install the trough: I and Chrysanthemum will share the room.

[FENG JINHUA tries to run off but UNCLE DOGGIE notices her. He looks surprised.] Dahu, your mother, she's at the fair, not back, is she?

CHEN DAHU No.

FENG JINHUA *[trying to regain her composure]* Well, how are you?

UNCLE DOGGIE You are . . . Wanjiang's wife? I'm so grateful to you, you saved me. . . . You better go, Brother Wanjiang should be home now.

FENG JINHUA Let me, . . . let me help Xiaomeng fix up the room for . . . the horse . . . one more time.

UNCLE DOGGIE No. Come over here, Xiaomeng. Do you remember the courtyard in the old days?

QI XIAOMENG Not really. I remember my father talking about it though. Inside the arch there was a screen wall, and as you went further in, on one side there were lilac trees, and on the other side the vats for the lotus—

UNCLE DOGGIE Right! Right!

QI XIAOMENG In front of you would be the main hall, and on the sides were the rooms.

UNCLE DOGGIE *[remembering]* Right, right! Then the people who were allotted these rooms simply dismantled them and built their houses elsewhere with the bricks, and what we had was the arch. The arch is the facade! With a facade, you can rebuild the courtyard. Dahu, how are we doing for cash?

CHEN DAHU What do you have in mind?

UNCLE DOGGIE What do I have in mind? If the Qis could build a courtyard, so can the Chens! Are we good for nothing?

CHEN DAHU Nothing. Not a penny. You're talking in your sleep!

FENG JINHUA Dahu, you're talking to your dad, watch your language!

[SU LIANYU enters with the framed business permit.]

SU LIANYU Oh, the old man is back!

UNCLE DOGGIE *[truculently]* Yeah, waiting to buy more land from you.

SU LIANYU Crazy as ever.

FENG JINHUA Su.

SU LIANYU Oh, you're . . . back, too.

FENG JINHUA I knew he was coming back, so I came over to have a look. Who'd have thought . . . He's still not all there. Didn't recognize me.

SU LIANYU *[relieved]* In that case, let's talk business. We've got the business permit and everything. Work begins tomorrow, and, when the factory is built, you'll be the general manager, Dahu, and Xiaomeng the assistant manager. Now, your Uncle Su here should be at least a deputy, right? As soon as the bulldozer arrives, I promise you, we'll pull down the arch!

UNCLE DOGGIE *[explodes]* What! Pull down the arch! What's all this nonsense? You . . . you are going to pull down the arch?

SU LIANYU *[trying to placate him]* It's like this, the arch is old. Look at it this way, since you are old, the arch is surely old too. We'll pull it down, to welcome Jinhua back from the fair—

UNCLE DOGGIE *[suddenly overcome with sorrow]* No, she'll never be back! Just now, as I was tying the horse to the jujube tree, our neighbour, old Granny told me all. Su, you have been deceiving me all my life!

[LI WANJIANG enters.]

LI WANJIANG Old Brother, come with me to my place. The two of us are going to have a heart-to-heart talk! *[Sees JINHUA, surprised]* You are here too?

UNCLE DOGGIE Brother Wanjiang, take your wife home. My Jinhua, Mother of Dahu, is not coming back any more. If she's become an immortal, I'll build her a temple; if she's turned into a ghost, I'll build her a grave, all in my heart. But the lot of you here, you're going too far! You, Li Wanjiang, you're the head of the village, are you going to pull down my arch, pluck out my heart?

CHEN DAHU Dad—

UNCLE DOGGIE Who is your dad? You have forsaken all of your
ancestors!

CHEN DAHU No, I have not. I never learnt anything about my
great-grandfather, I just know grandfather died because
he ate a puppy alive in order to win a bet for some
land; and I know my Dad was crazy for land. Wasn't it
all because we wanted to build up a family fortune?
Your son here, he's going to build up that fortune!

UNCLE DOGGIE You're going to do it? Pah! When I was young, I got
up before dawn everyday to pick up manure. Have you
ever worked that hard? This courtyard here, such a tidy
place, has turned into a pigsty in your hands. And
what's happened to the stepping-stone at the front
entrance for horse riders?

CHEN DAHU We've used it as the cornerstone of the factory.

UNCLE DOGGIE The factory, my arse! Is the factory your father? What's
going on in that head of yours? Are you possessed by
some demon? Why won't you put your mind to tilling
the land? Have you forgotten what I've always taught
you? Gold comes from the land. Money earned from
easy ways will be lost just as easily! Get that into your
head, you whelp!

CHEN DAHU [with infinite patience] Dad, look around you, what an
ideal place we have! A highway in front, and the rock
slope right behind. Look at the slope, it's pure white
marble. A treasure trove. In foreign countries, when
they build those huge buildings, they need this stuff.
They want every bit we can produce. It's an easy job,
we'll just quarry and cut it to size, and, see, the rock
becomes hard cash! We can't just stare at the old arch
and go on scraping for a living out of the earth.

QI XIAOMENG That's right, Dad. The bit of land allotted to us, you
can look after without sweat. And if you are tired of it,
why, we can hire labour to do it. After we have pulled
down the arch, we'll build the factory. We'll also put
up a little room at the entrance, and when there is not
much to do in the fields in winter and spring, you can
take care of the reception office, maybe grow some
flowers, keep some birds, take a few telephone calls.
We'll give you double pay, and you will receive bonuses
every month.

UNCLE DOGGIE Ha, you two make a perfect pair! The two of you are
scheming to throw me out, aren't you? What a good
son I've got! Why did I risk my life to reap the

sesame, with the life of your mother thrown in? Had
I known you'd turn out to be such a freak of nature,
I would have strangled you at birth! And you, such a
sweet, kind-hearted innocent girl. Who'd have thought
you had such venom in you! Now at last you've shown
your true colours, a child of the Qis through and
through! *[Raising his voice]* Qi Yongnian!

[QI YONGNIAN's apparition enters.]

QI YONGNIAN Here.

UNCLE DOGGIE Your daughter, isn't she?

QI YONGNIAN A dragon will beget a dragon, and a phoenix a
phoenix.

UNCLE DOGGIE You never miss a chance to foul things up!

SU LIANYU There, out of his mind again.

UNCLE DOGGIE *[to the apparition]* This is a trick you thought up! You
couldn't work it in the open, so you did it on the sly.
You send your daughter to ruin my household! I earned
this arch with blood and sweat, I got it because there
was a new society. Li Wanjiang can testify to that, and
you, *[To SU LIANYU]* you barber, and you, *[To FENG
JINHUA]* the lady here—all of you can testify—was it
easy for me to build up this family fortune? Am I now
to stand by and allow this spendthrift son of mine to
ruin it?

CHEN DAHU *[with finality]* Dad, the arch is sold.

UNCLE DOGGIE *[stunned]* Sold?

CHEN DAHU You were sick, you had to have injections, medical
treatment, we had to borrow right and left, and now
we have to pay up.

UNCLE DOGGIE Sold to whom?

SU LIANYU To me!

UNCLE DOGGIE *[shaking his head and stamping his foot]* Oh Su, you grew
up with me drinking water from the same well, we are
supposed to be brothers! So you sold me that land of
yours and now you are buying my arch! For how
much?

SU LIANYU Three bushels of sesame seed! No, no, the price has yet
to be decided on. Tomorrow, yes, tomorrow we'll make
the final decision. Tomorrow.

UNCLE DOGGIE Tomorrow?

CHEN DAHU Tomorrow.

UNCLE DOGGIE *[seeking help]* Oh! Head of the village, aren't you going
to do something about it?

LI WANJIANG I will, I will, but what can I do? You've come back to
the village only just now, you have no idea what I have
had to face. As things stand now, nobody can tell
anybody what to do anymore. The couple of hundred
people in this village, everyone of them is a genius;
each is into private enterprise. I'm the only idiot. I've
done you wrong, and I'll make it up to you. But about
the demolition of the arch, I have no say. I dare not say
anything, and I can't say anything. The only thing you
can do perhaps is to go to the head of the township.

UNCLE DOGGIE You are an official, and you wash your hands of it?

LI WANJIANG From tomorrow onwards, I will no longer be an official.

UNCLE DOGGIE So what am I supposed to do?

LI WANJIANG The township leader is way above my rank. He should
have a better idea.

UNCLE DOGGIE All right, I will go then, and once I get to see this
high ranking leader, I'm going to sue all of you for
conspiracy.

SU LIANYU Oh Brother Doggie, don't be silly, I just came back
from town, and they told me that the township leader
was entertaining two Japanese visitors, having a drink
with them.

UNCLE DOGGIE What? Even the township leader has become a
collaborator? We're doomed, doomed!

CHEN DAHU Dad, don't worry yourself about these things.

UNCLE DOGGIE I would worry even if I were dead!

CHEN DAHU We'll provide you with everything you want: food,
drinks of your choice. We'll serve you, we'll be filial,
we'll treat you like one of the gods, what more do you
want?

UNCLE DOGGIE You're going to be filial?

CHEN DAHU Yes, we'll be filial.

UNCLE DOGGIE Filial to me?

CHEN DAHU Yes, to you.

UNCLE DOGGIE So the arch, you won't pull it down?

CHEN DAHU It's in the way, we'll have to.

UNCLE DOGGIE *[slaps him hard]* You traitor!

[Everyone on the stage freezes.]

BLACKOUT

SCENE FIFTEEN

[Time: a short time later.
The arch. QI XIAOMENG*'s giggling and* CHEN DAHU*'s laughter can be heard offstage.* UNCLE DOGGIE *and the apparition of* QI YONGNIAN *are together as they were in the opening scene. After a moment of silence, the action begins.]*

UNCLE DOGGIE *[gathering his things and lighting the torch]* Tomorrow, tomorrow, tomorrow. You have your tomorrow, and I have mine.

QI YONGNIAN But I don't have any tomorrow. Oh well, my daughter will have her tomorrow.

UNCLE DOGGIE *[finding* QI YONGNIAN *at his side]* Go away, I don't want to see you, ever.

QI YONGNIAN Ha! After today we have tomorrow, and tomorrow there will be fun and games. Ha ha ha! *[Disappears]*

UNCLE DOGGIE Tomorrow . . . there'll be fun and games. . . . *[Shouting]* The arch—my arch! *[Hurls the torch]*

[Spotlight on UNCLE DOGGIE, *who has thrown himself on the ground in front of the arch]*

THE END*

---

* In the Chinese text, the play ends with a short scene in which Chen Dahu discovers the fire, tells Qi Xiaomeng to put out the fire so that the construction work scheduled to begin in the morning will not be delayed, and then rushes out to look for his father. Ying Ruocheng, while directing the play for stage production in America, thought that the play should end where its dramatic climax occurs, i.e. in Scene 15. After consultation with the playwright, Scene 16—the last scene—was omitted from the translation.

THE OTHER SIDE

A CONTEMPORARY DRAMA
WITHOUT ACTS

1986

By
GAO XINGJIAN

Translated by
JO RILEY

— ABOUT **THE PLAYWRIGHT** —

GAO XINGJIAN (1940–) graduated from the French Department of the Institute of Foreign Languages in Beijing in 1962 and worked as a translator at the Foreign Languages Press for several years before being sent down to the countryside during the Cultural Revolution. In 1977, he was transferred to the Foreign Affairs Unit of the Writers' Association of China and resumed his work as a translator. In 1978, his writings began to be published. In 1981, he was transferred to the Playscript Division of the Beijing People's Art Theatre and became a full-time playwright. Between 1982 and 1985 he wrote a number of controversial plays (*Absolute Signal*, 1982; *Bus Stop*, 1983; *Wild Man*, 1985). These earned him the suspicion and wrath of the authorities (*Bus Stop* was banned soon after it opened at the Beijing People's Art Theatre) but he also won high international acclaim and was credited by the Mainland drama critics for having started the experimental theatre movement on the Mainland. In 1986, he was rehearsing *The Other Side* when the order came that performance of the play was to be banned. In the following year, he went on a lecture tour in Germany and France, and decided to settle down in France. In 1990, another of his plays, *Escape*, was again singled out for criticism by the authorities, and since then his plays have not been seen on the Mainland stage. In 1992, he was nominated *Chevalier* in *Ordre des Arts et des lettres* by the French government. He now writes in both Chinese and French, directs his own plays, paints, and conducts theatre workshops in Europe.

Gao Xingjian has written several novels, one theoretical work on novel-writing, and one on modern drama, as well as some twenty-five plays, ten of which he destroyed during the Cultural Revolution. Many of his plays have been translated—into French, English, German, Italian, Japanese, Swedish, Hungarian, Polish, and Dutch. They have also been performed in Sweden, Germany, France, Austria, Britain, America, Australia, Italy, Poland, Taiwan, and Hong Kong. *The Other Side*, banned in 1986, had its world premiere in Taiwan in 1990, in a Mandarin production directed and performed by the staff and students of the National Institute of the Arts in Taiwan. In 1995, at the invitation of the Hong Kong Academy for Performing Arts, Gao came to Hong Kong and *The Other Side* was performed, with Gao as the director.

ABOUT **THE PLAY**

The Other Side is a deliberate attempt by Gao Xingjian to break away from the 'socialist-realist' mould of drama in mainland China. It is a daring piece of avant-garde writing that defies conventional assumptions about plays and play-acting, about the theatre and theatre performance. In this piece, a group of men and women undertake a journey. Their destination? The 'other side'—the Buddhist's 'other shore'.

In the course of the journey, the characters engage in various, seemingly arbitrary and spontaneous activities. They play games, gamble, pray, fight, dance, and play with language. There is no conventional storyline or structured plot—the men and women on stage are just acting, re-acting/reacting, interacting/inter-acting; playing, paying, p-a-ing; talking but not communicating, communicating but not talking; speaking but not with words, uttering words but not speaking. . . . For this is what the playwright is exploring—the potential for drama in the most mundane everyday event, in the simplest body movement, and in apparently nonsensical words. And when this dramatic potential is borne out by innovative performing skills, the effect can be mesmerizing.

Gao Xingjian seeks to push the definition of drama beyond the limits of *hua ju* ('speech plays') to include other elements of the performing arts, such as dance, singing, acrobatics, and mime. His aim is to liberate drama from excessive reliance on language. While Western dramatists have long been experimenting with this notion, this was still uncharted territory for the Mainland dramatists in the 1980s, and represented a radical departure.

Gao Xingjian has found traditional Peking Opera—which emphasizes, more or less equally, skills in singing, chanting, martial arts, and acting—a rich source of inspiration for his approach. *The Other Side*, Gao says, is written with the aim of training the actors to be more versatile in the art of performance. The play requires them to explore fully the acting potential of every part of their body, and to learn how to realize it—instinctively and spontaneously.

DRAMATIS PERSONAE

WOMAN
MAN
MOTHER
GIRL
CARD-PLAYER
ZEN BUDDHIST MONK
YOUTH
FATHER
OLD WOMAN
QUACK DOCTOR
MAD WOMAN
SHADOW
SHEPHERD
ACTORS

There should be at least ten actors who play all the other
parts, including CROWD, CARD-PLAYERS, WALL, NUNS and MONKS, and
MANNEQUINS.

Time: Unknown
Place: From the real world to the non-existent 'other' world.

PRODUCTION NOTES

1. Modern theatre in China has long been dominated by the spoken word. It is important to free theatre from such a limitation, and restore to it the multiple performance elements of total theatre, including recitation, singing, mime, and movement.

2. This play aims at a non-conventional, non-restrictive, non-formulaic performance. It relies rather on fresh, spontaneous interaction of the actors with one another, and with objects concrete or imaginary.

3. The important dialogue in the play is the relationship between the characters and the situation. All the sounds and noises produced by the actors in the play are part of its language of sounds.

4. Other than a few simple objects, the play does not require any scenery or props. Much depends on training the actors—and the audience—to exercise their imagination to observe relationships in concrete as well as imaginary contexts.

THE **PLAY**

[This play can be performed anywhere—theatre, hall, rehearsal room, warehouse, gymnasium, temple, circus tent, or patch of ground—as long as there are facilities for lighting and sound. If performed in daylight, there is no need for lighting. The actors can be among the audience or the audience can be among the actors. The ACTORS *gather together at the start of the performance.]*

ACTOR Here is a rope. We're going to play a game, a serious game, the way children play. Our performance begins with a game. *[Addresses another* ACTOR*]*

Right, you take one end of this rope. Look, now there is some kind of relationship between us. Before that I was I, and you were you, but the rope has bound us together and now it's you and me. *[The two* ACTORS *perform the following actions as they are described.]*

Now if we both run in opposite directions, you'll pull me and I'll pull you, we're like locusts on a string, neither can get free. Or, we're like man and wife. *[Pauses]* No, that's a bad metaphor.

If I were to pull hard on the rope, then we should see who the stronger was. The stronger one would pull, the weaker one would be pulled, like a tug-of-war. It's a competition of strength. There'd be a winner and a loser, victory and defeat.

If I threw the rope over my shoulder and dragged you along, you'd be no better than a dead dog. If, on the other hand, you took up the strain, then I'd be like a horse or an ox, a beast of burden harnessed to your command.

So, the relations between you and me can never be constant. We could go on and build some even more complex relations. For example, you circle around me, taking me as axis. Now you're my satellite. If you don't want to revolve around me, I could turn on the spot and make believe that everyone is really turning around me. Is it you revolving around me, or me turning on the spot? Am I revolving around you or are you revolving around me? Or are we both turning on the spot, or *[indicating another* ACTOR*]* are we both revolving around him, or are they revolving around us, or are we all revolving around the Supreme Being or is there no Supreme Being, just a millstone in the universe revolving by itself? Now we're moving into philosophy, let's leave that to the philosophers. Let's get on with our game.

You can take a rope and make all kinds of patterns, and there are an infinite number of patterns. And you can use the rope to reflect all the different kinds of relationships that can exist between people. The rope game is just such a game.

[ACTORS divide into pairs and each couple takes a rope. The pairs can constantly re-form as they like, or they can establish brief contact with other couples and then break away naturally. The game should become increasingly lively, intense, and noisy, and is accompanied by all kinds of shouts and calls.]

ACTOR Stop. Stop a moment. Now let's extend the game a little, make it even more complex. For example, each of you give me one end of your rope and keep the other end in your hand as before. Now I can establish all kinds of relationship with you, tight, loose, distant, close, and your reactions will influence me differently. For we are each of us pulled into this complicated, ever-changing human world. *[Pauses]* As if we had fallen into a spider's web. *[Pauses]* Or as if we were the spider itself. *[Pauses]* The rope is like our hands *[He lets go of one rope, the actor holding the other end does the same, and the rope falls to the ground.]* or like an extended antenna *[He drops another end, the actor opposite does the same.]* and it's like the language we use: 'Good morning', 'How are you!' *[Another rope falls to the ground.]* Like a look between us *[Another rope falls.]* and like our thoughts. You might ache for her, but she's longing for another. *[He brushes past a female actor's shoulder; she looks aside at another.]* These ropes bind us all.

Look.

[As ACTOR with rope speaks, the other ACTORS mime the following actions and relationships as if they are linked by imaginary ropes.]

We watch.
Stare intently.
There is attraction, fascination.
Command and obedience.
Conflict.
Mutual affection.
Exclusion.
Entanglement.
Desertion.

Succession.
Avoiding.
Driving out.
Running after.
Revolving.
Gathering.
Splitting.
Scatter!
Rest!
Now there is a river, not a rope in front of us, we
must cross the river to get to the other side.

ACTORS *[in succession]* Ah, to the other side! *[The following lines
are spoken by different* ACTORS *as they mime crossing a
river.]*
To the other side, to the other side, to the other side,
to the other side, to the other side!
Such clear water!
Ah, so cool!
Careful, there are stones underfoot.
The water feels so good.

[Gradually the sound of a river is heard.]

It splashes all over your skirt!
Is it deep?
Swim across!
Don't go it alone!
Ah, look how the spray sparkles in the sun!
Beautiful, like a waterfall.
Like a dam, with the water slowly flowing over it.
There's a long line in the middle of the river.
Further away the water's dark blue, dark blue and deep.
The fish are swimming between my thighs.
Nice.
I'm losing my balance.
Don't worry, hold on to me.
There's a whirlpool.
Help each other out, hold hands.
Against the strong current.
To the other side!
No one can see the other side.
Don't get poetic! I'm losing my balance.
Hold on, follow on, one after the other.
The water is green over there.
Oh, it's up to my waist!
I feel faint.

Close your eyes a moment.
Look ahead, all of you, look ahead, everyone look
ahead!
Look towards the other side.
Why can't I see anything?
We might all drown.
Food for the fish.
If we're going to die, let's die together.
Silly girls, don't talk such nonsense, concentrate.
The current is strong, walk in the shallow parts,
against the current!
I can't make it, I really can't make it.
Where is the other side?
It seems so hazy.
Is there light on the other side?
There are flowers. The other side is a flowery paradise.
I'm afraid I can't make it, don't desert me. *[Sobs]*
Can you feel it too, we're floating in the water.
Like corks.
Like water weed.
What will we do on the other side? I don't know.
Yes, why are we going there?
The other side is simply the other side, a place you can
never reach.
But you still yearn to go, to see what it's like.
We can't see anything.
No oasis, no light.
It's like . . .
In the underworld.
No, I can't make it.
We must make it!
We simply must!
But why?
To satisfy that longing for the other side, the other side.
No, I can't make it, I want to go back!
We can't turn back now.
None of us can.
No one can.
Ah . . .!
Who was that?
I don't know.

[Silence, just the sound of water]

Who called out? Did any of you hear it?
Someone must have heard it, why don't you answer?

[*Silence. Sobbing can be heard.*]

This is a River of Death.

A River of Oblivion.

[*The* CROWD, *as if in a trance, slowly, mechanically, step out of the River of Death. Soft music. The* CROWD *mime climbing up the shore, utterly exhausted, and collapse there.* WOMAN *appears in the murky darkness. She studies the crowd of people who have forgotten everything. She drifts among them, touching them, swiftly waking them up. The* CROWD *gradually open their eyes, look up and turn towards her as if they are trying to say something but cannot.*]

WOMAN [*raising her hand*] This . . . is a hand.

[*The* CROWD *make indistinct gurgling noises and utter nonsense words.*]

This is a hand.

CROWD [*still indistinctly*]

Th . . . thai . . . thei . . . i . . . is . . . hind . . . hand . . .

WOMAN Hand.

CROWD Hand, hund, hond, hand.

WOMAN This is a foot.

CROWD Th . . . th . . . this . . . i . . . is . . . f . . . fo . . . foot

WOMAN [*pointing to her eye*] Eye.

CROWD E . . . ey . . . eye . . . eye . . .

WOMAN [*gesturing*] Your eye looks at your foot!

CROWD [*chaotically*] Eye . . . locks . . . locks ate door . . . more . . . fate . . . fight . . .

[WOMAN *laughs, and the* CROWD *laugh too, foolishly.*]

WOMAN [*biting back her laugh, a little sorrowfully*] This is a hand . . .

CROWD [*severally*] This is a hand, this is a hund, this is a hond, this is a hand . . .

WOMAN This is a foot.

CROWD This is a fate, this is a fight, this is a fot, this is a foot.

WOMAN This is a body . . . your body.

CROWD This is a body, this is a body, this is a body, your body, this is your body this is a body is this is your body . . .

WOMAN [*shaking her head and gesturing patiently*] My hand . . . my body . . . my foot . . . this is me.

CROWD My hind, my hand, my body, my fate, my hand's body's foot's my fate's hand's foot's body this is my body it's me.

WOMAN Say me.

CROWD Say me, say me, say me, say me, say me.

WOMAN *[shakes her head, points to her body, from eyes to lips, from chest to foot]* Me.

CROWD *[almost in unison]* Me.

WOMAN Good!

CROWD *[in unison]* God! Goad! Good! Gade!

WOMAN *[stops gesturing, thinks a moment, points to someone in the crowd]* You.

CROWD *[pointing to the same person]* You.

PERSON *[looks around, then points to himself]* You.

WOMAN *[shakes her head, helps him point to another]* You.

CROWD You.

WOMAN *[gesturing]* Me and you.

CROWD Me and you.

WOMAN *[smiling]* Good!

CROWD *[also smiling]* Good!

WOMAN *[as the music increases in tempo]* Me and him!

CROWD Me and him!

WOMAN Them and me.

CROWD Them and me.

WOMAN Me and all of you.

CROWD Me and all of you.

WOMAN You and us.

CROWD You and us.

WOMAN Now, look. Use your eyes as you repeat after me.

CROWD Look . . .

WOMAN Tell me, who do you see?

CROWD *[in succession]* I see him, I see you, I see me, I see them, they see you, you see us, we see them . . .

WOMAN Now say touch, say give, say like, say love, then you won't feel so lonely.

CROWD *[becoming lively]* I touch you, you give me, I like him, he loves you, you touch me, I give him, he likes you, you love me . . .

[MAN emerges from the CROWD.]

MAN Who are you?

WOMAN I'm one of you.

MAN Where are we?

WOMAN We're on the longed for, never to be reached, other side.

MAN Are you the one that drowned as we crossed the river?

[WOMAN shakes her head.]

Are you her ghost?

[She shakes her head again.]

Or do you only exist in our thoughts, do you only come when we think of you? Or are you a kind of force taking us to the other side so that we wouldn't get lost?

CROWD *[speaking to each other, severally or in unison]* I've had enough of you.

You touched me!

I'll hit you!

Do you hate me?

I tormented her.

He deceived me.

You scolded him.

I'll tell against you.

You punished him.

He's scheming against me.

I hate you!

You cursed him!

I'll kill you . . .

MAN *[to WOMAN]* You're kind.

CROWD *[in succession, slowly turning towards WOMAN, playing with language]*

You're truly generous.

You're absolutely wonderful.

You're downright contemptible.

He's a bastard.

You're a liar and a cheat.

You're a double-dealing rascal!

She fawns on you, but actually she's jealous of you.

You're a schemer. You teach people language just so you can get round them!

You seem so gentle, who'd have thought you're a wanton whore!

She seduced our husbands!

She caused trouble among our brothers.

She's so charming, look, look at her.

Don't let the women have anything to do with her, she'll contaminate them!

Don't be fooled by her appearance, underneath she's more rotten than a common prostitute.

It's her fault, she frightened us, the world will never be at peace now.

[WOMAN shrinks back, the CROWD surround her, becoming increasingly excited by their own ever more poisonous words. WOMAN can't escape their accusing stare. WOMAN turns to MAN for help, hides behind him.]

Slut!
Viper!
She-devil!
Shameless whore!

[WOMAN clings desperately to MAN, seeking his protection. The CROWD become mad.]

Look, look,
Aah . . .
Throw her out!
Kick her out!
Catch her!
Strip her!
Strangle her, shameless whore!

[The CROWD rush at her and pull MAN aside. In the chaos, WOMAN is strangled. MAN pushes his way into the CROWD, and brings out her body. The CROWD are startled.]

Dead!
Dead?
She's dead.

[They quickly disperse. Lines are spoken in quick succession, sometimes in unison.]

Strangled?
You did it . . .
No, he made the first move.
You started shouting!
You were all shouting, I just joined in.
Who shouted first? Who?
Who shouted 'grab her', 'strip her', 'strangle her'?
Who?
We all did.
I was only shouting because you were.
You were all shouting so I shouted too.
But she's dead! Strangled!
I didn't kill her.
I didn't kill her.
I didn't kill her.
I didn't kill her.
I didn't kill her.

I didn't.
I didn't.
Didn't.
Didn't.
Didn't.
She's really dead. So attractive, even in death.
So beautiful. You just have to look at her to fall in
love with her.
Skin smooth as jade, pure and flawless.
And those fine, delicate hands—indescribable, soft.
Christ, she's a Madonna!
Pure, dignified.
She gave us language, brought us knowledge.
She was murdered.
That's unforgivable! Oh, you beasts!
Who are you calling names?
You murderers! You! I mean you!
How dare you accuse me? You bastard!
Scoundrel!
Hooligan!

[The CROWD *exchange blows.]*

MAN Have you finished? We all killed her. You did, he did,
I did, we all did it together. Here, on this desolate
shore, she gave us language. We didn't appreciate it.
She gave us knowledge. We didn't know how to use it!
We've shocked ourselves with what we've done, it's
disgusting, but we're too weak even to feel ashamed.

CROWD *[in succession]* So, what should we do?
We need a leader. A flock of sheep needs a shepherd.
We'll follow you.

MAN I despise you. I despise myself. We'd better go our
separate ways.

CROWD No, don't abandon us.
We've decided to come with you.

MAN Where to? Where can I lead you? *[Turns to leave, the*
CROWD *follow behind him.]* Don't follow me. *[Distressed]*
I don't even know where I'm going myself.

[He stands still, unable to think what to do next. The
CROWD *wait behind him at a distance.* MOTHER *enters and*
approaches him.]

MOTHER Do you remember me?

MAN Ah, Mother.

MOTHER I thought you'd forgotten me!

MAN *[kneels]* Mother. *[Clings to* MOTHER's *legs]*

MOTHER *[stroking his head]* Find yourself a nice girl, you should start a family, settle down.

MAN I want to achieve something.

MOTHER You're too ambitious.

MAN *[bows his head]* Well, I'm your son.

MOTHER *[indicating* the CROWD*]* Are they following you? Where are you going to take them?

MAN I don't know. All I know is, we have to keep going, don't we, Mother?

MOTHER Follow your instinct, my son. *[Hugs his head close to her]*

MAN Your hands are icy cold! *[Shocked]* Mother! Is this the underworld? A different world?

MOTHER There's nothing to be frightened of. It's just a bit dark and damp.

MAN *[stepping away from her]* How do I get out of here? I want to live, Mother—

*[*MOTHER *turns and exits.* MAN *hesitates a little, then hurries after her.* GIRL *blocks his way.]*

Who are you? I've seen you somewhere before but I can't remember your name. Didn't we live in the same street years ago? I used to try and catch a glimpse of you on my way to school each day, even if it was just your shadow, or just the sight of your long pigtails. Didn't you use to wear a dark red dress? My heart would beat wildly at the first sight of your dress and the long pigtails.

I used to follow you, follow you all the way to your door, hoping that before you went in and closed the door, you would turn round and say something to me, or maybe just smile. But you just looked at me, quietly. Ah, I can see those eyes again. *[Rubs his eyes. When he looks up again,* GIRL *has disappeared into the* CROWD. *He turns to the* CROWD.*]* We should get out of this ghostly place, away from this darkness. There may be light ahead. Where there's light there may be people. We can dry our clothes round the stove, have some tea. *[Persuasively]* And we can all go home and see our families again. Wives, husbands, sons, daughters, fathers, mothers. Our loved ones, the ones who love us!

*[*GIRL *appears again from behind the* CROWD.]*

Who are you? [*Blocks her way*] Wait! Your name is on the tip of my tongue! I think I used to write poems to you; didn't we once go to the cinema together? I held your hand in the dark, your tiny, fragile hand; you looked at me, I looked at you.

[GIRL *turns, taking her hand away from his, and eludes him. He turns, but can't find her, no matter where he looks.*]

She used to appear in my dreams and torment me whenever I was confused and couldn't find a way out. But I just can't remember her name, I can't picture her face clearly, can't quite grasp her; she still torments me. [*To the* CROWD] Why are you pestering me? I need peace and quiet, I need to be alone, I don't want a crowd of people staring at me, I don't need you and you don't need me. What you need is a leader to show you the way, but as soon as you have found a way, or think you have, you run away like frightened rabbits, and desert him without so much as another look. Like throwing off a pair of worn-out shoes. I know I don't need you. I don't need you! I just need love, I just want a wife. You've all loved someone and been loved; possessed someone and been possessed. I have the right to love too, to love a woman, possess a woman, and to be loved and possessed. I'm just like you, full of desires, ambitious, eager to excel in everything; sometimes weak, but upright, sympathetic, self-sacrificing . . . [*He rolls about on the floor and sobs.*]

[*The* CROWD *is stunned. They wait until he has cried himself out and is utterly exhausted. Then he rises to his feet and walks on. The* CROWD *continue to follow behind him, silently. Lights fade. In the darkness a table and chairs are set out. On the table there are drinks, cards, and an oil-lamp. A light appears which gradually increases in brightness. Under the light of the oil-lamp,* CARD-PLAYER *sits alone drinking and playing cards.* MAN *mimes knocking at the door and the* CROWD *clap three times to produce the sound of knocking.*]

MAN Excuse me, sorry to disturb you—

CARD-PLAYER [*without looking up*] Come in. Sit down.

MAN Excuse me—

CARD-PLAYER [*puts down the cards in his hand, looks up*] Do you play?

MAN I used to.

[*The* CROWD *press outside the door.*]

CARD-PLAYER Come in. Come in. Do you want to play? Close the door for me, the draught bothers me and makes the flame flicker, and that's bad for my eyes. Sit round in a circle, I'll sit at the head. Each of you takes a card and I'll do the same—just one card, that's fair. My card shall be trumps, because you can't have a game without a trump. And it's better that we begin with a trump card—that way it's easier for you. *[Taking a card from the top of the deck and looking at it]* I've got the two of clubs, but that's not so bad, as we card-players say, just blame it on luck. Now, if any of you draw a club, then it will be higher than mine, and I shall have lost and you'll be the winner. But if you don't pick any clubs, then what you've got is worthless and isn't even as good as my two of clubs. Are the rules clear?

MAN What does the winner get? And what does the loser get?

CARD-PLAYER The winner gets some of my wine.

MAN And the loser?

CARD-PLAYER Pays a forfeit.

MAN I haven't got any money. I've no land, no house, no wife.

CARD-PLAYER But you have your self-respect and you have your face.

MAN I don't understand.

CARD-PLAYER You soon will. You see, whoever loses gets a slip of paper stuck on his face.

CROWD *[severally]* That's easy.

How big a slip of paper?

Will any kind do?

The thing is, is there really any wine in your flask?

CARD-PLAYER *[offering his flask]* You can have a sip now.

CROWD *[taking turns to drink]* Mmmn, really good.

A full aroma.

An expensive wine.

I want a taste too.

Card-games are fun.

CARD-PLAYER It's your turn now to pick a card. I've already put mine on the table for all to see. But each of you is only allowed to look at your own card and not at the others'. That's a rule.

CROWD *[each hurriedly taking a card in turn]* Fine, no problem.

Each man plays for himself.

Even if someone shows me his card, I shan't look.

I'm honest.

It doesn't matter if I win or lose. I'll show my integrity, that's what counts.

[Those who have taken a card fall silent.]

CARD-PLAYER *[to the first who drew a card]* Show me your card. You lose.

1ST PLAYER *[nods]* What's the forfeit?

[CARD-PLAYER takes a slip of paper, spits on it and sticks it on 1ST PLAYER's face who shivers upon contact. The CROWD watch, laugh. 1ST PLAYER is relieved and also laughs.]

CARD-PLAYER *[turning to another player]* And you, friend? *[He shows his card.]* Ah, you lose too.

2ND PLAYER The forfeit?

CARD-PLAYER Stick it on your chin.

[2ND PLAYER takes a slip of paper, wets it with his tongue and sticks it on his chin, a little embarrassed. The CROWD laugh and he relaxes.]

3RD PLAYER *[a girl]* What fun!

CARD-PLAYER *[turns to her]* And you?

[She shows him her card and quickly hides it again.]

CROWD *[severally]* Did you win?

Yes!

No?

[She bashfully shakes her head.]

Then why don't you take a slip of paper?

Stick one on her face! Stick it on.

That's the rule. No exceptions.

If she can get away with it, so can we.

3RD PLAYER I don't want to.

CROWD *[in succession]* None of us does.

Come on, stick one on your ear.

Yeah, stick it on your ear.

Stick it on your nose!

Everyone must be different. Don't put it in the same place.

No one can get away with it.

[3RD PLAYER sticks the paper on her face. CARD-PLAYER looks at another player who shows him the card in his hand and then neatly sticks a slip of paper on his cheek. Everyone in the CROWD now start sticking paper to their faces.]

It's only fair.

Fair's fair.

If we lose, we'll accept the penalty.

Everyone gets a penalty, we've all got a slip of paper on our faces.

If you don't stick one on your face you'll look so odd people will be afraid of you.

[The weird, papered faces turn to MAN.*]*

Dear friend, your turn.

MAN I'm not playing.

CARD-PLAYER Everyone else is, why aren't you?

MAN It's a stupid game. Besides, I've got to be on my way.

CROWD Yes, yes, we should all get going.

Don't go by yourself.

Where are we going?

Yes, where are we going?

MAN I must go.

CARD-PLAYER I've lit my lamp and got some wine just so we could play a game of cards. I've never heard of anyone coming here and then leaving without playing. Why bother coming in the first place?

CROWD *[pulling at* MAN*]* Play with him!

Come on.

Just one game.

Then you can go.

MAN Can't you see? Don't you understand? It's no card-game: the game's on you. Your card, your card, yours and yours are all no-trumps. All those cards still in the pack are no-trumps, only the club in his hand can trump. His is the only club in the pack! *[*CARD-PLAYER *laughs.]* Let's go! Why waste time?

CARD-PLAYER There's no such thing as time here. *[Blows at the flame of the oil-lamp slowly, it becomes brighter]* There's just the eternal light. *[He takes the lamp and holds it under each person's chin in turn so that each face looks like a ghost.]* I like fun and games. Are you frightened?

MAN You are the devil.

CARD-PLAYER Why don't you stroke their arses, they've all got hairy tails. *[Points to their behinds and laughs loudly, puts the pack of cards in front of* MAN*]* Take a card, let everyone see if it's a club or not. *[Picks the top card—not a club—and shows it quickly to* CROWD*]* What do you say, is that a club or not?

CROWD MEMBER I didn't see clearly.

CARD-PLAYER And you?

2ND CROWD MEMBER I think . . .

CARD-PLAYER You saw it quite clearly.

3RD CROWD MEMBER I think it was . . . clubs.

CARD-PLAYER That's right. You, young girl, what did you see?

GIRL Clubs.

CARD-PLAYER Very good. You're my kind of girl. You, sir, what did you see?

OLD MAN Clubs. It couldn't be anything else.

CARD-PLAYER A most venerable gentleman indeed! [Suddenly angry] How could he say there are no clubs? Eh?

CROWD It was clubs.
Of course it was clubs, no doubt about it.
It was clearly clubs.
We all saw it.
We can all bear witness.

CARD-PLAYER [to MAN] Did you hear that? Now why did you lie and say there were no clubs in the pack? You're scared. Have you ever eaten the flesh of a snake, or rat? A little, live rat, jumping and biting inside your mouth, squeaking, so young there's no fur on it yet and its eyes are still closed, a baby rat dipped in sauce on a piece of bread? If you had, you'd have had the guts to speak the truth. I'll give you one more chance to speak the truth. Speak up, are there clubs in the pack or not?

MAN No clubs.

CARD-PLAYER Stick-in-the-mud! You're a real spoilsport. You've spoilt everyone's fun. What do you others say, isn't he a pain?

CROWD [passing the wine flask around, each taking a sip] A real pain.
A real pain.
A real pain.
A real pain.
A real pain.
A real pain.
A real pain.

CARD-PLAYER [taking the flask from them] What do we do with people like him?

CROWD [surrounding MAN] Kick him out!
Tell him to push off!
Upsetting everyone.

A real pain in the arse.
Trouble-maker, doing us out of a drink.
Teach him a lesson, teach him a lesson!
Whack his bum!
Strip him!
Pull his trousers down!

[*The* CROWD *try to pull* MAN's *trousers down.*]

CARD-PLAYER Think about it, think again.

MAN [*holding up his trousers*] But I think . . . I thought . . .
there were no clubs in the pack!

[CARD-PLAYER *picks up the wine flask, turns to leave. The*
CROWD *pull at* MAN, *as if playing with a bird on a*
string.]

CROWD Tell him to fly!
What? What?
Fly like a bird!
Man's no bird, why try to fly like a bird?
But it's great!
Fly!
Drop your head, let your arms fly!

CARD-PLAYER [*to* MAN] Friend, I hope you're not a stubborn man?

GIRL [*feeling sorry for* MAN] You can't say there are no trump
cards when we saw the clubs. Why talk such nonsense?

MAN I'm so confused, perhaps there were clubs . . .

GIRL Then why did you say there were none?

MAN I suppose there might be some clubs.

GIRL 'There might be' is not the same as 'there are'.

CARD-PLAYER You suffer because you're so pig-headed. Why say
'might be'? Either there are or there aren't, there's no
'might be'.

MAN Why is there no 'might be'?

CARD-PLAYER [*getting angry*] Might be what? It should be yes there
are, or no there aren't.

CROWD [*pulling at* MAN] We don't want any 'might be's!
We want yes or no.
We want clubs, we don't want no-trumps.
Down with no-trumps!
Long live clubs!

MAN Per . . . per . . . haps, there were . . . clubs.

CROWD [*angrily stamping their feet*] Speak clearly!
Speak up!
It's no good if you don't speak up!
If you don't speak up, we won't let you off!

MAN Clu . . . clu . . . it was clubs. *[Collapses on to his knees, defeated]*

[CROWD leap around CARD-PLAYER in a strange and awkward dance. Then they exit. Lights dim. WOMAN enters in a white cotton robe which she uses to cover MAN. She bows down and then hides under the robe herself so that all we see is a white mass. Lights fade out. Sound of a drum offstage. MAN and WOMAN exit in the darkness. The drum becomes deafening. A wiry monk, beating a drum with his fingers, palms, elbows, and knees, enters, leaping like a crazy spirit. ZEN BUDDHIST MONK enters, in time to the drum. He is wearing a ceremonial patchwork gown, his right shoulder is bare, his hands are held together before his chest, palms touching. A CROWD of monks and nuns in grey-coloured gowns enter in single file after ZEN BUDDHIST MONK, chanting 'Amitabha' as they walk. The chanting is totally free, each singing his own melody, at his own pitch. As one voice falls, another rises, and yet the voices blend in with the drum to become a harmonious chorus. MAN follows behind the CROWD, also chanting and frequently looking around. The CROWD put down prayer mats and sit cross-legged. MAN also sits cross-legged on a prayer-mat. The drum ceases and is replaced by the sound of wooden prayer-block and chime.]

ZEN BUDDHIST MONK *[kneels with his right knee on the ground, palms together, and recites from the 'Vajraccedika prajna paramita sutra']* It is said that Tathagata is mindful of all holy ones, and guides all holy ones. But master, should virtuous men and women wish to lead an untarnished, unparalleled life, should they wish to see things correctly, acquire great wisdom and the loftiest sentiments, how should they begin? How should they adhere to their intention? Buddha answered: You spoke true. Tathagata is mindful of all holy ones, guides all holy ones. Listen and I shall tell you . . .

[During the lesson, incense rises and the CROWD sit in meditation with their eyes closed. MAN also slowly closes his eyes. GIRL appears and crouches in the corner. With eyes closed, she meditates as if she were in a transparent shell, her hands and feet pressing againt the walls of the shell. YOUTH, sitting behind MAN, slowly stands and, fascinated by GIRL, very carefully, step by step, approaches her. The CROWD begin to leave and the sound of chanting becomes weaker, but it remains audible in the background. ZEN BUDDHIST MONK recites quietly so that the conversation between GIRL and YOUTH can be heard over his voice.]

Virtuous men and women, you shall lead an
untarnished, unparalleled life, see things correctly,
acquire great wisdom and the loftiest sentiments if you
do as I say, if you honour those above as I say. Then
the disciple said: We attend your teaching with a
cheerful heart. Buddha said: To attain great wisdom
you should . . .

*[YOUTH touches GIRL's fingers. GIRL immediately draws
back her hand, startled.]*

GIRL Why did you touch me?

YOUTH Are you meditating?

GIRL Yes, don't disturb me.

YOUTH May I ask what kind of meditation you are doing?

GIRL It's called 'Short as the Day', but I don't know what it
means.

YOUTH Is there a 'Long as the Day'?

GIRL I don't know.

YOUTH So you're doing something you don't really understand?

GIRL *[nervously]* Don't ask me, don't ask me!

YOUTH *[mischievously]* You probably don't even know what 'I
don't know' means. *[Suddenly grabs hold of her hand]*

GIRL Hey, you can't, you can't do that—

YOUTH Why not?

GIRL I'm frightened.

YOUTH What's there to be frightened of? Have you never seen
how a chick hatches from its shell? It just cracks the
shell—

GIRL Don't crack me.

YOUTH And if I pull you out?

GIRL Then I shall suffer.

YOUTH Aren't you suffering now?

GIRL *[in pain]* I can't explain . . .

YOUTH *[roughly grabbing her hand]* Then you must suffer some more!

GIRL *[imploring, struggling]* Ah, no, I don't want—

*[FATHER puts up his umbrella and enters. ZEN BUDDHIST
MONK stops reciting, and exits, leaving MAN sitting alone
on the prayer-mat meditating with his eyes closed.]*

YOUTH Father!

FATHER Don't get into any more trouble. Come home with me
at once!

*[He grabs hold of YOUTH and tries to pull him away. GIRL
exits.]*

YOUTH *[turns round to look, absent-mindedly]* It won't rain today.

FATHER It might.

YOUTH But it hasn't rained yet, has it?

FATHER It will, soon.

YOUTH And if it doesn't?

FATHER It will eventually. Otherwise, why would I put up my umbrella?

YOUTH You're just glad for something to do.

FATHER I've been putting this umbrella up all my life.

YOUTH Just because you want to.

FATHER Don't speak like that to your father!

YOUTH Then I won't say anything.

FATHER Get out! Go far away and don't come back! I disown you! *[Exits angrily]*

[YOUTH is at a loss. MAN is still sitting on the prayer-mat with his eyes closed. The chanting begins again offstage.]

SOUND OF The Buddha said: It is good. Let us enjoin all people
RECITATION to follow his teachings in this way. All living creatures, whether born of egg, born of womb, born of water, born of cocoon, born with form, born without form, born with intellect, born without intellect, all beings shall enter Nirvana.

[YOUTH turns, from behind him appears a wall of people formed by the CROWD. He looks troubled, for he cannot get over the wall. Then he sees OLD WOMAN appearing through a crack in the human wall.]

OLD WOMAN Boy, do you want to cross over?

YOUTH I just want to take a look.

OLD WOMAN Just want to take a look. They all just want to take a look. Do you have any money?

YOUTH *[feels in his pockets and finds a coin]* Yes!

OLD WOMAN *[laughs]* And you think I'll be satisfied with that small amount? Haven't you got anything of value your mother might have given you?

YOUTH *[suddenly remembering]* I've got a fountain pen with a gold nib. My mother gave it to me for my birthday. *[Holds it out for her to see]*

OLD WOMAN *[takes it and looks closely at it]* Hmm, it's not bad. *[Puts it in her pocket and steps aside so that the crack appears again]* You can go through.

YOUTH *[hesitating]* What if my mother finds out . . .?

OLD WOMAN Will she beat you?

YOUTH Don't know. What shall I tell her?

OLD WOMAN You can fib, say you lost it. You know how to fib, don't you?

YOUTH My mother says I mustn't tell lies.

OLD WOMAN You're still young. There isn't a grown-up on earth who doesn't lie. If there were no lies, life would be miserable. Enough, be off with you.

[YOUTH *crawls through the gap in the wall of people, looks up and sees, on the other side,* GIRL *with her hands over her face crying silently. He has just got to his feet when two* CROWD *members step out from the wall and begin to beat him.* GIRL *disappears and the sound of recitation fades. The wall becomes a* CROWD *again.* MAN *remains sitting on the prayer-mat, meditating with his eyes closed.*

QUACK DOCTOR *enters, his chest bare, a sash tied at his waist with a sword tucked into it at his back. He beats a cymbal, and walks in a circle the way a Peking Opera actor does. The* CROWD *quietly approach and surround him.* YOUTH *lies in a heap on one side.*]

QUACK DOCTOR Wonder plasters! Wonder plasters for sale! A secret prescription passed down over generations. A cure for internal wounds, external wounds, contusions, heart attacks, rabies, love-sick youths, infantile convulsions, geriatric strokes, and the possessed. Just stick on a plaster and you'll be cured. If one plaster doesn't do it, stick another one on. Wonder plasters! Wonder plasters for sale! If you've tried a home cure, or taken the wrong medicine, if a woman can't conceive or her man's impotent, try it. Give it to those who corrupt public morals, the treatment is quick! Ah, if you stutter, if your mouth is all crooked, if your woman is jealous, or your husband seeks revenge, if father won't dote on mother, if a child won't obey his father, if you have a spotty face, or corns on your feet, if one plaster isn't enough, slap on another, satisfaction guaranteed or your money back. Wonder plasters! Wonder plasters for sale! Don't miss your chance, it'll never come again!

[YOUTH, *beyond the circle of the* CROWD, *finally scrambles to his feet.* MAD WOMAN *enters.*]

MAD WOMAN [*goes up to* YOUTH] They say I am a whore, but they don't mention the fact that it's the men who sidle up to me to sleep with me. They say I'm a fallen woman, as if they'd never done anything wrong, as if they'd never had pleasure with another.

[YOUTH *draws away from her. The* CROWD *turn to them.*]

CROWD The mad woman's here!
The mad woman's here!
The mad woman's here!

MAD WOMAN You're the mad ones!

CROWD Look, look!
She's talking crazy again.

MAD WOMAN You're the ones talking crazy.

[*The* CROWD *laugh wildly.*]

QUACK DOCTOR If you've got the cash, let's see it, if not, give me a round of applause. Wonder plasters! [*Throws a handful of plasters to the ground*] No expenses spared, all items must go, pay what you like. Selling cheap! [*Draws back in revulsion as* MAD WOMAN *approaches him*] You foul prostitute!

[*Picks up the plasters and exits*]

MAD WOMAN Sell yourself cheap!

[*The* CROWD *laugh again.*]

What are you laughing at? Laugh at yourselves! You'll do anything to sleep with a woman. Don't think just because you look human you are human. You're all dogs, dogs, wild dogs!

MEN IN THE CROWD [*to the women in the crowd*] Don't let her talk such nonsense. Take her away.

MAD WOMAN What are you afraid I'll say? Got a bad conscience, eh? You try and get as far away from me as you can now, but I know too well what's in your minds! [*Laughs foolishly*]

MEN IN THE CROWD Take her away! Take her away!

[*The* CROWD *move forward and pull her away.*]

MAD WOMAN Are you afraid too? Afraid I'll let on that your husbands have slept with me? Are you afraid you'll be dropped like me when they're done with you? Afraid they'll find out you've been having affairs with other men? Afraid people will find out you lost your virginity long before you married?

CROWD Gag her!
Stuff her mouth with horse shit!
With bull shit!
Gag her!

MAD WOMAN *[struggling with the women]* Have you never seduced a
man? You're just like me, you can't part with the men
you've slept with.

[The CROWD *approach her and use a rope to tie her up and
then they gag her. She becomes hysterical, crying, and
howling.* CROWD *exit with her.* YOUTH, *surprised, watches
and follows them off.* MAN, *sitting with his eyes closed on the
prayer-mat, also exits. Immediately following,* MAN *re-enters
from the other side followed by his* SHADOW. *The* SHADOW
is wearing black, with a black hood over his face. MAN *and
his* SHADOW *stand next to each other but do not look at
each other, and each speaks only to himself. Their steps and
movements, however, are alike.]*

MAN A seed falls on the soil.

SHADOW A child is born into the world.

MAN A gust of wind blows through the forest.

SHADOW A horse gallops across the plain.

MAN A grain of sand blows into my eye.

SHADOW Tears fill my eyes.

MAN And flow on to the dry desert.

SHADOW It's like entering a lively market town.

MAN Watching the bustling people, but not being able to
see their eyes.

SHADOW All you can see are dead fish.

MAN It's a lonesome town.

SHADOW Pop stars yelling themselves hoarse with all that
shouting.

MAN Only the stars above can hear the sound of the windchimes.

SHADOW But it's not the sound of their hearts.

MAN It's a nerve-jangling electric guitar.

SHADOW You dance freestyle, but you feel a fool.

MAN Because you are a coward.

SHADOW It's more like a vulgar farce.

MAN A trumpet playing out of tune—treee, squee, deeee . . .

SHADOW The conductor, though, is all right.

MAN They all say they live in pain most of the time.

SHADOW Pleasure lasts but a minute.

MAN And it's not when you're drinking beer.

SHADOW Chicago, Nuremberg. . .

MAN Were ravaged by a war.

SHADOW But only the sparrows got killed.

MAN The soldiers didn't fight, they just stood on guard.

SHADOW The ones that stood on guard won medals.

MAN Who's that talking to me?

SHADOW It's your shadow, speaking your thoughts.

MAN You're always following me—

SHADOW When you lose yourself.

MAN —to remind me of things, make me more confused . . .

SHADOW You look so distracted, are you looking for something?

MAN Thanks for reminding me! Yes, I've lost something, but I don't know where to find it.

SHADOW [*scornfully*] I don't think you know what you're looking for.

MAN I think . . . well, aren't we all looking for something?

[*The* CROWD *enter. Like children playing a game, they make a circle, and bend down, searching for something on the ground.*]

SHADOW Why don't you ask them what they're looking for? [*Moves away and exits*]

MAN Excuse me, what are you looking for?

ACTOR 1 A needle: a needle with an eye for a camel to pass through.

MAN [*to another*] Excuse me, can you tell me what you're looking for?

ACTOR 2 I'm looking for a seat, a strong, comfortable seat, and once I'm on it, I shan't get up again. [*Whispers*] I've got piles. I can't just sit on any old seat.

MAN [*to another*] What are you looking for?

ACTOR 3 [*stammering*] I . . . I . . . I'm looking for a m . . . mouth . . . that I . . . can . . . that I can . . . can . . . can talk with. . . . I have so . . . I have so much . . . so much . . . so much . . . to say . . . every . . . every day.

MAN And how about you, young lad?

ACTOR 4 I'm looking for a living. You've all got one, but I haven't!

MAN Yes, a living is important, keep looking, keep looking. [*Treading on someone's foot*] Sorry, I didn't mean to . . . [*Pulling his foot back*] What are you looking for?

ACTOR 5 I'm looking for a pair of shoes that fit. No matter what I do, these shoes really pinch. I wonder . . .

MAN I'm looking for something too . . .

ACTOR 5 Do your shoes pinch too?

MAN No, my shoes don't pinch, but I don't know which way my feet should go!

ACTOR 5 Just follow someone else's footsteps.

MAN *[to another]* Are you looking for someone else's footsteps?

ACTOR 6 *[jokingly]* I'm looking for a tunnel so I can get through without anyone seeing and come out at the other end triumphant.

MAN *[to another]* How about you, friend? You don't look like someone who cares to go into a tunnel.

ACTOR 7 Correct.

MAN So what are you looking for?

ACTOR 7 I'm looking for my childhood dreams.

MAN I'm sure they were beautiful. *[To another]* And you? Are you looking for your dreams?

ACTOR 8 No, I'm hunting for a sentence.

MAN Are you writing a poem?

ACTOR 8 Anyone can write poetry, it's as easy as making love.

MAN Then, you're looking for . . . ?

ACTOR 8 A thought! Everyone has a brain, but not everyone can think.

MAN That's true. Then you must be looking for an epigram.

ACTOR 8 I can't say for sure if it's an epigram. The problem is, if I can't find it my thoughts will be interrupted, and an interrupted chain of thought is like a kite on a broken string—it'll never come back. If I can't find my sentence, I can't find my thought, because a train of thoughts is like the links on a chain, you see?

MAN You, young lady, what are you looking for?

ACTOR 8 Guess!

MAN It must have something to do with love.

ACTOR 8 Absolutely right! I'm waiting for a pair of eyes, soft, deep, burning . . .

[He leaves the girl and bumps into another person.]

ACTOR 9 You're treading on my toe!

MAN Sorry.

ACTOR 9 Do you always go around like that?

MAN I didn't see you, I'll go over there.

ACTOR 9 Everyone else is looking here, what are you going over there for?

MAN The thing I'm looking for isn't here.

ACTOR 9 What are you looking for?

MAN *[vexed]* I don't really know.

ACTOR 9 Hey, look, here's a weird one. He doesn't even know what he's looking for.

ANOTHER ACTOR Perhaps he's already found it.

>[The CROWD surround him.]

MAN No, really, I haven't. *[Steps away]*

SHEPHERD *[standing away from the CROWD]* Where are you going?

MAN Over there.

SHEPHERD Have you found anything yet? Why go over there if you haven't?

MAN I'm not looking anymore, I'm just going over there.

SHEPHERD We're all still looking here. Why do you insist on going over there? What do you say, friends, shall we let him go?

CROWD No.
Of course not.
He can't go.
Wait till we've all found what we're looking for and then he can go!

MAN Let me explain—

CROWD You don't need to, we understand.
You're looking, I'm looking, we're all looking.
No one's found anything yet, but you insist on going over there.
It won't do.
It just won't do.
If you're not looking any more, then we won't either, and you can go. But right now we're all still looking, you can't just go over there, like that. How could you? Either we all look together, or we don't. Right?

MAN But I have nothing to do with you.

SHEPHERD Friend, for you are still our friend, you don't see the light, do you? *[To the CROWD]* Let's tell him again. Let's make it quite clear to him in advance.

CROWD *[severally]* Either we all look together or we don't. Everyone's looking, or no one's looking. Not looking is simply not looking, looking or not looking, not looking or looking, looking not looking or looking . . .

MAN And if I don't want to look?

CROWD *[speaking over each other, the words descend into nonsense.]* If you don't want to, that's fine, we can't force you. But if you don't want to look it doesn't mean no one else can look, and if everyone's looking you can't not look, when no one's looking, then you can stop looking; if everyone is looking and you're not looking, everyone's looking for everyone, you're not looking for everyone, if you're

looking everyone will be looking. Are you looking, if
you're not looking everyone will be looking for if
you're not looking everyone will not be looking but
looking for you.

MAN *[angrily]* I go my way and you go yours! Leave me
alone, let me go!

SHEPHERD No way! How could you have found something when
we haven't?

MAN But I haven't found anything!

SHEPHERD Then you'd better go on looking.

MAN I don't want to look here any more. I . . . want . . . to go!

SHEPHERD Don't you understand the rules? We've explained to
you so many times, why do you have to be so
stubborn?

CROWD What's this?
What's all this?
Let's beat him up!

SHEPHERD No, that's not a good idea, that's not civilized. Even if
he still won't change his mind, we won't make things
difficult for him. We'll just make him crawl under
here. *[Points between his legs]* What do you say?

CROWD *[loud laughter]* Yeah!

*[Silence. MAN unexpectedly bends down and crawls between
SHEPHERD's legs. The CROWD is startled, then they disperse
and exit. As MAN crawls through he picks up a key from the
ground. SHADOW immediately enters.]*

SHADOW A key? Yes, weren't you looking for something similar?
Yes, yes, that's it, you were looking for a key!

*[Kneeling, MAN looks at the key in his hand, stands up and
goes to the centre, puts the key in an imaginary lock, opens a
heavy imaginary door, and goes in. SHADOW exits. A
moment of silence.]*

MAN *[testing]* Hey!

ECHO Hey . . . hey . . . hey . . . hey . . . hey . . . hey . . .

MAN Oh!

ECHO Oh . . . oh . . . oh . . . oh . . . oh . . . oh . . .

MAN Anybody there?

ECHO Anybody there? . . . anybody there . . . anybody there . . .
anybody there . . .

MAN Nobody? Nobody at all?

ECHO *[now sounds like men whispering]* Nobody. Nobody at all.
Nobody. Nobody at all . . . at all . . .

[MAN *looks around and sees that something is hidden under a black cloth. He very carefully pulls out the naked arm of a female shop mannequin from under the cloth.*]

MAN *[amazed]* Oh!

ECHO *[now sounds like the breath of a woman's sigh, quickly]* Oh . . . oh . . . oh . . . oh . . . oh . . . oh . . .

[*This intrigues him all the more, and he searches under the cloth. He finds the mannequin's leg.*]

MAN *[excited]* Ah!

ECHO *[like women's voices, calling rapidly]* Ah . . . ah . . . ah . . . ah . . . ah . . . ah . . . ah . . .

[*He discovers the mannequin under the cloth. He takes it out and examines it, turning its hands and feet as he looks at it appreciatively. He twists the mannequin into various poses and turns its head and moulds its face to give it different expressions: joy, pain, surprise, a bland stare. Each change he makes is accompanied by instruments simulating women's voices.*

He pulls out other mannequins of men and women, whose faces are veiled, and arranges them into a particular formation. After a moment's thought, he gives the first model a veil too. The music grows louder and louder, and he stamps his feet to the rhythm as he arranges the formation of mannequins. And now the formation begins to re-arrange itself. Soon, MAN is drawn into the formation and becomes entangled and unable to extricate himself. The voices of the mannequins grow louder than his. Finally, with difficulty, he crawls, exhausted. The mannequins pass slowly by him, turning around him, hooting and jeering, and then slowly exit.

SHADOW *appears again and keeps a certain distance from* MAN. *As* SHADOW *speaks,* ACTORS *enter dressed in dark mourning clothes. They stand like trees in a forest.*]

SHADOW *[speaking calmly]* Then winter came. There was a heavy snowfall that day and you walked barefoot in the snow to experience the cold. You thought you were like Christ and you suffered alone. You thought you were filled with the spirit of self-sacrifice although you didn't know who you were sacrificing yourself for. Yes. You left your footprints in the snow, and in the distance lay a deep, labyrinthine forest.

[*In a state of utter exhaustion,* MAN *enters the forest of people.* SHADOW *follows him.*]

You walk into that deep dark forest. The trees have shed their leaves, and are stretching out their bare branches like naked women. They stand alone on the snowy ground, forbidding, solitary and silent. You can't help wanting to tell them about your sufferings. You remember the days of your youth, how you once stood at the side of the road waiting and waiting for her. That day it snowed too, and all you wanted was to open your heart to her. You want to tell them you were naive then and now you're full of sin and can never return to those days again. You lost faith in people ages ago and your heart has aged, you can never love again. You just want to walk quietly in the dark forest, on and on till you're exhausted, and then collapse somewhere, never to be found.

[MAN *leans against a 'tree' to rest.* SHADOW *comes closer, watching him.*]

Actually, it's nothing more than self-pity. You're not done with your life yet. You're a vain, ambitious man. [*Exits*]

TREE AGAINST WHICH [*in a human voice*] Ah, so here you are.
MAN LEANS

[*The 'trees', like weird beings, slowly move towards him. They take on human form and become the* CROWD.]

CROWD [*gesturing and speaking monotonously, one after another*]
We've been looking for you everywhere.
Buy us a drink.
You're the host, why did you run out into the snow?
You're our hero, our pride and joy.
You're a giant. We really look up to you.
You're so famous, we're a bit in awe of you.
We admire you but we won't turn you into an idol.
You're nothing but a cheat, but we're not deceived.
Get up, come with us.
You should help us with the Child Welfare Services.
You know the children need money.
It's amazing, you walked through the forest, not even ghosts would dare as much.
You're a pioneer, you took an untrodden path, led people astray.
It's just good luck, not everyone can be so lucky.
It's not that you're more talented than others, it's just that others don't get the chance to prove themselves.

You're really something. You deserve a slap on the back.

[The CROWD *laugh derisively, some start to pull at him. Then they stop suddenly as* SHADOW *enters.]*

There he is!
Talk of the devil.
Make way!

*[*SHADOW *enters limping weakly. The* CROWD *make way for him. He stands beside* MAN *with his back to the audience.]*

MAN *[feebly]* Who's there?

SHADOW *[even more feebly]* Your soul.

[The CROWD *stare as* SHADOW *silently leads* MAN *away. The* CROWD *follow and exit.* ACTORS *enter from another side.]*

ACTORS *[talking, sometimes in union, sometimes one by one]* We set out before dawn, in the thick morning dew. We could hear the breath of the cows chewing cud on the hillside nearby. In the distance the deep blue light of a river bend shone brighter than daylight.
He told us a fairy tale.
I dreamt an elephant's tusk had grown from my belly. It scared me to death.
Have you ever, have you ever wanted to be a bird?
Why be a bird? I'm happy like this. He says he loves me.
Faulkner.
I like Emily's roses.
I telephoned you many times.
Can you read palms?
You don't need to explain, you don't need to explain ever again!
What a sweet kitten.
Where have I seen you before?
I have a sweet tooth, I love yoghurt.
Your hair looks nice, is it a wig?

[The sound of a baby crying]

Sweetheart, O, I forgot to change your nappy.

[The sound of a motorbike starting up]

Why are you going back?

Hey! What sort of a play is this?

What are you doing tomorrow? Shall we have supper together?

[The sounds of a baby crying, of vehicles starting up and driving off, bicycle bells, water gushing from the tap, and the distant wailing of an ambulance siren.]

THE END

THE LEGEND OF
OLD BAWDY TOWN

A PLAY IN FOUR ACTS

1988

By
MA ZHONGJUN

Translated by
JANICE WICKERI

— ABOUT **THE PLAYWRIGHT** —

MA ZHONGJUN (1957–) completed his secondary school education in Shanghai in 1974, after which he was assigned the job of a road-construction worker at the Shanghai Municipal Council, and he started writing in his spare time. In 1978, he was posted to the Writing Team of the Shanghai Municipal Workers Union. After two award-winning plays, *There is Warmth Outside the House* (1980) and *Road* (1981), he was transferred, in 1983, to the Culture and Arts Institute, Jiangsu Province, and became a full-time writer. Two more nationally acclaimed plays, *Trendy Red Dress* (1984) and *Red Room, White Room, Black Room* (1985), which he also adapted into award-winning film scripts, brought him another posting, this time to Beijing. Since then, he has been working as full-time playwright at the Chinese Youth Art Theatre. He has also written a number of television drama scripts.

Ma is one of the younger generation of playwrights in the Mainland who are keen to explore modes of writing and drama production other than the socialist-realist model which has dominated the contemporary Chinese theatre for decades. *The Legend of Old Bawdy Town*, first performed by the Chinese Youth Art Theatre in 1989, is his most daring and ambitious attempt so far.

ABOUT **THE PLAY**

This play is a radical, often subversive, interrogation of authority in its many different manifestations. The story takes place at a time when the ruling dynasty had banned all trade and association with foreigners, and presents a conflict between the prostitute Virtue, whose only wish is to help the people of Bawdy Town, and the army general who represents authority and the emperor. The result is an ironic and powerful critique of traditional Chinese notions about discipline, loyalty, honour, chastity, self-sacrifice, bravery, and wisdom.

With carefully researched material based on folklore, legends, ancient myths, and surviving local customs which celebrate the pleasures of the flesh, the play reveals and highlights an aspect of Chinese culture all too often suppressed or even erased by the canonized Confucian culture. The tension between Virtue and the general is not only a conflict between two individuals with powerful personalities, but is also a dramatization of the battle between the sexes. At the same time, the discord and drama between these two characters reveals the friction between two different modes of consciousness, two opposing systems of values, and two completely different attitudes towards life.

The play is a deliberate attempt to move away from the socialist-realist and slice-of-life drama which represent the mainstream in Mainland theatre. The playwright's introduction of the surreal into the action, his careful enwrapping of the action in a mood and an atmosphere that turns from the ordinary everyday to the dreamy to the nightmarish, his use of a quasi-archaic, quasi-elevated style of language to convey thoughts that are unmistakably feminist and therefore distinctly modern—all these reveal a consciousness and an imagination deeply committed to experimentation and innovation. As such, the play marks a determined attempt to break new ground in the Chinese theatre.

──── **DRAMATIS** PERSONAE ────

FAN WUCHEN, male, aged 35, Governor-General of Lianghuai* and
   Brigade General of the south-eastern coastal towns
VIRTUE, aged 30, alias Huaman, a resident of Bawdy Town, a lady of
   pleasure, a business woman, and later, a 'comfort woman' in the camps
GEOMANCER WU, aged over 60, Bawdy Town's itinerant Taoist priest
GRANNY TEA, in her 50s, proprietess of the town teahouse
LOTUS, in her 20s, village embroideress
YOUNG SEVEN, in his 20s, village cotton-fluffer who prepares cotton
   for spinning
BUTCHER, in his 50s, village butcher
OIL VENDOR, in his 30s
LI LAICHUAN, in his 60s, the town headman
LI BENYI, in his 40s, the town scholar
LI CHITIAN, in his 50s, the town squire
MADAM FAN, aged 28, wife of FAN WUCHEN
FAN JUAN, aged 12, FAN WUCHEN's elder daughter
FAN ZHEN, aged 9, FAN WUCHEN's younger daughter
FAN WU, aged 19, FAN WUCHEN's servant boy
LI ZHIYONG, in his 40s, Colonel, right wing of FAN's army
WANG HUI, in his 50s, Colonel, left wing of FAN's army
LIU YUAN, in his 30s, Captain of FAN's army
ANTONIO, 40-ish, Spanish Special Envoy, trader, owner and captain of ship
LUIS, 30-ish, Portuguese Special Envoy, trader, owner and captain of ship

SOLDIERS:

BUG-EYES, in his 30s
HATCHET-FACE, in his 20s
BIG BEARD, in his 20s
FATTY, in his 20s
SKINNY, in his 20s
RATTY in his 30s
SPROUT, in his 40s
BUTCHER'S BOY, in his 40s

Townsfolk, constables, squires, beggars, travellers, officers, and soldiers
   of the Garrison
Time: Some time in the Middle Ages
Place: Old Bawdy Town
Music and sound effects: harness-bells, kettledrums, flutes, and bamboo
                        flutes. A modern electric band can be used.

* Region between the Yellow River and the Yangtze River in Anhui and Jiangsu Provinces.

ACT 1

[The faint, mysterious jingle of a harness-bell is carried on the breeze from afar. It's nearly here, crisp and charming, but a moment later the sound gradually fades away.

Waves can be heard gently lapping the shore.

The curtain rises on a corner of the square in the centre of the town. There is a stage off to the right, but it is empty and bare. The sun of a March morning filters weakly through the mist, casting a ray of red light on to the stage. To the left, a section of the street is visible: wineshop, rice shop, dogmeat shop, oilshop, carpenter's, bamboo worker's, and so on, all cheek by jowl. Crowds of people come and go, lots of hustle and bustle. There is a teahouse upstage left, with an arched bridge beside it. Water can be heard flowing underneath. The cabin roofs of small boats are visible on the water. Green mountains rise in the distance.

Two men emerge from a boat. One is dressed as a general—red helmet, gold armour, a sword at his waist, high boots. He is about 35; his face long, thin, and swarthy. He usually squints; his eyes are seldom wide open, except in reproach. Obviously he is someone who knows how to control his emotions. He is FAN WUCHEN, the Governor-General of Lianghuai and Brigade General of the south-eastern coastal towns. Having gained the bank, he takes up a map and studies it, comparing it from time to time with the scene before him. The other person is his servant, FAN WU, a slender, agile, and pleasant-looking young man. He wears a patterned purple tunic over white trousers, a short blue skirt, white socks, black cloth shoes and black cloth cap.

Sounds of hustle and bustle reach them from the town.]

FAN WUCHEN *[puts down map]* So this is Bawdy Town.

FAN WU *[curiously]* Excellency, do you come from around here?

FAN *[shakes his head]* I was here fifteen years ago.

FAN WU What a busy place!

FAN Summon our men and wait for orders. I'll try and find out whether people here really do fraternize with barbarians. Don't enter the town without a signal from me.

FAN WU Yes, Excellency. *[He returns to the boat as FAN exits.]*

[The teahouse is the busiest place in all Bawdy Town. The upper floor is given over to a wineshop with alcove seats. It is completely empty. Downstairs is the teahouse with its rough-hewn tables and stools. The villagers are there: sitting, squatting, feet up on the stools, or perched cross-legged on the tables. Most are bare-chested and barefoot, only a few are respectably dressed. They're downing bowls of tea, shelling peanuts and melon seeds, laughing or wailing in despair, making a real din. GRANNY TEA strolls among them, busily filling up teapots and replenishing the nuts and seeds. The

wine tipplers open their mouths wide, pouring wine down their throats straight from the gourd, then calling loudly for more. Tea drinkers savour their tea while airing their vocal cords to hum a few verses of southern-style opera from 'The Jade Hare'.

Enter FAN, disguised as a scholar. He drifts casually into the teahouse through the stream of townspeople. He wears a long robe the colour of jade, its wide sleeves trimmed in dark green, and has on a scholar's headcloth. The tassel of his fan dangles from his hand. His manner is debonair, completely at ease. Something catches his attention, his eyes flash. Four men are seated at the first table. One, wearing the garb of a Taoist priest, is a little old man with short white eyebrows and red tipped nose; this is GEOMANCER WU. A detached smile plays across his face, and he has the other-worldly air of a rustic hermit. The other three—YOUNG SEVEN, the cotton-fluffer, OIL VENDOR and BUTCHER—are all dressed in clothes typical of tradesmen in a small market town. Their discussion draws FAN's interest. He chooses a table nearby, quietly sits down and listens to their talk.

A harness-bell jingles softly.]

YOUNG SEVEN Me, I've got the foresight of the mastermind Duke Zhuge: this morning's Flower Queen will be Lotus. If you don't believe me, I'd be willing to lay a little wager—the loser stands the winner a jug of wine.

[A moment of silence, then they all talk at once, some sneering.]

GEOMANCER *[dubiously]* Lotus?

BUTCHER *[disdainfully]* Oh, the embroideress from Squire Chi's Textile Factory. She's not bad. Got something of a reputation with the boys.

YOUNG SEVEN Huh? Listen you dog butcher, eaten too many dog penises, have you? Overdose of heat got to your eyes? Not bad? Lotus? Hear this, she's ten times prettier than Xishi, or Chang E, or any of them famous beauties. If all the fellows in love with her were stacked up on top of each other, they'd reach to the moon!

BUTCHER *[coldly]* Pretty? Yeah. Like one of them vases from the government kiln at Jingdezhen. I've got some twenty years on you—now, maybe in all that time I haven't eaten as much rice as you, or as much salt, but girls I've seen more of! In Chang'an, Kaifeng, Jinling,*

* An old name for Nanjing.

Linan . . . I've seen them all, but not one could hold a candle to Virtue. What a looker! And there's that story about her, and what happened when she turned up at the port the day the Emperor banned maritime trade with foreigners. The port had high city walls and fisherfolk anxious to go out to fish were all crowded at the city gate. The soldiers arrived to stop them, and started shouting, scolding and kicking the crowd. Then suddenly, there was a whiff of fragrance in the air and splash, splash, splash—

OIL VENDOR *[curiously]* Huh?

BUTCHER The soldiers fainted dead away and fell into the sea!

OIL VENDOR How come?

BUTCHER Intoxicated by the sound of Virtue's footsteps!

GEOMANCER *[a heartfelt sigh]* Ah! This town of ours with all its droughts and floods, its alkaline land, bitter water. If it hadn't been for Virtue's trampling the embargo and letting the fishing boats out to sea, why, today—

[Finding the stranger FAN WUCHEN *eavesdropping at the next table, he shuts up.]*

YOUNG SEVEN *[unconvinced]* That's past history.

BUTCHER Past history? Has the Emperor lifted the embargo? If it wasn't for Virtue would we have such a grand contest today?

*[*GEOMANCER *takes another look at* FAN WUCHEN. FAN *notices, but continues to act as if there's nothing amiss.]*

YOUNG SEVEN *[sighs]* Aw, ten years ago, Virtue was a raving beauty, none like her . . . I would gladly have carried her chamber pot for her! Now—

BUTCHER You're not good enough even to carry her chamber pot! Up your granny's! Ungrateful swine! Dog! You run drooling through the streets; it's all one to you, any bitch'll do. If it wasn't for Virtue, you little cotton-fluffing cur, you would have snuffed it long ago. You'd be a goner. Would you still be running through the streets sowing your oats?

YOUNG SEVEN *[furious with shame]* You dog butcher, any more of your nastiness and I'll slice off your family jewels!

OIL VENDOR *[smoothing things over]* You two stop shooting your mouths off. I say we have a bet on it. Win or lose, five taels of silver. My money's on Lotus. If I lose, I'll stand you two a jug of wine.

YOUNG SEVEN I'll bet five taels.

BUTCHER It's a bet.

GEOMANCER Now, now I really shouldn't. We Taoist priests
shouldn't care for material things; but since you two
will favour me, I will have to accept.

[The soft lapping of waves can be heard.]

*[A man from another province, seated across from FAN, leans
over curiously.]*

STRANGER Can you tell me, sir, what is this contest?

FAN Sorry, this is my first visit here, I must ask you to
enquire elsewhere.

STRANGER *[bows, walks over to YOUNG SEVEN and raises clasped
hands in greeting]* Excuse me, I heard what you said just
now with interest. I wonder if you would tell me what
this contest is?

YOUNG SEVEN Have a seat, sir. Ah, this . . . well, there's a custom
here; we hold a contest each year on the third day of
the third month. All women, married and unmarried,
collect underwear from their husbands and all the men
they've slept with and string them up on bamboo
poles. All sorts of underpants, big ones, little ones,
short ones, long ones, coarse ones, fine ones, wide ones,
narrow ones. Then they get up on stage and parade
their spoils. Whoever has the most and the best variety
wins the title of Flower Queen.

STRANGER Oh? Doesn't that mean that the biggest slut wins?
Interesting, interesting! Why hasn't it got underway yet?

YOUNG SEVEN We're waiting for someone. Thick fog today, the roads
are bad.

STRANGER Who are you waiting for?

YOUNG SEVEN Who else? The reigning champion, Virtue.

STRANGER Ah, amazing! Amazing!

*[A light fog permeates the scene, cloaking the day. After a
moment, it clears. Gentle waves can be heard.*

    *GRANNY TEA emerges from a room and sees FAN from a
distance, then scurries over.]*

GRANNY TEA What an idiot I am, sir! I must be getting senile to
neglect a guest such as yourself.

FAN No harm done.

GRANNY TEA Honoured sir, my humble teashop is a lowly one
serving poor tea and indifferent wine. We seldom have
the opportunity to serve a guest so refined as yourself;
today is truly a red-letter day. If it's wine you wish, please
come upstairs, we have *Huadiao* and *Zhuangyuanhong*—

FAN Tea will do nicely.

GRANNY TEA Good. We have West Lake Dragon Well and Eastern Hill *Biluochun*—

FAN Mmm, thank you. There's a famous tea from Fairy Maiden Cliff in this province. They say local girls pick the leaves with their lips before the spring showers, and so it's called 'Red Maiden'. I'd like that one.

GRANNY TEA Ah? You've lived here, sir?

FAN Old Bawdy Town is famous, its reputation drew me here. The tea should be brewed with lightly boiled water from the Small Dragon Pool, and never with water from the stream—

GRANNY TEA *[eyeing FAN suspiciously]* Sir, you really must be from these parts.

FAN *[rather pleased with himself, but soon realizes that GEOMANCER is watching him, and grows serious, regretting his lapse, then smiles expansively]* Old Bawdy Town lies within the boundaries of the kingdoms of Wu and Yue. As recorded in the village chronicles: 'To the east the sea, to the west a mountain, low but precipitous, called Mount Wu. A spring rises from Small Dragon Pool in Mount Wu. It never runs dry. It gurgles into a stream, a clear, shallow stream, full of fine fish. Where the water flows out of the mountain it is called *yin* water, which is bitter. Mount Wu is rich in flora, and its famous tea has round leaves, a white calyx around the bud, red petals with dark streaks and small citrus fruits. Whoever eats the fruit will have innumerable children. Thus, families in Bawdy Town have many sons and grandsons. One woman gave birth to nine sons at one time. The tea leaves are light as feathers, tender as new grass. Steeped in water from Small Dragon Pool, it is like dew . . . Mount Wu is rich in animal and bird life. There is a bird there with a body like a wild duck, but with only one wing and one eye; where it flies, there will be flood.' Ha ha, I have glanced through the village chronicles, but I might have got it all wrong.

GRANNY TEA Incredible! Fifteen years ago these old eyes saw the *manman* bird fly out of Mount Wu, and all Bawdy Town was flooded.

[A harness-bell jingles briefly, mysteriously. FAN WU enters and goes quietly into the teahouse.]

What would the honoured sir like to nibble on with
his tea? We have fresh lotus seeds, new walnut meats,
fresh water caltrop, fresh water chestnuts, assorted dried
fruit, almonds, pickled goose web, meat floss, *muxi*
salted fish, salted chicken wings—

FAN Just tea, thank you.

GRANNY TEA Ready in a moment, sir. *[Exits]*

FAN WU *[sits down quietly and speaks in a low voice]* Excellency,
there's a bold woman on the highway, riding a fine
horse, with two foreigners in tow. They're heading
towards the village!

FAN *[looks pleased at this report]* Oh?

FAN WU These ignorant peasant women do not know that they
can be beheaded for fraternizing with foreigners.

FAN *[indifferently]* Rather well-timed. Don't alarm them.

*[GEOMANCER glances at them again. FAN WUCHEN looks
away and ignores him, cool and composed.]*

FAN WU *[has a brainwave]* Excellency, I'll take a turn through
the streets.

FAN No harm in taking a stroll.

*[FAN WU goes. GEOMANCER ponders for a moment, then
approaches FAN.]*

GEOMANCER Sir, you got all that by just flipping through the
chronicles? You really have a good memory.

FAN *[graciously]* Thank you.

[The two men silently size each other up.]

GEOMANCER Ah, the gentleman has a broad full forehead, a
prominent nose, bold eyebrows—altogether a noble
face. Poor Taoist cleric that I am, I know something of
geomancy and the hexagrams, I practise astrology and
physiognomy, for which I have quite a reputation here
in Bawdy Town. Shall I do a reading for you?

FAN I wouldn't presume to impose on you, sir.

GEOMANCER If I'm wrong, it won't cost you a penny; if I'm right, it
still won't cost you anything.

FAN Interesting.

GEOMANCER In fortune-telling, if the will is strong, it will become
manifest in the physiognomy; if there is good fortune
in the physiognomy, but no will to match it, the
physiognomy will lose its promise. Looking at you, sir,
I see a round head, short neck, long hands, straight
arms: without doubt you are the stuff of heroes. The

space between your eyebrows is red, which means that
in your youth you suffered cold and hunger, and your
parents died early. Your eyebrows slant downwards,
showing that you have been in reduced circumstances
and have had to beg for food. Then with the help of
your benefactor, your career blossomed and all roads
were open to you. You are able with brush and sword,
wielding the brush with the flourish of a sword, and
the sword with the finesse of a brush. You are a learned
warrior, a brave scholar. A man of fortune and high
degree, a pillar of the nation! If I am not mistaken,
you are an official of the ninth rank and today you are
travelling in disguise on a secret inspection—

*[FAN is startled, but his demeanour does not change. The two
men look at each other. GEOMANCER strokes his beard and
smiles. They break into laughter.]*

FAN You flatter me. If fortune should smile on me, I won't
forget our meeting today.

*[The two look at each other again and laugh. GRANNY
TEA approaches with the tea.*

*A crowd of people surges up the street. FAN and
GEOMANCER both look in that direction. In front of the
crowd are the town headman LI LAICHUAN, the local squire
LI CHITIAN, and the scholar LI BENYI. Dressed in fine
clothes and wearing headclothes of different styles, they are in
high spirits, each waving a fan. Behind them comes a group
of followers carrying three vermilion plaques, lettered in gold:
'Resplendent Virtue', 'Number One Woman of Virtue Under
Heaven', 'Paragon of Virtue', followed by a band of trumpeters
and drummers. A brief jingling of the harness-bell.]*

LI BENYI Reporting, Headman. Everything is ready for the
contest, all that's missing is the main attraction. We're
just waiting for Virtue's gracious presence.

LI LAICHUAN *[strokes his beard]* Excellent. Virtue is the goddess of
wealth for our towns around here. We had better
proceed with caution. Her ladyship's a touchy one—if
anything's the least bit amiss she says what she feels.
No respector of persons, that one.

LI BENYI *[hesitantly]* But Lotus . . . she insists on competing for
the title.

LI LAICHUAN Oh? Can she beat our Virtue?

LI BENYI My dear sir, all the young men around here are smitten
with her. She'll have collected a lot of underwear from
her sweethearts. Could be that—

LI LAICHUAN *[furious]* Could be, could be trouble all right. If Virtue doesn't win, we'll be in deep trouble. Spread the word that there's a hundred taels of silver in it if Lotus doesn't show up.

LI BENYI *[trembling with fear]* But she will!

LI LAICHUAN Fool! Get going! Tell those flunkeys, whoever steals a pair of her fancy men's shorts from Lotus gets a reward of ten taels of silver.

[LI BENYI acquiesces. A constable runs up huffing and puffing.]

CONSTABLE Most honoured Headman, Virtue is coming.

LI LAICHUAN Sound the trumpets!

[Instantly drums and trumpets raise a din all around. People turn toward the south.]

CONSTABLE *[bowing]* I dare not keep it from you, Headman. Virtue has two long-nosed red-beards with her.

LI LAICHUAN Stop the music!

[The music stops.]

Oh what a mess. What a mess! I've heard from the capital that the new Governor-General of Lianghuai, the Brigade General of the towns along the south-east coast, Fan Wuchen, has already taken up office and is headed here!

LI BENYI Aiya! I heard that when General Fan was serving in Ji and Liao, in Yunnan, and in Guangdong and Guangxi provinces, he was brilliant in battle, and slaughtered lots of people. This big shot, the Emperor's favourite, will not tolerate anything irregular, not even a speck of dust. When he was serving in Ji and Liao, one of his favourite officers fell in love with a Nuzhen barbarian maiden and Fan sliced off his head just like that!

LI CHITIAN I've heard the talk too. General Fan makes no exception for family or friends. He sticks to the strict letter of the law. He has a reputation in this dynasty as a righteous official. Sending him to the south-east here is a way to allow him to start a fight.

LI LAICHUAN Fraternizing with foreigners is a very serious offence. If someone informs . . . what's to be done?

LI CHITIAN What's to be done?

LI BENYI What's to be done?

LI LAICHUAN Stupid pigs! I'm asking you! Well?

*[Silence. A harness-bell jingles. On the bridge a woman
appears.* It is VIRTUE. *She wears a white satin cloak, with
a dull gold skirt, her hair twisted into a bun. She is
extremely seductive, a peerless beauty. Her eyes are particularly
expressive—'talking eyes'. Her generous moist mouth, a fresh
red, brings to mind her life of prostitution.*

    *Two foreigners in Chinese dress, high nosed, hollow-eyed
and red-whiskered, stand one on either side of her.]*

[flustered] Music!

[A cacophony of instruments. VIRTUE *and the foreigners stroll
leisurely down from the bridge towards the teahouse. All eyes
are drawn to them—gasps of admiration and cheers from the
teahouse.]*

*[The squires scurry up, bowing and scraping and humbling
themselves.* VIRTUE's *proud glance sweeps over them to* FAN.
Their eyes meet, clash—finally FAN *tears his eyes away.]*

[bowing] Our paltry town is a mere rural wasteland, but
today, by favour of Virtue, Mr Luis, and Mr Antonio,
its humbleness is raised to glory.

VIRTUE Once a year this poor woman comes home and every
year there are changes in the old place. Headman, you
really know how to flatter a girl—the streets of the
village are swept clean, couplets pasted up on the
doorways to catch my fancy, and the bamboo bridge
has been replaced by a stone one—But Headman, you
old sweetheart, you're so miserly. Why did you kick all
our brothers, the beggars, out of town today?

LI LAICHUAN Uh, it wasn't me who gave that order.

LI BENYI *[hangs his head]* I'm afraid I'm responsible.

VIRTUE I've invited them back. Mr Scholar dear, how many
years did you have to beg for a living?

LI BENYI Five.

VIRTUE *[smiles]* You see, it's the beggars who make pillars of the
nation. You're illiterate, Scholar, you bought your merit
with silver. *[Pauses over each word]* Fifteen years ago a
very young man came here begging, and today he's—

LI LAICHUAN Governor-General of the Lianghuai Region and Brigade
General of the south-eastern coastal towns, Fan Wuchen!

VIRTUE Obviously there's something to be said for begging.
Give each one a scholar's robe and silver to buy himself
a rank or a title. One fine day they'll all be generals.
Put the lot on my account.

[A crowd of beggars surges forward; LI BENYI *leads them off.]*

LI LAICHUAN Virtue, your favour to the town here is great as a
mountain. In fact, you are like mother and father to
the folks in Bawdy Town. Each tile and brick of the
town, every bit of silver and gold, each grain of rice,
has been bestowed by you. If you had not broken the
embargo to trade with the foreigners, Bawdy Town
couldn't have held on this long. All the people, young
and old, of Bawdy Town join me in expressing our
good wishes to you.

*[Another burst of music. His followers raise high the three
red plaques.]*

VIRTUE *[applauding and laughing]* 'Number One Woman of
Virtue Under Heaven', 'Resplendent Virtue', 'Paragon
of Virtue'! I'm so pleased, Headman, to see these
plaques. Fifteen years I've been a prostitute, a purveyor
of smiles, a harlot in the Spring Garden. I served wine
on the Qinhuai River, walked the streets at the
Embankment, and was fondled by the soldiers guarding
the harbour. I've had hundreds and thousands of men. I
am truly worthy of the honour of Number One Woman
of Virtue Under Heaven, a paragon of virtue!

[General laughter]

LI LAICHUAN *[bowing and speaking over-anxiously]* Don't misunderstand,
Virtue. Throughout the ages, we have known it's
impossible to be both loyal and filial; both virtuous
and righteous. In your case, why bother with small
virtue; yours is the greater Virtue, the greater
righteousness.

LI CHITIAN Resplendent Virtue—you are certainly worthy of the
name.

LI LAICHUAN Number One Woman of Virtue Under Heaven, you
have no peer in the world.

TOWNSFOLK *[raising their voices high]* You are worthy . . . worthy. . . .

*[Exhilarated, VIRTUE greets those around her; her searing
gaze once again meets the icy stare of FAN WUCHEN.
      FAN once more drops his gaze.
      The two foreigners are also infected by the merry
atmosphere.]*

ANTONIO Mistress Virtue. A missionary from my country wrote a
book about China. The woman who sleeps only with
her own husband and has no secret liaisons with other
men is the chaste wife honoured by Confucius in his
Moral Precepts—but—

VIRTUE Wrong! What Confucius decreed was modest virtue. When a woman's dalliances with men are exceptionally numerous, hot, and tempestuous, that's resplendent virtue. That alone is true virtue.

ANTONIO Oh, so that's how it is.

LUIS How terribly interesting. I must spread these wondrous moral precepts of your great country among the women of Portugal, so they can learn from Chinese women.

VIRTUE I'll take them under my wing.

[The squires beam.]

There are now six houses of pleasure in Bawdy Town and a prostitute's quarter. Recently sister prostitutes have come from Suzhou, Songjiang, and Shanghai. Three plaques for six houses of pleasure—not enough to go round. Headman, dear, could I trouble you to make three more plaques, so every house can have one?

LI LAICHUAN *[hesitantly]* As for that—

VIRTUE *[angry]* The girls in these houses are in the same business as I am.

LI LAICHUAN *[flustered]* As you wish, as you wish, up they go. We'll make three more and hang them immediately.

[Music blares. The followers raise their plaques, take a turn around the stage and exit. LI BENYI enters, followed by a crowd of beggars dressed in shiny new scholars' robes. They swagger on to the stage, take a turn around, then sit and begin eating and drinking. As VIRTUE slowly makes her way nearer to the teahouse, the townsfolk all around cheer. She responds repeatedly, until without realizing it, she has reached FAN. Her incisive glance takes him in, sizing him up. The harness-bell jingles ominously.]

VIRTUE What a man!

FAN What a woman!

VIRTUE The festivities have completely taken over the town. Colour! Drinking! Eating! With his cup of green tea, this gentleman stands out from the crowd.

FAN Your compliment is misplaced. I am one for whom tea is life. A cup of green tea, contemplation of the vagaries of the world—these are my everyday pleasures. Having heard tales of Bawdy Town's beauties, and seeing you in the flesh today, truly, one look is worth a thousand words!

VIRTUE *[smiles faintly]* The gentleman must be quite familiar with Bawdy Town?

FAN [*courteously*] Not at all, I simply heard of it along the
    way.

[*Their eyes meet again.*]

VIRTUE May I ask the gentleman's name?

FAN [*bows*] My name is Wu Xiaotu from Qiantang in
    Zhejiang; I am also known as Youfeng.

VIRTUE And I am—

FAN Your reputation precedes you. Meeting up with you
    today is good fortune enough for three lifetimes.

VIRTUE [*laughs*] I see that you're interested in the foreigners I
    brought along, sir. I'll introduce them to you.

FAN You're too kind.

ANTONIO [*perceives that there is more to* FAN *than meets the eye*] I am
    Antonio, Spanish trader and owner of a shipping
    company. [*Meaningfully*] What an honour to meet you,
    Mr Wu. I'm delighted. I'd appreciate your goodwill
    and guidance.

LUIS [*jovially*] And I'm Luis, a Portuguese trader, and owner
    of a shipping company. The more Chinese friends I
    make the better. I'm delighted to meet you!

FAN The pleasure is mine, gentlemen.

[*Pause.*]

Our Emperor has decreed the seaports closed. Soldiers
are stationed all along the coast to form a blockade
tight as an iron net. You two must be infinitely
resourceful to come and go from my country as you
please.

LUIS Ha ha. We have Chinese friends. There are many
    channels, it's extremely convenient. In Chinese you say:
    With money you can even get the devil to push the
    millstone for you! There's also this saying: Heroes
    always fall for beauty's charms. Ha ha.

[FAN, *shaken, tries to suppress his anger.*]

ANTONIO [*glossing things over*] My friend is given to exaggeration
    and sensational blabbering. We're extremely fond of
    Chinese customs, so we just blunder along to watch the
    excitement.

FAN [*sees the looks on the faces of* VIRTUE *and the others, and*
    makes an effort to relax] Of course. Once you've seen the
    excitement in Bawdy Town, nowhere else holds any
    attraction. No wonder the two of you are so bold, I'm
    truly impressed.

LUIS Taking risks is our greatest pleasure.

ANTONIO In pursuit of the novel and the exotic. We are good friends of China. We do not need to fear our friends, do we?

[*FAN smiles enigmatically,* VIRTUE *and the foreigners smile too. The squires look confused.*]

VIRTUE Mr Wu, won't you come and take a cup upstairs?

FAN [*considers a moment, bows*] Why thank you Ma'am. I am a wanderer down on his luck. This is my first time here. I have yet to get acquainted with this place. It is not proper for a stranger like me to trespass upon your hospitality. But do not let me keep you from your pleasure.

VIRTUE Please suit yourself. [*Spotting* GEOMANCER] Geomancer, you old Taoist rogue, why have you been hiding from me?

GEOMANCER [*ingratiatingly*] Where there's wine, this poor Taoist shows up, invited or not.

VIRTUE Thick-skinned old rogue. You give me a good reading on my face, say something lucky, and I'll offer you a drink.

GEOMANCER Your signs are good. Very good.

[*The harness-bell jingles.*]

Virtue's face beams with joy. Joy brings luck to whatever befalls; even prison seems like the bridal hall. A good reading.

LI LAICHUAN You old Taoist rogue, you spoil Virtue's happy mood. I'll rip your tongue out.

VIRTUE [*laughs it off*] It's a good reading. My treat. Some wine for the geomancer.

[*FAN continues silently sipping his tea; he seems to have fallen into a reverie.*
    Fog fills the sky, bearing down on them, blotting out the light.]

Let the contest begin!

[*LI LAICHUAN, the headman, bustles around gesticulating, and music fills the stage—strings and woodwinds. A band of women in red tops and green trousers, carrying bamboo poles, begin the bamboo-pole dance. From their poles flutter every size, quality, and colour of men's underwear. They raise their voices in sweet song.*]

Third day, third month, our ancient contest ply
as for the winner's crown we vie.
Aiyo, aiyo, aiyoyo . . .
Bamboo poles lifted high
and from the curved tips,
our lovers' shorts sigh.
Little sister takes the lead,
Older sister follows nigh
If not one the other tries,
blushing, blushing aiyoyo—
to win the flowery prize.

[Cheers go up from the tables in the teahouse. FAN *fans himself, a stratagem in mind.* FAN WU *slips into the teahouse carrying a cloth-wrapped bundle.]*

FAN WU *[in hushed tones]* Colonel Li Zhiyong has sent me to request instructions, General. We have Bawdy Town surrounded, when should we make our move?

FAN They're trapped—like a turtle in a jar—what's the hurry?

FAN WU They're drinking and merry-making like there's no tomorrow. What a riotous lot!

FAN Fan Wu, tell me, why are they so brazen?

FAN WU They have a backer. Must be a high official.

FAN *[smiles]* I'll soon be invited for a drink.

FAN WU I see. The General wants to cast a long line to catch a big fish, to feel along the vine until he finds the plumpest melon—

FAN Soldiering is like farming or weaving, you have to judge your moment. When the time is ripe, the water will flow into the channel, the melon will fall.

[The dance has intensified, several women bedecked with jewels also come on stage carrying bamboo poles with men's underwear hanging from them.

Upstairs, in the wineshop, merriment reigns. VIRTUE *glances sideways from time to time, as if casually, checking up on* FAN *downstairs. As* GRANNY TEA *goes down to make more tea, she comes to a halt. Thereupon,* FAN WU *deliberately raises his voice.]*

FAN WU *[opens his bundle]* Sir, this piece of dogmeat smells so good. It's called dogmeat in prime sauce, a secret recipe handed down from the family of General Fan Kuai under Emperor Gaozu, of the Han dynasty. The meat is simmered in an age-old tortoise broth and is very fragrant, tender and delicious. The name, dogmeat in prime sauce, came down from Emperor Gaozu too. Please sir, when do you want to eat it?

FAN Later, wait until we get home.

GRANNY TEA *[returns to wineshop]* There are secret agents downstairs.

[The squires are dismayed. Only VIRTUE *and the foreigners continue talking and laughing as if nothing has happened.]*

GEOMANCER *[strokes his whiskers and grins]* Would that it were only secret agents. I read the heavens at night, the skies are heavily overcast, yet Mars shines bright. Fan Wuchen, Governor-General of Lianghuai and Brigade General of the south-eastern coastal towns is already here on a secret mission.

[The squires are pale with shock, their wine cups fall to the floor, they're at a loss what to do. Downstairs in the teahouse cheers ring loud and riotous.]

YOUNG SEVEN Hey, look, Squire Li's old lady has the underpants off that lowlife Scholar Li. Ha ha.

OIL VENDOR Ha ha. And Squire Li's shorts have fallen to the Scholar's old lady.

BUTCHER And the underwear of those two has all been collected by the headman's wife.

VIRTUE *[beside herself with delight]* The headman is such a darling! And all the women are up on stage now. I'm having such a good time!

LI BENYI *[berates the squire,* LI CHITIAN, *through closed teeth]* Dog!

LI CHITIAN Swine!

LI LAICHUAN *[extremely worried]* Governor Fan is here. What shall we do now? Virtue, say something, quick!

GEOMANCER When things are this bad, they can only get better. All is vanity.

LI CHITIAN Aiya, my worldly goods are as good as gone!

LI BENYI Worldy goods? What about, what about fraternizing with foreigners? That's the death penalty for the whole family.

GEOMANCER One thing is as bad as the other.

[The squires prostrate themselves before VIRTUE.*]*

TOGETHER Please save us, Virtue!

VIRTUE *[laughing]* On my way into town, I heard no horses' hooves or bird song, not on main roads or small ones, not by the sea nor the rivers; the soldiers have hidden themselves in the thick fog. But it was obvious they were all drawn by the excitement of this contest. So, when I was halfway here with these red-haired barbarians, I thought to myself, come what may we've got to make it. There's going to be so much fun! That gentleman on his secret mission is waiting for the headman to treat him to a drink. Go, invite him!

GEOMANCER Fortune—disaster; disaster—fortune. Let this Taoist go to greet his lordship. *[Goes downstairs]*

[Silence]

[A single bell jingles. In the midst of the music and singing, it is particularly ominous.]

LI BENYI *[relieved]* Virtue and General Fan are—

[LI LAICHUAN gives LI BENYI a scornful look, VIRTUE smiles but says nothing, the company listen to the goings-on downstairs.]

GEOMANCER *[bows to FAN]* I am the poor Taoist Wu Yifeng of Bawdy Town; I'm also known as Yexiang. By order of the headman, I humbly beseech Mr Wu to come upstairs for some wine and honour us with the pleasure of his company.

FAN The honour and pleasure are all mine.

GEOMANCER After you.

FAN After you, priest. *[Mounts the stairs grandly, his manner dripping self-satisfaction and arrogance]*

[The moment the squires see FAN, they're all aflutter, abject and frightened. VIRTUE continues to smile as always.]

I'm Wu Xiaotu. Today, thanks to the celestial bounty of our Taoist worthy, I have the chance to be introduced to you honoured gentlemen.

[The squires immediately begin to wax verbose and pedantic.]

LI LAICHUAN I am Li Laichuan, also known as Jiuquan. Priest Yexiang holds you in high regard. To be able to make the acquaintance of one as revered as yourself is a long-awaited honour. A great honour for me.

FAN *[laughing]* I am a simple wanderer, a nobody. You all do me too much honour.

LI LAICHUAN Sir, your great aspirations and fame are everywhere known.

LI BENYI Mr Laichuan is our headman, and head of our Li clan.

FAN Honoured.

LI CHITIAN I'm from Bawdy Town, my humble name is Li Chitian.

FAN Honoured.

LI BENYI This unworthy one is Li Benyi.

FAN Honoured. *[His eyes meet those of* VIRTUE, ANTONIO, *and* LUIS.*]*

*[*VIRTUE *smiles graciously;* ANTONIO, *on his guard, falls silent;* LUIS, *a hostile look on his face, sizes* FAN *up.* FAN *smiles. The harness-bell jingles.]*

I'm delighted to meet you again.

LI LAICHUAN *[flustered]* Please, sit down. Drink . . . have a drink.

[They all slowly sit down.]

LUIS *[provocatively]* Mr Wu, we Westerners like to get straight to the point. What kind of business are you in?

FAN I'm a curious sort. I heard that there were many amazing things in Bawdy Town, so out of curiosity, I came.

LUIS Then—

VIRTUE People in my country value subtlety. There's no need to spell everything out.

LI LAICHUAN Drink up, drink up.

*[*FAN *and* VIRTUE *clink their cups. Their eyes meet again.]*

FAN Drink . . . drink . . .

*[*FAN *and* VIRTUE *laugh,* VIRTUE'*s laugh is a prolonged one.* GEOMANCER *realizes that* VIRTUE *is behaving strangely.]*

VIRTUE Mr Wu, I seem to have met you before.

FAN *[feigning astonishment]* Really?

LI BENYI *[pleasantly surprised]* Yes, yes. Mr Wu is . . . the number one talent in south China and Virtue is the number one beauty. How can talent and beauty remain strangers?

VIRTUE *[acting serious]* I entertained you in the house of pleasure. You were drunk that day, and in the middle of the night you came groping to the door—

[The squires are in stitches; they're beginning to feel more hopeful.]

FAN *[carefree and leisurely]* Your memory fails you, Virtue. I have a good education in proper behaviour. I do nothing that offends propriety.

[The squires begin to feel uncomfortable again.]

VIRTUE Oh, I remember, I do remember. Mr Wu sailed up the Qinhuai River for an assignation to drink with me. I sang a little ditty.

FAN [*unruffled*] I lead a virtuous life. I keep myself unsullied.

VIRTUE Oh, well then, was it when I was soliciting on Embankment Street that you turned up?

FAN [*coldly*] You are joking, I suppose?

VIRTUE Ooh, many's the scholar I've kept company, from as high up as ninth rank officials to poor students in cotton robes. Please don't misunderstand, Mr Wu. Anyway, scholars have ever been gentlemen of false refinement. Even the ancient sages never forbid men to enjoy sex! Old Confucius said: 'Three things are unfilial, and the worst of these is to have no progeny', or words to that effect. A woman is just a vessel for bearing children. Was there ever an emperor who didn't have scores of concubines stashed among his palaces and gardens? Is there a wealthy man who doesn't have a few concubines in his house? Is there a poet or gentleman of letters who doesn't down a few glasses, wax poetical, and take his pleasure where he finds it? The barbarians say that we Chinese are the world's most advanced society when it comes to womanizing and aphrodisiacs. That's right on the mark. The Grand Secretary Zhang Juzheng, the most famous prime minister of his time and an excellent judge of talent— how did he die? From debauchery. Tan Lun, Minister of War and a battle-hardened hero—he's as proud a soldier in bed as in the fields. Had he not passed on Tang dynasty Sun Simao's 'The Art of the Bedchamber' to Zhang Juzheng, he would not have won his appointment as Minister of War and would have had to stay at home to instruct his three-year-old grandson in military principles. Even Qi Jiguang, the Ever-victorious General of Ji and Liao, and a notoriously hen-pecked husband—even he took three concubines and had five sons. Until his sons were grown, his shrewish wife didn't even know he had an heir. And the reason he always stayed on top and was never out of favour was because he bought the beauty, Precious Gold, as a gift for Prime Minister Zhang. As for Fan Wuchen, Governor-General of Lianghuai and Brigade General of the south-eastern coastal towns—

FAN [*alarmed*] What about him?

VIRTUE [*howls with laughter*] He's got wax for balls.

[*Silence. The squires, dumbstruck, begin to speak but think better of it; not wanting to offend either side.*]

VIRTUE Women the world over were made to give pleasure.
Men the world over take their pleasure. It's just that
some do it openly while others sneak around. Bawdy
Town is one big whore house: virgins from good
homes, pretty girls from humble ones, and harlots like
me all get up on stage. So honest, so direct. It seems
to me . . . that . . . compared to the likes of the Grand
Secretary in Peking, or the Minister of War, or the
General of Ji and Liao and what not, compared to those
. . . those . . . wax-balls, we're so much more wholesome!

FAN *[enraged]* You?

VIRTUE *[grinning]* What about me?

FAN *[forced laughter]* You're very clever. But perhaps General
Fan knows that intolerance of small annoyances may ruin
the whole plan. General Fan controls Lianghuai and the
south-eastern coast, if you should fall into his hands—

VIRTUE *[offhandedly]* I look forward to that.

FAN *[suspiciously]* You have a score to settle with him?

VIRTUE He has shown me great favour, I have nothing but
praise for him.

FAN He may reward you for your praise with a stroke of the
sword.

VIRTUE No need for that; a pair of underpants would be reward
enough!

[The squires turn pale, and hasten to smooth things over.]

LI LAICHUAN Drink up, drink up, let's enjoy the contest.

*[Silence prevails for a time. FAN suddenly roars with
laughter and recovers his composure as if he has a plan up
his sleeve. The squires heave a big sigh of relief.]*

FAN With her unrivalled beauty Virtue moves among
officials like a fish in water, a bird in the forest. No
wonder she's so daring. I am prostrate with admiration!
This contest today has given me the good fortune of
seeing the graceful and elegant Flower Queen. Cheers!
[Empties his glass]

[All drink.

*On stage the bamboo-pole dance has reached fever pitch;
suddenly the town maidens on stage form two lines. An
especially beautiful young woman in a top and a skirt the
colour of lotus leaf comes leisurely on stage. It is* LOTUS. *Her
appearance calls forth a wave of cheers.* LOTUS *has a beautiful
singing voice, like a songbird on a bough. She sways in her
dance like a breeze among flowers. The crowd falls silent.]*

LOTUS *[sings]*

> Dust along the road does fly,
> Where sisters in their contest vie.
> Old shorts and breeches Big Sister's load,
> Torn from lovers young and old.
> Her sweat between her shoulders flows,
> Into a river along the road.

[VIRTUE leads the loud cheering and everyone joins in.]

VIRTUE *[singing in a loud joyful voice]*

> Dust along the road does fly,
> Where sisters in their contest vie.
> Old shorts and breeches Little Sister's load,
> Torn from lovers young and old.
> In heaps along the road they lay,
> And Little Sister's lost her way.

[Cheers like tidal waves. Then the women file silently from the stage, leaving LOTUS alone. She bows to the audience while tossing defiant glances at VIRTUE in the teahouse. The cheers intensify.]

VIRTUE Enough! Enough! I see I'm going to meet my match today. But I'll show my mettle and put up a good fight. *[Leaves teahouse]*

[The crowd parts for her to pass, pressing close and cheering as she mounts the stage. After VIRTUE leaves, the squires immediately start fawning on FAN. ANTONIO and LUIS watch the stage with interest.]

LI LAICHUAN *[ingratiatingly]* Mr Wu, this contest has a long history in Bawdy Town. According to our forebears, Bawdy Town was the home of the legendary Emperor Yan. When Yan started his reign, the people of Bawdy Town were sterile, so Yan cried out to Heaven, and a wizard relayed Heaven's will. A snake in the body of a woman instructed the people of Bawdy Town to cut their hair, tattoo their bodies, and worship the snake. Women were ordered to hang men's underwear from bamboo poles on the third day of the third month and dance the dance of the god Fang Feng. Heaven was moved and thus the progeny of Bawdy Town prospered—

FAN *[meaningfully]* Aaah.

[VIRTUE mounts the stage; she and LOTUS silently face off, sizing each other up.]

VIRTUE [*smiling*] You're amazing, Lotus! You've outdone all the other girls, haven't you?

LOTUS Every last one.

VIRTUE Looks like I won't be Flower Queen this year.

LOTUS I've been waiting years for this.

[*A roar goes up from the crowd.*]

VIRTUE So how many pairs of men's drawers have you got?

LOTUS [*proudly*] 365 altogether.

VIRTUE Whew. That settles it, I've only got 363 pairs, two pairs less than you. But, ah, you should count up—

LOTUS All right then, think I'd cheat you? [*Counts*]

[*In the wineshop,* FAN *and the two foreigners and the assembled squires watch with fascination the proceedings on stage.*]

LI BENYI [*toadying*] Mr Wu, sir. There is a legend behind this contest in Bawdy Town. It's most fascinating!

LI LAICHUAN [*interupts to tell the legend himself*] Oh, Mr Wu, sir. There is a legend. The story goes that Emperor Wu, named Fuchai, in the eleventh year of his reign, led his navy to attack the kingdom of Ji. Returning victorious, his ship met with a great wind which blew him here. Emperor Wu led his men ashore and stationed them on the bank where they built a fortress. When the soldiers came ashore they harassed the countryfolk and the villages and towns were in uproar. Our forebears, on the third day of the third month, thought of a plan: they revived an ancient custom and offered their women to Emperor Wu. The lovely maids of the town danced and sang by day and sported with the Emperor by night. The Emperor was so pleased he restrained his troops and order was restored. As the Emperor was about to leave, he presented all the women with gold, but they thanked him and refused, taking instead his underwear as mementos. The Emperor was greatly moved and with his own hands hung his shorts from the banner pole and named the fortress Bawdy Town. From that day forward, the contest has always been held on the third day of the third month.

FAN Mmm. Very interesting.

[*On the stage,* LOTUS *has finished counting.*]

VIRTUE How many pairs then?

LOTUS *[frowning mightily]* I counted them several times before I left home, how did it get to be 360?

[Below stage, a roar goes up among the townsfolk, there are cheers as well as cries of foul.]

VIRTUE Ah, well somebody snitched your shorts. But if I win I want to win fair and square; or lose honestly. *[Goes to the front of the stage]* Scholar, old sport, give Lotus back the five pairs of drawers you stole from her.

LI BENYI I——

VIRTUE Give them to her!

[LI BENYI sighs and leaves the wineshop. The townsfolk all spur him on with cheers.]

[turns] Lotus, you have a total of 365 pairs in all. I have 363, looks like I'm short by two pairs. But I came prepared for setbacks. Two more pairs came with me—on those two red-beards! I have a liaison with them, if I get theirs, does that count?

LOTUS It does.

VIRTUE *[leaves stage]* You two red-bearded devils, I need to make use of your underpants.

ANTONIO Most happy to oblige.

LUIS Delighted.

[LI CHITIAN leads them from the wineshop.]

VIRTUE Looks like we're tied, Lotus. We have to compete in something else to see who's won.

LOTUS What'll it be?

VIRTUE *[smiles]* Whichever one of us can get the pants off that wax-balls will be the winner.

LOTUS It's a deal!

[A lone harness-bell jingles, advancing rapidly. It sounds like the mysterious knock of destiny at the door. Amid cheers, VIRTUE and LOTUS leave the stage hand in hand. The people in the wineshop are at a loss.]

FAN Who won, Mr Headman?

LI LAICHUAN Ah, Mr Wu, it's not settled yet. Let's drink—

FAN Mr Headman. I'm not sure I should ask . . . But the Emperor has decreed an embargo, and, I hear that Governor-General Fan is a just, strict, upright man—

LI LAICHUAN *[alarmed]* Governor-General, honourable sir—

FAN I'm Wu Xiaotu, a mere citizen.

LI LAICHUAN Oh, Mr Wu. Virtue . . . but I know nothing, nothing.

FAN It must be that someone in the noble Fan's employ is backing you? Otherwise fraternizing with foreigners would cost you your heads!

LI LAICHUAN *[seized with trembling]* I, I know nothing . . . nothing at all.

[VIRTUE and LOTUS have entered the teahouse. The foreigners and the squires have returned as well. The townsfolk, too, squeeze in and the teahouse is absolutely packed.]

FAN *[changing the subject]* All right . . . all right. Let's see who will be Flower Queen today after all.

[LOTUS comes forward and salutes FAN.]

LOTUS Sir, I'd like to challenge you to a match in couplets, line for line. If I should lose, I lose the contest. Should you lose, you have to give me a little something of yours. What do you say?

FAN Ha ha. Whether you win or lose is up to me? But I'm an expert at matching couplets. If you lose, don't be too upset.

LOTUS Listen now.

FAN *[full of himself]* No harm in trying.

LOTUS   Bawdy Town on a bawdy hill; her people bawdier still.

FAN *[ponders]*

    Flower maid with flowers crowned; in her radiance flowers drowned.

[A cheer goes up from the teahouse.]

LOTUS Okay. Let's do another. A descriptive one this time. Listen carefully:

    The high street north with south does link. . . .

FAN *[looks at the street, then, nonchalantly]*

    East and west, shops line its brink.

[Wild cheering. The people have been all but won over by FAN, the squires even more so. As LOTUS departs in chagrin, YOUNG SEVEN and LOTUS's other supporters sigh and shake their heads. VIRTUE strolls up; the people cheer her wildly. All their hopes now rest with her.]

[complacently] Take your time, Virtue. Writing poetry and matching couplets is my speciality; I'm afraid you won't find it easy to beat me. How about this? I'll

change places with you. I'll set three lines and if you can match them, I'll admit defeat and you shall have whatever you want.

VIRTUE *[smiles]* Agreed.

FAN The first one's a play on things medicinal. Listen now:

He goes, she goes, but indigo won't go.

VIRTUE *[ponders a moment]*

In the zoo there are male lions, female lions; but no dan-de-lions.

[A roar goes up.]

FAN *[unruffled]*

Books at dawn, Kungfu at night; I'm a man of virtue bright.

VIRTUE *[tit for tat]*

Early a beggar, late a mandarin's cap; all freely falls into your ample lap.

[In the teahouse, people are all craning their necks, they seem drunk with excitement, their cheers have a metallic ring. FAN feels amazement, admiration, frustration. He turns anxious, his eyes glaze over, he racks his brains. A moment of silence.]

FAN Heaven's net encompasses it, as earth's net does the ground;
where the two at their borders meet, two nets in one are found.

[For some time, VIRTUE can't find words, her face turns red, she mumbles to herself and keeps shaking her head. FAN begins to chortle, well pleased with himself.]

VIRTUE A coffin's made with talent; talent makes a scholar swell.
Put the scholar in the coffin—talents together dwell.

[Thunderous laughter. Wild cheers. Suddenly someone begins to beat the drum. VIRTUE waves a hand and there is silence.]

Mr Wu has lost. There's nothing I want, except that Mr Wu remove his underpants and give them to me.

[Laughter fills the room.]

FAN *[admiring]* I lost indeed. But I lost in order to win.
I played deaf and dumb to pursue my secret
investigation. I can see that you really are extremely
bright, you already realize that I am the Governor-
General of Lianghuai and Brigade General of the south-
eastern coastal towns. *[Smiles, then suddenly serious]* Take
these traitors away!

[Cries of alarm go up from the crowd.]

VIRTUE Wax-balls!

*[The fog rolls in like gunsmoke, obscuring the sky over
Bawdy Town. The sun is lost in the fog. Muffled metallic
sounds are heard, the clash of weapons, sobs and shouts of
alarm and harness-bells jangle nearer, growing more urgent as
they come.]*

CURTAIN

ACT 2

[The beat of a kettledrum is heard; the sound is like some wild beast biding its time, howling in spite of itself as the scent of fresh blood comes to it on the wind. Next the muffled sound of an ox-horn. One long blast, one short, like sobs; and then a powerful blast like the very bellow of an ox—a soul-quaking sound. Then harness-bells begin to jingle. Note that from now on the single harness-bell becomes many, a fleeting jingling which rises over all other sounds. As before, the sound swells and fades as full of mystery as before.

The curtain rises on a fog-shrouded night. Dark clouds envelop the Military Garrison. It is brightly lit by red candles and hanging lanterns, as if it has been washed in dark red blood. In the hall, flanked on either side by formidable armed guards bearing pikes and spears, FAN sits in full armour on a raised seat. Commotion from the street is dimly heard. An officer kneels before FAN to make his report.]

OFFICER Reporting, Commander. Dense fog today and, along with the fog, rumours thick and fast. The shops have closed, the common people have rolled up their mats and fled their homes. People in the streets are anxious with fear. They say 'His Excellency has arrested Virtue and the red-bearded barbarians are coming.'

FAN I know.

[OFFICER exits.]

Bring the female prisoner.

SOLDIER Bring the female prisoner!

[Amid shouts, VIRTUE, a heavy wooden yoke round her neck, hands tied with thick rope, enters the hall in the custody of soldiers. Her step is still as lithe and graceful as before. She seems unaffected. Silence.]

FAN On your knees!

[The soldiers make her kneel.]

If you have been wronged, you may appeal for justice; if you have a complaint, you can give it voice; if you know you are guilty, you must admit your guilt.

[Silence]

I act to enforce the law, I act according to the law. The accused need have no fear. I harbour no desire for revenge just because you trifled with me while I was on my secret investigation. But have a care. If the crime is not yours, you need not take this heavy burden upon your shoulders; if it is yours, then you must not implicate others.

VIRTUE What crime am I supposed to have committed?

FAN *[expression hardens]* Fraternizing with the enemy!

VIRTUE Your Excellency, this person does not understand: what
is fraternizing with the enemy? Please enlighten me,
your Excellency. With the emperor's order for an
embargo, how can the common people go out to the
deep sea to fish? If fisherfolk cannot fish, how can they
survive? Silk weaving is controlled by the Textile
Bureau, salt making by the Salt Monopoly, and grain
selling by the Tribute Office. All the means of
livelihood have been usurped by the officials. Bawdy
Town sits on alkaline land. How can the people make a
living?

[Shocked, FAN *is silent for some time.]*

FAN *[lightly]* I wouldn't have guessed it. You see yourself as
a saviour of the people.

VIRTUE Eighty or ninety per cent of the so-called bandits are
the folk in this town.

FAN *[taken aback]* What do you mean?

VIRTUE People who sneak out to sea have had their boats sunk
by you officials. They have nothing to eat, that's why
they become bandits. As for those barbarians, they've
come to do honest trade with us. But our boats are
impounded by you officials, our cargoes confiscated. You
people have driven us into the sea. If we don't become
bandits, what can we eat? The wind? You say your
soldiers are here to put down bandits. And yet, it's
only because you put them down that the people
become bandits. Bandits all. But the real bandits are
the officials and soldiers!

FAN What gall! Failure to find out what is going on,
ignorance of the people's trials and tribulations, failure
to show solicitude for the people's plight, failure to
make the sufferings of the masses known to those that
rule, failure to protect the people and act on their
behalf: these are the crimes of officials derelict in the
duties of their office. The embargo is a dynastic
principle and national policy. From the Emperor and
ninth rank officials down to the common man, all must
obey the laws. There may be some truth in what you
say, but you cannot use that as an excuse to flout the
nation's laws. Ants and insects boring their tunnels can
undermine an embankment miles long. To counter a
mistake with another mistake is to combat crime with
crime. If criminal responsibility is not clear, the nation

will never know a day of peace. This official has taken
upon himself a mission to make the laws and precepts
clear, to enforce the embargo for the benefit of the
people. You womenfolk are ignorant, you have no
vision, that's why you're so reckless, so benighted. But
more vile still are your cohorts, traitors who know the
law but break it, who should enforce the law, but
violate it. The aim of my secret mission is to get to
the heart of the matter. If this traitor is not exposed,
there will be endless trouble.

[Silence]

As long as you wholeheartedly repent, this official can
consider dealing leniently with you. Speak: which of
my officials did you buy with sexual favours?

*[*VIRTUE *shakes her head.]*

If you didn't have somone on the inside, the Bawdy
Town embargo would have been impregnable. Even if
the barbarians grew wings, they couldn't have got in. If
there wasn't anyone on the inside, you couldn't have
been so brazen. Those who suit their actions to the
times are wise, you'd better confess. This official here is
determined to expose those scoundrels.

VIRTUE What if you can't?

FAN *[smiles]* I don't wear this official's black gauze cap for
nothing.

VIRTUE And if I confess?

FAN You escape death.

VIRTUE And if I don't?

FAN You die. The serious tortures will be applied, slowly,
until you confess.

VIRTUE Everything you say is one big fart. There's not a word
of truth in it. I won't believe you.

FAN This excellency has never uttered a false word.

VIRTUE All right. If you remove the underwear you lost to me
and hand them over, then I'll believe you.

FAN *[smiles]* A gentleman's word is his bond. I come
prepared. Guard!

*[A soldier enters from the back room bringing the garment in
question.]*

[handsomely] Virtue, please accept your prize.

*[*VIRTUE *takes the drawers and breaks into loud laughter.*
FAN *is puzzled by her laughter.]*

[VIRTUE *continues to laugh, her laughter is naughty and lively, fearless and untroubled, especially at odds with the cold stern atmosphere, and especially charming.*]

What is there to laugh about? Confess.

[VIRTUE *continues to laugh.*]

[*angry*] How dare you trifle with this official?

[VIRTUE *continues to roar with laughter.*]

[*furious*] Brazen criminal, what have you got to laugh about? Confess.

VIRTUE Hold your anger, your Excellency, this slave wishes to laugh. Anger is a habit of high officials, tears and laughter are the provenance of common folk. Please proceed with your anger, Excellency.

FAN What cheek!

VIRTUE What stupidity!

FAN You . . . you!

VIRTUE The angrier you get, the more it makes your slave laugh! You're a fool, Excellency. You said I consorted with the enemy, that shows what a stranger you are here. What's more, I happen to know each and every one of those under your command, and I know each and every one well. You are the stranger. Which one of them would you have me accuse? You can rage on, Excellency.

FAN Take the prisoner away and torture her!

[*Soldiers rush towards her. She continues to roar with laughter.*]

Apply all the thirty-six tortures. Keep it up until she confesses.

VIRTUE I've tasted all the dissolute joys of life, with the exception of prison, torture and execution. Now I can try even these.

SOLDIERS To the torture chamber! [*They lead her away.*]

[*The hall regains its austere atmosphere. An officer enters.*]

OFFICER Reporting, Excellency. The barbarians have taken advantage of the fog to capture Mount Wu. They also have the sea sewn up. Bawdy Town is surrounded.

FAN [*smiles*] This Garrison has already sent Captain Liu Yuan to see to the sea defence and get rid of the traitors in league with the enemy. Captain Liu Yuan should be back by now.

[*Clamour is heard in the street.*]

OFFICER The people have heard that the barbarians are on the rampage. Popular feeling is running high. There's a band of scholars who want to become soldiers.

[A weird blast on an ox-horn.]

FAN [smiles] For scholars to exchange their writing brushes for the sword when the nation is in danger is an admirable aspiration and should be commended. Bid them enter.

SOLDIERS Enter, scholars.

[A band of beggars in scholar's dress surges in to the rhythm of the kettledrum. FAN's smile turns wooden. He recognizes them as the beggars he saw outside the teahouse.]

FAN [strikes the gavel block for silence] Away with you!

[The head beggar leads them in kneeling down.]

OLD BEGGAR I beg your indulgence, Excellency. We unworthies are all beggars. Because the garrison has blockaded the port, our Bawdy Town benefactors found their sources of wealth completely cut off, and now they are standing in line to become our apprentices and goodness knows what else. Our little band has grown. But people these days are in such difficult straits few can afford to be charitable, and we don't know where our next meal is coming from. All things considered, being a soldier is a better guarantee of the next meal. We sincerely beg your Excellency to bestow a bowl of rice upon us—

BEGGARS ALL If the Commander does not deign to do so, we will beat our heads against the floor until we die.

FAN Lies! Can this be your only recourse?

OLD BEGGAR There is one other. . . .

FAN Speak!

OLD BEGGAR We can become bandits.

[FAN strikes the gavel block.]

It's the last thing we want.

[Silence]

FAN [shakes his head and sighs] This is all the doing of those red-bearded barbarians. If we don't subdue them, the people will never be able to raise their heads. That you should be beggars is a shame to this official. I shall speak plainly with you, if I allow you to be soldiers, from this day, you must bear the same responsibility as I do. As soldiers, in normal times you get your rations and pay. Even if there is nothing for you to do, you get your three meals and three fen of silver per day. The silver and grain is levied on the common people. It is their toil that keeps you, they look to you only to win a few battles. If you are not willing to kill bandits to protect the people, why should they support you? Go along to the mess and eat, think things over. If you really want to be soldiers, then stay.

BEGGARS ALL Thank you, your Excellency.

FAN Off you go.

[The beggars exit the great hall. A soldier kneels to report.]

SOLDIER Reporting, Excellency. The thirty-six tortures have all been applied. The female criminal laughed all the while and still hasn't confessed.

FAN *[startled]* Oh? Continue the tortures.

SOLDIER The female criminal has fainted.

FAN Bring her around with cold water and continue the torture.

SOLDIER Yes, Excellency. *[Exits]*

[The kettledrum begins to beat, the sound of the ox-horn soars and pierces the fog. To the drum beat, a strong and vigorous young captain of military bearing hurries into the hall. He is Captain LIU YUAN *of* FAN's *command.]*

LIU YUAN Captain Liu Yuan reporting, your Excellency. The barbarians have taken advantage of the thick fog to capture Mount Wu. They also tried to launch a surprise attack under cover of the fog, but, seeing that our defences were strong and our morale high, and that we stood ready for combat, they changed their minds. However, they now have Bawdy Town surrounded.

FAN *[alarmed]* Send for reinforcements at once!

LIU YUAN I have successfully sent a messenger through the lines.

FAN Good.

LIU YUAN I have discovered the details of the townsfolks' collusion with the enemy.

FAN Speak.

LIU YUAN They brazenly broke the embargo, gathering for the barbarians large quantities of silkworm cocoons, silk reels, fabric, tea, and medicinal herbs; and undertaking large-scale smuggling. This illegal trade was carried on by a group of eighty-five townsfolk who were in personal contact with the barbarians; three members of the gentry in particular, were on such good terms with the foreigners that their daughters were married to them. There were thirteen evil traitors who repaired the barbarians' boats for them and divulged secret information. That was how the barbarians were able to capture Mount Wu. I've already rounded up the whole lot.

FAN Very good. Have a seat.

[He sits.]

Bring in the traitors, I wish to interrogate them personally.

LIU YUAN *[stands]* The traitors defied orders and tried to escape. They have been beheaded.

FAN Not even one was spared?

LIU YUAN All beheaded.

FAN All beheaded? *[He is upset and lapses into silence. Suddenly something occurs to him, the mystery comes clear and he laughs out loud.]* There is one left.

LIU YUAN No one escaped.

FAN The chief culprit is left—the harlot Virtue.

LIU YUAN *[sighs]* There is one left!

FAN Except for her, you haven't left any.

LIU YUAN To spare them would have been to invite trouble.

FAN Well said. Even the imprisoned gentry have been wiped out?

LIU YUAN They were plotting to escape.

FAN Beautiful. You've cut down the grass and pulled up the roots. Killed them to stop them talking.

LIU YUAN What do you mean, Excellency?

FAN A pity your cleverness has defeated itself and unmasked your plot. Your lust will cost you your life. You left one alive—

LIU YUAN *[kneels]* Spare me, Excellency.

[The assembled officers plead for mercy.]

FAN *[silences them]* When officials are lascivious and the people seek personal gain, how can the nation survive? If a bamboo fence is not secure, the wild dogs can breach it. The barbarians, those scoundrels, were invited in! You are an official and depend upon the Emperor's favour, you . . . what should be your punishment?

[Silence]

LIU YUAN To die a thousand times!

FAN A million merits could not atone for this crime! Let your death be a warning to all other officers. Whoever betrays his lord and breaks the law shall be executed on the spot with the full authority of the law.

LIU YUAN I die here without regrets. I have only one favour to ask of your Excellency.

FAN Speak.

LIU YUAN Allow me to see Virtue one last time.

FAN *[startled, thinks for a while]* You're about to die and you're still under her spell?

LIU YUAN In my life, I rode into battles north and south following your Excellency, braving dangers untold, engaging in outstanding military exploits—I have no regrets in life! And if my death be for that eternal peerless beauty, Virtue, then I have no regrets in dying either. An ardent life, a lusty death. I have not wasted my encounters with life and death. Please grant my wish, Excellency.

[Silence]

FAN *[sighs feelingly]* Captain Liu Yuan—*[Suddenly it's as if all the things he wants to say well up, yet he cannot speak, but sighs continually and waves his hand to give the command.]* Go.

[Harness-bells ring and their music is like a love song. LIU YUAN is led away by soldiers.]

[FAN feels he has lost something, his heart is empty.] Clear the hall!

[A soldier enters and kneels to report.]

SOLDIER Reporting, Excellency. The two barbarians arrested in Bawdy Town several days ago beg to see Your Excellency.

FAN *[hesitates, stands and strides about, then sits again]* Tell them to come in and wait. *[Stands and leaves the hall]*

[SOLDIER exits. Soul-shaking beats of the drum, shrill blasts of the ox-horn. Marching to the rhythm of the drum, SOLDIER leads ANTONIO and LUIS into the hall. The armed guards follow them in, holding their weapons aloft, whose blades glisten silver-white. Several SOLDIERS light candles and hang up lanterns. The scene is bathed in an ominous red light.

ANTONIO and LUIS are ill at ease. One thing about their heads stands out: each has his left ear bound up in a white bandage.]

ANTONIO Special Envoy from Spain Antonio begs to see General Fan, Governor-General of Lianghuai and Brigade General of the south-eastern coastal towns. I bring gifts and letters to your Emperor from my King, and a map of the world, a clock, a crystal prism. I ask His Excellency to cast his eyes upon them.

LUIS Special Envoy from Portugal Luis begs to see General
Fan, Governor-General of Lianghuai and Brigade
General of the south-eastern coastal towns. My King
has entrusted me with letters and gifts for your
Emperor, a map of the world, an hour-glass, and a
concave sundial. I ask His Excellency to accept them.

*[Two SOLDIERS receive the gifts and carry them into the back
room. Silence.]*

Mr Antonio, are we taking too great a risk? The first
time we met the General, we lost one ear, this time we
may be parted from our heads. I'm afraid the only way
we can speak to General Fan is with cannon and
battleships.

ANTONIO We came to China in peace and friendship. To my
knowledge, the Chinese are a peace-loving race, without
the slightest curiosity about the rest of the world, even
less the desire or ambition to overrun it. Just look at
our buildings in Europe and compare them with those
in China. European buildings rise toward the clouds
upon foundations sunk deep in the earth, with spires
that pierce the very skies, reflecting an expansionist and
warlike ambition. In China, on the other hand, there
are no tall buildings. Everything is on one level,
spreading out across the ground, be it the closed
courtyards of the Emperor or village dwellings; the
quadrangular courtyards of the north, or southern
houses with their closed-in clusters of rooms and halls.
The aim is self-encirclement: the outer parts are quiet
and peaceful, showing that there is no conflict with the
world; the inside is intricately designed, with complex
relationships strictly ranked. To each its courtyard
where flowers, grass and trees are grown, where
sunlight and rain, snow, wind and fog are allowed to
fall inside the high walls to moisten the peaceful
Chinese soul. This, I suppose, is the aesthetic
realization of what Chinese philosophers call 'the
harmony between man and heaven'. The best way for
us Europeans to relate to a people so zealous in their
love of peace is to employ the olive branch and the
smile.

*[Obviously he is not only speaking for the benefit of his
companion. Colonel LI ZHIYONG enters from the back
room, followed by two SOLDIERS, who are returning the
gifts.]*

LI ZHIYONG Special Envoys, sirs. His Excellency says that the sky is round, the earth is square, and China is the centre of the universe. The map received from your respected country has placed China on the periphery. Clearly you harbour evil intentions, your lies are preposterous. Please take your leave.

ANTONIO Wait, Colonel. In deference to Chinese habits of mind, we will take back these two factual maps of the world and exchange them for two others. In the new maps, China will be placed at the centre. I think that might satisfy the General.

[Colonel LI ZHIYONG *and the two* SOLDIERS *exit to the back room carrying the gifts. A short while later,* COLONEL *and* SOLDIERS *return with a large bundle wrapped in red cloth.]*

LI ZHIYONG This is a gift from His Excellency General Fan, he invites the two of you to examine it.

ANTONIO Thank you, thank you.

*[*COLONEL LI *exits to the back room.* ANTONIO *and* LUIS *open the red bundle to find a head dripping with blood. It is the head of* CAPTAIN LIU YUAN. *They recoil in terror.*
The lanterns cast their red glow, the candles sputter as they burn, the dark shadows of the swords and spears appear now short, now long, a menacing sight. The two soldiers stand like wooden figures. It is inordinately quiet and still.]

ANTONIO *[shaken]* Captain Liu Yuan!

LUIS *[furious]* Is this the way General Fan demonstrates his prowess?

ANTONIO *[ponders in silence a moment, then following Chinese etiquette, places* CAPTAIN LIU's *head respectfully upon the bench, kneels and bows deeply]* Captain Liu Yuan, our motive in coming to China has been misunderstood and this misunderstanding has brought you misfortune. This moves us to deep sorrow and disquiet. But the wise General Fan should realize that we came not out of ambition to invade or expand our territory, but to engage in friendly trade. From now on, may there be no further tragedies like this. May your soul rest in peace. *[He bows deeply three times more.]*

*[*LUIS *also bows to show his respect.*
There is a lovely jingling of harness-bells.
Colonel LI ZHIYONG *enters from the back room.]*

LI ZHIYONG His Excellency General Fan has prepared another gift for you.

[The two SOLDIERS *escort* VIRTUE, *bound and bleeding, into the hall; she moves with difficulty, but a smile still hovers on her face.* LI *exits to the back room.*

ANTONIO *and* LUIS *are shocked and horrified, their mouths hang open, but no words come out. This has brought their own plight home to them.* VIRTUE'*s gaze remains fixed throughout upon the head of* LIU YUAN *sitting on the bench; her eyes glisten with tears.]*

ANTONIO Virtue . . . you've been tortured.

VIRTUE *[waves a hand]* Pshh *[Approaches the bench step by step, gently picks up the head and lets it rest in her bosom]* Let no one speak. Let Liu and I have a few quiet moments together.

[A crescendo of beautiful harness-bells]

Liu, Liu, I'm fortunate to have one person in life who truly understands me! Liu, Liu—*[Like a mother, she cradles the head and strokes it.]*

[The beautiful music of the harness-bells fades away.

    Suddenly, to several loud blasts on the ox-horn, a wave of drum rolls approaches; soldiers come in swishing glinting swords and spears which they hold aloft. Attended by his officers, FAN *comes striding into the hall from the back room. His bearing is stern, his bright glance sweeps the scene and falls on* VIRTUE *and the head she cradles. At a glance from him, the soldiers take* VIRTUE *and* LIU YUAN'*s head away.]*

*[*FAN *sits on the raised chair and the officers sit around him.]*

FAN How wonderful it is when friends come from afar. We're old friends. Please sit down. Bring on the feast.

[They sit. Armed guards leave the hall. SOLDIERS *bring on long tables, and fine wine and delicacies are swiftly spread before the company.]*

You can relax, Special Envoys, the Chinese are very hospitable. In dealing with friends who brazenly break our embargo and barge into our country, I take an ear to show them my respect. As for Special Envoys, I will not ask them to forfeit their heads. Drink up. Please. *[Raises a cup]*

[The assembled officers and ANTONIO *and* LUIS *raise their cups.]*

ANTONIO General Fan, we came to—

FAN *[cuts him off]* I understand your purpose in coming.

[From the street come sounds of voices and singing.]

[smiles] Hmm. Sounds like there's an opera troupe in the street. Gentlemen, China is strong and her people prosperous, there is peace in the world. In their spare time, our people enjoy themselves in singing and dancing. Every day is a festival. A country as rich as ours is sufficient unto itself, self-supporting; we have enough to keep our people content. We have no need to trade with the outside world, it only upsets our people. Let's have some songs, it will help the wine along and show you what I mean.

[Exit SOLDIERS. *After a while, the Bawdy townsfolk, miming a dragon boat, surge into the hall. They carry lanterns and their bodies sway as they begin to dance.* GEOMANCER *and* GRANNY TEA *are the head and tail,* YOUNG SEVEN *and* LOTUS, *among others, make up the body. They sing as they dance 'The Famine-fleeing Song'.]*

TOWNSFOLK *[sing]*

> Fleeing famine is merry and begging is fun,
> The best of pleasures for everyone.

*[*FAN *is taken aback and frowns.]*

YOUNG SEVEN *[solo]*

> When the sun warms your backside,
> You stretch and get off the ground,
> You stumble and stagger as you look around,
> Then the coins tumble streaming in your palms.
> To taverns to restaurants boldly you stride,
> For good food and wine to warm your insides.
> Then opera at the whorehouse, you beat the time,
> And silver in your pockets jingles a rhyme.

TOWNSFOLK *[chorus]*

> Fleeing famine is merry, and begging is fun,
> The best of pleasures for everyone.

LOTUS *[solo]*

> No labour no toil, you get two meals of rice,
> A roof o'er your head too, now ain't that nice?
> Get a donkey, a wife, what can be the harm?
> Bring up your kids too, with an open palm.

TOWNSFOLK [chorus]

>Fleeing famine is merry, and begging is fun,
>The best of pleasures for everyone.

FAN [smiling] Look at this lot—innkeeper, geomancer, cotton-fluffer, dog butcher, embroideress. They have so much time on their hands they make a game of begging. Ha ha ha—The good life has unbalanced their minds.

GRANNY TEA General, we really are beggars. Begging is the good life for us. There's a saying: 'Three years of begging and you wouldn't trade places with the Emperor.' It's true!

GEOMANCER General, you've bound up Bawdy Town tighter than a drum—

LUIS [interrupting] Of course there's no business to be done.

[While they were talking, the soldiers have been setting off fireworks, filling the air with excitement.]

ANTONIO [in wonder] What beautiful fireworks. Ten times more beautiful than fireworks in Paris, London, Rome, Lisbon, or Madrid.

FAN [complacent] They're nothing compared to those in the capital.

LUIS [coldly] Your honoured nation uses its compass for geomancy, we install it in our battleships to guide their route. Your honoured nation uses gunpowder to set off fireworks. We make ammunition out of it.

FAN [as coldly] Have you come to provoke me?

ANTONIO No, no. We've come to engage in friendly trade.

FAN Buying and selling is something both sides enter into freely. The two of you sail here in your battleships to discuss trade—that's like someone holding a sword to my neck and asking me to buy and sell. I call this trade by coercion.

LUIS General Fan, this is all very easy. Just agree to trade with us and our battleships will leave your shores at once.

FAN How can there be preconditions for buying and selling? Your esteemed country wishes to trade. Our revered Emperor has ordered an embargo, and will allow no trade with the outside. One nation's laws cannot be changed by another at will, and after all I am the one charged with enforcing the law. You two should be aware that Cathay is a land of courtesy and humanity

and has respected friendship down the ages. There is a
saying in China: 'If buying and selling doesn't work
out, there is still humanity and justice.' There will
always be disagreements in trade, but humanity and
justice endure. You two have come from afar, I raise a
cup to you in welcome. But as the two of you must
soon be on your way, this cup is also a farewell toast.

[They all drink.]

Let us have another song.

GEOMANCER Shall we sing Your Excellency a song of a sage?

FAN What kind of sage?

GEOMANCER A peasant woman.

FAN How can a peasant woman be a sage?

GEOMANCER Your Excellency, the ancients said: 'Actions cannot
depict a sage, for virtue leaves no trace. Words cannot
depict a sage, for virtue does not speak. Ability cannot
depict a sage, for virtue is not strained. Appearance
cannot depict a sage, for virtue has no form.' And *The
Book of Poetry* says:

> Although the kingdom be unsettled,
> There are some who are wise, and others who are not.
> Although the people may not be numerous,
> Some have perspicacity, some have counsel.
> Here is a wise man:
> His views and words reach to a hundred *li*.
> There is a stupid man:
> He on the contrary rejoices in his madness.*

Astute observations indeed. Though a country be small,
it will have both genius and fools. Intelligent people
perceive things a hundred *li* away, while fools are merry
even as disaster hangs right over their heads. A sage is
an intelligent person. There are sages of medicine,
painting, books, chess, poetry, and wine. There are
sages among emperors and ministers and there are sages
among the ordinary people. Metal is tempered to make
swords, boats are built to sail on water, all craft is done
by sages. Why can't a peasant woman be called a sage?

FAN I bow to your eloquence. You might as well get on
with your song.

*[The townsfolk once more mime a dragon boat and begin,
slowly, to dance.]*

* *The She King, or The Book of Poetry*, James Legge, tr. (Hong Kong: Hong Kong University Press, 1960),
pp. 332, 525.

GEOMANCER *[to the tune of 'Lianhua luo']*

> The *manman* bird flies southward, circling slow,
> Bawdy Town is flood-locked, how tears flow.
> Officials in fast boats flee, gentry sail quickly away,
> For boats poor commonfolk like us cannot pay.
> To Heaven and Earth we plead. There's no reply.
> What other recourse have we but to cry!

YOUNG SEVEN *[dressed up as the young FAN during his years of hardship sings to the tune of 'Lianhua luo']*

> A scholar I, bound for the Imperial Examinations,
> To bandits forfeit are all my worldly possessions;
> Rain pelts down, thunder rumbles beside,
> Drenched to the skin, in a hollow tree I hide.
> Wails of flood victims ring in my ear,
> As inch upon inch the waters rise ever nearer;
> Fever-racked, starving and in pain,
> I'm dizzy and faint, life seems to drain,
> Water drowns my spirit, I can barely stand.
> Pity the poor scholar, his life at an end.

LOTUS *[in the role of VIRTUE, back to the year when she saw FAN, the young student, in dire straits, and was moved to pity for him. Song: 'Lianhua luo']*

> My name is Huaman and I am but fifteen—

FAN *[as if waking from a trance, cuts her off]* What did you say?

LOTUS My name is Huaman.

FAN You are Huaman?

LOTUS I am Lotus, playing the part of Huaman.

FAN *[beside himself]* And Huaman is who?

LOTUS Huaman is Virtue, that's who.

FAN Repeat that!

LOTUS Huaman is Virtue's childhood name, and Virtue is Huaman grown up.

FAN Where did she live in those days?

LOTUS Third hut on the left, by the old hollow tree at the foot of the bridge into Bawdy Town.

FAN What family did she have?

LOTUS No parents, she was alone.

FAN And where does she live now?

LOTUS In your garrison prison.

> *[Silence]*

FAN [*emotions in a tumult*] Virtue—

[*The sound of harness-bells comes on the breeze, it seems to be bringing memories, nostalgia. Now short, now long, now light, now heavy, it comes clip-clopping beautifully from afar.*]

[*sighs deeply*] Don't sing anymore, each of you will get ten taels of silver. Go now.

[*The harness-bells slowly fade. The townsfolk dance out of the headquarters, and their distant song can be heard:*

Fleeing famine is merry and begging is fun,
The best of pleasures for everyone.]

LUIS I really don't get it. How do you Chinese think? Trade is clearly beneficial for both sides, but you refuse to do what would benefit you. I really can't understand it!

FAN What do you mean by beneficial? Cathay has had relations with the barbarian nations since ancient times, and the lessons have been blood and fire.

ANTONIO [*sincerely*] General Fan, we have come loaded with goods. If we go back home with them, we will be bankrupt.

LUIS If General Fan is willing to trade with us, we can teach you the art of using gun powder to make ammunition. How about it? Our battleships haven't met an enemy they can't defeat. Destroying broad swords and spears can be easier than shooting birds. Since we have come, we can't be got rid of that easily.

FAN [*controlling himself with effort*] I am well aware of your purpose in coming here. And I have made our principles clear. The great sage Mencius said: 'Heaven's favourable weather is less important than Earth's advantageous terrain, and Earth's advantageous terrain is less important than human unity. . . . It is not by boundaries that the people are confined, it is not by difficult terrain that a state is rendered secure, and it is not by superiority of arms that the Empire is kept in awe. One who has the Way will have many to support him; one who has not the Way will have few to support him. In extreme cases, the latter will find even his own flesh and blood turning against him while the former will have the whole Empire at his behest. Hence either a gentleman does not go to war or else he is sure of victory. . . .'* Through the ages the people of Cathay

* Mencius, *Mencius*, Book II, Part B, 1. D. C. Lau, tr. (London: Penguin, 1970), p. 85.

have disliked war, but they in no way fear it. The morale of all our soldiers and generals is high. With good faith and unity, our long swords and spears can destroy all enemy soldiers and weapons of war. Whoever dares to break our embargo and invade our rivers and mountains will not leave our country alive! Last time we met, I took from each of you an ear; this time, I present you with a head; next time, you may leave *your* heads behind! I will see you on the field of battle! Conduct the visitors out.

ANTONIO I am extremely disappointed! *[ANTONIO and* LUIS *exit.]*

[FAN looks distinctly irate. It is obvious his anger is related to knowing the truth about VIRTUE's *origins. It is clear, too, that he is suffering from a troubled conscience and great emotional turmoil. The anxious beating of the kettledrum and the uneasy sound of the horn seem like a reflection of his mood.]*

FAN *[in a loud voice]* Clear the hall!

[Exit SOLDIERS *and officials. The garrison is as silent as the grave.]*

Tea!

[FAN WU approaches silently and pours tea.]

Cold tea. No, no, make it hot tea.

[FAN WU waits to one side, not daring to speak. FAN hums for a while, staring vacantly ahead.]

Fetch . . . Virtue.

FAN WU Yes, Excellency. *[Exits]*

[The sound of harness-bells, now pressing nearer, now fading, now jingling, now silent, floats into the garrison.

FAN seems beside himself, he keeps trying to control his racing emotions by drinking tea, sipping it very slowly. From time to time he looks towards the door, his whole being concentrating on listening to the silence. Finally footsteps are heard. He takes a long deep breath, pulls himself together and recovers his composure.

A long silence. Then FAN lifts his head to see VIRTUE kneeling on the floor, her white satin skirt blood-spattered, her dishevelled hair lying across her face. Her wild, unfettered boldness has gone, and she seems a completely different person. She is inordinately, preternaturally still and in the glow from the lights and the reflection from the floor, there is a beauty about her that is sacred and inviolable.

FAN dismisses FAN WU and the soldiers.]

FAN Virtue . . . please rise.

[Silence]

Miss Huaman . . . please rise.

[Silence]

I am Fan Wuchen, the scholar who met with misfortune that year at the hollow tree in Bawdy Town.

[Silence]

[gets off his chair and approaches VIRTUE *slowly, step by step. He gazes at her for some time, then slowly kneels and bows his head.]* My benefactress, allow me, Fan, to pay my respects. Fan knows that his benefactress recognized him long ago, but though he half-suspected that Virtue was his benefactress, Huaman, he would not let himself believe it. You have been cast into prison, you are covered in wounds and spattered with blood, your bones broken. All this is due to the brutality of Fan Wuchen, Governor-General of Lianghuai and Brigade General of the south-eastern coastal towns, it has nothing to do with the scholar whom you rescued when he had fallen on hard times on his way to the examinations. Without your help, Fan would not be here today. When Fan was a boy, he lost his parents, and he was destitute. Lonely and miserable, he and his grandfather depended upon one another to survive. He studied at his cold window for fourteen years, and was lucky to meet with his benefactress and escape the flood. Fan's life was given to him by his benefactress. And yet it is Fan who brought you to this sad day. Without Fan, you would never have suffered in the brothel, nor stood on the street corner selling your favours, nor been a trader breaking the embargo and running afoul of the Emperor's law, nor would you be wearing the wooden yoke and facing execution. Your life has been encumbered by Fan. Had Fan known this day would come, he would have rejected scholarly honour, service to the Emperor and the hand of a young lady of good family. He should have killed himself so his benefactress would banish the thought of selling herself to the brothel to rescue him. He should repay what his benefactress has done for him by caring for her to the end. A drop of mercy should be repaid with the abundance of a fountain. Your beneficence to Fan was as great as the mountains. He should serve you

even with his life, and beyond the grave. What a despicable wretch he is to have treated you like this! But the scholar and the Governor-General of Lianghuai are two different people! The humble scholar wishes to repay your kindness, to be your faithful servant. The General is above personal feelings, heeding only the good of the state. The scholar and the General are two persons in one body, the soul pursuing two extremes. Oh Benefactress! The scholar dares not ignore the weight of office bestowed upon him by the Emperor. He must cast his benefactress into the death cell to wait for the order of execution from the palace. There's fresh water in the river and salt water in the sea. So to each his constraints. But, with all sincerity Fan begs you for your forgiveness. *[He kowtows deeply, and does not rise from his kneeling position.]*

[VIRTUE, who seems to have sunk into a state of meditation all this while, suddenly breaks into laughter. There is a burst of crisp harness-bells.]

CURTAIN

ACT 3

[Muffled thunder. There is a cacophony of sound: horses stamping, soldiers talking, harness-bells jangling, the kettledrum beating, the ox-horn blaring, creating a feeling of battle readiness.

The curtain rises: fog spirals and rolls. There is a vague suggestion of a corner of the city wall and a rough wooden fence with arrows stacked under it. Beside the wall is the door to a crude wooden hut which seems to be a makeshift prison constructed by the soldiers. In the open area in front of its door a cauldron boils over a fire. FAN and VIRTUE kneel facing each other on either side of the cauldron. VIRTUE appears to be lost in meditation. It is now very quiet all around. FAN is playing soft music on a reed flute. After a while, he stops playing, draws his sword deftly from its sheath, opens his armour, rips open his trousers and hacks off a piece of flesh from his thigh which he drops into the cauldron. When the flesh has cooked awhile, he spears it out with his sword and offers it to VIRTUE, who makes no move to take it. Her eyes are closed, she appears to be in a trance, her lips softly moving, as if reciting.

FAN has been kneeling a long time when a few blasts on the ox-horn, some short, some long, are heard from afar. The sound is urgent. He hesitates a moment, then reluctantly puts away his sword, kowtows three times to VIRTUE and rises to leave.]

VIRTUE *[laughs aloud]* Wonderful, truly wonderful. Don't go away, my dear General, I want to go on playing nun.

> *[FAN is beyond earshot.*
>
> *A soldier named BUTCHER'S BOY and another called SPROUT come out of the prison entrance. Before long, a soldier enters from the left, leading GRANNY TEA.]*

SOLDIER General Fan has given instructions that this old lady should speak with Virtue.

> *[BUTCHER'S BOY and SPROUT exit.]*

GRANNY TEA *[enters the open area of the prison and sits to one side of the cauldron]* Virtue.

VIRTUE Granny Tea.

GRANNY TEA I hear tell that wretched General's been kneeling before you for three months and more. Wax-balls wants to bare his heart to you, stir up old affections, but you have not spoken to him. So this old bag of bones thought of a clever trick. I told him I knew how to convince you, and he at once let me come to see you . . . hee hee hee. The folks worry about you—

VIRTUE Are they well?

GRANNY TEA *[looks all around]* That's why I'm here. Bawdy Town is in a bad way. The red-haired barbarians have taken

Mount Wu and their battleships are at sea hidden in
the heavy fog. For three months now, the General's
army has had Bawdy Town barricaded tighter than a
drum against barbarian invasion. No one gets out, no
one gets in, we have no more food. The soldiers,
damned pirates, barge around town turning up every
vat and bottle, looking for food. The place has been
plucked bare. The women, desperate to feed their
children, offer themselves to the soldiers, but when the
soldiers are through with them they still have nothing
to eat. Lotus was the most pitiful of all. Every day she
gave herself to over a hundred soldiers who lined up to
have her. They kept her at it the whole day, for
nothing more than three turnips. . . . Well, they've done
with her now.

VIRTUE *[startled]* She's dead?

GRANNY TEA Dead, dead, they're all dead. What's to be done? The
men, young and old, are ready to risk everything. With
Young Seven in the lead, they burst into the garrison
like a pack of crazed dogs and begged Fan to release
you and let you go to the red-haired barbarians to
make it up. The General had a fit and threw Young
Seven into prison. But the threat of death didn't stop
the men—they put on more pressure. The Oil Vendor
tried to assassinate Fan and was beaten to death!
Things are bad. The peace and quiet of Bawdy Town
has been shattered—it's been devastated! What do you
say we should do, Virtue?

[Silence. A coarse, untrained voice can be heard singing:

> *My love, you marched with the soldiers,*
> *While I stood and watched you go.]*

Hurry up Virtue, think of something. I don't know
what to do.

[A note of raucous laughter enters the coarse voice:

> *Night after night with you—*
> *As the moon climbed the willow.]*

[gazing at the cauldron] He's been kneeling here
everyday, for three months or more now. He's in love
with you.

VIRTUE I saved him that year he had a fever; he was so weak. I
cooked chicken in boy's urine, and fed him with flesh
from my own thigh. And now, having tortured me, he

comes and cooks chicken in boy's urine for me and feeds me with flesh from his own thigh to make me strong. I played him music on a bamboo flute that year and now he does the same. One good turn leads to another, no less!

GRANNY TEA *[face wreathed in smiles]* This is wonderful; he really does love you.

VIRTUE Granny Tea!

GRANNY TEA And you still snub him?

[Silence]

GRANNY TEA Be nice to him! If he cares so much for you, it means he loves you. He wants to make it up with you so he can sleep with you and feel the warmth of old dreams. Be nice to him, then you can beg him to—

VIRTUE Granny Tea!

GRANNY TEA Take him to bed—for our sake. I've said what I came to say.

[Silence. The coarse singing draws nearer:

> *Everynight I beg you not to go,*
> *My tears soak the pillow.*
> *Such breasts and all to keep you here,*
> *As the sun sinks low in the west, my dear.]*

VIRTUE *[moved]* Granny Tea, if sleeping with Fan would save Bawdy Town, I'd do it a thousand times. But what Fan wants is to have his cake and eat it: to screw me and still be seen as a man of true virtue and principle. Bawdy Town is doomed! The folks must fend for themselves!

[Long silence]

GRANNY TEA *[sighs]* I'll say goodbye then. Take care of yourself, Virtue.

VIRTUE You keep well, Granny Tea.

[She leaves. The soldiers SPROUT *and* BUTCHER'S BOY *enter and take* VIRTUE *back into the prison hut. Silence envelops Bawdy Town. A group of soldiers enters from the left.]*

SOLDIER A Hey, they say the Flower Queen is locked up in this shed. She's plump, white and tender; every pinch a juicy mouthful. The General's been kneeling some three months before her. Now, I'd like to feast my eyes on that!

SOLDIER B Just thinking about it gives me a hard-on. Come on.

[SPROUT and BUTCHER'S BOY come out at the sound of their voices. They shut and lock the door and, spears held across their chests, call the group of soldiers to a halt.]

SPROUT Clear off! The town's under siege. You should be guarding the fort. What the hell are you doing loitering around the prison? Tired of living?

SOLDIER A Shit! We've been guarding the wall for three months and more and we ain't seen nary a hair of a red-haired barbarian. We seen nothing but fog, fog, and more fog. That there fog's just about made its way right into me old bones. We're not standing watch today, and we want us a peep at the Flower Queen. How about it?

BUTCHER'S BOY Sod off! General Fan's orders. Private visitors to the prison will be punished. Now beat it!

[The soldiers dart angry glances back and forth and they advance fiercely. SPROUT suddenly raises the ox-horn and the soldiers react as if they've seen a fiend, turning tail and running, cursing and shouting as they disperse. SPROUT and BUTCHER'S BOY look at each other and break into laughter.]

[The sounds of harness-bells, ox-horn, and kettledrum all start at once, mingling and clashing, stopping and starting, like the gong and drum in a comic scene of traditional opera. Two soldiers, one fat, one skinny, enter warily to the rhythm of the comic gong and drum, making their way furtively along the wall.]

FATTY Sprout, you on the watch today?

SPROUT Yep.

SKINNY *[with a lecherous grin]* Tsk, tsk, tsk. Sprout, Butcher's Boy, ain't you the lucky ones? And you two good old boys get to stand watch over the Flower Queen for another two weeks yet! I've seen you coming swaggering back to the hut after a watch, that pleased, as if you'd been in seventh heaven! It makes me sad, it does. And I thinks to meself, no damn luck. Can't even feast my eyes on that beauty! Now, I'll make you an offer—this month's pay. My three fen of silver are yours!

FATTY Butcher's Boy, you can have my pay for wine!

[SPROUT and BUTCHER'S BOY take a moment to calculate, exchange a look and nod their heads.]

FATTY *[overjoyed]* I'll get the money!

[*The opera music ceases. Footsteps.* FATTY *and* SKINNY *make a quick get away.*

The footsteps draw nearer. They belong to MADAM FAN, *a woman of 27 or 28, calm and collected, pretty in a delicate sort of way, with the genteel air of one from a respectable family. She stands there uncertainly, her expression half sad, half anxious.* SPROUT *and* BUTCHER'S BOY *kneel in greeting.*]

SPROUT Greetings, Madam. Does Madam have instructions for us?

BUTCHER'S BOY Greetings, Madam. At your service.

MADAM FAN Bring Virtue to me.

[VIRTUE *is brought out of the prison shed.* SPROUT *and* BUTCHER'S BOY *quietly exit.* VIRTUE *silently kneels, again as if in meditation. There are sad notes from the ox-horn and a light flurry of harness-bells.*]

[*gazes at* VIRTUE *for some time*] Please rise, Virtue.

[VIRTUE *does not move.*]

[*hurriedly kneels*] Benefactress, this unworthy person before you is General Fan's wife.

[*Silence*]

So, you really are an unusually intriguing woman.

[*Silence*]

[*as if talking to herself*] Ever since the General met his Benefactress again, he returns each evening to a sleepless night. He stands alone at the window, drinks alone, sleeps alone, wakes alone. Often, holding the scented silk handkerchief the Benefactress gave him that year, he sighs aloud: 'She won't talk to me; she hates me; she hates me for a heartless, merciless small man. I have destroyed her, yes, I have! Why does she say nothing to me? Even if she upbraids me; that would be something. Why doesn't she? I don't understand. And I've played "All the water is moonlight" for her on the flute.' Day after day he questions himself this way, as if he's lost his wits. He's wasting away before my eyes. I'm beside myself with worry.

[*Silence*]

If this goes on, even if the enemy doesn't destroy him, the General will destroy himself!

[*Silence*]

Benefactress, the General likes you, and you must have liked him too. In the town, you made a fool of him, in the garrison you mocked him, now you torment him with silence. You did all this out of love! But the General cannot endure your silence, Benefactress. He is troubled by the siege, he has to be alert to enemy attack. Even a small mistake could lead to death and defeat and the gates of the country would be forced open. To allow the General to engage the enemy unencumbered, and to free him from hurt and distraction so he can meet death with a smile, I beg you to take pity on the General and talk to him. Even if you upbraid him!

[*Silence*]

[*tears in her voice*] Benefactress, if not for the General, then for the security of the nation, for the people of Bawdy Town, talk to him. Believe me, Benefactress, the General has not abandoned his Benefactress and married this unworthy one for fame and fortune. What happened was the workings of fate. And now, I stand abashed before you whom I have unwittingly wronged. If the Benefactress will talk to the General, this unworthy woman promises to accede to the Benefactress's every wish. Please, I beg you!

VIRTUE [*slowly*] All right.

MADAM FAN Oh thank you.

VIRTUE [*pausing after each word*] I want Captain Liu Yuan alive; I want Lotus alive, the Oil Vendor alive, all those who died wrongly alive; I want General Fan to call off his soldiers. Can you manage these things?

MADAM FAN [*dumbfounded*] Benefactress—

VIRTUE You're no fun at all, General Fan wants to make a nun of me and so do you. Play some other game with me!

MADAM FAN [*pleading*] Benefactress!

[VIRTUE *shuts her eyes again.* MADAM FAN *has no choice but to leave.* VIRTUE *returns to the prison shed.*
    Sorrowful blasts on the ox-horn and soft quick harness-bells are heard and gradually fade. Then the ox-horn, kettledrum and harness-bells blend into a comic gong and drum song again. Two soldiers, HATCHET-FACE *and* BUG-EYES, *tiptoe on stage to the rhythm of the comic opera music.* SPROUT *and* BUTCHER'S BOY *enter.*]

HATCHET-FACE Sprout, Butcher's Boy, congratulations to the both of you.

SPROUT *[suspiciously]* What for?

BUG-EYES Fortune knocks. Us two want a look at the Flower Queen, so we'll give each of you four fen of silver to switch duties.

SPROUT No way. Not even for a mountain of gold.

HATCHET-FACE *[takes out gleaming silver]* five fen of silver—

BUTCHER'S BOY No! I've promised someone else.

BUG-EYES I got altogether six fen of silver, all yours. I'm that hot for it. Will you switch? If you won't, we'll switch with somebody else tomorrow.

[SPROUT and BUTCHER'S BOY stare at the silver being waved before their eyes, and change their minds.]

SPROUT It's a deal.

BUTCHER'S BOY Done! *[Takes the silver and weighs it in his hand]*

[After the money has been pocketed, the four soldiers all stick their heads into the prison shed.]

BUG-EYES *[shoves SPROUT and BUTCHER'S BOY]* Go on, get out of here. If you don't leave, we'll take back that silver.

[SPROUT and BUTCHER'S BOY reluctantly exit. BUG-EYES and HATCHET-FACE stick their heads into the prison shed again. Wanton laughter rings in the still air.]

HATCHET-FACE Those two black-hearted foxes, six fen of silver! It was worth it, though. It's worth a whole tael.

BUG-EYES Hey, come on, our eyes have had their fill, it's time we earned that silver back.

HATCHET-FACE Eh? What do you mean?

BUG-EYES We can't be the only ones who want an eyeful, everybody wants a look at her, and they will pay.

HATCHET-FACE Brilliant!

[To the opera-style music of horn, drum and harness-bells, a band of soldiers led by BIG BEARD and RATTY enter in stylized marching fashion.]

HATCHET-FACE Speak of the devil!

BUG-EYES *[an idea dawns]* Hey, fellers, this here is a prison area, clear off. Come tomorrow, General Fan is going to chop off her head, and he wants us two to keep a good eye on her. You fellers get lost.

BIG BEARD She's going to be executed tomorrow?

BUG-EYES Oh, yeah, that flower-like, jade-like head of hers will roll tomorrow. Pity! Hey, do you know how beautiful she is?

HATCHET-FACE She's a beauty all right, a look at her is sweeter than honey candy; warms the cockles of your heart.

BUG-EYES What makes her so beautiful?

HATCHET-FACE A melon face tender as bean curd fresh from the pan, eyes like stars, nose like crystal, and her mouth—big and red like a plump date out of the steamer. A whiff demands a taste, a bite makes you yearn for another whiff. . . .

BUG-EYES What else?

HATCHET-FACE Fine fingers like new scallions, dainty little feet like wine cups.

BUG-EYES What else?

HATCHET-FACE Breasts so white and tender, so soft they'd melt on your lips, so fragile they'd break in your hands.

[The soldiers are enthralled by these words.]

RATTY Well then, give us a look!

BUG-EYES Sure, two fen of silver a go. Pay and step right up; otherwise, on your way.

BIG BEARD Bug-eyes, old buddy, that's a bit pricey, can't you come down a little?

BUG-EYES What's good ain't cheap and what's cheap ain't good.

HATCHET-FACE Okay, okay. Since you're all soldiers same as us, we'll make it one fen of silver a look. That's cheap, lads, tomorrow there'll be nothing to see.

[They think it over a minute. A few grit their teeth and hand over their money first; the rest follow one at a time. To a quicker rhythm of the three instruments joined opera-style, the soldiers form a line and file by the prison shed door to take a look at VIRTUE. Now and then one lets out a sigh of admiration.

FATTY and SKINNY come hurrying up from far away.]

SKINNY Move aside, move aside. Where's Sprout? I've brought my silver to switch duties with him.

BUG-EYES Get lost. I'm on watch today.

SKINNY You are not. I'm with Sprout and Butcher's Boy. I made a deal with them to switch duties for three fen of silver.

BUG-EYES *[guffaws]* For three fen? Are you dreaming?

[While they're talking, FATTY squeezes up to the door of the prison shed for a look, but is shoved aside by HATCHET-FACE.]

HATCHET-FACE Move it. Want a look? No problem, one fen of silver!

FATTY Jackass. This is our post. Why do we have to pay?

BUG-EYES *[gives him a shove]* You arsehole, you useless piece of crap, you looking for a cuff on the ear?

FATTY Damn you! You snatched my post and I'm not done with you yet!

SKINNY You old fool. Me, afraid of you?

BUG-EYES You two are rocks out of the cesspool—you're hard and you stink. I'll teach you a thing or two.

[BUG-EYES and FATTY start to fight with HATCHET-FACE and SKINNY. The other soldiers continue to wait their turns to look at the Flower Queen.
Two more soldiers enter.]

SOLDIER Sprout, Butcher's Boy, time's up, we've come to take the watch. Beat it, all of you! *[The two soldiers start shoving those at the prison shed door and soon start fighting with those watching there. More soldiers enter, and somehow or other get drawn into the mêlée. The fight proceeds to the rhythm of the opera-style music. A farcical fight that goes on for some time.]*

BIG BEARD Stop it! The General's coming.

[They quickly drop their fists, but they soon discover it was a false alarm. A wet cool quiet prevails in the heavy fog.]

Why do we get at each others' throats over a woman? It's not worth it!

FATTY Shit! Women are a disaster.

RATTY Right, I didn't even know what the fight was about.

SKINNY *[shame-facedly]* No man can be untouched by beauty.

HATCHET-FACE The Flower Queen really is a looker.

SOLDIER A I didn't even get a look!

SOLDIER B And she's going to die tomorrow. It's a crying shame!

SKINNY Why don't the lot of us form a friendly little line and each take a good look?

HATCHET-FACE And when we're done, we'll just, just—let her go!

FATTY Let her go?

SKINNY Yeah, let her go! I think it's a dirty shame to kill her.

BIG BEARD But if the General should find out, he'll have our heads!

SOLDIER A I say we should let her go too.

[Shouts of 'Yeah, let her go!']

BUG-EYES I agree. Her beauty has no match on earth or heaven. If the General happens to find out, I'll take the blame. It's worth dying for a beauty like this. But, how'll we get her out of here once we let her go? Come on, let's think it over, and when we've come up with a good plan, we'll write it on our palms and then we'll follow the best one.

SOLDIERS Agreed! *[Each of them begins to rack his brains. After a while they form a circle and put out their palms to find that they've all come up with the same phrase: 'Kill her!']* 'Kill her!' *[They cover their mouths, frightened into a cold sweat.]*

[A long silence]

BUG-EYES There's no escaping the will of Heaven!

HATCHET-FACE The gods want her home.

SKINNY A beauty like that belongs to heaven.

BUG-EYES In my opinion, to kill the Flower Queen is to do her a favour. We're giving her away to the gods in heaven. Hey, we should make a wedding celebration out of it.

SOLDIERS A celebration?

BUG-EYES Live it up. Make merry. We can ask Geomancer to conduct the ceremony.

[BIG BEARD nods and exits.

HATCHET-FACE opens the door to the prison shed. The soldiers instinctively form a line. They cast nervous, excited and frightened looks toward the door of the shed.

VIRTUE comes slowly out of the prison shed. She takes off the wooden yoke and the heavy ropes. Her face is wreathed in pure smiles. She takes tiny, sliding steps from left to right across the ranks of soldiers as if reviewing them. The soldiers' heads turn this way and that and then, as if by unspoken consent, they raise swords that glint with a cold light.]

VIRTUE *[laughs]* I've been wanting to find out what it's like to lose your head. What fun! Thank you all!

[Silence. BIG BEARD enters with GEOMANCER, who is wearing armour and carrying a gourd and his ritual sword.]

BUG-EYES *[salutes]* Revered Geomancer, we all wish to take Virtue as wife. Unfortunately there's only one Flower Queen like her and no way to share her out, but our love is so great that if we can't have her alive, we'll have her dead. We ask Geomancer to conduct a wedding ceremony.

GEOMANCER In *The Book of Changes*, there is record of Cathay's ancient custom of bride-snatching. But who are you common folks to dream of marrying the Flower Queen, a woman as beautiful as the Goddess Nüwa?

VIRTUE Don't be pedantic, dear old Geomancer. I'm willing to be wife to each and every one. It'll be fun to play at bride-snatching. Go on with the ceremony please!

GEOMANCER As you wish!

[The ritual begins. Unusually beautiful jingling of harness-bells accompanies the ceremony.]

Sound the ritual horn.

[Horn. The soldiers begin a rough dance.]

Beat the great drum.

[The kettledrum sounds loud and strong.]

Bow.

[The soldiers begin the sacrificial dance to the rhythm of Geomancer's sword. Their dance grows wilder and wilder.]

Present the offering.

[The soldiers lift VIRTUE *up and circle round beneath the swords and pennants. Then all kneel together with* VIRTUE *held aloft, motionless.]*

[chants]

> At the creation of heaven and earth,
> The four pillars of heaven collapsed, Oh!
> Heaven's curtains rent asunder,
> Showing great depths within, Oh!

SOLDIERS *[sing chorus]*

> Heaven covered not the earth;
> Nor earth supported the heavens, Oh!
> Vast and furious the waters flow,
> Birds and beasts sprang on man, Oh—

[The horn plays wedding music. The soldiers rise to their feet and stand respectfully at attention. After a pause, harness-bells are heard slowly approaching, as if a bride-snatching party is approaching on horseback. The soldiers dance to the rhythm of the bells and horn. Their dance is beautiful.]

GEOMANCER *[still chanting]*

> Men in white on white horses gallop,
> Bride-snatchers, not brigands these.

SOLDIERS *[take up the chorus]*

Handsome men on handsome horses,
Hooves a-ringing,
Proud heads tossing.
'Tis no kidnapping.

[Harness-bells fade, becoming a soft tinkle. Some of the soldiers pretend to be bride-snatchers, and draw stealthily nearer to VIRTUE.]

GEOMANCER *[still chanting]*

They halt, they move, they hesitate,
Bride-snatchers,
No brigands they.

SOLDIERS *[take up the chorus]*

Horses slowly trotting,
Riders lightly wheeling,
Quietly steal the lady away,
While her family is sleeping.

[Some of the soldiers close in on VIRTUE. The harness-bells ring merrily.]

GEOMANCER *[chants]*

Homeward the horses go,
But blood and tears will flow.

SOLDIERS *[chorus]*

Gently their way they steer,
But the lady will not go.
In her struggles a stream of tears,
Endless tears, as blood, do flow.

[VIRTUE is laughing with abandon. The soldiers dance around her, making a merry noise.]

[Suddenly, the horn and the kettledrum erupt joyously together, pushing the ritual to its high point. Four soldiers lift the recumbent VIRTUE high overhead. Her hair cascades down, the soldiers lift their swords, and advance towards her step by step.]

GEOMANCER *[chanting the incantation]*

So Nüwa refined coloured stones to mend the sky,
With sturdy tortoise feet she set earth's axes high,
Slew the black dragon to save the people at Ji,
Piled reed ash to stop the waters and restored peace.

Mended the sky.
Righted the earth.
Tamed the waters.
Peace restored.
The serpent slain.
The people survived,
With land at their back,
Their faces to the sky—

VIRTUE I don't want to mend the sky!

[*Harness-bells jingle easily and smoothly. The soldiers raise their swords toward* VIRTUE.
   Suddenly FAN *enters and hurries to the scene.*]

FAN Stop it!

[*Silence*]

You devils!

[SOLDIERS *kneel.*]

BUG-EYES Stay your anger, General. The Flower Queen must die!

FAN How dare you!

BUG-EYES We've guarded the city, enduring cold and hunger, braving foreign cannon, but rumours are rife. They say the Flower Queen is a rare beauty. And now, no one can concentrate on their duties, they all want to see her. If this keeps up, the ranks will be unsettled and they'll have no will to fight. If the Flower Queen does not die, it will be tough on our morale. Please judge fairly, General.

SOLDIERS General, please execute the Flower Queen!

[*Colonel* LI ZHIYONG *hurries onstage.*]

LI ZHIYONG Reporting, General. The countryfolk are rebelling, they want the Flower Queen released. What are your orders?

[*Silence*]

FAN [*decisively*] Release her.

[*The* SOLDIERS *are stunned.*]

The criminal shall become a comfort woman to serve the soldiers; all those who are brave in battle can enjoy her!

[*The* SOLDIERS *cheer.*]

SOLDIERS Thank you for your favour, General.

FAN [*in a sudden rage*] Be gone all of you.

[*The* SOLDIERS *exit, frightened.*]

[*gazing at* VIRTUE *in despair, to himself*] The town is fog-bound, the arrogant barbarians threaten at our door, the people are in an uproar, the relief troops haven't arrived, there are hardly any provisions left for the troops, the rations are depleted. There will be hard times ahead, we have only our morale to sustain us. Nothing else.

[VIRTUE *laughs out loud.*]

And you laugh! Do you think that Fan enjoys this? Do you really think he's no better than an animal? Loyalty comes before filial piety, virtue, or righteousness. When the nation is in danger, there's no better policy. I have no alternative but to sacrifice my benefactress. I am, after all, Governor-General of Lianghuai, Brigade General of the south-eastern coastal towns!

[VIRTUE *laughs long, turns and walks slowly away.* FAN *kneels, following* VIRTUE *with his eyes as she slowly disappears from view. Tears course down his face.*

Suddenly, the horn, kettledrum, and harness-bells sound madly, like a thunderbolt, earth-shattering; with the hoarse shouts of the soldiers, the sound reverberates a long time under the fog-shrouded sky.]

CURTAIN

ACT 4

[Deathly stillness. The curtain rises on a hazy dusk; the fog is thick and wet, rows of fog banks hang in mid-air. Beside the city wall is a military tent. On the desk inside, an oil-lamp burns with a flickering yellow-blue flame. To either side, weapons cast their shadows all around.

FAN WU comes out of the tent carrying an armload of firewood and walks slowly along the city wall. FAN is returning from an inspection of the defences.]

FAN *[hears something, draws his sword and, demands]* Who's there?

FAN WU Your servant Fan Wu. *[Quaking, he doesn't dare raise his head.]*

FAN The firewood is for military use, how can it be taken home? *[Goes into the tent]*

FAN WU *[follows, head down, muttering a complaint]* There's not a scrap of firewood at home; the chairs, stools, tables, cupboards, trunks and desks—what wooden furniture or utensils there were—have all been burnt. Your wife and daughters have gone hungry for days, and not even a drink of hot water. They spend the days shivering in their quilts. And your wife has forbidden me to tell you. *[Still muttering, he brings the firewood to the back of the tent and out.]*

[A soldier enters, helps FAN remove his armour and serves him green tea. FAN turns up the wick on the oil-lamp and sits deep in thought. In the weak lamplight, his face appears drawn and tired. Colonel LI ZHIYONG, Colonel WANG HUI and other officers silently enter. They stand there, silent and still, not wanting to disturb FAN.]

FAN What activity at the front?

LI ZHIYONG Morale is as usual, the men are on the point of starvation.

WANG HUI The soldiers have gone for days without food now, when will the reinforcements arrive?

FAN Enemy activity?

LI ZHIYONG None.

[Silence]

FAN *[sighs]* It's not long past noon, why is the sky so dark? *[They are silent.]*

FAN WU *[seeing that the officers haven't been forthcoming, makes bold to speak]* General, the fog has swallowed up the sun.

LI ZHIYONG *[stuttering]* The fog has lingered for months, this has never happened before. It is difficult to tell what this omen forebodes.

FAN *[his glance rakes the officers]* Midsummer should be scorching hot, why is it as cold as the depths of winter?

[The officers remain silent, they're all shivering.]

It's freezing!

FAN WU General, I'll light a fire to keep you warm.

FAN *[shakes his head]* Colonel Wang Hui, order the soldiers to light fires to keep warm. Tell them to gather round the fire and exercise their muscles so they won't get frostbite. If they're warm, they can ward off hunger.

WANG HUI At the general's command. *[Exits tent]*

FAN Why isn't there any noise? Where's the horn? The harness-bells? The sound of horses' hooves? The soldiers' voices? Why is it so quiet?

[Silence]

[stands suddenly, leaves the tent, stands lost in thought awhile, goes back inside] Ah, the fog is like a wall, it has swallowed all sound.

[Far off the lights of camp fires appear, one after another.]

Strange! The campfires are lit, you can see them, so you should be able to hear sounds too . . . why isn't there any sound?

[Silence]

Why don't you say something?

[Silence]

Speak up! I really don't understand. Our men like to look at Virtue, so I make her serve the troops. Day and night she waits on them, yet even this hasn't raised their spirits! I thought that once I gave her to them their shouts would resound like thunder and make the enemy quake in their boots. Why isn't there any noise? Not a peep!

[Silence]

Well, speak up.

[After a while, LI ZHIYONG breaks the silence.]

LI ZHIYONG I know the General cares for his troops—

FAN *[cuts him off]* Speak plainly, Colonel Li.

LI ZHIYONG General, the soldiers are afraid of Virtue.

FAN Afraid of her?

OFFICERS ALL Yes, afraid of her!

FAN Why?

LI ZHIYONG Wherever she goes, they fall silent. When she passes
    by, she leaves a frozen stillness behind.

FAN Mmm. The soldiers don't dare to touch her. Fear of her
    is fear of me—

LI ZHIYONG No, General.

FAN Then, why fear her?

LI ZHIYONG She doesn't laugh.

[Silence]

FAN *[laughs]* Not laughing is a cause for fear?

GENERALS It's too frightening!

FAN Why?

LI ZHIYONG Because she used to laugh a lot, and now when she
    doesn't—

FAN Ridiculous!

LI ZHIYONG I thought it was ridiculous, too. But the soldiers are
    afraid of her because she doesn't laugh.

FAN Joy and anger, sorrow and happiness are like the
    seasons, one cannot always be laughing. What is there
    to fear in this? Tell me!

LI ZHIYONG Her laugh was entrancing, the soldiers all loved it
    when she laughed. Suddenly, she stops laughing, and
    everyone feels as if they've lost their soul. She stops
    laughing, and her glance is cold as ice, oppressive gusts
    of cold, so cold that the heart quakes. When the
    soldiers see her coming, they quickly duck and
    prostrate themselves. They're afraid they'll be frozen to
    death by her look!

FAN Preposterous!

[Silence]

Leave me.

OFFICERS Yes, General. *[All except* FAN WU *exit tent.]*

FAN Bring Virtue.

[Soldier exits. FAN *sits silent; anxious, perplexed.]*

FAN WU What's more, General, everyone is hungry. They haven't
    eaten for days, they're so hungry they've collapsed.
    Besides there is something the officers don't dare tell
    you. Everyone pities Virtue. They think that there's no
    point going to war with foreigners over trading, that's
    why their morale is low—

FAN Shut up!

FAN WU Yes. I'll go home now.

FAN Take a silk and fur quilt for Madam.

FAN WU I don't dare, or I'll get a scolding when I get home.

FAN Go!

[FAN WU *gets the quilt, kowtows and exits. After a short while,* VIRTUE *appears, clutching a flute to her breast.*]

[*gazes long at her, finds nothing at all to fear and repeatedly shakes his head*] The fog is everywhere . . . the cold pierces the bones, it's a hardship for the Benefactress to serve the troops. Sit down, please.

[VIRTUE *sits. She is expressionless.* FAN *sees the flute and his eyes light up.*] Is that the flute?

[*Silence*]

[*moved*] Yes, yes! It's the very same one. Copper-coloured, twelve holes. That moonlit night, with the flood water shimmering below the hollow tree. I stood beneath the tree, you sat upon a branch. Then you began to play. The flute conjured up the moon and a myriad moons danced on the shimmering water. [*Remembering, his faced suffused with the light of youth. It's as if a different* FAN *has entered his body.*] Your beauty and your music were magic. You looked so lovely even when you were not smiling, even when you cried! How can they be frightened? [*Lost in reminiscence*] Benefactress, give us a tune.

[VIRTUE *plays the flute, the same melodious tune of fifteen years before.*

FAN, *his emotions taking over, picks up his sword and begins to dance, and his dance is a joyous one. After a while, memory pierces his heart and soul, and his sword dance becomes a wild whirl of white light. With the music, the fog recedes and the translucence of the setting sun reveals the beauty of nature. The music brings a crescendo of harness-bells. Subsequently, all sounds return. The harness-bells, the ox-horn, the kettledrum, voices in song, noise, all ring through the air.*]

[*with deep emotion*] Huaman, you have forgiven Fan Wuchen at last.

[VIRTUE'*s face is a picture of desolate sorrow. She looks at* FAN *with immense pity.* SOLDIER A *rushes into the tent and prostrates himself to report.*]

SOLDIER A Reporting, Excellency. A miracle has happened.

FAN What miracle?

SOLDIER A The troops were on the brink of starvation when
suddenly a tune was heard, and then no one was
hungry any more, or cold. Everyone was beside
themselves with joy, laughing and carrying on, like it
was Spring Festival. Colonel Li Zhiyong begs you,
Excellency, to ask Virtue to play another tune.

FAN *[overjoyed]* All right.

[SOLDIER A exits. SOLDIER B comes into the tent.]

SOLDIER B Reporting, Excellency. The situation is not good.

FAN What's wrong?

SOLDIER B The soldiers aren't hungry any more.

FAN Can that be bad?

SOLDIER B The soldiers have all stripped naked and are dancing
and singing for joy. Colonel Wang Hui fears that since
the soldiers have thrown down their spears and swords,
thrown off their clothes and armour, should the
barbarians attack, the situation will be serious.

*[The singing grows louder. A troop of half-naked soldiers
snakes by along the city wall.]*

FAN Fools! Devils! They're deliberately stirring up trouble!
Why aren't they punished according to military
regulations?

SOLDIER B They've gone crazy. They can't help themselves.

FAN Ah, Benefactress, no more music for now.

*[SOLDIER B exits. The fog once more swallows up all sound
and shuts out the sky. Silence once again envelops everything.
    FAN, beside himself with agitation, gazes at VIRTUE and
shakes his head over and over again. THREE SOLDIERS rush
into the tent in a panic and kneel and kowtow.]*

SOLDIER C Reporting Excellency. The entire Regiment on the Left
Flank has fainted.

SOLDIER D Reporting Excellency. The majority of the Regiment on
the Right Flank has fainted.

SOLDIER D Reporting Excellency. The greater part of the Central
Regiment has fainted.

FAN *[pales in amazement]* But why?

SOLDIER A Because she stopped playing.

FAN Nonsense!

SOLDIER A The General can see for himself.

[Silence]

FAN *[staring at VIRTUE]* Ha ha ha . . . you hold in your
hands the fate of thousands of soldiers. If you don't

play they'll starve to death. When you do play, they
shed their clothes and dance and leap about. What
good is an army of madmen who divest themselves of
their armour and discard their weapons? What good are
they to the Governor-General of Lianghuai and the
Brigade General of the south-eastern coastal towns?
Preposterous, utterly preposterous!

SOLDIER A All the troops beg your Excellency to permit Virtue to
play, so at least we can save the soldiers' lives!

FAN Dismissed!

[Soldiers exit.]

[riveting VIRTUE *with his stare, fatigue and age once more
apparent in his face. His agonizing worries plague him, he
feels more and more perplexed. In the midst of his puzzlement,
he senses a kind of fatalistic force, and thinks of using
spiritual forces to solve his dilemma.]* Fetch the Geomancer.

[A soldier immediately exits the tent. Dead silence]

*[agitated, the more he thinks the angrier he gets, until
suddenly he has a revelation.]* You whore! You're making
use of witchcraft to get back at me. Why bother? I
would gladly die to repay your kindness in saving my
life, as long as the peace and stability of the country is
not threatened. You shouldn't do this! You shouldn't
toy with the peace of the nation! Say something! Why
don't you say something? Smile! Laugh! You love to
laugh, to tease and taunt people. Speak! Laugh!

[Silence]

No, no, no! You are not Huaman, you are not Virtue,
you're not human! You're a sorceress, a demon!

*[GEOMANCER enters the tent, still dressed for battle. He
carries a ritual tray of sand for divination.]*

[as if he's seen his saving star] You are a wise man. In
the face of a national crisis, you certainly would not
stand by and allow the people to be plunged into
despair. I ask you, Taoist priest, who is she?

GEOMANCER Virtue.

FAN Is she human or a demon?

GEOMANCER She is human.

FAN If she is human, why does she resort to witchcraft?

GEOMANCER I do not understand.

FAN When she plays the flute, the soldiers shed their clothes
and dance; when she stops, they faint right and left. Is
that not witchcraft?

GEOMANCER Excellency, fainting is brought on by hunger. These men have gone without food for days; of course they're starving. If Virtue really could use witchcraft, Bawdy Town could have been saved.

FAN If she's not using witchcraft, then what makes the soldiers take off their clothes and dance when they hear the music?

GEOMANCER The flute. The flute was created by the primal goddess Nüwa. Nüwa created the world, fixed the earth's axes, covered the earth with soil, made man and woman, invented the flute, created music and let mortals live and love and multiply. Nüwa dislikes war; that's why the soldiers forget their hunger, forget the cold, and begin to dance when they hear the music, as if they've been reborn.

FAN *[doubtfully]* Really?

GEOMANCER Excellency, you've wronged Virtue.

FAN *[silently kneels to* VIRTUE*]* Fan apologizes for his misplaced accusation. Benefactress, please show your magnanimity towards him. You are free to go now, Benefactress.

*[*VIRTUE, *who has retained her equanimity throughout, drifts out of the tent.]*

Priest, this heavy fog has been with us for months, covering the sun and engulfing the moon; does it bode good or ill? When will it disperse? Please do a divination for us.

GEOMANCER *[smoothes the sand in his tray, lights incense, cleanses his hands, then writes in the sand with a lily branch, and mumbles an incantation]* Fog. Fog belongs to water. When water gathers, it fills; when the heart is filled, it lacks room and loses what it cannot take; when a mind is full and does not take in the new, there is disaster.

FAN *[anxiously]* I am untutored in these oracles. I beg the master to explain.

GEOMANCER Fog. If you see fog, then there is fog; if you see it not, it's not there.

FAN *[ponders a while]* Please do another divination, Master. When will the reinforcements arrive?

GEOMANCER *[waves the branch]* Reinforcements gather round you. So an embankment is round, or a lake, or a barrel—all of them store up water. If the water inside does not get out; the water outside does not get in. When water does not flow it stagnates.

FAN Please explain, Master.

GEOMANCER Heaven's secrets may not be revealed. This poor priest bids you adieu. *[Clasps hands and bows, then exits with his tray]*

FAN *[laughs heartily]* Ha ha ha. Fraud, fraud! You old rogue, you and that whore are in it together! You're in cahoots. Did you think the General wouldn't find you out? What a laugh!

[Colonels LI ZHIYONG *and* WANG HUI *enter the tent.* FAN *falls into an abrupt silence and the two Colonels keep quiet, too. Fog mounts up; there is a deathly quiet.]*

[after a pause] Have the soldiers come to?

LI ZHIYONG No.

WANG HUI Most of them are breathing very feebly.

FAN Any enemy movement?

LI ZHIYONG Not a sound.

FAN *[sighs]* It's too quiet, the big battle is about to take place.

LI ZHIYONG There's not a speck of grain left. The only way to save the men is to kill the horses. I ask permission to slaughter the horses.

WANG HUI All my officers also request permission to slaughter the horses.

FAN Kill the horses?

LI ZHIYONG Kill the horses.

WANG HUI Kill them.

FAN *[muttering to himself]* The battlehorse is the transport of the warrior; a mount is essential equipment in pursuing and killing the enemy! How can we kill the horses?

LI ZHIYONG I make bold to speak plainly: the soldiers are dying, what good are live horses?

[Silence]

FAN If there are no horses in the city, no sound of horses' hooves, the enemy will know that the city's defences are weak, that this general is bluffing. They will surely take advantage of our weakness and launch an attack. The gate of the nation will be breached at once. We can't kill the horses! No! Colonels, let me have a moment to think about this.

[They exit. FAN *stands still and gazes into the heavens. His hand comes into contact with his sword. He is startled by his own thoughts. He draws the sword, it glints coldly.]*

Kill the people, kill the people and eat their flesh . . .
ah, would that raise their spirits? *[Plunges into thought
again]* Heaven is against Fan! Fan is useless, utterly
useless *[He's confused and dispirited, he waves the sword in
the air, then resolutely shoves it back into its sheath.]* Bring
my wife and daughters to me!

[A soldier enters.]

SOLDIER Yes, General. *[Exits]*

*[The music of harness-bells, lyrical and dreamy, drifts in.
     After a pause, MADAM FAN and their daughters FAN
JUAN and FAN ZHEN follow FAN WU into the tent. FAN
JUAN is about twelve or thirteen, FAN ZHEN around eight
or nine. When the two of them spot FAN, they let go of FAN
WU's hands and, calling out 'Father', run to FAN's arms.
FAN gazes at MADAM FAN and says nothing for a long
time. Filled with conflicting emotions, he pats the girls' heads.]*

FAN JUAN Father, I'm hungry!

FAN ZHEN Father, I'm hungry too!

*[FAN nods, not knowing what to say. FAN WU leads the
girls to one side.]*

FAN Madam.

MADAM FAN General.

FAN Madam.

MADAM FAN General.

*[FAN WU quietly turns up the oil-lamp. FAN lets the tears
course silently down his face.]*

FAN JUAN Father, you're crying!

FAN ZHEN Don't cry, Father.

FAN I'm not crying, I'm not. Fan Wu, take the children out
to the kitchen and see if there's anything left to eat.
We'll have a family banquet shortly.

[FAN WU takes the girls to the kitchen. Complete silence.]

This has been hard on you, Madam.

MADAM FAN It's you who has suffered, General.

FAN *[hesitantly]* Ah, Madam . . .

MADAM FAN *[thoughtfully]* General, I have prepared a sleeping
potion—

FAN *[taken aback]* Madam!

MADAM FAN I am a General's wife. I can offer my worthless carcass
to the General, to express my loyalty to the Emperor.
That will be my honour!

FAN *[moved, takes* MADAM FAN *into his arms]* Madam is a
truly virtuous wife! The only one who understands me.

[A long bleak silence]

Lay the banquet.

*[A loud drum beats, an ox-horn sounds. To the bleak music,
the soldiers set up a table, chopsticks, cups, and bowls.* FAN,
MADAM FAN, FAN JUAN, FAN ZHEN, *and* FAN WU *take
their places. Lanterns are lit and hung by the soldiers.]*

SOLDIER *[gloomily]* Excellency, there aren't even any vegetables
left. There are a few biscuits, left over because the
General didn't want any more privileges than the men.

MADAM FAN Biscuits are nice.

FAN Serve the food.

MADAM FAN Fan Wu, fetch the wine.

[The music of the harness-bells is sweet and joyous.]

General, your humble wife has kept some Red Maiden
all this time.

FAN Red Maiden . . . that's wine you made yourself. It's my
favourite. Madam is truly thoughtful . . .

[FAN WU pours the wine. They raise their cups.]

Madam, the reinforcements will be here soon, and we
will have victory over the barbarians. When the soldiers
know how devoted to our cause Madam was, their
spirits will be lifted. Their high morale will make the
barbarians beat a retreat. Here's a toast to our victory
over the barbarians, and to Madam. Drink this cup.

[They all drink.]

MADAM FAN Today our family is together. But if the nation were in
ruins, it would be impossible for families to stay
together. To help keep families united in days to come,
I am glad we have today together. I invite the General
to drink to family reunion.

[FAN drinks slowly. The soldier brings the biscuits.]

General, look well on your children, and look again . . .

*[FAN fixes his gaze on FAN JUAN and FAN ZHEN,
suppresses his sorrow with a smile, takes the children into his
arms and covers them with doting kisses.]*

Eat the biscuits children, you're weak with hunger.

*[MADAM FAN gives the biscuits to FAN JUAN and FAN
ZHEN. The two of them are fed in their father's arms. They
eat hungrily and soon fall asleep.]*

The children are asleep, they'll have pleasant dreams. They'll dream of their father's victory.

[Harness-bells, sounding like a lullaby, come gently, dreamily.]

General, this third cup we drink to our marriage. *[Soft jingling of harness-bells, softly fading]* Your humble wife is glad that she has placed her life in your hands. But since I will no longer be here to serve you, please take good care of yourself. Dress warmly and eat regular meals. Please drink this cup with me, General!

[Loud drum beats. Blasts on the ox-horn. FAN and MADAM FAN kneel facing each other and slowly drink in silence. LI ZHIYONG and WANG HUI burst into the tent and fall to their knees.]

LI, WANG *[together]* General, please, whatever you do, you mustn't—

FAN *[without turning round]* Leave!

[The two officers exit, much troubled. The rhythm of the drum picks up.]

MADAM FAN Your sword, General.

[FAN slowly takes out his sword. MADAM FAN silently takes the sword, and with FAN WU carries FAN JUAN and FAN ZHEN to the back of the tent.]

FAN *[takes a few hurried steps after them]* Madam, since ancient times no mortal has escaped death—

[MADAM FAN reaches the curtain at the back of the tent, turns and once more bids farewell to FAN. Exits. The curtain slowly closes. After a while, FAN WU parts the curtain and comes out.]

FAN WU Madam and the girls are gone.

FAN Send to the kitchen. Make a stew to serve the troops.

[SOLDIERS carry the corpses of MADAM FAN, FAN JUAN, and FAN ZHEN from behind the curtain and past FAN, and then out of the tent and around to the back. All of a sudden, FAN lifts his face to the sky and gives a long wail, then laughs wildly and uncontrollably.

LI ZHIYONG and WANG HUI, leading all the officers under their command, come solemnly into the tent and rustle to their knees. Soldiers come carrying a dozen or so cauldrons and set them down outside the tent.]

LI ZHIYONG General, the womenfolk of all the officers of my Regiment are in the cauldrons.

WANG HUI General, the womenfolk of all the officers of my
Regiment are in the cauldrons.

FAN Beat the great drums.

*[The drums boom, each beat sounding like a crash of muffled
thunder.*

*Row after row of exhausted soldiers enter one after
another, faces drawn with hunger; spear-bearers, shield-
bearers, halberd-bearers, trident-bearers trudge heavily up,
and sway to a halt. FAN WU and a soldier carry a large
cauldron out from behind the tent and set it with the others.
The soldiers realize what is happening.]*

Serve it out to the troops to assuage their hunger.

*[Soldiers lift the lids of the cauldrons and steam rises up,
bowl after bowl of soup made of human flesh passes from
hand to hand, down endless lines.]*

SOLDIER *[mumbles]* The General, the officers, have given
everything they have, if we don't guard the city well,
may lightning strike us dead!

SOLDIERS ALL So long as we live, there will be no surrender. We
swear to live or perish with Bawdy Town!

*[Morale runs high. Banners whip in the wind. Music plays.
FAN solemnly reviews his troops. The men slowly disperse.*

*Once again, dense fog swallows everything. Once again,
deadly silence. The crisp light sound of a flute is heard, an
old husky voice is singing a jolly ditty and laughing. The
voice stops suddenly.]*

SOLDIER *[softly]* The Geomancer is dead. He died singing and
laughing.

[VIRTUE drifts in, like a spirit.]

VIRTUE Geomancer is dead, Lotus is dead, Young Seven is dead,
Oil Vendor is dead, Butcher is dead, Granny Tea is
dead. . . . Captain Liu Yuan is dead. . . . Bawdy Town is
dead—

FAN Madam Fan is dead, the girls are dead.

VIRTUE Now it's your turn. Fifteen years ago, I played you a
song of rebirth on the flute. Today, fifteen years later,
I've played you a dirge. It's your turn to die. Listen,
listen, your end is near, their spirits are weeping,
wailing, laughing, they're coming for you.

FAN *[alarmed]* Why is there no sound? Where are the
harness-bells? The ox-horn? Voices? All gone?

VIRTUE There are sounds everywhere. They fill heaven and
earth: unquiet spirits crying and wailing, the King of
Hell laughing, the sound of footsteps of officers from
the underworld, ghosts calling—calling for you—

FAN You're insane!

VIRTUE It is insane to eat human flesh. It's your turn to die!

FAN To die? Fan is ready to die. But sounds? Sounds?
Nothing. It's all your doing! Where have the sounds
gone?

VIRTUE *[laughs]* You ate them!

FAN *[insanely]* Yes, yes. But first, I'll eat you. *[Grabs her and
pulls her into his arms]* Fan is so tired! Let him have a
moment of bliss!

[Silence]

Fan has always hungered for you; it's driven him crazy.
But he cannot have you, not while he is in his sane
mind. Now he can. Now he can. You see? Ha ha. Then
Fan will be at peace, then he can die, Fan can die.
[Begins kissing VIRTUE *hungrily and it is a long long time
before he releases her]*

[All is silent again.]

VIRTUE *[murmuring]* I do not want to see the General die!

FAN *[moved]* Benefactress, you do care for Fan!

VIRTUE General, please grant me death as well.

FAN No no no! You cannot die.

VIRTUE You toy with us women, then you devour us. My flesh
is delicious, it will serve—

FAN No no, no one shall eat of the Benefactress' flesh.

VIRTUE *[desolate]* Mine is the flesh of a prostitute, not fit even
for staving off hunger.

FAN Forgive me, Benefactress.

*[*VIRTUE *laughs loudly, doubles up with laughter.* FAN *is
bewildered. She exits laughing.]*

[Colonels LI *and* WANG *have been waiting a long time.]*

LI ZHIYONG Your Excellency, I have already had all the womenfolk,
young or old, of Bawdy Town slaughtered and eaten.
But the soldiers still haven't had enough to fill their
bellies and many have died. All the soldiers under my
command beg the Commander's permission to kill the
horses!

WANG HUI The soldiers under my command are desperate. They
have eaten the bodies of their starved comrades, yet

many are still on the point of death. They all beg the Commander's permission to kill the horses.

[Silence]

FAN *[suddenly ready to risk everything]* Kill the horses!

LI ZHIYONG Kill the horses!

WANG HUI Kill the horses!

[A chorus of 'Kill the horses!']

FAN Once the horses have been killed, remove the harness-bells. Tie them to our legs and dance, and the jingling bells will deceive the enemy.

LI ZHIYONG Right, Excellency!

WANG HUI Yes, Excellency!

[They exit. After a while, they return to present FAN with a pair of harness-bells.]

[A wave of soldiers surges forward. FAN sets the example and they tie harness-bells to their ankles and legs and begin the dance of the harness-bells. The dance formations keep changing, surging and billowing like waves, ebbing and whirling, stirring the thick fog, never still. Gradually, the rhythm slows. Then the soldiers stay in formation and stamp rhythmically on the ground with strong, powerful movements. This sets the harness-bells dancing, jingling loudly. In the dance of the harness-bells, one group of soldiers is especially lively and cheeky—it's the beggars.]

SOLDIER A Hey, you're going strong and you haven't even had any horse meat!

SOLDIER B This is fun! We beggars are used to going hungry. The dance will work up an appetite.

[VIRTUE appears, like a flower goddess wandering among the flower glades, she floats among the dancing troops, chanting.]

VIRTUE *[chants]*

The phoenix returns at the sound of tiger drums.
So many are the brave immortals there.
Is this misty vision real or illusion?
Can you, from a tortoise shell, pluck hair?

[The dance quickens. It's like a dream, like a hallucination. The sound of harness-bells, ox-horns, drums surges forwards with an earth-shattering roar. The lights go out, the tent collapses, the horizon dims. The dance slows. The harness-bells, horns and drums fade. The soldiers slow into their death throes. They keel over in droves.]

The rising sun burns off the clouds and fog, and lights up a blue sky. The scene lies tranquil in the bright light. VIRTUE's solitary figure stands motionless and alone. Before and behind her lie countless corpses of soldiers. She picks her way through them, walking forward. The way before her seems endless. White banners come floating down from the sky, made golden by the light of the radiant sun.]

VIRTUE *[sotto voce]* The sun shines, the fog has lifted. It is said that there is hair on the tortoise's back, but the truth is there is nothing. There were no battleships, no cannons, not even a red hair from the head of a barbarian out there. Nothing. But fog . . . just fog. Now everyone here is dead. Killed. Eaten. Starved to death. They tied on harness-bells and danced, for five days and nights, ten days and . . . danced themselves to death.

[Lights slowly fade. Harness-bells jingle into a frenzy, then stop.]

[Lights go up.]

[One morning in the late 1980s, a throng of men and women dressed in all the latest fashions—denim suits, flowered dresses, thigh-high boots, Western-style suits, and Mao suits— kneel in front of the City God's Temple, as incense burns and the gong strikes softly. It is a solemn scene. The City God on the altar is FAN, his lady is VIRTUE. The unique Chinese imagination has joined them in marriage.

CURTAIN

THE END

OLD FOREST

1991

By
XU PINLI

Translated by
MARTHA P. Y. CHEUNG &
JANE C. C. LAI

— ABOUT **THE PLAYWRIGHT** —

XU PINLI (1953–) graduated from Shanghai Institute of Theatre Art, and taught drama there for a number of years before leaving to pursue a career in the entertainment business. A prolific writer with diverse interests, she has written playscripts, film scripts, television drama scripts, as well as Shaoxing opera scripts. Her play, *Ye Zi* ('Leaves') has been translated into English, and was included in the German 'KARAGA' Theatre Yearbook of 1990. It was also performed in English at the Illinois State University in America in 1992. *Old Forest* was first performed, to rave reviews, by the Shanghai People's Art Theatre in 1991 and drama critics in Shanghai generally regard her as one of the most promising playwrights on the Mainland. She is now owner and general manager of Shanghai Golden Elephant Film and Television Company Ltd and part-time scriptwriter at the Shanghai Shaoxing Opera Theatre.

ABOUT **THE PLAY**

Old Forest is a story about a man, his dog, and their common enemy, the wolves. It is a powerful moral tale about suspicion, distrust, and betrayal. According to Xu Pinli, the play also examines deep-seated and disturbing elements in the psychological make-up of the Chinese people—their vindictiveness, and their perverse need for real or imaginary enemies to give meaning to their life. This is a provocative premise which some will recognize as truth, and others might contend.

Revenge is a familiar theme to most Chinese audiences. 'Kung Fu' novels, an integral part of mainstream popular Chinese culture, almost invariably feature a revenge-oriented plot. But the concept is not culture-bound. With this play Xu Pinli has, perhaps unwittingly, written a story that transcends culture, and may touch a universal chord in the human heart.

Like *The Other Side*, *Old Forest* also explores the notion of drama as performance, although Xu retains some of the more conventional elements of plot, characterization, and dialogue. The dog is played by two actors: one serves as a voice relating the dog's thoughts; the other portrays the dog's actions through mime. Lighting, sound effects, and props—all highly suggestive and symbolic—also work to highlight the performance aspects of the play, making it a powerful theatrical experience.

─── **DRAMATIS** PERSONAE ───

NARRATOR, Male. He speaks the thoughts of the dog, ARROW, and
appears as the plot requires. Sometimes, he is also part of the plot.

ARROW, Male. A tawny wolfhound. (The actor should portray the part
by acting rather than relying on costume or make-up.)

BLACKIE, A man in his mid-thirties

IVY, A woman in her mid-twenties

A PACK OF WOLVES

THE **PLAY**

[Total darkness on stage. Sounds but no images.

A bitch is moaning. As the moaning grows louder, there rises also the sound of a hurricane lashing at the land, and the occasional howling of WOLVES. These sounds evoke a sense of the wilderness—the background against which the bitch is in labour.

NARRATOR appears in a corner downstage. In a deep voice, he begins the story.]

NARRATOR I'm a dog, a tawny wolfhound with sharp ears. I've lived in this world for over thirty years. Has any other dog ever lived as long? Yes, over thirty years! Makes you wonder if I'm really a dog or not, doesn't it? Am I really a dog, then? I . . . I'm not sure myself! Maybe it's time I took stock of my life.

[The sound of a bitch moaning and gasping.

A large black cloth can be seen wrapped round an amorphous shape. Part of the cloth is lifted, revealing a red light within. The black cloth and the red light make up the cross section of the bitch's uterus, inside which a few actors playing the pups are rolling in pain, pushing against each other, struggling to get out.

Amplified heartbeats of a dog.]

I was yelping in mother's womb. Oh yes, I could bark even when I was in her womb. I couldn't breathe. The spasms of the soft bag I was in oppressed me and choked me. There were a few others together with me, though I didn't know how many. I couldn't count then . . . We were yelping, rolling, kicking, fighting for breath. But things just got worse . . . Oh, where had I been before all this agony? Could I feel at all? Was I in pain? Could I bark? I don't know, I'll never know. But as the spasms grew more and more tortuous, I could feel . . . that I existed . . . It was a terrible feeling! I couldn't keep still. I lurched from side to side, I fought desperately for a way out. So did the others. Poor mother, she must have been exhausted! All of a sudden, we found a narrow passageway, soft and slippery. I pushed blindly into it and I smelt blood. The smell of blood has stayed with me all my life, a life of endless struggles and fierce battles.

[The moaning and gasping of the bitch grows more urgent.]

I was almost out; I felt like I was dying. Birth pangs and death throes seem so alike. But I didn't care whether it was life or death, I just wanted to be out, out!

[Red light fades. The black cloth is lifted at two points to form the outline of two gigantic mountain peaks.]

I made it! I was out! Out of the bag, away from the heartbeat. The world is so big, so boundless! The air so fresh, so sweet! I was born! Into the world! I existed!

[The lights emphasise the outline of the peaks in radiant gold. The NARRATOR rushes up to the mountain.]

I love those warm round shapes! I want to go to them to suckle, to nestle against them. Instinct tells me they're female. I'm sure they are. Later on, of course, I learnt that people called them mountain peaks. People can call them what they like, but we dogs know at birth that mountains are female! They are female!

[The green eyes of the WOLVES begin to flicker on the stage.]

What are they? Stars? Or green eyes? The world is big, beautiful and sweet! Oh, how wonderful it is to be alive!

[The WOLVES howl.]

What's that? My ears are ringing! Ah, I hear my loving mountain sigh. She is saying, in a language only we can understand, that it is the wolves crying! Mother is trembling, holding her breath in fear!

[A dog barks.]

Ah, I understand. Mother is saying, 'This is the end, my darling puppies! We're done for, my angels!' She barks, she springs at the stars. No, at those beautiful green eyes.

*[A flash of white light.
Sound of WOLVES howling and a dog barking.
Green eyes flickering and moving on the stage.
Sound of a dog fighting ferociously with the WOLVES.]*

The world is not beautiful, not at peace. It's full of sound and fury, noise and confusion! In the mad ravishing of those eyes I smell my mother's blood, the same as that I'd smelt in her womb. A pack of black creatures have fallen upon her . . . This is what remains!

[Fragments of a dog's skeleton appear on the stage.]

Is this you, Mother? Where, where is that warm soft
bag that has kept us safe? And the loud heartbeat? Is
this the last I'll see of you? But why? Mountain, tell
me why! Ah, you're crying too, my mountain!

*[Silence returns. Once again pairs of green eyes, gentle and
beautiful, flicker about in the dark.]*

And now the world is all quiet and beautiful. No! It's
no longer beautiful! Look at those green lights. They're
flickering with cruelty, ruthlessness, and violence.
They're stealing up on me, inch by inch! Close! Close!
But now he appears. Blackie, my master-to-be,
appears—

*[BLACKIE enters, shouting at the WOLVES, a lighted torch in
his hand.]*

BLACKIE Woohoohoo—Woohoohoo.

*[The mountain reverberates with echoes of BLACKIE's
shouting and the WOLVES' howling. Slowly, the eyes
disappear.]*

NARRATOR What is he holding in his hand? It spreads, and yet is
so soft. It burns. Ah, it's a red-faced drunkard, a living
monster. It's name is fire! Blackie has set the mountain
ablaze and driven off those eyes. When he picks me up
in the blazing fire and walks into the blazing valley,
the mountain peaks, beautiful and feminine, tremble;
the naked earth, too, trembles.

*[Sounds of hurricane, earthquake, landslide, and of mud and
rock crashing down from the mountain. The trembling
mountain gradually becomes a range of rolling hills. All this
time, BLACKIE is holding an imaginary pup in his arm,
shielding it from the turmoil.]*

The naked earth trembles, the beautiful and feminine
mountain peaks are no more, new folds are formed.
In the violent throes, a new world is born. The blaze,
blood-red and like a drunken monster, has engulfed
my innocent mother and my brothers. I survive, safe in
Blackie's arms. But the wolves, too, survive—

BLACKOUT

S C E N E   T W O

[Lights rise on an old forest made of a steel frame with pillars of gauze or fabrics.
BLACKIE enters, holding one end of a long rope, the other end of which
remains inside the wings.]

NARRATOR Blackie and I have started a new life. I follow him
everywhere, treading on the fallen leaves, smelling the
scent of the earth, licking the sweat trickling down his
body.

BLACKIE *[looking towards the other end of the rope, offstage]* Come,
Arrow, come. You don't mind this name, do you? I
know it doesn't sound like a name for man or dog. But
we hunters love arrows! *[Pulls the rope which is now
stretched taut]* Why are you trembling? And staring at
the trees like that? Don't be afraid, this is just an old
forest, a forest too old to die. . . . Ah, you're afraid of
the trees; you think they're beasts! No. Let me tell you,
my pup, the last earthquake turned them into such
weird shapes, but they're held to the ground by their
roots. They won't come after you. . . . That's right,
come on. Take your time. Good, I'll tell you something
more. *[The rope becomes slack. BLACKIE, still holding it,
walks on.]* My name's Blackie. Don't know why I'm
telling you this, you can't talk, and there's not a damn
soul around. Still, dogs and cats have names, you might
as well know that I've got one, too—

*[The howling of a wolf. The rope suddenly goes taut. Sound
of a dog gasping.]*

NARRATOR *[on another side of the stage]* What is that thing hanging
from the tree? It's reeling, kicking, clawing, and biting
at the air . . . bleeding and staring at me . . . I know
those eyes—ruthless, and now pathetic. They're the eyes
of those creatures that ate my mother.

BLACKIE *[towards the wings where ARROW remains offstage]* Yes, it's
a wolf, a baby wolf. About your age. I've tied him up
there.

*[The movement of the rope suggests that the dog is struggling
to get away.]*

Hey! You fool! That'll strangle you! See, it hurts. Now
listen to me, Arrow—

NARRATOR *[still apart]* You're going to feed me to him, I know. I
go near that tree and you'll set him free to kill me.

BLACKIE *[towards the wings]* Look at you. You think I'll let him
    feed on you? You idiot! You're a dog, not a wolf. A
    dog is a man's best friend. I'm your friend, always. So
    listen, in a minute I'll set you free, but not him. Get
    him, fight him, tire him out, tear him up, and feast
    upon him. Treat him the way his kind treated your
    mother.

    [The howling of WOLVES *in the distance]*

NARRATOR *[still apart]* No, no, I can't do it! He's got my mother's
    flesh in him. I can't!

    [Another round of howling]

BLACKIE From now on, I'll feed you only with baby wolves.
    You'll have to eat them or starve. When you grow
    bigger, you'll eat big wolves. By the time you grow up,
    you'll hunt for the wolves yourself . . . Are you
    listening?

NARRATOR *[apart]* Master, I don't understand why you are doing
    this. I'm scared of those green eyes and that blood-red
    mouth. I'm scared of all the green eyes and blood-red
    mouths in the world. I'm scared! Scared!

BLACKIE Don't be such a coward, Arrow! Be brave! Take your
    revenge now!

NARRATOR But why? Why must I take revenge just because they
    killed my mother?

BLACKIE *[almost simultaneously]* I shall teach you. From now on I
    shall teach you to become an arrow worthy of your
    name.

NARRATOR Mother brought me into this world, but why can't I
    just play with the mountain, have fun in the old forest
    and frolic with a female pup that I like?

BLACKIE Everyday you must learn to run and bite and attack.
    And I'll hang a wolf from this tree every day to bend
    its trunk and shape it into a perfect bow.

NARRATOR Why should I avenge a wrong even Mother herself
    couldn't handle?

BLACKIE With that bow, and with you as my arrow, I can wipe
    out all the wolves in this forest.

NARRATOR I won't do it! I won't! I won't!

BLACKIE Let me tell you. There are thirty-seven wolves in this
    old forest now. Yes, thirty-seven. I'm not trying to
    scare you. Every night I count their eyes from behind
    the trees. One day, I'm going to shoot them one by
    one. So you must do as I say. Now, go! Get the wolf!

What? Trying to sneak away? You coward! Are you a
dog? All right, I'll carry you there, okay? Why do you
look at me like that? Do you hate me? Hah! So you do
know what hatred is. Then why don't you hate the
wolves that killed your mother? Stupid dog, you can't
tell right from wrong! Listen, if you spare a wolf that
comes your way, there will be one more wolf to eat you
alive! Believe it or not, if I set this one free, it'll tear
you into pieces this very minute!

[WOLVES howl in the distance.]

That's life in this old forest. Either you eat him or he
eats you . . . What's the matter? You're shaking . . . It
has frightened the shit out of you, eh? What are you
afraid of? I've tied him up, he can't get you. All right,
all right. Come, I'll give you a hug.

[BLACKIE rolls the rope into a large ball.]

I'll tell you a story about me and the wolves. *[Looks at
the ball]* Are you listening? *[Rolls the ball from tree to
tree]* I had a beautiful wife and a lovely boy. Her long
dark hair was like a beautiful cascade. When she
combed it, it went swish—swish—like a gentle
rustling wind, like a murmuring stream. Listening to
its intoxicating murmur, your heart leapt, and you felt
light as the wind. Then one day, believe it or not, her
hair charmed even a kite from the sky and it fell
tumbling down. . . . *[Gently rocking the ball]* One day, I
killed a wolf. When I slashed open its belly, I saw four
baby wolves inside. I felt the shivers down my spine.
But it was too late for regrets. So I quickly finished the
job, put away the hide and threw the carcasses into the
backyard. That night, the wolves laid siege to the
house, and killed my wife and son. But I lived because
I suddenly remembered I could chase them off with
fire. Fire, that amazing monster, drove them away. In
the past, human beings used to be my enemies. We
had fled to the mountain in fear of them. . . . But from
that day, the wolves became my sworn enemies. I didn't
run away. I stayed in this old forest, with the remains
of my beloved ones. I killed any wolf that came into
sight, and they tried to kill me. There were thirty-
seven of them. I fought them all by myself. . . . And
now, I have you. . . . It's hard to live in hatred and
enmity. But damn it, they killed my wife and my son!
How can I not take revenge on them? They killed your

mother too. If you are a good dog, you too must take your revenge! No one is born with hatred. But once you're in this world, you grow to know hatred, whether you like it or not.

[The WOLVES *howl.]*

I've always thought you were no ordinary dog. When you were born, the mountains trembled and the earth shook. When you let out your first cry, your mother and your brothers lost their lives. But you survived. That's Providence. There's greatness in you, don't you see? Go now, take your breakfast, finish that baby wolf.

*[*BLACKIE *throws the ball towards the wings, keeping hold of one end of the rope. The rope leaps up and down. The sound of a dog fighting with a wolf offstage. The rope is stretched so taut that* BLACKIE *nearly loses his balance a few times. He lets go of the rope. It flutters and disappears into the wings.]*

Good, Arrow, Good! You've done it. You've tasted the blood of a wolf! That's what you'll live on. Yes, jump higher, and higher! Aim at its eyes. Gouge them out! And now the tongue. Bite it off, drink its blood. Well done! You are strong!

*[*ARROW *barks ferociously offstage.]*

Great dog, Arrow!

SCENE THREE

[The black cloth is lifted at one corner to make a cottage. Beside the cottage stands a big tree with a curved trunk. It looks like a totem-pole. BLACKIE *and the actor playing* ARROW *are under the big tree, staring intently at each other's eyes.* NARRATOR *enters.]*

NARRATOR I'm a big dog now. Leaping, attacking, biting, gouging, I've grown agile and fierce. I polish off two young wolves in one meal. And I can hunt. I can pick up their scent miles away and go straight for them, like an arrow.

*[*ARROW *jerks his head.]*

BLACKIE You lost, Arrow. You moved first, I've outstared you. Come, let me scratch your nose. *[*BLACKIE *scratches* ARROW's *nose.]* Okay, we'll start again.

*[*ARROW *looks impatient.]*

Don't go. We'll do it one more time. Remember to keep still.

[ARROW and BLACKIE stare intently at each other's eyes again.]

NARRATOR I've learnt to hate the wolves. They're so ugly, black all over. No, not even that, but smeared with grey and blotches of the ugliest dirtiest colours. And the way they howl! As if they're mourning for all their dead. But I hate their eyes the most. They're stupid, deceitful.

[ARROW twitches again.]

BLACKIE You've moved again, Arrow! Come on, let me scratch your nose.

[ARROW runs away.]

Trying to run away? No, I'll scratch your nose. I'll get you.

[BLACKIE runs after ARROW.]

NARRATOR Master used to hang the wolves up on this tree. It has grown, its trunk bent into a beautiful curve like a bow. Master says we can soon use it to shoot arrows at the wolves . . . The other night, we counted thirty-nine pairs of eyes. That's strange! Everyday I gobble up two of them but their numbers are growing.

[ARROW, still running, suddenly finds something in the bush, digs it up and pulls it out.]

BLACKIE Got you. Two legs are as good as four. *[Catching sight of what ARROW has pulled out]* What's that? . . . A kite. Where did you find it? *[Perplexed, he looks around but finds nothing.]* That's strange! Something's happened. For years, there has been just me, a dog and a pack of wolves in this old forest. How come there's a kite? I've seen this kite before.

[BLACKIE is deep in thought.]

Oh, why bother! Strange things happen everywhere. Nothing makes sense anyway.

[BLACKIE tries to scratch ARROW's nose. ARROW turns away.]

Okay, I'll let you off this time. But we'll practise again, just one more time. I promise. You know, man or dog, you need a pair of sharp eyes for the wolves. Matching eyes is just the right exercise for us. You want to be quick, sharp, and deadly accurate, don't you? Come on.

[BLACKIE and ARROW resume staring at each other's eyes.]

NARRATOR How well I know those eyes, my master's eyes. Happy, they shine like the sun. And they turn misty when he's sad. Today, I see something I've never seen before. It's an abyss, a bottomless ocean. Ah, he's longing for something, yes, he is.

[The wind rustles, swish—swish. BLACKIE has moved. ARROW leaps at him, trying to scratch his nose.]

BLACKIE Listen. What's that noise?

[ARROW pricks up his ears.]

NARRATOR That's the wind.

BLACKIE That's a woman combing her hair.

[Swish—swish—goes the wind.]

NARRATOR You hear it everyday in this old forest, hundreds of times. Nothing special.

BLACKIE That's a woman combing her hair. Arrow, maybe . . . maybe there's someone . . . Let's go and have a look. See what we can find.

[BLACKIE and ARROW search through the bushes and the undergrowth. They find nothing.]

Forget it. Better get back to our eye-match. *[They do so.]* Hang on. No, this doesn't count. I'll tell you something, then we'll start . . . You know, Arrow, it's no fun living with people. There are so many things you can't do. You can't pick your nose, for example. Bad manners, they say. But you'll still do it when you're alone, right? That's how we keep our noses clean! Then, you can't shit anywhere you like, you've got to go to a particular place to do it. And you can't just eat anything you like, even though it's right under your nose. Why? Because it belongs to someone else. Anyway, the human world is full of can'ts and don'ts. But when a man lives with a dog, then all's well. When I want to laugh, I laugh. *[Makes faces]* If I want to box my ears, I can do it at once. *[Boxes his ears, and ARROW's too]* . . . And if I want to cry—*[Bursts into tears]*

[ARROW tries anxiously to comfort him.]

BLACKIE Isn't this just as good? Why bother with people? A man and a dog—that's life. Good, very good. Come on, *[Wipes his tears]* we'll match eyes.

[BLACKIE and ARROW resume their eye-match once again.]

NARRATOR I don't understand you, my master. But I can see your
eyes are still an abyss, a bottomless ocean. And tears
are streaming down your cheeks. I've licked those tears
before, they tasted like salt. You're unhappy, I know,
because dogs cry too when they're unhappy. Not so
long ago, I ran away for three days with a young bitch.
When I came back you beat me up. I cried, too, all by
myself. But how can I make you happy? I've tried so
hard. You wanted me to jump and leap, I did it. You
wanted me to eat the wolves, I did it. I don't like
matching eyes, it hurts, but I did it with you all the
same. Right now, I need a break, my eyes are sore, I
want desperately to blink, but I can't. You'll be mad
with me if I lose again. Oh, Master, I've tried so hard
to obey you and please you, why are you still crying?

[Swish—Swish—
      BLACKIE *and* ARROW *stare stubbornly at each other's
eyes. Swish—Swish—]*

BLACKIE *[losing his concentration]* I want to call a halt again,
Arrow. No, this doesn't count either. I've given you
notice. *[Relaxes at once]* That's the sound of a woman
combing her hair. I know it, even though I haven't
seen a woman for seven years. I remember the sound—
'swish—swish—'. That's it. Why do you look so glum,
Arrow? I know, you've never seen a woman before.
[Excitedly] You have no idea what a woman is! I tell
you, a woman can make wine, and sing, and whisper
sweet words in your ears. No, a woman is the wine,
the song . . . *[Overcome with disappointment all of a sudden]*
But there won't be one here . . . Come, we'll match
eyes.

*[ARROW reluctantly stares at BLACKIE's eyes.
      Swish—Swish—. BLACKIE and ARROW do not move.
Swish—Swish—]*

NARRATOR Looking at my master's eyes, I suddenly discover
something new—a flash of light I've never seen before.
It grows brighter and brighter, filling the abyss, the
bottomless ocean, shining through the tears in his eyes.
And now it has turned into a fire, a fire that burns,
that scorches the earth, ravages the mountains, that
looks like a red-faced drunken monster. Yes, it's
burning, burning—

[Swish—Swish—]

BLACKIE I've moved. I lost. Come, Arrow, scratch my nose.
[Grabs ARROW's *paws to scratch his own nose, getting excited]* You know why I moved? I'm certain there's a woman here, Arrow!

*[*BLACKIE *and* ARROW *hide themselves at one corner downstage, facing the audience.* IVY *enters, carrying a golden vine. Although* BLACKIE *and* ARROW *have their backs turned towards her, they can see her movements, as if in reflection.*

IVY *draws out the full length of the vine she is holding. It is tied with many knots. Mementos such as windchimes and dried flowers are tied to the knots. These are her thoughts and memories.*

BLACKIE *and* ARROW *watch her stealthily, still with their backs turned towards her.]*

IVY *[looking for something and suddenly finding it]* Here it is. The kite I've lost. Who has hung it up?

NARRATOR This is the first time I've seen a woman. Ah, she's female, just like the mountain peaks I saw when I was born . . . Strange, we dogs have sharp ears, how come I didn't know a woman was here. My master's ears are dull; he can't even tell when the grass, trees, and ants are talking—how did he detect her first?

*[*IVY *trails the knotted vine as she walks around on stage.]*

BLACKIE Arrow, do you know what she's doing? She's airing her thoughts and memories. Only lonely people do that. And only lonely people, like me, can know what she's airing. Look at those knots. They're windchimes, windmills, kites—her childhood memories. And look at those flowers and dandelions—they must be her girlhood memories. They tell you so much about her life. Isn't this exciting? Look, she's going to tie up the kite we've dug up and turn it into her memory too!

*[*ARROW, *still with his back towards* IVY, *watches with amazement. After a while, he loses interest and turns his attention elsewhere. Finally, he picks up one corner of* BLACKIE's *clothes with his teeth and drags him away.]*

Keep still, Arrow! I know, the human world, our world, is too alien for you. But watch carefully, you'll learn much about our secrets.

*[*IVY *spreads out the knotted vine, golden in colour, for airing. The thoughts form a beautiful pattern. A net overgrown with creepers descends on* BLACKIE *and* ARROW. *They are not aware of it.]*

But we can't let a woman stay with us. We have to match eyes everyday, work on the bow, and kill the wolves, our common enemy. How can we take in a woman who has nothing in common with us? Go, Arrow, chase her away.

*[*ARROW *is ready to spring at* IVY *but finds that he is trapped by the net.* BLACKIE *also attempts to rise.]*

Oh, we've been crouching here too long. Look, the creepers have grown all over us. The damp is so strong, moss will soon grow on us. Let's go! *[Struggling to disentangle himself from the creepers]*

*[*ARROW *manages to break free and heads straight for* IVY, *growling ferociously.]*

IVY Whoa! What a fierce wolf! And howling as if it means business! *[Catches sight of* BLACKIE*]* Is it yours? Why don't you keep an eye on it. Such a fierce wolf! You should keep it on a leash.

[As she says this, IVY *helps to disentangle* BLACKIE *from the creepers.]*

BLACKIE It's not a wolf. It's a dog. He's my best friend. His name is Arrow. He hunts wolves—

IVY Dog or wolf, they're pretty much the same.

BLACKIE Well, yes, they're alike in some ways. But, mind you, wolves are cruel and fierce while dogs are brave and loyal.

IVY I see, you hunt wolves. But don't try to persuade me. I don't want to keep dogs and hunt wolves. Anyway, they're all the same to me.

BLACKIE You've come into my old forest. What do you want?

IVY Your old forest? Huh, does it belong to you?

BLACKIE Yes. I've lived here for seven years. No one has ever come here before.

IVY This is my forest, the forest that exists in my dreams. Every night I dream that I'm in this forest, strolling, playing, airing my thoughts and memories. *[Continues to spread out her thoughts on the golden vine for airing]*

BLACKIE What? This is the forest that exists in your dreams?

IVY Yes.

BLACKIE Are you dreaming now?

IVY I am.

BLACKIE And I'm in your dream?

IVY That's right.

BLACKIE What's your name? Where do you live?

IVY My name's Ivy, but I don't know what I'm called when I'm awake, or where I live.

BLACKIE *[deeply perplexed]* Am I awake or in a dream then? *[Bites his finger]* Ouch! It hurts! So I'm awake. . . . Of course I am. I don't sleep much, and I never have dreams. But how can we talk if you're dreaming and I'm awake?

IVY Aren't we talking now? Isn't it nice? If you like, you can come and look at the thoughts I'm airing. Hm, this is my memory. . . . That's my imagination. . . . That one there is my longing.

BLACKIE *[enchanted, but trying to remain clear-headed]* Sorry . . . I, erm, I've got things to do. I'm not interested in what you're airing. Arrow, come here. We'll match eyes.

[BLACKIE and ARROW stare at each other's eyes. IVY looks on curiously.

NARRATOR enters.]

NARRATOR Mountain, my beloved mountain, I have grown up in the joy and comfort of your arms, I stand guard over you like a loyal soldier.

IVY What's the matter with the two of you? Are you bewitched?

NARRATOR I can understand your incantation, your thundering rage, your gentle murmurs. I can understand, too, your silence and your stillness.

IVY Hey! What's the matter with you? I'm talking to you. Can't you hear me?

NARRATOR My beloved mountain, you've told me the story about the third tree from the furthest end of the old forest, how it tore up half of its roots from the ground when it strained to catch another glimpse of the bluebird that flashed through the air, and how it died not long after—

IVY *[trying to pull ARROW away]* Hey, wolf. Oh no, your master says you're a dog. Well, you were growling like crazy just now, why so quiet all of a sudden?

NARRATOR And the story about the tree overgrown with red creepers, how a clap of thunder split its trunk into two, but the creepers remained just as red, blood red. That made me believe there is such a thing as hatred in this world.

[IVY picks a dandelion 'clock' from the thoughts she is airing, holds it up before BLACKIE, and blows at it. The white dandelion gently caresses BLACKIE's face.]

Master has said, a man who doesn't take revenge is not a true man; a dog who doesn't take revenge is not a good dog. For years, I've been chewing on those words. They're like some tough gristle. I like it too much to spit it out, but I have yet to swallow it.

[IVY *keeps blowing at the dandelion.* BLACKIE *finally moves.*]

BLACKIE Why do you want to muck up our plan?

IVY Muck up your plan? I don't know what you mean. I just want to play with you.

BLACKIE We don't have time to play with you.

IVY Why not?

BLACKIE We've got to train our eyesight and make a strong bow to kill all the wolves. We want revenge!

IVY Kill all the wolves? All the wolves in this old forest? Ha! Ha! [*Bent double with laughter*]

BLACKIE What are you laughing about?

IVY You seriously think you can have your revenge?

BLACKIE Why not? My dog polishes off two wolves a day. I've made many many arrows. With each arrow, we can kill a wolf. One day, I'll wipe them all out!

IVY There are so many cats in this world, but they can't kill all the rats. There are so many wolves in this world, but they can't eat up all the sheep. And as for all the hunters dead set on killing the wolves, not a single one will ever kill them all. Forget your revenge.

BLACKIE [*stunned*] Why did you say that?

IVY That's what my thought here tells me. This one . . . Listen!

[IVY *flicks her finger at the vine. It tinkles.*]

BLACKIE What about this one? What does it say?

IVY This one? [*Flicks her finger at the vine again, the thought also tinkles.*] It says, why do you want to keep a dog? Isn't it the same as a wolf?

BLACKIE A dog is a man's best friend. It's brave, alert, fierce—

IVY So are wolves.

BLACKIE Dogs are loyal and obedient, but wolves are not.

IVY You're wrong. Where I live, people long ago used to keep dogs, feed them and give them shelter. In the end, the dogs all turned against their masters. Men, women, children—all were badly injured. Later on, our people drove away all the dogs. They fled to the

mountains and joined the wolves. God knows how
many dog-wolves they produced. Years later, they
returned and laid siege to our place. None of us could
tell the dogs from the wolves. Anyway, in the dark,
they all have bright green eyes.

BLACKIE *[feebly]* But, but the wolves killed my wife and my son.

IVY They didn't kill you. They can't wipe us out, just as
you and your dog can't wipe them out.

BLACKIE Oh!

[The WOLVES *howl.]*

IVY Listen to what this thought tells you.

*[*BLACKIE *leans his ear against a windchime tied to the vine.
The howling of* WOLVES *becomes cheering on a football
pitch.]*

Did you hear that? Maybe they are not howling at you.
Maybe they're just having fun playing among
themselves. Forget the wolves! Forget your revenge!
There are better things to do.

BLACKIE But I've never thought about what I could do if I don't
hunt wolves.

IVY Oh you can air your memories with me, your thoughts,
your longings.

BLACKIE I don't long for anything, and I have no thoughts. I
used to have some memories, but I just left them in a
heap, never aired them. They must be a hopeless mess
now, and mildewed all over.

IVY That's all right. I can help you. *[Takes a long hairpin
from her hair]* This is the hour hand on a clock. You
can use it to string up your memories.

BLACKIE I haven't got that many memories.

IVY Don't worry. Yesterday is today's memory, today will be
tomorrow's memory. Soon you'll have a nice long string
of memories. What I've said just now could turn into
your memory, right? You're young and strong, why
don't you do something to make your memories more
beautiful?

BLACKIE Like what? Can I have you in the first memory I'm
going to create?

IVY Come and catch me then. I walk on clouds, I can fly,
ha, ha . . .

*[*BLACKIE *runs after* IVY *in slow motion. Every time they
touch a thought, it tinkles.* ARROW *looks on in
amazement.]*

NARRATOR Ah, that white bitch with curly hair that came out of nowhere rushed away. I ran after her, breathing heavily, wanting nothing so much as to follow that scent. It smelt of grass, the naked earth, and dew drops. The scent went straight to my head. I longed to catch up with her, kiss her, lick her belly, feel her curly hair.

[BLACKIE has caught up with IVY. Laughing, she picks some dandelion 'clocks' from the thoughts she is airing and blows them at BLACKIE. Wisps of dandelions drift about on the stage.]

How I yearn to see her again, run after her, crawl up to her nest, just like last time, and let that scent overpower me. I know that scent well, I can pick it up at once. But since that day, I've never caught a whiff of it anywhere. I want to go and find it, to leave my master for three more days again.

[The sound of fierce wind sweeping through the stage. BLACKIE and IVY hold each other's hand to keep their balance. Against the wind, ARROW stands, his ears pricked up, gazing straight ahead.]

What's going on? Oh, why has the world changed so suddenly? The sun has snatched away those lovely bright arrows criss-crossing the trees. The leaves are falling in cascades. The trees have lost their sharp teeth and fierce claws. Oh, it must be because of that white bitch with curly hair. Thinking about it has turned everything upside down! I must chase it away. Let me howl! Let me tear it up! Come, hatred, come! Help me destroy it!

[The howling of WOLVES is followed by their flickering shadows.]

BLACKIE *[unsure what to do]* Look! They're there!

IVY *[excitedly]* Listen to what my thought tells you. Listen!

[BLACKIE listens. The howling of WOLVES becomes a cheering sound. ARROW barks, somewhat hesitantly. He turns to look at his master and breaks off barking, then gazes at the distance again, and growls instinctively again.]

They're cheering! Maybe because they've slept well, or found some food, or given birth to some baby wolves. They've got so many things to cheer and wail about. I'm surprised you keep thinking they're howling at you.

NARRATOR Here they come, bold and brazen, sneering at me because of that moment of weakness I've shown for that white bitch. They've come to trample my soil and foul it with their horrible scent. But they've forgotten one thing: I live only to fight, to growl, to kill!

[*The green eyes of* WOLVES *flickering about on the stage.* ARROW *springs at the* WOLVES.]

BLACKIE [*stopping him*] Stop! Arrow! Stop!

[ARROW *ignores* BLACKIE's *order. He wrestles with the* WOLVES. *A song rings in the air:*

I'm a wolfhound with sharp ears. I've lived long. Day in, day out, I go up and down this old forest, jumping, leaping, hunting, killing, locked in a life-long battle with that damn old fool Providence.

ARROW *has finally driven away the* WOLVES. *He goes up to* BLACKIE *and* IVY, *breathing heavily. They stare at him.*]

IVY Look at the blood on his mouth! How horrible!

NARRATOR Why doesn't he pat me and ruffle my hair as he used to? Why doesn't he say: Well done, Arrow, you're a good dog!

BLACKIE [*to* ARROW] Do you know what your first duty is?

NARRATOR [*apart*] To kill the wolves.

BLACKIE No, your first duty is to obey me. I'm your master.

NARRATOR [*apart*] Aren't they the same thing?

BLACKIE They are. But not always. Under some extraordinary circumstances, I may order you not to kill the wolves, then you mustn't do as you please.

NARRATOR [*apart*] But you've never ordered me not to.

BLACKIE It may be different from now on. From now on I will. So do what I tell you.

NARRATOR [*apart*] I will, even though killing the wolves has always been the same as obeying your words. I can't tell the difference, but I will try my best, my master.

IVY [*staring at* ARROW *all this time*] I have another thought, Blackie. It's rising up in me. This is what it says: the wolves are not your enemy, they are not threatening your life, the real threat to your life comes from your companion.

BLACKIE My what? What do you mean? Who's that? There's only you and my dog, how could either of you threaten my life?

[*The sound of the sea is heard, indicating the rise of* IVY's *thought.*]

IVY Hold me, Blackie, I think I'm going to wake up. . . .
What shall I do? . . . *[Yawns]* When new thoughts
come lapping at me and I yawn, then I'll be awake
soon. *[BLACKIE hastily grabs IVY's arms.]*

BLACKIE Oh no! Please don't wake up! You haven't yet told me
everything. Wait, I'll go and get you a bunch of
flowers to tie you to memories of me . . .

IVY I don't want to wake up either. But . . . even if I do,
I'll come to you again next time I dream.

BLACKIE Oh, I'm afraid I'll never see you again!

IVY This is my forest, the forest that lives in my dream. I
dream the same dream all my life. I'll come back to
this old forest everyday.

BLACKIE But I don't dream. I live in a real forest. Things never
come back once I lose them. Please don't go!

IVY I'll try not to wake up then.

*[The two hold tightly on to the memories, embrace each other
and wind the long vine round their bodies.*
   The shadows of WOLVES on the backcloth. No howling.
   *ARROW dashes about anxiously and impatiently. Finally,
he starts to bark ferociously.]*

[startled] Oh!

*[The golden vine tied with her memories snaps. IVY wakes
up.]*

BLACKIE Ivy! Ivy! *[To ARROW, furious]* Who told you to bark?
Your first duty is to obey me, haven't I just told you?
You did it on purpose!

IVY Where am I? *[Catching sight of BLACKIE and the dog]*
How come I'm here with the two of you?

[ARROW slinks away to one side, hurt and aggrieved.]

[picks up the memories] What are these?

BLACKIE Oh, Ivy! My dear Ivy!

IVY Keep your hands off me! Who's your Ivy? My name is
Wu Mei. Oh, I know, I must have walked in my sleep
again. That's why I'm here.

BLACKIE You've been here a long time.

IVY I must have slept for a long time then. Did I dream?

BLACKIE Yes. Look, these are your memories, your thoughts,
your longings. I and the dog here are the man and the
dog in your dream.

IVY But that's a wolf!

BLACKIE You called him a wolf too in your dream. But he's a dog.

IVY Did I really? I can't remember now.

BLACKIE Try, try and see if you remember something, anything, from your dream.

IVY *[thinking]* No I can't. I can never even remember whether I dreamed or not, let alone what happened in my dream.

BLACKIE *[flicking at a knot on the vine with his finger]* Look, these are your thoughts, your memories. We've been running about in the forest, hand in hand. You held up a dandelion 'clock' before my face and blew at it to tickle me. I entered your thoughts and you entered my memory.

IVY *[looking intently]* Every time I wake up strange things like this happen, but I can never figure out how and why. Anyway, they occur so often I'm no longer amazed. *[Tears off a flower carelessly from the knotted vine]* I don't want these. I'll have others next time I dream.

BLACKIE *[heart-broken]* Oh! How can you do this to me!

[ARROW, sensing his master's agony, springs at IVY, barking fiercely. She flees, screaming for her life.]

IVY Help—! Help—!

BLACKIE *[in a sad voice]* Oh stop it! Arrow.

[ARROW stops chasing IVY, but still growls.]

IVY Kill it! It's a wolf! Kill it please!

BLACKIE Clear off, Arrow!

[ARROW goes grudgingly to one side, still growling.]

IVY I don't understand, why do you keep a wolf?

BLACKIE *[snaps at her]* It's a dog!

IVY A dog?

BLACKIE *[forcing back his anger]* I told you already . . . in your dream.

IVY It scared the life out of me! You ought to hang him.

[ARROW springs at IVY again, snarling.]

NARRATOR Hatred burst in me. Why should there be a white bitch with curly hair and a scent like dew drops and the naked earth? Why should both man and dog have memories, and dreams that are so much like memories? Oh, I want to hate, scream, kill, run wild, suffer, and offer my blood to the mountain, freely and without regrets!

BLACKIE Oh stop it, Arrow!

[ARROW is barking wildly.]

Arrow!

[BLACKIE snatches up a length of the broken vine and lashes at the ground with it, giving full vent to his grief and sorrow. ARROW mimes being whipped on another side of the stage, rolling about in pain.]

[lashing and crying] Hah—!

[A pack of WOLVES howl loudly in echo, Aooo.]

[even louder] Hah—!

[The WOLVES howl louder still, Aooo.]

IVY Look! They . . . the wolves . . . they're going to attack us!

BLACKIE *[lashing hard]* Didn't you say they were just playing?

IVY I never said anything like that!

[BLACKIE, crestfallen, throws down the vine and stares at IVY.]

I really can't remember having said anything like that.

BLACKIE *[glances at ARROW]* All right, go and kill the wolves now! I order you!

[ARROW looks at BLACKIE timidly. BLACKIE's every movement gives him a start.]

Why do you look at me like that? Why do you hang your tail so miserably? Why don't you bark now? You want to settle the score and do me in? Go! Get the wolves!

[The WOLVES are approaching.]

IVY Quick! Help! Help!

BLACKIE Ivy! Ivy! My Ivy!

[The WOLVES leap on to IVY, surrounding her completely, they strike, bite, and tear. When they disperse, only IVY's dress remains.

The WOLVES now encircle BLACKIE. At this, ARROW regains his courage and fights fiercely with the WOLVES.

The song rises again: I'm a wolfhound with sharp ears, I've lived long. . . .

Dog and WOLVES fight; soon the WOLVES begin to retreat.

ARROW looks at his master who has collapsed on the floor. Ignoring his own pain, he snuggles down under his master's head to let him rest on his own body. BLACKIE slowly wakes up, not aware that his head is resting on ARROW's body.]

Ivy! Ivy! Oh my Ivy! *[Catches sight of IVY's dress, holds it with both his hands]* Ivy!

[BLACKIE cries disconsolately, picks up the mementos and flowers scattered about on the ground, ties them back on the vine and ties her dress to the vine as well. Then he hangs up the vine and watches the dress flapping in the wind.
BLACKIE *is overcome with emotions. He turns round and sees* ARROW*, who is watching him quietly.]*

Did you drive them away?

[ARROW looks at him and remains motionless.]
You saved my life?

[ARROW continues to look at him, still motionless. BLACKIE *holds out his arms.]*

Oh, you're a good boy!

[ARROW, wincing with pain, totters up to BLACKIE *and lies quietly beside him.]*

I must have hurt you! *[Stroking him gently]* Here? Or here? It's here, I can see it *[Stroking him apologetically]* Come on, hit me. It's all my fault! *[Grabs* ARROW*'s paws]* Hit me again, and again. Oh! I've been such a fool!

NARRATOR I can see your eyes again, so closely, too. Ah, now your eyes see only me, your good boy, your faithful follower!

BLACKIE *[looking at* ARROW*'s eyes]* Let's start all over again! We'll match eyes, bend the tree, make a bow, kill the wolves, just like the old days. But Ivy said that we'd never wipe out the wolves. That the cats in this world would never wipe out the rats just as the wolves would never wipe out the sheep. But what can we do if we don't seek revenge? When hatred is no more, what can a man and his dog do? Oh, let's forget that dream, Arrow. It's someone else's dream—I just stumbled into it. Pity, it was a beautiful dream. Ah, I know, we can learn to dream. Come, Arrow, we'll close our eyes and dream together!

[BLACKIE lies down on ARROW's body, then they both close their eyes.]

NARRATOR *[in search of something]* Where is the dream? Up in the tree? Amongst the fallen leaves? Or hidden in the bushes? But there's only an abandoned bird's nest in the tree, it won't be big enough for a dream! And the fallen leaves are so light, they can't carry a dream! As for the bushes, I saw only a caterpillar when I passed them just now.

BLACKIE Arrow, are you still awake? . . . So am I. Those who
have let hatred grow in them will probably never be
able to dream. What shall we do if we don't dream?
Without hatred, without anything to do, without
dream, what . . . *[Leaps to his feet all of a sudden]* I've
got it now! You brought the wolves here! I'm sure you
did! They don't know this place. Your barking brought
them here. . . . You killed Ivy! If you could save me,
why couldn't you save her, too? What a fool I am to
say you're a good dog!

*[ARROW just looks at him quietly. BLACKIE returns his
stare, reminiscent of when they used to match eyes.]*

Maybe you're a wolf after all. Maybe when that bitch
was in labour years ago and the mountains were
trembling, the earth shaking, I made a mistake and
carried away a wolf. And since then I've simply taken
you for a dog, trained you like one, played with you
and grown close to you.

NARRATOR But I've fought and killed and eaten so many wolves!
Isn't that the best proof of my loyalty to you?

BLACKIE *[looking intently at* ARROW's *eyes again]* No, you never
wanted to do it: I forced you to. I had to force you to
do everything. Who knows what's really in your mind?
At first, it scared you; later on, you just got used to it.
It's not in your nature to eat wolves, it's a habit I've
trained in you.

[ARROW, greatly hurt, avoids BLACKIE's *eyes, slinks away
to one side, and listlessly paws the ground.* BLACKIE *stares at
him.]*

Oh, I don't know. Maybe you're a dog, just a dog, and
I think too much. In this old forest now, there is only
a man and a dog. As for Ivy, she's just a dream. Gone
now, leaving me a string of memories. Oh well, dog or
wolf, you're the same to me. We aren't doing too badly,
are we? Come, *[To* ARROW*]* let's match eyes.

[ARROW looks at BLACKIE *but does not move.]*

What else can we do? Kill the wolves? When I'm not
even sure whether you're dog or wolf? What if I get
this gigantic bow done and wipe out all those vicious
green eyes one night, only to be killed by you the next
day? Hah! That will be a story to go round the old
forest! A hunter spends all his life hunting wolves—in
the end, he finds that what he's been hunting are wild

dogs, and he's been living with a wolf all the time. How's that for a story, Arrow? Do you think I'm going to be that hunter in that story?! Like hell I will! Come, we'll match eyes.

[ARROW scratches and paws the ground listlessly, heart-broken. BLACKIE shouts at him.]

I said match eyes, do you hear me?

[ARROW still does not move. BLACKIE rushes at him, pulls him up and smacks him on the head.]

Match eyes!

[ARROW, forlorn and dejected, stares at BLACKIE.]

NARRATOR His eyes used to be the brightest stars in the dark sky . . . . But tonight, they have lost their lustre, their brilliance. They're an endless stretch of dark marshland. How can they regain their light? Master, I miss the old days, the forest of the old days and the hatred that used to sustain me. Yes, the hatred!

[ARROW is still staring at BLACKIE, but tears are now trickling down his eyes.]

BLACKIE You're crying, Arrow! This is the first time I've seen you cry. *[Flings his arms around ARROW, deeply moved]* You lost, Arrow. . . . I'll . . . I'll scratch your nose. *[Breaks into tears, too]*

[A gust of wind makes the windchimes tinkle. BLACKIE turns round to look at IVY's dress. He lets go of ARROW.]

Ivy! My Ivy is calling me! *[Facing the mountain]* Ivy! Ivy!

[All quiet again. BLACKIE returns to ARROW.]

Come. *[With determination]* We'll match eyes and not think about anything else.

[They match eyes. Suddenly, BLACKIE finds ARROW's eyes becoming a pair of wolf eyes. Equally suddenly, he sees ARROW's eyes again. This happens a few times.]

Damn it! Are you dog or wolf?

[ARROW, startled, goes timidly to one side.]

Maybe you really are a wolf. *[Holding his head in his hands]* Oh! Go, go away! I'll be digging my own grave if I let you stay. Sooner or later, you'll devour me. Go!

[ARROW does not move. BLACKIE hurls a stone at him. Then another stone, and another stone.

  Sound of stones rolling down a deep valley. It sounds as if the mountain was wailing, pleading.

ARROW *leaves reluctantly. Soon he turns again, and runs
towards* BLACKIE, *who hurls more stones at him. He stops,
unsure what to do. Finally he tears himself away.*
Sound of stones rolling down the deep valley.]

He's gone. I'm all alone, with a string of broken
thoughts that belong to someone else, and an old
forest. Oh well, let it be, I don't need anyone! When
you're with people, there are too many things you can't
do—you can't laugh when you want to, you can't cry
when you feel like it—so what's the point? Living with
a dog is just as bad. He doesn't talk. Even if you pour
out your soul, he just stares at you. And you never
know what he really thinks. He lets you do what you
like—beat him, kick him, rest your head on his body.
But maybe he is saying to himself, 'Just you wait!
Sooner or later I'll devour you.' Why live in danger?
It's best as it is. All alone by yourself, with a string of
memories and an old forest. If I want to talk to
someone, well, I can talk to the thoughts here.

[BLACKIE gently shakes the vine and the windchimes tinkle.]

They're talking to me. They're saying, look at the trees,
they're a bunch of drunken men dancing; look at the
moon, that's the ball we've been playing with. You
want to embrace and caress someone? There, *[Winds the
vine round his body]* it's embracing me, holding me
tight, whispering into my ears, 'There, there. Hold me
tight. Like this, forever.'

*[BLACKIE is lost in happiness. After a while, he unwinds the
vine, hangs it up, and sits down dejected.]*

Who will match eyes with me? Who? *[Loudly]* Who
will outstare me? *[His voice echoes.]* Who will outstare
me?

[Suddenly the stage flickers with WOLVES' eyes.]

Eh! *[Frightened]* Arrow! Arrow! Help me! *[WOLVES' eyes
disappear.]* I shouldn't have let him go! I brought him
here as a pup, rocked him in a cradle I made from a
rope, fed him and trained him. How could I have let
him go just like that? If he really is a dog, I should
have kept him. If he was a wolf, I shouldn't have let
him go either. I should have killed him, shot him with
this big bow that'll soon be ready. Yes, I should have
either kept him or killed him! What a fool I was! But
it's not too late. He won't have gone far. I could still

take him back, or get rid of him for good. But I must
make up my mind now. . . . *[Thinks, then makes up his
mind]* No, I don't want him back. He's so strong, so
fierce, he can kill a wolf in no time. Only he is
invincible in this old forest. I'm afraid of the wolves.
The wolves are afraid of him. But what is he afraid of?
Nothing! He's so strong he could make the wolves
obey him, make me obey him. Then why should he
take orders from me? But he has never disobeyed me.
He has always let me kick him, beat him. No, there is
something wrong with him. There must be a snag
somewhere. Dog or wolf, he is so much stronger than
me, so much more fearless, why would he accept me as
his master? No, he must be harbouring some evil
designs on me!

[WOLVES' eyes once again flicker on the stage.]

Here they come again . . . Maybe he's among them. *[He
goes behind a tree and picks up a huge bow.]* But I'm still
strong, still good for a fight. All right, Arrow, I'll use
this to match eyes with you!

*[Lights dim. A slide with images of bows is projected on to
the stage. ARROW is weaving his way with difficulty
through this forest of bows.*
    Sound of arrows swishing through the air.
    ARROW is surrounded by green flickering eyes.
    Sound of arrows swishing through the air.
    *The song rises again: I'm a wolfhound with sharp ears,
I've lived long . . . ARROW pushes his way through the bows
and springs at the green eyes. There is a fierce battle, and the
green eyes become fewer and fewer.]*

NARRATOR Wounded, I drag myself up to your hut. I yearn to let
you rest on my body once more, match eyes with you
once more. I know that the creepers and vines on the
old trees make merciless whips, but I long to come to
you, offer myself to you.

[Sound of arrows swishing through the air.
    *An arrow hits ARROW's front paw, pinning him to the
ground. ARROW, wincing with pain, tries to pull out the
arrow with his teeth, but fails.*
    Pairs of flickering green eyes are closing in on ARROW.
    *ARROW barks wildly, desperately. Finally he manages to
bite off his front paw. He writhes in pain.*
    Green eyes closing in on ARROW.

ARROW *springs at the green eyes and drives them away.
Then he turns round to look with longing towards the wings,
from where the arrows have come. Suddenly, he is hit in the
left eye by another arrow.* ARROW *gives an agonizing cry,
rolling and writhing. Finally, he snarls at the wings.*
NARRATOR'*s voice is overcome with rage]*

Woa! Woa! Woa!

*[Blackout. The auditorium rings with the sound of a dog
barking with grief, fury, and hatred.]*

SCENE FOUR

[A huge bow stands on the stage, just out of reach of where BLACKIE *sits.*

BLACKIE, *an old man now, sits like a statue inside an enormous net overgrown
with creepers, holding a long string of memories in his hands. His body is also
covered with creepers.*

A gust of wind sweeps through the forest. BLACKIE *remains motionless.*

Green eyes flicker everywhere. The WOLVES *are launching an attack on*
BLACKIE.

BLACKIE *struggles to reach the bow, but is held back by the net. He tries to
disentangle himself.]*

BLACKIE *[in an aged voice]* Damn these creepers! You are my real
enemy!

*[*BLACKIE'*s movements are much slower than before, and his
voice trembles.]*

My first enemy was a man who borrowed money from
me and beat me up. Then my enemies were the wolves.
They threw me into eternal loneliness. Later on,
somehow or other, my enemy became a dog. It brought
me grief and desolation. Now, my enemies are these
damn creepers, these green, unsightly, aggressive
monsters! But of all my enemies, I still hate the wolves
the most. I don't know why.

*[*BLACKIE *is worn out by the struggle with the creepers. He
looks up, watching the* WOLVES *in despair.]*

All right. You can come for your meal now. A bit late
though—I'm just a bag of old bones. What now? Put
off by these creepers? All right, I'll just try a bit
harder to free myself. But if I'm rid of these creepers,
I'll shoot you all with my bow and arrows. *[He really
has no more strength left to disentangle himself.]*

[The WOLVES *are about to attack when the sound of a dog barking desolately and with subdued anger rises in the distance.*

ARROW *enters, blinded in his left eye.*

The WOLVES *recede, howling, becoming pairs of green eyes. The green eyes weaken into dark flickering shadows.*

ARROW *limps towards* BLACKIE, *every step an effort. Then slowly and laboriously, he tears away the creepers entangling* BLACKIE.]

Aren't you that tawny wolfhound with sharp ears? I hardly recognize you. I thought you were dead. I remember two arrows hit you—one in your front paw, the other in one of your eyes. Well, I can see I wronged you. You won't bear a grudge, will you?

*[*ARROW *is still working to disentangle* BLACKIE. *Eventually* BLACKIE *staggers up to the bow.]*

I'm so glad you've come. Here, I'll let fly an arrow. When it hits a wolf in the eye, you go and eat it up. Today we'll exterminate the wolves, finish the job we wanted to do when we were young; we'll let loose all our hatred. There's no holding back now. Come.

*[*BLACKIE *is too old, he does not have the strength to draw the bowstring. He turns to* ARROW *in amazement.]*

Am I that old?

*[*ARROW *does not answer. He goes up to the bow, holds the bowstring with his teeth, tries to draw it for* BLACKIE. *But he does not have the strength either. Half-blind and limping, he, too, is weak and old.*

BLACKIE *looks at* ARROW. *He sees that they are both defeated.*

The dark shadows become flickering green eyes again. The eyes are pressing up on them.]

They're here. What shall we do? We're no match for them now. Oh well, let them come. At least we still have the strength to count their eyes. No matter who drops dead first, the two of us must count how many pairs of eyes there are. *[In an aged voice]* One, two, . . . five, six . . . seventy. Seventy pairs of eyes in all. Oh no, more like seventy-one. Let's do it again. One, two . . . Yes, seems like there are seventy-one pairs. No, we'll do it again. No, no, I haven't got it right. One, two, three . . .

NARRATOR We'll never get it right. Seventy or seventy-one. But they've grown in number, that's for sure. I remember when we were young, there were only thirty-seven pairs, and we couldn't have got it wrong in those days. Strange. How is it that we've grown so old? Too old to draw the bowstring, too old to count, too old for anything. And yet the wolves just grow in numbers, why? Why? Old as I am, I still don't understand!

[BLACKIE *is still counting, though his eyes are bleary and he can't see clearly.* ARROW *watches the* WOLVES *lazily, motionless. Green eyes flicker everywhere on the stage.*]

In his life my master has directed his hatred at many different enemies. I have not. I've only known one enemy. Ever since my master taught me to hate the wolves, I treated them as my enemy. But perhaps it's time I changed that. Perhaps my real enemy is the mountain, the beautiful feminine mountain. It has suckled me and Blackie, it has suckled the wolves, too, and the creepers. With its rich plump breasts it has given feed to me, to us, to all the enemies we may come to hate. . . .

[*Sounds of hurricane, earthquake, landslide, and of mud and rock crashing down from the mountain. Lights fade out.*]

THE END

BIRDMEN

A DRAMA IN THREE ACTS

1993

By
GUO SHIXING

Translated by
JANE C. C. LAI

— ABOUT **THE PLAYWRIGHT** —

GUO SHIXING (1952–) was born into a middle-class family—his grandfather was a grandmaster at chess and his parents worked in a bank. He had just completed his primary schooling when the Cultural Revolution broke out, but the political upheavals did little to deter his interest in literature. When the Red Guards dispersed the library holding in the city where he lived, he managed to salvage copies of translations of famous classics by such authors as Tolstoy, Turgenev, Dostoyevsky, Gogol, Balzac, and Stendhal, and his avid reading of these works more than made up for his lack of formal education. He was assigned to work in the fields in Heilongjiang Province in the far north. Later on, he worked as a technician before being transferred back to Beijing, where he was assigned a job at the *Beijing Evening News*, as a reporter on the arts, especially on drama. From 1980 to 1993, he attended more than a thousand drama performances, and interviewed over a hundred writers, playwrights, directors, actors, and other theatre personalities. He reads extensively, and is much influenced by Zen Buddhism, and by the dramatist Friedrich Dürrenmatt. His knowledge of and his passion for drama prompted Lin Zhaohua (director of *Uncle Doggie's Nirvana* and of Gao Xingjian's controversial plays, *Absolute Signal* and *Wild Man*, in the 1980s) to encourage him to turn to playwriting. *Birdmen* was his first effort. When it was staged in 1993 by the Beijing People's Art Theatre, it was a roaring success and attracted much international media attention. It has seen over a hundred performances in China, and fifteen performances in Taiwan. *Birdmen* is the first of a trilogy on what Guo calls the 'idlers' on the Mainland. The other two are *Anglers* and *Chessmen*.

Guo now works full time as Resident Dramatist at the Central Experimental Modern Drama Troupe in Beijing.

ABOUT **THE PLAY**

Bird-fanciers, as many people may know, are strange creatures: demanding animal trainers, boastful collectors, and heartless slave-masters all rolled into one. They speak a language of their own and practise a rigid code of behaviour that often strikes an outsider as fussy, pedantic, patronizing, inflexible, and somewhat bizarre. Certainly this is how the group of bird-fanciers in this play impress their observers—in particular an overseas Chinese psychiatrist who has a pat Freudian explanation for everyone's foibles except his own.

The play is replete with puns, witty repartee, and verbal and psychological one-upmanship, and features amusing caricatures of familiar urban types. It belongs to the tradition of 'slice-of-life' drama that has brought international fame to dramatic works from mainland China. It differs, however, from such works (Lao She's *Teahouse* being the most memorable example) in two important aspects. It does not rely simply on the racy Beijing dialect and the use of topical wit for its linguistic effect. The playwright is equally inventive in the use of bird-fanciers' jargon, psycho-babble, and the highly-mannered language of traditional Peking Opera. The result of this medley of styles, registers, and diction is an extravaganza of linguistic fireworks that brings new vitality to this popular genre.

More importantly, *Birdmen* does not present the usual critique of the pre-Liberation 'old society'. Instead, it offers a delightful range of reading possibilities. The birdmen's chatter is loaded with political overtones, and the play can be read as a clever lampoon of gerontocracy in China. Scholars in cultural studies will, depending on their theoretical positions, regard the play either as a hilarious/tongue-in-cheek or sobering/cynical study of what happens when two cultures meet, and clash. Others may simply enjoy the play as an amusing social comedy, or an outrageous parody of the game called psychotherapy. And, to keep the authorities happy, the play can also be read as a rebuttal of the influence of Western 'bourgeois liberalism' on the Chinese people—a triumphant assertion of their belief in doing things their own way, with Chinese characteristics.

DRAMATIS PERSONAE

SUN, a company manager, in his 40s

'FATS', male, from Tianjin, about 40, amateur Peking opera singer

XIAO XIA, a maid from Anhui Province, aged 18

'LARKMAN' ZHANG, male, in his 70s, bird-fancier

PAUL DING, male, psychoanalyst, in his 40s

'GRANDMASTER', in his 60s, bird-fancier, Peking opera singer, used
    to sing 'Painted Mask' (*hualian*) parts

DR CHEN, ornithologist, in his 40s

CHARLIE, Observer from International Council for Bird Preservation,
    in his 30s

LUO MAN, guide and colleague of CHARLIE's, in her 20s

GUARD, in his 20s, a factory worker, a prankster

HUANG MAO, aged 20, a farm lad from Anhui Province

HUANG DAN, male, a factory worker, bird-fancier

MA, male, disabled, bird-fancier

XI, male, bird-fancier, 'private enterprise' trader

ZHU, bird-fancier, a cadre

Bird-fanciers

Workers

Sellers of birds, birdseed, cages, etc.

Guards

Peking Opera musicians

ACT *1*

[*For performance in a small theatre in-the-round: As the audience enter the auditorium, they see workmen putting the finishing touches to a huge bird cage, large enough to encase the acting area and the surrounding auditorium seating.*

For performance on a proscenium stage: The effect of a stage encased in a cage can be created at the back of the stage.

As the house lights dim, lights go up stage centre. The workmen are gone, leaving an unfinished cage. Bird-fanciers, sellers of birds and cages enter in twos and threes. The place soon becomes a bustling bird market. Birdsongs and bird calls of larks, thrushes and other birds fill the air.

Centre stage stands a round stone table with stone seats around it. A few men have put down their lark cages on the table and are seated around it. As they listen to their birds chirp or sing, they glance now and then expectantly in one direction. Sellers of birds, of cages, of bird-feed, insects and spiders, position themselves around the edge of the acting area. The ground is dotted with trees and bushes. Bird cages hang on the branches of some. Bird-fanciers wander among the vendor stalls, some striking a bargain, others chatting. This is a world of leisure. A middle-aged man, SUN, kicks at a small tree rhythmically. A fat man, FATS, carrying a lark cage walks up to him.]

FATS Excuse me. Move over. [*Reaches up to hang his cage*]

SUN There's plenty of room. Must you hang it here?

FATS What are you doing here?

SUN Exercising.

FATS Exercising? Go over there. This is the bird corner.

SUN I was here first.

FATS Going by seniority, are we? This is not a promotion exercise. Have you got permission from the Forestry Department to kick that tree?

SUN I *am* the Forestry Department.

FATS When you've kicked it to death—make sure it's dead— why don't you get in touch with me, eh?

SUN You're—?

FATS I sell timber. We're a bit short on supply.

[*The two shake hands, and introduce themselves. SUN looks pleased.*]

SUN And I thought we were heading for a fight. You've got style.

FATS All bird-fanciers have style. He never fights who carries a cage. You know why? We don't want to startle the birds. They cost hundreds. Can't afford to lose our tempers, can we?

SUN Keeping a bird can really help you to mellow?

FATS Try it. Get a bird that's easy to care for, that sings—

SUN I've never kept one before. Don't know how to. And I don't have time.

FATS Keep a yellow siskin then. You don't have to train it. Just feed it a few seeds and some catkins, that's all. Easy.

SUN But what if the family objects?

FATS The Government has set aside a Bird Week. How can you observe it if you don't keep a bird? You should support the Government's plans. Go and pick one for yourself.

[*SUN hesitates and exits.* FATS *takes his cage and goes to the stone table.*

  A girl in red is standing near the stone table. She is XIAO XIA, *a maid from Anhui Province looking for work.*]

XIA Could anybody use a housemaid? I can do the laundry, cook, and look after babies.

[*The larks in the cage are startled and flap around nervously. The bird-fanciers glare at her.*]

ZHANG Keep away!

XIA [*aggrieved*] Did I do something wrong?

FATS [*conciliatorily*] Larks don't like anything red, my girl. If you startle them, you can't afford to pay for the damage.

[XIA *wipes away a tear and wanders off to a corner.*

  DR CHEN, *the ornithologist, enters. He eyes the cages sharply as if looking for something. He squeezes his way to the edge of the stone table.*]

ZHANG Mind your birds all!

[*The bird-fanciers turn round to stare at* DR CHEN.]

DAN What are you doing?

CHEN Just listening, all right?

ZHANG Who knows what you've brought with you? All you need is to bring a toad that croaks, and it'd ruin all our larks.

CHEN Why would I carry a toad?

ZHANG All right, all right. He's been milling around here for days and hasn't done any harm. He's a beginner. Let him stay.

[FATS' *thrush suddenly calls out loudly.*]

ZHANG [*to* FATS] Hey! Thrushes over to that side.

FATS *[puzzled]* What? Aren't I allowed here?

ZHANG You're from Tianjin, aren't you? Here in Beijing, our larks mustn't sing thrushsong.

FATS Not sing thrushsong! Then it's an incomplete repertoire! You can't call your bird a lark!

ZHANG Well, your Tianjin larks have to sing thrushsong. Not ours in Beijing. Our 'Repertoire of Thirteen' doesn't include thrushsong. The gentlemen here all keep 'repertoire larks'. You will excuse us.

FATS What 'Repertoire of Thirteen'?

ZHU He doesn't even know about the Thirteen. Calls himself a bird-fancier!

FATS Go easy there, will you? Customs vary with places. Not all rules apply. Why don't you tell me about your rules, I may learn something.

ZHU Can do. But first I'll ask you a couple of questions, to see if you know anything. If you can answer them, we'll tell you the rules, if you can't—

FATS Move over.

XI I'll ask the first question. Why do you line a lark cage with sand?

FATS That's a question? The lark's natural home is in the sand. Born and bred in sandy land. Never can survive far from sand. East, west, home's best. Life may be great abroad, but I'm happy with my lot. Love my humble cottage too much to find another spot.

MA *[to XI]* Go on. Why ask kindergarten questions? Listen. Answer if you can. Why build a pedestal in a lark cage?

FATS Larks can't get a firm grip on a perch. They're born to walk on sand. Where would you find a tree to perch on in the desert? It's not like us people, always trying to climb up and up. So you give a lark a pedestal, put it on a stage to perform.

ZHANG Don't treat him like a beginner. Let's ask him a tough one. What's the worst thing that can happen to a lark?

FATS When he won't get on the pedestal, but sings offstage.

DAN So he sings offstage. What's wrong with that?

FATS If he sings offstage, he is a mere amateur! Only when you sing on stage can you be a star!

CHEN I've been an ornithologist for years, but I never realized how cruel and merciless you can be in dreaming up ways to torment the poor creatures! You bird torturers.

Call yourselves bird lovers! Do you think these creatures of freedom that fly in the sky would willingly submit to your torments?

DAN We let you stay, we didn't ask you to criticize. Who is tormenting the birds? Huh? Look at this little bowl here. Fine Jingdezhen blue and white bone china, painted with five blessed children offering the peach of longevity. And inside? Millet mixed with egg yolk. In its desert days it would never dream of such food and service. Really!

CHEN Come on. That's going too far the other way. When we studied overseas, we lived only on instant noodles—

ZHANG Going too far? Larks don't eat well at all. Bluethroats eat meat, you know. The best lamb chops, with all the gristle removed. Then, the meat is sliced and chopped into a fine purée, so no strands of meat will tangle up their tongues and ruin their voices.

CHEN But food like that should be for people.

ZHANG For people? If I give you the food, can you sing the 'Repertoire of Thirteen' for me? You do the bird a favour, then he does you a good turn. That's the way it goes! By the way, what do you do?

CHEN I'm an ornithologist. A bird specialist.

ZHANG That's news. A bird specialist not knowing what you feed birds.

CHEN I don't keep birds.

FATS What kind of specialist are you if you don't even keep birds?

CHEN I study birds. Their history, habitat, ecology . . . You wouldn't understand.

FATS I know. You watch wild birds. Go to the forest. This is a bird market! *[To his friends]* I've answered your questions. Now tell me about the 'Repertoire of Thirteen', won't you?

CHEN What Thirteen?

FATS I'll tell you. Larks are smart. They can imitate thirteen different calls. That's the 'Repertoire of Thirteen'.

CHEN Thirteen is an unlucky number!

FATS That's for foreigners. I was chef in an embassy once, so I know. Twelve foreigners gather for dinner, and one more turns up. What do you think the twelve do?

DAN Get up and go.

FATS No way. The twelve have ordered the food. If they up
and go, they leave all the food for the one man!
Foreigners are no more fools than you or me. The
twelve gang up and drive the man away. And do you
know why? Because their Jesus had a meal with
thirteen at table, and then he was taken away.
Foreigners are scared of thirteen. We're not. Thirteen is
a good number. Thirteen-Herbs Potion, thirteen
unrelated cards at mahjong—

MA We're on to mahjong, are we?

CHEN But how do you limit its repertoire to thirteen? No
more? No less?

XIA Will anyone hire a housemaid? Do the laundry, and
look after the baby?

[PAUL DING enters.]

DING Can you manage nursing?

XIA I don't know how.

DING You'll manage, I'm sure. Come on. Let's take a look
over there.

XIA No. They said I'm in red, and that scares the birds.

DING They have a point. Come, put this on. *[He takes off his
own tracksuit top and puts it on her.]* That should do.

XIA *[pulling on the jacket]* It's too big. Is it Addi-
something?

DING Adidas! You know about that too?

XIA My cousin said if someone gave me a tracksuit, I
should insist on Adidas.

DING This is Pacino. A good brand. Just as good.

XIA Thank you, sir.

DING What did you say just now? Do the laundry, cook, and
look after the baby?

XIA Yes. I can do all that.

DING Can you feed birds as well?

XIA Yes.

DING Say it all out loud!

XIA Do the laundry, cook, look after babies *and birds.*

DAN *[to XIA]* Come over here. This is excellent! It's the first
time I've heard of help with looking after birds!

XIA *[to DING]* You're really something. You read them like
a book!

DING Yes. I mean to study them. They're going to be my
patients. When I've set up the clinic, I'll take them all
in, and you shall be the head nurse.

XIA Good. It's always good to have a head.

[XIA *pulls* DING *along with her to the stone table.*]

ZHANG The girl looks familiar.

FATS Isn't she the girl in red? Now she's dressed to play a male lead! Anyway, tell me more about the Thirteen.

ZHANG [*indicates* DING] And who's this?

DING I'm just watching.

ZHANG That's strange! Why is the whole world here today?

ZHU [*to* DING] You haven't brought anything you shouldn't, have you?

DING What do you mean?

DAN Things like toads, cicadas, chirpers.

DING What are those?

XI Things that make a noise. If they croak or chirp and the larks imitate them, that ruins the birds and you can't keep them anymore.

DING I don't own anything like that, let alone bring it here.

FATS [*disdainfully*] Overseas Chinese. They would have searched him at the Customs. Now the Thirteen. I've waited longer for this than for the grand ending of the opera *Lianhuantao*.

ZHANG Who goes to the opera these days? Sure, a few people can sing a little, but how many are really good? If you were to pay good money to listen to them, they would die of joy. As to the Thirteen, there's just this one bird here that can do it! [*To* ZHU] You, tell him.

ZHU Allow me! [*Clears his voice*] They are: The home bird rousing the woods, magpie landing in the woods, the marsh tit hopping across boughs, the baby swallow returning to nest, the kitten playing with its dame, the sparrow-hawk circling, the bluethroat pining for home—I can't remember the rest.

FATS [*engrossed*] Oh, you don't have 'the water cart running over the dog'—'*zhizhiqiuqiu-de-wangwang*'?

ZHANG That is only for the 'clear voice larks' from south Beijing. 'Pure voice larks' from north Beijing aren't allowed to do that, or they'd be labelled 'foul mouth'. There are lots of fine distinctions. The Thirteen have to be sung in the proper sequence. Mix them up and you're called 'dead mouth'. Even in the magpie song, 'over the woods' is different from 'landing in the woods'. 'Over the woods' is '*ga-er—ga-er ga-er*'; but 'landing' is '*ga-er—jijijijiji, ga-er—jijijijiji*'.

CHEN This is an important revelation. *[Takes out a small notebook and makes notes]*

XIA They're crazy!

DING These people will be our patients. I call them 'birdmen'. These birdmen feel only for the birds, they have little feeling for human beings; and if they have any, it usually manifests itself as antagonism.

XIA How do they get to be like this?

DING It's very complicated. Have you heard of psychoanalysis?

XIA You mean like schizophrenia?

DING No, no. That's different. There you're talking about madness. But many people who appear quite normal, not mad, suffer from psychological problems. Psychoanalysis is a way to cure such problems. Through psychoanalysis we get to know why people are the way they are, and so help to change them and make them nicer people.

XIA Are you some sort of doctor?

DING I'm Paul Ding, a psychoanalyst. What's your name?

XIA Xiao Xia.

DING Ah. Xiao Xia. I've come back from America with all that I've learnt to save the countless victims of mental problems in China.

XIA Where is your hospital?

DING I'll set up a tent here. I won't call it a hospital. Don't want to scare off my patients, you see. I'll call it 'Birdmen Mental Rehabilitation Centre'. What do you think?

XIA What do I know! I can only do the laundry, cook, look after babies . . . and birds.

DING That will do.

XIA What about salary?

DING Two hundred yuan a month.

XIA So much? Done!

DING Good. Now you should join me in observing these birdmen, pick the classic cases and persuade them to come to the centre.

[The two merge into the crowd.]

ZHANG And now! *[Gets ready to uncover his cage]*

[All the BIRDMEN *put their cages under the table, leaving only* ZHANG's *cage on the table.]*

ZHANG Wait a minute—

FATS What now?

ZHANG What about your thrush?

FATS I can't very well kill it!

ZHANG Watch it then. Don't let it chime in. If it so much as squeaks—let me warn you, you won't have to kill it—I'll flatten it for you!

FATS This should do it. *[Takes up from the table a water-jug for feeding birds, takes a mouthful of water, uncovers his cage, sprays the bird with the water from his mouth and covers the cage again]*

ZHANG Fine. That's the proper thing to do. Now—

[ZHANG uncovers his cage, takes up a fine bamboo stick, and waves it like a conductor's baton. His lark begins to sing.]

[GRANDMASTER enters. He is in his 60s and dressed in a Mao jacket and matching trousers, very spruce and sprightly. He carries a bird perch on which sits a marsh tit, known to bird-fanciers as hongzi.*]*

FATS *[listens to the bird sing a series of calls, and murmurs the name of each call in identification]* Home bird rousing the woods. Magpie. *Hongzi.* Hens scrambling for feed. Swallow. Kitten. Big Magpie. Sparrow-hawk circling. Hey, why has it stopped?

ZHANG That's the first half. You get an intermission even at the opera, don't you?

FATS What's in the second half?

ZHANG The bluethroat's trill, flight from the reeds, the siskin's song, mating call of the shrike.

GRANDMASTER That first set is not impressive. Your bird lacks sophistication of melody.

BIRDMEN *[suddenly aware of GRANDMASTER's arrival]* Grandmaster! *[They bow to him.]*

GRANDMASTER Too kind! Too kind!

ZHANG Grandmaster! It's far from perfect. Nobody has a *hongzi* as good as yours. What bird can match it? Oh, you haven't brought that one along? We're all waiting to hear it practise.

GRANDMASTER This one is not bad. He sings even when tied to the perch.

ZHANG Right. I'll cover mine up.

GRANDMASTER Not doing the second half?

ZHANG No. Grandmaster, let's not lose time. We've been waiting for you all morning. *[Covers his cage and puts it under the table]*

GRANDMASTER *[studies the bird on his perch]* Don't underestimate this
    young lad. *[Sits down and gestures to the others to sit]* Sit,
    sit, sit. He has a good voice. He is a southern *hongzi*.

CHEN *[studies* GRANDMASTER's *bird]* A marsh tit. Insect-
    catcher, protects crops.

GRANDMASTER *[glances disdainfully at* CHEN*]* And why do we call him
    a southern *hongzi*? To answer that we need to know
    about the eastern *hongzi*.

BIRDMEN Yes, yes.

GRANDMASTER The eastern *hongzi* comes from Shandong Province. It
    has no melody, no tunes.

CHEN *[writing in his notebook]* Tunes?

GRANDMASTER There is a lot to learn. Pitch, timbre, energy,
    projection, grace notes. All have to do with tune and
    melody.

CHEN I'm not getting all of this.

GRANDMASTER How does the eastern *hongzi* differ from the southern?
    The eastern *hongzi*'s voice is crisp, but low. The
    southern red's voice trails, but is feminine, alluring: '*xi-
    xi——gun-er, xi-xi——gun-er*'. They come from Henan.
    Why are they so good? The quality of the land and the
    water has a lot to do with the creatures that live there.
    Anybody can tell that Henan opera far excels Shandong
    opera. Why? The south is better than the east.

DING *[to* XIA, *pointing at* GRANDMASTER*]* He can be their
    group leader.

XIA He is handsome. I like handsome old men!

DING Mind you, no emotional entanglements with the
    patients. Go on. Do as we planned.

    *[*XIA *exits.* SUN *enters carrying a cage. He pulls* FATS *from
    the group.]*

SUN Look, I bought one.

FATS A canary?

SUN Lovely colour!

FATS *[somewhat exasperated]* This is a canary! What serious
    fancier would keep a canary?

SUN But it looks so lovely.

CHEN The canary. Discovered by the Spaniards in the
    fourteenth century on the Canary Islands north-west of
    Africa. They named the bird after the islands. Hence,
    Canary. *Serinus Canarius*. Once much prized at European
    courts. Quite a lot of sub-species bred now in Germany,
    Japan, and America. Some mixed breed sub-species in

China, mainly in Shandong and Yangzhou. I favour keeping canaries. They can be bred artificially, so their natural numbers in the ecosystem won't be affected.

FATS This bird has no language. It just gurgles. Real fanciers keep clear of them. A canary's call makes a lark 'foul mouthed'. Don't you let the lark people hear it, or they'll—

GRANDMASTER *[goes on regardless]* Those from south of Xingtai can be called southern. Where does this one come from? Where the famous general Lin Xiangru turned his chariot round.

ZHANG That makes it Handan? Hebei Province, south of Xingtai.

GRANDMASTER Aye. Larks from around here don't sing '*qiuqiu-er*'. But that doesn't mean that *hongzi* are necessarily better the further south you go. They're bringing Anhui *hongzi* into Beijing these days, so you've got to be careful. By the time they start selling Vietnam *hongzi* in Beijing, you might as well give up. They get everything wrong.

ZHANG *[indicating* GRANDMASTER's *bird]* Isn't he ready for the cage yet?

GRANDMASTER This lad is all right as far as speech goes. No bad habits. But of the five faults in movement habits, 'flap, shiver, roll, peck, and somersault', he's got three. I have to chain him. How else can I train him?

ZHANG The expert hand, eh? Ready?

GRANDMASTER Go. *[Points at the bird on the perch]*

[The bird sings pleasantly: 'xi—xiguner, xi—xiguner. Xi— xi'.]

BIRDMEN Ah, wonderful!

[A green-eyed, blond foreigner enters with a Chinese woman. The foreigner is CHARLIE. *The woman is his guide and colleague,* LUO MAN.]*

CHARLIE *[to* LUO*]* What bird has he got there?

LUO *[to* FATS*]* What bird is that?

FATS A *hongzi.*

LUO A *hongzi.*

CHARLIE *[with a strong foreign accent]* A *hongzi*? *[Shakes his head]*

CHEN It's a marsh tit.

LUO *Parus major.*

CHEN No, that's a Great Tit. The proper scientific name is *Parus palustris.*

FATS Do foreigners keep *hongzi* too?

LUO This is Mr Charlie, an official Observer from the International Council for Bird Preservation. He's here especially to observe our country's progress with the preservation of birds.

CHARLIE Why does he chain the bird?

FATS I know how to talk to him—*[Imitates* CHARLIE's *accent]* No chain, fly away.

CHARLIE *[wondering]* Why do some use cages, and others chain the birds? It's cruel. Terrible!

FATS No, its good! That's a silver chain. Made by a jeweller. It costs almost a hundred yuan.

CHARLIE What if the bird gets its neck tangled up in the chain?

FATS On this chain, there are thirteen links that turn freely on pivots. Guaranteed safe.

CHARLIE Won't the chain strangle it? What if the bird drops off the perch and there is no one around to help it?

FATS No one around! Anything can happen in China except that. There are always people around. Grandmaster is out all day holding up the perch.

CHARLIE *[amazed]* All day? Doesn't he do anything else? Doesn't he work for a living?

FATS You don't understand. If he didn't have his perch to hold on to, what would he live for?

CHARLIE I mean, if he doesn't work, what does he live on?

FATS Does it matter what a man lives on? It's the bird that matters. You've got to treat it properly. Besides his work is special, he can go to work with his birds.

CHARLIE He works in a zoo?

ZHANG Better than that. In an opera troupe.
Our Grandmaster sings. Does nothing else.

CHARLIE Does he put on performances?

GRANDMASTER I don't, and nobody else does.

CHARLIE What do you mean?

FATS Nowadays, if you put on a performance, you lose money. You put on more performances, you lose more money; you put on fewer, you save money.

CHARLIE But why?

FATS Nobody goes to the opera.

CHARLIE Why?

FATS Why? You foreigners have mucked it up for us! Last year a fat guy came, fatter than I am. What's his name? With a beard. Ah, Papa Lorry!

LUO Pavarotti!

FATS That's him! Ten yuan a ticket. The People's Hall was full, all ten thousand seats sold! And it went on for days! Who'd go to the Chinese opera! And the venerable Yuan Shihai was selling for only two yuan a ticket!

CHARLIE *[shrugs]* You haven't answered my question. Why do you chain the marsh tit?

FATS Not a tit, a *hongzi*.

GRANDMASTER *[seeking consent from the group]* Shall we let a foreigner in on our professional secrets?

ZHANG Sure, tell him. He won't know what to do with the information. Besides, even if he could find a *hongzi* in his country, it would probably say '*qiuqiu*' and nothing else.

GRANDMASTER *[holds up his fists together in front of him in a gesture of polite salute to* CHARLIE*]* Sir! There are ten things a *hongzi* mustn't do. First, enunciation. He mustn't say '*qiuqiu*', he should say '*xixi*'. He can say '*xi-xi-gun-er*', or '*xi-xi-hong-er*', but not just '*xi-xi*'. He mustn't ever say '*hu-hu*'. He mustn't recap, and he mustn't slur.

*[*CHARLIE *is bewildered.]*

Recapping is repeating a syllable. For instance, for '*xi-xi-gun-er*', he says '*xi-xi-xi-gun-er*', that's recapping. It won't do. And what is slurring? It's leaving out a syllable, like instead of '*xi-xi-gun-er*', he says '*xi-gun-er, xi-gun-er*'. These are grave mistakes.

LUO Why, that happens when you're fluent in English. It's called elision. Necessary economy of effort.

GRANDMASTER Yes, I know. You can add a syllable too, in any language. It's called stuttering. Only it is not allowed in a good songbird, nor in Peking opera. Enunciation is vital in opera, and in birdsong as well.

CHARLIE You still haven't answered my question.

GRANDMASTER What I said just now has to do with language. Now for faults in movement. These are: flapping, shivering, rolling about, pecking at tail-feathers or the cage, and somersaulting. The first two are symptoms of sickness.

CHEN Deficiency in Vitamin D and B1.

GRANDMASTER The last three are just temper. The chain is corrective treatment for bad temper.

CHARLIE But why?

GRANDMASTER When we perform on stage, there is a correct form for every movement and gesture, for standing, for sitting down. Any deviation has to be corrected. You can't do just as you please. In China, there's a rule for everything.

FATS Please don't get the wrong impression. What he says applies only to what is done here in Beijing. These rules came from inside the palace.

CHARLIE The palace?

FATS Yeah. Where the emperors lived. They made lots of rules and were most particular. Not only about birds, but about opera too. Peking Opera has so many rules, so many restrictions. But outside the capital, in Shanghai and other provinces, anything goes. In Peking Opera, generals with full armour are not allowed to do somersaults. But in Tianjin, we have them stand on three tables stacked high, and jump off in a backward somersault. Shanghai opera too, has acrobatics. You're welcome to come to Tianjin and visit our bird market. Our lark cages are not as small as here, but tall as a man. And the larks fly up and down as they sing. *[Imitates a Tianjin lark]* And you put a cage at each end of a pole and you carry them everywhere with you. Beautiful!

CHARLIE All this is a bit confusing.

[LUO nods in agreement. DING *and* CHEN *shake hands and exchange greetings.]*

CHEN I'm Chen Daozhong, ornithologist.

DING Paul Ding, psychoanalyst.

CHEN You don't sound like a Mainlander.

DING I was born overseas. I've come back to serve my country. A psychoanalyst, or psychiatrist, has a future only in his own country.

CHEN Shall we go over there? *[Indicates direction]*

DING Are you working on a project?

CHEN I'm looking for a bird.

DING What bird?

CHEN *[whispers in* DING's *ear]* Do you know, there is only one such bird left in China. It's rumoured that it has been captured and smuggled into Beijing for the bird market. As soon as it shows up, I can take custody.

DING Custody of what? Man, or bird?

CHEN The bird, naturally. The man—well, he can't get away either.

DING I wish you success. As for me, I'm glad I've found my niche, a place that really needs me. As I said, a distinguished psychiatrist can only do his best work in his own country.

CHEN You mean—

DING These birdmen must have had early memory imprints. The fact that so many of them want to spend their lives with birds is a reflection of the subconscious problems embedded in the deep structure of the psychology of our entire race. If I can make a breakthrough, it would save not just a few bird-fanciers, but this race of people with its long and glorious history.

CHEN Is it that important?

DING It is not easy to understand the commitments of other people's professions. I'll treat my patients for free. I'll use my assets overseas to set up a Birdmen Mental Rehabilitation Centre.

[The hongzi *keeps singing pleasantly.*
    A few workmen enter, and continue to build the big cage.
    A workman enters carrying a board with black lettering on a white background. He hangs the board on a tree. It reads: 'Birdmen Mental Rehabilitation Centre'.
    XIA enters with a man wearing a 'Security Guard' armband. They begin to disperse the people assembled on stage.]

GUARD Go on! Get a move on!

FATS What do you mean?

XIA This place is now a hospital. See, it says so here.

GRANDMASTER *[reads the board]* Birdmen Mental Rehabilitation Centre. Rather insulting, isn't it? Who are they calling 'birdmen'?

GUARD Don't talk rot. Birdmen can stay here in hospital with their birds. If you're not a birdman, scram!

FATS Do you take patients with fatty liver?

[DING jumps on to the stone table, and claps his hands for attention. BIRDMEN are outraged and clutch their cages protectively.]

XIA The world-famous psychoanalyst Mr Paul Ding will talk to us.

DING Friends. Psychoanalysis has a history of over seventy years in the West. But here, on the Mainland, it is virtually unknown. What is psychoanalysis? It is a treatment that, through talking and chatting, will help you to understand your past, relieve your mental burdens, so that you can live a normal life.

GRANDMASTER They've known about chatting for only seventy years? That's rather backward.

DING The establishment of the centre here is a result of my observations over the last few months. Birdmen reflect a bird culture. And the subconscious activities of this bird culture provide ample ground for psychoanalysis. Initially we'll invite six patients to stay in the hospital. Actually it's not really hospitalization, more like staying together, chatting and keeping birds, and relaxing.

FATS Can one claim expenses? Our unit would not reimburse us for treatment at the Sino-Japanese Hospital.

DING There is no charge. It's free.

ZHANG Still. I won't go.

GUARD I repeat. This piece of land has been assigned to a joint venture. From now on, only those hospitalized can come here and play with their birds. Non-patients are not allowed. Sorry. Please go away.

GRANDMASTER Doesn't that make it concession territory?*

DING The centre offers not only free treatment, board, and lodging, it offers assistance with keeping birds.

DAN This is too good to be true. Count me in. What have I got to lose? Can't be worse than the 731 Bacteriological Unit the Japanese set up during the war, can it?

DING As I said, This is only the beginning of psychoanalytic treatment here. We can only take six patients in the first round. *[Points at DAN]* You are the first to apply. Accepted. Now we take into consideration self-recommendation and our research finding to enrol others. Miss Xia, please help with the registration. *[Jumps off the table, opens a file, takes out a pen and puts these on the table]* Please refer to the list we made.

[XIA sits on a stone stool ceremoniously.]

XIA Line up, Line up. Don't push. Please have your identification ready. When I call your name, come and register. If you don't hear your name—goodbye! Ready? Larkman Zhang.

* In the late Qing dynasty, in treaties signed with Western countries after military defeat, the Chinese government agreed to set aside sections of cities such as Shanghai as territories under the rule of Western powers.

ZHANG Show a bit of respect. Say 'Mister Zhang'.

XIA Well, we've picked you.

ZHANG I'll have none of your fancy tricks. The Americans built the Xiehe Hospital with the Indemnity money we paid them in 1900 after the Boxer Rebellion. No doubt you'll think that was nice. But they gave this Dong chap an X-ray for free, and they X-rayed him to death. Broke his head as well. I'd rather die in the bird-market and not do you weirdos a favour.

XIA There's no need to be insulting.

GUARD *[grabs hold of ZHANG]* Trouble-maker? What's the name of your unit?

ZHANG Oh? You want to report me to my unit? You'll need an appointment.

GUARD Well, which unit?

ZHANG The crematorium. Go there and tell them.

GUARD Damned fool! Your smart answers won't get you anywhere!

GRANDMASTER I see. If one doesn't sign up, one can't come here with one's birds.

GUARD Right.

GRANDMASTER Is one free to do what one likes?

DING Within the law. Anything.

GRANDMASTER You don't want to make money?

DING We subsidize the whole thing.

GRANDMASTER If you used your subsidy to revive Peking Opera, that would be something.

DING Then you'd have to revive Shanghai Opera, Shaoxing Opera. There are so many of them. Which one could you help? If we revive our spirits, then there is hope.

XIA *[writing down his name]* Grand-mas-ter.

GRANDMASTER All right, I'll see what it's about. Sign me on.

FATS Is my name there?

DING We'll consider you for the next round.

FATS I've got to be with him. *[Pointing at GRANDMASTER]* You don't understand. I worship him. Besides, since Mr Zhang won't come, I can take his place, can't I?

DING All right.

FATS Thank you, sir. This is great. I'll learn to sing opera in the hospital.

DING *[pointing at CHEN]* We've accepted you too.

CHEN You must be joking! There's nothing wrong with me.

DING Impossible! You've got problems.

CHEN I know about your psychoanalytic methods. I've read Freud.

DING You know too that you can't analyse yourself.

CHEN I've got an assignment. I have to locate that Category One protected bird.

DING All right. But no excuses next time.

[CHARLIE whispers to LUO.]

LUO Mr Charlie asks whether your centre is a clinic for birds.

DING No. It's for people who keep birds.

CHARLIE I hope there will be a hospital for birds some day.

[SUN's canary suddenly breaks into a shriek, which is abhorred by all bird trainers.]

ZHANG Idiot! *[Rushes over, grabs hold of SUN's cage, dashes it to the ground and stamps on it]*

[All the lark-fanciers run away.]

CHARLIE *[rushes forward to identify the dead bird on the ground]* A canary. Not wildlife. Not protected by the International Council. But still, this gentleman is rather rash and violent. What gives you the right to interfere with others' freedom?

ZHANG Damn! Foul-mouth canary!

SUN *[shaking with rage]* You . . . you . . . *[Faints]*

FATS Hey, Mr Sun! What's the matter? Help!

[ZHANG's lark breaks out loud and clear in imitation of the canary's cry.]

GRANDMASTER He sure learns fast!

ZHANG *[in a rage]* I've trained birds for three years and never a foul-mouth. Now, I—*[Takes his lark from its cage]* I'll be damned if I ever keep another bird again! *[Dashes his lark to the ground, killing it in front of everyone, and exits]*

CHARLIE A lark. Miss Luo. Please bear witness for me. In your country, people wilfully destroy wildlife species such as marsh tits and larks, and it often happens that such birds are killed at whim.

LUO Yes, sir.

DING *[agitated]* You . . . you people, and that includes this Mr Charlie. You care only for the birds, and feel nothing for people. Look, this man has fainted dead away and nobody cares! Will somebody get an ambulance?

[Some of the BIRDMEN scatter.]

FATS I'll go! *[Runs off]*

[Excitement begins to grow among the bystanders.]

BIRD-FANCIER 1 When you foreigners run a hospital, you too, favour people with connections.

BIRD-FANCIER 2 I want to be hospitalized as well!

OTHERS Yeah. We want to stay in the hospital too!

[The crowd begins to jostle and push. The GUARD takes out a whistle and blows on it. GUARD 2 enters and begins to drive away the crowd. The crowd is pushed back, leaving SUN, who has fainted, DR CHEN, DING, XIA, GRANDMASTER, DAN, ZHU, CHARLIE, LUO, and the GUARDS. The siren of an ambulance from afar.]

GUARD The ambulance is here! Move back! Make way!

[The workmen have completed tying the cage frame. They begin to drop canvas sheets one by one to cover the frame. Lights out.]

ACT 2

[A sheet of canvas covering the big cage that is the acting area is pulled apart to let in the sunlight. All the canvas sheets are then removed, revealing the bright blue sky above. In the central acting area, besides the stone table and stools, there are three reclining chairs. The ground is covered with green grass.

GRANDMASTER is reclining in one of the chairs. Behind his chair are the backstage paraphernalia of a Peking Opera troupe: a costume rack full of costumes, a props rack with swords and spears, a table and a chair, and assorted stage props. GRANDMASTER is holding, in one hand, the perch with his bird hopping and chirping merrily on it, and in the other hand, a small teapot.

FATS, and other BIRDMEN, DAN, MA, XI, and ZHU are standing in a line on the lawn, their birdcages hanging on the trees nearby. XIA, in a tracksuit, is leading FATS and the others in physical exercise. DING watches them with interest.]

XIA One, two, three, four. Good. Hands behind your head. Five, six, seven, eight. Good. Stretch both arms. Kick right foot high at the head.

[FATS raises his right foot to kick DAN in the head.]

DAN Hey! Kick your own head!

FATS Don't be silly. I'm too fat to do that. It's tough enough trying to kick yours.

XIA Stop! What's the matter with you? And Grandmaster, why aren't you joining in?

GRANDMASTER Never heard of stars exercising with walk-ons. I'll work out on my own, later.

FATS Grandmaster, do us a favour. Do a turn for us, please.

GRANDMASTER Since you are so keen, *[Stands up, revealing in full his black Kung Fu trousers, Kung Fu exercise shoes, and a white jacket]* I'll do a short piece.

XIA Group dismissed. Free activity. *[The people gather round GRANDMASTER in a semi-circle.]*

FATS Which piece will you do, Grandmaster?

GRANDMASTER *Chaining the Five Dragons.**

FATS I'll get the chain and shackles.

GRANDMASTER Isn't that too much trouble?

BIRDMEN You're taking the trouble to sing for us!

[FATS takes a chain and shackles, special props for Peking Opera, from the props rack. He goes over to GRANDMASTER and puts the chain on him.]

* A Peking Opera set just before Li Shimin set himself up as the first emperor of the Tang dynasty. GRAND-MASTER is playing the part of Shan Xiongxin, who is brought before Li in chains for refusing to support him. Shan is enraged to see that his friend Luo Cheng, whom he has helped many times, has sided with the enemy.

FATS Not going to paint your face?

GRANDMASTER What is this, a paid performance? You expect too
    much.

FATS Your first performance in twenty years! Didn't expect to
    see it in a hospital.

GRANDMASTER So it is. Hold on to the *hongzi*. You play the
    executioner.

FATS Xiao Xia, take the teapot.

    [FATS *takes the perch in one hand, and with the other takes
    the teapot and hands it to* XIA.]

XIA Shall I play Ah Xing's wife?

FATS In this piece Li Shimin kills Shan Xiongxin. What's Ah
    Xing's wife got to do with it?

XIA I've played that part in Shaoxing Opera.

FATS Forget it. There's no place even for me, let alone you.
    Oh, Grandmaster, you look just like the celebrated
    actor Jin Shaoshan! The spitting image!

GRANDMASTER [*saddened by the thought*] Too much of a compliment!
    There is no one like him today, or in the next life!
    [*Grows a little melancholic*]

FATS Sir, is something wrong? Did I say something wrong?

GRANDMASTER Nothing. Ah, the opera. [*Sighs*] Not much time left!

XIA You say he looks like Jin-something. But I say he looks
    rather like a bird.

FATS What do you mean?

XIA See for yourself. The stance, the chain round the neck.

GRANDMASTER [*looks down at the chain, touches it, making it rattle*]
    You're right, my girl. We chain our birds to make
    them sing. Now I wear the chain, so I sing!

DING [*gets up*] One question. Why this particular piece?

GRANDMASTER Good question. There is a passage in the fast *xipi*
    mode. In it is a lovely phrase, inspired by birdsong.

DING How's that?

GRANDMASTER Jin Shaoshan learned the phrase from listening to his
    bird.

DING That's interesting.

GRANDMASTER Did you know that, Fats?

FATS This hospitalization is most rewarding. Do please sing
    for us now!

GRANDMASTER Come, give me a hand!

FATS [*straightens himself, holds the perch in front of him, and
    gives* GRANDMASTER *a push in the back*] Hah!

[GRANDMASTER *uses the momentum, takes a few stumbling steps, steadies himself, takes a stance in classic Peking Opera fashion, then rattles his chain.*]

GRANDMASTER [*sings, eyes glinting, with a good strong voice*]

When I see Luo Cheng it stirs a rage in me.
You're a shameless ingrate and villain mean.
Your stronghold's fall and ruin—do you recall?
Your escape to Luoyang—do you recall?
And how I built you a mansion with high walls,
Gave you a fortune, gave you all!

BIRDMEN Hao!* [*Thunderous applause*]

GRANDMASTER [*bows with clasped fists in acknowledgement*] Thank you. Thank you.

FATS [*goes forward to remove the chain for* GRANDMASTER] Thank you so much, sir.

GRANDMASTER Not at all. Who can tell me which phrase was inspired by birdsong?

XIA I don't think it sounds like a bird at all, more like a tiger, tethered and still trying to kill!

GRANDMASTER Ah, there's a true aficionado! The hero Shan Xiongxin is like a tiger. When he sees the ingrates who betrayed him, he flies into a rage, trying to kill them all before he himself is killed. I don't teach women *hualian* roles, otherwise, my girl, I'd teach you.

FATS Xiao Xia, drink.

XIA What?

FATS Give him a drink.

[XIA *hands the teapot to* GRANDMASTER, *who takes a sip, and lets his bird drink out of the teapot.* FATS *hangs the chain round his own neck and strokes it lovingly.*]

GRANDMASTER Fats, did you spot the phrase?

FATS No.

GRANDMASTER 'Gave you a fortune, gave you all.' That's the phrase Jin Shaoshan learned from his bird.

FATS What kind of bird?

GRANDMASTER A *hongzi*.

FATS A *hongzi*?

GRANDMASTER Jin Shaoshan was inspired by the rise in pitch. His pitch went up on [*Sings*] 'gave you all'.

FATS How did he figure it out? It's perfect.

* Bravo!

GRANDMASTER Jin Shaoshan was a true master, unsurpassed. None like him now!

FATS Teach me this piece, sir. Please.

GRANDMASTER You flatter me. Stick with your bird, it sings better than you do.

FATS I don't believe that I cannot learn. I'm willing to work hard at it.

GRANDMASTER What if you do learn? There's plenty of mediocrity, but Jin Shaoshans are rare.

DING *[attempts to change his attitude]* You have to understand that the past, however wonderful, is passed; and the future, however imperfect, will be with us—

FATS You won't pass on the art? You'd just watch the art of the brass-hammer *hualian* role die out?

GRANDMASTER That will do. *[Referring to the chain]* Take it down.

FATS You've brought all the props and things here, just for show?

GRANDMASTER I feel good having them around.

FATS How about giving a few lessons to an amateur then?

GRANDMASTER I never waste my time with amateurs.

FATS You'd rather see Peking Opera go from bad to worse? And never produce another Jin Shaoshan?

GRANDMASTER If there is a man with what it takes, he won't escape me. I'll hang on to him even if I have to chain him.

FATS That's it then. That's the end of Peking Opera, if it were up to you. You might as well send all your opera paraphernalia to the crematorium at Eight Treasures Hill!

GRANDMASTER You're right. And if you can't pull a few strings, they probably won't take the stuff either.

DING Let's sit down. Anywhere.

[GRANDMASTER reclines in his chair. FATS sits down by him on the ground. DAN and MA each occupy one of the remaining chairs. XI and ZHU sit on the stools.]

We'll have a session now. Miss Xia, please give the eye-shades to the patients.

[XIA takes out six sets of eye-shades and distributes them to the patients.]

GRANDMASTER I can do without. I don't even want to open my eyes.

DING This is to meet the conditions of analysis. It's best to wear them.

[All six put on the eye-shades.]

XIA No peeping, Fats.

[FATS *quickly adjusts his shade.*]

DING You wear these so you can ignore me, and relax. We'll do a group session today. We'll do private sessions later. You can say what comes to mind.

DAN My bird—

MA Time to give it some water.

XI They can do without food, but must have water.

ZHU Or they are done for.

FATS Mr Ding, you heard that?

DING Yes, I'm listening.

FATS Are you doing anything about it?

DING I mustn't interrupt. The point is to let you talk and reveal all your anxieties and worries.

FATS Our birds, that's what's worrying us. Give us back our cages!

DING In analysis sessions in other countries, one doesn't go and do other things.

DAN This is China.

FATS You should amend the regulations according to the special conditions in China.

DING Oh, I give up. Miss Xia, give them their cages.

[XIA *hands back the cages one by one to* FATS *and the others.*]

DAN [*at one touch of the cage*] This is a thrush cage. Your *huamei*, Fats.

FATS Steady on. You scare him and he'll have 'chin-up' trouble. Whose *hongzi* is this? Xiao Xia, take it away.

[XIA *redistributes the cages as instructed by the* BIRDMEN.]

MA I say, can I take off the shade to feed him water, then put it on again?

XIA What a troublesome lot you are.

FATS Well we can't see.

DING Oh, all right. Take them off for the moment.

[BIRDMEN *take off their eye-shades.*]

XI That's much better.

FATS [*sings*] 'The liberated sky is a clear bright sky.'

DAN O, my! Where is my *hongzi*? Xiao Xia, did you open the cage?

XIA I didn't.

DAN My *hongzi* sings four different pitches, and has two sets of repertoires! Oh, you might as well kill me! Someone has to pay for this!

FATS And you turned down a good offer for him. Serves you right!

DAN He is worth eight hundred yuan at least. But money aside, where could you find one like him? *[Grabs hold of* XIA's *hand]* This is not the end of it.

XIA *[sobs]* I didn't do anything, honestly.

[The crisp chirp of a hongzi *is heard.]*

MA He's up in the tree.

DAN *[frantic]* Come down, come down here. *[Runs to stand under the tree, takes some grubs out of his pocket and puts them in the cage, hangs the cage on a branch, and kneels down]* My precious great-grandfather, please come down!

XIA Mr Ding, I resign. It's bad enough looking after old people without having to put up with this nonsense. One could get killed here!

DING It's all right. Much safer than at a mental home. They'll improve with treatment.

DAN *[pleads]* My honourable ancestor, please come down!

[MA, XI, and ZHU all go over to watch DAN.]

Don't stand there. You'll scare him away.

[They all squat down.]

XIA I want to go home.

DING Are you married?

XIA *[shakes her head]* I was hoping to make some money in Beijing and then go home to get married.

DING Is he nice to you?

XIA *[nods]* Mmm. *[Starts sobbing again]*

DING How long have you been away from home?

XIA Three months.

DING In America, if husband and wife don't live together for three months, it would imply that the marriage was over.

XIA Really?

DING If two people are in love, they can't live apart.

XIA Once we have money, we won't live apart.

DING Who knows.

XIA Beijing is all right but for these people. I sometimes think that if my Huang Mao could open a small restaurant in Beijing, we would live very well.

DING Has he written recently?

XIA He wrote about a month ago, to say that he'd come to join me in Beijing. Since then there has been no news. What about you, Mr Ding? Where is your family?

DING I was married once. It didn't work out.

XIA Why?

DING She was a patient of mine. After our marriage, she objected to my work. She couldn't stand the thought of me doing analysis for other women.

XIA I don't understand your work either. To spend so much money looking after these people, and having to chat with them.

DING Everyone has a unique history. Analysing a person is like reading a book, a book full of wonders. You get hooked on it. When you have finished analysing one person, you want to know about another. And so the search goes on, like a habit and then an obsession, and nothing can stop it.

XIA Have you ever analysed yourself?

DING One can't analyse oneself, just as a judge cannot sit in judgment over himself.

[As the BIRDMEN *wait intently for the bird to return to its cage,* CHEN *enters.]*

DAN Don't come near us. You'll scare him!

*[*CHEN *is slow to respond. He keeps walking.]*

DAN Are you deaf or something? I told you not to come, but you had to come. Look, it's gone! You stupid fool!

CHEN Look who's talking!

DAN Do you want a good beating?

MA Forget it. Let's go after the bird.

DAN Wait till I get back! *[Runs off, followed by* BIRDMEN *except* FATS *and* GRANDMASTER*]*

XIA Don't go too far. Dinner will be ready soon.

DING Welcome, welcome.

CHEN I'm here for the bird.

DING The Category One protected species?

CHEN Hasn't it turned up?

DING There's nobody here but my patients and me.

CHEN This is the first bird market from Shanxi to Beijing. I expect the bird will turn up here first. I plan to station myself here and wait for it.

DING You can stay here, on one condition—

CHEN What's that?

DING Be my patient.

CHEN There is nothing wrong with me.

DING That's impossible. I'm not saying you are mentally ill, but you have psychological problems, like everybody else.

CHEN I have no psychological problems.

DING Yes, you have.

CHEN What problems?

DING Voyeurism.

CHEN *[pauses]* How do you know?

DING Stay. I'll give you a few sessions, and alleviate your pain.

CHEN And if I won't?

DING Then you can't stay and wait for your bird.

CHEN Is everything free?

DING Of course. And since you are a senior official, you'll get senior intellectual preferential treatment.

CHEN And that is?

DING You eat better.

CHEN Surely you know that a lot of scientists forget to eat. And . . .?

DING You live better. You have your own room, modern facilities, and privacy.

CHEN That's better than what I'm getting.

DING You'll get preferential intellectual treatment. You can read banned books like *Jin Ping Mei* and *Rou Putuan*, and even watch porn movies.

CHEN Not the expurgated version of *Jin Ping Mei*, I hope? Not much in that.

DING A facsimile of the original, with illustrations.

CHEN There's a porn movie called *Men and Beasts*, all about men and animals. As a zoologist, I have to understand—

DING You will be satisfied. That will be part of your professional study.

CHEN You look after the needs of intellectuals better than the State.

DING We can't let the State do everything.

CHEN The conditions are fine. Oh, I forgot. Can I conduct my own research here?

DING Of course.

CHEN One is better off here than at the Science Institute. I'm beginning to wonder whether there isn't something wrong with you.

DING You agree to stay then?

CHEN Agreed. But this place is set up for bird-fanciers, and I don't keep birds.

DING In the army, it is the foot soldier that is armed to the teeth; the highest commander doesn't even carry a gun. You are an ornithologist. What is a mere bird-fancier compared with you? If there are no more birds, what will they fancy? They cannot exist. But even if all the birds in the world die off, the ornithologist can go on, in fact, will grow in importance. Jurassic creatures are all extinct, but Jurassic research centres have prospered.

[FATS is snoring.]

CHEN Somebody is having a nap.

DING Our analysis session was interrupted and they have fallen asleep.

XIA I'll wake them up.

DING Don't. When they wake up, I can analyse their dreams.

CHEN Why is the fat man wearing a chain?

DING Sympathetic identification. It's a subconscious process. To imitate someone he admires, and transfer that admiration from the person to the things used by that person. The chain is a Peking Opera prop that belongs to this man he admires. Wearing it, he consoles himself with the thought that he *is* the man he admires.

CHEN That's pretty obvious. You don't need analysis. Any fool could tell you that.

DING What we do is to tease out the mass of early memories related to his complex, and remove the source of his anxieties to make him normal again.

[FATS wakes up slowly.]

Close your eyes. Answer my questions.

[FATS closes his eyes.]

Where were you just now?

FATS Doggone-it.

DING Rude even in his sleep. That's resistance to analysis.

CHEN Doggone-it? That sounds familiar. Ah, I remember. It's the name of an eatery that sells special buns.

DING Really? I don't know much about restaurants in China. What were you doing there?

FATS Eating, drinking.

DING Was there anybody with you?

FATS Not much fun eating alone. A few friends.

DING Who were they?

FATS I know the names of my superiors, and those of my subordinates.

DING Can you tell me?

XIA Do you think I would betray my comrades? Never!

DING Why did you barge in?

XIA He was quoting a line from Jiang Jie.

DING Who is Jiang Jie?

CHEN The heroine in a popular revolutionary novel. This is a quotation from a scene where she is interrogated by the enemy. They made a film of it, starring Yu Lan.

FATS My compliments to Yu Lan.

XIA You know her?

FATS No. But I'm a fan of all stars.

DING He is obsessed with imitating heroes.

XIA Perhaps not. These Peking Opera fans will imitate anybody, heroes and villains. They imitate anything done well. I heard Fats imitating Hatoyama singing too.

FATS Compliments to Yuan Shihai. Tell him: Pavarotti doesn't know how to paint his face. He just stands there with nothing on him and sings. Tell him: don't do that.

DING Who is Hatoyama?

XIA Head of the Japanese Secret Service in *The Red Lantern*.

DING And Yuan played the part?

XIA Don't you know anything?

DING America is very parochial and uninformed.

FATS No wonder you came back.

XIA [to FATS] Why did you open your eyes?

FATS Every time I hear people say that America is no good, and the Chinese there all want to come back, I feel so good.

DING You are much too clear-headed for analysis. Miss Xia, help him put on the shade.

XIA [helping FATS *with the eye-shade*] We'll use two this time.

DING You are too excited. Were you drunk in the restaurant?

FATS [sings] 'I can down ten thousand cups.'

DING Well done.

FATS That's good? Nowhere near what Hao Liang can do.

DING Knows too many people. Why did you drink?

FATS *[sings]* 'Ask Li Yuhe for the secret code.'

XIA He is getting confused.

DING Ssh—Shall I take the chain off?

FATS No. When Wang Jinlu . . . waits for a bus, he . . . stretches his leg . . . on the bus-stop stand.

DING Why?

FATS To practise. You need that for Kung Fu, *[Does a few Kung Fu moves with his hands]* and for singing.

DING Don't get so worked up. Lull yourself into a semi-conscious state.

FATS When I think about opera, I can't even sit still.

DING What do you do when your birds are restless?

FATS I spray them with water.

DING Miss Xia. Spray him.

[XIA pours the tea from GRANDMASTER'*s teapot on to* FATS. *But finding the flow too weak, she takes off the lid and throws the contents on* FATS' *head.]*

FATS Good jasmine tea, Grandmaster's Fragrant Cloud Tea. Hey, I don't want tea leaves on my face! What do you take me for? A bird?

DING Well? A little calmer now?

FATS *[sneezes]* If I catch cold, my voice will be hoarse. It'll ruin me.

DING What liquor did you have?

FATS It cost thirteen cents a tael.

DING That's cheap. Brandy costs more than a thousand yuan.

FATS Who can afford to drink that? Even Ma Lianliang earned only seventeen hundred a month and he was a star.

DING Were you drunk?

FATS Yes. You go faster with cheap liquor.

DING Then why did you drink it?

FATS You drink to get drunk, why else? You can get drunk for a thousand yuan, or for thirteen cents. Which is more cost efficient?

DING Then what happened?

FATS Went to the Fortune Theatre.

DING Where is that?

FATS Next to Donglaishun. Opposite United.

DING What did you do?

FATS Watched opera.

DING What was on?

FATS *Chaining the Five Dragons.*

DING The excerpt played with the chain?

FATS Good stuff.

> [FATS *gets up suddenly.* XIA *quickly pushes him down again.*]

DING Can't you keep still even after the spraying?

FATS You have to cover up after the spraying. Oh, why did I tell him? Making trouble for myself.

DING Cover him.

XIA What with?

DING Get a bedsheet.

> [XIA *gets a bedsheet and covers* FATS *from head to toe.*]

FATS Ready with the obituary?

XIA What obituary? This is no memorial service for you.

FATS Shan Xiongxin sings before he is beheaded, otherwise he'd be booed off stage.

DING Sing then.

FATS *[sings]* 'Where, pray, is Qin, my brother?'

XIA I've heard this so often I can sing it: 'He is out with the ration convoy and not yet returned'.

FATS Ah. *[Sings]* 'My good brother—' *[Speaks]* And his wife?

XIA Why do you keep asking for his wife when he's out?

FATS That line's not in the script!

XIA You make things up too.

DING All right. Let's get back to the Fortune Theatre. What about audience response? Did they like it?

FATS There was only one person there.

DING A woman?

FATS You were there too?

DING Mmm.

FATS She was pretty, wasn't she? But lay off her.

DING Do you know her?

FATS I saw her photo once.

DING What photo?

FATS Grandma showed it to me and said, 'This is your mother'.

DING How many people were there in the photo?

FATS Two.

DING Who was the other one?

FATS Gran said it was my father.

DING Did he look like you?

FATS Couldn't tell. He had a mask painted on.

DING Your father was an opera singer, a *hualian*?

FATS Must have been very good. Why else did my mother marry him?

DING Where is he now?

FATS Gone to father somebody else.

DING And your mother?

FATS Died.

DING So your father took you with him?

FATS If he had, I'd have become a star. No, Gran kept me. She said my father was a good-for-nothing.

DING Is he still alive?

FATS Who knows? Hey, are you done asking?

DING *[pleased, mops his brow, turns to* XIA*]* Note this, Miss Xia. A successful analysis. Classic case of the Oedipus Complex.

*[*GRANDMASTER *stirs on the reclining chair.]*

FATS *[to Ding]* You've been on at me for ages, like interrogating a thief. You've got to do something for me. Walk my *huamei*.

DING Why do you keep a thrush, a *huamei*?

FATS To vent my frustration. *Huamei* has a strong voice, as good as Jin Shaoshan. He has pride. He stands on the perch, cocks his tail, spreads his wings and sings until blood comes out of his beak. He's that bent on out-singing all other birds. If he can't out-sing them, he somersaults off the perch, utters not another note and dies.

*[*FATS *stirs under the sheet, rattling the chain. As the rattling dies down, he begins to snore.* DING *takes* FATS' *cage for a stroll with* CHEN.*]*

CHEN *[points at* GRANDMASTER*]* He is quiet. Doesn't even stir.

DING This type is most uncooperative. Most difficult to analyse.

CHEN Why?

DING Specialists are the most bigotted. He spends all his energy on one small area, and knows nothing about anything else, and so lacks the power to see the whole, to synthesize and analyse. There is an old saying:

'specialists are bound to be fools'. He is quiet now, but if he gets a chance to show what he is good at, he'll lose all control.

CHEN What is he good at?

DING He is a maniac at training. He wants to pass on his expertise at Peking Opera, and is never at peace because he can't find the right person to train. So he trains birds for pupils. The strange thing is, why do the birds sing better when they are chained? Their singing is louder, more disciplined, and more varied than in the wild.

CHEN There is a slavish side to all animals. Material well-being confuses us all.

DING Not necessarily human beings. Don't heroes die for their principles?

GRANDMASTER *[sits up]* Birds too. Food alone doesn't entice them all. You have to know what they like. The bluethroat likes to bathe, so you have to give him water to bathe as soon as he starts to preen himself. Or, when you have a new bluethroat, if you don't know how he feels, you'll never get him to eat anything, and he'll starve to death. You have to stay close to him, and wait. When he takes a liking to you, he'll take a tiny morsel of lamb, and live. Actually you know this better than I do, the way you make a living is no different from tempting bluethroats to feed.

DING So even birds have to be psychoanalysed, let alone bird-fanciers.

GRANDMASTER And because I know birds, I know people better than you do. Your methods don't work so well on me.

DING We can try them.

GRANDMASTER Do. But I'm not Fats.

DING Lie back and relax.

GRANDMASTER Relax? I'm almost asleep.

DING Did you sleep just now?

GRANDMASTER For a while.

DING Did you dream?

GRANDMASTER I wanted to. But I didn't.

DING What did you want to dream about?

GRANDMASTER Whatever is good.

DING What is good?

GRANDMASTER A spread of blue, a patch of purple, a band of jade, and the god of fire.

DING What is that?

GRANDMASTER A bluethroat.

DING Birds again. Substitutes for real pupils. Would finding a bluethroat satisfy you?

GRANDMASTER That depends on what he could sing. If he croaked like a frog, he'd be worthless. But if he could manage a cicada chirp or two, then he would be superb.

DING What's so special about the chirp?

GRANDMASTER On the coldest days of winter, when snow drifts outside the window, and bare trees look desolate against the dying sun; inside, a warm fire, a cup of *biluochun* tea freshly brewed, and a cicada chirp from a bluethroat. It would be like sitting by a verdant pond, on a willow bank.

CHEN I'm an ornithologist, but I never knew this mystery about birds.

GRANDMASTER Not the cicada chirps of the height of summer, but the chirps of late autumn. What we call 'autumn cool'. As the days grow cold, and the cicadas wait for death, the call is tinged with sadness. *[Imitates the cicada's cry: 'fu—tianer—']*

DING Ah—

GRANDMASTER Desolate and forlorn, like Yang Baosen's mournful wail.

DING What other bird is good?

GRANDMASTER The *hongzi*. A bluethroat is perfect at imitation. There is nothing he can't learn. But the *hongzi* has pride. He doesn't imitate other birds, he is imitated by others.

DING Never changes its principles.

CHEN Like the French refusing to speak English. They do all their diplomatic papers only in French.

DING Let me sum up. You live in the past. When it is winter, you yearn still for autumn, and torment yourself with the desolation of loss. It is clear that the days of the Peking Opera are over, yet you, like the *hongzi*, cling proudly to what you have.

GRANDMASTER You certainly know how to hurt.

DING You like beautiful women too. The blue, and purple, and band of jade. You got through to them as well, perhaps through your performance. You were good. But then one day, you blew it, like the bluethroat that croaked like a frog. You became worthless, you lost everything, you lost your place on the stage. So you keep birds, stubbornly turning back to past glories, to the late autumn cicada, to your loss, so forlorn. The worse things get, the more appealing the autumn scene: the fruit, the applause, the money, the women.

[GRANDMASTER grows agitated.]

DING You are old. You will never make a come-back on the stage. So you keep birds. You don't go near the theatre. You think nobody can sing, and they get everything wrong. But you can't prove yourself. You keep birds as a substitute for yourself. If they sing well, they would be as you once were. You train birds because there is nobody you can pass your expertise to. If you found that person, you'd train him like you train your birds, to prolong your dream.

GRANDMASTER No more!

DING The worst is that physiologically, as a man, you can't, not anymore.

[Silence. A cicada cries.]

GRANDMASTER Huang Zhong, at seventy, killed Xiahou Yuan.

DING On the battlefield perhaps, but no good in bed. You're not likely to kill anybody, perhaps not even yourself.

GRANDMASTER One wouldn't want to make mistakes again just because of one's pride. A hero doesn't dwell on past glories.

DING But you still want to try and prove yourself. Perhaps give a sort of farewell performance. When that's done, you're probably done as well.

CHEN *[pulls DING aside]* Mr Ding, perhaps you should be more cautious in talking to old people like him. The shock may drive him over the edge, don't you think?

[GRANDMASTER sits in pained silence.]

XIA Did you mean to do this?

DING Psychoanalysis is supposed to lay things bare. Once you come clean, it's easier to look life in the face.

GRANDMASTER Go away. Don't confuse me.

FATS Walk my bird.

[DING hurriedly swings the cage. The huamei calls.]

DING *[to XIA]* Keep an eye on Fats. He may kill somebody.

[XIA glances at FATS in fear.]

CHEN How do you know?

DING Did Oedipus know?

CHEN The Greek king of Thebes who killed his father and married his mother?

DING Fats wants to become a famous *hualian* actor to gain
the love of the one person in the audience, his mother.
Note that *hualian*, the painted mask, masks the
intention to kill and replace his father. The
subconscious, when restrained by social and ethical
considerations, rationalizes itself in some acceptable
form. In Fats, the rationalization takes the form of a
performance, and the aim of the performance is the
courtship of his mother.

CHEN Amazing.

DING Do you remember what he said about the photo? His
father's face was just a painted mask. So Fats' face can
also be a mask, a *hualian*, and he can then replace his
father. If Freud knew about this trick of the
subconscious, he would jump for joy.

CHEN You said Fats might kill somebody?

DING Not might, but will. From worship of authority to
imitation to annihilation to replacement.

[*The sound of people approaching in great excitement.*
BIRDMEN, DAN, MA, XI *and* ZHU *enter with a young man
in his twenties, from out of town. He is* HUANG MAO. *He
carries a large metal cage, covered with a cloth.*]

MAO Is this really the bird market?

XI That's right. Only it is now called 'Birdmen Mental
Rehabilitation Centre'.

MAO Will you pay me? I won't give it away.

ZHU Show us then.

DAN I just lost a *hongzi*. If this one is good, I'll keep it.

[MAO *lifts part of the cover.*]

MA Isn't that a chicken?

ZHU Who'd spend good money on a chicken?

MA Is it for keeping or eating?

MAO Whatever you like. Just give me my train fare.

XI How much?

MAO One hundred.

DAN Are you mad? No chicken is worth a hundred.

MAO This is a *maji*. The only one in the area.

CHEN Don't let him get away!

[CHEN *dives forward, grabs* MAO *and holds on to him.*]

Put the cage over there. You and the *maji* are under arrest.
I've waited for you long enough in this loony bin!

[*The group rush to see what has happened.*]

XIA Huang Mao! It's you!

MAO *[cries out loud]* Xiao Xia! I've found you!

> *[MAO's voice wakes up* GRANDMASTER. *He stands up, removes the eye-shade and looks intently at* MAO.*]*

DING Do you know each other, Xiao Xia?

CHEN You have violated the law. The brown *maji* is found only in China, and only in Shanxi Province. Where did you get this?

MAO In Wenshui county, Shanxi.

CHEN That belongs to the Pang Spring Natural Reserve. This is probably the only one left. It is a Category One protected species.

XIA How do you know it's the only one?

CHEN Scientific observation.

XIA What will you do to him?

CHEN He will be sentenced.

XIA *[to MAO]* Run for it!

CHEN You can't get away with it!

DING The bird belongs to the Centre.

CHEN Nobody is allowed to touch it! Hey, Fats! Wake up, Fats, and come over!

> *[FATS jumps up and pushes away the sheet.]*

Take off your chain.

FATS *[hesitates]* Why?

CHEN In the name of the State, take it off!

> *[FATS takes off the chain, and moves over.]*

Tie him up.

FATS Can he do it? He's got to learn to sing first before the stage movements.

CHEN Tie him up!

FATS *[grudgingly]* I was here first. *[Ties up MAO]*

CHEN Keep an eye on him. I must examine the bird to see if there is any injury. *[Opens the cage, takes out the brown maji]* One feather missing behind the left ear. One tail feather missing. Trace of faeces in the anus.

XIA *[rushes forward to MAO and grabs him by his arms]* Why did you do it?

MAO I didn't catch it. I bought it off a hunter for twenty yuan. He said I could make big money for it in Beijing.

> *[DING snatches the maji from CHEN and tries to hand it to MAO.]*

DING Take your bird, and stay.

CHEN How dare you? This is the most precious creature in the country!

DING The most precious creatures in the country should be human beings! If it can make a person whole, what is the sacrifice of one bird?

CHEN If these precious creatures are extinct, there will be no more. But human beings . . . there are plenty!

DING If this young lad were extinct, he would be no more.

FATS [*to* MAO *and* XIA] Hey, you two. Not so close. [*Tugs at the chain*]

GRANDMASTER Bring him over here. [FATS *leads* MAO.] Call out and let me hear your voice.

MAO I can't.

GRANDMASTER Say 'Ah—'. Don't be nervous.

MAO [*looks to* XIA, *who nods*] Ah—

GRANDMASTER His voice is better than yours, Fats.

FATS But his hair is sandy, yellow.

GRANDMASTER That's deviant plumage.

XIA What's deviant plumage?

GRANDMASTER What colour is a sparrow?

XIA Brown.

GRANDMASTER Aye. If it were white, that would be deviant.

XIA Is that good?

GRANDMASTER It's rare, and therefore good.

XIA Foreigners have yellow beards as well.

GRANDMASTER That is not desirable. A white face doesn't look good with a yellow beard. A green face with a red beard looks much nicer.

DING Is there anyone with a face like that?

GRANDMASTER Yes. Douerdun, the *hualian* bandit.

FATS You haven't heard this lad sing.

GRANDMASTER Fats, sing a line from *Chaining the Five Dragons*. Let him sing after you.

FATS [*sings*] 'When I see Luo Cheng it stirs a rage in me.'

MAO I can't sing Peking Opera.

GRANDMASTER Just sing along. I just want to hear your voice, enunciation, and projection.

MAO [*sings in style of* Huangmei *Opera*] 'When I see Luo Cheng it stirs a rage in me.'

FATS Hey, that's *Huangmei*!

GRANDMASTER Not bad. Stay here and learn to sing.

DING *[claps his hands in excitement]* Good, I'm getting more and more patients.

MAO *[appeals to* XIA*]* Xiao Xia, I'd rather die than learn to sing. Let's go home. It doesn't matter how poor we are, or how tough life gets, we can bear it.

XIA Don't be so silly, Huang Mao. If we can stay in Beijing, I'll do anything. It's so backward at home.

CHEN You keep an eye on him. If he escapes, I'll hold you responsible.

GRANDMASTER What are you talking about? Do you think I'd let somebody with his potential get away? What would the opera do without him? We need good *hualian* now!

MAO Please, Mr Chen, take me to jail. That's better than training for opera.

CHEN *[finds himself in a difficult position]* Well, it's not so easy. I don't know anybody who runs a jail. Why don't you stay here for a few days—bear with it. It's not a proper jail, of course, but it will get better. See, you already have the chains reserved for real criminals. Beside, this *is* a sort of jail.

DING I object to your statement. That's incitement!

GRANDMASTER Never mind him, Dr Ding. If one can keep birds, and rehearse operas, what does it matter if it is a jail?

FATS Grandmaster is right!

GRANDMASTER *[to* XIA*]* Raise his right leg.

*[*XIA *raises* MAO*'s right leg.]*

GRANDMASTER *[taps* MAO*'s left leg with a thin bamboo stick]* Stand up straight.

FATS *[pats the small of* MAO*'s back]* Straighten up!

DING This is wonderful. You work at this. *[Takes over* GRANDMASTER*'s bird perch]* I'll walk your birds for you. *[Exits, carrying the* hongzi *in one hand and* FATS' huamei *in the other.]*

*[*CHEN *picks up the metal cage with the* maji *inside, and starts to leave. The* maji *shrieks.]*

MAO Mr Chen, you've got your bird. What about me?

CHEN You are all right. The bird will be all right. I'll put it under my protection forever.

MAO Bear witness. It was all right when I gave it to you.

CHEN That is neither here nor there. The point is we mustn't let this bird be smuggled out of the country. It must stay in our country forever. I will tell posterity that, once upon a time, we had this beautiful living creature in our land!

[The sheets covering the big 'cage' drop down quickly. The maji *bird gives a terrible cry. Lights out.]*

[The 'cage' cover is raised. Lights up in the acting area. On the stone table, MAO, in chains, is striking a Peking Opera pose to establish his presence on stage. XIA stands in attendance on one side holding a teapot. GRANDMASTER reclines in a chair facing the table, with FATS standing beside him.]

GRANDMASTER *[to MAO]* Again.

MAO *[sings with accompanying gestures and movement]*

> When I see Luo Cheng it stirs a rage in me.
> You're a shameless ingrate and villain mean.
> Your stronghold's fall and ruin—do you recall?
> Your escape to Luoyang—do you recall?
> And how I built you a mansion with high walls,
> Gave you a fortune, gave you all?

GRANDMASTER Not so heavy on 'mansion'. Save a bit of energy for the high turn in the next line.

[DING enters, carrying the hongzi in one hand and the huamei in the other.]

DING This is yours. And this is yours. *[Giving the birds to GRANDMASTER and FATS]*

[FATS takes out of his pocket a plastic bottle fitted with a drinking straw, and tops up the water in the drinking cups for both the birds. XIA feeds MAO a sip of tea from her teapot.]

GRANDMASTER *[to XIA]* Be careful when you offer tea. Take a sip to test the temperature first. Not too hot, and not too cold. Then let him drink. Not too much either. Just enough to wet the throat. That will do. Fats, you attend to him. I have to see to the bird. Did you say your *huamei* can't get the *hongzi's* song right?

FATS Grandmaster, don't just fuss over the birds. Watch me rehearse.

GRANDMASTER When you sing, you can't get the beat right. When you move, you don't have the basic techniques. Why don't you just fool around a little? Why strain yourself?

FATS I want to learn and you won't teach me. Yet you insist on teaching someone who doesn't want to learn.

XIA *[takes a sip from the teapot]* Have another sip.

MAO *[sips]* This is no life for a human being. I'd rather go and build pigsties.

XIA Be patient. Didn't Grandmaster say he would teach you a hundred operas? Fats would give his eye-teeth to have this chance. You learn a trade and it's yours.

MAO I don't understand this. You don't work, you sing all day, and somebody pays for your food and lodging!

[GRANDMASTER points at the hongzi, *and it sings. He points again, and it stops.]*

GRANDMASTER Why has he lost the slow notes? The notes are flat.

FATS You've been busy with Huang Mao, and the birds are out of practice!

GRANDMASTER Huang Mao has talent, and I want to make more of him. *[To* MAO*]* Come down. Lie down to rest for a little. Fats, help him down.

[FATS goes over reluctantly.]

DING *[looking at his watch]* They've made him stand there for four whole hours, from 4 to 8 this morning. A classic example of a compulsive mental state. They are filled with a sense of responsibility and mission, to turn everyone into obedient birds. They'd make distinguished teachers and educationalists.

[FATS and XIA *help* MAO *down.* MAO *walks shakily to the reclining chair.* GRANDMASTER *stands up to help him sit down.]*

DING Between kindness and intimidation, they force their subject into a mould.

[CHEN enters carrying the stuffed carcass of the maji *bird, covered with a red cloth. He puts it down carefully on the stone table. The larks, the* hongzi, *and the* huamei *all shriek with horror.]*

CHEN I've decided that the brown *maji* should stay here forever, for the benefit of all ornithologists and birdmen.

DING This gesture of support is deeply appreciated. Thank you, Mr Chen.

CHEN And I have a piece of good news. A representative of the International Council for Bird Preservation will be here for a visit today. We will hold a ceremony in honour of a threatened species—the brown *maji*.

DING *[applauds]* I sincerely hope that Mr Chen will stay here with the *maji*.

CHEN Thank you for the invitation. But an ornithologist today has many tasks to attend to. He belongs to the world, not to a country, or a unit.

DING Suit yourself.

CHEN You said earlier that Fats might kill somebody?

DING Not so loud.

CHEN That prediction is not going to come true, is it?

DING His desire is artfully disguised, but it's about to break out.

CHEN How are you going to cure him?

DING Bring out what's in his subconscious. Point out the problem, and dispel the wish.

CHEN I wish I could prove by scientific means that your analysis is correct.

DING Do you want me to stand by and watch him kill?

CHEN People will only believe an earthquake forecast after the earthquake's happened.

DING There's a very strong streak of voyeurism in you.

CHEN What do you mean?

DING Have you ever felt the urge to peep at a woman bathing?

CHEN Well, I—

[GRANDMASTER *strolls with his teapot.* FATS *and* MAO *are talking about opera.*]

GRANDMASTER Well, my learned friend, what are we analysing now?

CHEN You shouldn't analyse me in public.

DING It's all right. Once the subconscious thought is exposed, it no longer exists. [*To* GRANDMASTER] I was asking him whether he has ever felt the urge to watch a woman bathing.

GRANDMASTER That depends on how old the woman is.

CHEN [*pointing at* GRANDMASTER] You see. He has.

DING Answer me. Have you or have you not?

CHEN I'd have to think.

DING When a woman in a skirt steps on a glass-panelled escalator, have you ever stood under it and waited for the escalator to go up?

CHEN I'd rather go to the ballet.

DING You see. What do you like about the ballet?

CHEN What does anybody like about the ballet?

DING Same as you.

CHEN But do the dancers know? If they knew our thoughts, that would be rather, erm—

DING Of course they know. That's why they do all those beautiful turns.

CHEN Isn't that like fighting fire with fire?

DING On the contrary. They twirl up their skirts and you even see their pants. So the curiosity dies, and then you begin to appreciate art.

CHEN And if they didn't show their pants?

DING You'd probably want to sneak into the orchestra pit.

CHEN Is that why conductors sometimes miss a beat or two?

DING That is why ballet music is never entirely satisfactory.

CHEN Does this prove your point about the obsession?

DING The obsession in itself isn't serious. Just not very respectable. What is socially dangerous are the various disguised manifestations of voyeurism.

CHEN Disguised?

DING Like prying into people's privacy, reading people's mail, spying on your neighbours' visitors, especially of the opposite sex, and spreading rumours about them. In the workplace, causing dissension, spying—

CHEN Why did you say I suffer from this obsession?

DING You are different from other people.

CHEN In what way?

DING When a peacock spreads its tail, everyone stands in front to watch it. Only you'd stand behind.

CHEN So?

DING Voyeurism. Peeping.

CHEN I don't even miss a chance with a peacock?

GRANDMASTER You'd sure know where to look.

CHEN He is being sarcastic.

DING When you got the brown *maji*, which part of it did you examine most carefully? The anus.

CHEN That's my work.

DING Watching *Jin Ping Mei*, *Rou Putuan*, and other porn movies is also your work?

CHEN You offered me those.

DING Did I offer to let you watch Fats kill?

GRANDMASTER What? Is Fats going to kill somebody?

CHEN He will kill—

[DING quickly gestures CHEN not to tell.]

GRANDMASTER I don't believe it. Fats is not very smart, but he's nice. He couldn't do it.

CHEN I don't believe it either. That's what we're arguing about. According to Mr Ding's analysis, Fats will kill a figure of authority whom he admires.

GRANDMASTER That would be none other than me!

[Silence]

FATS *[teaching* MAO *to sing]* 'When I see Luo Cheng it stirs a rage in me.' That's how you sing it, with a lot of fire. Get it?

GRANDMASTER Suppose I left the hospital?

DING You would have even less protection. Nobody outside would believe our analysis. Besides, Fats could discharge himself too.

GRANDMASTER Suppose I report him to the police?

CHEN You only have a case when somebody has been killed. There is no case without a killing, and Fats has no previous record.

DING Actually you don't really want to call the police. You have a death wish.

GRANDMASTER What does that mean?

DING I hope you don't mind. Put plainly, it means you want to die.

GRANDMASTER Huh? Explain.

DING What happened to this Shan Xiongxin that you play?

GRANDMASTER He had his head chopped off.

DING By whom?

GRANDMASTER Li Shimin.

DING No. By the executioner. Fats.

GRANDMASTER But that's just the opera.

DING There are plenty of operas. Why this particular one? This is not just chance.

[Silence]

FATS *[indicating* MAO*]* Grandmaster, perhaps you should explain to him.

GRANDMASTER *[diffidently]* You explain. You do it, please.

FATS Why are you so polite to me?

GRANDMASTER No, no. You're doing so well.

*[*FATS *continues to discuss points about opera with* MAO.*]*

GRANDMASTER I've heard enough about your analysis. Are you sure you don't make mistakes?

DING It is a science.

GRANDMASTER What science? It's just like a court trial. I know how to do it too.

DING You do?

GRANDMASTER We do it without your imported chatting technique. We do it in Peking Opera. We can get to the bottom of things just as well.

CHEN That would be interesting.

DING Analysis by amateurs can be dangerous.

GRANDMASTER I don't analyse. I judge. *[Makes to go]*

DING Where are you going?

GRANDMASTER To prepare the stage. *[Exits]*

> *[A Peking Opera orchestra comes on to one side of the stage, settles down. The orchestra plays* jijifeng—*fast music which heralds the entrance of a major character on stage. It then plays* daoban—*a few phrases which lead in to the singing.* GRANDMASTER *sings offstage: 'Judge Bao sits in his courthouse'. He then enters, dressed as Judge Bao, his face painted over with a mask.*]*

GRANDMASTER *[to* BIRDMEN*]* Move the table and chair over here and then play the court attendants.

> *[*BIRDMEN DAN, MA, XI *and* ZHU *move the table and chair used in opera sets to centre stage. They place on the table ink-brushes, an ink-brush stand, a seal of office, a cylinder with sticks standing in it, and a block of wood which serves as a gavel. Then two of them stand to attention as guards, staff in hand.*
>
> *The other two also stand to attention, each holding an oar-like staff—a ban. The flat end of the ban is used to beat the buttocks of recalcitrant defendants to extract confession, or as punishment for contempt of court.]*

FATS Grandmaster, are we performing? Can I join in?

GRANDMASTER You be Wang Chao, my officer.

FATS *[pointing at* MAO*]* What do I do with him?

GRANDMASTER Let him stretch his legs while he watches. One learns from watching.

> *[*FATS *pulls* MAO *to his feet, unchains him, and places one of* MAO's *feet up on the branch of a tree to stretch his leg.]*

MAO Ouch! That hurts. I can't stand like this.

FATS And you think there's nothing to the art of performing.

> *[*FATS *chains* MAO *to the tree.]*

GRANDMASTER Don't chain him. Chain Mr Ding.

> *[*XIA *rushes to help steady* MAO *on his one foot.* FATS *takes the chain off* MAO, *and, with a very deft movement, puts the chain on* DING, *and leads him by it.]*

BIRDMEN What about our birds?

---

* Judge Bao—Bao Zheng (999–1062)—was an upright judge who became a legendary figure in Chinese culture as a symbol of justice. Many operas were written based on cases he had tried in court. The pace and rhythm of the dialogue in the court scene is set by the orchestra, as in a Peking Opera court scene. GRANDMASTER's singing and recited opera lines can be pre-recorded.

GRANDMASTER Hang them up in court.

> [BIRDMEN *hang up the cages near the Judge's table.*]
> Court in session.
>
> [*Orchestra plays music with drums and gong appropriate for a court scene.* BIRDMEN, *as attendants, growl* 'wei—wu' *a ritual cry to establish the solemnity of court and to intimidate criminals.*]

>> FATS Kneel. [*Giving the chain a sudden jerk*]
>> DING Why?
>> FATS This is a performance. Just kneel down.

>> [DING *kneels down reluctantly.*]

GRANDMASTER [*takes the gavel block in hand and strikes the table with it*] Who kneels before Judge Bao?

>> FATS Answer him.
>> DING Me?
>> FATS Yes.
>> DING Paul Ding.

GRANDMASTER Bold, brazen Paul Ding. Look up.

>> [DING *is about to look up.* BIRDMEN *all growl* 'wei—wu'.]

>> FATS [*pushes* DING'*s head so that he looks down*] Say 'I dare not'.
>> DING He told me to.
>> FATS That's the convention. You have to say you dare not first.
>> DING All right. I dare not.

GRANDMASTER Your discourtesy is forgiven.

>> FATS Look up.

>> [DING *looks up.* BIRDMEN *all growl* 'wei—wu' *again.*]
>> Quick. Bow your head.

>> [DING *bows his head.*]

GRANDMASTER Why do you say your surname after your personal name?

>> DING Westerners all put their surnames after their personal names.
>> FATS Don't think that Westerners know it all. We Chinese sometimes say our surname last as well.

GRANDMASTER Well said! You tell him!

>> FATS 'Butcher' Chen, 'Baker' Wang, 'Wonton' Li.

GRANDMASTER 'Dough-sculptor' Tang [*Emphasized by a sharp rap on a small gong*], 'Potter' Zhang [*Sharp rap on small gong*], and 'Wine-maker' Chang [*Sharp rap on small gong*]!

FATS Grandmaster knows everything.

DING They're all smarter after therapy.

GRANDMASTER What do you do?

DING I'm a psychoanalyst.

GRANDMASTER Who is your teacher?

DING Sigmund Freud.

GRANDMASTER His place of origin?

DING Born in Freiberg, in the Austro-Hungarian Empire. Lived later in Vienna.

GRANDMASTER Summon this 'Freud'.

DING He's been dead a long time.

GRANDMASTER Why do you follow the teachings of a master who has been dead a long time?

DING Karl Marx has been dead a long time too. But your honourable country follows his teachings still. Isn't that so?

GRANDMASTER Hah! The comparison is outrageous. Answer my question. This idea of killing one's father and marrying one's mother, is it advocated by Freud?

DING Yes.

GRANDMASTER Why do you bring to our illustrious dynasty such abhorrent bestial behaviour?

DING But . . . but . . .

GRANDMASTER [*strikes the gavel block on the table*] Guard!

BIRDMEN Your Lordship.

GRANDMASTER [*picks four 'order sticks' from the cylinder*] Beat him forty times. [*Throws the sticks on the ground before the table*]

[*The* BIRDMEN *carry out the order.*]

DING Hey, you're doing this for real? Oh, that hurts!

BIRDMEN Ten. Twenty. Thirty. Forty.

[*The* BIRDMEN *return to their former positions.*]

FATS At this point you should do all the stylized movements: writhe in pain, rub hands in frustration, rub the buttocks, and twirl your long hair to show anguish.

DING I should have let you play my part.

GRANDMASTER Did you, as a child, contemplate marrying your mother?

DING I don't rightly remember.

GRANDMASTER [*strikes the gavel block on the table*] Bring in the instruments of torture.

DING I remember. I remember. The thought did occur to me.

GRANDMASTER Mmm . . . How old were you at the time?

DING About three.

GRANDMASTER At three years old. No wonder you grew up to be such a fool. Do you make it a habit to stand under glass-panelled escalators watching women in skirts? Answer.

DING *[aside]* How does he know about that?

GRANDMASTER Ever wanted to be conductor of an orchestra?

DING Yes, certainly.

GRANDMASTER Ever peeped at decent women bathing?

DING Yes. And watched striptease as well.

GRANDMASTER Where were these offences committed?

DING In America. *[Corrects himself]* What offences? These are not offences. The cinema shows women bathing, and striptease shows are operated under licence.

GRANDMASTER Brazen villain! Who is asking about public affairs? I asked if you peeped.

DING I can't remember.

GRANDMASTER Bring in the royal guillotine!

[DAN and XI exit and then return with the guillotine.]

DING What is that for?

FATS To chop you in two if you don't confess.

DING These birdmen are mad!

GRANDMASTER Did you, or did you not, peep?

DING Yes. Yes.

GRANDMASTER At whom?

DING I can't remember.

GRANDMASTER Call Xiang Lian!

FATS Xiao Xia. Fill in for the part. Quick!

XIA *[comes over]* What are my lines?

FATS Got some tissue paper?

XIA Here.

FATS Take it in your hand. Go in and say: Xiang Lian humbly presents herself before your lordship.

XIA *[goes forward with tissue paper spread out in her hands]* Xiang Lian humbly presents herself before your lordship!

GRANDMASTER *[sings a greeting in* jiaoban *mode to address* DING*]* 'Prince Consort!
[Sings fast-tempo—kuaiban] There is no need for excuses and lies.
We have proof to testify.
Bring me the plea that she supplies.'

[FATS takes the tissue paper from XIA and hands it respectfully to GRANDMASTER.]

GRANDMASTER *[raises the tissue paper in one hand. Sings in fast-tempo—* kuaiban*]*

> 'Prince Consort approach, observe.
> Xiang Lian hereby you accuse;
> That you deny you're wed to her,
> To wed another, the royal princess.
> You have betrayed both god and man.
> This appeal has come to my court,
> Here justice will defeat your plot!'

Did you peep at her bathing? *[Pointing at* XIA*]*

DING Yes. How does he know?

XIA *[stylized weeping movement of female lead role—qingyi]* Wu—oa—!

GRANDMASTER *[strikes the gavel block on the table]* Brazen voyeur! How dare you project your own depraved inclinations on to others? Did you not say just now that Fats intends to kill?

FATS You what?

DING That I did say.

GRANDMASTER Have you any proof?

DING It's based on analysis.

GRANDMASTER Whom, did you say, does he intend to kill?

DING An authority in Peking Opera.

GRANDMASTER What do you mean by authority?

DING An expert.

GRANDMASTER What is an expert?

DING One who knows more and more about less and less, until he is absolutely sure of things that cannot be proved.

GRANDMASTER In that case, is an ornithologist an expert?

DING Yes.

GRANDMASTER And a psychoanalyst?

DING Certainly.

GRANDMASTER How do these experts compare with Peking Opera experts in status?

DING Higher.

GRANDMASTER Higher than an opera expert. Then these higher authorities should have precedence in being killed. Why me?

DING Er . . .

[CHARLIE and LUO enter, conversing excitedly. BIRDMEN *growl: 'Wei—wu'.]*

GRANDMASTER Who is causing a disturbance outside?

    FATS A woman of our country brings a barbarian to the presence of your lordship.

GRANDMASTER Throw them out!

    FATS This year is designated 'Golden Year for Tourism', your Lordship. Courtesy would be in order.

GRANDMASTER Let them approach.

        [CHARLIE *and* LUO *walk towards* CHEN.]

    CHARLIE Hello, Mr Chen.

    CHEN Sh—

    LUO What time does the welcoming ceremony start?

    CHEN There is a trial going on here!

GRANDMASTER Who stands there?

    FATS He means you two.

    LUO Oh, a rehearsal? May I present the Observer from the International Council for Bird Preservation.

GRANDMASTER The same gentleman who asked me about bird language and movements, Mr Charlie?

    LUO Yes.

GRANDMASTER And you are keeping his company again?

    CHARLIE She's my wife now.

GRANDMASTER Oh, the inconstancy of barbarians! Young woman, you should be careful. Take heed!

    LUO I don't intend to stay married to him for life.

GRANDMASTER Now that you have married him, stay with him. As poulterers stay with poultry, birdmen with birds. In our country, it is important to keep faith.

        [BIRDMEN *growl*: 'wei—wu'. GRANDMASTER *looks around him.*]

    FATS Your Lordship, shall we proceed with the trial, and not chatter with this woman?

GRANDMASTER What official business have you here?

    LUO Charlie's here for Mr Chen's celebration of the brown *maji*.

GRANDMASTER Call Chen Daozhong.

    CHEN I've been here the whole time.

    FATS There is no such line in any opera. Announce yourself!

    CHEN Doctor of Ornithology Chen Daozhong pays his respects, your Lordship.

GRANDMASTER Where is the brown *maji* at present?

    CHEN On the stone table.

GRANDMASTER [*to* DING, *indicating* CHEN] And what do you call his problem?

DING Voyeurism disguised as mania for collecting. There is only one way to collect living things, and that is what Dr Chen did.

CHEN Mr Ding, that's unfair!

GRANDMASTER Bring the brown *maji*!

[FATS brings the stuffed bird over.]

GRANDMASTER Lift the cover!

CHEN Unveiling the bird is a solemn ritual. Would your Lordship perform it jointly with Charlie?

GRANDMASTER As a minister of the first rank, I do not trouble myself with such triviality. Tell Charlie to unveil it.

[CHARLIE solemnly unveils the bird. He strokes the life-like stuffed bird. A lark suddenly gives a magpie call.]

CHARLIE *[withdraws his hand quickly]* Is it still alive?

CHEN No.

LUO Ah, it's beautiful.

CHARLIE To honour your important contribution to the preservation of rare bird species in the world, I present to you, Mr Chen, on behalf of the International Council for Bird Preservation, the Birdman Medal.

[CHARLIE hangs a medal round CHEN's neck. The two shake hands.]

BIRDMEN What? Him, a birdman? He killed the bird! We are people who look after birds. We are birdmen!

GRANDMASTER Arrest Chen Daozhong. Chain him.

FATS We have only one chain.

GRANDMASTER Chain them together. One killed his father and married his mother, the other killed the bird when he was supposed to care for it. These cases will be reported to His Majesty the Emperor, and the offenders will be executed.

CHARLIE I protest. This is a blatant violation of human rights!

FATS Your Lordship, we cannot be seen to discipline our children in front of our guests.

GRANDMASTER Wait till the foreigners have left then. You will not be dealt with lightly. Now hear ye, barbarian emissary. Return to your tribe and report to your chief. Tell him that the affairs of our Central Plain do not require the attention of outsiders. If you should return to award another such Birdman Medal, it will be on pain of being turned into a stuffed specimen!

CHARLIE What does he mean?

[LUO whispers to him.]

We live in a global village now!

GRANDMASTER Silence! Were it not for the diplomatic immunity you enjoy, you would be in peril of your life! Throw them out!

[BIRDMEN drive CHARLIE and LUO out with their staffs.]

Ha ha . . . ha ha ha . . . *[Blasts of sound from a harsh trumpet and percussion to signal the end of an episode]*

BIRDMEN That's all, folks. Let's walk our birds.

[BIRDMEN throw down their staffs, etc., to pick up their cages, stirring up a wave of birdsong. GRANDMASTER takes the chain off DING and CHEN, rattling it. FATS holds out his hand for it, but GRANDMASTER chucks it at MAO. XIA hangs the chain on MAO. FATS hands GRANDMASTER his hongzi. GRANDMASTER exits with dignity in stylized opera style to the sound of the gongs and drums of the orchestra.

CHEN, DING and FATS watch as GRANDMASTER exits. MAO removes his foot from its position on the tree, sits down on the ground. XIA hugs him, sobbing.

In the midst of birdsong, a spotlight goes up on the stuffed maji bird.

The orchestra exits.

BIRDMEN exit.

XIA helps MAO to one side of the stage, dragging the chain behind them. FATS picks up the end of the chain and follows them off.

CHEN exits.

DING stirs, walks to where the guards stood, picks up a staff, looks at it, drops it, and it falls noisily. Silence. DING goes towards the 'judge's table', walks behind it, stands a moment, and sits down staring before him. He picks up the gavel-block, looks at it and brings it banging down on the table.

A hongzi cries twice.

A magpie calls once.

DING bangs the gavel-block again.

Silence, only the reverberation of the gavel's sound.

A brown maji's shriek.

DING clutches his head.

Lights fade out.]

THE END

PLAYS FROM

TAIWAN

FLOWER AND SWORD

1977

By
MA SÊN

Translated by
DAVID E. POLLARD

— ABOUT **THE PLAYWRIGHT** —

MA SÊN (1932–) is very much a citizen of the world. He moved from mainland China to Taiwan while he was still at secondary school. After graduating from the National Taiwan Normal University, he moved again, this time to France, to take a degree in Drama and Film at the Institut des Hautes Études Cinémathographiques in Paris. After graduation he took up a teaching post at the Centre of Oriental Studies at El Colegio de Mexico, and headed the Chinese Studies section. After five years in Mexico, he was on the move again, this time to Canada. In 1977, he obtained a Ph.D. in Sociology and Anthropology from the University of British Columbia. From 1979 to 1987, he taught at the School of Oriental and African Studies, University of London. During this period, he spent a year in Taiwan, as Visiting Professor at the Department of Theatre of the National Institute of the Arts. He also travelled extensively in mainland China, and lectured at a number of universities there. In 1987, he returned to Taiwan, and has since been Professor of Chinese at the National Ch'êng Kung University. From 1988 to 1989, he was also Chief Editor of a prestigious literary journal in Taiwan, *Unitas* ('Lienhê Wênhsieh').

Ma Sên started writing when he was still at university. In addition to plays, he also writes novels, short stories, drama reviews, as well as critical works on films, East–West drama, and cultural studies. His novels have been translated into English and French. He is also a translator himself, proficient in French, Spanish, English, and Chinese. *Flower and Sword* (1974), one of the nine plays he has published to date, was written when he was in Mexico, but a number of experimental theatre groups in Taiwan, seeing it as a work with strong relevance for the people of Taiwan, have put it on stage. In the 1980s, university drama groups in mainland China, Australia, and Canada also regarded Ma's plays as interesting specimens of the experimental theatre, and *Flower and Sword*, as well as his other plays such as *A Bowl of Cold Congee*, *The Weak*, and *Frogs* (all written in the early 1970s) have been performed.

ABOUT **THE PLAY**

The Chinese diaspora as a topic for serious academic research rose to prominence in the mid-1980s. This play, written in 1977, is strikingly prophetic in its voicing of the concerns of many overseas Chinese intellectuals today. The play tells the story of a young person's return to his homeland to visit his father's grave. In an intricate series of events that are unfolded in a dream-like, symbolist manner, the play depicts the child's desperate attempt to free himself from the voice that has been haunting him all through his adult life.

The play is heavily symbolic in its use of matching pairs of ideas such as flower and sword, husband and wife, husband/wife and his/her lover, father and mother, male and female, parent and child, and the play can be interpreted on many levels. But what emerges most clearly is the tormented consciousness of the child. This serves as a parallel for the experiences of Chinese emigrants who have strong but ambivalent feelings towards the culture, tradition, and moral and ethical values that have 'fathered' them. In this sense, the play is the dramatization of a painful attempt to deal with the history of one's origins.

This play typifies the effort of many Taiwanese dramatists who sought to produce plays that would not be mere extensions of the tradition of realist drama established in mainland China during the 1930s and 1940s, and subsequently in Taiwan in the 1950s and 1960s. It is an example of the early experimental works that appeared in Taiwan in the 1970s: social reality is set aside and the focus is on the state of the individual mind. The rejection of the conventions of realism and naturalism can be seen in the set, costumes, and acting style, all of which are deliberately stylized. The use of masks is central and reminiscent of Sichuan Opera, which features stunning and split-second mask changes. This, together with the music and lighting, creates the ominous feeling of phantasmagoria which hovers about the play.

── **DRAMATIS** PERSONAE ──

THE GHOST, wears a long black or brown gown of cotton or wool, of the kind that men used to wear before the Qing dynasty. The gown is tied at the waist with a cord. The ghost wears straw sandals, and a mask with four layers:

Outer layer (MOTHER), gives the appearance of an old lady, but not too old; her mouth is marked by suffering; her complexion is creamy overall, with pink highlights, something like the make-up for the respectable young women in Peking operas, but not as red on the cheeks, and without the slanting eyes and eyebrows.
Second layer (FATHER), his appearance should be as close as possible to that of the CHILD.
Third layer (FATHER'S FRIEND), as described in the play: bright eyes, white teeth, black beard.
Fourth layer (GHOST), a death's head.

THE CHILD, wears a light blue or long white gown of silk, with a matching silk sash; long hair, no mask; aged 26 or 27; could be either sex. Make-up and clothing should give one the impression of youth and beauty. Can be played by an actor or actress, but should combine the valour of a man and the alluring charm of a woman.

DIRECTOR'S NOTE

The set, costume, and acting style in this play cannot be treated realistically. Colours should be strong and bright, and movements larger than life, but not exaggerated as in a farce. Actors should deliver their lines fluently, with passion, emphasizing their pace and rhythm. The actor who plays THE GHOST *should have a voice with a wide range. The play should be accompanied by music.*

THE **PLAY**

[Setting: There is a grave to the right and another to the left of centre stage. Next to each grave there is a tree in full bloom. Between the graves, to the rear of the stage, there is a small cottage. The cottage is wreathed in mist, and can be seen only dimly. In the further distance there is a background of mountains and woods.

Time: Dusk. In the sky there is a brilliant sunset glow; from time to time crows returning to their nests flit across the space.

When the curtain opens, the GHOST *wearing* MOTHER's *mask (hereafter the* GHOST *will be named according to the mask it is wearing) is standing downstage centre in an attitude of silent prayer. A crow flies over, cawing.* MOTHER *looks up to the sky, and makes as if to chase it away, calling 'Shoo, shoo, shoo!'. Then she looks into the distance, and gestures in surprise.]*

CHILD *[sees* MOTHER *and approaches her]* Excuse me, madam, would this be the Two Hand Grave?

MOTHER *[looks* CHILD *up and down]* By Two Hand you mean the left hand holding a flower, the right hand holding a sword?

CHILD *[taken aback]* Why yes! *[Aside]* How could she know that the left hand held a flower, the right hand held a sword? You must be . . . you must be . . . you are my mother!

*[*MOTHER *does not speak.]*

[looks closely at MOTHER, *then approaches her quickly, speaking doubtfully]* Are you my mother?

*[*MOTHER *still does not speak.]*

I am sure now! *[Goes forward and embraces her]* Yes, you are mother, mother, my mother!

MOTHER Why have you come back?

CHILD *[somewhat crestfallen, lets* MOTHER *go]* I don't know.

MOTHER Didn't I tell you not to come back? Never to come back as long as you lived?

CHILD You did! I still remember your words, remember the icy tone of your voice. Whenever I thought of those words of yours I shuddered and gave up all thought of coming back here.

MOTHER Then tell me why you came back all the same.

CHILD I don't know, I really don't know. In the years I was away I went to many countries, met a lot of people and had a lot of experiences, but through all this there seemed to be a voice from the deep that kept whispering in my ear, 'Go back! Go back! Go back to where your father is buried!'

MOTHER *[coldly]* And that's all you came back for?

CHILD *[perturbed]* Mother, don't reproach me! I know I
shouldn't have come back. But there was a kind of
force drawing me, pulling me; it wouldn't give up
until it had dragged me back here. You don't know
what a fearful struggle I've put up these last few years.
That voice kept nagging me, whispering in my ear, 'Go
back! Go back! Go back to where your father is
buried!'

MOTHER *[gnashing her teeth]* That was his ghost! *[Calms down]*
Didn't I tell you? However hard, however painful the
going was, you had to stick it out, and you were not
to come back, not now, not ever!

CHILD Oh mother, God knows I tried. I tried everything, but
in the end that voice was too strong for me; I had to
come back here, as if it was written in my fate that I
should come back, and there was nothing I could do
about it.

MOTHER *[sighs helplessly]* Ah! So he is proved right. Twenty
years, twenty years on, you have come back to where
you started from!

CHILD True, it's been twenty years. *[Goes forward again to
embrace* MOTHER*]* Mother, mother, I hardly recognized
you. I remembered you as so young, so pretty. *[Holds*
MOTHER *at arm's length, looks her up and down again]*

MOTHER *[calmly]* And now I'm old.

CHILD Not really old, just not as young as I remembered.

MOTHER *[reflects]* Time leaves its mark! When you left home
[Gestures] you were only so high, now you are so tall.

CHILD Look, mother, this is the gown you made for me. I
wore it specially today, to come back to the Two Hand
Grave.

MOTHER I didn't make it for you; it was once your father's.

CHILD *[surprised]* My father's? I thought he left only two
things behind, the flower and the sword, nothing else.

MOTHER No, this is the one thing he left, besides the flower and
the sword. Didn't I tell you when you left home? By
the time you were twenty, you would be as tall as your
father; then you could wear this gown.

CHILD I have never worn it, though. Look, it's still brand new.
I couldn't bring myself to wear it, the material and the
workmanship were so good. I decided not to wear it
until I returned to the Two Hand Grave, so that you
would be able to tell at a glance that it was me.

MOTHER You were right, I did recognize the gown at a glance, but I never thought you would have grown so tall!

CHILD It's been twenty years, mother!

MOTHER Twenty years, all of twenty years!

CHILD Have you been here all these years? You've never left Two Hand Grave?

MOTHER Never. How could I leave? Your father's two hands are buried here, *[Pointing to the grave on the left]* one on this side, *[Pointing to the grave on the right]* the other on that side.

CHILD *[rubbing his/her own hands]* Father's hands. Apart from father's hands, I don't remember what he looked like at all. I can only see father's hands in my mind's eye. Mother, what did father look like?

MOTHER *[scrutinizes* CHILD *closely]* Why do you ask?

CHILD Because . . . because . . . I want to know that I had a father, a whole person, and not just a pair of hands. Mother, everyone has a father, don't they? Why can't I have a father?

MOTHER You did have a father.

CHILD But why don't I remember what he looked like, apart from his hands?

MOTHER Because he was very busy. He was writing his books.

CHILD That's right, I remember, he was writing his books. He was never-endingly writing his books. When I knocked at his door, he would just open the door a crack. It was all dark inside. He would stretch out his hand and stroke my head. Then he would close the door again. I didn't know who he was, I only knew his hands. Mother, did he ever hold me in his arms?

MOTHER Yes, he did. You were very small then, you probably don't remember.

CHILD But as far back as I can remember he never held me in his arms again, never played with me. I so much hoped that one day father would take me for a walk, like I had seen other fathers do, and would put a hand on my shoulder, or around my waist, as if we were pals. I longed too for father to join me in skipping, playing chess, bike riding . . . but he never did. I didn't know how to play when I was small, I just stood there by myself watching other children jumping about and shouting. I didn't know how to play, and I didn't want to, because all I thought about was my father.

MOTHER He was very busy, with his own affairs: he was writing his books.

CHILD I know he was very busy. Every father is very busy, but every child needs his father, longs for his father to take him on his knee, cuddle him, be loving. Mother, I sometimes doubt that I ever had a father.

MOTHER Of course you had a father.

CHILD But my impression of him is so vague, apart from his hands. . . .

MOTHER Haven't you got a photograph of him?

CHILD You mean the one and only photograph of him? The one with him holding a flower in his left hand, a sword in his right hand? The one you placed in my hands when I left home?

MOTHER Yes.

CHILD I was still very little then, mother. I was toying with that photograph while I sat on the deck of the ship as it sailed away. Suddenly a gust of wind blew it into the sea. If it were now, I would jump into the sea without a second thought and retrieve it. But then I was too little: I just watched in horror as the waves carried it away. From then on I could never remember what father looked like. I only remembered his hands: the left hand holding a flower, the right hand holding a sword.

MOTHER The flower and the sword are what your father left you.

CHILD Perhaps it was because I had the flower and the sword that I remembered the hands that held them.

MOTHER Do you still have those things?

CHILD Mother, didn't you say I was to give them as a present to my lover?

MOTHER It was your father who said that before he died.

CHILD So I kept them with me, right up to when I met Juliet.

MOTHER Who is Juliet? A foreigner?

CHILD Yes. I travelled across dozens of lands before I met a girl I really loved. She had golden hair and sea-green eyes. Her skin was as white as snow, as smooth as silk, as fragrant as honey. But the main thing was she said she loved me. We sat facing each other, her hand in mine, my hand in hers. I looked into her eyes, she looked into my eyes. We sat like that, never saying a word all day.

MOTHER You fell in love with her?

CHILD I fell deeply in love with her. So I gave father's flower to her. It had long before faded, but it still had a striking scent.

MOTHER You didn't settle down with her?

CHILD I think I would have stayed with her, if I hadn't met Julian.

MOTHER Who is Julian?

CHILD Julian is Juliet's brother. He had black hair, a black beard, and rode a big horse. His skin was tanned bronze by the sun. When he laughed he showed a set of pure white teeth, his eyes were as bright as the stars at midnight. He said he loved me.

MOTHER You fell in love with him too?

CHILD Yes, I fell in love with him, madly in love. So I gave father's sword to him. The sword was green with age, but it was still very sharp.

MOTHER You didn't settle down with him?

CHILD I think I would have stayed with him, if it wasn't for Juliet.

MOTHER You didn't know who to love?

CHILD No. If I stayed with Juliet, Julian would die of grief. If I stayed with Julian, Juliet would not live long, either.

MOTHER So you couldn't choose between them?

CHILD Oh, mother, love is such a painful thing! Why can we only love one person?

MOTHER Poor child, you really are your father's child!

CHILD Why do you say that, mother? Why, why?

MOTHER You shouldn't have come back, child. You should have obeyed me and not come back here, not ever!

CHILD I didn't want to come back, but that voice was saying in my ear, 'Go back! Go back! Go back to where your father is buried!' If I hadn't come back, I couldn't have gone on living.

MOTHER Why? If you loved Juliet you could have settled down with her; if you loved Julian you could have settled down with him.

CHILD I love them both: how could I settle down with both of them? Oh mother, if I had just had father's flower, I would not have loved Julian; if I had just had father's sword, I would not have loved Juliet. I don't understand why father should have held a flower in one hand and a sword in the other—and given me both.

MOTHER *[agitated]* No, don't ask that question! Don't ask that!

CHILD I want to know, I want to know, mother! I can't go on living otherwise.

MOTHER *[evasively]* Don't ask that question! Don't ask that!

CHILD Mother, that voice whispered in my ear the whole day long: 'Go back! Go back! Go back to where your father is buried!' My purpose in coming back was to sort this business out. *[Goes over and catches hold of* MOTHER'*s sleeve]*

MOTHER *[angrily tugs herself loose]* Let go! Let go of me! Is that all you came back for?

CHILD *[pressing his suit]* Yes, mother! I want to know how father died, and why only his two hands are buried here, the one on the left and the other on the right.

MOTHER *[shrilly]* Heavens, heavens! After twenty years he has truly come back to ask these questions!

CHILD Mother, why are you keeping things from me? Shouldn't I know about my father?

MOTHER Dead and buried the man, dead and buried the matter. Why bring this up now?

CHILD *[imploring]* You must tell me, mother! You must! This is my business. It doesn't matter how many countries I went to, I still ended up back here. I have to find out who my father was, and what he did, in order to know who I am, and what I can do.

MOTHER Do you mean to say you don't know who you are yourself?

CHILD No, I don't, I don't, because my father is just a blur to me. I don't know anything about him—whether he was handsome or ugly, brave or cowardly, kind or vicious, any of those things.

MOTHER *[helplessly]* Child, what do you want from me? What can I tell you?

CHILD Everything! I want to know everything about my father! How did you come to marry? And how did you come to have me?

[A crow settles on one of the trees in front of the graves and caws.]

MOTHER *[angrily claps her hands at the bird]* Shoo! Shoo! *[The crow flies away.]* Detestable creature! Vile black crow!

CHILD *[persistently]* Tell me mother, please!

MOTHER We married because our parents wanted us to, and somehow or other we had you.

CHILD And my father? What kind of a man was he?

MOTHER Your father was a strange man.

CHILD How do you mean?

MOTHER [*talking to herself*] He was a strange man . . . a strange man.

CHILD In what way was he strange? Did he love you?

MOTHER [*startled*] Love? What is love? In our day we didn't use words like that. We didn't need to speak, we just looked at each other and understood all there was to understand.

CHILD But why did he always shut himself up in his dark room?

MOTHER That was after you were born. To begin with everything was perfectly normal. It was after you were born that your father changed. He began to avoid me, I don't know why.

CHILD Didn't he love you any more?

MOTHER He was very busy, he began to write his books. After that he just ignored me, as if I was a total stranger.

CHILD Was he really writing his books? If so, why have I never seen any of the books he wrote?

MOTHER Because he burnt them when he had finished them. He wrote three books, and burnt all three, so nothing is left.

CHILD He really was a strange person.

MOTHER Yes, he was a strange man. At the time I didn't understand him. I think he rather hated me.

CHILD Hated you? why?

MOTHER I couldn't say. He was so cold and distant, as if he didn't know me. He didn't want anything to do with me any more.

CHILD Did you hate him?

MOTHER I . . . I . . . why should I go into all this now?

CHILD [*forcefully*] You have to tell me, you have to! There's no one else to hear, just you and me. If you don't speak now, I will have no way of knowing my father. Waters cannot flow without their source, trees cannot grow without their roots. If I do not know my father, I cannot go on living.

MOTHER It's a dreadful story—do you really want me to tell it?

CHILD I can bear it no matter how dreadful it is! I've been to so many countries, met so many people, had so many experiences, I can bear it no matter how dreadful it is! Tell me straight, mother!

MOTHER *[casting her mind back]* Where should I begin?

CHILD You were saying he rather hated you, and you rather hated him too.

MOTHER Yes, he hated me, and I hated him too, but we could not live apart.

CHILD Why?

MOTHER I don't understand it myself; perhaps it's only when you cannot even hate anymore that you can't go on living. He made me suffer; I made him unhappy.

CHILD Oh, mother!

MOTHER So in tormenting each other we also got some satisfaction. I think his greatest pleasure was in waiting for me to take a lover, so that he could kill me!

CHILD Did you have a lover?

MOTHER I? hmm . . . no. But one day your father brought a friend home. He was strong, warm, and lively. He had black hair and a black beard, his skin was tanned bronze by the sun. When he laughed he showed a set of pure white teeth, his eyes were as bright as the stars at midnight. He kept watching me . . . watching . . . watching . . .

CHILD Did he fall in love with you?

MOTHER I don't know . . .

CHILD Did you fall in love with him?

MOTHER Don't ask me that! I don't know, I don't know; why do you press me?

CHILD I want to know. I want to know everything about you, about my father, and about that man.

[In the following sequence the actor playing the GHOST *should differentiate the two roles as far as possible.]*

MOTHER One day your father suddenly came up and caught my hand *[Changes position and imitates* FATHER's *voice]*: 'Now you have a lover, you don't blame me any more?' *[Reverts to original position, in her own voice]* I said: 'What should I blame you for?' *[Takes up opposite position and imitates* FATHER's *voice]* 'For being cold toward you.' *[Reverts to original position, in her own voice]* I said: 'Blame doesn't come into it, it's a matter of fate!' *[Takes up opposite position, in her own voice but imitating* FATHER's *actions]* Then he lifted up my hand and smelt it, then smelt it again, smelt it time after time. *[Reverts to original position, in her own voice]* 'What are you smelling?' *[Takes up opposite position, imitates* FATHER's

voice] 'Ah! I can smell a special scent!' *[Reverts to
original position, in her own voice]* 'Do you like the
scent?' *[Takes up opposite position, imitates* FATHER's *voice]*
'It goes to your head, it really goes to your head!'
[Reverts to original position, in her own voice] I asked him:
'What scent is it?' *[Takes up opposite position, imitates*
FATHER's *voice]* 'It's his scent, I can tell, there's no
doubt it's his scent!' *[Reverts to original position, in her
own voice]* 'How do you know it's his scent?' When I
asked this his face blanched. He turned and left *[Lifts
her head as if watching* FATHER's *departing figure]* without
saying another word. The next day the dreadful thing
happened.

CHILD What was that?

MOTHER Your father and his friend both disappeared, but a pool
of blood was left in his room.

CHILD *[exclaims in alarm]* Ah! My father killed him? Or did
he kill my father?

MOTHER No one knows. A month later, over there *[Points into
the distance]* in the ravine, they found two corpses.

CHILD My father's and his friend's?

MOTHER Heaven only knows!

[Another crow alights on the tree to the left and caws.]

[chases away the crow, in a shrill voice] Shoo! Shoo! Evil
spirit! Fiend! It was these evil spirits who picked your
father and his friend clean. I only recovered a pair of
hands; otherwise only a pile of bones was left.

CHILD Those were father's hands?

MOTHER One hand held a flower, the other hand held a sword,
just as you saw in the photograph.

CHILD Father, oh father, only a pair of hands was left of you!
But you were also a man, a man of flesh and blood.
You knew desire, you knew love, you knew passion,
you knew hatred. . . . Father, I want to know, did you
ever love me?

MOTHER *[imitating* FATHER's *voice]* Of course I loved you!

CHILD Mother, I was addressing my father!

MOTHER But I am your father! *[Strips off the first mask, revealing
the second]*

CHILD *[dumbfounded]* What? You are my father? Hasn't my
father been dead these many years?

FATHER It wasn't me who died, it was your mother and her
lover.

CHILD *[staggers back]* You . . . you . . . I don't follow! How can this be? My father's bones must have rotted away by now. Look, here is his grave, with his left hand buried on one side, and his right hand buried on the other.

FATHER *[laughs out loud]* Ha ha ha! You've let your mother fool you! It's not me who's buried here, it's your mother and her lover.

CHILD Why would mother fool me?

FATHER Because she didn't want you to know the truth. It was she who sent you abroad and told you never to come back, don't you remember?

CHILD That's true.

FATHER She was afraid, you see, afraid one day you would learn that she had done me wrong.

CHILD Mother did you wrong?

FATHER After you were born your mother treated me very coldly.

CHILD Because of me?

FATHER All day long she hugged you and cuddled you, smiled at you and spoke to you; I ceased to exist for her!

CHILD So you were jealous of me?

FATHER I don't know if I was jealous of you or not, I just felt she was a different person, she was so cold to me.

CHILD So that's the reason you never paid me any attention, never took me in your arms—because you were jealous of me!

FATHER Perhaps; or perhaps it was because of my will to possess, possess your mother. I didn't want her to spare the least bit of love for anyone else.

CHILD So you began to hate her?

FATHER I hated her and she hated me; I tormented her and she tormented me.

CHILD All because of me?

FATHER No! No! Not all because of you. Hatred had already taken root in our hearts. Love and hate are twins: once there is love there is also hate. I not only hated her, I hated myself, only more so.

CHILD Why did you hate yourself?

FATHER I blamed myself for not being able to love her as I loved myself.

CHILD You loved yourself so much?

FATHER Sometimes I thought I did, sometimes I thought I didn't. Sometimes I could forget myself entirely; at such times I was supremely happy. But as soon as your mother stood before me, I came back to myself. It was she who made me unable to forget myself: she was she and I was I, two quite separate people. However much I loved her, I could not become her, and she could not become me. I think I loved her too much, beyond my capacity for love, so I grew weary. *[Bitterly]* But I blamed myself for not being able to give her more.

CHILD So you hated her?

FATHER Yes. But then, she hated me too. We tormented each other.

CHILD Why didn't you simply part company?

FATHER Part company? That never crossed our mind. The fact is, the emptiness of a life without torment is even harder to put up with. Then one day your mother suddenly said to me *[Takes up a position opposite, imitates* MOTHER's *voice]*: 'How can I make you happy, make you contented?' *[Reverts to original position, in his own voice]* I said: 'There's no way you can make me contented, make me happy, because we love too much, hate too much!' But she laughed coldly and said *[Takes up opposite position, imitates* MOTHER's *voice]*: 'I know what would make you contented. Your greatest satisfaction would be to have me take a lover, and then to kill me. Here, tell me what this scent is.' *[Reverts to original position and raises his wife's imaginary hand to his nose]* 'Ah, I can tell it's his scent, the scent of my best friend. I take your meaning, you are in love with him.' *[Takes up opposite position, imitates* MOTHER's *voice]* 'That's right, I'm in love with him. You can kill me!' *[Reverts to original position, in his own voice]*: 'I have no intention of killing you: if I killed you, I would be even more unhappy!' *[Takes up opposite position, imitates* MOTHER's *voice]* 'If you don't kill me, I shall kill him, your best friend!' *[Reverts to original position, in his own voice, fearfully]* 'No, no! Why would you do that?' *[Takes up opposite position, imitates* MOTHER's *voice, grinding out the words]* 'Because I know you love him. You love him more than you love yourself!' *[Reverts to original position, in his own voice, imploringly]* 'Don't do that, I beseech you!' When I said that, her face blanched, and she went away. *[Lifts his head as if watching the imaginary figure departing]* The next day the dreadful thing happened.

CHILD What was that?

FATHER Your mother and my friend both disappeared. A pool of blood was left in your mother's room.

CHILD *[horrified]* Ah! My mother killed him? Or did he kill my mother?

FATHER No one knows. A month later, over there *[Points into the distance]* in the ravine they found two corpses.

CHILD My mother's and her lover's?

FATHER Heaven only knows!

[Another crow alights on the tree to the right and caws.]

[driving away the crow, in a shrill voice] Shoo! Shoo! Evil spirit, fiend! It was these evil spirits who picked your mother and her lover clean! I only recovered a pair of hands; otherwise only a pile of bones was left.

CHILD Whose hands were they?

FATHER One hand was clasping a flower, the other hand a sword.

CHILD Weren't they yours, the flower and the sword?

FATHER I had given the flower to your mother, and the sword to my friend.

CHILD Heavens! You did the same as I did, father. Does that mean you also loved them both, and could not choose between them?

FATHER Yes, yes, I loved them both, and could not choose between them!

CHILD Oh, father, tell me what I should do.

FATHER *[mysteriously, in a leaden voice]* Kill one of them, and settle down with the other!

CHILD Kill Julian? Or kill Juliet?

FATHER Either one will do!

CHILD But I still don't know how to choose between them. How did you choose in the end, father?

FATHER You really want to know?

CHILD Of course!

FATHER I chose to kill the two of them!

CHILD *[shocked]* What? It was you who killed them?

FATHER *[categorically]* Right, it was me who killed them!

CHILD *[distressed]* You didn't love them!

FATHER I did love them!

CHILD *[vehemently]* You're lying! You're lying! You don't love anybody, me included, you never loved me!

FATHER Child, it was just because I loved you that I chose the way I did.

CHILD No! No! You don't love me! You never cuddled me, hugged me, patted me, soothed me. How can I believe you loved me?

FATHER I gave you life. To love you was to love myself.

CHILD You are you and I am I. You're cruel, father!

FATHER All fathers are cruel! But I loved you because you are my child, an extension of my life. You took my love away with you, and my hate, my everything. I am now an empty shell, bereft even of life; that is why I summoned you back.

CHILD So it was you? It was you who whispered in my ear all day long 'Go back! Go back! Go back to where your father is buried'?

FATHER Yes, it was me! I had vowed that after twenty years you must come back, come back here and understand everything. If you want someone to blame, blame your mother, don't blame me. It was all her fault!

CHILD Enough! Enough! I am back now, but I no longer want to understand everything. I only want to know one thing . . .

FATHER What?

CHILD I want to know if my father ever loved me.

FATHER Of course I loved you. The only thing was you were too young then; I didn't know how to tell you.

CHILD Oh, father, you didn't have to tell me! You only had to pat me, soothe me, cuddle me, hug me. It is too late for you to tell me these things. Look at how big I am, how tall I am; the time is past for you to pat me, soothe me, cuddle me, hug me. You can say you love me a thousand times, it would all be pointless!

FATHER [approaches anxiously] You don't mean it!

CHILD [recoils] Don't come near me! Don't come near me! When I was little do you realize how often I looked forward to you taking me for a walk, putting your arm round my shoulders—like this—telling me what you liked and what you hated, teaching me how to make my way in the world, how I should live my life? Do you realize how often I looked forward to us skipping together, playing chess together, riding our bikes together, looked forward to you taking me on your knee, hugging me, all warm and affectionate. . . . But none of this, none of this ever happened!

FATHER [approaches hesitantly] Perhaps we could even now—

CHILD *[shrinking back]* Now? Now I'm not a child any more, as you can see. Now I am as tall as you, as big as you, I don't need those things now.

FATHER *[pained]* Child! Tell me what I should do. I want you to know . . .

CHILD Know what? Know that you love me? Oh, father, what good would it do to know? It is my feelings that count. It is all too late.

FATHER *[disappointed]* Too late . . . too late! You are right! Too late . . .

CHILD Still, there is one matter you might yet be able to help me with.

FATHER *[excited]* What? Tell me, what is it? I'll do anything in my power.

CHILD I just want you to tell me, should I also kill the two of them, Julian and Juliet?

FATHER *[hesitates]* Er . . . er . . .

CHILD *[pressing him]* Didn't you say you yourself killed mother and your friend?

FATHER It's precisely because I killed them that I am unhappy now.

CHILD Why? Hasn't killing them made you free? All doubt and hesitation is behind you, and you don't have to make any more choices.

FATHER Free? *[Laughs hysterically]* Ha ha ha ha. . . . That's wishing for the moon! Dead they may be, but the love lives on.

CHILD You still love them?

FATHER Of course, *[Points to his heart]* they are still alive in here!

CHILD *[dispirited]* Then there is no hope for me!

FATHER Hold on, look! *[Strips off the second mask, revealing the third]*

CHILD *[recoils in amazement]* Who are you?

FRIEND I am your father's friend, your mother's lover.

CHILD Didn't you die long ago?

FRIEND Actually it wasn't me who died!

CHILD Who was it?

FRIEND It was your father and mother.

CHILD I don't understand. My father and mother both told me they had killed you, and your body had fed the crows in the ravine.

FRIEND They were having you on! The truth is, your father and mother were once very much in love, but then they both fell in love with me.

CHILD So the three of you were in a quandary?

FRIEND Even if one of us was got rid of, the other two still would not be happy.

CHILD Why didn't the three of you settle down together?

FRIEND How could all three of us be always watching for one of the others to make a move? You can't have three mouths kissing at once.

CHILD You don't have to tell me that!

FRIEND So we decided it would be better if we all died together. One day we went to the ravine over there. *[Points into the distance]* Your father held a sword in his hand, your mother a flower in hers. They stood eyeing each other for a long time, then finally your father thrust his sword into your mother's heart, then turned it on himself and pierced his own heart!

CHILD *[shrieks]* Oh, heavens! Don't go on! Don't go on!

FRIEND Two pools of blood soaked into the bare soil.

CHILD Heavens! What a frightful way for them to die! But what about you? How come you did not die?

FRIEND *[smugly]* Ha ha! Me? I had no life to begin with, what need was there for me to die?

CHILD What do you mean? I don't understand!

FRIEND The fact is, I have never really existed. I am half your father, half your mother. Actually I am a second self of your parents.

CHILD *[sternly]* Who are you? Tell me straight! Who are you?

FRIEND I am your father, and also your mother, and also your father's friend, your mother's lover. Your mother was a fool: on no account would she have you come back here, but she didn't realize that to be kept in the dark would only be harder for you to bear. All right then, let me tell you the true facts!

CHILD I don't want to know any more true facts! I just want to know what choice I should make myself.

FRIEND *[whispers]* You shouldn't make any choice at all! Because you have never loved at all: you never loved Julian, you never loved Juliet. The truth is you are not yourself at all!

CHILD Then who am I?

FRIEND You are your father's son, your mother's daughter; you model yourself on them in every way. Since they never loved you, how could you have any love to give to another?

CHILD [*shocked*] That's a lie! I am quite sure I love deeply, madly—

FRIEND If you are truly in love, you don't need to make any choice: you go ahead and kill them both, and they will live forever there! [*Points to* CHILD*'s heart*]

CHILD [*angrily*] No! No! You are talking nonsense, nonsense! If anyone is to die, it can only be me.

FRIEND [*egging on*] Go on, follow your father's example, go and kill Julian and Juliet!

CHILD [*defiantly*] No! No!

FRIEND [*coaxingly grasps* CHILD*'s hand*] Go on! If you love me, you will do this for me!

CHILD [*struggling*] No! No! Who are you? What man are you? Who are you really?

FRIEND Take a look, take a close look and tell me who I am.

CHILD [*looks at him closely, bewildered*] You look like my father, and at the same time like my mother, then again like Julian, then again like Juliet. Oh, [*Plaintively*] who are you, who are you really?

FRIEND [*laughs hysterically*] Ha ha ha! I am love, I am hate! I am your heart!

CHILD [*angrily*] Ah you . . . you . . . who are you really? [*Goes over and rips off the third mask, revealing the last layer, a death's head*]

[*At this point the sun suddenly sinks, and the moon shoots up into the sky. The stage lighting abruptly changes from the dazzling sunset to an eerie moonlight. The* GHOST *slowly retreats and gradually disappears into the mists that wreathe the cottage. A crow flies over, cawing.*]

CHILD Heavens! Heavens! Where am I? Who am I? I've come such a long way to get here. Oh, father, you called me back here, but what did I meet with? I should have listened to my mother and never come back. I should have gone my own way. But father, why did you whisper in my ear all day long: 'Go back! Go back! Go back to where your father is buried!' Was it just to say you loved me? You killed my mother, but you said she is living in your heart! [*Painfully*] My heart is beating fast, my throat seems to be on fire. [*Puts his hands round his neck]* There seems to be a pair of hands squeezing me here. . . . *[Struggling]* I want to cry out! I want to shriek, I don't want to love any more, love just brings me grief. . . . I have lost my way. No one has ever told me what way I should take, how I should live my life.

[A red lantern suddenly appears in front of the cottage.]

FATHER'S VOICE *[hollowly]* Come! Come!

CHILD Is that you, father? Is that you calling me? You have been calling me like that for all of twenty years! Enough! Enough! I won't obey you any more. I am already big and tall.

FATHER'S VOICE *[hollowly]* Come . . . come . . .

CHILD *[runs forward a few steps, in a choking voice]* Tell me, father, tell me you love me! You loved me. . . . No! No! Don't say anything! It's too late, everything's too late! I know you never loved me. My heart is so empty, so cold; I really haven't loved anyone. You were right, I never loved Julian, and I never loved Juliet, because no one ever loved me! Yet there is a fire burning here, *[Points to heart]* I am sure of that. I want to love, I want to love! I want to love Julian, and I want to love Juliet. I gave the sword to the one, and the flower to the other: how can I choose between them? Look, even this gown is yours! Does that mean I am fated to take your way? No! No! *[Rips the gown off his/her back]* This belongs to you! *[Throws it at the lantern]* Take it back! Take it back!

FATHER'S VOICE *[hollowly]* Come! Come! Come with me . . .

CHILD *[goes forward another few paces, then stops. The red lantern floats slowly towards the back of the stage, as if being carried further and further away.]* Oh, father, I have lost my way. But I can't go along with you! I can't! *[Wheels round. A crow flies over, cawing bleakly.]* Where is my way?

[Curtain falls.]

THE END

PINING . . .
IN PEACH BLOSSOM LAND

1986

By
LAI SHÊNG-CH'UAN

Translated by
MARTHA P. Y. CHEUNG

— ABOUT **THE PLAYWRIGHT** —

LAI SHÊNG-CH'UAN, STAN (1954–) was born in Washington, DC to Taiwanese parents. He moved to Taiwan with his family at the age of twelve, and lived in Taipei for many years before going back to the States in 1978 to study Theatre at the University of California, Berkeley. In 1983, he obtained a Ph.D. in Dramatic Art. At the invitation of the National Institute of the Arts, he returned to Taiwan and taught at the Institute, where he is still a professor. He also chaired the Department of Theatre at the Institute for five years and was founding Head of the Graduate School of Theatre.

Soon after his return to Taiwan, in 1984, Lai Shêng-ch'uan co-founded the 'Performance Workshop' and has since been its Artistic Director. The plays he wrote and directed are all attempts to blend high art and popular Taiwanese culture, and are characterized by an innovative and provocative treatment of themes about life in contemporary Taiwan. They were so well received that the 'Performance Workshop' soon won the support not only of regular theatre-goers but also of the general public. This brought new energy and vitality to the burgeoning theatre movement in Taiwan and the excitement generated by Lai and the 'Performance Workshop' led to the establishment of new theatre groups and a surge of interest in the theatre. Over the past decade, he has created thirteen original plays—all premiered in Taipei—including successes such as *Plucking Stars* (1984), *Chinese Comedy in the Late Twentieth Century* (1985), *Pining . . . In Peach Blossom Land* (1986), *Circle Story* (1987), *The Island and the Other Shore* (1989), *Look Who's Cross-talking Tonight* (1989), *Strange Tales of Taiwan* (1991), and an opera, *Journey to the West* (1987), based on a classical Chinese novel of the same title. Overseas tours to places like Hong Kong, Singapore, and the United States have won Lai and the 'Performance Workshop' international acclaim. For his theatre work, Lai was awarded Taiwan's 'National Literary Prize' in 1988.

Lai makes extensive use of improvisation in collaboration with his actors. *Pining . . . In Peach Blossom Land*, like most of Lai's other plays, is the result of a collective creative effort, with the framework and central ideas provided by Lai and the lines by the actors and actresses during rehearsals. It was first performed by the 'Performance Workshop' in Taipei in 1986. In 1992, the play was made into a film, *The Peach Blossom Land*, which Lai directed. The film won the 'Silver Prize' at the Tokyo International Film Festival Young Cinema Competition, the 'Callgari Prize' at the Berlin Forum, and the 'Best Film', 'Best Director' and 'FIPRESCI' awards at the Singapore International Film Festival. Lai's second film, *The Red Lotus Society*, completed in 1994, has also enjoyed stirring reviews in Toronto and Kyoto, and at the New York Film Festival.

ABOUT **THE PLAY**

Complex in structure and rich in meaning, *Pining . . . In Peach Blossom Land* is one of the best experimental works produced in Taiwan in recent years. *Pining* is a tragic love story set in Shanghai at the end of the Second World War; *In Peach Blossom Land* is a love comedy in ancient period costume and a tongue-in-cheek adaptation of Tao Yuanming's utopian classic, *Peach Blossom Land Chronicle*. The two plays are being rehearsed at the same time in the same theatre. The actors find themselves cross-acting, their lines interweaving, and the plays commenting on each other.

Each of the plays can stand as a separate and independent work, but they can also be explored together since both contain similar themes of love, relationships, and separation. Together they provide an encapsulation of the experience of many of the older generation in Taiwan—those who left China during the war or after the Communist take-over, for whom the experience of loss is still an incurable scar, and nostalgia a mood that torments them. Furthermore, they create a parable revealing what happens when people keep on pining for the 'Peach Blossom Land' when they are already there—an important element in the consciousness of a whole generation in Taiwan.

When the two plays are juxtaposed on stage, something more emerges. The cacophony and incongruity in styles produces an amazing theatrical experience as the dialogues fuse, separate, and comment on one another. This hilarious rapid-fire comedy of errors is also a comedy of infinite possibilities. At the same time, the play draws on a host of artistic and historical sources: impromptu comic scenes in traditional Peking Opera, Tao Yuanming's classical work, and the sentimental soap operas so popular in Taiwan in the 1960s and 1970s. The play can thus be regarded as Lai Shêng-ch'uan's attempt to blend his home culture with his acquired culture. It certainly is a dazzling *tour de force.*

DRAMATIS PERSONAE

CHARACTERS IN PINING
CHIANG PIN-LIU
YÜN CHIH-FAN
MRS CHIANG
NURSE

CHARACTERS IN PEACH
BLOSSOM LAND
T'AO
CH'UN-HUA (WOMAN IN WHITE)
YÜEN (MAN IN WHITE)

CHARACTERS OUTSIDE THE
PLAYS-WITHIN-THE-PLAY
DIRECTOR
SHUN-TZŬ
STRANGER, a woman
STAGE-MANAGER
WANG
CARETAKER

THE **PLAY**

[From the darkened stage rises the sound of CHIANG PIN-LIU *singing the song 'Seeking'.]*

CHIANG *[sings]*

> 'You are a wisp of cloud in the sky,
> You are a meteor flashing through the night . . .'

[The curtain rises. The lights come up slowly. Setting: an evening in Shanghai after World War II. It is late, but the lights of the metropolis are still shimmering in the background. Downstage, the young lovers CHIANG PIN-LIU *and* YÜN CHIH-FAN *are in the Bund Park sitting side by side on a pair of swings, swaying gently.* CHIANG *has on a Western-style suit of the 1940s,* YÜN *wears her hair in two long plaits. In this scene, they should both adopt the traditional acting style of a sentimental romance.]*

CHIANG *[goes on singing]*

> 'Your tenderness enthrals my heart,
> Your love light brightens my heart . . .'

*[*YÜN *rises slowly and moves towards* CHIANG, *who goes on singing.]*

YÜN *[looking around]* How still it is! I've never seen Shanghai so still before. It's as if the two of us are the only people in the whole city. The rain just now makes me feel so good. *[She sits on the swing again, and sways gently.]* There is something indescribably wonderful in the air.

CHIANG *[goes on singing]*

> 'How can I endure any longer?
> How can I wait any longer . . .'

YÜN *[pointing her finger forward]* Pin-liu, look at the lights in the water—It's beautiful.

CHIANG *[stops singing and watches intently]* Like a painting.

YÜN Everything seems to have come to a standstill.

CHIANG *[looks at* YÜN*]* Do you like it?

*[*YÜN *nods, and smiles. They quietly watch the lights in the water.]*

YÜN *[feels a draught]* It's getting chilly.

[CHIANG, *concerned, rises and removes the scarf he is wearing, goes behind* YÜN, *and puts it round her neck.*]

[*feeling the warmth of his scarf with her hand*] I'm so happy this summer! I still remember the last few years, when the war was on, I never even dreamt that life could be so wonderful. Now people are so full of hope, like us, don't you think?

CHIANG [*starts singing again, in a softer voice*]

'Seeking the love that knows no bounds,
Seeking the life where love abounds.'

[CHIANG *puts his hands on* YÜN's *shoulders and rocks the swing with loving tenderness. They watch the night scene in silence.*]

YÜN Pin-liu, will you write to me when I'm in Kunming?

CHIANG I've written already.

YÜN [*surprised*] Have you really?

CHIANG I've timed it perfectly. You're leaving tomorrow morning by boat; in ten days, you'll be home; the minute you walk in, my letter will be there waiting for you!

YÜN [*smiles, incredulous*] No kidding?

CHIANG I didn't post it though. [*A mischievous smile*]

YÜN [*also smiles*] Go on.

[CHIANG *takes out a letter from his pocket, kneels on one knee before* YÜN, *takes her hand, and puts the letter on her palm.*]

CHIANG Now I can be sure it reaches you.

YÜN Can I read it now?

CHIANG Wait till you get home.

[*Appreciating his meaning,* YÜN *puts the letter into her pocket.*]

CHIANG [*returns to his swing*] Chih-fan—

YÜN Mm?

CHIANG I miss Kunming.

YÜN Well, to think that you spent three years in Kunming studying at the University—I just can't believe it! My home is right next to the University, and we never even met! And yet, we meet here in Shanghai! Such a vast city, Shanghai; you don't run into people easily. [*Pauses*] I wonder what would have happened if we hadn't met in Shanghai.

CHIANG [*with absolute certainty*] We were destined to meet in Shanghai.

YÜN Are you so sure?

CHIANG Of course! I can't imagine how empty life would be if we hadn't met in Shanghai.

[*They look at each other, both startled by the realization of what a mystery it is that they should have met each other.*]

You know, even if we had missed each other in Shanghai, in ten years' time we'd meet in . . . [*Reflecting a moment*] in Hankou! And if we didn't meet in Hankou in ten years' time, then in thirty years we'd meet . . . [*Reflecting a moment*] we'd meet abroad. That's for certain!

YÜN But we would both be old by then, what would be the point?

CHIANG It would be just as beautiful!

[*Their eyes meet. They remain seated, looking at each other in silence.*]

YÜN Pin-liu, close your eyes.

CHIANG Why?

YÜN No questions, just close your eyes!

[CHIANG *closes his eyes,* YÜN *takes out a sweater from a shopping bag and holds it up against* CHIANG. CHIANG *opens his eyes, greatly surprised.*]

I saw this in Wing On Company today, I thought it would look nice on you.

CHIANG [*lost for words*] My . . . [*Takes the sweater and examines it*] How much did it cost you?

YÜN Never mind the money! Put it on. See if it fits.

[CHIANG *takes off his jacket and puts on the sweater.*]

CHIANG [*still full of surprise and delight*] Well, this is . . .

YÜN [*studies him up and down as she smooths out the sweater for him*] Perfect, don't you think?

[CHIANG *too, studies himself in his new sweater.*]

You can wear it when I'm in Kunming, then you'll always remember me. [*Returning to her swing*] I also bought two pairs of nylon stockings for my younger sister. Stockings are very expensive in Kunming. And two lengths of dress material for my mother—

[*While* YÜN *is chattering away,* CHIANG *suddenly feels an attack of loneliness.*]

CHIANG *[with a heavy heart]* It's great to be able to go home!

YÜN *[replying happily, not aware of the change in* CHIANG'*s mood]* Yes, it is! This is our first family reunion since the War! Even my eldest brother and his wife will join us, and they live in Chongqing! Oh, I love spending Lunar New Year in Kunming! Pine needles all over the floor, delightful scent! That's what the New Year should be like! *[Getting carried away]* Pin-liu, when I come back from Kunming, I'll bring you some camellias, shall I?

CHIANG *[still with a heavy heart]* It's great to be able to go home—

YÜN *[noticing his sadness]* What's the matter? You're homesick again? *[Comforting him]* You'll be able to go home to Manchuria one day! The Russians won't be there forever.

CHIANG You can't just jump on to a train and be off to Manchuria just like that!

YÜN *[goes up to* CHIANG*]* The day *will* come when you can spend New Year in Manchuria! *[The more she tries to comfort him, the sadder he grows. She squats down, holding his hands.]* Pin-liu, the war is over. We're lucky to be still alive. Why keep thinking about unpleasant things?

CHIANG There are things one just cannot forget!

YÜN But you must, you must. Look around you, is there anyone who isn't scarred and hurt?

CHIANG There are things we can never forget, for as long as we live.

YÜN *[patiently, like coaxing a child]* But you must! You must learn to forget!

CHIANG What about the time we've spent together? Can we forget that?

YÜN Come on! I didn't ask you to forget that! I just mean those unpleasant memories—the war; evacuation. You must put them behind you to start a new life. Please!

[CHIANG begins to calm down.]

When I come back from Kunming we can go and look for a house.

CHIANG Yes, let's do that! We want a place that's convenient, and not expensive. It won't be easy, but I'm sure we'll find one, don't you think?

[They gaze dreamily into space, thinking about the future.]

YÜN *[dreamily]* Pin-liu, if you had the choice, where in the
world would you choose to live?

CHIANG Me?

YÜN Yes, and I mean anywhere in the world.

CHIANG Isn't Shanghai good enough?

YÜN You know something? In 1939, when the war was
raging, a rumour broke out that Kunming would be
bombed the next day, by over a hundred Japanese
bombers. Everybody fled. Overnight, Kunming became
a ghost city. We fled for our lives, too. Mother took us
from Dianchi to Gaoqiao, and from there we went on
foot for two days until we came to a very special place
deep in the mountains. *[Completely lost in the idyllic
world evoked by her memories]* The wild flowers were
blooming gloriously; the people there spoke a language
we didn't understand, but they were so friendly. We
spent a whole month there, and had the most
wonderful time! Talk about fleeing for our lives! Later
on, we learnt that the rumour was just a scare, so we
came out of the mountain. Even now, I still think
about that place every so often.

CHIANG Does such a place really exist?

YÜN I'll take you there when we have a chance, shall I?

CHIANG Let's go together if we have the chance.

YÜN *[quiet all of a sudden]* Pin-liu, what will you do when
I'm in Kunming?

CHIANG *[having considered the question seriously]* Wait for you.

YÜN And?

CHIANG *[turns to* YÜN, *gazing into her eyes]* Wait for you! *[He
reaches out his hand, and holds* YÜN's.*]*

YÜN And then?

[They look at each other. Lights fade out.]

SCENE TWO

[Lights brighten suddenly. Actor CHIANG PIN-LIU *and Actress* YÜN CHIH-FAN
*are still sitting on their swings, but standing between them is an elderly man whose
hairstyle and clothes are modern, and completely at odds with Shanghai in the
1940s. About sixty years of age, he is the* DIRECTOR *of Pining. He is staring
blankly out front, as if lost in memories.]*

DIRECTOR It . . . it wasn't like that as I remember it. *[Pauses]*
There's something wrong . . . But I just can't put my
finger on it!

ACTOR CHIANG But where and what exactly is the problem?

[The actress playing the NURSE *enters in her uniform, not knowing what is going on. Seeing that the rehearsal has been interrupted, she glances around and goes out.]*

DIRECTOR Chiang Pin-liu, you must try and understand Chiang Pin-liu's background. And you've got to remember that this scene is the key to the whole story! This is what leads to the pain and anguish you have to suffer for the rest of your life!

*[*ACTOR CHIANG *tries to understand the meaning of* DIRECTOR's *words.]*

Chiang, this is the quintessence of all your memories. The moment your fingers are entwined in hers . . . *[He takes* YÜN's *hand.]* is also the sweetest and saddest moment of your life.

[The actress playing MRS CHIANG *comes on stage, still busy with her make-up.]*

ACTOR CHIANG Director, could you be more explicit?

[Seeing that she is not wanted just then, ACTRESS MRS CHIANG *goes off quickly.]*

DIRECTOR What I mean is, you don't seem to have got the picture yet. *[He is lost in memories again.]* Shanghai in those days was the busiest and most prosperous city in China! How can you not see that?

ACTRESS YÜN But you can't blame us! We've never been to Shanghai! We've tried our best to do what you tell us—*[Points her finger forwards]* this is the Bund Park, in front of it is the Huangpu River—

DIRECTOR The Huangpu River? *[Pause. He scowls at them.]* You act as if you're facing the Tamsui River. Look, Chiang, if you don't get it right in this scene, by the time you go to the next one and you're an old man, you'll have no memory to fall back on!

ACTOR CHIANG *[suppressing his resentment]* Well, what now?

DIRECTOR Let's take it again! From the sweater.

[The two return to their swings and try to get into the mood. DIRECTOR *shouts at the Control Room.]*

Cut the lights!

[Lights fade.]

SCENE THREE

[Lights come up slowly, revealing once again the swings and the night scene in Shanghai. CHIANG PIN-LIU *and* YÜN CHIH-FAN *are to start again from the part about the sweater.* YÜN *smoothes out the sweater for* CHIANG *and studies him up and down.]*

YÜN Perfect, don't you think? You can wear it when I'm back in Kunming; then you'll always remember me. *[Returning to her swing]* I also bought two pairs of nylon stockings for my younger sister. Stockings are very expensive in Kunming. And two lengths of dress material for my mother—

CHIANG *[with a heavy heart]* It's great to be able to go home!

YÜN Yes, it is! This is our first family reunion since the War! Even my eldest brother and his wife will join us, and they live in Chongqing! Oh, I love spending Lunar New Year in Kunming! Pine needles all over the floor, delightful scent! That's what the New Year should be like! Pin-liu, when I come back from Kunming, I'll bring you some camellias, shall I?

CHIANG *[still with a heavy heart]* It's great to be able to go home—

[Several figures dressed in casual, contemporary clothes appear one after another upstage left. They have with them bags, large and small, and are carrying some props and bits of ancient period costumes in their hands. They stand there, quietly watching the rehearsal.]

YÜN What's the matter? You're homesick again? You'll be able to go home to Manchuria one day! The Russians won't be there forever!

CHIANG You can't just jump on to a train and be off to Manchuria just like that!

YÜN *[goes up to* CHIANG*]* The day *will* come when you can spend New Year in Manchuria!

[Looking puzzled, the group upstage start whispering among themselves as they watch the performance of the two on the swings.]

Pin-liu! *[She squats down, holding his hands.]* The war is over. We're lucky to be still alive. Why keep thinking about unpleasant things?

[The group have come to a decision. One of the men moves cautiously downstage, stops just a little behind CHIANG *and* YÜN, *midway between the two swings, and waits for a convenient moment to interject.]*

CHIANG There are things one just cannot forget!

YÜN But you must, you must. Look around you, is there anyone who isn't scarred and hurt?

[The sound of DIRECTOR *roaring in the wings.]*

DIRECTOR *[offstage]* What's going on upstage?

*[*CHIANG *and* YÜN *carry on unperturbed. The others have no idea who is yelling at them and are looking round trying to locate the voice.]*

CHIANG There are things we can never forget, for as long as we live.

YÜN But you must! You must learn to forget!

[The intruders are now gathered around the swings. Some are even standing between CHIANG *and* YÜN *and watching their performance with baffled expressions.]*

CHIANG What about the time we've spent together? Can we forget that?

YÜN Come on! I didn't ask you to forget that! I just mean those unpleasant memories—the war, evacuation. You must put them behind you to start a new life. Please!

[The sound of DIRECTOR *roaring again in the wings.]*

DIRECTOR *[offstage]* What are you people doing there?

[The lights brighten suddenly. DIRECTOR *storms in, furious. Everyone is taken aback.]*

What the hell is going on?

ACTRESS YÜN *[resentful of the interruption]* What now?

*[*DIRECTOR *heads straight for the leader of the intruders. The man is from the theatre company that is going to do* In Peach Blossom Land. *He plays* YÜEN, *the shop owner.]*

DIRECTOR What are you doing here?

ACTOR YÜEN *[innocently]* Are you talking to me?

DIRECTOR Yes!

ACTOR YÜEN *[rising to the challenge]* What are *you* doing here? Please clear the stage, we're about to start rehearsal!

DIRECTOR What rehearsal? We've booked this place!

ACTOR YÜEN You've what? Impossible! Our play opens tomorrow evening. Tonight is our dress rehearsal. There's a poster outside—*In Peach Blossom Land.* Didn't you see it?

DIRECTOR I did, but I'm damn sure I've booked this place!

ACTOR YÜEN You must have got it wrong! *[Not wanting to argue anymore, he turns to his group.]* Shun-tzŭ, take away the swings!

*[*SHUN-TZŬ *goes up to the swings.]*

ACTOR CHIANG *[stops him]* Hey! We're rehearsing!

ACTOR T'AO *[has been watching them all this time, and now speaks]* Excuse me, there must be a misunderstanding. But we do need the stage.

DIRECTOR You must be joking! I've booked this place!

ACTOR T'AO Who is joking?

ACTOR CHIANG *[incredulous]* Wait a minute. Are you sure you've booked it?

ACTOR YÜEN *[with absolute certainty]* Yes!

ACTOR T'AO Positive!

ACTOR CHIANG How can that be? This evening is ours! We've filled in all the forms!

ACTOR YÜEN *[to* CHIANG*]* What are you rehearsing?

ACTOR CHIANG *Pining. . . .* The play opens the day after tomorrow. We've got to have a run-through tonight.

ACTOR YÜEN That's where you're wrong. *[Self-righteously]* Look, we open tomorrow. We have to have a dress rehearsal! *[He pays no more attention to the* Pining *lot.]* We have no time to lose! *[To his team]* Bring in the props!

[Dressed in ancient peasant-woman costume, the actress who plays CH'UN-HUA *in* Blossom Land *comes up to* ACTOR YÜEN.*]*

ACTRESS CH'UN-HUA Which scene first?

ACTOR YÜEN Let's begin with 'The Triangle in Wuling'.

ACTRESS CH'UN-HUA *[reminds* ACTOR YÜEN*]* Go and get changed!

[The Blossom Land *crew begin to bring in the props— ancient-looking furniture that includes a screen, a table, and a few stools.]*

ACTOR CHIANG *[furious]* What went wrong with the booking, Director?

DIRECTOR You think I've mucked it up?

ACTOR CHIANG How come there's a problem?

DIRECTOR All right, all right! I'll go and see. *[Strides towards the wings]* Damn! I don't need this!

ACTOR YÜEN Yeah! You go and see!

DIRECTOR *[not stopping]* We have little enough time as it is. Damn!

[The props of both plays are scattered over the stage.]

ACTOR T'AO *[to his team]* Let's hurry!

ACTOR YÜEN *[giving orders]* Shun-tzǔ, take away the swings!

[SHUN-TZǓ, a young man, comes over.]

[indicating the swings] Take them away!

ACTOR CHIANG *[protesting]* No! We're rehearsing!

ACTOR YÜEN Look, your director isn't even here. Come on. *[To* SHUN-TZŬ*]* Get moving! We don't have much time!

> *[*SHUN-TZŬ *pushes the swings towards the wings and exits.]*

ACTRESS YÜN *[to* ACTOR CHIANG, *still not quite sure what exactly is going on]* Are we really done?

ACTOR CHIANG No idea. I don't know what the director has done with the booking.

ACTOR YÜEN *[seeing that the two are still hanging about]* Sorry! Could you stand aside? We're starting now.

ACTRESS YÜN *[at her wits' end]* Oh, what's going on? *[She looks around, then goes off reluctantly.]*

> *[*ACTOR T'AO, *dressed in a short jacket and fisherman's trousers, has taken up his seat on the set for* In Peach Blossom Land.*]*

ACTOR T'AO *[to* ACTOR YÜEN, *resentfully]* I've told you I can't stand being interrupted at rehearsals!

ACTOR YÜEN *[placating him]* Okay, okay! No problem! Just relax.

ACTOR T'AO No problem! You kept telling me there was no problem last time, but it was absolute chaos!

ACTOR YÜEN When was that?

ACTOR T'AO Look at that stupid swing we had to move off the stage. Last time I had to move a giant ark, remember?

ACTOR YÜEN What do you mean 'You moved the ark'? *I* moved the ark!

ACTOR T'AO What do you mean 'You moved the ark'? *I* moved the damn ark!

ACTOR YÜEN Well, I assure you, this time there'll be no problem. We'll have the stage all to ourselves this evening, I promise!

ACTOR T'AO *[repeats emphatically]* I can't stand being interrupted!

ACTOR YÜEN *[soothingly]* You won't be interrupted!

ACTRESS CH'UN-HUA *[taps* YÜEN *on the shoulder]* Where do I—

ACTOR YÜEN *[flies into a temper]* I can't stand being interrupted! *[Pulls himself together]* What is it?

ACTRESS CH'UN-HUA Where do I make my entrance?

ACTOR YÜEN Just a sec! *[He turns to speak to the technician, then to the Control Room.]* Give me some light! There . . . *[Points to the screen behind him]* I want some light there too!

> *[Sound of Chinese music]*

> *[impatiently]* I said light, not music! *[Music breaks off.]*

ACTRESS CH'UN-HUA Where do I make my entrance?

> [*ACTOR YÜEN takes ACTRESS CH'UN-HUA to one side of the wings.*]

ACTOR YÜEN [*indicating one of the entrances*] From there! [*He turns round to find ACTRESS YÜN and ACTOR CHIANG back on the stage.*] Could you clear off please!

ACTOR T'AO [*shouting from one side of the stage*] We'll start with 'The Triangle'.

> [*Lights fade out.*]

SCENE FOUR

[*Lights come up slowly. At centre stage stand a small bamboo table and three stools, one on each side, leaving the side nearest the audience clear. Not far behind the table is a stand with a vase and some props on it. Further back upstage is a bamboo screen, beyond which is another space.*

T'AO, in fisherman's costume, is sitting at the table and struggling to remove the cork from a wine bottle, in vain. He takes a cleaver from the stand behind him and tries to pry the cork from the bottle. No luck.]

> T'AO [*muttering*] Home sweet home indeed! What sort of a home is this? Does it take the whole day for her to get me some herbal medicine? [*Still unable to remove the cork, he slams the wine bottle and the cleaver down on the table.*] All right, no wine. I'll have a bun. [*Picks up a big bun from the table—his mind elsewhere*] Wuling is such a horrible place! The mountains are barren, the rivers are treacherous. The men mean, the women fierce. Here birds don't sing and flowers have no fragrance. I'm supposed to make a living catching fish. But the damn fish all stay away. It's a conspiracy! And my wife, the slut, is out all day! What a horrible place! [*Puts the bun into his mouth, but cannot bite into it*]
>
> [*After a long struggle, he snatches up the cleaver to cut a slice of the bun. He cuts and cuts, but the bun remains intact. He snatches up the cleaver again and chops at the bun ferociously. It still remains intact.*]
>
> Damn! This is no cleaver! [*He flings away the cleaver with a backward toss of his arm, then scowls at the bun.*] And this is no bun! [*Throws it on to the floor, then snatches up a bunch of dried vegetables from the table*] And this is no vegetable. [*Throws it on to the floor, then stamps on the bun*

with one foot and the vegetables with the other, like an exotic dance. Having given vent to his feelings, he walks away, but swings round at once, shouting at the things on the floor.] Don't you move! What are you laughing at? *[Plucking up courage]* Gone for the whole day! Does it take you the whole day to get me some bloody herbal medicine? Where the hell are you? *[Picks up the cleaver and, all of a sudden, aims it at the bun and the vegetables]* Damn! *[He furiously hacks away at the bun and the vegetables on the floor. Then he gives up in exasperation and throws away the cleaver.]* Damn! This is no cleaver! *[Close to despair, he goes helplessly towards the front door of the house at the wings.]* Why isn't she home yet? *[He takes a few steps, then suddenly dashes back centre stage, in one leap jumps on to a stool, then off the other side, and lands right on the bun and the vegetables. He speaks hysterically.]* It doesn't take a whole day, does it? Does it? Does it? Huh! Huh!

[In a fit of uncontrollable temper, he tramples the objects on the floor, wrings them and twists them about. Then, he does a comic acrobatic routine to show his exasperation. Palms pressing down on the floor and supporting himself on his arms, he swings his leg round and round, round and round. Then he stands on his head and, pushing himself up and down with his forearms, bangs and knocks his head on the floor angrily, mercilessly. He breaks into a chant.] I'll crush you! Crush you! Crush you! Crush you all!

[CH'UN-HUA enters, dressed in a red bodice and skirt, a packet of herbal medicine in one hand, a bunch of flowers in the other, humming and singing, a dreamy look on her face.

T'AO *is still standing on his head. At the sight of* CH'UN-HUA *he puts his feet down, squats on his heels, snatches up the bun his groping hands have found, and starts scrubbing the floor energetically with it. When he realizes how ridiculous he looks, he picks himself up and stares at the enraptured* CH'UN-HUA.]

[He is driven to confront her by his suspicion alone. There is not much conviction in his voice.] Where the hell have you been the whole day? Does it take you the whole day to get me some medicine?

[Ignoring him, CH'UN-HUA *carefully arranges the flowers in the vase, puts it on the table, sees the wine bottle, picks it up absently and puts her hand on the cork. 'Pop'—the cork is out, she pours herself a cup and downs it at once.* T'AO *is flabbergasted.*

Her eyes still on the flowers, CH'UN-HUA *picks up the vase from the table, turns round, puts it on the stand, and admires the flowers from different angles.* T'AO *grabs the wine bottle and tries to open it. But the cork remains stubbornly in place, frustrating him no end.]*

[*indignant*] I asked you where you'd been the whole day? Didn't you hear me? Where did you go to get the medicine? Answer me!

CH'UN-HUA [*annoyed*] Why are you shouting at me? Can't you speak more gently?

T'AO [*with feigned gentleness*] Ch'un-hua, you've been gone the whole damn day to get me some damn medicine. Where have you been?

CH'UN-HUA [*with feigned politeness*] Oh, your medicine! [*Turns on him suddenly*] It's here!

[CH'UN-HUA *snatches up the packet of medicine and hurls it at* T'AO. *He ducks it, and then stamps on it, not bothering to hide his feelings anymore. When he has done stamping on the packet, he sits at the table again.* CH'UN-HUA *picks up the packet of medicine from the floor and slaps it down on the table.]*

[*impatiently*] It's got everything you wanted—sea dragons, sea horses, seals' penises—

T'AO [*petulantly*] What about toads? snakes? stags' penises?

CH'UN-HUA Yes, yes, I got everything. And now we have no more money left!

T'AO [*nodding with approval*] Good . . . Good . . . Take it to the kitchen and brew it. Then, drink it.

CH'UN-HUA [*astounded*] What? Me? Isn't this your medicine?

T'AO Is it me or you who can't produce a child?

CH'UN-HUA The doctor said there was nothing wrong with me! So there must be something wrong with you!

T'AO [*furious*] Something wrong with me? Nonsense! What can be wrong with me? [*Looking as if there is indeed something wrong with him*] Nonsense! What's wrong with me? What can be wrong with me?

CH'UN-HUA What the hell is the matter with you? You don't go fishing, you stay at home all day, you asked me to get you the medicine and now you won't take it. Well, you're the one dying to have a child, not me. I don't care whether you drink it or not.

[T'AO *studies the packet of medicine carefully.]*

T'AO [*deliberately perverse*] This is not medicine!

CH'UN-HUA [*anxiously*] What do you mean? Yüen, the shop-owner, said it would work wonders.

T'AO [*got her at last*] Yüen? How would he know?

CH'UN-HUA [*somewhat guiltily*] He means well!

T'AO [*furious*] How does he know we can't have a child? You tell me, tell me!

CH'UN-HUA [*lamely*] He was just being nice, he means well!

T'AO Means well? How come he knows we can't have a child? Tell me! How?

CH'UN-HUA Are you going to drink the medicine or not?

T'AO [*raising his voice*] How does he know?

CH'UN-HUA Are you going to drink it or not?

T'AO How does he know? Tell me!

CH'UN-HUA Yes or no?

[CH'UN-HUA *picks up the packet and dashes it to the floor. Then both she and* T'AO *stamp on it with one foot. They are still glowering at each other when* YÜEN, *the shop owner, walks in. He is dressed in a short robe and trousers, with leggings.*]

YÜEN Hello!

[T'AO *and* CH'UN-HUA *quickly pull themselves together.*]

T'AO Hi!

YÜEN How are you, T'ao?

T'AO [*half-sarcastically*] Fine, thank you! My marital life is fine!

YÜEN Good!

[*As soon as* T'AO's *back is turned,* CH'UN-HUA *goes up to* YÜEN *in great delight and they start winking and ogling at each other.*]

CH'UN-HUA [*putting on a show of politeness*] How nice to see you, Yüen. Come and sit down!

YÜEN Look! I've got a present for you [*Realizing he is being indiscreet, he hastily adds a word.*]—both.

[YÜEN *unfurls the quilt he has brought with him and shakes it out.*]

CH'UN-HUA Oh, a new quilt! How beautiful!

YÜEN Isn't it?

T'AO [*standing at some distance from them*] A quilt for a present! Never heard of such a thing!

YÜEN Come on! Yours is torn and tattered. You ought to throw it out.

CH'UN-HUA You're right!

T'AO How did you know our quilt was torn and tattered?

YÜEN [realizing his blunder] Don't be so sensitive, T'ao!
[Laughs emptily] This quilt is from Suzhou, I had it
specially brought all the way here to me!

[To placate T'AO, YÜEN and CH'UN-HUA go up to him
and hold up the quilt for him to see. T'AO throws a sulky
look at the quilt, snatches it from YÜEN, holds it up himself
and peers at it. YÜEN and CH'UN-HUA, protected from view
by the quilt, take the opportunity to embrace and caress each
other. All of a sudden, T'AO lowers his hands. YÜEN and
CH'UN-HUA part at once.]

T'AO [cantankerously] What sort of a quilt is this? Look at
it yourself. Never seen a quilt with a front and an
underside like this one! [Muttering to himself] Never!

[Still muttering, he turns the quilt over and then over again
to show them the front and the underside. CH'UN-HUA
absently holds up the other end of the quilt for T'AO, and the
quilt is drawn like a curtain in front of them with YÜEN in
the middle. Only their heads are visible.]

YÜEN [looking down and pointing his finger at the front of the
quilt] T'ao, I don't need to tell you how good the
material is. As for the embroidery—

[CH'UN-HUA takes the opportunity to caress YÜEN's cheek
with her right hand. YÜEN keeps kissing CH'UN-HUA's
hand as he remarks on the quilt. Sensing something wrong,
T'AO looks up from the quilt and stares at YÜEN. CH'UN-
HUA quickly points her finger at various parts of the quilt as
YÜEN comments on them, making it look as if it is YÜEN's
finger that is moving.]

Look what it's got here! An embroidered dragon and a
phoenix.

[T'AO follows the direction of CH'UN-HUA's finger and looks
at the quilt. CH'UN-HUA takes the opportunity to caress
YÜEN's cheek again with her hand. YÜEN cannot resist
pecking CH'UN-HUA on the cheek. T'AO looks up again at
the noise, only to find YÜEN yawning mightily. CH'UN-
HUA's hand, looking like YÜEN's hand, is patting YÜEN's
mouth as he yawns.]

T'AO Why get so excited about a quilt? You only use it
when you go to bed. No big deal!

YÜEN *[CH'UN-HUA's hand, playing YÜEN's hand, gestures emphatically as he speaks.]* But that's the whole point— going to bed!

[T'AO looks at YÜEN, a strange expression on his face. CH'UN-HUA's finger again points excitedly at the quilt. Again, it looks as if it is YÜEN's finger.]

Why look at me? Look at the quilt!

[T'AO looks down again, and YÜEN smiles sweetly at CH'UN-HUA.]

Take a good look at the eyes of this dragon! Such bright and piercing eyes! As to the phoenix, have you ever seen such an exquisite figure?

T'AO I don't like it! *[Flings down the quilt and walks away]*

[As the quilt hits the floor, YÜEN is seen embracing CH'UN-HUA round the waist with both his hands. The two give a start and YÜEN lets go of CH'UN-HUA at once.]

CH'UN-HUA *[picks up the quilt]* T'ao, put it away!

T'AO I don't care for his quilt!

CH'UN-HUA *[coaxingly]* Ours is old and worn. Take it!

[Muttering to himself, T'AO takes the quilt and goes out. Strolling idly about, YÜEN notices the packet of medicine on the floor.]

YÜEN *[contemptuously]* He thinks that will give him a child! Ha! Ha! *[Kicks the packet away]*

CH'UN-HUA *[lowering her voice]* Haven't we just spent the day together? Why are you here again?

YÜEN *[ever so tender]* Where are the flowers I gave you, my love?

CH'UN-HUA *[indicating the flowers]* Over there!

[Intoxicated with love, they look tenderly at the flowers.]

[becoming clear-headed all of a sudden] Never mind the flowers. You must go now. He's getting suspicious!

YÜEN *[in the melodramatic tone of a love-tormented hero]* No! I can't wait any more!

CH'UN-HUA *[helplessly]* But we must!

YÜEN No! I can't! Oh, how I wish I could take you away at once! Away from this place!

CH'UN-HUA *[despairingly]* But where could we go? Where?

YÜEN Anywhere! *[Takes CH'UN-HUA's hand]* As long as we love each other, we can go anywhere, to the ends of the world, *[Gazing dreamily into space, so does CH'UN-HUA]* and call it home!

CH'UN-HUA *[waking from the dream]* But . . . , but . . .

YÜEN *[gallantly]* No more 'buts'! *[Takes two steps downstage, narrows his eyes and peers into space, his face glowing]* I have a dream! *[Pointing out front]* I can see, standing in that far off place, our sons and grandsons, hand in hand, side by side, all of them just—[Measuring out a height with his thumb and index finger]* this tall.

CH'UN-HUA *[elated at first, becoming puzzled all of a sudden]* Why just—[Imitating YÜEN]* this tall?

YÜEN *[factual]* Because of the distance. *[Returning to his dream again and gesticulating extravagantly]* With grapes in their left hands, cups of the finest wine in their right hands, pineapples in their mouths—

CH'UN-HUA Doesn't that make them look like roast pigs?

YÜEN *[eloquence momentarily checked]* What I mean is, they have an endless supply of fresh fruit!

CH'UN-HUA *[elated again]* Is there really such a place?

YÜEN *[exaggeratedly gallant]* Trust me.

CH'UN-HUA *[pointing at where T'AO is inside the room]* But he—

YÜEN Don't you worry, I can handle him!

CH'UN-HUA Can you really? *[They embrace.]*

[The sound of T'AO coughing in the room.]

[They give a start and then embrace again, in a different posture. Then it dawns on them that they are forgetting themselves. They quickly draw apart. T'AO walks in. An embarrassing moment for all.]

T'AO Yüen, you never just drop in for a chat. You've given us the quilt, what do you want now? Sit down and tell me.

YÜEN *[reflecting a moment, then takes a stool and sits down]* Yes, I would like to talk to you! It's about your catch from the river. Lately, it's been getting smaller and smaller.

[CH'UN-HUA takes a wine cup, YÜEN removes the cork from the bottle effortlessly, to T'AO's great surprise. YÜEN pours some wine for CH'UN-HUA, then for himself, and puts the cork back. T'AO is beside himself with amazement.]

YÜEN But let's have a drink first. Cheers!

T'AO *[looking at the empty cup in his hand]* Well I—

[YÜEN and CH'UN-HUA finish their drinks in one swig, T'AO looks on pathetically.]

YÜEN Good wine!

T'AO *[echoing emptily]* Good . . . wine!

YÜEN I say, T'ao. Your fish are getting smaller and smaller, I can't sell them. You know as well as I do that there are twenty, thirty of you whose catch I have to sell. Why should I give you special treatment?

T'AO I know you've treated us very well all these years and I'm grateful. But fishing is a tricky business, very tricky business! You may be good, but there's just no guarantee how big your fish will be, is there?

[CH'UN-HUA *removes the cork again to pour herself and* YÜEN *some more wine. She is about to replace the cork when* T'AO, *still speaking, covers the mouth of the bottle with his hand.*]

[*lifts the bottle as he speaks, ready to pour himself some wine*] Everyone wants the big fish. You can't blame me if those I catch are small. [*Helplessly*] I didn't make the fish smaller and smaller, did I?

[YÜEN *holds out his cup to* T'AO, *who fills it absently.*]

So much depends on luck! Every day I go out hoping to land some great big fish. Hoping and hoping—

[T'AO *puts down the wine bottle distractedly,* CH'UN-HUA *replaces the cork and* T'AO's *hope of getting a drink is once again dashed. By the time he turns his eyes on the bottle, staring helplessly at it, it's too late.*]

But I just can't land them!

YÜEN Well, there are many tricks you can use. But let's have another drink.

T'AO [*staring at his empty cup*] Well I—

[YÜEN *and* CH'UN-HUA *again finish their drinks in one swig.* T'AO *pretends to drink from his empty cup.*]

YÜEN [*wiping his mouth*] Hm, that's good!

T'AO [*wipes his too*] Yeah, very!

YÜEN Listen, T'ao. One must work hard and think big. [*Points his finger forward*] There are plenty of big fish up the river. Why don't you go upstream and try your luck?

T'AO How could you say such a thing, Yüen? We all know the big fish are up the river. But I only have a small boat. If I go, it'll be for good. I won't be coming back any more!

CH'UN-HUA [*unable to restrain herself any longer*] If you were a man, you would go!

[*Silence.* CH'UN-HUA *and* YÜEN *are watching* T'AO's *reaction.* T'AO, *in his turn, is staring at* CH'UN-HUA.]

T'AO *[breaks the silence as he says with self-pity]* I'll go, all right? I'll go straight up the river now, and I hope I'll never come back!

[Before he finishes the sentence, T'AO dashes towards the door. YÜEN quickly moves to stop him.]

YÜEN Come on! Come on!

T'AO Don't stop me! I'll go now! *[He dashes towards the door again.]*

[YÜEN locks his elbow into T'AO's. T'AO swings round and stops.]

CH'UN-HUA Look at you! Look at you! I just said a few words and you want to walk out on me. You're worthless!

T'AO *[accusingly]* I'm worthless, am I? I never see you! This is no home!

[YÜEN plays the peacemaker, soothing and pacifying both.]

CH'UN-HUA All right then, I'm worthless! I'll leave! *[Storms out]*

[T'AO locks his elbow into CH'UN-HUA's. She swings round and stops.]

T'AO Where will you go? Won't you miss him?

YÜEN *[dissuading her tenderly]* Don't go, please don't! *[Losing his temper all of a sudden and flinging off T'AO's arm]* All right, if I'm in the way, I'll go! Let me go! *[Storms out]*

[CH'UN-HUA locks her elbow into YÜEN's. He, too, swings round and stops.]

[The three are standing in a line with their elbows locked, and reduced to silence for a moment.]

T'AO Yüen, let's not play dumb anymore. Sit down. Let's sort things out.

YÜEN All right!

[They all return to their seats, each preoccupied with what tactics to use.]

T'AO Now, let's get things off our chests. For a start, we're all reasonable people!

YÜEN Correct!

T'AO And there are just the three of us in the house!

YÜEN Just the three of us!

T'AO There's nothing to hide!

CH'UN-HUA Nothing to hide!

T'AO Out with it then!

YÜEN Out with it!

T'AO It's no big deal!

CH'UN-HUA No big deal!

T'AO Good! *[Pointing at* YÜEN*]* You start!

YÜEN Good! *[Pointing at* CH'UN-HUA*]* You start!

CH'UN-HUA Good! *[Pointing at* T'AO*]* You start!

T'AO Good! *[Pointing at himself, his voice shaking a little with guilt]* Why me?—*[Plucking up courage]* Okay, if it's me, then it's me. I'll start!

YÜEN Tell us what's on your mind!

T'AO I will!

CH'UN-HUA Well, tell us then!

T'AO I will, I will!

YÜEN, CH'UN-HUA *[together]* Out with it! Out with it!

T'AO The truth is,—

YÜEN, CH'UN-HUA *[together]* Yes? Go on.

T'AO The truth is . . . I . . . *[His courage fails him and he speaks dejectedly.]* But if I tell you the truth, won't it be a bit, um . . . *[Looking for words]* a bit much? *[Sits down]*

CH'UN-HUA It'd be a bit much if you didn't!

YÜEN Well, I can see it's a bit too much for you, T'ao. Let me, um, . . . let me start. *[Stands]*

T'AO Sure!

YÜEN Well, for a start, the way you treated her—*[Indicating* CH'UN-HUA *as he picks his words]* wasn't it a bit . . . um *[Breaks off to look for the right words]* a bit much!

T'AO All right, maybe the way I treated her was, um . . . a bit much. So what? It's our business! As to *you* . . .

YÜEN What about me?

T'AO The way *you* are treating us—it's—it's too much!

YÜEN So you think *I'm* too much! But *you* . . . *you* . . .

[Both men have risen to their feet in exasperation.]

T'AO *[rapid-fire exchange]* What about me?

YÜEN *You* . . . *you* . . .

T'AO When . . . ? When . . . ?

YÜEN In the beginning . . .

T'AO In what beginning?

YÜEN In the very beginning!

T'AO In the very beginning . . . *[thinks]* neither of us was anything much.

[Pause. Both men sit down quietly.]

*[*YÜEN *is exasperated.]*

YÜEN That's not saying much! But . . . but it's too much! Much too much! Far too much!

[From now on, their control over language disintegrates and they start gesticulating accusations at each other.]

T'AO Come on, it's nothing much!

CH'UN-HUA Who's nothing much? You're too much!

YÜEN Yeah, who's nothing much? Who? Whooh? Whoo-ooh?

T'AO *[not to be outdone]* Wow! Wow! Wo-ow!

CH'UN-HUA Ow! Ow! Ow!

T'AO Hah! Hah! Hah!

YÜEN Ah! Ah! Ah!

CH'UN-HUA A—ah! A—ah! A—ah!

[T'AO and YÜEN are standing face to face and jabbing accusing fingers at each other's noses in a strange kind of rhythm.]

T'AO, YÜEN *[together]* Huh! Huh! Huh!

CH'UN-HUA *[screaming to break the deadlock]* Aa—h! Aa—h! Aa—h!

YÜEN *[bellowing]* Oooh! Ooo-ooh!

T'AO *[roaring above the din]* Stop it!

[Complete silence. At a loss what to do, they all sit down and stare blankly into space.]

[calmly] How about this? I'll go and kill myself.

[Silence again, broken only by a sudden loud burp from YÜEN]

YÜEN Hup!

T'AO *[seeking a definite answer from YÜEN]* Didn't you hear what I said? I'll go and kill myself!

[YÜEN burps again.]

YÜEN Hup!

[T'AO stares long and hard at YÜEN. Then, as if he has got an answer, he rises and moves to one side.]

T'AO *[exploding]* Fine! I'll kill myself! I will! Then you'll be rid of me! [Starts strangling himself histrionically]

[CH'UN-HUA and YÜEN move at once to stop him.]

YÜEN, CH'UN-HUA *[together]* Come on! Come on! *[They seize T'AO's arms, but he refuses to let loose his grip on his throat.]*

CH'UN-HUA *[explodes in frustration]* All right, I'll go and kill myself! *[In an equally histrionic manner, she pinches her nose and covers her mouth, as if she is going to suffocate herself.]* I'll kill myself! Kill myself!

YÜEN *[playing the peacemaker again, soothing him and calming her]* Come on! Come on! *[Explodes in frustration]* Stop it! You just want me out of the way, don't you? *[Snatches up the rope used to tie the quilt, loops it around his neck and starts pulling it at both ends histrionically]* I'll kill myself! Let me die!

[Having positioned themselves at stage left, centre, and right, they start killing themselves and screaming hysterically, in as melodramatic a manner as they can manage. Eventually T'AO *gives up strangling himself and starts swinging his hands back and forth between his knees, as if he was dancing.]*

T'AO Let me die! Let me die!

[CH'UN-HUA does the splits, baring her teeth and puckering her face.]

CH'UN-HUA Let me die! Let me die!

[T'AO wags his forefingers frantically in front of his face, then jabs at his eyes. YÜEN *turns his back towards the audience all of a sudden. When he turns round again, the rope has been knotted into the shape of a bow tie.]*

YÜEN Let me die! Let me die! *[Jumps as he notices the neatly knotted bow tie on his neck]*

[CH'UN-HUA springs up from the floor. She and YÜEN start wagging their fingers at each other.]

CH'UN-HUA, YÜEN *[chant in unison]* Let me die! Let me die! Let me die! Oh!

[YÜEN bangs his head on the table while CH'UN-HUA flits about the stage like a ballet dancer. T'AO, in the meantime, hits and slaps himself loudly. Soon, the actions merge into a single Peking Opera comic acrobatic routine, with each slapping his/her shoulders, hands, forearms, chest, head, legs, and feet rhythmically and in unison. Then they leap simultaneously into the air while slapping the soles of their feet. When they land on the floor again, they bow to the audience, then freeze. Lights out at once.]

SCENE FIVE

[From the darkened stage rises the sound of T'AO *singing a fisherman's song.]*

T'AO Heigh—Ho—Heigh!

[Lights come up slowly. T'AO *is standing, feet apart, and holding an oar. Behind him a canvas is hanging painted with a colourful river scene.* T'AO *mimes rowing a boat in stylized Peking Opera fashion, moving across the stage.]*

[*solemnly quoting from* A Record of Peach Blossom Spring, *one of the best-known pieces of utopian writing in classical Chinese literature*]

'In the Taiyuan period of the Jin Dynasty there was once a native of Wuling, who lived on fishing.' [*Pauses*]

[*helplessly*] Driven to distraction and bitter cynicism by a difficult wife and a broken family—up the river I go!

[*'Rowing', he disappears behind the canvas, from where the fisherman's song rises again.*]

Heigh—Ho—Heigh—!

[T'AO *appears from behind the canvas at stage left. The canvas is drawn back like a curtain, revealing another canvas with another river scene.*]

[*'rowing' into the scene, quoting solemnly*]

'One day he rowed upstream, and soon forgot how far he had travelled.'

Yes, forget is the word. What's her name? 'Ch'un-hua'—she is forgotten! And what's his name? 'Yüen'—he, too, is forgotten! Forgetting is all!

[DIRECTOR *of* Pining *enters from the wings and stares at* T'AO. *He is followed by the actress playing the* NURSE.]

Oh, shouldn't the rapids be here? [*Pauses*] Oh well, I'll carry on! Heigh-Ho! [*Starts 'rowing' again, turns round, catches sight of the intruders, gives a start, comes out of his role, and calls to* ACTOR YÜEN, *director of* Blossom Land]
Hey! They're back!

[*House lights come up instantly.* DIRECTOR *approaches* T'AO, *a document file in his hands.*]

DIRECTOR Here's the agreement. Read it!

ACTOR T'AO [*turns round and cries out again*] They've even got an agreement!

DIRECTOR The place is ours for tonight. Is that clear now?

[ACTOR YÜEN *enters in a rage.*]

ACTOR T'AO [*to* ACTOR YÜEN] I told you I can't stand being interrupted!

ACTOR YÜEN [*to* T'AO] Relax! Relax!

DIRECTOR [*to* YÜEN] This is the agreement. Read it!

ACTOR YÜEN [*not paying him much attention*] Just a sec. I've got some urgent business, I'll talk to you later. [*Calling one of his crew*] Shun-tzŭ! Shun-tzŭ! Could you come here please?

DIRECTOR Hey, don't make things difficult for me, okay? This play is very important to me. It's the summation of my life. I don't want any trouble from you!

ACTOR YÜEN [not listening] Shun-tzŭ! Come here!

ACTOR T'AO [takes up the debate] In Peach Blossom Land is very important to us too!

ACTOR YÜEN [impatiently] Shun-tzŭ! Come here at once!

[SHUN-TZŬ appears. He goes up behind YÜEN and taps him on his back. When YÜEN turns round, SHUN-TZŬ slips to the other side, still standing behind YÜEN.]

ACTOR YÜEN Shun-tzŭ, where's the main backdrop?

SHUN-TZŬ I've loaded it on to the lorry!

ACTOR YÜEN Have you? Why hasn't it arrived then?

SHUN-TZŬ You mean . . . arrived here?

ACTOR YÜEN Hm. [Pauses] Where else do you think it should go?

SHUN-TZŬ I thought it was going to Kaohsiung.

ACTOR YÜEN [trying to control himself] Tell me, why do you think it should be going to Kaohsiung?

SHUN-TZŬ Didn't you tell us we'd be playing in Kaohsiung day after tomorrow?

DIRECTOR Is there a problem?

ACTOR YÜEN No! [Turns round, suppressing his anger] Shun-tzŭ, I'm glad you remember that we'll be playing in Kaohsiung day after tomorrow. But, if I may put the question to you, shouldn't we be playing in Taipei first?

SHUN-TZŬ [reflects a moment] Yes.

ACTOR YÜEN [insistently] Yes?

SHUN-TZŬ [with certainty] Yes!

ACTOR YÜEN [agreeing] Yes!

DIRECTOR Look! Come what may, I've got to start now!

PINING ACTORS [offstage] Shall we bring in the props?

[Everyone on stage starts to stir. ACTOR YÜEN and SHUN-TZŬ remain where they are.]

ACTOR YÜEN Shouldn't you run along and see if the lorry has left?

SHUN-TZŬ Yes! [He does not move.]

ACTOR YÜEN Yes! [Melodramatically] Shall I go and stop the lorry? [No response from SHUN-TZŬ] Shall I go all by myself to stop the container lorry?

SHUN-TZŬ Sure! But, what do you want me for?

ACTOR YÜEN [swings round and storms up to SHUN-TZŬ] You're damn right! What do I want you for? [Close to tears]

[ACTRESS CH'UN-HUA bustles in with a question. On seeing that her team is not rehearsing, she reluctantly leaves. Taking advantage of the disarray the Blossom Land *team is in, the* Pining *crew have prepared the set for the next scene and quietly removed the backdrop, the table, stools, and bamboo screen left behind by the* Blossom Land *team. The stage now looks like a hospital room with a hospital bed, a drip stand, a wheelchair, and a door frame.]*

DIRECTOR Come on, don't waste time. Show me the slides!

[On the plain backdrop is projected a slide of CHIANG PIN-LIU, MRS CHIANG *and their only son. The picture was taken in or around 1971.* CHIANG *looks close to fifty,* MRS CHIANG *about forty and their child about ten.*

While DIRECTOR *and* STAGE MANAGER *are discussing the slides, the actors and actresses of* Pining *are either preparing themselves for their parts or busy with the props. One or two are staring blankly at the slides flashing on the backcloth. None notices the* STRANGER—*a young woman in eccentric clothes—who has slipped in and is now looking around her.]*

[shouting to STAGE MANAGER*]* Not this one! We're doing the 'Advertisement for Missing Person' scene. Not this one!

STAGE MANAGER *[shouting from backstage]* Not this one?

DIRECTOR No. This is the family picture of the Chiangs after he comes to Taiwan.

[Another slide flashes up, a close-up of CHIANG PIN-LIU *and* YÜN CHIH-FAN *in a photo studio in Shanghai. The photo, taken in 1948, is yellow with age.]*

No, not that one either.

STAGE MANAGER *[shouting]* Isn't that his wife?

DIRECTOR No, she's the woman he met in Shanghai.

STAGE MANAGER *[a little confused about the plot]* Didn't he marry her?

DIRECTOR *[sarcastically]* If he did, he wouldn't be like this today! Next one!

STAGE MANAGER *[thoroughly confused]* Hey, Director, would you mind numbering the slides for me?

DIRECTOR Okay, I'll do that.

[Another slide. It shows the 1948 photo of YÜN *as it appeared, yellow with age, in an 'Advertisement for Missing Person' printed just underneath the masthead of a recent copy of the* Central Daily News.*]*

DIRECTOR That's it! Get ready, everybody! *[About to go]*

[STRANGER suddenly goes up to DIRECTOR.]

STRANGER *[shyly]* Excuse me! Have you seen Liu Tzŭ-chi?

[DIRECTOR is taken aback. The others who are getting ready are used to such interruptions.]

DIRECTOR Who?

STRANGER Liu Tzŭ-chi. We've arranged to meet here.

STAGE MANAGER *[shouting from backstage]* You're sure it's this one, right?

DIRECTOR *[his attention back on the slide]* Yes. Let's get ready!

[DIRECTOR is about to go when he is accosted by the young woman again.]

STRANGER *[anxiously]* I've got to talk to him, it's urgent! Could you please find him for me?

DIRECTOR What's his name again? Liu—?

STRANGER Liu Tzŭ-chi.

[SHUN-TZŬ appears.]

[in a sudden fit of anxiety] I must see him. He promised to come and sort things out with me!

[DIRECTOR is at a loss what to do when he catches sight of SHUN-TZŬ.]

DIRECTOR Hey! This lady here is probably looking for you!
[Shepherds her over to where SHUN-TZŬ is]

SHUN-TZŬ *[surprised]* Looking for me?

STRANGER *[to SHUN-TZŬ]* I'm looking for Liu Tzŭ-chi.

SHUN-TZŬ *[takes her away as he questions her]* Who?

STRANGER Liu Tzŭ-chi.

SHUN-TZŬ Liu Tzŭ-chi. *[Pauses]* What's his surname?

[Exit SHUN-TZŬ and STRANGER.]

DIRECTOR *[seeing that they are gone]* Okay. On we go.

[Lights fade out.]

SCENE SIX

[The lights come up on a hospital room. In the middle of the room, directly facing the audience, there are a hospital bed and two bedside tables, one on each side; on the bedside tables, a telephone and other daily necessities; at one side of the bed, a drip stand and a wheelchair. A free-standing door at upstage right opens into the room. A chair for visitors is placed in front of the bed, at a little distance from the door.

*On the backdrop is projected a slide of the 'Advertisement for Missing Person',
on which is a photo of* YÜN CHIH-FAN *as a young woman.*
*CHIANG PIN-LIU is sitting in bed reading a newspaper. His hair has turned
white and he looks old and gaunt. The door opens and the* NURSE *comes in, a copy
of the* Central Daily News *in her hands. She is young and lively, a recent
graduate from a nursing school.]*

NURSE Did you sleep well? *[Goes up to* CHIANG *with the paper,
only to find that he has a copy already]* You've got the paper!

*[*NURSE *looks at the paper in her hand, not knowing where
to put it, or what to say. In silence,* CHIANG *hands her his
copy.* NURSE *takes his paper, turns round to put it on the
bedside table to her left, and begins to prepare medication.]*

Time for your medicine. *[Hands him some pills]*

CHIANG *[grumpily]* Why these red pills again?

*[*NURSE *moves the wheelchair up to the bed.]*

NURSE Nice day today. Shall we get up and sit over there?

[She helps CHIANG *into the wheelchair—a laborious task.]*

CHIANG *[sitting in the wheelchair but still grumbling]* Everytime I
take these red pills, my urine turns red!

*[*NURSE *pushes the wheel chair downstage.]*

NURSE They do you good. *[Looking outside the window]* What a
nice day!

[Prompted by NURSE'*s remark,* CHIANG *looks outside the
window.* NURSE *at once draws from her pocket the newspaper
she has brought with her and starts stealing glances at the
front page.]*

CHIANG *[after a little pause]* What a fine day.

NURSE Did you really put the ad in the paper?

*[*CHIANG *hardly responds.]*

[overcome with excitement] I can't believe it! You're the
first person I know who has put an ad for a missing
person in the papers! *[Reading aloud from the paper]*
'Yün Chih-fan: It's been over forty years since we last
parted in Shanghai, my health is deteriorating by the
day . . .' *[To* CHIANG*]* Oh, honestly! Why say things
like that in the paper? *[Goes on reading]* 'I learnt from a
friend that you came to Taiwan many years ago. I hope
you will come and see me as soon as you have read this
advertisement. I am in Chang Keng Hospital, Taipei,
Room 1120. Chiang Pin-liu.' *[Excitedly]* Who is she? Is
she a relation? Do tell!

CHIANG *[calmly, tapping the sweater he has on]* See this sweater? She gave it to me. In 1948. In Shanghai. I still wear it, even today.

NURSE She's no ordinary friend then, am I right? *[No reply from CHIANG]* What's the matter? *[Still no reply]* *[imploringly]* Come on, tell me!

CHIANG When were you born?

NURSE *[proudly]* 1970.

CHIANG *[sighs, shaking his head]* You wouldn't understand!

NURSE *[shakes CHIANG by the shoulders]* Try me! You tell me and I'll understand!

CHIANG *[recounts the story slowly]* In the summer of 1948 we met in Shanghai. That summer—that was the happiest summer of my life. *[Pauses]* In September, she had to go home to Kunming. We said goodbye in the Bund Park in Shanghai, thinking it was just a brief separation and we'd meet again in a few months. It turned out that we had parted for life—

NURSE Weren't you really close? How could you let her go?

CHIANG 'Let her go?' *[Shaking his head slowly]* You can't understand. There was confusion and chaos everywhere. In a world like that, one was so small, so helpless. . . . You wouldn't understand.

NURSE And for over forty years you've been thinking about her?

CHIANG There are things one just cannot forget!

NURSE Says who? You know my . . . my boyfriend Ch'ên? You've met him, remember?

CHIANG What about him?

NURSE *[naively]* We broke up two weeks ago. The last couple of days I've been trying to remember what he looks like. But I can't!

[CHIANG lapses into silence. NURSE notices how sad he looks.]

[steers the wheelchair aimlessly, stops after a few steps] Why didn't you look for her earlier? Why wait till today? What happened?

CHIANG I left the Mainland in 1949 when the Communists took over the country. I'd always thought she was left behind. You know we've been forbidden to communicate with relatives and friends all these years. The restrictions were relaxed only recently. But then I fell ill. So I asked Han, someone from my home town, to go and look for her in Kunming.

NURSE *[interjects]* You mean Mr Han? The one who often comes to see you?

CHIANG *[trying not to show his pain]* She, too, left in 1949. I never knew that. Maybe she's been here all these years.

NURSE What? She's been in Taiwan all these years?

CHIANG I don't know. I just heard she'd left China. Where she is now, whether she's still alive, I don't know!

NURSE Does your wife know about all this?

[CHIANG says nothing.]

It's a big ad you put in the *Central Daily News.* On the front page too. How much did it cost you?

CHIANG *[looking quite pleased with himself and eyeing the paper in NURSE's hand]* That photo—isn't she beautiful?

NURSE Very beautiful. But then . . . it's a bit faded!

CHIANG That's the only photo of her I have. Taken in Shanghai. I keep it in my wallet. It's gone yellow with age. In those days, she wore her hair in two long plaits. *[Pauses]* In those days, we were so young. *[Pauses]* Do you think she'll come when she's read the paper?

NURSE It's been so long. . . . *[She had wanted to be frank but decides to encourage a bit of optimism.]* If she sees the ad, I think she probably will. It's so romantic!

[A noise at the door brings their discussion to an abrupt stop. They turn round and see MRS CHIANG *stepping into the room. Neatly dressed, carrying a handbag and a newspaper, she is an ordinary housewife of about fifty.]*

[hides the newspaper] Good morning, Mrs Chiang!

MRS CHIANG Morning.

*[*NURSE *goes hastily to attend to her work.* MRS CHIANG's *cheerful behaviour seems a little forced. She seems to be hiding something.]*

MRS CHIANG Did you sleep well?

CHIANG All right!

*[*MRS CHIANG *forces a smile and goes to the bedside table to pour herself a glass of water.]*

CHIANG *[suddenly]* Mei-ju—

*[*MRS CHIANG *stops and turns towards* CHIANG, *a slightly nervous expression on her face.* CHIANG *says nothing. It is quite a while before* CHIANG *waves his hand to indicate that he does not want to speak.* MRS CHIANG *goes up to the bedside table and picks up the flask. It is empty.]*

MRS CHIANG *[to* NURSE*]* Look at you! The flask is empty!

NURSE I'm sorry! *[Hurries over to fill the flask]*

MRS CHIANG This can wait. You better bring me a basin of water. I'd like to give him a wash now.

NURSE Of course.

*[*MRS CHIANG *waits until* NURSE *is gone before she turns to look at* CHIANG *again.]*

MRS CHIANG I'll take you back to bed.

CHIANG I'd like to stay in the sun a bit longer.

MRS CHIANG The sun is too strong. You'll soon complain about getting a headache or something.

*[*MRS CHIANG *steers* CHIANG *back to the bed and helps him up. Putting him into bed is an equally difficult task.* NURSE *returns with a basin of water.]*

CHIANG Put it over there. I can handle the rest.

*[*NURSE *puts the basin of water on the bedside table. When she has settled him in bed,* MRS CHIANG *puts a towel in the water and wrings it out.]*

MRS CHIANG Your secretary's wife rang up and said she wanted to come and visit you.

CHIANG Better not. Tell her not to!

MRS CHIANG *[wiping* CHIANG*'s face and neck as she speaks]* Well, people are just being nice.

CHIANG Tell them not to bother. What's the point anyway? My days are numbered. Why all this fuss?

MRS CHIANG Oh, come, come! *[Stops wiping him]* Look at you! Why do you have to talk like this? Oh, well, if it makes you feel better, don't let me stop you.

*[*CHIANG *closes his eyes and becomes quiet.]*

[wiping CHIANG*'s hand]* I got a letter from our son yesterday. He said he was worried about you and wanted to come home to see you. I told him what you said. I said, don't interrupt your studies, wait until term ends and then we'll see. *[Seeking his approval]* What do you think?

*[*CHIANG *keeps his eyes shut and does not speak. A little put out,* MRS CHIANG *lifts the basin of water and puts it down on the floor at the other side of the bed. Then she squats down to clean the towel and wring it out.]*

[gently probing] I heard that Han is back.

*[*CHIANG *still keeps his eyes shut and does not speak.]*

[continuing to wipe CHIANG's *hand]* Did he really go to Shanghai? Rather foolhardy of him really, just because he holds a foreign passport!

*[*CHIANG *continues to ignore her, his eyes closed.]*

[haltingly, not looking at CHIANG*]* I wonder . . . , I wonder what Shanghai is like!

*[*CHIANG *remains quiet. He seems to have fallen asleep.]*

[starts wiping CHIANG's *feet]* Why do you just keep quiet every time I talk to you these days? If something is the matter, tell me. I can take it.

*[*CHIANG *remains quiet.* MRS CHIANG *turns round to look at her husband, a sick old man who has fallen asleep. She lifts the basin and hands it to* NURSE. *Then she stands beside the bed looking at* CHIANG. NURSE *comes up and smooths out the blankets. A little embarrassed,* MRS CHIANG *hastens to help her.]*

Nurse, looking after my husband is a lot of hard work. We're lucky to have you all this time. I don't know what I'd do without you!

NURSE All in a day's work, really! Besides, I've seldom come across a patient as nice as Mr Chiang. Some patients are impossible. They ring the bell all the time, scream and shout at you, and some even try to take advantage of you—

MRS CHIANG Mm. Mm. *[Directs the conversation to what's on her mind]* Have you noticed lately that something seems to be troubling Mr Chiang?

NURSE Maybe there is. But then all patients are like that!

*[*MRS CHIANG *forces a smile, and nods. Pause.]*

MRS CHIANG *[getting more and more agitated, finally she asks point-blank]* Have you seen today's *Central Daily News*?

*[*NURSE *does not know what to say. There is a pause and the atmosphere suddenly becomes tense.]*

NURSE *[warmly]* Mrs Chiang. . . . *[Searching for the right words]* Mr Chiang is a very nice man!

MRS CHIANG *[agreeing]* Oh yes, he is. Nice and quiet. He doesn't say much even when he's at home. Sometimes, he'll sit by the window, cup of tea in his hand, and stay there the whole day. At first, I didn't dare to disturb him. Later on, even our son didn't dare to disturb him. *[Pauses]* What I can't figure out is, how could a person have so much on his mind?

NURSE How long have you been married?

MRS CHIANG Many years. I married him in Tainan in 1959. Then we came up to Taipei and have lived here since.

[NURSE and MRS CHIANG go on talking as a song popular in Shanghai in the 1930s rises faintly. The song seems to have come from a dream; CHIANG, too, seems to be in a dream as he slowly sits up in bed.

The music continues, and the swings used in the earlier scene are quietly brought in and placed downstage right. YÜN CHIH-FAN, young and beautiful, dressed as in Scene 1, appears, also like someone from a dream. Wordlessly she drifts into the room, moves downstage, and strolls from left to right in front of the swings. CHIANG sits in bed and watches in a daze. NURSE and MRS CHIANG go on talking.]

[looking through the window] In those days, Taipei was so different. There weren't so many cars, and not so many people. It has changed so much!

NURSE How did you get to know each other?

MRS CHIANG [recollecting] Oh, we . . . we got to know each other through a match-maker. Ridiculous, isn't it?

NURSE No, not at all! What was Mr Chiang like in those days?

[CHIANG gets out of bed and walks to the clothes rack beside the door. Though old and gaunt, he acts like a young man getting ready for a date. Silently he changes into the suit he had on when he was in Shanghai, hangs up his hospital clothes, looks at himself in the mirror, brushes his hair, and goes slowly to join YÜN CHIH-FAN on the swing. NURSE and MRS CHIANG are still talking in the background.]

MRS CHIANG In those days he was tall and slim, at least ten years older than me, and considered to be quite respectable. In those days I found him—[Looking for the right adjective] very reliable.

NURSE [doing a bit of mental arithmetic] So Mr Chiang had already been in Taiwan for about ten years when you met him?

[MRS CHIANG is lost in her own thoughts. She sits on the visitor's chair.]

MRS CHIANG [talking to herself] Actually, I shouldn't complain. All these years, he's been very good to me, to our child too. But what's been on his mind all these years? [Breaks helplessly into tears] What has he been thinking about all these years?

*[*MRS CHIANG *sits in the visitor's chair gazing into space as* NURSE *works quietly. The music of the 1930s continues.* CHIANG *once again sings the song 'Seeking'.]*

CHIANG *[singing]*

> 'You are a wisp of cloud in the sky,
> You are a meteor flashing through the night.
> Your tenderness enthrals my heart,
> Your love light brightens . . .'

YÜN How still it is. I've never seen Shanghai so still before. It's as if we two are the only people in the whole city. *[Pauses]* The rain just now makes me feel so good. There is something indescribably wonderful in the air!

[They sway gently on the swings.]

[pointing her finger forward] Pin-liu, look at the lights in the water—

[Suddenly, the telephone in the hospital room rings, both MRS CHIANG *and* NURSE *are startled.]*

MRS CHIANG I'll get it.

*[*MRS CHIANG *acts as if* CHIANG *is asleep. She tiptoes to where the phone is, picks up the receiver, and stands beside the bed speaking in a soft voice.* NURSE *is still at her work table.*

The scene in the Bund Park in Shanghai and the scene in the hospital room in Taipei now take place side by side, sometimes simultaneously and sometimes in alternate order.]

CHIANG Like a painting.

MRS CHIANG *[speaking into the phone in her native Taiwanese dialect]* Hello! Yes. Who is it?

YÜN Everything seems to have come to a standstill.

MRS CHIANG *[into the phone]* Haven't seen you for a long time. Yes, yes. Yes, we're now trying a new medicine.

[The ever-popular Mandarin song by Zhou Xuan, 'When will you come again?' is heard.]

CHIANG *[looking at* YÜN] Do you like it?

*[*YÜN *nods, and smiles. They quietly watch the lights in the water.]*

MRS CHIANG *[into the phone, thanking the other party]* No, no, there's no need. Don't worry, I'll manage. . . . Yes, I have everything. . . . There will be side effects, of course. . . . Yes . . . I know—

*[*YÜN, *still sitting on the swing, suddenly feels a draught.]*

YÜN It's getting chilly!

[As if reacting instinctively to YÜN's *remark,* CHIANG, *as in Scene 1, rises, removes the scarf he is wearing, and puts it round* YÜN's *neck. He stands there as if spellbound, glancing at* YÜN *and his surroundings in the park with a look of wonder, like a dreamer who has suddenly realized that he is in a dream and has stepped out of it to watch on the sidelines.]*

[feeling the warmth of CHIANG's *scarf with her hand]* I'm so happy this summer! I still remember the last few years, when the war was on. I never even dreamt that life could be so wonderful! Now people are so full of hope, like us, don't you think?

*[*CHIANG *turns his attention to* MRS CHIANG *in the hospital room.]*

MRS CHIANG *[into the phone]* I know, I know. . . . Mm? . . . Yes, the doctor said . . . um . . . said he's got three months left. *[Forcing herself to remain calm]* It's all right, it's all right, I'm fine. I will. . . . Sure. . . . Thank you.

*[*CHIANG *stands there, leaning against the swing, watching his wife put down the receiver in a daze and then return to her seat, still in a daze.]*

YÜN What's the matter? I'm talking to you. Something on your mind?

*[*CHIANG's *attention returns to* YÜN, *he shakes his head at once.]*

Are you thinking about Kunming?

*[*CHIANG *does not reply.]*

I just can't believe it, you know. You spent three years in Kunming studying at the University. My home is right next to the university, and we never even met! *[*CHIANG *turns his head round and glances at* MRS CHIANG.]* And yet, we meet here in Shanghai! Such a vast city, Shanghai; you don't run into people easily. *[Pauses]* I wonder what would have happened if we hadn't met in Shanghai.

CHIANG *[speaks with his eyes fixed in the distance, as if he is in a dream and repeating something sharply engraved on his memory]* We were destined to meet in Shanghai.

YÜN Are you so sure?

CHIANG Of course. *[delivering his words one by one, each laboriously]* I can't imagine how empty life would be if we hadn't met in Shanghai!

*[*CHIANG *looks at* YÜN, *a tortured expression on his face;*

she is still smiling her ever beautiful smile. MRS CHIANG *is sitting quietly in her chair and the* NURSE *quietly going about her business. A long silence, with only Zhou Xuan's song still playing in the distance.*

Suddenly, DIRECTOR *roars, shattering the mood and all the emotions that have been gathering in the silence.]*

DIRECTOR *[from the wings]* Stop!

[The lights come up instantly. Those on stage all shade their eyes from the glare with their hands. DIRECTOR *storms in and heads straight for* ACTOR CHIANG. *The rest look on in a daze.]*

[losing control of himself] Haven't I told you Chiang Pin-liu isn't like this? How many times do I have to tell you? *[Gesticulating extravagantly to make his point]* He's the orphan of orphans. He grew up against all odds, at a time when the bloody Japs were brandishing their bloody swords all around him! *[Anger turning into sorrow]* He left home, drifted from place to place . . . drifted one day to . . . Shanghai. And there in Shanghai he met the woman he'd never forget for the rest of his life—Yün Chih-fan. *[Pauses] [To* ACTRESS YÜN*]* And you—you're not Yün Chih-fan! Yün Chih-fan is a white camellia *[Developing the metaphor]* that blooms in the night sky. *[Rapt]* The most charming, most beautiful white camellia! *[Completely lost in his dream world]*

ACTRESS YÜN Look, you keep saying 'a white camellia'! It's not easy to play 'a white camellia', you know!

*[*ACTRESS MRS CHIANG *and* NURSE *exchange a look, resigned to another bout of nostalgic sentimentality from* DIRECTOR.*]*

DIRECTOR *[absorbed, not listening]* Chiang Pin-liu, this is the most beautiful and most moving memory you have in your entire life, you know that! But, that feeling—as I remember it, the feeling wasn't like that.

ACTOR CHIANG *[defiant]* But we're talking about the play now! Can't you draw a line between 'you' and 'Chiang Pin-liu'? You've got to remember that we're dealing with a problem in a play!

*[*DIRECTOR *is hopelessly lost in his own memories.]*

DIRECTOR I . . . I don't think you two can ever capture the feeling!

[ACTOR CHIANG and ACTRESS YÜN stare at him with incomprehension.]

But it's a feeling I'll never ever forget!

ACTRESS YÜN *[coaxingly]* Director, we know it's your story. But you must put aside your personal feelings when you're working. It happened over forty years ago. There's no way you can put the clock back. You must forget the whole thing!

DIRECTOR *[full of self-pity]* How can I?

ACTRESS YÜN *[takes DIRECTOR's hand and urges him gently]* But you must forget about it when you're at work!

[Enter the Peach Blossom Land *team in their costumes. They survey the scene with interest.]*

You must get this into your head. I'm playing 'Yün Chih-fan'. I am me, she is she! I can no more become the real Yün Chih-fan than she can turn up on this stage! Don't you see?

[DIRECTOR is stricken with grief.]

Look, we get stuck every time we come to this part! What do you want us to do?

[ACTOR YÜEN has been observing this for some time. He now interjects.]

ACTOR YÜEN Excuse me. Our set has arrived. We must start at once!

ACTOR CHIANG *[impatiently]* We're rehearsing! We're rehearsing now!

ACTRESS YÜN *[still consoling DIRECTOR]* Let's take a break. Let's go for a cup of tea first, shall we?

[ACTRESS YÜN escorts the disheartened DIRECTOR over to the wings and exits with him, watched by ACTOR CHIANG. He is still deep in thought when someone claps him heartily on the shoulder.]

ACTOR YÜEN *[speaks as he claps CHIANG on the shoulder]* Thanks a lot, mate! *[Shouting instructions to the* Blossom Land *crew]* Quick! Get the set ready.

[The stage-hands come in with a huge backdrop rolled up like a carpet and start busying themselves with mounting it to the batten that has been half lowered to the floor. The electricians, too, are busy checking the lights. The stage is humming with the usual hustle and bustle.]

[to ACTOR T'AO] Can't believe our luck! I stopped the lorry driver in the nick of time! Good thing I did, or else Shun-tzŭ would have let them take the backdrop all the way to Kaohsiung!

ACTOR T'AO What's the matter with their director? Is he all right?

ACTOR YÜEN Never mind him. We have no time to lose! *[To the crew]* Take these things away!

ACTOR T'AO Yes, quick! Come on! Come on!

> *[The actors and actresses weave their way in and out of the crew, the props and the scenery batten, discussing among themselves as they step aside for the crew to pass. And now STRANGER—the young woman who appeared earlier— wanders in again, still looking for someone.]*

MRS CHIANG *[bewildered]* What's up? Are we done?

ACTOR CHIANG *[watching in resignation]* What can we do?

> *[STRANGER goes up to ACTOR YÜEN.]*

ACTOR YÜEN *[to STRANGER, unwittingly]* Give me a hand, will you?

STRANGER I'm looking for Liu Tzŭ-chi.

ACTOR YÜEN *[to her, without seeing her]* Okay! Good! *[Turns his head round]* Shun-tzŭ!

> *[Everyone is busy except SHUN-TZŬ, who is looking idly on.]*
>
> *[patiently]* Please take this swing away, okay?

SHUN-TZŬ Okay!

ACTOR YÜEN *[watches SHUN-TZŬ move the swing, shakes his head and mutters to himself]* A swing on stage! What next?

> *[ACTOR CHIANG hurries over to protect the swing.]*

ACTOR CHIANG Hey! What are you doing there? Careful! Careful!

> *[Exits with SHUN-TZŬ and the swing.]*

STRANGER *[will not let ACTOR YÜEN go]* Have you seen him? I'm in a hurry!

ACTOR YÜEN So am I!

STRANGER *[raising her voice suddenly]* Is he trying to avoid me?

ACTOR YÜEN *[surprised, turns round to look at her for the first time]* Who?

STRANGER Liu Tzŭ-chi!

ACTOR YÜEN *[with a touch of mockery]* Did he tell you that?

STRANGER *[overcome with agitation]* What's come over him? How could he be so irresponsible? I don't care! I must see him! It was he who said he wanted to sort things out face to face!

> *[ACTOR T'AO comes up to them.]*

ACTOR YÜEN *[whispering to ACTOR T'AO]* Who's she?

ACTOR T'AO *[replying in a whisper]* Don't know. She's probably from the other company.

ACTOR YÜEN They've got all sorts, haven't they?

STRANGER *[hysterically]* I don't care! I will have everything out with him today!

[*ACTOR CHIANG enters to remove their last prop—the wheelchair.*]

ACTOR YÜEN *[catching sight of ACTOR CHIANG]* Hey! Mate! [*Indicating STRANGER]* This woman here is probably looking for you!

ACTOR CHIANG *[puzzled, he turns around and sees STRANGER.]* What?

STRANGER *[lost all control]* Why do you hide him from me? [*Everyone is speechless with amazement.]* Where are you keeping him? *[Not a word from anybody]* What am I to do?

[*STRANGER flings her arms around ACTOR CHIANG and breaks into tears.*]

ACTOR CHIANG Come! Come! Don't cry! *[STRANGER sobs inconsolably.]* My dear girl!

STRANGER I'm not a girl, not anymore!

[*SHUN-TZŬ enters to find ACTOR CHIANG and STRANGER in an embrace.*]

SHUN-TZŬ *[pointing at ACTOR CHIANG, an enlightened expression on his face]* So you are Liu Tzŭ-chi! I'm pleased to meet you! Really pleased! *[Realizing that ACTOR YÜEN is glowering at him, he attends to his duties at once. Then, as if something has come to his mind, he turns round and says to ACTOR CHIANG.]* Oh, just now there was a woman looking for you!

[*Exits*]

ACTOR CHIANG *[perplexed]* What!

STRANGER *[still crying]* How can he do this to me?

ACTOR CHIANG Relax! *[Beginning to lose his patience]* Now, let's go and sort things out. *[Ushers STRANGER towards the wings]* It's been a very hectic day. If you're looking for anybody, you'd better come backstage with me. *[They exit.]*

[*The Blossom Land backdrop has been mounted and is now waiting to be hoisted.*]

ACTOR YÜEN Fly it now!

[*The backdrop slowly rises, revealing a huge Chinese landscape painting the width of the stage and the height of the proscenium arch. It is painted with rolling clouds and heavy fog patches—an endless expanse of mist and haziness. Perched high on a tall mysterious mountain is a small village, picturesque and dreamlike; everywhere on the*

mountain, there are peach blossoms. The backdrop continues to
rise, foot by foot, before its audience.]

Higher ... A little higher still. *[To* ACTOR T'AO,
smugly] How do you like it? Good, eh?

ACTOR T'AO *[looking at the painting]* Yes. Very good!

ACTOR YÜEN You see, when the lights hit it, it'll look like a piece of
embroidery!

ACTOR T'AO It's magnificent!

[The backdrop continues to rise, then at the bottom of the
painting there suddenly appears a large blank patch with
nothing painted on it. Surprised, ACTOR YÜEN *goes up to*
examine it and is overcome with amazement.]

ACTOR YÜEN Hold it! Hold it! Hey, what's the matter here? What
... *[Crying out aloud]* Call him! What's his name? Chap
who did the painting!

ACTOR T'AO Wang!

ACTOR YÜEN *[close to panic]* Wang! Come here!

[WANG comes rushing on and nearly slips.]

[pointing at the blank patch on the painting] What the
hell is the matter here?

WANG Didn't you want it that way?

ACTOR YÜEN When did I tell you I wanted it that way?

WANG Couple of days ago when I was doing the painting,
Shun-tzŭ said you liked this kind of 'look'.

ACTOR YÜEN *[livid]* Shun-tzŭ said I liked this kind of 'look'?

WANG *[innocently]* That's right! Shun-tzŭ said you wanted to
give this patch here an 'empty look'.

ACTOR YÜEN 'Empty look'? *[Controlling his anger]* Wang, come over
here! *[He draws WANG aside and the two stand looking at*
the painting together. Then he forces himself to speak calmly.]
Well, now. . . . Never mind what I've said, okay?
[WANG nods.] And never mind what Shun-tzŭ has said.
Judge for yourself—*[Indicating the blank patch]* This
patch here, what do you think?

WANG But—

ACTOR YÜEN *[speaking in exactly the same way as* YÜEN *in the play and*
using exactly the same words] No more 'buts'!
[Gesticulating] We open tomorrow. *[Anger beginning to*
get the better of him] And now you give me this—this
'empty look'! Shall we open or shall we not? Can't you
fill it in for me now?

[ACTOR T'AO takes WANG to one side, urging and coaxing
him.]

ACTOR T'AO All right! All right! Go get your gear now! *[They exit.]*

[ACTOR YÜEN is on the verge of hysteria.]

ACTOR YÜEN Damn! What a screw-up! *[Anger rising as he broods, he plonks himself down on the wheelchair that has not yet been removed.]* Shun-tzŭ? *[Irate]* Who the hell does he think he is? *[Bellows into the wings]* Shun-tzŭ!

SHUN-TZŬ *[from upstage left]* Coming!

ACTOR YÜEN *[letting out a thunderous roar]* You're fired!

SHUN-TZŬ *[obligingly, from backstage]* Okay!

ACTOR YÜEN *[in a storm of hysterical rage]* Okay? It's not okay! *[Swivelling the wheelchair round to where SHUN-TZŬ's answer has come, he jerks the wheels into motion with his hands and the wheelchair speeds off.]* Who wanted that 'empty look'? You or me? Answer me! Answer me! Don't let me catch you!

[ACTOR YÜEN, still in costume but seated on a wheelchair, exits. As he goes, the canvases painted with different river scenes are brought in and the lights slowly fade.]

SCENE SEVEN

[From the darkened stage rises the sound of T'AO *singing a fisherman's song again.]*

T'AO Heigh—Ho—Heigh!

[Lights come up slowly. T'AO *enters, 'rowing a boat' in Peking Opera-style mime from left to right. Behind him hangs a canvas painted with a river scene, the second one used in Scene 5.]*

Heigh—Ho—Heigh!

[Starting from the line just before the interruption occurred in Scene 5]

[recites]

'One day he rowed upstream, and soon forgot how far he had travelled.'

[Reminding himself as he rows] Yes, forget is the word. What's her name? 'Ch'un-hua'—she is forgotten! And what's his name? 'Yüen'—he, too, is forgotten! Forgetting is all! *[A thought strikes him.]* Oh, shouldn't the rapids be here? *[Peering about, suddenly letting out a loud cry]* Here they are! The rapids! Oops! Ough! *[The

canvas is drawn back quickly like a curtain, revealing painted rapids and a whirlpool. T'AO *jumps and leaps about, then swings round, stands still, and reports calmly to the audience.]* And a whirlpool!

[Again, he jumps and leaps about, then exits to the right.]

[The canvas is drawn back again, revealing another canvas painted with another colourful river scene, this one peaceful, with peach trees in the distance. T'AO *enters again from the left, still 'rowing'.]*

[standing firm and steady, then to the audience] Made it! What a narrow escape! *[Carries on 'rowing', then recites]*

'Suddenly he came upon a grove of peach trees.' *[He looks left and right about him.]*

'They flanked the banks of the stream for hundreds of paces, and there were no other trees to be seen.'

[He breaks off, reflecting, then suddenly turns to the audience.] Can you believe it? *[Carries on rowing]* Hang on! *[Closes his fingers on an imaginary bunch of grass growing by the river, leans forward and inhales deeply]* Mm!

'The soft grass, fresh and sweet.'

[He looks up, and acts as if he is showered with a cascade of falling petals.]

'Here and there falling blossoms danced gracefully in a thousand hues.'

[Delighted]

'He went on!'

[Sings again] Heigh—Ho—Heigh!

[Exit T'AO, *still 'rowing'. The canvas is again drawn back to reveal another scene.* T'AO *enters, 'rowing'.]*

T'AO *['rowing' as he sings]* Heigh—Ho—Heigh!

[Recites]

'The grove came to an end where the source of the river was, at the foot of a mountain with a narrow cave-like opening.'

[Peering warily]

'It looked as though light was coming from within.'

[Looks, then thinks] what do they mean by 'looked as though'? There *is* light coming from within. Definitely! *[Makes up his mind]*

'So he left the boat!'

[Breaks off abruptly to consider the line] The word 'so' is not in the original. *[Corrects himself]*

'He left the boat!'

[Mimes the movement of leaving the boat in a leap and lands on the shore. T'AO *now seems unsure how to proceed.]* I reckon I could 'enter the cave'? *[Ventures in courageously and exits from right]*

[The canvas is drawn back again to reveal the scenery on land.
After a while, T'AO *enters from the left, in the style of a Peking Opera actor with a martial arts role: he turns a full somersault mid-air, lands neatly on his feet, and strikes a pose.]*
[Reports in a loud, resounding voice]

'A broad vista suddenly opened up before him.'

[Facing right and staying on the same spot, he walks in mime, while the background scenery starts to move to the left continuously, creating the illusion that he is walking.]
[Looking at the scenery] It's nothing much!
[Reciting]

'The level plain stretched far and wide ... well-built houses ... foot-paths criss-crossed the fields. Cocks crowed, and dogs barked. Men and women busied themselves in the fields and were attired—'

[He comes to a stop. The background scenery, too, stops moving. Then, facing right and gazing straight ahead, he steps forward in actual steps.]

'in the same way as the people outside!'

[Exits to the right. Lights fade out.]

SCENE EIGHT

[From the darkened stage rises the sound of flute music evocative of a beautiful and idyllic by-gone era.
The lights come up on the main backdrop. As more lights rise on this huge landscape painting, the stage becomes vibrant with the mysterious power of the peach blossom grove, the mountain, and the river.

The stage is thick with mist. Pink peach blossom petals float down from above. In the middle of the stage stands an old well, behind it to the right a large boulder, in front of it to the left another large boulder. A woman in a long flowing white robe is sitting with her back to the audience on the boulder upstage right and playing a beautiful melody on her flute. One can just make out the outline of her figure in the mist.

T'AO enters from the left and is enchanted by the wide expanse of peach blossom grove and its stillness. The place fills him with fascination, curiosity, and apprehension.]

T'AO *[looking around him as he mumbles to himself]* What place is this? It's huge! *[The music drifts into his ears.]* Is it the wind whistling? Or the water murmuring? It seems so far away, yet so familiar. *[Bewildered by what he sees before him, he sits down on the boulder downstage left and soon sinks into his own troubles.]* I wonder how Ch'un-hua is now, all alone at home! *[Broods, then with jealousy in his voice]* Oh, she won't be alone! *[Shakes off this cursed thought]* Forget Ch'un-hua! In spite of her name, she's no spring blossom. And no match for these peach blossoms! *[Taking a leisurely stroll]* There is something indescribably wonderful in the air. I seem to have been here before! *[Finding it a little incredulous himself]* Impossible! There's no such place in Wuling! *[Takes a deep breath, completely enchanted]* Wonderful!

[He looks here and there, determined to enjoy himself, then goes up and down, carefully exploring the place. And now he discovers where the sound of the flute comes from. On first setting eyes on the WOMAN IN WHITE *upstage, he gives a start, then approaches her cautiously.]*

[stands tall and straight behind the woman, then addresses her politely] Excuse me! You play the flute wonderfully well. *[The woman goes on playing.]* The sound is so beautiful, so pure!

[The WOMAN IN WHITE *slowly turns her face round. She is played by the actress who plays* CH'UN-HUA *and the resemblance is clear.]*

[startled by the sight of CH'UN-HUA*]* So . . . horrible! *[They come face to face.* T'AO *cries out angrily.]* How come you're here too, Ch'un-hua?

[Frightened, the woman rises hastily and dodges to one side.]

*[*T'AO *goes after her with an insistent question.]* Ch'un-hua, how come you're here?

WOMAN IN WHITE *[gentle and tender, not a bit like the* CH'UN-HUA *in
                Wuling]* I beg your pardon. Is anything the matter?

T'AO Is anything the matter? Come on, don't play dumb!
      You can't fool me!

WOMAN IN WHITE You must have mistaken me for someone else. My
                name is not 'Ch'un-hua'!

T'AO How could I have mistaken you? I recognized you at
      once! I—

WOMAN IN WHITE You have, I'm afraid!

T'AO *[beginning to have doubts]* You're not Ch'un-hua? How
      could that be?

WOMAN IN WHITE You and I have only just met. *[Turning to comfort him]*
                You must be tired. *[Picks up a gourd ladle and draws
                some water from the well. She speaks gently.]* Have a drink
                of water!

[T'AO glances suspiciously at WOMAN IN WHITE *as he
drinks. He is feeling a little better now but still finds the
whole incident most bizarre.* WOMAN IN WHITE *is treating
him with infinite patience and loving tenderness.]*

WOMAN IN WHITE Are you looking for someone?

T'AO *[still full of suspicion]* What place is this?

WOMAN IN WHITE Peach Blossom Land!

T'AO Peach Blossom Land? *[Reflecting a moment]* Never heard
      of it!

WOMAN IN WHITE What are you doing here?

T'AO *[churlishly]* I've come here to fish! *[With a sudden surge
      of manliness]* I'm after the big fish!

WOMAN IN WHITE You were looking for someone called Ch'un-hua just
                now, weren't you?

T'AO *[abruptly]* Don't mention Ch'un-hua to me!

WOMAN IN WHITE Can I help?

T'AO What do you mean?

WOMAN IN WHITE Can I help you find her? Is she a relation?

T'AO She's my wife!

WOMAN IN WHITE What's the matter with her?

T'AO *[irascibly]* Don't mention her again!

WOMAN IN WHITE Why not?

T'AO The slut, she's unfaithful! *[Boxes his own ears in self-
      reproach for having told the shameful truth]*

WOMAN IN WHITE *[tenderly]* Come, come! Come and sit down! *[Gently
                ushers* T'AO *to the boulder downstage and sits him down]* Sit
                down and tell me what happened. Where are you from?

T'AO *[calming down]* From Wuling. *[WOMAN IN WHITE shows no sign of recognition. T'AO points his finger forward.]* Out there!

WOMAN IN WHITE What kind of a place is Wuling?

T'AO Haven't you heard of Wuling at all?

WOMAN IN WHITE *[ever so gentle]* I was born here. I've never left this place in my life.

T'AO And you've never heard it mentioned by anyone?

WOMAN IN WHITE None of us has ever left here.

T'AO *[incredulous]* None of you has ever gone out of this place?

WOMAN IN WHITE Where to?

T'AO To Wuling!

WOMAN IN WHITE What kind of a place is Wuling?

T'AO Oh—*[He is caught unaware by the question. All at once he is filled with pain, sorrow, bitterness, and resentment.]* Wuling—Wuling—Wuling. *[Gesticulating desperately, but the words won't come]* Wuling—! *[Buries his head in his knees disconsolately]*

WOMAN IN WHITE *[puzzled]* What has happened to your wife in Wuling?

T'AO *[calming down]* Might as well tell you. She . . . *[Slaps himself on the face]* she's having an affair!

WOMAN IN WHITE *[genuinely concerned]* Oh! Why? What's he like, the man?

T'AO He's—you won't believe it if I tell you. *[Getting very agitated]* I could draw him, but I don't think you'd have come across someone like him before! He looks . . . *[Gesticulating]* he looks like, like . . . like—*[Words fail him.]*

[A man in a white robe played by the actor who plays YÜEN *strolls in from the right.]*

Like . . . *[On seeing MAN IN WHITE, he recoils in fear, as if at the sight of an apparition.]* Oh—! *[He takes a closer look, then cries out in alarm.]* It's you, Yüen! How come you're here?

MAN IN WHITE *[gentle and tender, just like WOMAN IN WHITE]* I beg your pardon. My name is not 'Yüen'!

T'AO *[sharply]* Oh, come on, Yüen! You can't fool me!

MAN IN WHITE You must have mistaken me for someone else. My name is not Yüen.

T'AO Your name is not—? How could that be? You—

WOMAN IN WHITE *[coming up to comfort T'AO]* You have mistaken him for someone else.

[This is too much for T'AO. He shakes his head miserably in silence.]

MAN IN WHITE *[puzzled, directs question to* WOMAN IN WHITE*]* What's the matter with him?

WOMAN IN WHITE He's tired.

MAN IN WHITE *[to* T'AO*]* Are you tired? Have a drink of water!

[As caring and kind as WOMAN IN WHITE, *and with the same graceful movement, he picks up a gourd ladle, draws some water from the well and offers it to* T'AO. T'AO *drinks some water and begins to calm down.]*

[to WOMAN IN WHITE*]* He is—?

WOMAN IN WHITE He says he's from Wuling.

T'AO *[overcome with disbelief once again, flares up, points accusingly at the two persons in white]* Don't try to fool me! It's just possible that one of you would look exactly like one of them. But for the pair of you to look exactly like the pair of them—that's downright incredible! *[Fuming, stalks up to them. They move to one side.]* Did you arrange to come here together?

MAN IN WHITE, *[together, honestly]* Yes, we arranged to meet here!
WOMAN IN WHITE

T'AO *[advances step by step, interrogating them sternly]* Then how did you get here?

MAN IN WHITE We came here on foot!

WOMAN IN WHITE *[agreeing]* Yes, we came here on foot!

T'AO *[incredulous]* What? On foot? I came by boat and you arrived before me?

WOMAN IN WHITE No, I arrived before him.

MAN IN WHITE Yes, I came afterwards. I was held up at home!

T'AO *[another shock]* Home? You both have a family? What's your relationship?

WOMAN IN WHITE We are husband and wife. He's my husband!

MAN IN WHITE Yes, we're husband and wife!

T'AO *[hysterical]* You? *[Screams, like someone who has been driven mad]* Then I'll go and kill myself! *[Strangles himself as in Scene 4]* I'll kill myself! Kill! Kill! Kill!

MAN IN WHITE *[moving quickly and calmly to stop* T'AO*]* Easy! Easy!

[They seize T'AO's *arms.* T'AO, *as if hypnotized, soon calms down.]*

[to WOMAN IN WHITE*]* What exactly is the matter with him?

WOMAN IN WHITE I think he's very unhappy—because of his wife.

MAN IN WHITE *[turns round to* T'AO*]* What about your wife?

T'AO *[angry again]* I warn you! Don't mention my wife!

MAN IN WHITE *[turns round to* WOMAN IN WHITE*]* What's the matter with his wife?

WOMAN IN WHITE She's sleeping with someone else.

T'AO *[loses control again and screams hysterically]* I'll go and kill myself! *[Twirls his arms manically]* I'll kill myself! Kill! Kill! Kill!

MAN IN WHITE *[same reaction as before, saying patiently]* Easy! Easy!

*[*T'AO *calms down again.]*

[to WOMAN IN WHITE*]* How did he come to such a state?

WOMAN IN WHITE He mentioned something about 'the big fish' just now. Maybe the fish he caught were too small.

MAN IN WHITE *[turns round to* T'AO*]* Are your fish too small?

T'AO *[badly upset again, screams again]* Oh! I'll go and kill myself! *[Clasping his head with his hands, he mimes pushing and pulling his head into and out of his neck—a ludicrous attempt at suicide.]* Kill! Kill! Kill!

MAN IN WHITE, *[together]* Easy! Easy!
WOMAN IN WHITE

*[*T'AO *calms down again.]*

MAN IN WHITE *[draws a conclusion]* I see! *[To* T'AO*]* If you catch big fish, then your wife won't sleep around!

T'AO *[defensively]* They are two separate things! *[As in Scene 4, he wags his forefingers in front of his eyes in a comic routine.]* Totally separate things! The one's got nothing to do with the other! Absolutely nothing. . . . *[*T'AO*'s forefingers collide and he finds himself looking at his left hand with two fingers sticking up, and his right hand held in a fist. This drives him crazy.]* Heavens! They're one and the same! I'll kill myself! *[Begins to jab at his eyes]* Kill! Kill! Kill!

MAN IN WHITE, *[together]* Ea-sy! Ea-sy!
WOMAN IN WHITE

T'AO *[calms down again]* This place you live in is so weird—

WOMAN IN WHITE Is that how you see it? Why? It's wonderful here!

T'AO *[weakly]* How did the two of you get here?

MAN IN WHITE That's a long long story.

T'AO Why pick this place?

MAN IN WHITE Our ancestors brought us here.

T'AO Your ancestors?

MAN IN WHITE *[strikes an oratorical pose, identical to the one struck by* YÜEN *when he rhapsodized before* CH'UN-HUA *in Scene 4]*

Our ancestors had a dream! *[With evangelical zeal]* They led us, to this beautiful place, this land of plenty, so that we, their sons and grandsons, could, hand in hand, side by side—

T'AO *[chipping in]* Who were they—your ancestors?

MAN IN WHITE They . . . *[Momentary confusion]* They're not important now. *[Resumes his oratorical pose]* Because . . . because their dream—has been realized! And their aspirations have come to fruition here! *[Takes* WOMAN IN WHITE's *hand, the two breaking into a blissful smile]* That is why there are grapes in our left hands, cups of the finest wine in our right hands, and pineapples in our mouths—

T'AO Doesn't that make you look like roast pigs?

MAN IN WHITE *[his eloquence abruptly checked]* Well . . . well . . . *[At a loss for words, he changes the topic.]* Let's forget about these silly questions! You must be very tired now. Are you hungry? I'll get her to cook something nice for you. You'll have dinner with us, won't you?

T'AO *[stubbornly]* No, I'm not hungry!

MAN IN WHITE Come on!

WOMAN IN WHITE *[urging him too]* And if you like, you can come and stay with us!

MAN IN WHITE Yes, stay longer if you have problems at home. Relax and take things easy.

[MAN IN WHITE and WOMAN IN WHITE *close their hands on* T'AO's *arms and usher him towards the wings.]*

T'AO *[a sudden outburst]* Yüen! Ch'un-hua! How can I stay with you? How can I relax? How can I relax?

MAN IN WHITE Come on! Let's go!

T'AO *[crying out in dismay]* No! Yüen! No!

MAN IN WHITE *[dragging* T'AO *with him]* Forget Yüen!

T'AO *[cries again]* Ch'un-hua!

WOMAN IN WHITE Forget Ch'un-hua!

T'AO *[forgetting nothing, still whining]* Oh! What place is this?

MAN IN WHITE, *[together]* Peach Blossom Land.
WOMAN IN WHITE

[Lights fade as the three make their exit, only the puzzled voice of T'AO *can still be heard.]*

T'AO Peach Blossom Land?

BLACKOUT

SCENE NINE

[The graceful sound of flute music rises again on the darkened stage, evoking a quiet, mysterious, and other-worldly atmosphere.

The lights come on. The stage is bare except for the huge landscape painting at the back, and the sense of stillness that comes with it.

Mist everywhere, petals continue to fall gently. From amidst the thick mist the outlines of three figures can just be made out. T'AO *has changed into a long flowing white robe and is reclining in the peach blossom grove, happy and content, enjoying the colours and freshness of his surroundings.* MAN IN WHITE *and* WOMAN IN WHITE *are stealing up in slow motion on* T'AO, *both smiling serenely.*

WOMAN IN WHITE *covers* T'AO's *eyes with her hands.* T'AO *shows, in slow motion, that he is pleasantly surprised.* MAN IN WHITE *then goes up to behind* WOMAN IN WHITE *and covers her eyes with his hands. She, too, is pleasantly surprised. It is obvious the three are living in pure bliss and unadulterated happiness.*

The lights go out suddenly. They come up again at once. The three have already changed their positions. T'AO *and* WOMAN IN WHITE *are now standing downstage, to the left and right respectively,* MAN IN WHITE *is a few paces behind them, in the centre, a blindfold tied over his eyes, his hands raised in an attempt to catch the other two. They play out a game of blind man's buff in slow motion.*

The lights go out suddenly. They come up again at once. This time it is WOMAN IN WHITE *who is blindfolded. She is running after the two men in slow motion, her movements graceful and elegant, like a dance.* MAN IN WHITE *pushes* T'AO *with a shove, sending him into the arms of* WOMAN IN WHITE. *The three laugh heartily in silence.*

The lights go out suddenly. They come up again at once. T'AO, *blindfolded, is running after the other two in slow motion. The* DIRECTOR *of* Pining *is standing arms akimbo upstage centre, watching the performance. The* Blossom Land *trio, however, are not aware of the presence of this intruder and play out in slow motion the game of blind man's buff in the thick mist, amidst the enchanting flute music.*

The lights go out suddenly. They come up again at once. The Blossom Land *trio have taken up very different positions, each occupying one corner of the stage. This time they are all blindfolded, their arms outstretched, laughing and groping their way forward. Two more actors from* Pining—ACTOR CHIANG *and* ACTRESS YÜN—*are standing on either side of* DIRECTOR, *all looking very impatient. But the* Blossom Land *trio still have not noticed them and their rehearsal continues.*

The lights go out suddenly. They come up again at once. This time the entire Pining *team is there, crowding the stage.* ACTRESS MRS CHIANG *and* ACTRESS NURSE *are quietly watching the three blindfolded figures in their slow-motion dance,* STRANGER *is there too, staring blankly at the* Blossom Land *trio. In the thick mist and amidst the beautiful flute music, the trio, still blindfolded, are now standing in a line centre stage, facing the audience, hand in hand, a look of enchantment on their faces. Then they remove the blindfolds tied over their eyes, smile in slow motion, show delight, and then, still in slow motion, turn round in*

*gracefully synchronized steps to appreciate the scenery of the peach blossom grove
depicted on the painting. Only then do they notice the pack of intruders. The three
give a start. Suddenly all the floodlights are up, the sound of flute music breaks off
abruptly, there is confusion everywhere, with everyone talking all at once.]*

DIRECTOR OF PINING *[forthright, waving some document in his hand]* We must
    sort this out now!

> *[He springs at* ACTOR YÜEN, *but is held back by*
> ACTRESSES MRS CHIANG *and* NURSE.]

ACTOR YÜEN How? *[Still recovering from the shock]* I've never been
    interrupted like this!

ACTOR T'AO *[indignant]* Damn! They scared the shit out of me!

> *[*ACTOR CHIANG *and* ACTRESS YÜN *go at once to calm
> people down, but everyone is about to explode.]*

ACTRESS YÜN *[trying to be reasonable]* Let's talk things over. This play
    is really important to our director!

ACTOR YÜEN Isn't ours important to us?

ACTRESS YÜN *[patiently]* We've been rehearsing the whole day, but
    we've never had a moment's peace.

ACTOR YÜEN Don't blame us! Go and talk to the guy in charge. Did
    anyone go and talk to him?

ACTOR T'AO Yes.

ACTOR YÜEN Who?

ACTOR T'AO Shun-tzŭ.

ACTOR YÜEN Shun-tzŭ? *[Sighs in resignation]*

ACTOR CHIANG Let's find a compromise.

ACTOR YÜEN No way! I'm in a terrible fix! Under siege left, right,
    and centre! It's such a good comedy! But you've
    mucked it up!

> *[*ACTRESSES MRS CHIANG *and* NURSE *have been trying to
> calm* DIRECTOR, *but* ACTOR YÜEN's *remark makes*
> DIRECTOR *lose all control.]*

DIRECTOR All right! Now that you've said it, I won't mince
    words either! *[Delivering a personal attack]* Your comedy
    depresses me! I adore the writer of the original story,
    Tao Yuanming. How can you treat his work like that?
    He'll turn in his grave!

ACTOR CHIANG Come! Come! You'd better hold your tongue—

ACTOR YÜEN *[retaliates at once]* Well let me be frank with you, too.
    Your tragedy gives me the giggles. *[Everyone is
    astounded.]* Tell me, how do you play a 'white camellia'?
    Why don't you play it for me—play that white

camellia for me? Why don't you? Huh? *[Pointing at the pyjamas* ACTOR CHIANG *has on]* You've brought your pyjamas on stage as well, huh? And what about the swings? Might as well bring them in!

DIRECTOR *[sensing the deadlock]* Oh dear! Does he know what drama means?

*[*ACTRESS MRS CHIANG *tries to pacify him again.]*

ACTRESS YÜN Let's not argue anymore. *[To* YÜEN*]* Come on, can't we work something out?

ACTOR YÜEN Like what? *[Checks the wristwatch hidden under his long flowing sleeve]* Time's running out. . . . Now, how about this? *[Making a really desperate suggestion]* We'll take— *[Indicates one side of the stage]* this half of the stage and finish our run-through. You do what you like on the other half.

DIRECTOR What? Half and half? Never heard anything like it!

ACTOR YÜEN Neither have I!

ACTRESS YÜN *[to* DIRECTOR*]* We'll just have to make do!

[All eyes are turned on DIRECTOR, *who knows he has to decide at once.]*

DIRECTOR But—

[Everyone begins to move.]

[tapping at the document that has taken him so much trouble to find, and still reluctant to give in] Where's the guy in charge?

ACTRESS MRS CHIANG Never mind him! Let's get on with it!

[The Pining *crew are bringing in the props while the* Blossom Land *team are discussing what to do with their half of the stage.]*

ACTOR T'AO *[resentfully]* I've told you I can't stand being interrupted during rehearsals!

ACTOR YÜEN *[wearily]* What can I do? *[Draws a deep breath]* Let's take a break, collect ourselves and then start again, okay?

ACTRESS CH'UN-HUA Which scene shall we do?

ACTOR YÜEN *[reflecting a moment]* 'By the side of Peach Blossom Spring'.

[The Pining *crew have got everything ready.* ACTRESSES MRS CHIANG *and* NURSE *pick up their hand props and go off.* DIRECTOR *is carrying out a final check of his half of the stage, making sure everything is in place.]*

[ACTOR CHIANG, *wearing his pyjamas and the sweater from his Shanghai days, is trying to concentrate on his role and watching the meticulous* DIRECTOR *at work. When* DIRECTOR *is satisfied that all is in order, he gestures to* ACTOR CHIANG *to begin.*

WANG, the scene painter, has climbed up the stepladder he has just brought in and, paints and brushes in hand, begins to fill in the blank patch that stands out so awkwardly on the landscape painting of the peach blossom grove. ACTOR CHIANG *lies down on the hospital bed. Lights slowly fade.*]

SCENE TEN

[*Lights come up slowly. Stage right is crammed with the hospital furniture used by the* Pining *team in Scene 6—a hospital bed, a drip stand, two bedside tables, a wheelchair, and so on. The other side of the stage is empty.*

CHIANG, *old and gaunt, is lying on the hospital bed, listening quietly to a 1930s Mandarin pop song coming from the tape recorder on the bedside table—'A drifting water lily am I', by Bai Guang:*

'I *am a water lily, drifting in the sea of life.*
One peaceful evening and all alone,
I talked with the stars, and sang with the moon on high . . .'

The plain backdrop used for the hospital scene of Pining *is completely hidden by the huge landscape painting of the peach blossom grove. As a result, the slides for the hospital scene are projected on to the landscape painting, creating a strange overlapping effect.*

The slides are all scenes of Taipei in the 1980s. Panoramic shots of the city—bungalows, houses, and high-rise buildings—are followed by shots of the Chang Keng Hospital at a distance, and then by a series of corridor scenes inside the hospital, until finally there is a slide of an X-ray picture of CHIANG's *lungs. It seems incongruous for these slides to be projected on to the landscape painting, and yet in a subtle sort of way the images seem somehow to match.*

NURSE *opens the door and, as usual, walks briskly into the room. The song plays in the background:*

'The *gentle wind, the murmuring stream*
In a sweet duet entwined.
Oh—what an enchanting evening!
Oh—what an enchanting evening!']

NURSE You're awake? [*Hears the song*] The same song again! How often have I asked you not to listen to that song? It puts you in such a state. Let me switch it off! [*About to switch off the tape recorder*]

CHIANG No! I like the song.

NURSE What's so great about it? I've listened to it so many times and still I can't make out what she's on about!

CHIANG *[lapsing into a sentimental and nostalgic wistfulness]* She says: there is a man—he's been through a lot in his life—he remembers an evening that had him completely enchanted. *[Pauses]* That evening, the moon was singing, the stars were whispering; the gentle wind and the murmuring stream were entwined in a sweet duet. He thought that that evening was his to possess. Now that he is old, he discovers he is all alone. *[With a note of despair]* The only thing left for him is . . . to remember.

NURSE *[turns round to switch off the tape recorder]* Look at you. Every time you listen to that song you're like this! *[Reproachfully]* You shouldn't be thinking about that dreadful business all the time! Let's see, since you put that ad in the paper, it's been *[Counting on her fingers]* five days! And you're still waiting for her? I don't think there's any point! When Miss Yün didn't turn up the first day, I knew she wouldn't come at all. Besides, who knows whether she's still alive or not? Why punish yourself like this?

[CHIANG, crushed, looks up and throws a glance at NURSE, who realizes that she has been too blunt.]

[softening] Sorry! I didn't mean it! What I'm trying to say is—if Miss Yün did turn up, things might get even worse, because you might feel even more unhappy, right? *[CHIANG does not reply.]* So why not take things as they are and get on with your life? At least there's peace and quiet.

[CHIANG still does not reply. MRS CHIANG opens the door and walks in.

At the same moment, the Blossom Land *trio, in their long flowing white robes and carrying the prop boulders in their hands, march in and start preparing their half of the stage.]*

MRS CHIANG *[opens her mouth to deliver her lines, but is distracted by the sight of the* Blossom Land *team busying about the stage]* It's a strange place, this hospital you work in. They keep pestering me to pay the fees, when our patient here *[Patting CHIANG]* can't even run away!

[The Blossom Land *trio are discussing in low voices how to cram the props into half the usual space.]*

And when I went to pay the fees just now, the cashier
said it was time she got off work, and asked me to
come again tomorrow. Everyday I—

*[*ACTOR T'AO *is pacing his side of the stage sideways to
measure out the distance between the props.]*

I run round and round in this hospital.

[While MRS CHIANG *is speaking,* CHIANG *is reaching out
his hand for the wheelchair not far from the bed.]*

ACTOR T'AO *[taking charge]* Right, we're on.

MRS CHIANG *[to* NURSE*]* Nurse, I'm not blaming you. It's just that I
find this hospital—

[The Blossom Land *trio are ready.* WOMAN IN WHITE *is
sitting on the prop boulder placed near stage centre on their
half of the stage.* T'AO, *in his white robe, is strolling in
front of the boulder, looking at the imaginary river before
him, a serene expression on his face. It is as if, having lived
for a long time in Peach Blossom Land, he has become a
completely different person from the* T'AO *in Wuling.]*

MRS CHIANG *[looking at the* Blossom Land *team]*—a bit peculiar!

T'AO *[delivers his lines as he turns cheerfully to* WOMAN IN
WHITE*]* It's wonderful here!

*[*MRS CHIANG *turns round to find* CHIANG *straining to
reach the wheelchair, and goes up to him at once.]*

MRS CHIANG Why didn't you tell us you wanted to get up?

[She and NURSE *help* CHIANG *get into the wheelchair.* MRS
CHIANG *steers the wheelchair downstage.]*

CHIANG *[impatient with her attention]* I don't need you here.
You'd better go!

MRS CHIANG Why? I'll stay and keep you company.

*[*MRS CHIANG *is speaking with her head lowered, and the
wheelchair collides with the* Blossom Land *prop boulder.*
WOMAN IN WHITE *leaps to her feet, greatly alarmed.]*

T'AO *[reciting]*

'The soft grass, fresh and sweet!'

CHIANG *[to* MRS CHIANG, *indicating the boulder]* Look what
you've done!

MRS CHIANG *[indicating that there is too little space]* What can I do?

*[The two nearly break into a row. But both control their
temper, knowing that time is precious, and start again. The
atmosphere is tense as* CHIANG *returns to his bed and* MRS
CHIANG *leaves the room.* WOMAN IN WHITE *returns to her
seat, the boulder, and the rehearsal continues.]*

T'AO *[reciting the words from* A Record of Peach Blossom Spring, *as petals begin to fall gently from above]*

> 'Here and there falling blossoms danced gracefully in a thousand hues.'

[He sighs.]

WOMAN IN WHITE *[with her usual tenderness]* Don't be sad! Don't you like it here?

T'AO *[as if annoyed with himself]* I do! But I don't find what I really want here.

NURSE *[to* CHIANG*]* Where shall we start?

CHIANG From where you switch off the tape recorder.

WOMAN IN WHITE *[to* T'AO*]* What's the matter? I've never seen you unhappy since you came and stayed with us!

[The Pining *team have taken up their positions on stage right to go over the lines again. And now both teams are in action—one on stage right, the other on stage left.]*

NURSE *[to* CHIANG*]* Look at you. Every time you listen to that song you're like this!

T'AO *[to* WOMAN IN WHITE*]* I miss home!

NURSE *[to* CHIANG*]* You shouldn't be thinking about that dreadful business all the time!

WOMAN IN WHITE *[to* T'AO*]* You've been here so long. Why would you want to go back?

NURSE *[to* CHIANG*]* Let's see, since you put that ad in the paper, it's been—*[Counting on her fingers]*

T'AO *[to* WOMAN IN WHITE*]* How long has it been?

NURSE *[to* CHIANG*]* Five days!

WOMAN IN WHITE *[to* T'AO*]* Oh, a very long time!

[NURSE glances uneasily at T'AO *and* WOMAN IN WHITE.*]*

NURSE *[to* CHIANG*]* And you're still waiting for her? I don't think there's any point!

T'AO *[to* WOMAN IN WHITE*]* I don't know, maybe she's still waiting for me. I just want to see whether she wants to come with me.

WOMAN IN WHITE *[thinking for* T'AO*]* She might not!

NURSE *[to* CHIANG*]* When Miss Yün didn't turn up the first day, I knew she wouldn't come at all.

T'AO *[to* WOMAN IN WHITE*]* No, she will!

[Both teams are struck by this extraordinary coincidence. They exchange a look of amazement.
The rehearsals continue.]

WOMAN IN WHITE *[to* T'AO*]* She might have forgotten you!

NURSE *[to* CHIANG*]* Besides, who knows whether she's still alive or not? Why punish yourself like this?

T'AO *[to* WOMAN IN WHITE*]* How can you say that?!

WOMAN IN WHITE, *[speaking at the same time, another coincidence]* Sorry! I
NURSE didn't mean it!

> *[The way the lines of the two plays overlap and reverberate has stunned everyone on stage.* ACTOR T'AO *looks to and fro between* WOMAN IN WHITE *and* NURSE, *bewildered, not knowing to whom he should direct his reply.* NURSE *is vexed and frustrated.* CHIANG *is trying to cheer her up and to start again.* MAN IN WHITE *enters from stage left, and the* Blossom Land *rehearsal continues.]*

MAN IN WHITE Mean what?

T'AO Oh! You're here!

MAN IN WHITE What have you been talking about?

WOMAN IN WHITE I said something about his, um . . . you know who. He thought I was going too far. I'd say that if he turned up on her doorstep all of a sudden, that would really be a bit much.

MAN IN WHITE I see—Better not go back! If you go back now, you'll upset their lives!

> *[*NURSE *has recovered and the* Pining *rehearsal begins again.]*

NURSE *[to* CHIANG*]* What I'm trying to say is—if Miss Yün did turn up, things might get even worse.

T'AO *[to* MAN IN WHITE*]* How do you mean?

NURSE *[to* CHIANG*]* Because you might feel even more unhappy!

T'AO *[replying to* NURSE*]* No, I wouldn't!

> *[*MAN IN WHITE *smacks* T'AO *on the head.]*

MAN IN WHITE What are you saying?

> *[*T'AO *himself has no idea how he got it wrong. He keeps shaking his head and staring at the* Pining *team. The* Blossom Land *trio gather to discuss their lines.]*

NURSE So why not take things as they are and get on with your life? At least there's peace and quiet.

> *[*CHIANG *does not reply.* MRS CHIANG *enters.]*

MRS CHIANG It's a strange place, this hospital you work in. They keep pestering me to pay the fees, when our patient here can't even run away! And when I went to pay the fees just now, the cashier said it was time she got off work, and asked me to come again tomorrow.

[The Blossom Land *trio are ready to start again.* T'AO *and* MAN IN WHITE *pace to and fro.* MRS CHIANG *eyes them as she says her lines.]* Everyday I run round and round in this hospital. I'm not getting at you! *[A little embarrassed]* It's just that I find this hospital a bit peculiar!

T'AO I want to go back and see how things are!

[As before, CHIANG *reaches out his hand for the wheelchair, but* MRS CHIANG *and* NURSE *are distracted, and their attention has drifted.]*

MAN IN WHITE I don't think you should! What do you hope to achieve? I'm afraid you . . . you . . . *[Following his feelings through, he turns round and, seeing* CHIANG *straining to reach the wheelchair, points towards* CHIANG *and blurts out.]* You can't reach it! *[Realizing that he has got the lines wrong again, he smacks himself on the mouth.]*

MRS CHIANG *[suddenly alert, to* CHIANG*]* Why didn't you tell us you wanted to get up?

[As before, MRS CHIANG *and* NURSE *help* CHIANG *get into the wheelchair.]*

T'AO *[delivering his reply to what* MAN IN WHITE *should have said]* What more can I say?

MAN IN WHITE *[to* T'AO*]* If you are not really needed, you'd better not go!

CHIANG *[to* MRS CHIANG*]* I don't need you here. You'd better go!

MRS CHIANG Why? *[Steers the wheelchair downstage]*

T'AO *[to* MAN IN WHITE*]* I think I should just go and see how things are, then I'd have no more illusions!

CHIANG *[to* MRS CHIANG*]* You better go now!

MRS CHIANG I'll stay and keep you company!

[In a moment of carelessness, MRS CHIANG *has steered the wheelchair downstage and is heading towards the space between* T'AO *and* MAN IN WHITE*.]*

MAN IN WHITE *[to* T'AO, *but gazing at* CHIANG *in the wheelchair]* You'll get into trouble if you do. Don't go!

[The wheelchair has now stopped between T'AO *and* MAN IN WHITE*.]*

CHIANG *[to* MRS CHIANG, *but gazing at* T'AO*]* Go now!

MRS CHIANG, T'AO *[looking at each other]* I—

MAN IN WHITE *[his gentle voice becoming stern and harsh all at once]* You mustn't!

CHIANG *[contradicting* MAN IN WHITE*]* Go at once!

MAN IN WHITE No! You're not going!

[Both CHIANG *and* MAN IN WHITE *have forgotten their parts and are now using their lines to slam at each other. The others are at a loss what to do.]*

CHIANG Get the hell out of here!

MAN IN WHITE *[even more enraged]* I warn you, you're not going!

CHIANG *[waving his hand, fuming]* Go! Go! Go at once!

MAN IN WHITE *[quoting a line from the play haphazardly]* If you go, you can never come back!

CHIANG I said get the hell out!

MAN IN WHITE I'll be damned if anyone dares move an inch!

[All of a sudden, the DIRECTOR *of* Pining *storms in.]*

DIRECTOR *[barks]* Stop it!

ACTOR YÜEN *[resuming his role as director of* Blossom Land *and muttering helplessly to himself]* Not again!

[No one knows what to do. A long silence.]

DIRECTOR *[breaking the silence]* Yüen!

ACTOR YÜEN *[in a huff]* My name is not 'Yüen'!

DIRECTOR *[exercising great restraint]* My dear sir, how many more scenes do you still have?

ACTOR YÜEN *[trying to control his temper, too, takes a deep breath and points to* T'AO*]* He has to leave Peach Blossom Land and go back to Wuling. Just that scene and no more!

DIRECTOR *[making up his mind at once]* All right. We'll let you finish it first. Quick!

NURSE *[cries]* How can you give in to them like that?

DIRECTOR How can we carry on if we don't?

[Upon hearing this, the Blossom Land *team pick up their props and start repositioning themselves on stage. For a while, there is a flurry of activity, with the* Pining *team making their retreat and the* Blossom Land *team yelling out instructions and dashing about, and the props and furniture of the two companies getting lumped together in a state of commotion.*

Lights fade out.]

S C E N E   E L E V E N

[Light come up slowly on T'AO *and* CH'UN-HUA's *home in Wuling. The props are arranged as in Scene 4. But now there is a portrait of* T'AO *hanging on the bamboo screen 'in memory' of him.* CH'UN-HUA *is alone on stage sorting out a pile*

of diapers on the table. She is wearing the red dress she wore in Scene 4, but it's now old and tattered. She looks extremely unhappy and, as she folds the diapers one by one and stacks them up, resentment begins to rise.]

CH'UN-HUA *[muttering to herself]* Day in, day out, I do nothing but fold diapers! What sort of a life is that? *[Turns round and looks behind the screen]* And he does nothing but sleep. What sort of a man is he? *[Muttering and mumbling]* What did he say? 'I can see our sons and grandsons. . . . I can see our beautiful home'. . . . Rotten lies! *[Throws the diapers on to the floor one by one, just as* T'AO *threw things on to the floor in Scene 4]* To hell with them! *[Stamps on them]* To hell with them! *[Stamps]* To hell with them! *[Stamps and tramples]*

[Pause. CH'UN-HUA *stands there glowering at the diapers on the floor, still boiling with resentment. All of a sudden, she flares up again, jumps on to the diapers, and stamps, tramples, and grinds them under her feet. Her anger not quite spent, she drops on all fours, as* T'AO *did in Scene 4, and supporting herself on her palms, starts swinging her leg round and round, round and round, sending the diapers flying.*

YÜEN *enters, staggering from behind the screen, a wine bottle in one hand, the other hand rubbing his eyes. He has been woken up by the noise and is not pleased. His behaviour shows he is now a member of the household. He is wearing the same costume as in Scene 4, but it, too, is tattered. At the sight of* YÜEN, CH'UN-HUA *becomes aware of how foolish she looks, and scrambles to her feet.]*

Where were you last night?

*[*YÜEN *plonks himself down on a stool and tries to remove the cork from the wine bottle. But, like* T'AO *in Scene 4, he struggles in vain.]*

YÜEN Don't ask! Rotten luck! *[Tries again to pull out the cork]*
CH'UN-HUA You went gambling again!
YÜEN *[brusquely]* It's none of your business!
CH'UN-HUA If it is not my business, why are we living together?
YÜEN You mind your own business. I can handle mine!
CH'UN-HUA Can you? *[Well-intentioned]* I think you'd better get yourself a job or something!
YÜEN *[as if his dignity has been dealt a blow]* Get myself a job? Do people like me need a job? How many times have I told you *[Rises to his feet, strikes his usual heroic pose, and begins to expound on the grand aspirations he had enthused about in Scene 4]* I . . . I have a dream—

[Before he can go on, CH'UN-HUA *grabs some diapers and hits him hard on the head. A loud resounding 'thud', and* YÜEN *scurries aside.]*

CH'UN-HUA Cut that shit! To hell with your dream!

*[*CH'UN-HUA *throws all the diapers on to the floor. Then both she and* YÜEN *stamp on them and go through the same routine as at the end of Scene 4, and bow to the audience hand in hand. Then, realizing how out of place such a gesture is, they quickly let fall their arms.]*

YÜEN *[vexed and agitated]* That . . . that's too much! Why do you always treat me like that when things get . . . get too much for me?

CH'UN-HUA My fault again? Look at yourself! If you hadn't been so impossible, would we have come to such a state? Oh! You are too much, much too much, far too much—!

YÜEN Don't you much too much me! I tell you, you're thinking far too much, much too much about him!

CH'UN-HUA *[uneasily]* What about him? Haven't you said that he . . . that he's already had it, that it's all 'much of a muchness' for him now?

YÜEN *[something is bothering him]* Yes, yes, he's had it! But he *[Indicating the portrait of* T'AO*]* hasn't! And he *[Indicating* T'AO's *eyes]* is watching over me, haunting me day and night. Oh! It's too much!

CH'UN-HUA But I asked you whether you minded. And you said 'no'! *[Furious]* Okay! I'll take him down and throw him out! *[Takes down* T'AO's *portrait and smashes it on the floor]* Does that satisfy you? Are you happy now?

YÜEN What's the use? It's all . . . much of a muchness for me!

*[*T'AO *enters from the right, still wearing a long flowing white robe and carrying his oar. He is happy to be home.* YÜEN & CH'UN-HUA *are too busy shouting at each other to notice* T'AO. T'AO *does not notice them either, he is too excited.]*

[a tortured expression on his face] He's still there! Yes, in your heart!

[The joy and delight of homecoming is written all over T'AO's *face. He looks round, re-acquainting himself with the place.]*

Sometimes, I can feel his ghost is here, in this house, drifting up and down, up and down, *[Following the rhythm of his words, he points his finger up and down, and, unwittingly, at* T'AO *who is drifting up and down, up and down the place.]* up and down! *[Jumps as he sees* T'AO *in a long flowing ghostly white robe]*

T'AO *[greeting them in a gentle manner and with genuine happiness]* Ch'un-hua! Yüen!

YÜEN, CH'UN-HUA *[together]* Oh!

[They stare in horror at T'AO. *He has been away so long, and is so strangely dressed they are not sure whether he is a ghost or a man.]*

T'AO Ch'un-hua!

YÜEN, CH'UN-HUA *[together]* Don't, don't come near us!

[They fling their arms around each other, panic-stricken. T'AO *is a completely changed person, in bearing as well as temper. He speaks slowly and calmly, and with a gentleness that does not seem normal or natural.]*

T'AO I'm back!

CH'UN-HUA You're back?

YÜEN *[to* CH'UN-HUA, *in quick whisper]* I told you to burn more paper money for him but you never bothered!

[T'AO goes up to them. They back away in fear.]

CH'UN-HUA Why have you come back?

T'AO Ch'un-hua! *[Intimately]* I've come back to take you away!

CH'UN-HUA Away? You mean far, far away—*[Her legs give way,* YÜEN *catches her in time.]*

T'AO I'm sorry! I forgot to tell you what happened to me. I went up the river, do you remember? On the way, I got caught in the rapids. *[Concentrating on his recollection]* Later on there was a treacherous whirlpool—

YÜEN *[holding* CH'UN-HUA *and whispering into her ears]* That's where he kicked the bucket! *[Shivers]*

T'AO *[still recollecting]* After the whirlpool I came upon a huge peach blossom grove—an endless stretch of lovely pink!

YÜEN *[nodding his head and remarking to* CH'UN-HUA*]* That's right. They usually notice colours first.

T'AO *[talking to himself]* Then I left the boat!

YÜEN Of course! One has to leave everything behind! Everything! *[He looks like he is going to faint, but* CH'UN-HUA *gives him a timely punch with her fist.]*

T'AO And then I went into a dark and narrow cave—

YÜEN *[to* CH'UN-HUA*]* That's right! Dark and narrow!

T'AO I squeezed my way through and—Lo and behold, a broad vista suddenly opened before me!

YÜEN *[repeating dully, mechanically]* A broad vista . . . a broad vista!

T'AO And all my troubles were gone!

YÜEN [to T'AO, timidly] Was it . . . was it another world?

T'AO [reflecting a moment] Yes, you could call it another world.

YÜEN You . . . [In despair now] Must you take her . . .
[Indicating CH'UN-HUA] with you?

T'AO Yes, I've come to take her there! What? Do you want
to come, too, Yüen?

[YÜEN and CH'UN-HUA throw themselves on their knees.]

YÜEN [blaming himself and lamenting his fate] I knew he
wouldn't let me off so easily! [Scrambling away like a
fugitive fleeing for his life]

T'AO [automatically throws himself on his knees too and crawls
about the floor with them] Is this some new etiquette?
[Returns to his main topic] It's all right, I can take you
both with me! They can put you up. Plenty of room
there—

YÜEN I know, I know. There are eighteen levels in all. [His
voice is shaking so much his words can barely be heard.]
There are sword mountains, cauldrons of boiling oil—

T'AO What are you talking about?

YÜEN The Land of the Dead! Hell!

T'AO Oh! [Everything is clear.] You thought I . . . I was a ghost?

[YÜEN looks up sharply at T'AO.]

Well no! I'm still here! Alive and kicking! [Anxious to
prove it, he goes up to YÜEN and makes to touch him.] See
for yourself! Come on!

[YÜEN recoils in fear, and in the process touches T'AO by
accident. He realizes that he is alive. T'AO then goes up to
CH'UN-HUA to prove it.]

Ch'un-hua! Don't be afraid!

[CH'UN-HUA has taken refuge under the table and is now
shaking like a leaf. Only after T'AO has patted and touched
her does she begin to relax.]

See? I haven't gone 'there'. I've gone to 'Peach Blossom
Land'!

[YÜEN and CH'UN-HUA exchange a glance and begin to
look at T'AO differently.]

YÜEN [probing gently] What sort of a place is it?

T'AO It's a very unusual place—quiet, happy, and absolutely
wonderful! Most of the people—men and women,
young and old—have lived there all their lives and
never known the outside world!

YÜEN Have they been locked up?

T'AO *[too enraptured to pay much notice to the question]* Hmm! *[Recollecting]* And there's a couple who look exactly like the two of you!

YÜEN *[half-suspecting that* T'AO *is losing his mind]* How long have you been there?

T'AO *[trying to remember]* It seems a long time, and it seems not.

YÜEN *[convinced that his theory is correct]* So you can't remember, eh?

T'AO *[honestly]* No, I can't. But that's not important.

YÜEN *[like a sergeant leading a suspect on]* No. No, of course not. *[He nods to* CH'UN-HUA.*]*

CH'UN-HUA *[pointing to* T'AO's *clothes]* How come you're dressed like this?

T'AO Oh, I've been like this since I arrived there.

YÜEN *[nodding with certainty to* CH'UN-HUA*]* He must have had a blow to the head, poor thing!

CH'UN-HUA This robe—

T'AO *[rather pleased with his long flowing white robe]* They gave it to me. Helped me change into it as soon as I was there.

YÜEN *[to* CH'UN-HUA*]* You see!

CH'UN-HUA The people there—are they all like you?

T'AO Yes! *[Breaks off, reflecting]* No! They're in a higher state!

YÜEN *[explaining to* CH'UN-HUA*]* He's just a little cracked. And the others there are a lot worse.

T'AO Are you with me?

YÜEN, CH'UN-HUA *[together]* Yes! Yes!

T'AO No more misunderstanding between us now?

YÜEN, CH'UN-HUA *[ingratiatingly]* None at all!

[The three break into a genteel applause. Then they congratulate one another.]

T'AO *[behaving like the master of the house]* Very good! *[Indicating the table]* Please take a seat!

YÜEN *[agreeably]* Thank you! Whatever you say, T'ao!

*[*T'AO *takes the seat facing the audience.* YÜEN *and* CH'UN-HUA *carefully draw their seats back three paces away from the table before they sit down.]*

T'AO It's wonderful to be home! *[Looking about him]* Hm! Yüen! You . . . em . . . you come here often?

YÜEN *[taken by surprise]* I . . . I was passing by! *[Waxes lyrical again]* On this long and weary journey of life I have stopped by for a brief respite!

CH'UN-HUA *[springs to her feet, bitter and offended, and turns on* YÜEN *instantly]* For a brief respite! What do you take me for? An innkeeper?

YÜEN *[finding it impossible to back down, rises, too]* What are you talking about? *[The two break into a row before* T'AO.*]*

CH'UN-HUA Why did you say you'd just 'stopped for a brief respite'?

YÜEN Why is it that every time I say something you have to contradict me? Why do you always make me lose face?

*[*T'AO *is at first taken aback by this unexpected turn of events. He observes quietly, then realizes the nature of the relationship between* YÜEN *and* CH'UN-HUA. *He hangs his head in sorrow and helpless resignation.]*

YÜEN Why is it that every time an outsider is here—

CH'UN-HUA *[snapping back at once]* What do you mean by 'outsider'?

[Both break off abruptly, knowing that they have blundered, and look at T'AO *uneasily.* T'AO, *however, remains calm.]*

T'AO Do please sit down!

[The two pull up their stools and sit nearer the table.]

[choosing his words carefully and speaking gently, but not hiding the turmoil in his heart] Well I, um, I've been away so long, there are bound to be changes. I don't think I need to spell them out, but I can see—that the two of you are—*[He cannot bring himself to say it, so he gestures to suggest that they are living together.]*

CH'UN-HUA, YÜEN *[beating each other to it]* Having a chat together!

T'AO No! I mean, the two of you are—*[Knocking his hands together]*

CH'UN-HUA, YÜEN Working together!

T'AO No! What I mean is, I can see the two of you are— *[Making gestures of eating]*

CH'UN-HUA, YÜEN Having a meal together!

T'AO No! You're—*[He puts his palms together and places them under his ear to mime sleeping.]*

CH'UN-HUA, YÜEN Thinking about things together!

T'AO That's good! It never occurred to me that when you're . . . um *[Gesturing as before]* sleeping—you can still think . . . together! *[Pauses]* Well, you, too, are in a higher state.

YÜEN [*fumbling for an answer*] Oh, em, thank you very much!
T'AO Well!

[*Silence. When* T'AO *speaks again,* YÜEN *and* CH'UN-HUA *listen to him quietly, their eyes on the floor, occasionally exchanging a glance.*]

To be honest with you, even though I've been away for so long, I've been very happy and contented during that time, and I enjoyed my life there. But I missed Ch'un-hua. I've come back in the hope of [*Looking at* CH'UN-HUA] taking you with me. But now, seeing that the two of you are—[*Forcing back the words he had wanted to say and speaking gently, but not hiding the turmoil in his heart*] Well, no matter. We can still go together. It's such a wonderful place! Everyone there is so kind, so gentle, so considerate. Everything is delightful. Every sound that reaches the ear seems to have come from afar and is such sweet music.

[*All of a sudden, the sound of a baby crying rises from behind the screen. All three are startled. The crying grows louder.*]

CH'UN-HUA [*the instinctive reaction of a mother*] The baby's crying!
[*Hurries out and disappears behind the screen*]

[YÜEN *and* T'AO *sit face to face in acute embarrassment.* CH'UN-HUA *comes out from behind the screen, rocking a baby in her arms. Silence.*]

YÜEN [*flying into a temper suddenly*] Why the hell did you bring him out here?

CH'UN-HUA [*flies into a temper, too, making the baby cry even louder*] The baby's crying! What do you expect me to do?

YÜEN Such a nuisance! You should give him a spanking! [*The baby is crying at the top of his voice.*] Oh! Feed him! Shut him up!

CH'UN-HUA [*snaps back at him*] Look at the way he's crying. He's not asking to be fed!

[*The baby's crying becomes urgent and spasmodic.* YÜEN *and* CH'UN-HUA *break into a ferocious row.*]

YÜEN [*in a rage*] He is! When a baby cries, he either wants to be fed or to shit! That's all!

CH'UN-HUA [*even more enraged*] What do you know about babies?

YÜEN You think I don't know about babies? I was a baby once!

CH'UN-HUA Now you're shit!

YÜEN [*too angry to worry about* T'AO*'s presence*] Okay, now I'm shit! I've told you I didn't want any kids. You had to have one! The two of you are holding me hostage here. I can't go anyhere! I'm stuck, stuck.

[YÜEN *is banging the table furiously, yelling and screaming.*]

CH'UN-HUA Oh! Now you say it was I who wanted the child!

[T'AO *is listening, agonized by the row. He catches sight of the wine bottle on the table and picks it up absently. As the row continues,* T'AO *struggles in vain to pull out the cork.*]

Okay! [*Mad with anger now*] You find the child a nuisance? I'll throw him out!

[CH'UN-HUA *storms out, the baby in her arms, and is about to disappear behind the screen.*]

YÜEN Throw him out? How dare you! [*Runs after her*]

[*One can just make out the outlines of two figures engaged in a struggle.*]

[*offstage*] You're not going to throw my child out!

CH'UN-HUA [*offstage*] Oh yes, I am!

YÜEN [*offstage*] Oh no, you're not! If anyone is going to do it, I am! I'll throw him out!

CH'UN-HUA Don't you dare! You heartless bastard!

[*A loud and resounding 'smack'. The crying of the baby becomes even more piercing.*]

[*offstage*] You hit me! I'll go kill myself!

[T'AO *looks around, at this place, this home, at the couple behind him who are at each other's throats, at their baby, and at the wine bottle in his hand. He had never imagined his homecoming would bring him such pain and anguish.*

Behind the screen, YÜEN *and* CH'UN-HUA *are now screaming hysterically at each other and the crying of the baby is becoming unbearable.* T'AO *rises and leaves with a heavy heart. At the door, he turns round to take a look, then turns round again, throws his head back, heaves a big sigh, and lets out all his pain and sorrow in the fisherman's song he begins to sing.*]

T'AO Heigh—Ho—Heigh!

[*The farce has turned sour.* T'AO *picks up his oar, leaves the house, exits. Lights slowly fade. The fisherman's song, the crying of the baby, and the shouting and yelling also slowly die away.*]

SCENE TWELVE

[Lights come up slowly. The Blossom Land *crew, including* SHUN-TZŬ, *are clearing the props from the stage, the* Pining *team, including* DIRECTOR, *are busy getting their set ready. Everyone is working quietly and efficiently.*

T'AO, *still in his white robe and with an oar in his hand, enters from the wings on the left, and uses what time there still is to go over his solo performance that brings his play to an end.]*

> T'AO *['rowing' his boat]* Where's the buoy? I put it down to mark the way back. Where is it now?
>
> *[*STRANGER *wanders in again from the opposite direction, and plonks herself down on the visitor's chair used in the hospital scenes of* Pining. *Everyone is busy.* SHUN-TZŬ *enters from backstage.]*
>
> SHUN-TZŬ Director! The caretaker is here.
>
> *[*CARETAKER *enters, holding a bunch of keys in his hand.]*
>
> CARETAKER Time's up! Clear the stage! Off you go!
>
> DIRECTOR *[anxiously]* What? We're not done yet!
>
> CARETAKER What's that got to do with me? *[Looking exaggeratedly at his watch]* It's closing time now!
>
> DIRECTOR It's got everything to do with you! Why did you let two companies rehearse at the same time?
>
> CARETAKER I don't see two companies here! Where's the other one?
>
> DIRECTOR There! Look! *[Pointing to the* Blossom Land *team]*
>
> CARETAKER *[looking at* ACTOR YÜEN *with some surprise]* How come you're here?
>
> ACTOR YÜEN You told me to come today for our run-through. Do you have any idea what I've been through today?
>
> CARETAKER What do I care!
>
> DIRECTOR *[interrupting, his temper rising]* How can you talk like that?
>
> CARETAKER I've been here for years. I'd have to be out of my mind to let two companies rehearse at the same time!
>
> DIRECTOR *[hurrying after him]* But you can't deny there are two companies here!
>
> CARETAKER *[not wanting to argue with him]* I don't care! If you have any questions, talk to Miss Wang tomorrow morning at eight.
>
> ACTOR CHIANG *[puzzled]* Talk to Miss Wang tomorrow morning at eight? What for?
>
> CARETAKER I don't care! Clear the stage! Clear the stage! *[Turns to go]*

ACTRESS MRS CHIANG *[catching him by the arm, and pleads]* But, you know, this production is very important to our director.

CARETAKER *[indicating his watch]* This is very important to me, too! *[Turns to go]*

ACTRESS MRS CHIANG *[catches him by the arm again]* We've been rehearsing the whole day, and we open the day after tomorrow, but we're not through yet!

ACTOR CHIANG Just one more scene!

DIRECTOR Please! I beg you! I've been interrupted time and again today! Give me ten minutes, let me finish it. All right?

CARETAKER *[after a slight pause]* Exactly how much time do you need?

DIRECTOR Just ten minutes!

ACTOR YÜEN *[half-sarcastically]* Ten minutes isn't that precious to you, is it?

[STRANGER is still sitting in the visitor's chair, oblivious to everything. WANG is racing against time filling in the blank patch on the landscape painting.]

CARETAKER *[looking for some excuse to back down]* But I still have to lock up!

[Taking advantage of the commotion, SHUN-TZŬ sits on the wheelchair and plays with it.]

ACTOR YÜEN You go and lock up the other rooms first!

CARETAKER *[goes, after a few steps, says grudgingly]* Did you say ten minutes?

DIRECTOR *[nodding and bowing]* Yes! Yes!

CARETAKER *[muttering as he goes]* Ten minutes! Ten minutes! All my life I keep waiting for these ten bloody minutes!

[WANG has finished painting and is now putting away his paints and brushes.]

WANG *[announces]* It's finished!

[ACTOR YÜEN looks at the painting, but the rehearsal is already over. He waves his hand in resignation and sends WANG away.]

[The Pining team start to check the props, and take up their positions. The Blossom Land team make for the wings. SHUN-TZŬ has wheeled himself up to STRANGER and is trying teasingly to catch her attention. ACTOR YÜEN, on his way out, smacks SHUN-TZŬ on the head. Blossom Land team exit.]

[CHIANG lies down on the hospital bed, as in Scene 10. NURSE takes up her position beside the bedside table.]

[MRS CHIANG finds that STRANGER is occupying her seat.]

MRS CHIANG *[cautiously and politely]* Sorry! Do you mind—

[STRANGER rises and moves towards the wings.]

[anxiously] Hey! The handbag. It's mine!

[STRANGER calmly returns the handbag to her and exits. The Pining *trio have taken their positions.* DIRECTOR *exits. Lights slowly fade.]*

SCENE THIRTEEN

[Lights come up slowly. The set is the same as that in Scene 10 but since there is no need to share the stage now, everything is properly laid out. The hospital bed, drip stand, bedside tables, wheelchair, and visitor's chair occupy the centre of the stage. Upstage right is the door that opens into the hospital room. The huge landscape painting that serves as the backdrop for Blossom Land *is now complete and hanging at the back, forming the main backdrop for* Pining, *too.*

This scene repeats the first part of Pining *in Scene 10, and then carries on to the end.* CHIANG *is reclining on the hospital bed.* NURSE *switches off the tape recorder and turns round to* CHIANG.*]*

NURSE Look at you! Every time you listen to that song you're like this! *[Reproachfully]* You shouldn't be thinking about that dreadful business all the time! Let's see, since you put that ad in the paper, it's been *[Counting on her fingers]* five days! And you're still waiting for her? I don't think there's any point! When Miss Yün didn't turn up the first day, I knew she wouldn't come at all. Besides, who knows whether she's still alive or not? Why punish yourself like this? *[Realizing that she has been too blunt and that* CHIANG *is hurt]* Sorry! I didn't mean it! What I'm trying to say is—if Miss Yün did turn up, things might get even worse, because you might feel even more unhappy, right? *[*CHIANG *does not reply.]* So why not take things as they are and get on with your life? At least there's peace and quiet!

*[*MRS CHIANG *opens the door and walks in.]*

MRS CHIANG *[to* NURSE*]* It's a strange place, this hospital you work in. They keep pestering me to pay the fees, when our patient here can't even run away! And when I went to pay the fees just now, the cashier said it was time she got off work, and asked me to come again tomorrow. Everyday I have to run round and round in this hospital! Nurse, I'm not getting at you. It's just that I find this hospital a bit em . . . , peculiar!

*[MRS CHIANG is too busy talking to NURSE to notice that
CHIANG is straining to reach the wheelchair.]*

Why didn't you tell us you wanted to get up!

*[She and NURSE help CHIANG get into the wheelchair. Then
she steers the wheelchair towards the imaginary window in
front of her.]*

CHIANG I don't need you here. You'd better go!

MRS CHIANG Why? I'll stay and keep you company!

[CHIANG waves her away.]

[standing still] I've brought you some sweets. I'll get
you some.

*[CHIANG waves her away again. MRS CHIANG does not
move.]*

CHIANG The second drawer. *[Indicates the bedside table]* You'll
find a big envelope there. It's for you.

*[MRS CHIANG crosses over to get it and returns. CHIANG
puts on his spectacles and takes the envelope from her.]*
[taking out a sheaf of papers] It's all set down here.
[Indicating the papers and going through them one by one]
Ring Ch'ên at this number and ask him to put our
house into your name. Tell him to do it at once. *[Picks
up another document]* This is my—

MRS CHIANG *[too upset to let him go on]* Why talk about these things
now?

CHIANG *[impatiently]* Don't you understand? Now, this you
didn't know about. It's my insurance policy. I took out
this policy fifteen years ago. It matures in two years.
When the time comes . . . , you can show them this
policy and collect the money.

[MRS CHIANG is close to tears, but dares not stop him.]

[turns to yet another document] Oh! Yes, *[Blandly]* this is
the address of my ancestral home in Manchuria. I don't
know whether it's still there. . . . Someday, if you have
the chance, take our child to visit the burial grounds of
my ancestors and burn some offerings or something.

*[Forcing back her tears, MRS CHIANG snatches away the
documents and the envelope.]*

MRS CHIANG You take a good rest and don't bother about these
things!

*[MRS CHIANG puts the documents on the bed and returns to
steer the wheelchair.]*

MRS CHIANG Let me take you over there. *[Steers wheelchair to the left]*

CHIANG *[stopping her]* You'd better go now! I want to be alone. Go and do what I've told you to.

[ACTOR T'AO has changed out of his costume and into his casual clothes. He saunters on to the stage and is about to cross it when he is attracted by what is happening before him. He sits down in a dark corner upstage right and remains there for the rest of the rehearsal, watching quietly.]

MRS CHIANG *[ignoring CHIANG]* I'll take you over there.

[She pushes the wheelchair again. CHIANG stops the wheels with his hands and turns round to push away MRS CHIANG's hands.]

CHIANG You don't have to push me. Not you, not anybody, all right? Just let me sit here by myself. Okay? I don't want any company!

[CHIANG pays no more attention to MRS CHIANG and . wheels himself to one side. MRS CHIANG is at a loss, but can't bring herself to leave. After a while she approaches him.]

MRS CHIANG *[softly]* We can have a chat, or I can get you some candies, or we can—

CHIANG *[flies into a temper]* Can't you leave me alone?

[MRS CHIANG turns her back abruptly, hurt and crushed. There is a knock at the door. NURSE has all along been 'working' in the room. She now goes to answer the door. On the doorstep stands YÜN CHIH-FAN in a black overcoat, a fruit basket in her hand. She has aged, her hair, short and neatly cut, is silvery, her back slightly hunched. She looks a little ill at ease.]

YÜN *[softly]* Excuse me, is . . . is there a Mr Chiang Pin-liu staying here?

[NURSE turns round to look at the Chiangs. CHIANG is staring at YÜN in a daze.

As if driven by some inexplicable force, DIRECTOR has come quietly on to the stage and is now standing in a corner upstage left, anxious to watch the climax of the play at close quarters. It will also be the fulfilment of the unfinished dream on which he has built his own personal experience. For the rest of the rehearsal he stands there in the dark corner and watches intently.

MRS CHIANG *turns round, goes instinctively to* CHIANG, *stands behind him and puts her hands on his shoulders.*

NURSE, *sensing the significance of this moment for everyone present, invites* YÜN *in mechanically.* YÜN *remains at the door, gazing at* CHIANG. *Silence.]*

NURSE *[making an excuse to go]* Mrs Chiang, shall we go to the cashier now?

MRS CHIANG *[reacting instinctively]* I can do it tomorrow. *[After a small pause]* All right. Let's go.

[MRS CHIANG *picks up her handbag and walks wordlessly past* YÜN. *Exit* NURSE *and* MRS CHIANG.

At long last CHIANG *and* YÜN *are together.* CHIANG *in his wheelchair,* YÜN *standing. Silence.]*

YÜN *[breaking the silence]* I saw the advertisement in the paper.

CHIANG *[indicating the visitor's chair]* Have a seat!

[Silence.]

YÜN I brought you some fruit.

[YÜN *sits down on the visitor's chair normally used by* MRS CHIANG. *The two look at each other across the room. Silence.]*

Your health—

CHIANG Not very good. *[Pauses]* I . . . I didn't know you were in Taipei all these years.

YÜN I didn't know you were here either.

[Silence.]

[indicating CHIANG*'s sweater]* Isn't that the sweater—?

CHIANG Yes, I've kept it all these years.

[Silence.]

YÜN Have you been living in Taipei all this time?

CHIANG *[after a small pause]* I came here at the beginning of 1949. *[Pauses]* I kept sending letters to you in Kunming. But there was no reply.

[Silence.]

YÜN 1949. That year my brother and sister-in-law in Chongqing decided to take me out of the Mainland. We made our way to Thailand by the Burma Road, and then to Hanoi and Hong Kong. Two years later we came over to Taiwan and settled down.

[Silence.]

CHIANG When did you see the paper?

YÜN *[as if she hasn't heard him clearly]* Hm?

CHIANG When did you see the paper?

YÜN Today. *[After a small pause]* No . . . the day the ad appeared.

[Silence.]

CHIANG Are you . . . are you well?

YÜN All right. Had an operation last year—nothing serious—I'm getting on now. I became a grandmother the year before last.

CHIANG *[feelingly]* You used to wear your hair in plaits. Two long plaits.

YÜN I cut my hair the year after I was married—it's been a long time.

[Silence.]

Where do you live?

CHIANG I used to live in Chingmei.

YÜN *[after a pause]* I used to live in Chongqing South Road. Later on we moved to Tien Mu.

CHIANG *[after a pause]* A couple of years ago I moved to the Minsheng district.

[Silence.]

[rapt and intense] Shanghai is a vast city, and yet somehow we met. To think . . . *[After a small pause]* to think that a small town like Taipei should have kept us apart!

[Silence.]

YÜN *[glancing at her watch]* I should go now. My son is waiting for me downstairs.

[Slowly, YÜN rises and moves towards the door, opens it without looking back, and is about to go when CHIANG calls her.]

CHIANG Chih-fan—

[YÜN stops, her back towards CHIANG.]

[looking for the right words to express his feelings] All these years, did you . . . think about me at all?

[YÜN turns round. A pause.]

YÜN *[looking down, thinking about the past. Softly, she reveals her feelings for the first time.]* I wrote many letters to Shanghai . . . many many letters. . . . Later on, my brother said—*[Pauses]* I shouldn't wait anymore—*[Pauses]* Otherwise, I'd be too old.

[Silence.]

[murmuring] My husband . . . he's very nice . . . *[Pauses]* Yes, very.

[CHIANG holds out his hands silently. YÜN goes up to the wheelchair and gently takes CHIANG's hands. Then she kneels down and rests her head on CHIANG's lap. A long silence.]

[looking up and saying softly] I really must go.

[YÜN rises, goes slowly to the door, and exits. CHIANG remains in the wheelchair, staring blankly out front.

A long pause.

MRS CHIANG comes in and sees the pain on CHIANG's face. She turns round, glances at the door that has just been opened and then closed, and, looking relieved, goes to comfort CHIANG. To her surprise, CHIANG pushes her hands away. Embarrassed, she stands beside him helplessly. A pause. Suddenly, CHIANG waves his hand in supplication in the air. Looking at this hand, this stranger with whom she has shared her life for over thirty years, MRS CHIANG goes up to him without a word and takes his hand. Helplessly, CHIANG leans his head against this woman who has been standing beside him for some time. NURSE appears and stands at the door watching this small episode in the general drama of life. Then quietly, she goes about her business.

Lights slowly fade.]

SCENE FOURTEEN

[Lights come up slowly. The atmosphere on the stage is that of people packing and clearing up after a performance. The crew are removing the props. DIRECTOR is still in the dark corner he positioned himself in the previous scene. Completely swept away by the intensity and emotional currents of the play, he stands there, hanging his head, deep in his own memories. MRS CHIANG is slowly pushing the empty hospital bed. STRANGER has planted herself on the stage, waiting with determination and persistence for 'Liu Tzŭ-chi'.

The Blossom Land team are checking to see if they have left anything behind. ACTOR T'AO crosses the stage, throws a glance at DIRECTOR, waves goodbye to the Pining team, and goes off. SHUN-TZŬ is drifting about. Finding that he is not needed, he, too, goes off. WANG is sweeping the floor with a mop, cleaning up. DIRECTOR is so overcome with emotion he has difficulty pulling himself together. Enter CARETAKER.]

CARETAKER What? Still there! Come on, I've got to switch off the lights. *[To those still on stage]* I really must lock up. Off you go now.

[*Only* DIRECTOR *and* STRANGER *remain. At the stern voice of the* CARETAKER, *they both wake up from their reveries and slowly go off.*

The huge landscape painting of Peach Blossom Land is still hanging, bright, beautiful, mysterious.]

[*Lights fade slowly.*]

THE END

CATHAY VISIONS
(THE EMPTY CAGE)

1986

By
HWANG MEI-SHU

Translated by
HWANG MEI-SHU

— ABOUT **THE PLAYWRIGHT** —

HWANG MEI-SHU (1930–) received his secondary school education in mainland China before moving to Taiwan. After completing his BA at the Tamkang University and his MA at the National Taiwan Normal University, he took up a teaching post at the Tamkang University. Then he went to America for further studies and obtained a Ph.D. in Theatre from Florida State University in 1976. From 1976 until his retirement in 1995, he was Professor at the Graduate School of Western Languages and Literature, Tamkang University. He is actively involved in the drama scene and has contributed greatly to drama development in Taiwan. Apart from being a playwright, he is also a translator of plays, a theatre critic, and a founding member of the *Tamkang Review*, an influential literary journal in Taiwan. He has written eight plays. Of these, *The Fool Who Wins an Ass* (1973) was first performed in English at Florida State University, and *Cathay Visions* (1986) at Mankato State University in America. *Good Heavens!* (1981) was premiered in Korea in 1983, while *The Comedy of Mr Allman Yang* (1983) has been performed in Taiwan, Korea, and Malaysia. He won the 'Wu San-Lien Arts Award for Distinguished Achievements in Drama' in 1984.

Hwang Mei-shu is now retired but remains deeply committed to drama activities in Taiwan.

ABOUT THE PLAY

Cathay Visions is a typical example of the experimental work undertaken by a number of Taiwanese playwrights since the late 1970s. They are mostly writers who have received their education in the West, and are therefore well acquainted with Western drama and culture. Not content, however, with simply modelling their works on Western masterpieces, they create plays which allow them to embrace their own culture, their own literary and philosophical heritage. The result is a 'play of ideas', with ideas as the subject matter and in which ideas are played with, teased out, and examined from conflicting perspectives. In *Cathay Visions*, death and love, two significant aspects of human life, are under scrutiny. Employing the form of a 'dream-within-a-dream', historical and mythical figures from the West, such as Helen of Troy, Dr Faustus, and Hiawatha, are invoked to deliver their views, which are then commented on by the real-life characters—an old Chinese man and his family.

The playwright has said that inspiration for this work was drawn from a traditional Chinese story which took as its structural framework the form of a dream-within-a-dream. He is fascinated with this particular state— you dream that you are dreaming, and then think that you are awake when in fact you are still in a dream—and uses it to shape this play. The old man and his family take on the role of a chorus. The other characters come and go, like visions or like apparitions. And the overall unreal atmosphere of the play is enhanced by the way the lines are delivered— with 'some chanting quality'—by the arrangement of music, the use of mime and magic, and by the characters' movements and gestures.

——— **DRAMATIS** PERSONAE ———

MASKED CHARACTERS

CHINESE SCHOLAR, about 40 years old, dressed in the traditional
  Chinese-style robe
SWEET MAIDEN, his real/unreal lover, a charming girl in her late
  teens
HIAWATHA, the Indian hero, 'son of love and sorrow'
MINNEHAHA, HIAWATHA's wife
DR FAUSTUS, the learned scholar of Wittenberg
HELEN OF TROY, the great classical beauty of Greece

CHORUS (NO MASKS)

OLD MAN, about 60, the grandfather
HUSBAND, his son, about 24
WIFE, a young pretty woman about five years younger
BOY, about 10, son of HUSBAND's sister
GIRL, about 8, daughter of HUSBAND's cousin

The CHORUS should be able to play some simple musical instruments
  to accompany and/or punctuate the movement, dialogue and
  singing.

All the characters should try to include some chanting quality in the
  delivery of their lines, and some rhythm of puppetry in their
  movement and gestures.

The following parts should be played by the same actors:

CHINESE SCHOLAR	and	DR FAUSTUS
SWEET MAIDEN	and	HELEN
HUSBAND	and	HIAWATHA
WIFE	and	MINNEHAHA

Time and Place: The action may take place at any time and location.

Set: The stage is bare in terms of representational theatre, with only
  minimalist props such as rocks for the characters to sit or stand on,
  a few trees, and/or a painted backdrop.

Scene divisions in the script are for rehearsing convenience. There
  should be no break or intermission in actual production.

THE **PLAY**

PROLOGUE

[When the theme music fades out, lights come up. OLD MAN, wearing glasses and with a stick in his right hand, is walking to and fro slowly downstage, in a very dignified and stylized manner. He stops, bows towards the audience, then towards stage left, stage right, and upstage. He then turns to the audience again. He constantly makes gestures and murmurs to himself. GIRL enters stage right, runs up to him, and looks at him for a few seconds.]

GIRL What are you doing, Great Uncle?

[OLD MAN gestures her to be silent. He looks up at the sky, then takes out a watch and looks at it. He clears his throat, poses, then very slowly begins to address the audience, word by word.]

OLD MAN Evening / good // you / good?//*

GIRL No, Great Uncle, you should say 'Good Evening' and 'How are you?'

[OLD MAN looks at her, she nods confidently, and he turns to audience again.]

OLD MAN I / very sorry // good evening / how are you / every man sir / every woman sir //

GIRL No, no, no. You must say 'ladies and gentlemen.'

OLD MAN *[thinks]* West man / not made by their God / before woman?//

GIRL I don't know. People may say 'boys and girls,' but they always say 'ladies and gentlemen' in English.

OLD MAN You / sure?//

GIRL Sure!

OLD MAN Ha / interesting // when boy become man / he become gentle // and let woman above him // *[Pauses]* Maybe / like old Chinese say / good man not fight woman //

GIRL I don't know, Great Uncle. But you just have to say 'ladies and gentlemen' when you speak English.

OLD MAN When East man / talk to West man / polite / he must change / every thing's order?// Right?

GIRL I think so. Yes. But why do you speak English? What are you going to do?

OLD MAN I / go meet people // some speak English //

GIRL What people?

---

* The solidus is used to mark sense-group phrases in non-standard English. The double solidus indicates a longer pause and serves the function of a full stop.

OLD MAN Not know // man tell me last night / in dream // they come here / today //

GIRL In your dream?

OLD MAN Right // now you no speak // watch me //

[He turns his stick upside down, then puts his hands on the floor and pushes, as if attempting a handstand. GIRL watches in amusement. Just at this moment, BOY enters stage right, running. He stops suddenly when he sees what OLD MAN is doing.]

BOY What are you doing, Grandpa? Have you lost something?

OLD MAN *[stands up]* No // *[Pauses]* Yes //

BOY What have you lost?

OLD MAN *[pauses]* Face //

BOY What do you mean, Grandpa? Your face is on your face.

OLD MAN I can say / good evening / how are you / ladies and gentlemen // but I cannot turn my body upside down / like this stick // I learn no good / I have no face //

GIRL Oh, that's what you were trying to do, Great Uncle. But what for?

OLD MAN You say / I must change everything upside down / to talk English to / West man //

BOY No, you don't have to change the order of everything, Grandpa. Western people also have eyes below the eyebrows, a nose below the eyes; they also stand on their feet and sit on their arses.

OLD MAN They / do?//

GIRL They also eat with their mouths. Only we use chopsticks and they use forks and knives, and they have soup first and we have soup last.

OLD MAN I see / they also human // good // that make I feel / very much better // *[Thinks]* But also / very very much un-better // I not know / when put things upside down // when downside up / and when . . . when . . .

[A SCHOLAR's voice is singing offstage left. OLD MAN stops when he hears the singing and begins to smile happily.]

SCHOLAR

What's first, what's last?
What's up, what's down?
What's right, what's wrong?
What's East, what's West?

OLD MAN Ah, it is real // he / here / now //

[SCHOLAR walks in from downstage left, with a big cage in his left hand and a fan in his right hand. He is still singing.]

SCHOLAR   In every corner and every home,
Men may fear, men may love,
    Men may weep, and men may laugh.
And what would you like to become—
    A Buddha great and kind, or
A bum poor and dumb?
A mountain grand and high, or
    A feather light and numb?
It's all up to you—
    Your heart and your mind.

[OLD MAN goes quickly over to SCHOLAR.]

OLD MAN Ah, sir / I last night hear you / see you // you / this big cage // You now come // thank you // tell me where my wife // she / where / how?// *[Turns to BOY]* Run / run quick / fast // tell your uncle and auntie // come here / quick //

SCHOLAR You don't have to. They are coming.

[Continue into Scene 1]

SCENE ONE

[HUSBAND and WIFE are approaching from upstage right.]

OLD MAN Son / this morning I tell you my dream // you not believe // Now see / he come // so soon / other come / too //

HUSBAND Excuse us, sir. He is my father. This is my newly married wife. We are travelling with Father to look . . . er . . . for . . . for . . .

SCHOLAR I know. You and your lovely wife, your cousin's daughter, and the boy of your sister have been on the road with your father for the last seven days, looking for your mother. *[Whispers]* To you and your wife, she is dead; but to your father, she is trying to avoid him because of his long absence from home.

BOY Gee, how do you know all this?

GIRL How do you know us? I don't remember ever having seen you anywhere before, sir.

SCHOLAR Not even in your dreams?

BOY, GIRL *[together]* No.

SCHOLAR I suppose you are both right. Young people should not dream of the old. But you have always been in my dreams.

GIRL Really?

[OLD MAN pushes BOY and GIRL aside, goes over to SCHOLAR.]

OLD MAN So / you know my wife?//

SCHOLAR Yes, I do.

OLD MAN *[to HUSBAND and WIFE]* You see?// Old Mama not dead //

SCHOLAR But she is no longer in this world.

OLD MAN Where / she now?//

SCHOLAR *[looks at them all, then turns to OLD MAN]* Do you know Zhuang Zi?

[OLD MAN looks at his son.]

HUSBAND Yes, he was a great student of Tao and a great thinker.

OLD MAN My wife / now with him?//

SCHOLAR No. But I am going to tell you a story about this Zhuang Zi.

OLD MAN Not he / and my wife?//

SCHOLAR No. But this Zhuang Zi had a wife, too. *[To CHORUS]* You may sit down or stand as you like while I am telling the story.

[He puts down the cage by his side while he is talking. When BOY and GIRL lose interest in his tale, they go over to the cage and examine it with great curiosity.]

Now, the story says that Zhuang Zi had a wife. One day she died. Zhuang Zi's friend Hui Zi came to mourn her death. To his great surprise, he found Zhuang Zi sitting at the door, drumming on an inverted bowl and singing. So, Hui Zi was very angry and said, 'Your wife loved you, lived with you, and brought up your children. If you are not sorry for her death, at least you should not be drumming and singing, even before me. This is too much.' 'You misjudge me,' answered Zhuang Zi. 'I was as sad as any man could be when she died. Then, after some thinking, I told myself that Nature evolves from spring to summer, from summer to autumn, and from autumn to winter. Man's being has its seasons, too. If someone is tired and wants to lie down to rest, we should not disturb him with bawling and crying. My wife has lain down to sleep. To break in upon her rest with the noise of lamentation would only show that I know nothing of Nature's law. She would not like that. So I grieve no more.'

OLD MAN You mean / my wife dead / I / sing and drum / too?//

SCHOLAR Why not?

[OLD MAN *thinks for a while.*]

OLD MAN But I / no Zhuang Zi / no great //

SCHOLAR What's great, what's small! This great Zhuang Zi once thought he was a small butterfly dreaming of being a man.

OLD MAN I / also / no butterfly //

SCHOLAR Well, Confucius says that Tao, or the Way of Life, is so obvious and yet so subtle at the same time that every common man and woman can see it and are capable of living up to it, yet no sages or wise men can ever completely achieve it. Each of us is just as small, and great, as Zhuang Zi.

[OLD MAN *stands up and walks a few steps, stops.*]

OLD MAN No // long time ago / I and my wife / swear to Buddha // we say / we not born same year / same month / same day // but we die same year / same month / same day / together //

SCHOLAR Oh, I am ashamed of you. You believe in Buddhism and yet you do not know *yuan*, my old friend, if I may call you old friend.

[OLD MAN *seems to feel puzzled. He begins to meditate.* GIRL *moves over to* WIFE *and whispers to her.*]

GIRL What is *yuan*?

WIFE *Yuan* is said to be the destined meeting of people. It is said that people with *yuan* will get together even if they are thousands of miles apart, but people without *yuan* will not know each other even if they sit face to face.

SCHOLAR Yes. [*Smiles*] Life is made of *yuan*. The timely and untimely union and separation in life is *yuan*. So, when Zhuang Zi realized the great way of *yuan*, which is also an expression of Tao, he began to drum and sing.

GIRL What was he singing, sir?

SCHOLAR [*smiles at her for a second*] What do you think he sang?

GIRL I don't know. *[Thinks]* Maybe about his loneliness or something.

BOY No. I think he must have sung some lullaby to his wife, like this: *[He sings.]*

> My dear wife, wife dear,
> Sleep well, have no fear,
> I am here, by you near,
> Sleep well, have no fear . . .

GIRL You are inventing things again, Cousin dear.

[BOY stops singing. OLD MAN is still deep in thought. HUSBAND and WIFE go over to him. GIRL turns to SCHOLAR.]

Can I ask you something, sir?

SCHOLAR Certainly, my young lady.

GIRL We were just wondering why you are carrying this big *empty* cage with you?

SCHOLAR *[smiles]* To carry some emptiness in it.

BOY You mean emptiness is something real?

SCHOLAR Yes. Sometimes emptiness is more real than real. Your Grandpa could tell you that, I suppose.

[He looks at OLD MAN, who seems at the moment to begin to realize something.]

GIRL Emptiness is real—more real than real?

OLD MAN Yes / heavy / too //

BOY How heavy, Grandpa?

SCHOLAR Oh, as heavy as you think, I suppose.

GIRL You mean if I think it is very heavy, it is very heavy?

BOY But I think emptiness is nothing and not real. How can it have any weight?

SCHOLAR You are both right. The weight of emptiness varies with time and persons. You can all try out the emptiness in my cage and see how heavy it is, if you like.

[BOY and GIRL go over to the cage, curiously. BOY lifts it easily, then GIRL does so too.]

BOY I don't feel anything at all.

GIRL Me neither. Are you making fun of us because we are small, sir?

[SCHOLAR does not answer, but looks at HUSBAND and WIFE. Seeing his serious attitude, they also go over to lift the cage.]

WIFE *[lifting it easily]* Why, it is as light as spring air.
[Pauses] But strange, I didn't even feel the weight of
the cage.

BOY, GIRL *[together]* Yes, right. What is your cage made of, sir?

HUSBAND *[lifting the cage]* No. I can feel some weight—but I am
not sure if it is the cage or the emptiness in the cage.

SCHOLAR Very good.

*[He turns to OLD MAN, who hesitates a little and then
moves over to the cage.]*

OLD MAN Me / try too //

*[He tries to lift it with one hand, fails; then tries with both
hands, but still cannot lift it off the floor.]*

HUSBAND Let it go, Father.

OLD MAN But my hands / both grow on it //

*[SCHOLAR looks at BOY and GIRL, who feel puzzled and
look eager to help.]*

SCHOLAR Go and help him.

*[They do. The three together lift the cage about two feet off the
floor. They hold it in the air for a while and then put it down.]*

GIRL Strange. It is very heavy now.

BOY Yes, it is! Did you hold the cage down, Grandpa?

OLD MAN No // *[To SCHOLAR]* Thank you / sir / very much
thank // I see now // *[He turns to BOY and GIRL.]*
Thank you / too // these days I forget you all // Now /
come / we try again.

*[The three try again. They use too much strength and the
cage flies into the air. They are happy. OLD MAN catches the
cage and throws it to BOY, and BOY throws it to GIRL.
They continue playing for a while. Then suddenly, OLD MAN
stumbles when catching the cage. HUSBAND, who happens to
be near him, holds him up. BOY and GIRL run over quickly
to OLD MAN.]*

GIRL Are you all right, Great Uncle?

BOY *[simultaneously with GIRL]* Are you all right, Grandpa?

OLD MAN Yes / I all right // *[Pauses]* Only I wish / my old
woman here / with us //

*[Suddenly, the cage seems to become very heavy, making OLD
MAN almost collapse. BOY and GIRL hold him up.]*

GIRL Why is it so heavy again now?

SCHOLAR I told you it can be very heavy. But what else do you
feel besides its being heavy?

BOY I feel myself as strong as—as Superman!

GIRL I feel like Wonder Woman! *[Pauses]* But what have you really got in the cage, sir? Really only emptiness?

SCHOLAR Yes. Can you see anything else in it?

GIRL Can you show us what emptiness is like?

HUSBAND Could you tell us why you are carrying emptiness with you?

BOY You don't have anything better to carry, like a canary or some singing birds?

[SCHOLAR smiles when they are asking all these questions. Then, he waits for a little while.]

SCHOLAR I am very happy to have the *yuan* to meet you all today. I will sing you a little song, which, I hope, may reveal to you what emptiness is in life, what life is empty, what comes or goes with emptiness, and what life is not empty.

BOY I like songs; they are easy to learn.

GIRL Yes, and more fun than school.

[SCHOLAR gestures them to be silent.]

SCHOLAR Here is my song. You can play your music and sing with me, if you like. *[He sings.]*

> Many and many have said:
> Trust nothing but silver and gold.
> You have no hope when you have no silver;
> You have everything when you have gold.

HUSBAND, WIFE *[together]* Yes, it is true. When you are rich, people will hang upon you wherever you go. But when you are poor, nobody will come to your door.

SCHOLAR *[speaks]* But you know—*[Continues to sing]*

> Like ice and frost, silver and gold
> Are both very, very cold.
> But we need sweet dew and timely rain
> To bring life to the great plain.

GIRL, BOY *[together]* We love neither silver nor gold. We want knowledge and power to make life rich and colourful.

SCHOLAR *[speaks]* Yes, indeed. *[Sings]*

> Knowledge is wonderful,
> Power is admirable,
> Silver and gold may become capital.
> But knowledge and power of self-interest
> Will breed greed and tyranny
> And are just like the vulture.

HUSBAND, WIFE *[together]* But power often comes and goes with knowledge, silver and gold.

SCHOLAR *[speaks]* Yes, that is true. But wealth and power will only listen to the wise and generous and be their servants. What is more, if you trust them too much, they will become thieves that would empty your house even before your own eyes. Alas! *[Sings]*

> When many a man gets big money,
> He begins to live in agony;
> When many a man gets big power,
> He becomes a poor sleepwalker.

OLD MAN I see / sir / but . . . but . . . //

HUSBAND But what should people look for if it is not wealth, knowledge and power, sir?

SCHOLAR For what can be summed up in a single word— benevolence and love.

BOY But that is not one word.

SCHOLAR Love is benevolence and benevolence is love. And to love but not to be loved is no true love.

WIFE But, sir, what and how should we love?

SCHOLAR *[chants]*

> Love and live and live and love . . .

WIFE Love of what, sir?

SCHOLAR *[chants]*

> The Buddha of Mercy says to his disciples:
> The kaleidoscopic world is a void,
> The void is a kaleidoscope.

CHORUS Yes, we have all heard of that . . .

SCHOLAR *[chants]*

> Love the void in the splendid world of a kaleidoscope.

HUSBAND Love the void in the splendid world of a kaleidoscope?

SCHOLAR *[chants]*

> Love the splendid kaleidoscope in a void.

WIFE Love the splendid kaleidoscope in a void?

SCHOLAR *[chants]*

> If we look only for the splendour—the kaleidoscope . . .

BOY Isn't it good to look for the splendour?

SCHOLAR *[chants]*

>   We will one day become lost and blind.

GIRL Should we look only for the void?

SCHOLAR *[chants]*

>   No, no, that is against the true nature of mankind.

BOY We don't quite understand, sir, but we like your song and we like kaleidoscopes.

GIRL Would you show us the kaleidoscope?

WIFE Why is the kaleidoscope so splendid and yet a void? Because it is empty, sir?

HUSBAND Is love a kaleidoscope or a void?

BOY Please show us, sir. We like to believe in what our eyes see.

SCHOLAR *[smiles]* Very good—to believe in what you see with your own eyes. But there are many things you cannot see with your eyes. Think about it for a while, young friends. Now, I will show you some secrets of life—my life and the lives of some others. Take them as the kaleidoscope of love and marriage, or visions of an idiot, if you like. And if you can see both the splendour and the void in these lives, that is very good; if not, watch carefully what makes these lives so much admired, or so much pitied, or pitied and admired at the same time.

[All watch him closely with great curiosity, and react according to their age and life experience. SCHOLAR performs some simple gestures, a conjuring trick. He opens his mouth and a small figure comes out of it very slowly. SCHOLAR holds her gently in his hands. CHORUS hold their breath in amazement. Suddenly there is a burst of brightly coloured smoke. When it disperses, a life-size pretty girl is standing in front of him.]

OLD MAN Oh / I see you / too / last night //

BOY Wow! Is it magic?

SCHOLAR Yes, it is a vision of the kaleidoscope.

[The girl, SWEET MAIDEN, bows to SCHOLAR, then to OLD MAN and the others. She then turns to SCHOLAR.]

MAIDEN My Master dear, Sweet Maiden at your service. What is your wish today?

SCHOLAR Well, how about starting our time today with some dishes like phoenix-wings, lion-heads in brown sauce, dragon-eyes with lotus seeds . . .

BOY You eat the phoenixes and lions?

MAIDEN Oh, young man, don't you know what these dishes are? And do you think a girl like me would, or could, kill a phoenix or anything like a lion? Don't you know a phoenix is a euphemism for a chicken, and a lion-head is only a kind of meat-ball of ground pork with vegetables. *[Turns to* GIRL *who is smiling]* Little girl, you must know what these dishes are, don't you?

GIRL Yes. But I have always wondered why people call them phoenix-wings and lion-heads.

MAIDEN Oh, I guess beautiful names often make things nicer, isn't that so? You must have heard many girls named Graceful Phoenix, Bright Phoenix, Phoenix Bright, though they may not be all as pretty as a phoenix. Have you ever heard any girl called a Chicken?

GIRL No. But—

SCHOLAR Let's not waste any time on the names. The food is the real thing we want, isn't it? *[Turns to* MAIDEN*]* My Sweet Maiden, are you ready to serve the dishes now?

MAIDEN Yes, Master dear. And some wine, too?

SCHOLAR Yes, please.

[She moves to the empty cage, and, as if by magic, takes out of it a big sheet of silk cloth to spread on the floor. She mimes taking dishes of food, wine, cups, and chopsticks for two, and arranging them nicely on the cloth. She mimes pouring wine into the cups. The cloth can be real, but everything else is imaginary.]

BOY *[to* GIRL*]* Are they playing children's games?

GIRL I think so. I don't see any real food.

MAIDEN Oh, I am sorry. They are special dishes for my Master only. I should have served you first.

HUSBAND It's all right. We are not hungry.

BOY I'm starving. I'd like to have something like hot dogs or—

MAIDEN All right.

[She takes some wrapped things out of the cage and gives them to each of the CHORUS. BOY *opens the wrapping first.]*

BOY *[surprised]* Real hot dogs!

GIRL And still hot.

MAIDEN Of course, hot dogs must be hot. And what would you like to drink?

[Some say 'Coke,' some say '7-up.' MAIDEN, *still sitting there, makes some gestures with her hand in the air.]*

Here you are, ladies and gentlemen.

[Some canned drinks fly down to them. CHORUS *take the drinks and start eating and drinking. Gradually they begin to chat and dance around. This may last for two or three minutes.*

MAIDEN *begins to play the flute. The music is sweet but sad.* CHORUS *stop gradually and gather around her, beside* SCHOLAR, *who has fallen asleep.]*

OLD MAN What / become he?//

HUSBAND He has got drunk so easily?

MAIDEN *[stops playing]* Yes. When he is happy, he has an ocean capacity. But when he is unhappy, he cannot finish even a small cup of wine.

HUSBAND Why was he unhappy so suddenly? Was it because of something we did?

MAIDEN No, I think it must be because of the hot dogs. He doesn't like dogs, although hot dogs are not real dogs.

BOY Why does he not like dogs?

GIRL Are dogs not man's best friends?

MAIDEN I don't know. *[Pauses]* But I think he has good reasons not to like some watch dogs that look with fond eyes at their masters' rich friends, but bark at strangers and poor beggars.

GIRL Really?

BOY Yes. I don't like those watch dogs, either.

WIFE We are terribly sorry, Sweet Maiden.

BOY Could we wake him up and apologize?

MAIDEN No, that would make him even more unhappy, I am afraid. *[Pauses]* Besides, nobody can wake him when he prefers to sleep.

GIRL Will he be angry with you when he wakes up?

MAIDEN No. It is just that when he hears or sees something he doesn't like, he will escape to his dreams, like many other scholars.

WIFE Then why was your music so sad?

*[*MAIDEN *drops her head. Silence.]*

OLD MAN *[softly]* Anything / we / can do?//

GIRL Cheer up, Sweet Maiden. Tell us what has made you so sad?

MAIDEN I can't. *[Hesitating]* It is something very personal— something about my . . . my fate.

WIFE Do you mean he has another woman?

MAIDEN No.

WIFE Are you sure?

MAIDEN Yes, because I have long been in his heart. Only—only
. . .

[She stops and drops her head again.]

HUSBAND Only what? Tell us, Sweet Maiden. I know we are not
wise or learned, but, as people say, when three
shoemakers put their heads together they can work
wonders.

MAIDEN *[after some hesitation]* I cannot marry him.

WIFE Why? Is he married?

MAIDEN Yes, but that is no problem. Besides, his wife has been
gone for a long time.

GIRL You have already a husband?

MAIDEN No. I am a virgin.

BOY Do you mean you don't like him because he goes to
sleep so easily and leaves you alone?

MAIDEN I love him and he loves me, too.

GIRL Isn't it just wonderful you love each other like that?

MAIDEN I don't know. But I am a woman, you know. When I
was very young my parents said that I must marry the
man who first touched my hands and face. He was not
the first.

WIFE Does he know all this?

MAIDEN No. He doesn't.

BOY Why didn't you tell him?

WIFE No. You had better not.

GIRL Why? Isn't honesty the best policy?

WIFE You will know when you grow up, but you don't need
to know the reason now.

GIRL I don't want to grow up if growing up makes life so
complicated.

WIFE Oh, you will grow up and you will love—maybe you'll
love the complexity of love. *[She smiles at* GIRL *and then
turns to* MAIDEN.*]* Why didn't you marry the man you
wished to, then? He did not love you?

MAIDEN We were separated when we were younger than they
are now. *[She points to* BOY *and* GIRL.*]* Oh, I am
ashamed to death! The wine must have made me crazy
today to tell you all these things!

BOY, GIRL *[together]* Don't worry. We won't tell anybody, or him. *[Pointing to* SCHOLAR*]*

OLD MAN You know / your he / where now?//

MAIDEN No, I don't.

HUSBAND What's his name? We can help by asking around on our way, if you will tell us his name.

[MAIDEN thinks for a while. She makes up her mind and appears a little happier.]

MAIDEN Will you really help me?

[All say 'Yes'.]

Will you help me marry him if I can find him?

OLD MAN Gladly / gladly / very gladly //

MAIDEN Then I will try to find him and bring him here. *[She looks at* SCHOLAR *for a while.]* Thank you for all your care and love, my dear Master. But I am only a woman. Please excuse me. Your Sweet Maiden must see her sweet cousin now. *[She looks at* HUSBAND *and* BOY.*]* Would you gentlemen help me carry him to the back of that tree? *[Pointing to offstage left]* Though I am sure he won't wake up now, I must have the decency not to meet my sweetheart in his presence.

[While HUSBAND *and* BOY *carry* SCHOLAR *off the stage,* MAIDEN *mimes putting things back into the cage and takes it to where* SCHOLAR *is lying. They all return to the stage.]*

May I ask if any of you were born in the year of the rabbit or the chicken?

HUSBAND Yes, we were. I was born in the rabbit year and my wife in the chicken year. Can we be of any special help?

MAIDEN Yes. You see my magic power is small. If anybody born in those two years is within forty-nine steps of me, either my magic won't work, or those people will get hurt by my magic power. I don't want either to happen, you know. So . . . therefore . . .

HUSBAND We understand.

WIFE Can we watch at that distance?

MAIDEN You had better not. *[Pauses]* If you please, the farther you go the better, for the good of all of us.

[HUSBAND and WIFE *exit reluctantly at stage left.]*

[Continue into Scene 2]

SCENE TWO

[MAIDEN sits down in a ceremonial manner, like a Buddha, at upstage centre.]

MAIDEN *[to* CHORUS*]* Would you please keep watch that no stranger comes near me?

[They say 'Yes.' She closes her eyes and begins to murmur words like '. . . gods of heaven and earth . . . good spirits . . . come . . . please . . . lend me your power . . . help me . . .' Her voice is almost inaudible at first, then it becomes clearer, then inaudible again, then clearer again. The CHORUS *members speak over and in between her murmurings.]*

[OLD MAN walks around stage left; BOY and GIRL stay downstage right.]

BOY Who is her cousin?

GIRL We may see him soon, I hope.

MAIDEN . . . Come, Hi-a-wa-tha . . . good spirits of heaven and earth . . . help me . . . help me find Hi-a-wa-tha . . .

BOY Hiawatha?

GIRL Did she say Hiawatha?

OLD MAN Who / who he?//

GIRL Could it be the Indian hero in America?

BOY Must be. Anyway, that is the only Hiawatha I know, the son of love and sorrow.

OLD MAN Son of love / sorrow?//

BOY Because his mother Wenonah died in pain and anger when she was deserted by the heartless West Wind.

OLD MAN How you know him / son of love / sorrow?//

BOY Our teacher told us his story.

GIRL But how come he and Sweet Maiden are cousins?

BOY Our teacher said that his teacher's teacher said to him that the early Indians in America could have moved there from Asia or China.

GIRL Really?

[BOY nods. GIRL thinks for a second.]

Then why do these Indians all have red skin?

BOY I know why.

GIRL You do? Tell me, Cousin.

[BOY pretends he won't.]

Please, Sweet Cousin!

BOY All right.

[When he is telling the story, he sometimes acts out what he thinks interesting.]

My classmate has an uncle who knows everything about the world. He said that when those people moved from China to America, it was hot summer and their skin was burnt brown by the hot sun. And then, many, many years later the white men moved there, too. The white men tried to take the Indians' lands and drive them away. So the Indians became very, very angry. You know when people get angry their faces get red.

[GIRL nods in agreement.]

And the Indians were very, very, very angry and fought against the white men. But they had no guns, only arrows, so many of them were killed by the white men and their lands were taken away. So, they got more and more angry. They were angry day and night and night and day for a long, long time, and their skin became more and more red. At last they all became red-skinned men.

GIRL Poor Indians. I feel sorry for them.

OLD MAN Angry and sorry / no good / no use //

BOY But when—

[Suddenly, MAIDEN utters a cry of excitement. A red light beams down on her. The three stop talking. MAIDEN stands up and starts spinning, faster and faster. Lights begin to sparkle. When she stops, lights go back to normal, and HIAWATHA is standing in front of her, carrying a bow and some arrows.]

MAIDEN Hello, Cousin, long time no see. How do you do?

[They bow to each other, then MAIDEN sits down and asks HIAWATHA to sit.]

HIAWATHA Hello, Cousin, long time no see. What do you want to see me for?

MAIDEN Oh, nothing—nothing special. I just want to see you, Cousin dear.

HIAWATHA Then, goodbye now. I have to catch a deer for my people right away. I'll see you later.

OLD MAN Wait / please //

[HIAWATHA stops.]

[to MAIDEN] Not shy / speak //

MAIDEN *[hesitates]* But . . . you know . . .

BOY I'll speak for you. Hiawatha, your cousin wants to marry you.

HIAWATHA Marry me? No, Cousin. I am already married to Minnehaha, Laughing Water.

BOY Can't you marry her, too?

HIAWATHA But I can marry only one woman, young man.

BOY Why?

HIAWATHA Why, I don't know. That is the law, I think.

[MAIDEN begins to weep.]

HIAWATHA Don't cry, dear Cousin.

MAIDEN But Cousin dear of long-time-no-see, I've taken so much trouble to have you here. If you won't marry me, if you leave me alone, I will be shamed to death before these people. Besides, what do I live for if you don't want me? How do I sleep? What do I do when I wake up? For whom do I put on make-up? And for whom do I weep?

[She weeps louder.]

HIAWATHA Don't cry, please. *[He thinks.]* Look, like this bow, I already have a cord to bend me and draw me.

[She is still weeping.]

Sweet Cousin, if you stop crying I'll sing for you some lines by a poet named Longfellow, who is said to have had a long, long tongue.

[He makes faces trying to cheer her up. Slowly she stops crying.]

[sings]

> As unto the bow the cord is,
> So unto the man is woman,
> Though she bends him, she obeys him,
> Though she draws him, yet she follows.

My Cousin dear, a bow could not have two cords, and I have already one unto me.

MAIDEN But why could a bow not have several cords, especially when the bow is as strong as you are?

[HIAWATHA wants to speak, but she stops him.]

Let me sing a song for you, too, as of our old days, dear Cousin. *[She stands up and sings.]*

> When the world has more women than men,
> Plural marriage is not anti-civilization.
> When the world has more women than men,
> Plural marriage is a wonderful medicine:
> It will help kill syphilization,
> And save many a woman from prostitution.

HIAWATHA But Cousin dear, you know when one to one is married, the family will soon become more than two. If one marries more than one at a time, a family may breed faster than rabbits do.

[She starts crying again.]

GIRL Don't cry, Sweet Maiden. You know tears are salty, not sweet.

BOY And they cannot solve your problems.

MAIDEN But I have heard that lovers' tears can melt hearts of stone.

BOY What is your heart made of, Hiawatha?

HIAWATHA But friends, if I let this woman's tears melt my heart, another woman's tears will run like waterfalls.

GIRL You mean your wife Laughing Water may turn into Weeping Water?

[Right at the moment a loud laughing comes from offstage right, which stops their talking. The laughing continues into singing.]

MINNEHAHA *[singing offstage]*

> Ha ha—ha ha—
> My husband is bright as a star.
> Ha ha—ho ho
> I love him so.
> I will follow wherever he shall go,
> I will do anything for him, you know . . .

HIAWATHA Oh dear! Here she comes!

BOY What are you going to do, Hiawatha? Are you going to run away?

[MAIDEN stops crying.]

MAIDEN Is that Minnehaha? A woman with such a sweet voice must have a sweet heart, too. Let me talk to her, Cousin dear.

MINNEHAHA *[singing offstage]*

Ha ha—ho ho—
He is my soul.
When he says yes,
I will never say no.
When he says yes,
I will never say no—
Never no . . . never no . . .

[MINNEHAHA runs in from downstage right still singing 'never no'. She stops when she sees MAIDEN standing so near to HIAWATHA. She walks over to them, draws HIAWATHA to one side and plants herself between them.]

Dear husband, how could you leave me alone and run over here and stand so near and dear to another woman!

MAIDEN Hello. I am not just another woman. I am his cousin dear; so you and I are cousins, too.

MINNEHAHA Cousin dear? Never know!

[She turns to look at HIAWATHA.]

HIAWATHA Yes, Minnehaha, she is my Chinese long-time-no-see cousin.

MINNEHAHA What is this long-time-no-see here for?

[Both HIAWATHA and MAIDEN hesitate.]

GIRL She wants to be your husband's second wife, Laughing Water.

MINNEHAHA No. Never! What does he need a second wife for when he has me?

[HIAWATHA tries to explain, but MAIDEN stops him.]

MAIDEN Let me explain, Cousin Hiawatha.

[She walks over to MINNEHAHA and tries to hold her hand. MINNEHAHA refuses and withdraws from her.]

If he marries me, we will be good sisters, and then we can have—I mean I can help you keep a beautiful home.

MINNEHAHA Never! I can do that myself.

MAIDEN But when you two are out hunting, I can cook some delicious food for you and your children.

MINNEHAHA No! We have no children.

[Hearing this, MAIDEN seems to be very happy.]

MAIDEN Then, Sister Minnehaha, he has more reasons to marry me because I can give him many strong and brave sons and beautiful daughters to prosper and glorify *our* family—

MINNEHAHA Never! No!

GIRL Didn't you just sing in your song that you would never say no?

MINNEHAHA Who are you?

BOY But you said in your song you would do anything for your husband, didn't you? Why don't you let Hiawatha make the decision?

MINNEHAHA No. Never. Not now! *[She looks at* MAIDEN *and then at* HIAWATHA, *who says nothing but smiles awkwardly.]* Now, I know! *[She turns to stare at* MAIDEN.] You must be a fox spirit trying to bewitch my husband and steal him from me. I will show you, evil spirit! Yes, you are a fox.

[She begins chanting something unintelligible, and then attacks MAIDEN *in a dance-like movement, which should be primitively forceful and wild, suggesting a witch dance.]*

MAIDEN No, I am not!

[She dodges about, with graceful movements. Their movements become faster and faster, during which MINNEHAHA *shouts 'Yes, you are! Yes, yes . . .';* MAIDEN *responds with 'No, no, no, I am not . . .', both in the singing or chanting tone or rhythm.]*

[Continue into Scene 3]

SCENE THREE

[The loud, sharp sound of a bell pierces through the air, along with the loud laughter of an old man. MAIDEN *and* MINNEHAHA *are both frightened and withdraw to downstage right and downstage left respectively.*

An old man in Taoist dress, with a bell in his left hand and a long sword in his right, springs up in a cloud of smoke from the trap door (or rushes in from upstage centre if there is no trap door). He stops downstage centre, looking at MAIDEN, MINNEHAHA, HIAWATHA, *and the* CHORUS. *He feels a little puzzled.]*

FAUSTUS Where am I?

[Nobody answers but all look at him.]

Who are you? Are you some spirits from Hell sent to help me, or from Heaven sent to . . . to tempt me?

HIAWATHA We are not spirits. *[Pointing to* MINNEHAHA *and then* MAIDEN] We are Indians and she is Chinese.

FAUSTUS So I am in India, not far from Cathay. I did not know that my newly learned Chinese magic would bring me here.

MAIDEN You are dressed like a Chinese Taoist. Are you here to help me?

HIAWATHA Don't listen to her. She is an evil spirit.

FAUSTUS Both of your voices sound familiar to me. *[He walks two steps and thinks.]* I know. It must be your voices that interfered with my magic spell and brought me here. It is true that every pretty woman is a magician. Now, fare thee well. *[He walks a few steps and stops.]* Where am I going? What was I going to do?

HIAWATHA May we ask who you are, sir?

FAUSTUS You don't know who I am?

[All shake their heads.]

I see. Of course, you would not recognize me in this dress. You are forgiven. I am the famous Doctor Faustus of Wittenberg University—famous for my rich knowledge in theology, philosophy, and even magic arts, both Occidental and Oriental.

OLD MAN Good / good // you help us—no no / them / solve their problems // *[He points to* HIAWATHA, MAIDEN, MINNEHAHA.*]* Very serious problems // serious serious //

*[*FAUSTUS *seems to be interested and forgets about going away.]*

FAUSTUS Really serious problems?

[They all nod, except MINNEHAHA. FAUSTUS *starts walking to and fro and murmurs to himself.]*
Problems, problems. Problems always fascinate me! *[Suddenly he stops before* MINNEHAHA *and points his sword at her.]* What is your problem?

MINNEHAHA I want to get rid of this evil spirit.

[She points at MAIDEN.*]*

MAIDEN I am not an evil spirit.

FAUSTUS *[looking at her]* An old Chinese proverb says: A woman of great beauty is often the cause of tragedy. So, I am not sure if you are evil or not.

MAIDEN But being beautiful—if I *am* beautiful—is not my fault.

FAUSTUS That is also true. A young poet once said 'A thing of beauty is a joy forever.' Beauty may also give people pleasure—and inspiration, too. I've also heard another proverb which says: 'If a man dies under the peony'—I suppose you all know what the peony symbolizes? 'If a man dies under the peony his ghost is licentiously happy. *[He looks at* MAIDEN *and then at others.]* Well, what are your problems?

HIAWATHA Sir, to cut a long story short: This is my wife and this woman, my long-time-no-see cousin, wants to be my wife, too.

MAIDEN But I only want to be his second wife. I love him.

FAUSTUS Ha, the old, old problem of love and marriage. Interesting and complicated. And I can tell you the answers from various points of view. Now, find a seat and listen to me. *[He walks to and fro while talking.]* First, from the Christian theological point of view: God created Adam and then He created Eve to be Adam's wife. So, one man married one woman. That was simple—simple because there was no second man, or second woman at the time. Simple also because there were no ceremonial or legal formalities. *[Light pause]* You know such formalities may very often add difficulties to problems. *[Pauses]* Then, problems began to rise when man began to fall in love. Attention: Fall—in love. A good expression because it is simple and complicated at once. 'To fall—in love' means that when man loves he falls. Or man loves to fall? Some theologians beautify it as *felix culpa*—'The fortunate fall.' But in fact it is not always fortunate to *fall* in love—or fall out of love—that is the complicated part of the story. You see what I mean?

BOY, GIRL *[together]* No.

FAUSTUS No? Let me see. Ah, you are too young to fall yet. You just wait and see. Now love and marriage from the sociological point of view. *[Pauses]* Complicated, complicated, complicated. So, I had better not start it at all lest I do not know when and how to conclude. *[Pause. Stands still for a second]* But I could touch on it in my following analysis of love from the psychic-physical-linguistic point of view—and this term 'psychic-physical-linguistic' is worth a Nobel prize.

BOY Did you get the prize for it?

FAUSTUS No. And it was a pity that they didn't even know in which category to award me the honour. Ha! *[Pauses]* Back to my psychic-physical-linguistic point of view:

First, love *per se* is 'a-m-o-r' in Latin, the same in
Spanish; 'a-m-o-r-e' in Italian, and 'a-m-o-u-r' in
French. This suggests that love is an almost universal
feeling for mankind. And yet it has many names or
synonyms, such as affection, admiration, passion,
rapture, devotion, adoration, and idolization—to
mention just a few of the varieties of 'love' in English.
[MINNEHAHA raises her hand.]

You want to say: 'Isn't it beautiful that love has so
many names?'

[She nods.]

Yes and no. Because they sometimes may cause great
confusions; and what is more, some great confusions are
caused by something in the name of love.

[BOY and GIRL raise their hands.]

You want to know why love has so many names or
faces?

[They nod.]

This can be easily demonstrated from the interesting
changes and additions of the meanings of the word
'love,' which interestingly show man's changing
attitudes towards life. For instance, in the year 1589,
the expression 'love affair' was born and added a new
dimension to love in terms of sociological significance.
In 1613, love began to have a new definition: 'a
paramour'. Since the year 1714, love has been used to
mean 'no score' in games like tennis and cricket. This
deserves special attention—especially in relation to
marriage, which, in a very true sense, is an interesting
game, too.

Then, eleven years later, somebody invented a
finger-guessing game, and people loved the game so
much that they named it 'love' and so love itself
became a game too—a guessing game. Interesting, isn't
it? *[Pauses]* Since 1877, to some people to love is 'to
caress or embrace affectionately.' You see, the nature or
problems of love are physical, psychic, linguistical, and
sociological all at once.

[Pause. He looks around at them.]

BOY Do you know 'love' in Chinese, sir?

FAUSTUS Don't interrupt. I am coming to it. Now, last but not
least: love and marriage in Chinese are really

fascinating. The word, or to be exact, the Chinese character for 'love'—'*ai*'—is composed of symbols for heart, friendship, and giving and taking. The character for 'marriage'—'*hun*'—consists of two parts, one part meaning a woman, the other, dizziness, faint, or eve— not Adam and Eve's eve, but the poetic expression for 'evening.' This combination suggests to me an old Chinese saying that a married woman should not be too clear-minded or bright, but should make evenings joyful for her husband.

OLD MAN Old Chinese also say / woman / no talent / virtuous / good //

FAUSTUS Thank you. And one more afterthought: It is a pity that today many people only desire to 'make love'.

GIRL Why?

BOY Why is it a pity?

FAUSTUS Why, love is nature. If you have to make it, it means that you don't have love in you.

[GIRL *whispers something to* BOY.]

BOY Can people make marriage?

FAUSTUS Of course. Don't you know there are many, many match-makers?

HIAWATHA Can you make a happy marriage?

FAUSTUS That is a very complex question—complex because a) 'happiness' is a very relative feeling or mood, just like one man's dish is another's poison. Dish . . . poison . . . dish . . . [*Pause. Talking to himself*] An excellent image for marriage. Let's use it. So, b) what do you have for making a dish—butter or margarine, for instance? c) What are you trying to mix? Milk and water can blend together easily but water and oil will never mix. d) What do you expect of the dish? To taste delicious, or just to look splendid, or both? And do you have the right amount of salt in it? I mean love is the salt in life—I borrow it from *Lust for Life*, a book about a genius who loved sunshine and bright colours so much that he died of them—or for them—a beautiful love death indeed!

MAIDEN You must be a master of love and cooking, sir.

FAUSTUS Well, I certainly have done some research on recipes. But honestly I had never attempted, or been tempted, to try 'cooking' anything myself until quite recently.

MAIDEN According to your experience, sir, can one cook chicken, for instance, with more than one kind of vegetable and meat?

FAUSTUS Certainly. Yes. Why do you ask such a question?

MAIDEN Then, can you—can one man marry more than one woman?

FAUSTUS Ha, you are learning fast. Good. But to answer your question: Yes and No. It all depends on the type of recipe—I mean what religion or morality you will apply. According to Christianity, no—as I have perhaps already mentioned, though I have also been told that there have been exceptions in practice, both openly and privately.

MAIDEN Do you mean fathers and sisters cannot marry?

FAUSTUS You are right. But that is not what I mean by exceptions in practice and—

BOY Strange! How could they have children and become fathers if they don't get married?

FAUSTUS A stupid question! But an excellent example to show the stupidity of the English language. So I am delighted to give you a stupid answer; that is, this father is not the father you are thinking. Get it?

GIRL But why can't sisters get married?

FAUSTUS They do. They are all married to Jesus Christ.

MAIDEN Is this Jesus a man with great power?

FAUSTUS You are right again. A great man with great power.

MAIDEN So a man of great power can marry more than one woman. Hiawatha is powerful and he surely can marry me, too.

MINNEHAHA No. He is married to me. Me only.

[MAIDEN *walks towards* HIAWATHA, MINNEHAHA *tries to stop her. They begin to struggle.*]

OLD MAN What we do / Doctor?// They / fight again // you / wise // you help them / please //

FAUSTUS No, I can't.

GIRL But you have great magic power!

FAUSTUS Yes. But love is magic by itself, and, in fact, true love is the most powerful and most wonderful of all magic. So, what can my magic power do?

GIRL [*to* BOY] Can't we do something? What do you say, Cousin?

BOY I don't know. [*Pause. He thinks for a second.*] In a situation like this, I guess my parents would say: Wait

and see. When a boat comes to the narrow arch of a
bridge, it will go straight and sail through it all right.
[Suddenly FAUSTUS *shakes his bell. He feels kind of excited
and uses the bell to punctuate his lines when he comes to a
pause.]*

FAUSTUS Ha, why didn't I think of it!? Yes, when a boat comes
to the narrow arch of a bridge it will go straight and
sail through it all right. *[He gestures to* MINNEHAHA,
HIAWATHA, *and* MAIDEN.*]* Come. Come over here, you
three. I know how to help you solve your problems now.

[They do not move; BOY *and* GIRL *go over and pull them to
downstage centre.]*

Now, here is a boat. *[He draws a boat on the floor with
his sword, shakes his bell and murmurs something at the same
time. Then he says to* HIAWATHA.*]* Now, you jump into
the middle of the boat.

*[*HIAWATHA *does, and mimes the movement of the boat in
water. The rest of the group feel amused.* BOY *picks up a
pebble and throws it into the 'water' which makes a splashing
sound.]*

Be careful. The water is very deep. *[He turns to*
MAIDEN *and* MINNEHAHA.*]* When I say one, two,
three, the boat will start moving. If you really want
him, get into the boat. Ready? One, two, and . . . three!

*[*MAIDEN *jumps into the front of the boat;* MINNEHAHA
*into the back. The three mime the up-and-down rocking
movement of the boat, which becomes steady again gradually.]*

Now, you are all in the same boat! Remember the
water is very deep. Nobody can save you if you fall out
of the boat.

*[He shakes his bell and waves his sword and the boat begins
to move faster and faster.* MAIDEN *and* MINNEHAHA *both
try to get over to* HIAWATHA. *The struggling makes the boat
unsteady again and they almost lose their balance. So they
stop struggling, try to balance themselves and the boat.*
HIAWATHA *does not know which to help first during the
struggle. The boat circles the stage twice and exits upstage
left.]*

OLD MAN *[to himself]* In same boat // good / very good //

BOY Where are they going?

FAUSTUS To find their answers, of course . . . ha, ha, ha, ha . . .

*[*OLD MAN *joins him laughing. This lasts for quite a long while.]*

BOY Why are you two so happy?

GIRL Yeah, why?

FAUSTUS What?

BOY Why do you laugh so happily when they are struggling for love—I mean for life in the boat?

FAUSTUS Who? What boat?

BOY You know what I am talking about!

GIRL The people you just put in your magic boat!

FAUSTUS Did I? I don't remember.

BOY Are you joking, sir?

GIRL If you forget so quickly, how can you learn and remember so many things?

[OLD MAN *pats the heads and shoulders of the kids tenderly and smiles at them mysteriously. They feel more puzzled.*]

FAUSTUS Oh, that! Right. The more you learn the more you know, and the more you know the more you forget—or have to learn to forget. It is an interesting aspect of life; and it is sometimes a very good thing to forget, but it is sometimes so very difficult to forget. Right? You Chinese have an old saying: The honoured are easy to forget. And I have found it very true, and have made some modifications and put it into a formula: UIP is UFP, and vice versa.

BOY What are the UIP and UFP?

FAUSTUS Why are young people always so impatient? Of course I will explain. Now I presume you all know a VIP means a Very Important Person. But today the world has too many VIPs to make these Very Important Persons feel their importance or be honoured, just as there are too many millionaires and even billionaires now—so many of them that these billion-billionaires themselves feel that they are commoner than the common people. To satisfy the VIPs of VIPs of the million-billion VIPs, I substitute 'Ultra' for 'Very', and name them UIPs—Ultra Important Persons. [*Pauses*] However, my major contribution to the formula is not the U but the F in the UFP. The wonderful magic F, which happens to be the first letter of my own name: famous Faustus.

GIRL What does your F stand for, sir? Fortune and fortunate?

FAUSTUS Yes, famous and important persons are mostly fortunate. But that is not what I mean here.

GIRL What do you mean here, then, sir?

FAUSTUS 'Forget.' Of course.

BOY You forget again?

FAUSTUS No. *[Pauses]* Some people forget themselves; many forget others. And they are both UFPs, though very different in nature.

GIRL It's so very confusing, sir.

BOY Why don't you make two formulas, sir, one for the self-forgetting, and one for the other-forgetting?

FAUSTUS Yes, why not. Let me see . . . No. Great formulas should always be ambiguous. But I can tell you that to be Ultra-Self-Forgetting or Self-Forgetful is ultra difficult. One must, first of all, be Ultra Generous and Ultra Forgiving.

OLD MAN Yes, yes / old Chinese sage say // strict to you self / generous to other //

BOY It's hard to live up to that, but I'd certainly like to grow up to be such a UFP.

GIRL Me, too.

OLD MAN Me / three //

[*They all laugh.*]

Oh / oh / dear // we all become UFP now //

GIRL Oh, we have all forgotten the people in the boat!

BOY Oh!

OLD MAN No / no / they very safe / good // I mean / we forget your uncle and auntie // you two / go / run / find them //

[BOY *and* GIRL *run off stage left, calling 'Uncle,' 'Auntie' at the same time.*]

[*Continue into Scene 4*]

SCENE FOUR

[*As* BOY's *and* GIRL's *voices are fading out, there rises some sweet music, which comes nearer and nearer. The music is of some simple, classic style, with some modern romantic flavour.*

FAUSTUS *is immediately attracted by the music and he becomes more and more excited.*]

FAUSTUS Now, I remember what I was going to do.

OLD MAN You forget / some important thing?//

FAUSTUS I've just remembered something very, very important. I was trying to find my Helen, the greatest beauty of Greece, the Helen that some people say destroyed Troy. But she is *music*! Here she is, coming to me!

OLD MAN You sure / this is / that Helen?//

FAUSTUS Of course I am sure. I am not as forgetful as that, old man!

OLD MAN You sure / this Helen / not destroy you?//

FAUSTUS No.

OLD MAN You / not sure?//

FAUSTUS I said 'I am sure.'

OLD MAN You sure / she / destroy you?//

> *[At this moment,* HELEN *is in view. She is flying down centre stage, or sliding in from stage right.* FAUSTUS *is watching her and pays no attention to what* OLD MAN *is saying.* BOY *and* GIRL *run in from stage left, closely followed by* HUSBAND *and* WIFE. *They all see* HELEN *flying down.]*

HUSBAND   'Was this the face that launched a thousand ships . . .'

WIFE   'And burnt the topless towers of Ilium?'

> *[*FAUSTUS *moves toward* HELEN, *who is about to land on the floor. Her eyes are closed.]*

FAUSTUS   'Sweet Helen, make me immortal with a kiss.'

> *[*HELEN *kisses him, and they change positions while kissing.* FAUSTUS *flies up into the air after the kiss;* HELEN *stays.]*

HUSBAND *[dreamily]*

> 'Her lips suck forth my soul: see where it flies!'

WIFE *[holds her husband]* No, your soul is mine.

> *[*HELEN's *eyes are still closed.]*

HELEN Where are you, Paris? Oh, you are still so young and so naughty. But you are lovely. Come here. I will give you another kiss.

> *[A pause.* HELEN *opens her eyes, looks around, and sees the* CHORUS.]*

Who are you, ladies and gentlemen?

HUSBAND We are Chinese.

BOY Can I ask you something?

HELEN Yes, young man.

BOY You are so beautiful! Are you really Helen of Troy?

HELEN Yes, I suppose I am. *[Smiling at him. Light pause]* Now, can you tell me where my Paris is, who just kissed me?

GIRL We don't know where your Paris is, but I can tell you who kissed you just now.

HELEN It was not Paris?

GIRL It was Dr Faustus. Your kiss has sucked forth his soul, and body, and has made him fly away.

HELEN I am sorry!

OLD MAN No sorry // We say / not know / not blamed // He look very / very / more happy //

HELEN Thank you, Sir. *[Pauses]* Why are you people here, if I may ask?

WIFE We were on a journey to look for my mother-in-law, but then we started looking for something else.

HELEN Have you found it?

GIRL Yes.

OLD MAN No / I mean . . . //

BOY No? But . . .

GIRL But we found something very, very special.

BOY Yeah, something very interesting.

HELEN What is it? Can you tell me about it?

GIRL Yes, we found emptiness in an empty cage.

[HELEN smiles.]

HELEN *[jokingly]* What is this emptiness like, young lady?

GIRL I don't know. But we found it there.

BOY And it was sometimes very heavy, sometimes as light as nothing.

HELEN Really? Can you tell me how heavy or light this emptiness is?

OLD MAN As love . . . / and no love //

[Seeing everybody is serious, HELEN becomes serious too.]

HELEN You mean love is heavy, and, when there is no love, life is light?

OLD MAN Yes // no / no //

HELEN Love is light? And people in love will feel light, too?

[OLD MAN nods, then shakes his head.]

You mean there is no love in the world—no true love?

OLD MAN No love / empty //

HELEN *[as if to herself]* No love—empty . . . no love, no life? . . . and love is light and not light . . . heavy and not heavy . . . so love . . . is . . .

GIRL You know what love is?

HELEN I thought I knew, but . . .

WIFE Even you don't know love?

HUSBAND Have you never been in love?

[HELEN looks at them and heaves a sad, long sigh.]

HELEN I thought I had loved and been loved—and married,
     too . . . though not at the same time.

BOY Do you mean when you were married, you did not
     love; when you loved you did not marry?

HELEN *[thinks]* No, I think . . . the fact is: I was married to
     Menelaus, and then I fell in love with Paris and we
     . . . we . . .

BOY So you ran away together?

GIRL Gee! Love must be more exciting than marriage!

     [All look at her.]

BOY *[to GIRL, tenderly]* We will only love and never marry.
     So you cannot run away from me . . . or we can run
     away together. *[He turns to HELEN, seriously.]* Am I
     right, Miss Helen?

     *[HUSBAND, WIFE, and OLD MAN all laugh, and HELEN's
     face turns red. (Note: This might be done by changing masks
     or by lighting effect.)]*

     [looks at GIRL, and then at HELEN] Your face is burning,
     Miss Helen. *[He pauses and feels a little puzzled.]* Was it
     really your face that burned the City of Troy?

HELEN Love can be very hot. *[Pauses]* But I don't think love
     has ever made my face burn.

GIRL Do you know who really burned the city?

HELEN I don't know. Maybe some people who loved their own
     faces much better than anything else in the world.

BOY Can you tell us what has just made your face burn?

HELEN *[sighs]* I wish . . . But I have always been deeply sorry
     for the destruction of the city and its people. I did,
     still do, feel that this face of mine was the cause of
     many people's love for me or hatred against me. I feel
     really sorry that people think so much of the face. I
     always wish to be loved for what I am, not how I look
     . . .

OLD MAN I / very sorry for you / too // We say / great beauty /
     most ill-fated //

HELEN Thank you, Sir . . . and can you tell me some stories of
     the great beauties of your country?

OLD MAN Gladly / gladly // *[Pauses]* But my English poor // they
     can tell you story / better //

     [He points to HUSBAND and WIFE.]

HUSBAND But Father, you know the stories best.

GIRL Yes, I love Great Uncle's stories best. *[She turns to* HELEN.*]* What would you like to hear? How about the story of Lady Wang Zhaojun? How one evening her lute music led the Emperor to her side and then the Emperor led her to his room, and then how she killed herself because she refused to marry a barbarian king!

BOY No, no. I have heard too many stories like that: a pretty girl killing herself because she loved somebody she couldn't marry.

WIFE Father, sing us the song of the faithful wife Meng Jiangnü—about how she travelled ten thousand miles alone to look for her husband and how her tears broke down the Great Wall of China and she found his bones under the wall.

HUSBAND That story is too sad, though the song is lovely and popular. I like the story of Lady Chang E better, Father.

BOY I know that story. *[Narrating and miming with a feminine quality]* Once upon a time, there was a lady named Chang E, or Lady Chang the Beautiful. She wanted to live forever, so she stole the elixir-herb of immortality from her husband and ate it all. After a while, her body became lighter, and lighter, and lighter, and she rose in the air higher, and higher, and higher, and finally she got to the moon and so she became the Lady of the Moon.

HELEN Was she happy to be immortal in the moon?

BOY I don't know. Maybe. But a poet says she watches the earth from the moon every night and regrets . . .

GIRL Oh, Cousin, you have spoiled the best part of the story. I don't want to hear it again today.

[She goes over to OLD MAN *and whispers something into his ear.* OLD MAN *hesitates for a moment, then nods.]*

OLD MAN All right / the Song of Everlasting Sorrow //

GIRL But I call it Song of Everlasting Love!

WIFE I like the song, too, especially your own version, Father. I like it much better than the traditional one by Poet Bai.

HUSBAND So do I, Father. When you sing, don't worry about the English grammar.

BOY Use your own grammar!

OLD MAN That is good // *[Pauses]* But I fear / I / too / a UFP now //

BOY We can help you when you forget.

[When OLD MAN *is singing the story,* BOY *and* GIRL *mime out the lines.* HUSBAND, WIFE, *and* HELEN *react to the singing and miming.*

There should be some short music for transition between each two stanzas.]

OLD MAN *[chants]*

Long, long ago in T'ang dynasty,
Many, many things happen there.
My story not sing the heroic,
But the romance of a maiden.

[When he starts singing, the rest of the CHORUS *chants the refrains to the musical accompaniment.]*

[sings]

Her name is Jade Bracelet Yang,
A born beauty none can compare.
A pear blossom with dew of spring,
Shining with the sun of morning.
        [Refrain] She is lovely and fair,
                And who shall be her pair?

Clouds darken not the moonlight,
The moon not so bright as our Jade.
Since the Emperor make her his lady,
She wait on the Emperor day and night.
        [Refrain] She is his and he hers,
                They make their world paradise.

A phoenix she is when sing and dance,
With unmatchable beauty and grace.
The Emperor watch her with such zeal
He think not of his country, not of his meal.
        [Refrain] She makes the day short,
                She makes the moon speed.

On seventh day of seventh moon,
On this Lovers' Day they pray:
To be lovebirds when they live,
To become twin-boughs next life.
        [Refrain] He loves her and she him,
                Forever they swear to love.

So . . . so . . . much . . . the Emperor . . .

[To HUSBAND *or* WIFE*]* Quick / take over / . . . the line
/ I forget . . .

HUSBAND, WIFE *[continue the song together]*

> So, so much the Emperor loved our heroine,
> He granted great honour to all her family
>   and to all her kin.
> So, so many attentions to her were paid,
> Now, not for a son but a daughter
>   all families prayed.

[The mood of music suddenly changes.]

HUSBAND *[speaks]* But alas, one day—*[Continues to sing with* WIFE*]*

> Out of the blue a thunderbolt fell:
> War drums made heaven and earth yell,
> Made her melody and dance dispel . . .

*[*OLD MAN *gestures them to stop and takes over the singing after a musical interlude.]*

OLD MAN *[sings]*

> Some of her kinsmen not kind,
> Plotted for the throne and royal robe.
> Army gathered but would not move,
> Unless her ladyship be executed right off.

[Speaks] What could the Emperor do? He had no freedom of love. At the Mawei Slope, he saw her strangled . . . *[He continues to sing after a light silence.]*

> Dust rolled and winds blew,
> Tears and frost blurred his view.
> In muffled silence the army moved—
>   in silence and gloom.

[He cannot go on and his voice becomes very sad.]

HUSBAND Let me wind up the story, Father.

*[*OLD MAN *nods 'yes' and* HUSBAND *begins to speak.]*

The rebellion was put down, order was soon restored. But where was his Lady Jade Bracelet? The Emperor revisited and searched the Mawei Slope, but not a trace of her remains could he find. However—*[He sings.]*

> That made him happy, not sad,
> 'My Jade must have survived,' he said.
> Death parting became now live separation.
> He was so happy,
>   He was so sad,
>   He was sleepless at night.

He enquired,
　　He sought,
　　　　He searched until he died.
But his Jade was nowhere to be found.
Their love this life had come to its end,
They could only hope to be lovers again—
　　　　to be lovers again next life.

[Long pause. He speaks.] I did not believe that an emperor could be so foolish—I mean so deeply and madly in love. But I believe it now because my own father's story of looking for my dead mother has proved to me that a man can love a woman as deeply as that.

[Long silence]

HELEN I envy your mother. *[Silence]* I don't know who suffered, or regretted, more—the emperor or the lady. *[Pauses]* I used to think that true love might free us from all worldly cares whereas marriage would keep man and wife in bondage and make them compromise for each other—sometimes even compromise for somebody else or something beyond the marriage. Now I see that love enjoys less freedom—you cannot even compromise. What is more, it seems that the more sincere and deep love is, the more hopeless and foolish it may become. *[She turns to* OLD MAN.*]* Thank you very much for your song and teaching, Sir. And thank you for your wonderful performance, too, young friends. *[Pauses]* I think I should go now. Goodbye.

[Right at the moment, FAUSTUS's *voice comes from above— or from the direction he flew off. He soon flies down slowly.* CHORUS *stops to look at him.]*

FAUSTUS 'Come, Helen, come, give me my soul again,
Here will I dwell, for heaven is in these lips,
And all is dross that is not Helen.'

[He lands on the floor and goes to HELEN. *He seems a quite different person now.]*

BOY Where did you fly to just now, Dr F?

FAUSTUS *[thinks]* Did you call me Dr F?

BOY I did not mean—I mean Dr Faustus.

FAUSTUS Dr F? I like it. Well, I went to a timeless space.

GIRL What did you see there, sir?

FAUSTUS Wonderful things. I looked down at the earth, I saw
my own childhood, and those stupid years at the
university, and why I walked out of my study.

HUSBAND May we ask why?

FAUSTUS Do you want a straight answer or a metaphor?

BOY A straight answer.

OLD MAN I better like / metaphor //

FAUSTUS All right. I'll give you both. First, the straight answer:
I wanted to *experience* life and to really taste it. Now
the metaphor: I did not want to study recipes all my
life; I wanted to cook and eat the dishes.

BOY Are you hungry, Dr Faustus?

FAUSTUS Call me Dr F. But what has made you ask such an
interesting question?

BOY Why do you always think of eating and cooking and
dishes?

FAUSTUS I see. I have always been hungry—but not as you are
hungry, I think.

BOY No, I am not hungry. I just had some hot-dogs from
Sweet Maiden. You should have asked her for
something before you sent her away with Hiawatha and
Minnehaha.

FAUSTUS Thank you for your thoughtfulness, young friend. But
. . . how should I put it . . .

OLD MAN *[smiles]* No wrong want to eat / sir // long ago wise
man say / eating and sex / human nature //

FAUSTUS Did he say that?

[OLD MAN nods, and so does HUSBAND.]

Eating and sex are human nature! How simple and
true. It has almost summed up all I have said. Tell me
more of such sayings about man, and woman, too. I am
just hungry for more of such ingredients of wisdom!

HUSBAND Between man and woman, or to be exactly as is said,
between man and wife, the Way of Life is the same as
the Way of Yin and Yang, which forms the Universe
and all that live in the Universe.

FAUSTUS Another remarkable observation of a simple fact. Both
deserve some careful chewing. . . . *[He begins to think and
walk to and fro again, taking* HELEN *with him.]* Eating
and sex are human. . . . Yes, to people who live to eat,
eating is everything; to people who eat to live, eating
is also a basic need. And sex . . . and man and wife . . .
eureka! So love can be sex by nature; and marriage, sex

legalized and moralized. Excellent! Wonderful! Though
of course there is no rule without exceptions, especially
in the world today when love and marriage are so . . .
so . . .

GIRL So much like a game?

FAUSTUS Yes, I said that, didn't I?

BOY And a guessing game?

FAUSTUS I said that, too? Yes, I did.

HUSBAND Are you suggesting that we have to follow rules in love
and marriage?

BOY Do people always follow rules in games?

GIRL And who will be the referees if somebody cheats or
breaks the rules of the love game?

FAUSTUS Ha ha, very good and challenging questions. However,
I am afraid there is no standard answer. *[Pauses]* But
come to think of it, isn't it good that there is no
standard answer?

BOY Yeah! It would be no fun if everything had to go by
rule.

FAUSTUS Right! *[He gives* CHORUS *a look and turns to* HELEN, *very
gently.]* Now come, Helen. Let's go and love. As a poet
says: When there is wine, enjoy it—don't wait and
lament over empty cups.

OLD MAN *[chants]*

'Pick it when the flower is in bloom /
Don't wait till there is only the withered branch.' //

FAUSTUS, HELEN *[together]* Thank you, sir.

HUSBAND Miss Helen, may I ask you something before you go?

HELEN Yes, of course.

HUSBAND Do you Greeks believe that love is blind?

HELEN I do.

FAUSTUS So do I. And believe it or not, true love is always blind
simply because it is not rational or logical.

WIFE So love is dangerous?

FAUSTUS And yet most inspiring! *[Pauses. He thinks and smiles.]*
But danger is man, isn't it?

GIRL Danger is woman, too?

FAUSTUS Perhaps even more so—especially beautiful women. So,
it takes great courage to love a beautiful woman. *[He
turns to* HUSBAND *and* WIFE.*]* Tell me something, you
married couple. I've heard someone say: Marriage is like
a city surrounded by walls—from without, the

unmarried try to force a way into the walls; but from within, the married try to fight a way out. How do you two feel?

HUSBAND, WIFE *[together]* We like to stay inside the walls.

FAUSTUS *[pauses]* Yes, of course. You are newly married. So I think—

GIRL But Dr F . . . sir—

FAUSTUS Yes, my young lady?

GIRL Who built the walls?

FAUSTUS Who built the walls? Who? Who? Who?

> *[He turns suddenly to* BOY, *who is moving to* GIRL *and taking her hand in his.]*

> What do you think, young man?

BOY I don't know. But can't we just forget the walls?

FAUSTUS Forget the walls? *[Thinking]* Yes, why not. Yes. *[Pauses]* Yes, indeed. This is a magnificent discovery of the virtue of 'forget' I have learned today. Young man, and you too, young lady, are my teachers: teaching Dr F to forget. I want to honour you as the greatest UFP.

BOY, GIRL *[together]* We are?

OLD MAN Good / think not / what to wall in / what to wall out // good / good // and forget the void in kaleidoscope / forget the kaleidoscope in void.

FAUSTUS Did I say that, too?

> *[CHORUS look at each other.]*

> Never mind who said it. *[Turns to* HELEN*]* Let's go to the void in the kaleidoscope to find the kaleidoscope in the void. And don't let our 'native hue of resolution' be 'sicklied o'er with the pale cast of walls.' Farewell friends.

> *[He shakes his bell and sword which are both in his right hand now. He begins to dance with* HELEN. CHORUS *join the dance. Lights begin to change to strobe. Suddenly,* FAUSTUS *and* HELEN *both disappear in smoke.]*

> *[Continue into Epilogue]*

EPILOGUE

[When the strobe lighting and smoke are gone, FAUSTUS *and* HELEN *have both disappeared. Instead, there are among* CHORUS, MAIDEN, *and* SCHOLAR, *with the cage in his hand.*

BOY *runs to* SCHOLAR; GIRL *to* MAIDEN.*]*

BOY You missed a lot when you were sleeping, sir.

SCHOLAR Really? I had a wonderful experience in my dreams, too.

BOY Oh, what was your wonderful experience?

SCHOLAR I dreamt that I was a Dr Faustus, and he said he had dreamt that he was me.

[BOY *feels kind of puzzled and tries to reason it out with himself. He murmurs something to himself.* GIRL *draws* MAIDEN *to one side.*]

GIRL Where is your cousin?

MAIDEN My cousin, who?

GIRL Hiawatha. The cousin you want to marry.

MAIDEN Hiawatha? Oh, yes, he was in my dream.

GIRL Dream? I saw you go away with him and Minnehaha in a small boat!

MAIDEN [*smiles*] You did? Were you in my dream, too?

[*Now, like* BOY, GIRL *also feels puzzled and begins to think.* BOY *seems to have got some answer. He looks at* SCHOLAR.]

BOY But how is that possible that you dreamt of being Dr Faustus and then he told you he had dreamt of being you? You mean the impossible could be made possible through dreams?

[SCHOLAR *touches* BOY'*s head as a holy Buddha touches his disciples.*]

SCHOLAR Now you can be my disciple.

GIRL I would also like to be your disciple, sir, if you could teach me how to make dreams become real in life.

SCHOLAR I would like to, young lady. But I think your Great Uncle would be a better teacher for you.

[GIRL *looks at* OLD MAN, *who says nothing but smiles at her.*]

By the way, do you still believe that only what you can see with your own eyes is real?

BOY Yes.

[HUSBAND, WIFE *and* GIRL *all nod.*]

MAIDEN [*turns to* HUSBAND] Can you *see* my voice, sir?

HUSBAND No, Miss. But I can hear it with my ears.

MAIDEN [*to* WIFE] Can you *hear* the fragrance of flowers and grass?

WIFE No. But I can smell it with my nose.

MAIDEN [*to* BOY] Can you *smell* the air around us now?

BOY No.

MAIDEN But you *believe* it is there.

BOY Yes.

MAIDEN [*to* GIRL] Do you believe what he says?

GIRL Yes.

MAIDEN Can you tell me why you believe the air is there while you cannot smell it, hear it, or see it?

BOY Because it is a very simple fact.

SCHOLAR Good. But how do you know it is a simple fact?

BOY Because I can see it and feel it when there is wind.

SCHOLAR Very good. But how do you know the air is still there when the wind is gone?

[BOY and GIRL fail to answer.]

[turns to WIFE] Can you *hear* fragrance without using your nose?

[She shakes her head and thinks.]

[turns to HUSBAND] Can you *see* my voice without using your ears?

[HUSBAND shakes his head and thinks.]

[turns to OLD MAN] Can you see the void in a kaleidoscope? And the kaleidoscope in a void, now?

OLD MAN Some / yes / a little //

SCHOLAR Very good. Now, goodbye to you all.

[He and MAIDEN make some simple but graceful movements; then in a flash of light and/or smoke, MAIDEN becomes very small again—as she first appeared in the play. He holds her in his hands and slowly puts her into his mouth, and she is gone. SCHOLAR walks off downstage right, with the cage in his hand. CHORUS watch him go out of sight.]

BOY Grandpa, can you tell us now how to *see* voices and how to *hear* fragrance?

GIRL And how to make dreams come true, too.

OLD MAN Good / good // now you tell me / first // you see / what you dream // right?

[CHORUS all say 'Right.']

Now / your eyes open / or closed / when you dream?//

BOY Closed, of course.

GIRL Of course, closed. *[To BOY]* What a strange question.

OLD MAN But / how / do / you / see // then?//

[They look at each other, thinking. Lights begin to fade out gradually. Just before all lights go out, OLD MAN, who is now standing downstage centre, with his hands held up in front of his heart like a Buddhist, opens his hands, and a colourful magic light appears, as if from his heart.
The four cry out in excitement one after another, and the

voice is amplified by music. This must be done rhythmically, in the order of HUSBAND, WIFE, BOY, *and* GIRL, *in the following manner: a) hold up hands like* OLD MAN *does, b) take a few steps to stand by* OLD MAN—HUSBAND *on his left,* WIFE *on his right,* BOY *on* HUSBAND'S *left,* GIRL *on* WIFE's *right, c) close eyes, d) say 'I see!', and e) open up hands and lights appear. The lights should be different in brightness and colour.]*

HUSBAND I see!

WIFE   I see!

BOY   I see!

GIRL   I see!

[Then they begin to move clockwise around the stage, very slowly. They move in the order of OLD MAN, HUSBAND, WIFE, BOY, GIRL, *and* SCHOLAR *and* MAIDEN *come back and join them to bring up the rear.*

     When they turn their backs to the audience, each will light some small candles, magically. Then they move offstage down to the audience, and give the candles to members of the audience in different areas. When they disappear in darkness, house lights come up.]

[No Curtain Call. Music continues until the audience has all gone.]

THE END

NATIONAL SALVATION
CORPORATION LTD.

1991

By
LEE KUO-HSIU

Translated by
EVA HUNG

— ABOUT **THE PLAYWRIGHT** —

LEE KUO-HSIU, HUGH (1955–) was born in Taiwan and graduated from the World College of Journalism and Communication. One of the most prolific writers in Taiwan, Lee has written over thirty-five playscripts and close to a hundred television drama scripts to date. In 1984, together with Lai Shêng-ch'uan and Li Li-ch'ün, he founded the Performance Workshop. In 1985, he spent a year in Japan and America studying mainstream and non-mainstream experimental theatre movements in these two countries. On his return to Taiwan, he left the Performance Workshop to set up the Ping-Fong Acting Troupe and has since been its Artistic Director. Most of his plays are satirical comedies about urgent social and political issues of the day, and they are extremely popular with the Taiwan public. In just a few years, he turned the troupe, initially operating on a shoe-string budget, into one of the most successful theatre companies in Taiwan. With box-office success almost a matter of course, Lee is able to pursue his ideal of helping to 'lay a strong foundation for Taiwan theatre'. Over the years, he has spared no effort in promoting the growth and development of Taiwan drama by investing the profits made by the Ping-Fong Acting Troupe into the setting up of Ping-Fong branches outside Taipei and the running of training courses for aspiring dramatists.

National Salvation Corporation Ltd., first staged by the Ping-Fong Acting Troupe in 1991, was enthusiastically received by the audience and critics alike. At the invitation of the Chinese-American Arts Council, the production went on tour to New York in 1992. For this purpose, Lee substantially revised the script to enhance its relevance for the New York Chinese audience. The success of this first overseas performance established the name of the Ping-Fong Acting Troupe amongst the Chinese in America and paved the way for subsequent invitations. Since 1992, the troupe has brought productions of *Classified* (1993), *West of Yangkuan* (1994), and *The Taiping Heavenly Kingdom* (1995) to places like New York, Los Angeles, the Orange County, Singapore, and Hong Kong. In 1994, *Shamlet*, a parody of Shakespeare's *Hamlet*, was staged in Shanghai as part of the '1994 International Shakespeare Festival' and the 'Ping-Fong Acting Troupe' became the first contemporary Taiwan theatre troupe to perform on the Mainland. In 1996, *Shamlet* was performed in Los Angeles.

Zany in argument, irreverent in tone, and provocative in the questions it stimulates the audience to ask, *National Salvation Corporation Ltd.* revolves around a murder case and is a commentary on law and order in Taiwan. It is a social and political satire of great unsettling power, but it is also witty, fast-moving, entertaining, and punctuated with comments on the absurdity of life in Taiwan.

The playwright calls this work 'a rhapsodic comedy' and it certainly allows the imagination to run wild. There are no constraints on the way the plot develops, and the dialogue and action move constantly in and out of the realm of farce and of the absurd. The plot, however, is based on fact, and follows the disappearance in April 1990 of a Japanese university student. Lee Kuo-hsiu began his play several months later when the woman was still missing. The play had its first performance on 4 January 1991 and its last and seventieth performance on 3 March 1991. It was only afterwards that more information about the real-life case was released. The actual outcome turned out to be strikingly similar to the play when a man was said to have confessed to the crime, but the student's family were unable to identify the body. An interesting case, perhaps, not of art imitating life, but of life imitating art? Or was the play truly inspirational—for 'the authorities'?

The play is also an example of another type of experimental drama in Taiwan. There is no attempt to explore the resources of traditional culture, instead Lee Kuo-hsiu explores the resources of information technology, and examines its impact on a society dominated by the ethos of consumerism. A 150″ TV screen is lowered on to the stage at regular intervals and the playwright makes mocking use of the form of news bulletins and reports to expose the arbitrariness of the dividing line between facts and fabrication, news and publicity stunts, falsehood and truth. Then the illusion of life-likeness, much insisted upon by the realistic plays, is constantly broken by making the characters re-enact their past in a deliberately stylized fashion that highlights the notion of role and role-playing. The characters' past, moreover, does not help to explain the characters' present behaviour. The past is more like a figment of a character's imagination, or a fiction, or even someone else's fiction. The overall effect is of people leading puppet-like existences. 'As flies to wanton boys are we to the gods, they kill us for their sport'. The play strikes deep reverberations with these lines of Shakespeare. The question is: who are the gods?

DRAMATIS PERSONAE

LI HSI-CHIEH
KUO CHI-CH'IEN
CH'ÊN WEI-TSUNG
LÜ KUO-K'UNG
LIU JÊN-SHAN
CHANG SHAN-MAY
X HSI-CHIEH
CHANG A-MAY

CHARACTERS SEEN ON TELEVISION

SEKIMARU KIUKO
TV ANCHORMAN
NIHON DICKIRO
LI'S FATHER
LI'S MOTHER
REPORTER
FOREIGN REPORTERS
CAMERAMAN
MATZU HANAKO

LI HSI-CHIEH and X HSI-CHIEH are played by the same actor;
CHANG SHAN-MAY and CHANG A-MAY are played by the same
   actress.

THE **PLAY**

W A R M - U P

[Before the curtain rises, a TV set is placed on stage left, in front of the curtain, showing the main news of the day.]

P R E L U D E : T V N E W S 1

[Curtain rises.
150″ TV screen lowered on to the stage.
The screen shows photographs of Sekimaru Yuriko taken in front of the Presidential Palace and other Taiwan tourist attractions.]

SEKIMARU KIUKO *[Yuriko's mother, in Japanese]* My daughter Yuriko is still missing. I'm really worried . . . I don't know what's the matter with you people in Taiwan. You're just a small island with twenty million people—how can you fail to find a girl who speaks only Japanese? What's the matter with you Taiwanese? You call this a tourists' paradise? It's more like a den of vice! I'm disappointed in Taiwan! I'm disappointed in your government authorities! I'll never set foot in Taiwan again!

[PTV News Channel comes on screen.]

ANCHOR These are photographs of Japanese college student Sekimaru Yuriko travelling around Taiwan on her own in April 1990. The woman you heard denouncing Taiwan was her mother. The authorities' determination to crack the case resulted in the arrest of suspect Liu Ch'iang-hsüeh twelve months after the girl went missing. Liu admitted to the killing, and the authorities announced the successful closing of the case. This is excellent news! But don't rejoice yet. We now have bad news to report—on the X of X of this year, 1992,* Mitsubi-bi-bi—*[sneezes]* shit!—the largest industrial corporation in Japan, sent a 350-member delegation to Taiwan. When they arrived at Taipei International Airport yesterday evening, one Japanese woman—Matzu Hanako—went missing. The leader of the Mitsubi—*[sneezes]* shit!—tour group, Nihon Dickiro, has this comment to make:

[NIHON DICKIRO standing at a corner of the airport departure lounge]

* An optional date can be inserted here.

NIHON DICKIRO Another Japanese woman has gone missing. Now it's all up to the Taiwan government. If you mess this up, then as one of your sayings goes, 'It's a shaggy donkey story', no, 'it's a shaggy dog story, thereby hangs a tail', or . . . well, anyway, it's up to you. *Sayonara*—bloody fools!

[Back to the TV station]

ANCHOR Now, that is to be troubled in trouble. Law and order in this country is just like its economy and its politics—terrible, utterly terrible. But that is not important. The important thing is that the authorities have now set up 'The Matzu Hanako Search Unit 0808'. We want our citizens to be on the alert. We call on all the informers in the country to stand up—ah, no—to go into hiding, for if you stand up you might get killed. What's more, the authorities have come up with a sizeable reward though the exact amount is still confidential—not much, really *[Hears something in his earphone]* Oh—just a moment, just a moment—yes, Producer—yes, put him through—yes—well—really— good. Now that was a personal call to me from the authorities. They say they have already gathered crucial evidence. The authorities say: the suspect is a man—if not, then it's a woman. How's that? Now let us enjoy some commercials. After the commercials, a look at yesterday's weather. *Yester*day's weather? Shit!

[End of TV news. 150″ TV Screen is hoisted up.]

SCENE ONE: PERSUASION 1

[Secret Interrogation Office.
When the lights come on everyone is already on stage. LI *is handcuffed to a chair.]*

CH'ÊN Be a sport! Admit it—you killed Matzu Hanako.

LÜ Silence, hey? That's a tacit admission of guilt.

CH'ÊN He has the right to remain silent. Li, this is the chance of a lifetime for you. We're all going to die, it's just a matter of time! Look at it this way—you want to die, and we can provide you with a grand exit. All you have to do is change your way of thinking, cooperate with us and follow our plan—

LÜ Jên-shan dear, we need photos. Try to capture his expression.

[CH'ÊN continues talking. LIU *picks up a camera to take pictures of* LI.*]*

CH'ÊN We'll send a report to our superiors, and then the thing will come out on TV and in the papers. That'll satisfy the Japs—hey, what're you doing?

LIU Taking pictures for the file.

LÜ Jên-shan, capture his expression. Just look at his deadpan face. I think we should do a special on him— 'Super Murderer Contrite'. Now 'contrite' is a good one, don't you think?

CH'ÊN Does he look like he's contrite?

[LI blocks out the camera with his hand. LIU tries to push LI's hand away. LI struggles with her.]

Stop that! It's just a few pictures, what are you struggling for?

[LI beckons CH'ÊN with his hand.]

Now what?

[LI snatches CH'ÊN's gun from the holster under his shoulder.]

LI Freeze. One move and you're dead. I'm sorry, folks. I want to die, and whatever you do I'm a dead man. I'll gladly die in front of you all, so please be my witnesses. So long, folks—*[Puts the gun to his own head and pulls the trigger, but the gun is unloaded]* You people don't load your guns?

[LI hits his own head with the gun. CH'ÊN and LIU run up to stop him. CH'ÊN snatches the gun.]

CH'ÊN Chief—

KUO Kuo-k'ung, get him a safety helmet.

LÜ Yes, sir.

KUO Ch'ên, search him and get rid of anything he can use to harm himself.

[LÜ puts a safety helmet on LI.]

LÜ Is it too tight? Can you hear me . . . can you hear—

CH'ÊN He hears you all right!

[CH'ÊN takes off LI's watch.]

LI Hey, give me back my watch!

CH'ÊN Time is of no importance to you now.

[CH'ÊN takes away LI's watch and belt.]

KUO Jên-shan, put down the camera and see if there's anything else on him.

LIU Yes, sir.

[LI *tries to avoid being body-searched by her.*]
Turn around.

[LIU *unwittingly turns the body-search into body-massage.*]

LI Miss, are you searching or massaging me?

KUO That'll do. There's probably nothing else on him. Now,
Mr Li, do you want to die?

LI Yes, I do.

CH'ÊN Can't hear you!

LI I do!

KUO Listen, Mr Li. Why is society in such a mess? We have
laws, but no one respects them. We have rules, but no
one obeys them. We have good guys and we always
have bad guys—

[*While* KUO *is talking,* LÜ *is complaining to* LIU *about
family matters.*]

LÜ Society's in such a mess, of course he wants to
emigrate, right? Now where does he want to go?

KUO What do you think you're doing?

LÜ Who?

CH'ÊN You!

LÜ What about me?

CH'ÊN Just shut up!

[LÜ *finally twigs and shuts up.*]

KUO I don't deny that I'm partly responsible for the
lawlessness in society. But then who can say he is not
responsible? Can you really stomach the people we see
every day; and the things that happen; and all the
gossip and back-biting? Isn't it better for everyone just
to live in peace?

LI I've done her wrong.

KUO What're you saying?

LI I've done her wrong.

LIU Now that's better. Our Chief wants you to admit to
kidnapping Matzu Hanako.

LI Do you know who I'm talking about?

LIU The Japanese woman, of course. Now our Chief has this
plan—

LI I'm talking about May, the woman who lived with me.

LIU Well, you killed her anyway. That makes the case easy
to handle.

LI How?

LIU A life for a life, right?

CH'ÊN You're so eager to do away with yourself! If we let you go now, you'd just go somewhere and kill yourself. Now, that would be a great pity.

LIU We're talking about international homicide!

LI Just a minute. You want me to admit to having killed this woman? I don't even know who she is! What can I be guilty of? Hey, you—name?

LIU Matzu Hanako.

LI I mean your name.

LIU Liu Jên-shan.

LI Miss Liu. Listen to me, everyone. You want me to admit to kidnapping this woman, and then you say it's international homicide. Don't you see you're contradicting yourself? Now why don't you go inside and sort it out among yourselves first. Sure I want to die, but I'm not going to let you use me anyway you like. Tell me what exactly you are up to.

LÜ We're doing it for national salvation. How about that?

LI What a joke! What I'm—

LÜ It's five past nine.

KUO It's eight past.

LIU He isn't asking you the time!

KUO Mr Li, I want you to trust my watch—oh, pardon me—my sincerity. Our aim is simply national salvation.

LÜ We have a comprehensive National Salvation Plan. If we tell you you'll be astounded.

KUO That's enough. You'll only confuse everyone.

LÜ You must do your best to cooperate with us.

KUO Enough, you're just confusing him.

LÜ Don't let the stones and pebbles obstruct us on our way—

KUO That's enough!

LÜ We don't want—

KUO Enough, I said. Mr Li, what do you think of the law and order situation in Taiwan?

LI It's all right.

CH'ÊN Liar.

LI You said it, not me.

KUO As the Bureau Chief, I can tell you proudly—Taiwan holds the world record in solving criminal cases.

CH'ÊN Chief, I think you should tell the truth.

KUO Right. That also means we hold the world record in crime. Now I'm really in a fix. You want to know why? I'm about to retire, so what do I care? I can turn a blind eye to everything and I'll still get my pension—

[LÜ *tries to sneak away.*]

CH'ÊN Kuo-k'ung, where're you going?

LÜ I'm hungry. I'll go get some instant noodles. Anyone for instant noodles?

LIU Me. Vegetarian please.

CH'ÊN Do you think you're the only one who's hungry? Use you head.

KUO You must have died of starvation in your last life! Now where was I?

LIU Anyone for instant noodles?

KUO Did I mention instant noodles?

LI You were saying—'turn a blind eye to everything and I'll still get my pension.'

KUO That's it! Now see how clear-headed Mr Li is. Yes, I can close my eyes to everything and I'll still get my pension. But what about my conscience? Every time I lie down in bed and close my eyes, my bleeper calls: duty calls. I get up, put on my bullet-proof vest, strap on my revolver, get into my car, and off I go. I have to face up to villains carrying Uzi machine guns, assault rifles, and any number of hand grenades. Will I live? Will I die? Only God knows! Men should be able to live without fear, yet we live in fear every day of our lives. What kind of a place is this?

[LÜ *sees a piece of bread on the table.*]

LÜ Bread!

KUO Yes, we live in—'Bread'—what 'Bread'?

LÜ Toasted bread.

KUO Toast your arse. Can't you just shut up? Right! Now we live in fear in this jittery place, this Taiwan! You're an educated man, you're hot-blooded, you're patriotic, can you stand by and refuse to defend your country? Can you allow those villains to destroy our motherland? Can you turn a blind eye to things? That's why we need to think about national salvation! Let me tell you about our plan.

LI Please. . . . The problem is, I'm not what you think I am.

CH'ÊN That doesn't matter.

    LI If I don't matter, what do you want me for?

KUO Of course you matter.

    LI That's right, everyone has his own past—

      [LI, KUO and CH'ÊN all speak at once, their words overlapping.]

      I'll tell you why I killed the woman who lived with me—

CH'ÊN We've got your statement. There's no need for you to go over that—

KUO You've got to have a motive. We—

    LI *[to CH'ÊN]* You shut up.

      [LI, CH'ÊN and KUO are still speaking simultaneously.]

CH'ÊN Let me tell you, we'll build you up—

KUO Our plan is all worked out. You just have to—

    LI No, no, I want to tell you—

KUO *[to CH'ÊN]* Shut up!

      [CH'ÊN shuts up. LI and KUO continue to speak simultaneously.]

      I'll build you up as Taiwan's Number One Cold-blooded Killer.

    LI No! *[To KUO]* Chief, please shut up. I don't give a damn about your Number One. Just listen to me! It's about—the statement! The statement from your branch office is no good. They said they just wanted a 'rough account' because you wanted a 'rough solution'.

CH'ÊN Did I mention the statement?

    LI You just said over there that you had my statement.

CH'ÊN Don't you think I know what I said?

KUO You did mention the statement. I was standing next to you and I heard it clearly.

    LI Chief, since I was brought over here, no one has listened to me. I want to tell you the 'inside story' now. In your branch office where you took my statement—Excuse me, Chief, I must tell you my complaint. In the branch office someone beat me up, and I'm and bruised all over. Look.

KUO Who did it?

    LI Someone tall. *[Pointing at LÜ]* Him.

KUO Idiots! How many times have I told you not to hit or kick the villains during interrogation? Now who gave the order?

LÜ You did, Chief.

KUO Me? Oh, well that makes sense. Mr Li, though he hurt
you, he also sprained his own wrist while beating you.
That makes it even, so let's forget about the incident,
okay? Besides, beating you up has made him hungry
and now he has to buy himself some instant noodles.

LI I don't mind, Chief, really. I—

KUO That's good.

LI The 'statement'. I want to tell you about the
'statement'. When you took my statement you just
wanted to get the thing over with. You didn't care why
I killed the woman who lived with me. That's why I
must tell you now why I killed her. It's like your
National Salvation Plan—no one will ever know about
it, it's an 'inside story'.

LIU Chief, do we make a recording of what he's going to
say?

KUO Yes. All 'inside stories' must be recorded, and must
never be made public.

[LIU presses the RECORD button on the cassette.]

LI Miss Liu, you must make this clear in your 'statement'.
I'll tell you why I killed May. I'm six years older than
her, but age is unimportant. We split up because of—
incompatibility. *[To* CH'ÊN*]* Banal, isn't it? Seems all
lovers in Taiwan split up because of incompatibility.
The 'inside story' is—she cheated on me. She
committed an unforgivable act behind my back. Now
you may not believe me when I tell you that for the
four years we were living together I never touched
her—

[LÜ sniggers.]

I'm telling you the truth! Now where else on this
island would you find a man and a woman together
who can resist tasting the forbidden fruit? I did it. The
word 'Why' is written all over your faces. You can ask
questions.

[CH'ÊN is about to ask a question.]

No need for you to ask. I'll tell you why. Why—why
am I still carrying this chair around? Chief—

KUO I don't have the key.

LIU Chief, here's the—

KUO Release him.

LIU Chief, I don't have—

KUO You don't? So what's the use of getting out a whole bunch of keys? Where's the key? Release him.

LÜ I don't have it.

LI That's all right! Chief, just leave this to me. Now you brought me to this secret interrogation office in a car—where is this place?

CH'ÊN No idea.

LÜ The Trench.

KUO Mind what you say.

LÜ 142 Green Vale, third floor.

KUO Great! You told him the address, and you call this a secret office? Mr Li, please don't mind him. This is not The Trench, and this is certainly not Green Vale!

LI That's all right, I'll get to the truth. When we were in the car, I was blind-folded. Who was sitting in front of me?

KUO I was.

LI Who was driving?

LIU Me.

LI Who was on my left?

CH'ÊN Me.

LI [to CH'ÊN] So you have the key.

LÜ I was on his left.

LI So you have the key!

CH'ÊN I was on the left; you were on the right!

[The two men argue, speaking simultaneously.]

LI Hold it! That's fine, don't worry, I'll solve the case. I remember clearly—the man sitting to my left had a banana in his right pocket. That man has the key!

KUO Now who was it? Let's have it.

LÜ It was me.

KUO Give!

[LÜ takes a banana out of his pocket and hands it to KUO. Unthinkingly KUO tries to remove the handcuff with the banana and then flies into a rage.]

Do you use bananas for keys? Do you unlock your door with a banana? Now where's the key?

LÜ Can't find it.

KUO I'm sorry, Mr Li, but we can't find the key.

LI Never mind. I think you all want to know why I killed May, don't you? Good. I'll tell you the 'inside story'. I became engaged to her two weeks ago, and I regretted it the same night. Why? The question is written all over your faces again.

[CH'ÊN is about to ask.]

You need not ask. I'll tell you. It was because on that very night she went to bed with a stranger. She had premarital sex with him.

[Light change. Back to that night two weeks ago]

SCENE TWO: THE PAST 1

[LI plays himself. All the other characters from Scene 1 play the various parts in the flashback. Change of scene is represented by characters walking through a door frame. MAY enters from the wings pushing a door frame and walks through it.]

LI Why did you go to bed with him?

MAY I was under pressure. You put pressure on me.

LI We had just got engaged and you felt you were under pressure? And going to bed with a total stranger was supposed to take the pressure away?

[CH'ÊN tries to interrupt LI's recollection of the past.]

CH'ÊN She looks older than you.

KUO Shut your big mouth!

LI You thought I didn't care?

MAY Of course you cared. I knew how you felt—I just wanted to see how you'd react.

LI What? You just wanted to see how I'd react? How did you think I'd react? You knew I cared about your virginity, and you went to bed with a man just to see how I'd react! I turned pale, I was dazed, and I threw up—that's how I reacted. I couldn't believe that you'd go to bed with a total stranger. And, as if that wasn't enough, you had to tell me about it! You could have kept it a secret till you died; I wouldn't have known. How dare you tell me about it? If I can't even trust the person sleeping in the same bed with me, who can I trust?

MAY That's the lesson you should learn; that's what I tried to teach you—never trust anyone, not even me.

LI What was your real motive in going to bed with that man?

MAY 'Motive'?—I don't know.

LI You must have had one! Was it money? Was it because you wanted to dump me? Or because he was better looking? Oh, it gives me the creeps! I don't believe that in this day and age a woman dumps a man just because there's someone better looking. What about the man's virtues? I know: it was because you're dissatisfied, because I'm a nobody in Taiwan with no prospects; because you're dissatisfied with the air pollution, with the traffic congestion, with the political movements—

MAY What's that got to do with our relationship?

LI You're dissatisfied with this country, aren't you? You must have a motive! How am I to know if you don't tell me? *[To the others]* No, she never told me her real motive for betraying me. That night she sat at the window, and I stood at the kitchen door staring at her. It was stalemate for nine hours. We didn't speak—not one word. I looked at her; she looked at the moon; the moon looked at the two of us. At this point, I suddenly saw a picture in my mind: the twenty million people in Taiwan were all gone, leaving just the two of us on this little island. I felt I had been fooled—

[LI suddenly pulls out LÜ's gun.]

LI I thought, if I had a gun, I'd just pull the trigger and do away with her.

[LI points the gun at MAY and pulls the trigger.]

But then I'd never get to know her real motive for betraying me.

[LI returns the gun to LÜ, who is completely engrossed in LI's story. CH'ÊN tries to break through the time and space barrier by questioning MAY direct.]

CH'ÊN *[to MAY]* He wants to know your motive.

MAY *[slaps CH'ÊN]* Mind your own bloody business!

MAY, LI *[together]* I'd never get to know her real motive for betraying me, so I ran away from home.

CH'ÊN Li Hsi-chieh, where are you going?

LI To the toilet. I need a break.

CH'ÊN You're not going to run away, are you?

LI Have you seen a prisoner running away carrying a chair?

CH'ÊN Your shoelaces, hand them over.

LI I can't hang myself on a pair of shoelaces! *[Exits]*

[MAY takes up LI's first-person narration and continues with the story.]

MAY I needed to go somewhere to calm down, to think about what happened to May and myself. But in my mind I could see the face of that stranger May went to bed with.

[Light change. LÜ *comes in through the door, playing the part of* PROFESSOR.*]*

He was cultured, and he was learned. Maybe he was a university professor; there was nothing evil about him. They talked about many things, like the history of China, five thousand years of Chinese culture, the Chinese political system, Taiwan's ethnic history, its 100-year history as a colony, and the future development on both sides of the Taiwan Straits. May was probably fascinated by his wide knowledge. For the four years we had been living together, this was the one thing we never talked about—politics. We didn't talk politics, we didn't care about politics. And then that man asked her earnestly—

PROFESSOR Tell me honestly—you're not wearing a bra, are you?

CH'ÊN He asked her whether she was wearing a bra?

KUO What's so funny about that? Listen to Li.

MAY May's mouth curled up in a smile. She looked lascivious; they both looked lascivious. And then—

PROFESSOR May and I went to—the desk. I didn't want to do it in the bedroom. I was afraid my wife would find that the bed sheets were—untidy. No, to tell you the truth, my wife was asleep in the bedroom. But that didn't matter. She has a tumour on the right side of her brain which presses on the nerves of her right ear, which makes her a bit deaf. I don't think she heard us.

[MAY reverts to playing her own role.]

MAY He had his hand on my mouth, to make sure I didn't make any noise. In fact I didn't even know a woman was supposed to make any noise doing it.

PROFESSOR I changed my moaning to coughing, just in case. *[Coughs]*

MAY Something wrong with your throat?

PROFESSOR Seems blocked.

MAY Liar.

PROFESSOR Hush!

MAY At that moment I suddenly felt that sex was just like politics—full of lies, mutual deception, short-lived passion and irresponsible desires.

[MAY exits.]

PROFESSOR *[monologue]* I watched May leave my study with a touch of regret: she didn't even tell me her real name. I thought I'd never see her again. This would be our secret for the rest of our lives.

[Light change. LIU comes in through the door frame, playing the part of PROFESSOR'S WIFE.]

PROFESSOR'S WIFE *[monologue]* I, too, knew that secret. I knew about it when I was lying in bed, but I had to pretend not to know. I couldn't expose him, perhaps because he's my husband? Besides, he's going to be promoted soon. If I made a fuss, that would be the end of us in Taiwan.

PROFESSOR Haven't you gone to bed yet?

PROFESSOR'S WIFE Don't you think this cheongsam is a good fit?

PROFESSOR Mm, it looks nice. I'm off to bed. *[To himself]* Imagine trying on a cheongsam at four in the morning! *[Exits]*

PROFESSOR'S WIFE Great. I hurt like hell, and he didn't even notice.

[Light change. PROFESSOR'S WIFE walks in through the door frame. It is earlier that night.]

That night I went to a disco on my own. It meant nothing—I just needed to let myself go.

[Glaring lights of the disco. PROFESSOR'S WIFE dances with wild abandon. KUO, assuming the role of STRANGER A, walks through the door frame and enters PROFESSOR'S WIFE's past.]

STRANGER A *[monologue]* I sat in a corner watching this woman dancing hysterically. I knew she had a heavy heart, her melancholic eyes gave away her secret. I decided to go and chat her up. I have a way with women like her.

PROFESSOR'S WIFE I noticed the man coming towards me.

STRANGER A I think she still hasn't noticed me.

PROFESSOR'S WIFE One word was plainly written in his eyes: lust!

STRANGER A She'll never believe how good I am in bed.

PROFESSOR'S WIFE Let's face this with courage—come, I'm ready for all that you have to inflict on me.

STRANGER A Looking at her face, I became totally irrational.

PROFESSOR'S WIFE I lit the flame of desire in his heart.

STRANGER A I want this woman, but I must play it right.

PROFESSOR'S WIFE He opened his mouth and said—the most ridiculous thing!

STRANGER A Do you think we'll have a really clean general election at year end?

PROFESSOR'S WIFE Ha—*[Slaps the man in the face and exits]*

STRANGER A *[monologue]* After the woman left, I could only think of one thing: serves me right! There are just too many louts like me in Taiwan. It is only right that I have to go through this humiliation. But if it happens over and over again, who can take it? I can't! Really. Sometimes I want to kill myself. What's the point of living? So I went to Hsinying and bought a police revolver. I took the gun to a deserted dark alley and pointed it at myself—*[Points his gun at his head and makes to pull the trigger, then falls to the ground]*

[CH'ÊN, playing STRANGER B, enters through the door frame and helps STRANGER A up.]

STRANGER B Hey! Are you all right, mister?

STRANGER A *[monologue]* I didn't even have the courage to pull the trigger.

STRANGER B Mister, are you all right?

STRANGER A Push off! What's the matter with you? Can't I trip over? *[Drops his gun on the ground and exits]*

STRANGER B Hey, you dropped your gun! *[Picks up the gun]* A gun! Who'd have thought that you could pick up a gun in Taiwan just like that.

[Light change]

[monologue] It aroused all sorts of ideas in me. I wanted to take it to the police station—a most foolish idea! I could carry it with me while I went about my business negotiations; I could use it for blackmail and get millions of dollars. No! I'd use it to kill the person I hated most in my life—

[MAY walks through the door frame and assumes the part of STRANGER B'S WIFE.]

STRANGER B'S WIFE Don't you have any idea what time it is, still playing with that gun!

STRANGER B I'm polishing it—use your eyes. Now, you keep it safe for me.

STRANGER B'S WIFE Polish your arse! See if the police don't arrest you!

STRANGER B How will they know if you don't report it?

STRANGER B'S WIFE Do I have to? All your friends know you've got this gun. Show off! I bet you get arrested sooner or later.

STRANGER B You'd really like that, wouldn't you?

STRANGER B'S WIFE Sure I would. So what? A lout like you should have been locked up long ago.

STRANGER B Good, go on and shout. Do you want the whole
    neighbourhood to know I've got a gun—damn you!

STRANGER B'S WIFE Listen, everyone! My husband has a gun. Arrest him!

STRANGER B Arrest me, eh? Try shouting louder, and see if I don't
    kill you.

STRANGER B'S WIFE Oh I bet you would. Just show me!

STRANGER B You think I don't dare?

STRANGER B'S WIFE *[suddenly afraid]* Help, help! Wait! A-tsung is going to
    kill me with his gun!

STRANGER B Shut up. Damn you! I'll kill you!

STRANGER B'S WIFE Help! Murder! Help! *[Exits]*

> *[End of Scene 2. Gradual transition to Scene 3.*
> LÜ *enters.]*

LÜ Stop—don't shoot!

STRANGER B You're dead! *[Shoots him]*

> *[Light change]*

S C E N E   T H R E E :   P E R S U A S I O N   2

[Secret Interrogation Office.
  The door frame stands in one corner. KUO, LIU, *and* CH'ÊN *are standing
around.* LÜ, *in slow motion, lies on the floor, dying.]*

KUO *[to* CH'ÊN*]* Hey, buddy, what're you doing?

CH'ÊN I'm checking my gun for rust spots. *[To* LÜ*]* What're
    you doing there, Lü?

LÜ *[returns to normal]* I'm trying to figure out how to die
    gracefully if I get hit.

CH'ÊN Oh, quit it, will you! Where's Li Hsi-chieh?

> *[*LI *walks on to stage still handcuffed to the chair.]*

LI I'm here!

CH'ÊN Come, come and sit over here.

LI Never mind. I've got my own chair.

CH'ÊN Li Hsi-chieh, I'm really sorry. You told us a long story
    just now, but I didn't understand anything. There was
    no focus—you rambled on about the woman who lived
    with you, May, and then it was some professor, and
    then his wife, and then she met a lousy bum, and the
    bum met a stranger, and the stranger picked up a gun
    and tried to kill his wife . . . You jumped from one
    thing to another. What exactly were you getting at?

LI I was telling you about my past. I talked about May, so I had to tell you her background, and so I had to mention the professor who went to bed with her, and then of course I had to mention his wife—they just followed one after the other. That's the connection. What I mean is, who in Taiwan isn't connected to everyone else? We're all known to everyone. We're all interconnected! I just wanted to tell you more about myself. Do you think you'd do it differently if you talked about your past? Have you got no painful memories?

CH'ÊN Well . . . true . . . I didn't really get along with my wife. I remember it was at 4 p.m. on the 8th of August last year—

LÜ Hey, buddy, who's asking you? he's our man!

KUO Time is precious, let's get to the point. Mr Li, you were perfectly right about this connection business. Now I'll try to connect you to the disappearance of the Japanese woman Matzu Hanako. A Japanese woman has disappeared. You've got to connect this with: How many women disappear in Taiwan every year? How many men disappear every year? I've memorized all these figures. In 1989 the number of missing persons reported was—

LIU 3,990.

KUO Correct. In 1990 the number was—

LIU 2,304.

KUO Correct. In 1991 the number went up to over four thousand.

LIU The final figure hasn't been tabulated yet.

KUO If that's the case, the number must be even higher. In 1992 the number of missing persons already amounts to over six thousand.

LIU Chief, they're still counting.

KUO Still counting—I'm sure it's much more than previous years.

LI Chief, it seems that she's got a much better head for figures. Why don't you let her carry on?

KUO She's got a better head for figures . . . All right, you carry on.

LIU Yes, sir. Now who is responsible for these disappearances? Where have all the missing persons gone? Are they alive?

[LI *removes his handcuffs and walks away from the chair.*]

CH'ÊN Jên-shan, what's going on?

LIU What?

CH'ÊN Who took his handcuffs off?

LI I did—with the key.

LÜ *[pulls his gun]* Li Hsi-chieh, making a break for it again, huh? Raise your hands and stand over there! You've made three attempts already, isn't that enough?

KUO All right, you go and stand over there. Mr Li, how come you had the key?

LI I picked it up over there.

KUO How come the key was lying there?

LÜ Who dropped that key? Come on, own up. Now after we brought him in here, you interrogated him over here, and I was standing there to see if I could make the case more—Chief, I dropped that key.

KUO Easy, easy! Tell me, is there anything you will not drop?

LÜ I won't drop my gun. *[Drops his gun]*

KUO See? Now, Jên-shan, please carry on.

[LÜ sheepishly picks up his gun.]

LIU Right. I'll tell you a simple truth: our Chief's daughter has been missing for two years now. Even he has no idea where to find her. So you see—

LI Your daughter has gone missing, Chief?

KUO Not exactly. I haven't had the time to look for her. I've been too busy. It's not unusual for me to be kept away from home for two to three months at a stretch.

CH'ÊN I can fill you in on this incident. Two years ago, we were gambling at the Chief's place.

KUO Not gambling! Just playing mahjong.

CH'ÊN Not exactly gambling, but we had four mahjong tables going that day.

KUO Two tables. The others were eating.

LÜ I can testify to that. I was having congee at the table next to yours.

KUO Congee your arse! We were eating noodles!

LÜ Sorry, Chief, I got mixed up. Congee was another time, when we were sharing out the spoils in Ch'ên's place—

CH'ÊN Sharing out the toys.

LÜ Spoils.

CH'ÊN Toys.

LÜ Toys.

CH'ÊN Spoils! Be careful what you say.

LÜ Right! Ch'ên's right. That day KTV brought us NT200,000, the Chief took NT80,000, I took NT50,000, and Ch'ên took the rest.

KUO Now that's enough. That's not important.

LÜ No, Chief.

KUO Enough, I said. That's not important.

LI Chief, I think I have a fairly good grasp of such things. You really don't have to bring that up.

KUO But we must! I want you to understand my character.

CH'ÊN Allow me, allow me—

KUO I'll speak. You'll simply give everything away.

LÜ Ha ha ha!

KUO What's so funny? You're just the same. Mr Li, I must begin by telling you about my ex-wife. That day two years ago, my wife brought some friends home to play mahjong.

[CH'ÊN moves a chair over, indicating that LI should sit down. LI sits.]

CH'ÊN That day there were about sixteen or seventeen of them playing mahjong.

KUO Come off it! Not sixteen or seventeen, just six or seven of them playing mahjong. I was looking over my wife's shoulder at her hand. She was playing with Mrs Chang, Auntie Wang, and Miss Ch'ên. Now one of them discarded an '80K' and my ex mistook it for a '60K' and said she had won. The others didn't notice anything amiss . . .

CH'ÊN Chief, it wasn't a '60K', it was a '2 Strokes'.

KUO Right, '2 Strokes'. No, that was before. Anyway, she said she won with the '60K'. I was standing behind her, and I said: 'That's a sham. It won't do.' The other three at the table promptly applauded, saying I was fair and square. Oh my! It was joy to the world. They said whether they won or lost, they'd treat me to a midnight snack. Wasn't I thrilled! And when I turned around, my wife was gone! I said it was a sham, she got annoyed, walked out, and never came back!

LIU That's right. That night, Chief cried his eyes out at home. I'd never seen him cry like that before.

KUO I didn't cry.

LIU Yes, you did. Your face and nose were all red from crying. I felt so sorry for you.

KUO It was just the flu.

LIU No, it was because your wife walked out on you.

KUO Hey, you weren't there. How do you know?

LIU Ch'ên told me!

CH'ÊN No, I didn't. Chief, honestly I didn't.

LIU Yes he did. He told me!

LÜ It was me. I told her. Ch'ên told me, and I told you: the Chief cried like—

KUO Shut your big mouth! Whose side are you on, snitching on me like that? Mr Li, I didn't cry. I'm the Chief, how could I cry? Besides, what's the use of crying? Stand over there, all of you! Mr Li, I'm sure you understand.

LI Of course I do.

KUO I'm a police officer; I've got to uphold the law. It's true that gamblers cheat, but I couldn't allow anyone to cheat in my house, right?

LI Right.

KUO As for my daughter, my ex-wife didn't bring her up properly.

LI Right, her fault.

KUO Law and order is in a mess. That's what I'm responsible for.

LI Right, you're responsible.

KUO She was in charge of the house, in charge of the daughter. Now if the daughter turns out badly, is it my fault?

LI Right, your fault!

KUO No! Not my fault! I'm just responsible for law and order.

[The two speak simultaneously.]

I'll tell you why my daughter disappeared. It was 4 p.m. on the 8th of August last year—

LI No, Chief. None of you care about me. Let me tell you. I felt terrible after I killed May—

LÜ Li Hsi-chieh, how dare you interrupt the Chief when he's telling you about his past!

[LÜ stops LI and indicates that KUO can continue.]

KUO All right! I'll say no more. No one is to talk about the past. Mr Li, it is our intention to make you the number one murderer in Taiwan history.

LI That's a sudden turn in the conversation.

KUO Now listen carefully. We're going to build you up as a super-cool killer. You kill without mercy; you're also a kidnapper, a blackmailer, a bandit, a robber, and a slave trader; you smuggle guns, you own brothels and gambling dens, you have committed every crime under the sun; you have broken the crime record of the whole of Taiwan. You have the blood of three hundred people on you hands.

LI Three hundred?

LÜ *[moving a chair over]* Have a seat, Chief.

KUO Stay out of this!

LI Chief, there's a seat.

KUO Oh, is there? All right. *[KUO sits down.]* In our jargon this is 'ordering from the menu'. Whenever a suspect admits to one murder, before his execution we just ask him to choose a few more murders we can't solve. Now why don't you 'order from the menu' and pick three hundred cases?

LI Who'd believe that I could kill so many people?

CH'ÊN We would.

KUO That's right.

CH'ÊN You will be billed as an international murderer. You planned to assassinate the political leaders of a number of countries because you were unhappy about the international situation. But we found your assassination plan.

LI Have you gone out of your mind?

CH'ÊN No, you've gone out of your mind! You are a fanatic, you are a madman, you fantasize every day—

LI No, I don't.

CH'ÊN We say you do! Oh, no, he won't agree.

LI No, it's not that, but I don't know what you expect of me!

KUO Take it easy. We'll explain everything to you. It's a massive plan—but simple in execution. Mr Li, do you still want to die?

LI I do.

KUO Are you absolutely sure?

LI Yes.

KUO Good! Let me tell you, all you have to do is fall in with our plan. We—

LI Chief, let me tell you. That day after I killed May I saw the bathroom full of blood, I—

KUO Mr Li, listen to me. I'm now on a crucial point. Now listen, you—

LÜ Banana, anyone?

KUO Mr Li, would you like a banana? *[To LÜ]* Shut up! Behave yourself or else! You must get to know the plan as well as I do. Mr Li, well, politics and the economy are Taiwan's lifelines. *[Forgets the crucial point he was talking about]* Twenty years ago, the Japanese bought their bananas from us, now they go to South-East Asia, to Thailand, to Malaysia for their bananas. We must ask ourselves—what has gone wrong with our bananas?

LI Chief, Chief! I'm beginning to be interested in your plan, but I honestly don't know what you're talking about.

KUO It's bananas! *[To LÜ]* Sod off, you're mucking things up again—Now where was I?

LIU The crucial point—

KUO Crucial point? Why yes! The crucial point is: we want you to admit to the murder of Matzu Hanako.

LI Is that your plan? Then you've got it wrong right from the start. You want me to say I killed this Matzu Hanako. Now what does she look like? I don't know. Where did I kill her? I don't know. All right, even if I did kill her, where is the body?

KUO Where is the body? Let me tell you—it's the woman who lived with you; it's May!

LI I can see the devil in your eyes! May indeed! Why don't you use your head a little. May is May, Matzu Hanako is Matzu Hanako, they're two different people. When Matzu Hanako's parents come from Japan to identify the body, they'll know at once.

CH'ÊN Li Hsi-chieh, you can leave it to us. When they come to Taiwan, whose word will they take—yours, or the coroner's? You can plead guilty now, and a year later we'll announce that the case is solved. By then there won't be any body, just a skeleton. Do you think they'll be able to recognize that?

LI A skeleton? Oh please! Haven't you ever had a death in the family? The flesh of a dead body rots away underground, true, but what about the clothes? They were wearing different clothes!

LÜ We have a set of clothes identical to the ones Matzu Hanako was wearing when she died. *[LIU takes the clothes out.]* Her clothes, her knapsack, her hat—all these are evidence discarded by you.

LI So, you set a trap!

KUO What trap! Please don't make it sound so awful. Our aim is simple. We want to solve the case, to satisfy the Japanese, and to salvage our national dignity. Mr Li, what happened between you and Matzu Hanako was very simple. Now how should we put it? *[Pointing at* LIU*]* Suppose she is Matzu Hanako. Let me tell you what happened. You raped her, then murdered her by burying her alive. Then we'll satisfy your death wish by sending you to court. The judge will find you guilty and sentence you to death. You'll get a last bottle of wine and your last delicious marinated egg, and bang—you're gone. Now isn't that a proud death?

LI I . . . I don't look like a murderer.

LÜ You look exactly like one. No need for make-up.

LI I don't have a criminal record.

CH'ÊN Is there a rule saying only people with a criminal record can kill?

LI I . . . I suffer from a defect, a physical defect—

KUO What's that?

LI I suffer from piles.

KUO Excellent defect! Because of your piles you have a bad temper, and with a bad temper you lose control of yourself easily. No one dares come near you. If they do, you kill them. Because of this defect of yours, you become a merciless killer—you killed three hundred people.

LI Isn't that stretching it too far?

LÜ I think it's a bit far-fetched too.

KUO Come on, what's so far-fetched?

LÜ Killing three hundred people because of piles?

KUO Shut up! Where's your argument? You suffer from piles too, who's to say you won't kill someone? Moaning in the toilet every day!

LI Chief, may I ask a question? *[Indicating* LÜ*]* That man, is he on your staff?

KUO That's right. Don't worry. Sometimes he's not all there—his mind wanders a bit—sometimes a screw gets loose. But I give you my word: he's a loyal officer. Now how about it? Are you going to cooperate with us?

LI To tell you the truth, I'm not quite prepared for this.

CH'ÊN Shit! We've wasted hours on you and you're still unconvinced?

LI It's not a matter of being convinced. Chief, please sit down. To tell you the truth, I have a strange feeling that the four of you are salesmen, trying hard to sell me a product. But you don't tell me how to use it. And when I take the product in my hands I discover it's a bomb! Do you know what I mean, Chief?

KUO No, I don't.

LI That doesn't matter, just bear with me. I don't know whether I've got it right, but my feeling is that you have this company, and you are inviting me to become a shareholder.

CH'ÊN Precisely! It is our purpose to form a company, and the name of that company is National Salvation Corporation Ltd.

LÜ What do you think of the name?

LI Sounds foreign.

LÜ Ha! Exactly what I thought.

KUO Enough! Shut your big mouth! This is my decision. The whole plan hinges on your admitting to the murder of Matzu Hanako. So, to tally with the case in hand, and to fit in with the trend for internationalization, the name should sound foreign.

LI Excuse me, Chief, are you a native Taiwanese? I suppose everyone in this room is native Taiwan. Now as Taiwanese we've got to have our dignity. What do you want that kind of a company name for, to suck up to the Japs?

CH'ÊN Bullshit! Let me ask you, what's the brand name of your thermos at home?

LI Tiger.

CH'ÊN Your TV?

LI Sony.

CH'ÊN Your video?

LI Toshiba.

CH'ÊN Your motorbike?

LI Kawasaki.

CH'ÊN Chief, what car do you drive?

KUO Toyota.

CH'ÊN What car do I drive?

KUO Honda.

CH'ÊN What brand are your underpants?

LÜ Komizi! *[Everyone looks embarrassed.]*

CH'ÊN What bed do you sleep in?

LIU *Wasabi.*

CH'ÊN, KUO *[simultaneously] Tatami!*

CH'ÊN What's so different between living in Taiwan and living in Japan? Why all the fuss about sucking up to the Japs then?

KUO Mr Li, think this through carefully. Everything hangs on your decision.

LI Well, it's a tough decision. I know I want to die; I know I want to be famous before I die. And I know it's easy to be famous in Taiwan. But it never occurred to me to die the way you want me to.

LIU Whatever way you die, you die anyway. Since that's the case, why not make sure people will remember you? We'll build you a memorial; we'll build you a statue.

CH'ÊN That's right. We're great at setting up memorials and statues.

LI No, no, I don't want them. Don't you remember, Chief? A few years back Chiang Kai-shek's statues were all over the place—standing in the main streets and at roundabouts. And then they were all demolished.

KUO That was done to ease the traffic.

LI That's why I don't want statues. I don't think—

KUO All right, enough has been said. Now I want to concentrate on the essentials. What do you say, are you willing to be billed as a murderer?

LI Is there enough time?

LIU We can begin at once. It's never too late.

LI This is not a matter that can be settled in a few days.

LÜ If you don't do it now, you'll regret it forever.

LI I have my doubts.

CH'ÊN No more doubts. We love our country!

LI I'm struggling with myself.

KUO No more struggles. We must save our country!

LI I have to think about it.

LIU No more thinking. We need you!

LI I assume—

LÜ Do not assume, just agree!

[A moment's silence]

LI All right, I'll do it.

ALL Hurrah!

LIU Li Hsi-chieh, come over here and look at our National Salvation Manifesto.

LI A manifesto. So you had it all worked out.

KUO I'll leave the rest to you fellers.

LI Chief, wait! I'm from a good family; I care about my image. In Taiwan these days, all big enterprises are building their own CIS.* May I know if our company has a logo?

LÜ Oh dear, we forgot about that. Chief, what shall we do without a logo?

KUO Logo your arse! . . . On second thoughts, maybe we'll have to think about that.

[The logo for the National Salvation Corporation Ltd. is lowered on to the stage.]

LI There's another thing. I'm a law-abiding citizen, so I must ask you: have we registered with the Ministry for Home Affairs?

CH'ÊN We can't do that. We must follow the old example of the wartime anti-Japanese organizations, we must operate underground.

KUO He's right, but let's not discuss this anymore. Colleagues, allow me to make this important announcement: On this the tenth hour of the tenth day of the tenth month, 1992, we are formally incorporated.

ALL The National Salvation Corporation Limited!

LÜ You mean that's it?

[Lights dim.]

TV NEWS 2

*[150″ TV Screen lowered on to the stage.
PTV News Channel comes on screen.*

A picture card with the words 'Special News Bulletin' appears on screen. The anchorman appears.]

ANCHOR This is a Special News Bulletin. A week after the disappearance of Matzu Hanako of the Mitsubi-bi— *[yawns mightily]* shit!—car company, the authorities have arrested a suspect—Li Hsi-chieh. Li is a thirty-eight-year old native of Hsinchu, and he is single. He has one son and one daughter. The boy is eight and is a

* Corporate Identification System.

student at West Gate Primary School. The girl is one year old. At the moment she is in labour in Chung Shan Hospital . . . According to paediatrician Dr Ch'ên—Sorry, the wrong item!—*[Someone hands him the correct news item in front of the camera.]* Li Hsi-chieh is a thirty-eight-year old bachelor. As a result of the investigation, Li admitted to the killing of Matzu Hanako. Li has no criminal record, but he has admitted to the murder of three hundred people in Taiwan. It seems that the authorities have stumbled on this psychopathic killer quite by accident. The following is an exclusive interview with Li's parents.

[The screen shows LI's *mother weeping while his father talks to the camera.]*

FATHER *[with a Shandong accent]* That's impossible! They must've got the wrong man. I know my son. He comes home for dinner every night. He wouldn't have the time to kill anyone. *[To* MOTHER*]* Stop crying! Like I said, his mother and me are not even divorced; we have a happy family; we don't lack money—Stop crying!—Like I said, you've got the wrong man. My son may have the courage to kill a chicken, but he wouldn't dare kill a man. And you say he's killed three hundred! You must be crazy! You jerks just grab anyone you like—Stop crying—say something!

MOTHER *[in a Cantonese accent]* He did it! He did it!

FATHER What are you saying?

MOTHER I'll take the blame for what my son did.

FATHER Stop this nonsense! That's not true. My son didn't kill anyone. Enough, I tell you. Don't use any more tissue paper, it costs money. Look, we have no money, we are so poor—how would he kill anyone? You've got it wrong! Stop crying! I never curse—Bloody fool! Stop crying!

[The screen shows news studio shot.]

ANCHOR The suspect Li Hsi-chieh is being held at the Secret Interrogation Office for questioning. It is expected that the authorities will announce the successful closing of the case in a few days. What is intriguing is Li's 'motive' for killing the Japanese woman. Now let's turn our attention to the weather, after which we shall introduce you to some exciting commercials—*[Realizes he is talking nonsense]* Damn!

[TV screen is lifted.]

SCENE FOUR: MOTIVE 1

[Secret Interrogation Office.
Lights on. All characters are on stage.]

KUO I was on a study visit at the Yokohama Police Force
fifteen years ago, when they were investigating a case.
Now what case was that? A young Korean man raped
and killed a Japanese girl in Yokohama Harbour, but
he stubbornly refused to plead guilty. Why? He said:
'During the Second World War, the Japanese invaded
Korea and attempted to assimilate and wipe out the
Korean race.' He killed for revenge, and also for the
recovery of his national dignity. He told the judge in
court: 'I'm not guilty! You Japs had it coming to you!'
Now, repeat what I said.

LI I can't remember so much. I'll just repeat the last
bit—'I'm not guilty! You Japs had it coming to you!'

LIU That's your motive for killing Matzu Hanako.

LI Bit far-fetched! The Japanese and the Koreans have
been feuding for centuries.

KUO So have we. Remember our eight-year war against
Japan? Didn't you enlist?

LI No, not me. I was born in Taiwan.

KUO Born in Taiwan, eh? Well, that doesn't matter. I'll find
you a motive, and it's got to be righteous.

CH'ÊN I've got it, Chief. *[To LI]* Li, do you remember the
bank robber Li Shih-k'ê? This was what he said in the
courtroom: 'I didn't do no wrong. I took the country's
money, money that the country owes me!'

LI Li Shih-k'ê is from Shandong, isn't he?

CH'ÊN You're right, he's from Shandong.

LI But your accent wasn't right.

CH'ÊN How should I say it, you show me!

LI 'Ah didn't do no wrong. Ah took the country's money,
money that the country owes me!'

KUO Perfect! You had the right accent and the right voice!

LÜ And you sounded so righteous!

KUO Righteous your arse! This is not the right motive! It's
only the perverse act of a perverse individual. We are
patriots, we want to save our country, we can't do this!
Wait a minute—I've got it! Now you do as I tell you.
You have now been taken to the courtroom by the

guards, and you're going up to the witness box. Come on, go up to the box. And then—now this is the courtroom, you should all take up your roles as the judge, the portrait and the national flag. It's a law court, we must have the right atmosphere to make what we say sound authentic.

[The investigators follow their Chief's instructions and create a courtroom atmosphere. CH'ÊN *plays the judge,* LIU *carries a portrait of Sun Yatsen,* LÜ *unfolds a national flag; each occupies a corner of the stage.]*

You walk up to the box. The judge will ask you a last question—

CH'ÊN *[as judge]* 'What are your last words?'

[LI is speechless.]

KUO Hey, how can you look so depressed? You must show your courage; you must show your conviction! When you stand on that box you must look the judge in the eye and say to him: 'Although I am guilty of numerous crimes, although I killed three hundred innocent people, I killed one person justly. Why did I kill that Japanese woman? I did it as an act of defiance against Japanese colonial oppression of the people of Taiwan. I did it to avenge the Taiwanese comfort-women forced into prostitution in Japanese military camps. I did it for national pride, for national justice, for national integrity.' And finally you'll say to the judge: 'Fellow Taiwanese, you must show your dignity. The Taiwan people have stood up!'

[Applause]

Don't applaud! Stop applauding, judge. You too, national flag; and you, portrait. Mr Li, please repeat what I just said.

LI I can't remember all that. I'll just summarize. 'Your Honour, I must admit that though I killed one innocent person, I killed three hundred justly!'

KUO You're all mixed up! You killed three hundred innocent people, but you killed one justly!

LI That won't do. According to you people I'm in the triads, but I'm a good guy. I bump off the bad guys to rid society of their evil. Isn't that so?

LÜ Chief, he's got a point.

KUO Point your arse! You're just a national flag! That's not the point. The important thing is: why did you kill the Japanese woman?

LI You're right. Why did I do it?

KUO Right, let's see.

LI 'Your Honour, why did I kill that Japanese woman?'

KUO Why?

LI 'Because . . . because of the comfort-women.'

KUO That's it! He's got it!

LI 'The poor comfort-women! The Taiwanese comfort-women are so . . . em . . . so few that they dare not stand up and ask for justice from the Japanese.'

KUO He's got it, he's got it! We're saved!

LI 'Your Honour, why did I kill that Japanese woman?'

KUO Why?

LI Right. 'Because . . . because . . .' Because of what?

LIU Chief, it's hopeless!

CH'ÊN That's it, Chief! He's just not up to it!

KUO Relax. It may take a long time to straighten someone out, but to corrupt someone is a piece of cake. Let's be patient: everything is going to work out fine. Mr Li, can you pay a bit more attention to me? If you don't hear me clearly, you can always ask me to repeat. Why don't you pay attention? I'm not young anymore, you could be the death of me.

LI I don't mean to, Chief. It's just that things are going too fast. Trust me, I'm also a good organizer and I deserve some respect. I'm sorry to say that I think your plan is flawed. You can't have me on the stand from the start saying all those righteous things to the judge. What about the chronology of things? Chief, I have no idea how I met her, how I raped her, and how I killed her. Shouldn't these come first?

KUO First things first, eh? Let me tell you, we have taken care of all your worries. Come on, show Mr Li the scenario I devised two days ago.

[Following the Chief's instruction, everyone pitches in to create the right atmosphere.]

LÜ I'll get the backcloth.

KUO Now, this solves your problem, doesn't it?

LI Yes, I'll understand if you act the whole thing out for me.

LÜ Chief, it took me three days to paint this set.

KUO Not a bad job.

[LÜ and KUO roll out the backcloth which depicts An Ping Fortress. CH'ÊN plays LI; LIU plays MATZU HANAKO.]

CH'ÊN She plays Matzu Hanako, and the Chief wants me to play you.

KUO The time is 4:45 p.m. on 2 April this year. You meet for the first time outside An Ping Fortress in Tainan.

LI You mean I'm going to rape her in broad daylight?

CH'ÊN Only dogs do it regardless of time and place. Are you a dog?

LI Chief, he—

KUO I said you met for the first time outside An Ping Fortress. Just relax! We know how the whole thing started much better than you do. The rape comes afterwards. Jên-shan, carry on.

LIU 'Mister, are you from Tainan?'

CH'ÊN 'No, I'm from Laiyang in Shandong Province.'

LI That's wrong. I'm from Hsinchu in Taiwan.

CH'ÊN But your ancestors are from Shandong.

LI Well, my ID card says I'm from Hsinchu.

CH'ÊN Who changed that?

LI The Interior Ministry. Starting from 1 July this year they base their records on your place of birth, so I'm from Hsinchu.

CH'ÊN All right, all right, from Hsinchu.

KUO Come on, let's get on with it.

LIU 'Please can you tell me how many historical sites like An Ping you have?'

CH'ÊN 'There's just one An Ping Fortress. Which one do you want?'

LI Mr Ch'ên, may I know your family name?

CH'ÊN Nonsense! It's Ch'ên, of course!

LI Well, you were talking nonsense, too. 'There's just one An Ping Fortress. Which one do you want?' Absolute nonsense! Chief, you can't have him play me. His IQ is just too low.

CH'ÊN Murderers are stupid anyway.

LI A stupid murderer taking three hundred lives?

CH'ÊN Do you really think you could kill so many people?

LI Now, you tell me, who was the first person I killed? Did I use a knife or a gun? And where did I hide the body?

CH'ÊN That's all made up. The important thing now is to get on with the play.

LI Well, Chief, you see, you've picked the wrong man. You should have asked him to be the murderer.

CH'ÊN Ha! He's trying to wriggle out even before the show starts.

KUO What do you think you're doing? No more squabbles! Let's get on with it in peace.

LI You people just take me for a kitten when I don't roar.

KUO That's it! You have a murderer's temper. Come, kill him with the gun. *[Pointing at* CH'ÊN*]*

LI Chief, it's much better for me to play myself. If you have someone completely unlike me playing me, I'll have to adjust myself to him, and I'm sure as soon as I open my mouth in court I'd give the game away. It may not affect you if the thing is blown, but my reputation will be ruined. Who's going to take the blame except me?

LÜ There's something in what you say. As an outsider I could perhaps be allowed a fair comment—

LI Just a minute. When did you become an outsider?

LÜ Well, a spectator then; a spectator who has a perspective. You're right to say that you should play yourself. We just need to have a supervisory role.

LI That's right! Chief, yours is only a supervisory role. Now at last someone is being fair.

LÜ To be on the safe side, please follow the script. *[Hands* LI *the script]*

LI You have to play by the script for this kind of thing? I'm older than you. I know Taiwan better than you do. This kind of thing is simple. She plays her, and I play myself. She asks questions, and I answer them. That's all there is to it.

KUO Exactly! You really are a clever devil! The whole thing is made up, of course, but we've got to make it look real. Now, Jên-shan, you're still Matzu Hanako. You just ask the questions and he'll answer. *[To* LÜ*]* Throw away the script!

LIU All right. Shall I just ask any question?

LI Anything you like.

LIU 'Mister, I've been—'

LI Just a minute. What's he doing standing there?

CH'ÊN I'm a cop, plain clothes.

LI So I was followed the first time I met this Japanese woman?

CH'ÊN We've got lots of leads. Besides, you have a record.

LI I have a record, eh? It said on the TV news that I have no record—I've killed 301 people, and I have no record. My goodness! Your plan is full of contradictions. Honestly, this is too much! I quit.

CH'ÊN Look at him. He's the star now. Are we to dance attendance on him?

KUO Shut your big mouth. You've turned all the vital points into flaws, so stop wagging your tongue, and go back to playing the Fortress. Mr Li, TV news is just media report, they read out whatever we supply them with. To put it bluntly, we control the media. You're a fabricated murderer, and they get fabricated news. Two wrongs make one right, so fabrications turn real. The important point is: the news satisfies the public.

LI I'm sorry, Chief. I apologize to you all for shaking your faith in me.

CH'ÊN Do your best then!

LI I can't. I don't have confidence in myself now. I will follow your plan.

KUO You will? That's good. Hurry up then. You met outside of An Ping Fortress for the first time. How come you're still at the Fortress? It's a long play, hurry up!

LIU 'I've been to Taiwan several times now. There don't seem to be that many historical sites around.'

LI 'You're wrong there. We have a large number of them.'

LIU 'I've been to Lung Shan Temple and Lin's Garden. What else is there?'

LI 'Well . . . there's . . . a lot. Many of our old houses are listed as Grade I and Grade II buildings. We have a policy. Lots of historical sites.'

LIU 'Which ones are they?'

LI Chief, what historical sites do we have?

KUO Well, the average person in Taiwan doesn't know about historical sites.

LI How many are there anyway?

KUO Well, I don't know either.

CH'ÊN The Council for Cultural Development has published a book on it. Tell her to get one.

LI Miss, the Council for Cultural Development—Hey, you haven't bought one, so why should a Japanese buy one? Trying to cheat a foreigner?

KUO *[pointing at* CH'ÊN*]* Stop all this talk about books. You
never read anyway. Go back to playing the Fortress.
Mr Li—

LI I know, I know. I'm getting the act together. Now
what? Do I rape her?

*[*LI *makes a dash for* LIU.*]*

LIU Not so fast!

CH'ÊN What lust! What do you think you are? A Jap?

KUO What lust are you going on about? Your own, I
presume. Go back to being the Fortress. Don't worry,
you'll rape her in the next scene. What happens is—she
chats you up, and what she's going to say now, leads
up to the whole thing, all right?

LI Got it! What she says next leads me up to it.

KUO Exactly! Listen carefully. Jên-shan, now!

LIU 'If you don't have historical sites you don't feel
patriotic. You Chinese are always saying that nostalgia
comes from seeing old objects and old sites. That is
what history is all about. I think your government is
inept!'

KUO *[responds at once]* 'What was that you said? I dare you
to say it again!' *[To* LI*]* Repeat what I said angrily!

LI 'What was that you said? I dare you to say it again!'—
I think what she said makes sense.

KUO What sense? We know what's wrong with our
government. A foreigner has no business criticizing us!
You've got to stand firm.

LI I know, I know—And then? Do I rape her?

*[*LI *makes another dash for* LIU. *Everyone moves to stop him.]*

KUO I told you to just be yourself, and now I see there's
obviously a violent side to your character! The rape
comes afterwards. Jên-shan, carry on.

LIU 'If you don't have historical sites, you can't cultivate a
sense of identity, a sense of belonging.'

LI 'Miss, are you a history student?'

KUO Good question!

LIU 'No, I study human civilization.'

KUO Ask her whether she studies Taiwanese history.

LI 'Miss, are you a student of Taiwanese history?'—That
can't be right, Chief! I never studied Taiwanese history
at school.

KUO You were obviously no good as a student. Isn't *The
Secret Life of President Chiang* history?

LI You're right. 'Miss, *The Secret Life of President Chiang* is Taiwan history.' . . . And then? Do I rape her?

[LI *makes a dash for* LIU. *Everyone rushes to stop him. Lights dim.*]

SCENE FIVE: THE PAST 2

[*Secret Interrogation Office.*
   Lights come up.
   Only LI *and* CH'ÊN *are on stage.* CH'ÊN *acts out the role of an arrested murderer giving a statement to* LI.]

CH'ÊN 'That day Big Brother took me and a few other sworn-brothers to The Crown to settle a blood feud. I remember he looked absolutely deadpan, but his eyes were bloodshot. That look really scared me. We walked into the room with our guns pulled, and Big Brother was standing behind me when I shot. He started spraying bullets into everybody after I had fired. I was sure if I hadn't fired a shot first, he'd have killed me too.'

LI 'Your Big Brother is a nasty piece of work.'

CH'ÊN 'That's right. When he kills for revenge he never tells us the reasons. He'll tell me or some other chap to lay a trap—like telling the other side there's a drug deal or some smuggled guns, or sometimes that we need to talk things over or divide the spoils—and when these people come out, he wastes every one of them.'

LI 'And after that?'

CH'ÊN 'What?'

LI 'And after that?'

CH'ÊN 'What?'

LI 'What about the bodies? What does he do with them?'

CH'ÊN 'Oh, he's smart there. Most of the time he dumps the bodies in public cemeteries or in a wood. The site is prepared in advance; sometimes a big hole is dug in the ground to bury the bodies—I've dug a few holes for him myself. Each of these holes is five metres deep or more, and you can bury six bodies in it. Our record was burying seventeen. It's a good thing you've caught me, or else I could have ended up in one of those holes I dug.

[*Both men revert to their original roles.*]

LI Hey, you sure sounded like a villain.

CH'ÊN But I am a villain!

LI Really!

CH'ÊN Haven't you heard the saying? 'The three greatest social evils are: cops, reporters, and villains.' Well, maybe that's unfair. Anyway, when I was living in the village . . . Ah, well, forget it. Let's say I've handled so many cases of this kind I know only too well how they look. I'll show you. Just look at me: their faces are always deadpan, cold, calculating. Their eyes are always bloodshot; that's because they sleep very little, and they don't trust anyone. Remember, this one spent five nights in the mountains without any sleep.

LI I'm sorry, but your scenario must take my physical condition into consideration. The longest I went without sleep was two nights. I can't last five nights.

CH'ÊN But in our scenario you went without sleep for five nights!

LI This won't do! You'd better follow my plan.

CH'ÊN Oh, that doesn't matter, we can give you amphetamine.

LI I don't do drugs. Really, in all my thirty-eight years I've never done drugs.

CH'ÊN We have plenty of amphetamine. A little won't hurt.

LI If we do that we'll blow it. When they give me a urine test, they'll find that it's drug-free. Won't that blow it?

CH'ÊN Come on, urine tests are for schoolkids, not for you.

LI All right, let's forget that. Tell me, is there any poisonous substance in Taiwan that doesn't do any direct harm to the body?

CH'ÊN Of course there is! Water pollution, air pollution, noise pollution, traffic chaos—there's poison everywhere!

LI In that case I don't have to take any drugs; I'm already poisoned, right?

CH'ÊN So you see? Now I don't suppose it's a problem not sleeping for five nights, is it?

LI Piece of cake.

CH'ÊN Right. The killer has bloodshot eyes because he sleeps little and doesn't trust anyone. His only trusted friend is his gun.

LI That makes sense.

CH'ÊN Now imagine how you'd look when you set about to kill. You swagger along, keeping your eyes peeled, and when you see your deadly foe, you pull your gun and fire. *[Pulls his gun and pretends to kill]* 'Bang, you're fucking dead!'

LI I have a problem there. You see, someone as highly educated as I am doesn't swear.

CH'ÊN That's bullshit! You don't swear because you're educated? Well, I graduated from the police academy, and I swear like hell, so what does that make me?

LI Let's do it this way. Just show some respect for my opinion, all right? Please adjust my qualification to primary school level instead of college graduate.

CH'ÊN Why so?

LI Just think about this! I've only got primary school qualifications. I'm not educated; I have no expertise. I've been mucking around since I was a child, living with knives, guns, home-made bombs, smuggled rifles, hand grenades—

CH'ÊN That makes sense.

LI Of course it does.

CH'ÊN That's fine by me, but I've got to report to the Chief first.

LI It should be all right with him.

CH'ÊN Given so little schooling, when you're on the rampage you've got to swear—just to be in character.

LI Now, listen to me, forget about swearing.

CH'ÊN But you've got to swear to be forceful! Look—you pull your gun—'BANG! You're fucking dead!' Cool, isn't it? If you change that to something else, it won't sound right: 'BANG! You're ducking dead!' Does that make sense?

LI Well, I'll try my best.

CH'ÊN That's not good enough. You've got to do it.

[Hands LI *the gun, telling him to repeat what was demonstrated]*

LI A killer swaggers along. *[Walking unsteadily]*

CH'ÊN Have you been hit?

LI Well, that was the way you walked.

CH'ÊN I didn't look so bad!

LI And then, I keep my eyes peeled. *[Peers about exaggeratedly looking this way and that]*

CH'ÊN What are you doing? You're not a bloody pendulum!

LI Give me some time; I'll practise. And then, I see a deadly foe, I pull my gun—Screw—

CH'ÊN 'Your Mother'!

LI 'Your Mother'!

CH'ÊN Spit out 'Your Mother'!

LI 'Spit out your Mother'!

CH'ÊN Not spit out, 'screw'.

LI 'Not spit out, screw.'—It just won't do! It's too late to learn to swear at thirty-eight.

CH'ÊN Show a bit of fire when you're swearing! I've spent so much time training you, all for nothing. I could have trained a chihuahua to be a police hound in that time.

LI Just give me time to practise. I can't do it with you staring at me like that. Why don't you teach me how to fire a gun first? How do you release the safety catch?

CH'ÊN Don't fool around with it. It's loaded.

[CH'ÊN takes the gun from LI.]

LI Ch'ên, I'm curious about one thing. I've meant to ask you—

CH'ÊN Go ahead.

LI Why do you support the Chief's plan?

CH'ÊN Because of my wife.

LI So you're married! Congratulations!

CH'ÊN Not so fast! I'm divorced.

LI How come?

CH'ÊN She emigrated. You want to know about my past?

LI I guess I should get to know you a little better.

[Lights dim.

LÜ plays CH'ÊN, the husband; LIU plays his wife. The two walk through the door frame and appear at one corner of the stage, re-enacting CH'ÊN's past.]

CH'ÊN In fact I was the one with the problem. I didn't have a firm grasp of reality, and I had no plans and no goals for the future. I just wanted to plod on, one step at a time. I wasn't as rational as her; didn't have the foresight. I remember that day when I took her to Tao Yuan Airport, she said to me—

WIFE Aren't you going to say goodbye?

CH'ÊN I said—

HUSBAND Would I see you again if I did?

CH'ÊN She said—

WIFE You will forgive me, won't you?

CH'ÊN I said—

HUSBAND Your mind is made up. What more can I say?

CH'ÊN She said—

WIFE Forget me.

CH'ÊN I said—

HUSBAND I will as soon as I turn my back.

CH'ÊN And she actually—*[Claps his hands]*

[WIFE slaps HUSBAND.]

When she slapped me, she said—

WIFE I knew you'd say that.

CH'ÊN I thought to myself: 'You're leaving, and sooner or later you'll forget all about this place. And you want me to keep thinking about you so I can't even work, is that fair?' And finally she said something which was a blow to my pride. She said—

WIFE Ever since I married you, I've become even more of a neurotic than you are! You sleep every night with your gun up your nightshirt, what for? You just want a promotion, a fatter salary. Have you got it? How much are you making?

[CH'ÊN claps his hands. HUSBAND slaps WIFE in the face.]

CH'ÊN I—slapped myself.

[LÜ, who plays HUSBAND, is embarrassed that he has got it wrong. He slaps himself in the face.]

I slapped myself hard.

[HUSBAND slaps himself again.]

I thought to myself—

HUSBAND The day will come when you'll regret this!

[Lights dim.]

SCENE SIX: MOTIVES 2

[Secret Interrogation Office.
    Lights on. LI, KUO, CH'ÊN, LÜ, *and* LIU *are all on stage. They are simulating a court hearing.]*

LI 'That afternoon I took her to Cheng Ching Lake to take photos. And then I took her home for dinner. Your Honour, we didn't speak each other's language, so we used sign language. I pointed at the food on the table and said *Wasabi*—No! *Oshibori*—delicious! Try one.'

LÜ Hey, Li, what do you think you're going on about? *Oshibori* means napkin. How could she eat a napkin?

LI Oh, I wasn't inviting her to eat a napkin, I was asking her to try the fish. 'And she went to have a shower after dinner. After that I asked her to use my bed; and then I saw her knapsack, and I decided to sleep in it—'

LÜ How big is a knapsack? How can you sleep in one? Did you see any money in it?

LI 'Right! I decided to see how much money she'd got in the knapsack—All of a sudden, I stood behind her totally naked—'

LÜ No! You stood at the door totally naked! Do you think she's going to rape you? Chief, he's drifting away again.

KUO Mr Li, can you pay a little more attention and act according to the script?

LI It's not that, Chief. I just can't concentrate now.

LÜ You can't afford to make any mistakes in the court room.

LI I can't memorize all of this.

LÜ Try to remember the outline, all right? I don't even have to read the script to do it. Come on, let me show you. Pay attention, or you'll never learn.

KUO He'll demonstrate. Just pay attention.

LÜ 'That's right, Your Honour, I lay on her back, naked.'

KUO You were standing at the door and she was sleeping in bed! What a lousy demonstration this is!

LÜ 'Right, I was standing at the door naked. I felt a strong urge in me; an anti-Japanese flame was burning. In front of me lay a Japanese woman. Scenes of the Nanjing Massacre, the Marco Polo Bridge Incident, the hero Commander Xie of Sixing Warehouse, the warlord Zhang Xueliang who planned the Xi'an Incident— these all rushed into my mind.'

LIU The Xi'an Incident had nothing to do with the Japanese!

LÜ Didn't the Japanese Emperor issue an order for the arrest of Zhang after the Xi'an Incident?

LIU No!

CH'ÊN My goodness! However did you make it into the police academy?

LÜ None of your business! 'I looked at the Japanese woman, and deep inside I was screaming: Down with

Japanese Imperialism! Down with Japanese economic invasion! The Chinese have stood courageously! You Japs, lie down! People of Taiwan, you've got to live in dignity, live in dignity!'

CH'ÊN A great performance, Kuo-k'ung. But don't forget, he's the lead player. Who do you think you are? 'Lie down,' indeed!

KUO Enough. Go and 'lie down', both of you! No, stand to one side. Mr Li, what's on your mind?

LI I'm still thinking about May.

KUO What's the point? Think about the present. I'm trying to blow this case up as much as possible.

LI Blow it up, right. I'll fully cooperate. The question is—

KUO Right, you'll just follow my instructions and say to the judge—

LI I don't know. I have a very strange feeling. I don't know why I suddenly miss May so much. I'm running out of time, I'm afraid, so I'd better tell you. Chief, I had known her for seven years, and we had lived together for four years. The first three years of our courtship was really difficult. She was working in Tainan, and I was working in Taipei. At the beginning of every month we'd telephone to arrange for a place to meet at the end of the month. And it was a real headache—I didn't like the feeling at all.

KUO What feeling?

LI I prefer things and places to stay as they are, not to change. Like when I called May at the beginning of every month to ask, 'Where are we going to meet this month?'; she'd say at such-and-such a restaurant, and, when we turned up, the restaurant had closed down. Then another month I told her to meet at a noodle shop, and when we turned up the shop had been demolished! There was this one time which left a deep impression on me. I said: 'Let's meet outside such-and-such a Taipei toy factory. It's been there for over thirty years, it's not going to close down. We'll definitely meet there.' And when we got there, there was this poster on the door: 'We have relocated to mainland China.' I don't like this message of insecurity that society is sending us. It has become impossible to nurture a sense of 'roots'. Those three years were so painful for us. We kept thinking: 'Is there any place in

Taipei which isn't going to relocate, isn't going to be demolished, isn't going to close down, isn't going to disappear?' At last, it occurred to us that the best place for a date in the whole of Taipei was—

KUO Where?

LI The Presidential Palace. It won't be demolished; it won't be closed down; it won't disappear, will it?

KUO An excellent choice.

LI Chief, I didn't know until I looked up the records the other day that the Presidential Palace is the largest Grade III historic building in Taiwan.

LÜ Historic? You must be joking!

KUO Yes, historic. And the joke is on you. Mr Li, the Presidential Palace really is a Grade III historic building. Well, in fact it shouldn't have been considered historic for it was built by the Japs. During the Japanese occupation it was called 'Governor's House'. The architecture is mock-Baroque—

LI Chief, I've got it! The Presidential Palace is just like our organization—it's the biggest Limited Corporation in Taiwan!

LÜ What does *that* mean?

[Lights dim.]

T V   N E W S   3

[150″ TV screen lowered on to the stage.
PTV News Channel live report comes on screen.
A woman reporter is reporting at a street corner.]

REPORTER Here is the latest report on the Matzu Hanako case. Though the authorities have conducted a thorough investigation and arrested Li Hsi-chieh as the suspect for the murder, the case has now taken a sudden turn. The suspect Li Hsi-chieh has taken hostages in the Secret Interrogation Office, and is threatening to kill all the detectives. I am now standing outside the Secret Interrogation Office in question, and I am given to understand that Li has set up a so-called National Salvation Corporation Limited. This simple case of murder has now attracted the attention of the world media.

[Reporters from all over the world appear on screen—HKN from Japan, CNN from the USA, DDT from Saudi Arabia. Reporters from various countries speaking in various accents, each making up a story for their own report.]

Li Hsi-chieh is now the focus of world news. As the criminal with the worst record in our national history, he has tarnished our national image and affected our international status. He is the scum of our nation! The following is a report on the four detectives who died in the line of duty.

CAMERAMAN *[offstage]* They're still alive!

REPORTER Oh . . . who may die in the line of duty . . . Please stay tuned for further reports on the development of this case.

[TV screen is lifted.]

SCENE SEVEN: IN-FIGHTING 1

[Secret Interrogation Office.
LI enters, holding a gun, pulling CH'ÊN with him.]

CH'ÊN All right, loosen your grip a bit. This is not for real.

LI But we want it to look real, don't we?

CH'ÊN This is just as you predicted, Chief. The whole thing's getting bigger and bigger.

LÜ Marvellous! Big is good. I'm sure I'll get promoted.

KUO Calm down; control yourself. Success is not yours until it's in your hands.

LI You're really something, Chief! If you have any unsolved cases, charge them all to my account. I'll take them all on.

CH'ÊN I'll take them all on! Chief, we want to make it big, and we want to make a real stir. Let's add more twists and turns to the whole thing. Now I'm going to change your plan—

KUO You want to change it?

CH'ÊN That's right, I want to change it. Detective Ch'ên Wei-tsung of the Second Squad's Division 16 overpowers the fanatical criminal Li Hsi-chieh and brings him to justice. The whole nation rejoices! Then, in front of the TV camera, I admit to being the one who planned it all. I become the man of the hour! The lord of the manor! I'm the mastermind! You are now all my hostages! What's so funny? Raise your hands!

LI Hey, is this a script change?

[CH'ÊN points his gun at the rest of the group.]

CH'ÊN You too, old man.

KUO Ch'ên, what do you think you're doing?

CH'ÊN What do you think? Do you want a bullet in you? Hands up! *[To LIU]* You too! *[To LÜ hiding in a corner]* You—get out of there! You disgust me. Start doing the frog-jump. *[LÜ jumps as commanded.]* I'll definitely be taken to court, and I'll say solemnly in the court room—*[To LÜ]* Who told you to stop? Are you stupid or something?—And I'll say: 'The people of Taiwan must live in dignity!' I'll be taken to the execution ground; I'll be given my last cup of *gaoliang* wine and my last marinated egg, and then one shot—Kuo-k'ung, how about giving you that task? *[To LÜ]* What're you doing? You really like to frog-jump, don't you?

LÜ You think I'm nuts? No way!

KUO Ch'ên, what do you think you're doing?

CH'ÊN It's a joke! It's just a joke!

LI God! He really scared me. I thought it was for real.

CH'ÊN Relax. I was just joking.

KUO Don't fool around. Mr Li actually thought the script had been changed.

CH'ÊN *[to LÜ]* Does it matter whether you die or he dies? As the saying goes: if one of us gets to be an immortal, the whole gang goes to heaven.

LÜ But he didn't say he was quitting!

CH'ÊN You're chicken, that's all. I was only testing you out. If anything goes amiss, Chief, he's the one who'll sell us out.

LÜ What're you talking about? Say that again, and I'll belt you!

CH'ÊN Does it take so little to make you mad?

LÜ Go on, say it again!

CH'ÊN Tut-tut! Now everyone can see what you are!

LÜ Go on!

[Everyone suddenly chases one another in slow-motion. After a while, everyone's movements return to normal.]

LI Please, everyone! Listen to me. I'm a dying man, so just show me some respect and stop this nonsense.

CH'ÊN We've got to make one thing clear. We've got someone here who has been demoted from the Police Supervisory Unit.

LÜ Screw you!

[CH'ÊN still mistrusts LÜ.]

CH'ÊN Well if someone hasn't got what it takes, what's to be done about it?

LÜ That's right, that's right! Go on! *[LÜ pulls his gun.]* Go on!

CH'ÊN *[pulls his gun]* Your wife has emigrated. You have no home in Taiwan!

LÜ One more word and I'll shoot.

CH'ÊN You ain't got the guts.

LÜ All right, I ain't got the guts. You shoot first. My rank is only DC II.

CH'ÊN And my rank is DC I.

LÜ You're my senior, you go first.

CH'ÊN As the saying goes: the generous child takes the smallest pear. You first.

LÜ Bloody nonsense! What's it got to do with pears?

CH'ÊN What do you know?

LÜ What now?

CH'ÊN Just fire!

LI Good! Blast away to your hearts' content. If one of you doesn't die immediately, I'll make sure he gets another bullet.

KUO Bugger off!—What do you think you're doing? Letting off steam? All right, Why don't you fire at me? I'm an arsehole; I'm a moron! I shouldn't have dreamt up this stupid national salvation plan! I've thought it over: there's no point in staying alive. I've married twice, the first wife ran away with another man, and the second isn't much good either. Why don't you fire your guns and finish me off!

LI Right, that way you can make it big!

KUO Right, that way you can make it big!

LI I'll count to three, and we'll pull our triggers together.

[LI points his gun at KUO's head.]

LIU Li Hsi-chieh, stop it!

[LIU pushes LI's gun away. KUO snatches CH'ÊN's gun.]

KUO Damn it! Hand me your guns, all of you! *[LI makes to give up his gun.]* Not you! Jên-shan, yours too. What's the matter with you all? We're mates, why fight amongst ourselves?

[LÜ hands LIU his gun.]

CH'ÊN That's what I've been wondering.

KUO Give me your gun.

CH'ÊN I already did.

KUO Now!

[CH'ÊN *takes a second gun out from his back holster.*]

Jên-shan, spill the bullets.

LIU Yes, sir.

[LIU *takes the bullets out of all the guns except* LI'*s.*]

KUO Now that we have come so far, let there be no more fighting! It is far too early to count our chickens. Mr Li, now you take your gun and pull Kuo-k'ung over to the window. They'll definitely ask you what you want. Now you do this—Tell them you want a billion NT dollars deposited in your Swiss bank account.

LI I'm going to die. Why would I want money in my account?

KUO My bank account! *[Takes out his account book]* This is your Swiss bank account number. If they refuse your demand, you'll kill Kuo-k'ung.

LÜ In front of everyone?

KUO It's just acting. Don't worry! Now take him to the window.

LI I'm sorry, Chief. I need to clarify a couple of things first. Number one: Ch'ên, you just said 'Kuo-k'ung's wife has emigrated'?

LIU That's right! Kuo-k'ung just got divorced. I went with him to the airport to see his wife off.

LI That evening when you sat there telling me about your past, you said your wife had emigrated too.

CH'ÊN I . . . actually, I was telling you Kuo-k'ung's past, not mine.

LI *[points his gun at* CH'ÊN] I told you about my past, and you told me Kuo-k'ung's past? I opened my heart to you, and you lied to me? You rascal!

CH'ÊN Well, I really don't get along with my wife!

LÜ Don't get along, huh? Of course you don't! You have a mistress!

CH'ÊN That's nonsense!—Chief!

KUO Fire!

LI You heard the Chief. Sorry! *[About to pull the trigger]*

CH'ÊN Don't! Please don't!

[CH'ÊN *kneels down, pleading.*]

KUO Mr Li—

[KUO pushes LI's gun away and pleads on behalf of CH'ÊN.]

LI He didn't tell me the truth. He lied.

KUO Not exactly. We all keep some things private, that's human nature. Now, people out there have no idea what we are doing. But we in here should know our goal. It's national salvation we want! Why can't Chinese people work with each other in harmony?

LI There's another thing I want to clarify. A few minutes ago, I heard for the first time that you're blackmailing the people outside for a billion dollars?

KUO That isn't blackmail. The nation won't miss such a small sum!

LI That money won't be mine to spend! But each of you will get a quarter of a billion—

KUO I'll be honest with you. I'm going to retire soon, but I'm not ready to bow out yet! Law and order hasn't improved, and my aspirations remain unfulfilled. This case will be my stepping stone. I'm going to stand for the legislative elections as soon as I retire. And how am I going to do it without money? So you see, it's all for a good cause.

LI I want to know—what's your real motive for turning me into a murderer?

[Lights dim.]

[to himself] No, they've never told me their real motive for turning me into a murderer. *[To everyone]* Right, I don't have much time. Is there anything you haven't told me? Hurry up! I want the truth!

LIU I . . . can I tell you about my 'past'?

LI Will it take long? Do we have time?

[Lights dim.]

TV NEWS IV

[150″ TV screen lowered on to the stage.
PTV News Channel live report comes on screen.
A woman reporter reporting at a street corner.]

REPORTER This is the latest explosive turn in the Li Hsi-chieh hostage crisis. The lady standing next to me is the Japanese woman who has been missing for the last two weeks—Matzu Hanako. Li Hsi-chieh confessed to her killing but refused to say where her body had been buried. And now the lady is standing miraculously by my side. Would you like to say a few words?

HANAKO *[in Japanese]* I am Matzu Hanako and I'm still alive. I do not know Mr Li Hsi-chieh.

REPORTER So the case—

HANAKO *[in Japanese]* I have not been kidnapped—really I haven't.

REPORTER Really, this case is a mystery. What is Li's real motive for holding hostages in the Secret Interrogation Office? I'm sure the authorities will provide us with a reasonable explanation. Stay tuned for the latest reports on this case.

[TV screen is lifted.]

SCENE EIGHT: IN-FIGHTING 2

[Secret Interrogation Office.
Lights on. KUO, CH'ÊN, *and* LÜ *are on stage.]*

CH'ÊN Chief, what do we do now?

KUO Colleagues, I must admit that I may have overlooked something. But, a crisis is a turning point. 'We'll take on all cases which the authorities have failed to solve.'

[LIU enters, supporting MATZU HANAKO *played by* CHANG SHAN-MAY. LI *comes in after them.]*

LIU Chief, we've brought her.

LÜ How come she's here?

LI Chief, I turned everything around. Just now I went down to tell them that if they didn't hand her over, the four men up here were as good as dead.

CH'ÊN What do we do now, Chief?

KUO Fantastic! As I thought, you're not just clever, you're also wise. *[To* HANAKO*]* Now, we may have to sacrifice you, but we do have our reasons.

LIU Chief, she's Japanese.

KUO Oh—who speaks Japanese here? *[To* CH'ÊN*]* Come and interpret for me.

CH'ÊN What do you want me to do?

KUO I'll talk, and you interpret. 'We are all patriots here.' Ch'ên, interpret.

[CH'ÊN does not speak Japanese. He just makes things up.]

CH'ÊN *[in a Japanese accent]* We friends! No fear! It's all right—we're parrots!

HANAKO 'Parrots'?

KUO That's right. You are our pawn; he—

CH'ÊN Just a minute. *[In Japanese first]* Anatawa— You— *[Mumbles to himself]* You are a chess master's pawn!

HANAKO *[in Japanese]* What?

KUO He will shoot at you; he'll shoot you in the throat to stop you talking.

CH'ÊN Chief, you're speaking too fast. I can't keep up with you.

LÜ What're you saying to her anyway?

KUO All right! We won't talk to her. Come over here.

LI *Sashimi! Sashimi!*

[LI threatens HANAKO with his gun.]

CH'ÊN This is not a Japanese restaurant!

LI Oh, I got mixed up. How do you say 'bastard' in Japanese? *Bakayaro?*

KUO Ch'ên will teach you later. Now listen, with her in our hands the case is as good as settled.

LI Really?

KUO Sure. We'll make sure she loses consciousness and her power of speech, then we'll just carry on with our plan. Kuo-k'ung, fire!

HANAKO *[in Japanese]* I'm sorry. I've come to help you. It took a lot of courage to come and persuade this criminal to let you go.

CH'ÊN *[in Japanese]* Just a minute. *[To LIU]* Just a minute! Can anyone make out what she's saying? *Bakayaro!* Kuo-k'ung, fire!

LÜ Let her go!

KUO Kuo-k'ung, what're you doing? Shoot her! Show us you won't chicken out. Fire!

[LÜ fires a shot. Everyone moves around in slow-motion.
    After a while, everyone returns to normal. HANAKO has taken advantage of the chaos to escape. Everyone is at a loss what to do.]

LÜ Chief, I'm sorry. I just couldn't do it. I want out.

CH'ÊN Sorry, Kuo-k'ung, but we agreed before that no one is allowed to change his mind. We've got to see this through.

LÜ Sorry, Ch'ên, I'm just not up to it. I'm shaking all
   over. We're done for.

LIU Sorry, Ch'ên, but if we give ourselves up now, there's
   still hope. Chief, can't we call off the plan?

KUO Sorry, Mr Li. 'To err is human'. Do you think we can
   scale down this case?

LI Sorry, Chief! A while ago you wanted to 'make it big',
   and now you want to 'scale down'. Do you think I'm a
   football? Do you think you can kick me around? You'd
   better get your plan straightened out!

KUO I've thought it through. Since I planned the whole
   thing, I'm not going to let any of you get trapped. I'm
   going to take full responsibility for everything. Kuo-
   k'ung, I don't blame you. I understand how you feel
   about an unhappy marriage; I feel the same way. Ch'ên,
   I'm so sorry! I promise I'm not going to squeal on you.
   You'll get your promotion and your raise—the usual
   course.

CH'ÊN Sorry, Chief. But if I take the usual course, how long
   will it be before I get promoted?

LIU I'm sorry, Ch'ên! You're ambitious, you work hard.
   I wish you well!

CH'ÊN I'm sorry. I shouldn't just think about myself. I'm
   sorry, Kuo-k'ung.

LI Sorry, sorry . . . The whole darn place is saying 'sorry'.
   Get out! Chief, get out! There are reporters outside,
   you go and say 'sorry' to them. Why is it that you
   people in the establishment never say 'sorry' to the
   public when you've fouled things up?

   [Silence]

LÜ We've got to stick to our guns!

LIU Are you out of your mind?

LÜ Don't you realize that the authorities are lying? That
   Japanese woman, is she the real Matzu Hanako? We've
   been tricked! How come Li Hsi-chieh could get that
   woman to come up here so easily? We know better
   than anyone else the tricks played by the authorities—
   all they do is falsify things and set people up. They're
   unscrupulous! They're liars!

CH'ÊN That's a good twist! He's right, we mustn't be taken
   in. Chief, we must go ahead with the plan.

KUO No, there's something not quite right. Why would
   other units set us up? It's always been 'birds of a
   feather looking out for each other'.

LI Chief, times have changed. There's no more 'birds of a feather'! Just look at our country: the Nationalists have subdivided into the New Alliance; the Democratic Party has its factions; even the Communist Party is going to collapse. What 'birds of a feather' are you talking about?

KUO You're not just clever, you're also very wise.

CH'ÊN Well, that twist is a bit forced, but it sure makes everyone feel good! Kuo-k'ung, the fridge—

LÜ Mind your tongue!

CH'ÊN I'm not swearing at you. I mean there are two long ones in the fridge. Go get them.

LÜ More guns? Here I go. *[Exits]*

KUO Ch'ên, I told you to hand over all your guns.

CH'ÊN Sorry, Chief. That was just in case. I had to do it.

[LÜ enters with two M-16s.]

KUO Put the guns down.

CH'ÊN Mind your own business! Now I'll go with Kuo-k'ung and shoot at the crowd. It's you *[Pointing at* LI*]* shooting, of course. This will show them all hell has broken loose. Come! *[CH'ÊN and* LÜ *run offstage.]*

[Sound of semi-automatic firing offstage. After a while, CH'ÊN *and* LÜ *come back on stage.]*

CH'ÊN Ha ha . . . We finished the whole magazine of bullets. Reporting indeed! The reporters were the first to leg it.

KUO Ch'ên, what do you think you're up to!

CH'ÊN Shut up!

LÜ Ha ha . . . I hit a woman in the leg, and she ran off like all hell was chasing her! Ha ha! I don't give a damn about my wife emigrating. I'm better off on my own! Ha ha! Run, where did she think she was running to?

[Everyone moves around in slow motion. In slow motion LI *suddenly fires at* LÜ*'s chest.* LÜ *dies.*
Everyone returns to normal.]

LI Liar! Liar! He lied, didn't you hear him? He lied! 'I don't give a damn about my wife emigrating. I'm better off on my own!' Better off his arse. When our plan succeeds he's the biggest loser! He doesn't even have a home, what is there for him to live for? Life will just be endless pain for him. He was lying, everyone is lying to everyone else. People have lied to me since I was a child, and now that I'm going to die you're still lying to me. *[To* KUO*]* What are you doing?

KUO Mr Li, life is only a dream. Even if all this is for real, can you blame me for it? I'm an old fool; my mind's not clear. Just look at me and my loyal officers. Don't we look like a mother hen and her chicks looking for food? Life is so dull, we need a bit of excitement. Don't take things so seriously! Do you still care to know about me? Let me tell you something true—I found my daughter! When I retire my daughter will look after me. You know where I found her? A few days ago I went with some old commanders to a bar for a few drinks—she was working there. *[Snatches up a gun and pulls the trigger at* LI*]* You fucking—*[Discovers that the gun is not loaded]*

LI Chief . . . *[Imitating* KUO's *manner of speech]* 'Jên-shan, spill the bullets.'

*[*LI *fires at* KUO's *thigh.* KUO *collapses to the ground.* CH'ÊN *is frightened.]*

Liar! You're still lying! You lie so much it's become like the truth! You say I'm a murderer, all right, I can kill. It's all the same. I can kill one, or ten, or three hundred, it's just one death penalty for me! *[To* LIU*]* What are you doing?

*[*LIU, *in tears, is crawling over to* KUO.*]*

LIU I . . . I . . . want to watch TV.

*[*LIU *changes direction and goes towards the TV.]*

LI TV, TV, always watching that anaemic stuff. Everything on TV is fake, all the news media are fake! Listen, perhaps I haven't been cheated after all. I suddenly see this picture in my mind: on this island of Taiwan where twenty million people live, I am the last one left. But what's the point of being the only one left here? Miss Liu—

*[*LI *walks towards* CH'ÊN, *calling* LIU's *name in a sinisterly calm voice.]*

Miss Liu, look, look at this!

*[*LI *suddenly points his gun at* CH'ÊN's *crotch and pretends to pull the trigger.]*

'Duck'—I thank you for turning a chihuahua into a police hound. *[Almost hysterical]* Screw you! Screw your

Dad! Screw your Mother! Hey, I feel a strange sense of liberation. I must thank the authorities for turning falsehood into truth! *[Runs offstage]*

LIU Chief—

CH'ÊN Damn it! Chief . . . I've wet my pants!

[Lights dim.]

T V   N E W S   V

[150" TV screen is lowered on to the stage.
The studio of PTV News Channel appears on screen.]

ANCHOR Li Hsi-chieh, who is implicated in at least three hundred murders, has become the most wanted man in our country since his escape. However, there have been incessant rumours in the last year about Li. Rumour No. 1: To escape from the police, Li bought a fishing boat with his ill-gotten gains and sailed to New York, where he has now opened a brothel in a district where many Taiwanese gather. It is said that he gives a special discount to Taiwanese customers. According to Li: 'We're all from the same land!' Rumour No. 2: Li is hiding out somewhere in Xiamen in mainland China. The money he used to escape from Taiwan came from Chang Shan-may, the woman living with him. Rumour No. 3: According to a high-ranking police officer, 'Li Hsi-chieh and Chang Shan-may are Taiwan's Bonnie and Clyde, hiding out in an unknown place.' Rumour No. 4: Some informers have called up the police to say: I am Li Hsi-chieh—

[The anchor takes up a card on his desk: 'Anchor, LI HSI-CHIEH'. TV screen lifted.]

SCENE NINE: ONCE UPON A TIME

[A certain KTV Lounge.
Lights on. X HSI-CHIEH—played by the same actor who plays LI HSI-CHIEH—is polishing an M-16 in a corner. CHANG A-MAY—played by the same actress who plays CHANG SHAN-MAY—walks on to the stage carrying a pot of rice.]

MAY Hsi-chieh, dinner's ready. Where's the Chief?

X Burning paper money outside.

MAY Chief, dinner's ready!—What are these guns for?

X May, am I a good buddy or what? The Chief called last night to say that his bosses want performance, so this morning I got him three long ones and two short ones!

MAY I don't think you should have any more to do with him, or else you'll end up losing your life in the bargain—that's the long and short of it.

X I don't want to hear any of that!

MAY He's retiring soon, isn't he? What does he care about performance? *[Exits]*

X *[shouting after her]* What do you know, you fool! It's precisely because he's retiring that he needs good performance. Whether he gets a seat on the legislature will depend entirely on me. Let me tell you: I'm officially registered as a member of his election campaign team.

[COMMANDER KUO walks on to stage carrying a bunch of incense sticks. The logo of the National Salvation Corporation Limited is lowered on to the stage.]

KUO Hsi-chieh, have you offered any incense yet?

X Chief, have you found anyone to design the logo I need for my shop?

KUO It's all done. Just look behind you.

X Wow! Wonderful! How come there's no picture on the other side?

KUO It's not finished yet. I've only done half of it. My design is based on the Japanese flag.

X What's the picture on it? I can't make it out.

KUO Well, let me tell you. I've been a police officer for over thirty years; I'm no good at designing, but I had a sudden inspiration—the dove on my cap is now our logo.

X That's highly creative!

KUO Exactly. Hsi-chieh, I've found you a flat. It's in Chung Shan North Road, intersection with Chang An East Road.

X I'm not going to live there. Far too noisy and messy.

KUO Can you show me anywhere in Taipei that isn't noisy and messy?

X I'll tell you where I want to live.

KUO Where?

X Opposite the Presidential Palace.

KUO But there aren't any houses there.

X There's a large car park there. I want to put up a scaffold there, three storeys high. Put a tent on the scaffold, and mount a pair of 250x binoculars in that tent—

KUO What do you want them for?

X I want to watch the people in the Presidential Palace. I want to know what they do every day!

KUO What for? They go there to work every day, that's all. Now, come out with me to burn some incense.

[KUO exits.]

X *[to himself]* I think there is probably a pile of gold inside, and every day people carry it back and forth. Otherwise how come our foreign currency reserve is so high? And not a cent of that belongs to me!

[MAY comes on stage carrying two dishes.]

MAY Hasn't the Chief finished burning incense yet?

X He just went out. Didn't you see him?

MAY Hsi-chieh, that VIP room at the back, I think we should knock it down. It blocks the emergency exit. If they find out our license will be revoked.

X Oh, May! Someone with a conscience like yours shouldn't live in Taiwan.

MAY Nonsense.

X What are you afraid of? The Chief will take care of it. The VIP room stays!

MAY Take care of it indeed! How? He's not in charge of this area. *[Exits]*

X *[to himself]* What would you know, you idiot! The Chief has been in the force for thirty-odd years, he's been posted all over Taiwan. It's all his area. Just listen to him and you can't go wrong. He said: 'Those up above have policies; those down below have strategies!' You just mind your own business and live your life!

[KUO enters.]

Chief, dinner's ready.

KUO Eating, eating all day long. But then, if you don't eat, what meaning is there to life?

[A backdrop of the Presidential Palace is lowered on stage.
    X HSI-CHIEH and COMMANDER KUO sit eating at a table.]

[Lights dim.]

THE END

MOTHER'S WATER MIRROR

1995

By
LIU CHING-MIN

Translated by
JANE C. C. LAI &
MARTHA P. Y. CHEUNG

— ABOUT **THE PLAYWRIGHT** —

LIU CHING-MIN (1956–) was born in Taiwan and graduated from the Drama Department of the Chinese Culture University in 1981. Between 1976 and 1981, she was a key member of the avant-garde 'Lan Ling Theatre Workshop' that was regarded by critics to have started the 'Little Theatre' movement (i.e. experimental productions in studio theatres) in Taiwan. In 1981 she went to study Drama in New York. There she joined a workshop conducted by the renowned Polish director Jerzy Grotowski. During that year, her concept of theatre was radically changed. A remark from Grotowski—'You're a Western Chinese, not an Eastern Chinese'— also threw her into a deep identity crisis.

In 1985, Liu returned to Taiwan and began leading workshops for 'Lan Ling' and the National Institute of the Arts. She also acted in a number of productions, including *Pining . . . In Peach Blossom Land* (1986) and an all-night outdoor production of *Medea on the Mountain* (1987). In 1988, she went to Milan to attend another of Grotowski's workshops, where she reached a decision: 'I realized that I didn't want to be a Western Chinese, I wanted to be a Chinese Chinese'. Her identity crisis was over, and she returned to Taiwan.

In 1988, Liu founded the U Theatre ('U' is a free transliteration of a Chinese character which means 'excellent' and, in the ancient times, 'stage performer'). The group is well known for the training programme devised by Liu. This includes vigorous physical exercises, and the practice of traditional Taiwanese dance, drum playing, and Chinese martial arts such as tai chi chuan. Much of the training takes place outdoors, in the mountains on the outskirts of Taipei. Here, the group has built a small stage, where they rehearse in the evenings under candlelight, and the audience travel all the way up the mountain for their performances. Outside Taipei, they perform anywhere and everywhere—in the parks, on the streets, outside the temples—in order to bring theatre to the people. And the people love it.

Like Lai Shêng-ch'uan, Liu's plays also evolve from rehearsals. Keen to explore the performance dynamics of Taiwan folk art, festival rituals, traditional music, and classical Chinese stories, Liu will collaborate with experts to incorporate elements of these arts into the production, or adapt them to suit the thematic content of the plays, which are firmly focused on the historical and cultural influences that shape contemporary life in Taiwan. The lines, initially written by another writer, will also be revised during rehearsals.

Mother's Water Mirror, first performed by the U Theatre in 1992, is the second of a series of 'Water Mirror' plays by Liu. The others in the series— *The Story of the Water Mirror* (1992), *Desert · Water Mirror* (1993), and *Water Mirror* (1993)—have toured places such as Hong Kong, Philippines, Singapore, and New York.

A particularly fine example of the experimental theatre movement in Taiwan, *Mother's Water Mirror* tells the story of two women from different times, both of whom are victims of war. Forced to flee their countries, both have yearned for years to return home, but when the opportunity finally arises, each is torn by deep conflicts.

First performed in 1992, the play carries a strong anti-war message and a radical examination of the notion of home. Its validity and poignancy is made all the more effective by the current negotiations between Taiwan and mainland China on reunification, and by the present climate of uncertainty and tension on both sides of the Taiwan Straits.

The performance is a feast for the senses. The stage movements are beautifully choreographed and visually stunning; costumes are resplendent in colour and exquisitely embroidered; and the inventive use of percussion, stirring drum rolls, and other instruments form atmospheric background music. As a result the mood changes constantly—by turns frenzied, meditative, phantasmagoric, sober, eerie, desolate.

This play marks the attempt, by yet another Taiwanese playwright, to bring East and West together by blending traditional Western theatrical elements, such as plot and dialogue, with elements of traditional Chinese culture. Chinese kung fu and tai chi chuan are adapted for use in choreography; Chinese musical instruments are employed to enrich the texture of music; and costumes from traditional Taiwanese glove puppet shows are used as the models for the costumes of two of the characters in the play. The result is a uniquely powerful theatrical experience.

Mother's Water Mirror is the second of a series of 'Water Mirror' plays. The first, *The Story of the Water Mirror*, was conceived by Liu Ching-min, who then commissioned the writer Lin Feng-li to produce the script. The script was then heavily revised by Liu for stage performance. Further revisions were made when the U Theatre took the production on tour to the Philippines, and then to Hong Kong in March 1993, where Liu gave a solo performance and renamed the play, *Mother's Water Mirror*. Subsequently, she developed new themes for the play, and collaborated with two other writers, Chung Chiao and Liu Chên, to rewrite portions of the orginal *Water Mirror* script. By the time it was performed in Hong Kong in September 1995, the play had been expanded for six actors.

Because of the radical instability of the text and the play's heavy reliance on the dynamics of performance elements, Liu was at first unsure whether the work could be translated at all. After a trip to Taiwan in the summer of 1995, during which the translators held long discussions with Liu, it was finally decided that the expanded version of *Mother's Water Mirror* would suit the purpose of translation best. By September, however, when the play was performed in Hong Kong, the dialogue had been modified again. Liu shared the translators' view that, rather than pursuing a definitive script, it was better to produce a basic text upon which stage productions of this play could rest. Liu said that future revivals of the play would probably be based on this text.

Stage directions and production notes in this translation were added by the translators from information gathered at rehearsals and from the 1995 stage performance of the play.

DRAMATIS PERSONAE

MOTHER, in her sixties
CAI WENJI, a woman of great intelligence and beauty in the Han
   Dynasty in ancient China, she was abducted by the Huns, a
   northern barbarian tribe, and forced to marry the barbarian king.
PHANTOM GENERAL
EMISSARY
ATTENDANT
OLD ARTISAN
MOTHER's CHILDREN, three in all, in their early and late 30s
REFUGEES, three in all
Two ARTISANS accompanying the OLD ARTISAN

Time and place: The action moves freely amongst three different realms
   of time—the present, the recollected past, and the historical past—
   and also in and out of fantasy, dream, and reality. The stories of
   MOTHER and CAI WENJI are parallel stories, but the scenes
   interweave so that the stories provide implicit comments on each
   other. The stage is bare most of the time, with the change in time
   and place largely indicated by the change in costumes.

PRODUCTION NOTES

- There are six performers altogether. MOTHER and CAI WENJI are played by the same actress, PHANTOM GENERAL and EMISSARY by the same actor; the rest share the other parts, all playing at least two, and sometimes three roles.
- Emphasis should be placed on the evocation of atmosphere, to be achieved through the use of sound effects and music, and choreography of stage movements.
- The acting is stylized throughout.
- The embroidered costumes for WENJI and PHANTOM GENERAL are the proud creations of an embroidery specialist from Taiwan who works for the British Museum, and who has put together a team of garment-makers on the Mainland and spent three months on the job. These costumes should be made deliberately oversized to create new possibilities in rhythm of movement and to enable the actor and actress to give an extra touch of phantasmagoria to their movements.
- The performers' change of roles is indicated by their change of costumes, and, where suitable, their wearing and taking off of masks. These, on occasion, take place on stage, slowly, ritualistically. In most cases the performers stand with their backs towards the audience so that a sense of suspense and expectancy is created, thus making the transformation—from MOTHER to WENJI, or from EMISSARY to PHANTOM GENERAL—all the more dramatic.
- Scene divisions are for the convenience of rehearsals. There should be no break or intermission in the actual performance.

THE **PLAY**

[Lights go up. The stage is bare, but the occasional rumbling of aeroplanes in the background suggests an airport setting. MOTHER and her three CHILDREN enter, each pushing a large suitcase on castors. They are in loose fitting raincoats tied at the waist. MOTHER is about to set off on a visit to her homeland to see her relatives. She relives the memory of her hurried departure from home during the war. During MOTHER's monologue and the chorus of solicitous advice from CHILDREN, the group moves slowly across the stage, pausing occasionally.]

MOTHER It's been more than forty years. . . . That year they sealed up our house. Your sister Ping was only three, and I couldn't travel with a toddler. Your father and your grandma fled ahead to the city to get protection from the Kuomintang troops, and I took the child with me to seek refuge with your aunts and uncles in my mother's house. There was no news from your dad for a whole month. Then, one afternoon, Ping had a high fever. That night, your granddad, who had passed away, appeared in my dream. He said, 'I'm taking the child with me. You go ahead and look for her father.' The next day, before dawn, Ping died in her sleep. There wasn't even time for grief. Your aunts and uncles urged me to set off at once, to look for your dad. . . . They saw me to the road leading out of the village, and told me to come home if all was well. . . . I never thought . . . that I was going to be away for forty years . . .

CHILDREN *[speaking in turn, solicitously]* Mother, it's been forty years. Things have changed in your homeland. It's best not to think too much about the past.

And Mother, the weather is different from Taiwan. You must take care and not fall ill. Have you brought the medicine for your blood pressure?

If you cannot get used to the life there, come home, Mother. And don't cry when you meet your brothers and sisters. It will disturb you too much. You can't take that sort of thing anymore.

[together] Anyway, they have this open-door policy now. You can go there any time you want. So don't get too excited. Take care of yourself, you hear?

MOTHER *[remembering the bombing that drove her to flee her home]* I brought this little mirror with me when I left home. I just took what happened to be around. It has been with me for forty years. . . . Every time I look into the

mirror . . . *[Sounds of bombing]* I see images of the war,
of the evacuation . . . memories that won't go away.*
*[Sound effects create an aural background of fighting,
bombing, and people fleeing to safety. In the hubbub,
CHILDREN put on hats, kerchiefs, etc, to change into the role
of REFUGEES. Crouching over their suitcases, they rush
around, pushing and shoving, forming a picture of panic and
chaos, the castors of their suitcases making a screeching sound
that adds to the confusion all round. MOTHER, also
crouching over her suitcase and pushing it around, stops only
to deliver her lines.]* Such a big city. Full of people all
wondering what was happening. I didn't know where
your father and grandma lived. Where should I look for
them? Then I met an old friend who knew grandma.
He took pity on me and searched with me all over the
city. . . . We walked till our shoes fell apart. . . . *[Sounds
of bombing]* At last, the old man caught sight of
grandma. We found her, sitting on the doorsteps at a
distance, your dad behind her. He shouted with joy,
'Ping is here. Ping and her Mother, they're here!'. . .
Such memories. . . . At last we found her, sitting on the
doorsteps at a distance . . . and your dad shouting, 'Ping
and her Mother, they're here! . . . Where's Ping?' . . .
Then Tianjin was lost . . . the troops had to move south
. . . to Taiwan. Taiwan? Where is it? What is Taiwan?
It's very far away . . . an island . . . you had to go by
boat. *[REFUGEES slow down their frenzied movements.]*
   That night, your dad, your grandma, and I hurried
to the pier, and joined the troops on board the ship
headed for Taiwan . . . *[Sounds of bombing and gunfire]*
[Lights fade. All exit.]

SCENE TWO

*[Lights up. CAI WENJI, wrapped in a long red flowing robe and wearing the mask
of a genteel woman, stands where MOTHER has just been.*
   *Sound of a howling desert storm. Drum rolls suggesting the sound of horses
approaching.]*

EMISSARY *[offstage]* Cai Wenji! Beloved daughter of Grand
   Academician Cai Yung! Where can I seek you?

* In 1949, the Kuomintang (KMT, or the Nationalist Party) lost control of the Mainland to the Chinese
Communist Party. Government officials and the military, as well as many civilians, fled to Taiwan.

[EMISSARY, a long, loose, red cloak draped over his shoulders, a gentleman's mask on his face, enters the upstage area from one wing, moving swiftly in stylized Peking Opera fashion, then pauses as if in search, and exits swiftly by the other wing. He is followed by ATTENDANT, whose movements harmonize with his. ATTENDANT is in a Chinese jacket and trousers, and also wears a mask. WENJI remains standing, as if deep in a dream. Drum rolls fade.]

WENJI   The sands of the desert, how they shift and turn,
Fickle like fortune that flickers and burns.

I am Cai Wenji, but here I am wife to the barbarian king. *[Sighs]* I was Cai Wenji once. *[Chants mournfully and with bitterness]*

Barbarian hordes strained at the border,
Their alien banners covered the hills.
Their horses' hooves trampled the sun,
So many lives they destroyed at will.

I am no longer Cai Wenji. Not since the day the barbarian horses' hooves trampled the sun, and destroyed so many lives at will. The war has turned me into its ashes. I am not the Cai Wenji that I was twelve years ago . . .

EMISSARY *[enters as before, accompanied by drum rolls, but from the other wing, followed by ATTENDANT. He chants.]*

How the yellow dust rolls over the desert land,
How the scorching sun burns in my anxious heart.
Ride on my steed, ceaselessly,
Ceaselessly . . .

[WENJI is startled. She listens anxiously.]

Oh, Wenji! Beloved daughter of my learned teacher and mentor! Do you know how I, Zhou Yan, have journeyed thousands of miles, through scalding sandstorms, in the scorching sun, in search of you? Know you of my quest? Hear you not my heart's call? *[Chants]*

How the yellow dust rolls over the desert land . . .

[His voice, and drum rolls, fade as he moves away and exits, followed by ATTENDANT. Soft music fades up.]

WENJI *[ruminating dreamily]* Wenji? Cai Wenji? Who is that? Is that me? *[In confusion]* Who is calling me? Is he

calling for me? Am I Cai Wenji? I must be dreaming
again. Why do I dream such a dream so often? Why is
this voice so near? So disquieting?

*[Music becomes discordant—a prelude to the dream sequence
which follows. From behind the black mid-curtain,
PHANTOM GENERAL suddenly pokes his head out, a fierce-
looking mask covering his face. The curtain is made of a
light material responsive to movement. As PHANTOM speaks,
he causes the whole curtain to twist and twirl and ripple,
thus amplifying his ghostly presence, and allowing him to
dominate the whole stage.]*

PHANTOM *[shouting, apparently chasing somebody]* Tao Sheng! You,
master mirror-maker! Stop! You know that I cannot
rule the desert without the water mirror, and the Han
emissary is coming with the mirror to take Cai Wenji
home. The magic mirror you crafted a thousand years
ago is coming to the desert! I warn you. Do not
meddle in my affairs!

WENJI Who . . . who are you? How dare you trespass on to
forbidden ground! This is the palace of the King of the
Huns.

*[As PHANTOM speaks with WENJI, he pulls the curtain
forward and backward, and hovers around WENJI, above her,
beside her, taunting her, menacing her, cajoling her, his
presence enveloping her.]*

PHANTOM Forbidden ground? Cai Wenji, did you say I trespass?
I have ruled the desert a thousand years. I am the
Phantom General of the deserts. The Hun soldiers have
trespassed on my land. Your countrymen's war-horses
have trespassed in my domain. I rule the deserts of the
world. How could I trespass?

WENJI You . . . You mean, you are . . .

PHANTOM Yes. But there is no need for fear. You and I are both
victims of war. The difference is, I am dead, and you
live on.

WENJI What do you want?

PHANTOM I am here to tell you that you are going home, to the
Central Plain.

WENJI Going home?

PHANTOM Yes. Your Emperor has despatched an emissary to
ransom you and to take you home to the Kingdom of
Han in the Central Plain.

WENJI An emissary to take me home? Am I dreaming?

PHANTOM But, before you get too excited about the news, there is
        something you should know. The emissary is bringing a
        water mirror, a magic mirror engraved with water
        waves.

WENJI A water mirror?

PHANTOM It is a magic charm which helps the Han Emperor rule
        his kingdom. It makes the enemies lay down their
        weapons, and brings peace to the land. Without this
        mirror, the emissary cannot achieve his mission and
        take you home. But, if anything should happen to the
        mirror . . .

WENJI Stop. I know what you are going to say. You want to
        foil this mission, you want to seize the mirror, don't
        you?

PHANTOM Ha ha. You are as quick as you're reputed to be. But
        I am not going to foil the mission, nor do I want to
        seize the mirror. I am here to tell you that in three
        days, the emissary will stand here before you. Then you
        will have to decide: you will have to give up
        something you treasure.

WENJI What do you mean? What treasure?

PHANTOM Ah. Life is never as we like it. As a mother—

WENJI [interrupts] 'As a mother?'

PHANTOM You made me say this. As a mother, you will have to
        give up what you treasure most.

WENJI [in horror] Oh no! No!

PHANTOM Your barbarian sons are not permitted into Han
        territory.

WENJI My barbarian sons not permitted into Han territory?
        Why is life so cruel? No, no. It can't be like this! Not
        like this!

PHANTOM It's not for you to say, but for you to choose.

WENJI Do I have a choice? First, the war wrenched me from
        my homeland, from my family. Now, after twelve years
        of living in the shadows of war and carnage, I am to be
        ordered to leave my temporary shelter, to leave my flesh
        and blood. You who want to fight, to destroy—you
        should do your own fighting, and destroy yourselves.
        Why make us ordinary people suffer for your sake? In
        all this fighting, and killing, those who suffer and
        those who die are those who wanted no part of it!

PHANTOM Your rage is futile. In any case, my warning is a
        gesture of goodwill. After all, we can't fight against
        fate and destiny.

WENJI My barbarian sons are not permitted into Han territory! Will wars never cease?

PHANTOM So, Wenji, get me the mirror, and stay with your sons here in the desert. Besides, you are a concubine of the barbarian king, and your family is here in the desert. Is this then not your home? It can be your home for all eternity, if you choose to regard it so.

WENJI My home for all eternity? What do you mean?

PHANTOM Look you, there are thousands upon thousands of lonely, dead souls roaming the rolling yellow dust of the desert, without a home, or refuge, tormented by wind and storm. They await a power to guide them, to lead them, to protect them. Only the magic mirror can help me to help them. Don't you understand? For the thousands upon thousands of dead souls, stay for ever in the desert with the mirror, with me. Marry me, and the desert!

WENJI It can't be! It can't be true. You are making it up so that you can lay your hands on that mirror. I don't want to leave my children. I won't be sacrificed again for war.

PHANTOM Wenji, you are an intelligent woman. You would know how to choose. Come. Listen. That fool of an emissary is within a hundred miles of here. Listen to his voice carried on the wind. [Withdraws his head to behind the curtain]

[voice from behind the curtain] Protect your children, protect the mirror, marry me . . .

[Drum roll rises.]

EMISSARY [chants offstage, his voice carries as if on the wind]

> The yellow dust rolls over the desert land,
> The scorching sun burns in my anxious heart.
> Ride on my steed, ceaselessly,
> Ceaselessly,
> I must hurry . . .

Oh, Wenji! Do you know I have journeyed thousands of miles, through scalding sandstorms, in the scorching heat, in search of you . . . ceaselessly?

[EMISSARY enters, followed by ATTENDANT, and moves across the stage upstage, some distance behind WENJI, who is not aware of them.]

ATTENDANT Slow down, my lord. You ride hard in the day, you ride
even in your sleep. It's a wonder that you have not
collapsed. Perhaps if you did, I could catch a nap, and
have a proper meal. *[Sighs]*

EMISSARY I must hurry . . . Ride on . . .

*[Drum roll fades. WENJI rouses herself from the troubled
thoughts stirred up by PHANTOM and turns round to look,
but finds that PHANTOM is gone.]*

WENJI The Phantom General . . . the Phantom . . . It must have
been a dream! Or was it?

*[From under the black mid-curtain, and behind WENJI, OLD
ARTISAN creeps on to the stage, followed by two other
ARTISANS, also wearing masks. They are dressed in neutral
coloured ragged drapes which obscure their human form. They
move about in slow, fluid, and spectral movements adapted
from tai chi chuan—a form of Chinese martial arts—giving
the impression that they are amorphous, protean shapes rather
than humans, ideas rather than men.]*

Is a new exile about to begin? The generous bounty of
the Han Emperor heralds but a new catastrophe. Oh,
homeland! My homeland! Home? What does the word
mean?

ARTISAN *[from behind WENJI, in a soft, hypnotic voice]* Home is
always home. It is like the blood that flows in your
veins, it cannot be anything else.

*[The lines of OLD ARTISAN can be spoken by him and echoed
by the group, or spoken in unison with the group, or spoken
by members of the group in turn. The group performs a kind
of choric function to amplify OLD ARTISAN's role.]*

WENJI *[looks round, as if aware of a presence behind her, but does
not see OLD ARTISAN and is thrown into confusion]* Who's
that? Is that you, Phantom General? Why are you
hiding? General! Come out here and speak to me!

ARTISAN *[in a kindly voice]* Cai Wenji. The Phantom General you
are looking for is already a hundred miles away.

*[WENJI feels the kind presence of the ARTISAN and calms
down, but is still confused and dismayed. She looks around.]*

WENJI And who might you be? I cannot see you. Are you a
phantom as well?

ARTISAN You could say that. A phantom is a will that refuses to
die. Come to terms with your grief. Think of the past,
and the present, both as a dream. Start over again when

you get home to Han territory. Let the love and warmth of home heal your wounds and soothe your hurt.

WENJI I appreciate your kindness and your concern. Please tell me, who are you? Why are you so kind to me?

ARTISAN I am the master craftsman who made the water mirror. I have stayed with the mirror for centuries, to make sure it does not fall into evil hands. Make good use of this opportunity to reach safety, and you will suffer no more from ill fortune.

[During this exchange, the ARTISANS *advance towards* WENJI *and encircle her, confront her, and then retreat in group formation.]*

WENJI But . . . *[In anguish]* my children . . . *[She cries.]* My barbarian sons are not permitted into Han territory. How . . . how can I bear to part from my own flesh and blood? How can I welcome with joy such terrible grief?

ARTISAN *[the lines are chanted softly against eerie sounds produced on woodwind and percussion instruments]* Wenji. Look at the rolling sandstorms. There roam thousands upon thousands of spirits, wailing and howling in the wind. Their will to victory in battle, their will to a triumphant return, their will to fame through eternity have driven them to live on beyond the death of their mutilated bodies. Look! Look at their phantom shadows in the sandstorms. And listen to their battle cries, their wailing in the wind. I, too, am like one of these, living beyond my death. But now my mind is clear, and so is yours, I hope. Let us put aside our wills and desires, and be at peace. You should live for that which is to come, and forget that which has been. I will be the mirror when I see myself in it, and forget it when my image shifts from it.

WENJI *[murmuring to herself]* Live for that which is to come, and forget that which has been. That is a state not easily—

ARTISAN You share your father's intelligence. You know what it means.

WENJI But the children of my body—how can I forget them?

ARTISAN I must leave now, the Phantom General will be here soon. Remember! You must not let the tyrant of the desert take possession of the water mirror. Now I must go.

WENJI Old master craftsman, please don't go. I won't hand
over the water mirror to the Phantom General, but I
don't want to leave my children either. Please—

[OLD ARTISAN, and group, exit, as if vanished. Drum roll
fades in to herald the arrival of PHANTOM GENERAL.
PHANTOM suddenly pokes his head out from behind the
black mid-curtain, as if chasing ARTISAN.]

PHANTOM Tao Sheng! You old fool! Don't run away. You're a
coward if you do. Coward! Tao Sheng! Tao Sheng! [He
looks around, then speaks to WENJI.] It looks as though
the damned fool has been talking to you. Wenji, for
the sake of your children and your future, don't believe
a word he said. Stay here in the desert, marry—

WENJI Only if I can 'live for that which is to come, and forget
what has been' will I have peace of mind? [Sighs] I fear
I cannot do that.

PHANTOM That's right, Wenji. Your children are your flesh and
blood. How can you abandon those you love for a
dream of the past? I have done you a favour. I have
moved aside all obstacles with a sandstorm, the Han
emissary will be here soon. About the water mirror . . .
[PHANTOM vanishes.]

WENJI Is home always home? Live with that which is to be,
forget what has been. Forget my children, and return to
the land which is in my blood! No, I can't do it!

[Lights dim. WENJI exits.]

SCENE THREE

[Lights slowly up. MOTHER appears, dressed in a raincoat as in Scene 1, a
suitcase in her hand. She is followed by three actors, dressed as REFUGEES, each
holding a suitcase. MOTHER, still steeped in memories of her wartime experience,
recalls her experience of giving birth to a baby on board the ship to Taiwan. The
other actors, who play the REFUGEES sailing in the same ship, move in formation
to amplify her feeling and actions.]

MOTHER Has it been forty years? The ship that sailed for Taiwan
. . . it drifted for seven days and seven nights. There
was no water. . . . I was carrying your brother . . .

REFUGEE A I'm thirsty. . . . I'm in pain. . . . Give me some water . . .
oh, my belly hurts!

REFUGEE B Give me some water . . .

MOTHER I'm thirsty. My belly hurts! *[She stands astride over her suitcase, leans back, and strenuously pushes her suitcase forward from between her legs, miming a woman in labour. REFUGEES do the same. Background music rises, evocative of the panic of the terrified women.]* I want to throw up. . . . Give me some water. . . . The baby . . . the ship . . . we could not go ashore. . . . the baby . . . I'm going to throw up . . . the baby . . . on the ship . . . *[The suitcases/babies are pushed to the front. MOTHER and REFUGEES collapse in fatigue on the suitcases. Music fades out.*

   Lights dim.

   In preparation for the next scene, MOTHER squats down, opens the suitcase, takes out an elaborately embroidered robe— the costume of WENJI at court—and slips it on. Then she stands up, and with her back towards the audience, begins slowly to dress herself and put on a mask. Behind her and further upstage, the REFUGEES, men and women alike, also open their suitcases and each takes out a contemporary wedding gown. Still facing the audience, they start to change into their wedding gowns, but their slow, almost ritualistic movements are not intended to reflect the conventional romantic associations of the gowns.]

SCENE FOUR

[MOTHER, having transformed herself into WENJI, turns round to face the audience. She is now decked out in the full regal spendour of her elaborately embroidered, oversized robe. The other actors, in wedding gowns, drift desolately about the stage in formations as the scene unfolds—a visual contrast to WENJI.]

ATTENDANT *[offstage]* Madam Wenji, I announce the arrival of the Special Emissary from the Court of the Han Dynasty, His Lordship Zhou Yan.

   [EMISSARY enters, followed by ATTENDANT.]

EMISSARY My hearty congratulations, Wenji. Wenji . . . Madam, I have the pleasure to greet you at last. Wenji . . . I . . . I am . . .

ATTENDANT You are struck dumb, my lord. Read the Royal Decree!

EMISSARY Ah, yes. Yes. *[Clears his throat]* Cai Wenji, daughter of the Han Dynasty scholar Cai Yung, be present to receive this Royal Decree. By order of the Emperor of the Kingdom of Han: The scholar Cai Yung, by virtue

of his distinguished learning and talent, was fully
deserving of a place at Court to assist in the affairs of
State. The same personage was, however, pressed into
the service of the former minister Dong Zhuo, against
the interests of the Realm. Now that the truth of the
case has come to light, His Majesty, the Emperor, in
his benevolence, resolves to overlook the deeds of the
past, and being mindful of the well-being of Cai
Yung's sole surviving progeny, Cai Wenji, who was
abducted by the Huns and detained in their Court for
the past twelve years, now sends a Special Emissary
with a ransom of ten thousand taels of gold, one
hundred bolts of silk fabric, to appeal to the King of
the Huns, in consideration of the peaceful relationship
between both our Kingdoms, to grant the return of Cai
Wenji to Han territory.

WENJI *[kneels to receive the scroll of Royal Decree]* Wenji gratefully
receives the Royal Decree. Thank you, Your Lordship.

EMISSARY Furthermore, you are granted a treasure of the Han
Dynasty court: a water mirror.

WENJI *[almost indifferently]* I acknowledge the Royal Command.

EMISSARY Madam Wenji, you should be delighted! This water
mirror is amongst the rarest of treasures in the Royal
Court, used in prayers for rain and blessings for the
commonwealth. Only the magic powers of this water
mirror will see you and I through the parched
desolation, and the eerie dangers of the desert land, and
return us safely to our homeland. You should be
overjoyed at the gift, Wenji. *[Holds tightly on to the
water mirror]*

ATTENDANT My lord. How can the lady share your joy at the
mirror if you keep clutching on to it?

EMISSARY Oh yes, yes. My apologies, my apologies. Wenji.
[Hands her the water mirror] I . . . I . . .

ATTENDANT Say it, my lord, say it. Tell her. *[Mimics him]* 'I, Zhou
Yan, a scholar, have journeyed thousands of miles,
through scalding sandstorms, in the scorching sun, in
search of you . . .'

WENJI I am grateful to you. But this water mirror, will it
bring good fortune or ill? Will I be the mirror when I
see myself in it? Oh, my children!

EMISSARY Your sons will stay with their father. His Majesty the
Emperor has arranged for you another marriage—to me.
Your two sons will not enter Han territory.

WENJI My two sons will not enter Han territory!

EMISSARY That is so. Wenji, your father was my teacher and mentor, and at your residence, we have had the pleasure of meeting—

ATTENDANT My lord, why don't you just recite once more what you have been saying all the way here. It saves a lot of humming and hawing.

EMISSARY *[embarrassed]* Hah!

WENJI I remember you. Zhou Yan, from Zhengzhou, adept at military strategy, and divination, excellent at music. My father often mentioned you.

EMISSARY *[excited by the recognition of his merit]* Really? *[Now holds forth with some boldness]* When the Emperor wanted a special emissary to bring you home, I volunteered my service, to repay the debt of gratitude to your father, my mentor. I have pledged my life to protect you on this long journey and accomplish my mission.

WENJI Thank you, my lord. And my father? How is he?

EMISSARY *[sadly]* The truth is he passed away in his prison cell.

WENJI Oh, woe! *[Overcome with grief, she chants.]*

> The heavens above, know you no mercy?
> All was well ere I was born,
> Then ill fortune attended the realm of Han.
> Heaven is cruel in the gift of war,
> Earth is cruel to torment me more.

EMISSARY Wenji, control your grief in acceptance.

WENJI *[chants mournfully]*

> War turns life into peril, dangers attend the road.
> Men driven to exile, sorrow in tow.

EMISSARY Wenji, the Emperor thought highly of your late father's merits, and of your learning, that is why he has spared no expense to bring you home.

WENJI Let it be! My father is gone, I have no family in the Central Plain. This may be alien land, yet to leave it I would have to leave my sons. Let it be! *[Pauses]* I thank you for this long journey. But I am in truth confused. What makes a home? Is it not where one's beloved is?

EMISSARY Oh, indeed not. This is—

WENJI Why is it in every war, women are the spoils of war? Why is each exile another nightmare, a new marriage bond? What is this homecoming? Is it not the start of another exile?

EMISSARY Please do not confuse right and wrong. You must
understand the good intentions of the Emperor.

WENJI *[sighs]* When I set foot in the Central Plain, and cast
my eyes north to the desert land, and watch the
twilight set dusky over the lonely trail of smoke over
the wilderness, is not the pain in my heart a yearning
for home as well?

EMISSARY But madam, the trees grow tall by your father's grave.
Can you, his child, turn away in neglect and make
your home in a barbarous land? And his aspirations for
the good of the Realm, that too, is a legacy you cannot
refuse. What's more, the Emperor values your talents,
you must repay that kindness. You must not make your
captors your mentors. There is a difference between our
race and theirs!

WENJI I am sorry, my lord. I know too little of the world,
I cannot tell the difference between our race and theirs.
I know only I am the mother of two sons.

EMISSARY You . . . you don't want to go back! I have travelled
thousands of miles to take you home, and you don't
even want to go back! I . . . I . . . *[Breaks out in a
horrifying burst of laughter]* Ha . . . ha . . . ha . . .

WENJI What horror in that laughter . . . how familiar that
howling sounds!

*[EMISSARY swirls round the stage in fury, flings off his mask,
and with a backward somersault, retreats to the back of the
stage. He stands with his back to the audience as ATTENDANT
helps him change into PHANTOM GENERAL's costume.*

*There is a low, tense drum roll. OLD ARTISAN, and
group, enter.]*

ARTISAN Cai Wenji, the decision to go or stay is not for you to
make. You must know that thousands upon thousands
of phantoms wait eagerly for that water mirror in your
hand, longing for you to take them back to their roots.
When you set forth for home with that mirror in your
hand, your countrymen's spirits will follow your steps
and cast off the pain of exile. Go home, Wenji, take
them home to rest!

WENJI Even the dead want to return? Is that the truth? Is
there no choice in what to do? Is the only course to
take that of homecoming?

ARTISAN If you do not return, and the mirror falls into evil
hands, then all the dead souls in the desert will fall
within the Phantom General's realm, they'll be
condemned to exile for an eternity of anguish.

WENJI The mirror! The mirror again! It is the cause of all the
strife. It is the undying will and desire in man! Let me
destroy it, and so destroy desire in ghosts and man!

ARTISAN Destroy the mirror? Don't do that! I fashioned it with
my life.

*[EMISSARY, having changed into the costume of PHANTOM
GENERAL, breaks into a howling laughter and swings round
to face the audience. He is dressed in an oversized embroidered
garment suggestive of a warrior's armour, plus headgear
adorned with pheasants' tails, and wears a fierce warrior
mask. In stylized Peking Opera fashion, he rushes violently
about to deafening drumbeats and eerie percussion music, and
dashes towards WENJI.]*

PHANTOM How dare you destroy the mirror! It is my hope of a
thousand years!

ARTISAN What? The Phantom General! Wenji, give me the
mirror! *[Rushes forward to seize the mirror]*

PHANTOM Give me the mirror! How can you destroy desire in
ghosts and man? *[Joins the scuffle for the mirror. The
struggle is accompanied by violent music.]*

WENJI Master Craftsman, Phantom General, if you want to
fight, do it. Your battles have nothing to do with me!

*[PHANTOM succeeds in seizing the mirror, but at that very
instant, the water mirror vanishes. He and OLD ARTISAN
scream with desperation, 'The mirror!' They exit, as if
vanished.*

*Music changes, marking the transition from the violent
fight to sorrow and grief.]*

[chants]

> Times change. Dynasties change.
> So does the life of Cai Wenji:
> North, south, wandering in exile,
> From the Plains to the desert, from the desert
>   to the Plains.

*[The actors in contemporary wedding gowns sing in unison,
as chorus.]*

CHORUS
> Endless the rank weeds grew to the sky,
> Brute hooves trampled the city walls,
> No king to protect us from on high,
> The people grieved, the warriors died.
> By the city gates, see how the willows fly.

WENJI *[chants]*

>A reluctant widow remarried,
>A mother twice bereaved, my plight.
>Singing the sad song of my life,
>Breaks my soul in the dead of night.

CHORUS

>Endless the rank weeds grow to the sky,
>Brute hooves trample the city walls,
>No kings to protect us from on high,
>The people grieve, the warriors die.
>And Wenji's story stays alive.*

[Lights fade. All exit.]

SCENE FIVE

[Lights up. MOTHER, *still wearing a raincoat, is standing in the place where* WENJI *last stood. She is getting ready for departure.]*

MOTHER *[murmuring to herself]* Forty years it's been. That day, your aunts and uncles said, 'Go and look for him. Come back if all is well.' I never thought . . . that I would be away for forty years. *[Takes the mirror out of her suitcase]* I took this little mirror with me. I still have it with me today. Now what shall I do with it?

[Voices of her CHILDREN, *offstage]*

VOICE OF CHILDREN Take care, Mother.

We've sorted out your bags. You'll soon be home.

Don't forget that you've just had an eye operation, Mother. Don't tire yourself out.

It's been forty years, Mother. Do you think you will recognize them?

Mother, have you got your eye lotion?

And the little mirror you wanted to bring with you?

Rest well, Mother. If you're not used to life there, come home soon.

---

* In history Cai Wenji agreed to return to Han territory and remarried. Guo Moruo, a mainland Chinese dramatist, wrote a famous play based on this story entitled *Cai Wenji* (1959). In his version Wenji agrees, after much conflict, to abandon her husband—the barbarian king—and her children, and returns to serve her country. The play glorifies Wenji's selflessness and her willingness to put the needs of her country before herself.

Mother, phone us as soon as you get there. We'll be waiting.

[*Lights dim during the chorus of farewells.*]

MOTHER [*holding the mirror, stands in spotlight*] This mirror. Where shall I put it?

BLACKOUT

THE END

PLAYS FROM

HONG KONG

BEFORE THE
DAWN-WIND RISES

A CONTEMPORARY DRAMA
IN TWO ACTS

1985

Before the dawn-wind rises,
Before the shadow flees,
Return!

The Song of Songs 2:17

By
JOANNA CHAN

Translated by
JANE C. C. LAI

— ABOUT THE PLAYWRIGHT —

JOANNA CHAN graduated from the Chinese University of Hong Kong, after which she studied Theology in the Philippines, and Art and Design at the Art Institute in Chicago. She received her MA, M.Ed., and Ed.D. in Theatre and Communications from Columbia University, where she was appointed adjunct Associate Professor in 1982, and was honoured with a Distinguished Alumni Award in 1994.

Chan's theatre career spans more than twenty-five years in North America, Hong Kong, China, and Taiwan. She was co-founder and Artistic Director (1970–7, and 1983–92) of the 'Four Seas Players' in New York City, and Artistic Director (1986–90) of the Hong Kong Repertory Theatre. In 1992, she co-founded the 'Yangtze Repertory Theatre of America' to produce works for and by Asian artists. The forty-odd productions she has adapted and directed include *Othello*, *Cabaret*, *The King and I*, *Dream of the Red Chamber*, *Rickshaw Puller Camel Cheung*, and Raymond To's *Where Love Abides*, which she took to Guangzhou in 1987.

Chan began writing plays in 1975. Her major works include *Before the Dawn-wind Rises*, commissioned by the Hong Kong Urban Council for the Tenth Asian Arts Festival; *Crown Ourselves with Roses*—commissioned by the Sing Tao Newspapers—which toured North America in 1989; *The Soongs: By Dreams Betrayed*, a political drama published in Hong Kong in 1992; and *Forbidden City West*, a musical in English that examines one hundred years of the Chinese American experience.

In addition, Chan is author and designer of the books, *Children of the Yellow River*, *Towards a Distant Vision*, and *Oasis in the Night*. She has written extensively on drama and on issues relating to East–West communication. A member of the Dramatists' Guild in the United States, she is well known for her dedicated promotion of Chinese culture in America and in 1993, she was honoured at 'An All-Star Salute to Chinese American Cultural Pioneers' at City Hall, New York City.

Meanwhile Chan continues to show an interest in, and concern for Hong Kong by contributing frequently to Hong Kong magazines and newspapers.

Joanna Chan is also a Maryknoll Sister.

ABOUT **THE PLAY**

Realistic in style, this play deals with the subject of family separation, estrangement, and reunion that has touched many Chinese people's lives throughout the twentieth century. Set in Hong Kong in the early 1980s, it tells the story of two brothers from a Hong Kong family who have been estranged for years. The elder brother lives in mainland China while the younger brother lives in Hong Kong. The play focuses on the drama, conflicts, misunderstandings, and revelations about the past that ensue when the brothers and their families meet again.

In the last decade, following China's Open Door policy, there has been growing opportunity for interchange between China and Hong Kong in terms of trade, and, more importantly, for people to travel and meet. This meeting of people after many decades has generated excitement, as well as anxiety, about possibilities for renewal of contacts, re-establishment of ties, reunion, and reconciliation.

This play is one of the earlier attempts by a Hong Kong playwright to deal with the topic, and is important as a record of Hong Kong's socio-cultural history. The interaction between the two branches of the family reveals much about their different values, aspirations, tribulations, and achievements. At the same time, the play delineates the cultural and ideological burdens and affinities of the two brothers. Not only does it compare two ways of life, it delves more deeply to unearth earlier and persistent tensions between the brothers, giving an insight into the sense of responsibility, of resentment and guilt not only in the two men, but in the larger Chinese brotherhood on both sides of the border.

DRAMATIS PERSONAE

SI KA MAN (CARMEN), aged 35, a career woman

HO KEI CHEONG, businessman, owns a factory, CARMEN's husband.
   Appears at the ages of 18, 30, and 48

HO KEI WOON, CHEONG's elder brother, on a visit to Hong Kong
   from mainland China. Appears at the ages of 25 and 50

CHEUNG HEUNG MUI (MAY), WOON's wife, on a visit to Hong
   Kong from mainland China. Appears at the ages of 17 and 47

HO SHING KWONG, aged 30, son of MAY

HO SHING YEE, aged 17, daughter of MAY

LEE CHI CHUNG, aged 80, maternal uncle of WOON and CHEONG

MOTHER, Mrs Ho, mother of WOON and CHEONG. Appears at the
   ages of 42 and 56

Time: Mid-October 1985
Place: Hong Kong

If possible, each character should be played by the same actor
   throughout. Since there will be little time to change costume and
   make-up to indicate time changes, the age differences should be
   suggested by minor changes in costume, and accessories such as
   glasses.

SET

There are two levels to the set. The upper level recessed at least ten feet from the front of the lower level. There should be a hidden stairway behind the set for access to the upper level. There is a narrow staircase (with at least 16 steps) at stage right, facing the exit on stage right. If possible, when the action takes place on the lower level, the upper level should be screened off with a wall or curtain. The set and the lighting should be realistic. The lighting for the flashback scenes should be tinted sepia, as in a faded photograph.

The play is divided into 14 scenes, with an intermission of fifteen minutes after Act 1, Scene 5. Areas of the set used for each scene are as follows:

1. The HO family living-room (centre stage) and bedroom (stage left, slightly recessed). Below the landing is the front door, which faces the audience at an angle. In the bedroom, stage left, a door leads on to a bathroom offstage. Act 1, Scene 1, and Act 2, Scenes 4 and 9. Time: 1985.

2. LEE CHI CHUNG's home in a section of an old tenement flat in Shaukeiwan, a rather run-down residential area (upper level, stage right). Act 1, Scene 2 and Act 2, Scene 5. Time: 1985.

3. CHEONG's office in Causeway Bay (centre stage; same area as HO living-room). Act 1, Scenes 3 and 5, and Act 2, Scenes 1, 3, and 7. Time: 1985.

4. The HO family home in a small room in an old tenement flat in Nam Chong Street, Shamshuipo, a crowded area (upper level, near the centre). Act 1, Scene 4, and Act 2, Scenes 2 and 6. Time: Early 1955 and autumn of 1967.

5. A room in the Miramar Hotel (stage left, slightly recessed; same area as HO bedroom). Act 2, Scene 8. Time: 1985.

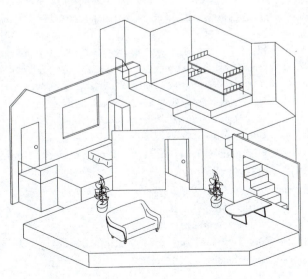

ACT *1*

SCENE ONE

[Evening. Mid October. The HO *family living room. The lights are on. The modern Western decor is stylish and elegant. Here and there in the corners are placed luxuriant bonsai plants of different sizes which look real from a distance.*

When the curtain opens, a hi-fi set is playing popular American music—a lyrical piece. CARMEN *is seated in front of her dressing-table in the bedroom doing her make-up, humming phrases of the melody. Dresses and clothes are scattered all over her bed, all very fashionable and brightly coloured.*

CARMEN *has just turned 35. She is poised, and elegant. She is also generous, with a touch of the romantic in her nature. She comes from a good family, has studied abroad, is a university graduate, and now holds a well-paid job. It has been smooth sailing for her all her life. She is not particularly intelligent, but she is quick, direct, and forthright in dealing with things and people. She has a lively mind and enjoys talking to anybody, or even to herself when there is nobody around.*

She has been married to CHEONG *for five years, long enough to have passed the phase of romantic enchantment, but something of that still remains. Just over three years ago,* CHEONG *decided to go into business. When her distinguished engineer husband, who was educated abroad, suddenly became a textile factory boss, she felt let down, and her disappointment adds a touch of contempt in her attitude towards him.*

Soon after the curtain opens, someone unlocks the front door from outside and opens it. CHEONG *walks in, carrying a briefcase and looking depressed. He is not quite 50, smartly dressed. He has worked hard to raise himself from his humble origins through studying abroad, and is proud of his achievements, yet he feels frustrated that he has not made his fortune and he is running out of time. This feeling has prompted him to take risks.*

He frowns at the music which greets his return. He loosens his collar as he walks to the hi-fi to turn down the volume. CARMEN *notices her husband is home.]*

CARMEN Hey! *[Pauses, waiting for her husband to come into the room]* Where were you? We all waited at the railway station. We called your office but you weren't there.

CHEONG *[puts down briefcase]* I was busy at the factory. *[Takes off jacket, goes into the kitchen and returns with a can of beer]* The maid's day off?

CARMEN Her kid was ill. Since we aren't eating at home I let her go early.

CHEONG *[opens the can of beer, sits on the bed and looks at the pile of clothes there]* Been shopping again? *[Blandly, not out of curiosity or resentment]*

CARMEN No, I picked out some old clothes for your niece.

CHEONG My niece?

CARMEN Yes, your brother's daughter. *[Pauses to look at him]* What's the matter with you? Your elder brother brings his whole family from the Mainland to see you, the first time in thirty years, and you didn't even turn up to meet him as you promised. What's wrong?

CHEONG Something went wrong with the shipment. *[Stands up]* I'll go and wash my face. *[Goes into bathroom, turns on the tap. CARMEN pauses for him to continue.]* Are they at the hotel?

CARMEN Yes, at the Miramar. I said they should have a rest, then we'd pick them up and bring them home for a chat, and then go out for dinner. But they said they'd come here by themselves. *[Getting no response from CHEONG, she goes on.]* It was funny when we met. They didn't know me, and I didn't know them, but I picked them out right away. Kwong looks just like you. No wonder they say nephews look like their uncles. Kwong is the spitting image of you. *[CHEONG stands at the bathroom door, pensive. Getting no response from him, CARMEN goes on.]* And May, your brother's wife, is so slim and elegant! Not like that woman deputy director of something from China that we took to dinner once. That was a real friendly neighbourhood housewife, ha. *[CARMEN laughs.]* May grew up in Hong Kong, didn't she?

CHEONG Yes. *[Walks away]*

CARMEN Have you met her before?

CHEONG Umm. *[Turns away]*

CARMEN Odd though. She's so young you don't expect her to have a son his age. *[Pauses. Sensing something in CHEONG's silence, she turns round to look at him.]* What's wrong with the shipment? Is it late?

CHEONG No. It'd be terrible if we were late with such a large consignment.

CARMEN Then what's wrong?

CHEONG I don't know. We had a telegram from America. Their agent here told them the shipment doesn't meet the specifications.

CARMEN Oh? *[Pauses]* Does Lam Bunn know?

CHEONG I don't know if he does. I can't find him.

CARMEN Lam is bound to know. It'll be all right.

CHEONG It'll be disastrous if it isn't. I've invested everything in this shipment.

CARMEN You can always count on Lam. It'll be all right. Don't imagine the worst. *[Stands up]* They'll be here soon. Why don't you change first. *[Indicates the outfit she has laid out for him. Takes clothes from the wardrobe, exits to the bathroom]*

[CHEONG stands in the middle of the room, thinking. Goes to take a look at the clothes laid out for him. Switches off the hi-fi in the living room, stands there a moment and returns to the bedroom. He stands looking at the outfit. CARMEN has changed and comes into the room, buttoning up and putting on her belt.]

CHEONG I don't like this outfit.

CARMEN No? Get something else then. *[Pauses]* Or go as you are.

CHEONG *[sits down and shakes his head as he looks at himself]* In this?

CARMEN Why are you so particular today? You're only meeting your brother. He's family.

CHEONG I don't want to overdress, but then I don't want to be sloppy.

CARMEN When have you ever been sloppy?

CHEONG You don't understand.

CARMEN Suit yourself.

[CARMEN ignores him, goes to do her hair. CHEONG picks a tie from the wardrobe, goes to CARMEN]

CHEONG Shall I just change the tie?

CARMEN *[turns to look at him in exasperation]* What's the matter with you? I know you've been troubled for months by your brother's visit, but he is here whether you like it or not. And this won't be the only time you'll see him. I know it's been thirty years, and you've been apart since you were twenty. But the excitement of your reunion will break the ice, and then there's bound to be a lot to talk about. I'm never at a loss for words.

CHEONG *[sits down again]* No. You could talk yourself silly just looking at the mirror.

CARMEN Yes, but, it's more fun if it's two-way traffic. You and I manage all right, except for this once. You're not quite yourself. Are you worried that they'll come and sponge on us?

CHEONG *[picks up the outfit, a disdainful look on his face]* They can't if I don't let them.

CARMEN Don't be so mean. Not everyone from the Mainland
sponges on people. If he had wanted to settle in Hong
Kong, he'd have discussed that with you in his letter.
He had to wait so long for his visa, and yet he only
applied for a week-long visit.

CHEONG Perhaps he's here to case the joint.

CARMEN How can you talk like that? We're doing all right and
he's your only brother, we should give him a hand.

CHEONG Well, he wanted to go to the Mainland in the first
place. It's not my fault.

CARMEN They're doing fine. He's a technician, she a teacher.
They have a fine son and a pretty daughter. *[Pauses]*
The girl will look so beautiful when I've taught her
how to dress. I'll give her some of my old clothes.
These won't be in by next season anyway.

CHEONG *[after a moment's silence]* What was he wearing?

CARMEN Your brother? He was in a suit. He's taken some
trouble to dress up. Not a good fit, of course. You
could tell at a glance it was made in China. But plain
and dignified. Not like some of our country cousins.

CHEONG *[sighs. Thaws a little]* My brother Woon was always
plain and dignified.

CARMEN *[glances at him through the mirror, half joking]* Not like you.
You sly sweet-talker, you could sweet-talk me into anything.

CHEONG *[turns to go to her]* I'm all upset. Don't tease me, please.
[Tries to embrace her, to get her to console him]

CARMEN *[stops him]* Get changed. *[CHEONG gives up and goes into the
bathroom.]* Have you paid the money back to Uncle Chung?

CHEONG Ye-es.

CARMEN Really. Your brother's family's one-week visit doesn't
even come to ten thousand dollars, and you only forked
out the money when Uncle Lee shamed you into it by
footing the bill. *[Getting no response from within the
bathroom]* Your brother wanted to come because he
wanted to pay his respects to your mother's grave. Why
have you never mentioned her grave all these years that
I've known you? *[No response]* I thought she was buried
in England. When we talked about it, Uncle Lee said
your mother never went to England. *[CHEONG has
changed. He comes out of the bathroom holding his tie, and
stands at the door but says nothing.]* Where is your
mother's grave? *[She pauses. CHEONG says nothing. She is
about to speak again when the doorbell rings.]* They're here!
[Gets up and walks briskly to open the door]

[CHEONG *hurriedly puts on his tie, and starts to walk out of the room. But on hearing the noise of people arriving he hesitates and stops.*

WOON *and* MAY *come in first, a little reserved and smiling a little timidly.* WOON *has just turned 50 and is dark and robust, perhaps more at home in the country than in a city. His face shows a generous and forgiving spirit. Unaccustomed to wearing a suit, he looks almost apologetic.* MAY *is more poised but strains to keep her dignity. She is gentle and at peace, with the quiet fortitude of a woman who has suffered. She has the look that appeals to male protectiveness. She is over 40 but neither old nor haggard. Although she is plainly dressed, it is obvious that her soft petite figure would look very beautiful in better clothes.]*

[warmly] Do come in! Please come in!

[The two greet her and enter. They are obviously taken aback by the decor which is more opulent than they had expected. The two move closer together. WOON *seems to be taking stock of the situation.*

Then the two children come in. YEE, *17 years old, has big bright eyes. She greets her aunt cheerily, and looks curiously at the surroundings with the confidence of a beloved spoilt child. She is in a Western-style dress, obviously brand new. She walks about smugly, but with some difficulty, on a pair of gold sandals with three-inch heels.*

KWONG *carries a bonsai plant, and greets his aunt politely. He is slim, looks younger than his 30 years, but staid and reserved, a contrast to the lively wilfulness of his sister. He quickly notices the plants around the room, and turns to his mother in slight embarrassment.]*

MAY *[smiles reassuringly at her son and turns to* CARMEN*]* We thought that since you have everything in Hong Kong, we would bring one of our bonsai plants for you. Now that we know you keep more and better plants, we are almost embarrassed to offer it.

[CHEONG starts at MAY's voice, crosses his arms in front of his chest to calm himself.]

CARMEN *[delighted with the plant and accepts the gift with both hands]* How beautiful! It would cost the earth to get one like this here. Thank you so much. *[Looks for a place to put it down]* All our plants are artificial—fakes. We had you fooled. Ha ha . . . *[Puts down the plant]* Please. Take a seat.

[They all sit down, perched as if ready to stand up again any moment. KWONG shows an interest in the artificial plants.]

YEE *[gets up again as soon as seated. Goes over to the hi-fi]* What a big hi-fi set you have!

CARMEN *[smiles warmly at YEE]* Yes. What would you like to listen to? I'll switch it on and you pick something you like. *[Switches on the hi-fi. Melodious Western music fills the room.]* Kei Cheong is changing. He'll be here soon. Make yourselves at home. I'll go and make some tea.

WOON *[bows slightly and mutters]* Eh. Don't go to any trouble.

[The moment CARMEN turns to go, MAY signals KWONG to switch off the hi-fi. KWONG finds the switch, YEE pouts in protest, but gives in after KWONG says something to her. CARMEN goes briskly into the bedroom, and, as she expects, finds CHEONG standing there.]

CARMEN What's the matter? Why are you still here? I'll get the tea.

CHEONG I'll get it.

CARMEN *[briskly and loudly]* Get what? You don't even know where the cups are. *[Goes out crossing a corner of the living room]*

[CHEONG goes to the door of the bedroom, leans against the wall, closes his eyes and takes a deep breath. Then with an effort of determination he gets out of the room into the living-room. All stand up. The children greet him as 'uncle'. CHEONG nods acknowledgement, his eyes on WOON.]

CHEONG Elder Brother! *[Hesitates a moment, goes forward and offers his hand. WOON, a little nonplussed, reaches out and shakes hands. CHEONG turns round and glances at MAY.]* Sister-in-law *[Turns away to look at KWONG]* Shing Kwong? *[KWONG responds cheerily and greets him as uncle. CHEONG offers his hand. KWONG hesitates, then, smiling, shakes hands.]* Take a seat, please.

[They all sit down. The brothers look at each other. MAY and the children look at CHEONG.]

CHEONG Got here this afternoon?

WOON Yes.

CHEONG Crowded, was it?

WOON Not too bad. *[Pauses]* The train was quite comfortable.

CHEONG Yes. Not bad. *[Pauses]* Through train, was it?

WOON Yes.

CHEONG Hm. *[Nods. Pauses]* Eh. Were there a lot of people?

WOON You mean the tour group? *[Pauses]* Scores of people.

CHEONG All tourists?

WOON *[nods]* And people meeting family and relatives.

CHEONG Hm. *[Nods again]* Staying at the Miramar?

WOON Yes.

CHEONG Are the rooms nice?

WOON Yes. *[Pauses]* Very nice.

YEE They've got colour TVs.

CHEONG *[turns to smile gratefully at* YEE *for helping him to break the ice]* Your aunt buys programmes for a TV station, and knows a lot of TV people. She can take you there for a visit. *[Turns and notices* MAY *observing him]*

YEE *[delighted]* Will she? Really?

[CARMEN has come in with the tea tray and now puts it down on the coffee-table. She hands a cup to WOON, *then one to* MAY. MAY *looks at* KWONG *who responds by thanking his aunt and taking a cup for himself, and one for* YEE. CARMEN *serves a plate of biscuits.]*

CARMEN Oh, yes. I know a lot of the TV artists. I'll take you to watch them shooting in the studio. *[*YEE *beams at her father who smiles at her, then she looks at* MAY.*]* Shing Kwong is probably not interested in TV stars, but I can take you to the Hong Kong University. Would you like that? I studied there. *[*KWONG *nods happily.* CARMEN *turns round and hands* CHEONG *a cup of tea.]* Don't you think Shing Kwong looks just like you?

[A clatter as MAY *drops her teacup and spills the tea.* MAY *is flushed with embarrassment, and bows her head. The children are startled to see this uncharacteristic clumsiness in their mother.* WOON *gets up and stands solicitously by his wife, his hand holding the teacup shaking noticeably.* CHEONG *stands staring at* MAY.*]*

[turns round and says graciously] Oh, it doesn't matter. *[To* CHEONG*]* Go and get some tissues. *[Nudges* CHEONG *who remains staring, then she quickly leaves the room to get a handful of tissues.* CHEONG *follows her. She comes back and mops up.]* No harm done. None at all . . . *[To* KWONG *and* YEE.*]* What else do you want to see? *[Pauses to think]* But we'll wait and see where the tour is taking you first. Have you got the itinerary here?

YEE We're going to Ocean Park* tomorrow.

KWONG And the Peak the day after.

YEE But I want to go to a disco.

CARMEN *[recalls something]* Ah. Are you allowed to go around by yourselves?

WOON We'll have to get permission first. But the most important thing is to visit—

[He is interrupted by the telephone ringing. CARMEN goes to answer it. CHEONG returns to the living-room and stands at the door.]

CARMEN Hello . . . yes? . . . Oh, Uncle Lee? *[They all look in her direction.]* Didn't you say you'd meet us here? . . . You're still at home? . . . Yes, just a moment. *[To CHEONG]* Uncle Lee wants you to pick him up—

CHEONG *[willingly]* Okay.

CARMEN Wait . . . what . . . yes. *[To CHEONG]* Uncle says to take Shing Kwong with you, and Elder Brother. . . .

CHEONG *[changes his mind]* Better tell him to come by taxi.

CARMEN No, go and pick him up. *[Gets back to the phone]* What? . . . It's all right. The three of them are coming together. See you later. *[Hangs up]* It's not easy to get a taxi where he lives. It's better to pick him up. *[WOON and KWONG stand up to go.]*

WOON Is Uncle still living in the old place?

YEE *[at the same time]* Dad, can I go too?

MAY They'll be back soon. Another time. *[YEE is disappointed.]*

CARMEN *[notices that CHEONG is about to leave without saying a word]* Yes, he is. You'll probably recognize it. *[To KWONG]* Although your great-uncle sells newspapers, he has read widely, especially the classics. He can talk about anything under the sun: the natural world and current affairs. He knows so much. You'll like him. *[Sees the three out of the main door, closes it, and turns to YEE]* Shing Yee, you don't want to go with them. There'll be other opportunities. Your Aunt Carmen has lots of pretty clothes for you.

[YEE's eyes light up. She turns to look at MAY, who seems unwilling to accept the generosity.]

[to MAY] Shall we go and chat in my room? *[Picks up the plate of biscuits and offers them to MAY]* Have one.

* Ocean Park is a theme park in Hong Kong.

[MAY takes one, thanks her. CARMEN hands the whole plate to YEE.] Take the whole plate. These are imported. *[Picks up YEE's cup, and the three go into the bedroom. To YEE]* Your outfit looks nice. Who bought it for you?

YEE Dad did.

CARMEN Can you get those clothes on the Mainland?

YEE Oh, you can get anything now. Even French watches. Look. *[Holds out her hand]*

CARMEN *[takes a look]* Cartier. Made in France. How much did you pay for it?

YEE Fifty yuan.

CARMEN Fifty yuan for a Cartier watch! It's a fake, silly. They cheated you. *[Goes out of the bedroom into the living-room, leaving MAY and YEE very embarrassed]*

MAY *[hurriedly but softly urges YEE]* If she offers you any clothes, don't take more than one or two things.

[YEE pouts, staring at her watch, and doesn't answer.]

CARMEN *[comes in with another cup of tea]* May, have another cup of tea. *[To YEE]* The famous brand products you get on the Mainland are mostly fakes made in Hong Kong. Hong Kong specializes in making fakes. The plants we have in our flat are all fakes. Ha ha ha.

[CARMEN laughs heartily. Although MAY is troubled, she can't help but admire CARMEN's openness, and breaks into a smile.]

[to YEE] I've only worn these once or twice. If you don't mind, take what suits you.

[YEE chooses from the clothes on the bed, and looks in the mirror to see which would look nice on her. But she cannot imagine herself in these clothes and cannot decide.]

[to YEE] Your father makes about a hundred yuan a month at the most, and he spent fifty on your watch?

YEE My brother's watch cost even more. *[Munches on the biscuits]*

MAY He saved up the money himself.

YEE I only get ten yuan a month pocket money. How can I save anything?

CARMEN Ten yuan? That's almost one tenth of what your father makes.

YEE You think that's a lot? A classmate of mine gets twenty, and she has a boyfriend who gives her money to spend.

CARMEN Do you have a boyfriend?

YEE *[shakes her head and makes a face]* None that I like.

CARMEN What type do you like?

YEE *[pouts]* Somebody who can take me abroad.

CARMEN Abroad? Would your parents let you?

YEE Why not if I had the chance? *[Turns round holding one of* CARMEN's *dresses against herself]* This one is nice.

CARMEN Yes. Try it on in the bathroom. *[Points to the bathroom door]*

[YEE goes in, comes out immediately and stands hesitant at the door.]

YEE This is the bathroom?

CARMEN *[looks at her for a moment, and then it dawns on her that the bathroom is different from what* YEE *is used to. Goes over]* Oh yes. *[Follows her into the bathroom]* If you want to used the toilet, push this to flush. *[The sound of flushing]* Show us when you've tried it on. *[Comes out, closing the door behind her. Stops at the door, shakes her head as if trying to get rid of an unhappy thought. Sees* MAY *watching her, smiles]* Yee is a lovely girl! *[Goes over to* MAY *and sits down]*

MAY You haven't got any children?

CARMEN I don't want any.

MAY *[very surprised]* Don't want any?

CARMEN *[shakes her head]* When I married Kei Cheong, we agreed not to.

MAY Agreed not to?

CARMEN *[laughs at* MAY's *surprise]* Nicer life for a twosome! A lot of career women in the States prefer that.

MAY Kei Cheong is doing so well. You don't have to work.

CARMEN *[laughs]* He has his business and I have my own career. That has nothing to do with him.

MAY Is that so?

CARMEN In these days of equality, we don't depend on our husbands.

MAY Then why get married?

CARMEN To build a family!

MAY If you don't have children, what will you do in days to come?

CARMEN It's not like it used to be. You don't have to count on your children being around you when you get old.

MAY It's easy to say that. Even now, isn't it a bit too quiet at home?

CARMEN We are both busy, dashing here and there.

MAY On your own?

CARMEN Why of course! Did you think we went everywhere together? That sort of thing is out of date.

MAY When Kei Woon was sent to the country, I used to long for him to come home. When he was home, I feared that he would be sent away again. We are old fashioned, I suppose.

[*The bathroom door opens.* YEE *comes out in the new dress. She goes over to look at herself in the mirror.*]

CARMEN Hm. Not a bad fit. But it makes you look a little too mature. [*Turns* YEE *round to face* MAY] What do you think, May? [MAY *looks but says nothing*] Try the yellow one. [YEE *takes the yellow dress into the bathroom.* CARMEN *turns to* MAY.] You know Kei Cheong has a son, of course. [MAY *looks up, startled.*] Half foreign. When I first met Kei Cheong—about ten years ago—he had been divorced a long time. His English wife had not yet remarried, and the son stayed with her. But the year I married Kei Cheong, she remarried, and the son took another surname. Things have a way of surprising us! [*She talks about this lightly, as if it has nothing to do with her.*]

MAY Did Kei Cheong see his son often?

CARMEN Perhaps he did. We seldom talked about it. Quite pointless. I dreaded meeting up with his son. If he called me 'mother' I would die! His son is twenty-something.

MAY Have you met his ex-wife?

CARMEN [*shrugs*] No. [*Pauses*] Probably quite a nice person. Kei Cheong has good taste in women. You used to know him!

MAY [*taken aback by the remark. Realizes that she has asked too many questions*] Oh . . . that was a long time ago.

CARMEN Hey, did he ever want to go into business when he was young?

MAY Go into business?

CARMEN Well, he studied engineering in England. I thought I married an engineer. But a year after we got married, he suddenly said he wanted to start a textile factory. Said it had always been his ambition to go into business and make money.

MAY When he was small, his mother insisted that he go to study in England.

CARMEN That he did. But I don't know why he suddenly quit his job to go into business.

MAY There's more money in business.

CARMEN Well, it's tough for me! He spends all his time mixing with business people. It's as if my husband has suddenly metamorphosed. Sometimes I really want to go and get myself another, but I haven't the time!

[YEE comes out in the yellow dress. She looks stunning. Even MAY approves.]

CARMEN Now this is more like it. *[YEE looks at herself in the mirror.]* But the shoes are wrong.

YEE They're new.

CARMEN Girls don't wear those kinds of shoes.

YEE Who says?

CARMEN Only women out to make some quick money wear those kinds of shoes.

YEE You make a lot of money, don't you?

CARMEN Not that kind of money. Besides, I'd only wear heels as high as those on formal occasions, with evening gowns. For day wear . . . hm . . . It doesn't look as though you can wear mine. . . .

MAY Don't put Aunt Carmen to any more trouble. Take these dresses back to the hotel and try them on there. We can return those that don't fit to Aunt Carmen later.

CARMEN That's all right. Try them on here. Have fun.

MAY Get back into your clothes, and fold these up.

[YEE does as she is told.]

CARMEN I'll get you some shoes another day.

[They fold up the clothes.]

MAY I thought people like you and Kei Cheong would not stay in Hong Kong.

CARMEN We love the place too much.

YEE You choose not to go abroad?

CARMEN What do you think living abroad is like, silly? You live in a foreign country. You're an outsider. Your views don't count when people debate big issues about the country and the lives of its people.

YEE But people say that if you run a restaurant abroad you can make a lot of money.

CARMEN So—you could buy whatever you wanted, you could fill your house with the things that money can buy. Fourteen hours a day, seven days a week, you and your wife and children would work in the restaurant—your kingdom. Deep in the night, you would close shop, and sit there counting all the money you'd made that day, and say to yourself what a success I am!

YEE Isn't that enough?

CARMEN When you see foreigners, you speak softly, you cower. When they do you wrong, and you want to scream at them, scolding them in their language doesn't feel half as good, and it's no use scolding them in your own language, because they won't understand.

MAY But if you were educated you could have a good career and do something useful.

CARMEN Then they respect you, praise you, use you to help build a better education system, economy, technological future. But the world that you help to build is not really your world.

MAY Still, you are part of that community.

CARMEN Yes. So you and your family live in an upper-middle-class suburb. You see only blue-eyed, blond-haired foreigners until you forget what your people look like. Then one day you see yourself in the mirror and get a fright: who is that Chinese in the mirror staring at you?

[MAY *and* YEE *look at* CARMEN *sceptically.*]

MAY So you will stay in Hong Kong then?

CARMEN [*shakes her head*] Yet one is afraid to stay.

YEE Afraid?

CARMEN Our generation grew up in Hong Kong. We used to think that politics and history were things that happened in books, and news about the Mainland had nothing to do with us. Our grandparents grew up during the war, but we've been lucky. We reap what they worked hard to sow. We live in peace, we travel on roads that they built, and know little of their hardship and struggle. Now Hong Kong has to change, and we panic. I used to think, especially when I was studying in England, that I didn't really belong anywhere, that I had no roots. Now that we have a country to call our own, I'm afraid. How ironic.

MAY On the Mainland, we envy you people in Hong Kong. We didn't know you'd feel like this.

CARMEN *[nods]* Actually, we feel like children abandoned at
birth. Now we've grown up, and suddenly we have to
go back to live with our natural parents and serve
them. True, there's the joy of reunion, but the feeling
of estrangement is there. And we don't know whether
our parents want us back only because we're doing
well. It takes time to get over these feelings, for trust
and affection to develop. And we're afraid it's going to
be tough. We're afraid that if we want to live well
then we'll have to make sure all China can live well.
It's such a heavy burden! Just the thought of it makes
you want to run away. *[Sighs]* Having a foreign
passport makes it easier to be patriotic.

MAY And many Hong Kong people leave because of this?

CARMEN Yes. *[Pauses]* I don't want to become like so many of
them living abroad: gloating over Hong Kong's fate.
'Hong Kong is not going to make it, not now, not in
the future. She's had it.' They take refuge in other
countries, and yet still yearn for Hong Kong's culture
and lifestyle, and busy themselves in movie magazines,
newspapers, and TV soaps from Hong Kong. They
come back for shopping sprees in Hong Kong and the
Mainland, and they say, 'You see, it's not going to
work, Hong Kong will go down with the Mainland'.
[Shakes her head] Hong Kong is my home. I don't ever
want to find myself saying that. *[Calms down]*

YEE *[breaking in abruptly]* Aunt Carmen, when you've
emigrated can you apply for us to go too?

*[MAY and CARMEN look at YEE, and then smile at each
other, shaking their heads.]*

MAY *[to CARMEN]* Shing Yee is so bent on going abroad,
I'm afraid she hasn't taken in what you said.

CARMEN Well, this is not the time to talk of emigration. First,
I'll teach you how to dress and look fashionable.

*[CARMEN stands up, takes YEE aside to teach her to dress
nicely. Lights fade.]*

SCENE TWO

*[Lights go up at stage right the upper level, and on the staircase at stage right.
This is Uncle LEE CHI CHUNG's home, in a corner of a tenement building in
Shaukeiwan. LEE is a news-vendor. He lives alone in this small and gloomy place
that is crammed full of books and magazines, old and new. Against the wall there*

is a rusty double-bunk bed. The upper bunk is piled high with clothes and bedding, the lower bunk is the old man's bed. In the middle of the room there is a square table covered with a faded blue-green plastic tablecloth. By the table, two chairs, different styles. By a cupboard are cooking utensils, thermos flasks, cups and glasses.

LEE *is about 80 years old, quite a strong build, not frail. He stands straight and has sharp eyes. His work out of doors gives him a healthy tan. He is almost bald, and has lost some of his teeth, revealing his age when he smiles. He has worked hard all his life, but now is content to amuse himself and others. When he sits still, he chews on nothing, and blinks as if he is lost in thought.*

When the lights go up, LEE *is standing at the top of the staircase, waiting impatiently, shuffling his feet and nodding to himself.*

CHEONG *walks forward in silence, followed by* KWONG *and* WOON. *It is evident that the three have important things to say but have not said them.]*

> CHEONG *[somewhat relieved that they have arrived]* Ah, here we are!
>
> *[*WOON *and* KWONG *look up. They have not expected* LEE's *home to be where it is.* KWONG *looks at his father.]*
>
> *[stands aside for* WOON *to go up first. Mutters an explanation half to himself, half to his brother]* I offered to find him somewhere else to live, and his folks in his home village asked him to go back, but he wouldn't. . . .
>
> *[Before he finishes,* LEE *sees them coming up the stairs and opens his arms in welcome.]*
>
> LEE Ah . . . Ah . . . Kei Woon . . .
>
> WOON *[rushes up to greet him]* Uncle—*[Looks at the old man, whom he is shocked to realize he does not recognize. Chokes with emotion.* LEE *holds him by both arms but is so eager to meet* KWONG, *who is standing behind* WOON, *that he does not notice* WOON's *reaction.* WOON *steps aside on the landing, rubbing his eyes]*
>
> LEE Ah . . . this is Shing Kwong?
>
> KWONG *[courteously]* Great Uncle!
>
> LEE *[holds* KWONG *for a closer look]* How tall you are! How old are you?
>
> KWONG *[laughs]* I'm thirty.
>
> LEE Your face. You look more like your uncle than your father.
>
> *[*KWONG *turns to smile at* CHEONG. CHEONG *looks at his nephew, wondering whether he likes the comparison.* LEE *leads* KWONG *into the room. The two brothers follow in silence.]*
>
> Come in, come in. Not married yet, are you?

KWONG *[laughs.* WOON *smiles.]* Not yet.

[LEE *points to the chair on his right for* KWONG *to sit down.* CHEONG *remains standing and notices that* LEE *is about to put the kettle on to make tea.]*

CHEONG *[definitely not going to touch the tea]* Don't bother with tea, Uncle. We should be going.

LEE Stay a little while. Whenever we meet, your wife opens her mouth, and nobody else can get a word in.

[They all laugh. CHEONG *gives in and stands near the door to wait.* LEE *puts the kettle on, sits down on the bed and gestures* WOON *and* KWONG *to sit down.]*

LEE *[takes a good look at* WOON*]* You haven't changed. Still a plain and simple man. I thought I'd never see you again. Who would have thought that a newspaper would bring us together?

WOON I thought Kei Cheong had gone to England and would never come back. Since there was nothing I could do, I never tried to reach him.

KWONG My sister Shing Yee was the one who found him. She read in the papers that a Hong Kong businessman had donated money to build a school in a village in memory of his mother. And there was a photograph.

WOON She thought the name a coincidence, and asked me what her grandmother's name was, and which village she came from.

KWONG *[looks at* CHEONG, *quite excited]* Everything fitted together, and we were able to trace Uncle Cheong!

LEE This is wonderful. Now you two brothers are reunited. *[To* WOON*]* You shouldn't have done that, back then, even if you were keen to serve your country! You knew Kei Cheong had left for England, and you just disappeared and left your mother all on her own. You were never that irresponsible! *[Sees* WOON *hang his head in silence]* What? Gave the best years of your life to your country, did you? And look what a roaring success it is now, eh? *[*WOON *looks up as if he wants to speak, but keeps quiet.]* Well, it is not so easy to explain, is it? We'll let that pass.

WOON *[haltingly]* To get us all here . . . the money you paid for our tour . . . we'll pay you back someday . . . your circumstances—

LEE Kei Cheong has paid me back.

*[*WOON *looks at* CHEONG *in surprise.]*

CHEONG Forget it. As a technician in a factory, you make about
a hundred a month at most. It'll take you a lifetime to
pay back a few thousand dollars.

LEE *[to save* WOON *from embarrassment]* It's nothing. Not a
lot of money. I don't mind paying for it myself. But
since Kei Cheong is rolling in it, and doesn't feel the
pinch—

WOON We won't be spending much in Hong Kong. My one
wish is to take the whole family to pay our respects at
Mother's grave. I don't mind if we don't do anything
else.

[All fall silent. LEE *turns to look at* CHEONG, *who looks
displeased. Getting no response,* WOON *looks up at*
CHEONG, *and then at* LEE.*]*

LEE *[as if he hasn't heard what* WOON *said]* Kei Cheong is
rolling in money—he won't feel the pinch. *[Pauses and
sighs]* When you were kids, you loved Kei Cheong and
pampered him. What's a few dollars to bring you here
for a few days?

WOON *[to* CHEONG*]* You and Carmen are busy. You don't have
to keep us company. Just tell me where Mother's grave
is and we can find it by ourselves.

LEE *[again as if he has not heard* WOON*]* Do you remember,
when you were kids, your mother taught you to save
money? Kei Woon wanted to save money to buy a bike
to ride to work in the Tsuen Wan textile factory. Kei
Cheong was at school then. He spent his money on
rubbish and managed to save only a few dollars. He
wanted to buy a camera to take pictures of the girls at
school, so he'd be popular. He borrowed a camera one
day, to show off. But he broke the lens. He was so
scared he didn't sleep all night. The next day, big
brother broke his piggy-bank and gave him all the
money. Kei Woon never did get his bike.

KWONG *[smiles]* Now we have three bikes at home. Dad doesn't
have to do without.

WOON Yes. I said to Mother at that time, 'We work so hard.
When I get my first pay packet, I'll buy us each a
chicken, cooked to our taste, and have a feast.'

LEE I had mine roasted.

WOON Kei Cheong did too. Mine was steamed.

[The three become excited at these thoughts of old times.]

CHEONG Mother's was baked in salt.

WOON We feasted until midnight, and still couldn't finish the food.

LEE But it put us off chicken for months!

[The three laugh heartily. KWONG watches in amusement.]

WOON Mother grumbled for days because I had splashed out. She said we should have saved the money for Kei Cheong to study abroad.

CHEONG That year—at the New Year festival—I wanted to play badminton. You went and bought us a set of racquets. We played on the rooftop, and the shuttlecock fell all the way down and landed on the street. You told me to keep shouting that it was ours, and you dashed downstairs to get it.

WOON Somebody pinched it anyway.

CHEONG It cost sixty cents. Enough for a matinee at the cinema. How it hurt!

[They all laugh. The kettle whistles, startling them. There is an awkward silence.]

LEE *[stands up]* The water is ready. *[Goes to make tea. KWONG follows to help him.]*

[WOON and CHEONG are still smiling at the reminiscences. Then the estrangement of thirty years takes over, and they look at each other awkwardly. CHEONG is annoyed with himself, and turns away.]

[senses the silence behind his back] Well, Shing Kwong, you'll learn a thing or two in Hong Kong, won't you?

KWONG *[smiles and nods. He has taken a liking to this great uncle.]* Some comrades who have been here said, 'They don't have to have meetings and political education every day and they manage very well indeed.' They told me to figure out how capitalism can bring 'wealth without corruption; stability without stagnation'.

LEE Good. Good. You figure it out! *[Makes tea]* Look, I know many people in the home country have a sudden craze for civilized progress, for material enjoyment, and are dying to come here. That's why I asked Uncle Kei Cheong to bring you here to see me. Look at me. I'm well read in the classics. You could say I'm erudite. But I've never made it rich. I've been selling newspapers here in Hong Kong for decades and I'm still here in this dingy place. I want you to know, the streets here are not paved with gold. If you see only Uncle Kei Cheong's Hong Kong, you won't see the full picture. *[Serves tea]*

CHEONG The wealth and prosperity here is bought at a price. People your age may have got a wife, a car, a flat, and a child. But, to pay the mortgage on a tiny flat, they have to keep a job in the day and another one at night. The wife has to work as well. They work so hard they don't even get to see the daylight outside. Your unemployed youths back home would rather die than work so hard.

LEE Yeah. Keep a few chickens, sell a few eggs and they want to become private enterprise millionaires overnight, eh?

WOON Shing Kwong is all right, but Shing Yee is a problem. She thinks of shopping day and night. And nothing but brand names will do.

LEE Well, it was the same here twenty, thirty years ago. People were crazy about imported things. Keeping up and showing off. Now that life is more stable, things have settled down. Most people have got it out of their system. Perhaps it will be like that too in the home country.

CHEONG But some of those people from the Mainland really annoy me! In early '84 I went to Qinghai province. That was when the '97 business nearly ruined Hong Kong. The Hong Kong dollar went down and down. It frightened the hell out of us. The moment we sat down to dinner in a restaurant, there was a crowd behind us, the unemployed youths, waiting to grab the leftovers the moment we stopped eating. When they learned that we were from Hong Kong they said, 'Hey, we're coming to take over. Just you wait!' *[Becoming more agitated]* You people made a mess of the Mainland, and we slog our guts out to make Hong Kong what it is. We don't mind sharing. But for such country bumpkins to stroll over and take charge! Who can stomach that?

LEE *[laughs. To* WOON *and* KWONG*]* Ha. Do you know what we call people from the Mainland?

[They both nod.]

You can tell them at a glance. Dark grey suits too big for them, always in groups of four or five, looking at everything, gaping at everything, and chattering among themselves. They live in high-class official dormitories, I bet they switch off the lights to watch TV the moment dinner is over.

KWONG But Hong Kong goes on prospering for all that!

LEE That's why you've got to hand it to us. Two years ago we thought the end was here, and that scared the shit out of us. By last year, the dust had settled and we believed that things would stay the same until '97. When things hit rock bottom where else can they go but up? So we started all over again. Perhaps life would get better, and there would be sharks' fins again for dinner. Call us spendthrifts, if you like, or optimists, or realistic. We're patient, we work hard, we don't whine or spread gloom or thoughts of doom.

CHEONG It's not easy to do what we've done. But it's a fragile prosperity. Since early this year, new US legislation has required certificates of origin for all our textile exports. If we can't cope with that we'll be plunged into depression again!

WOON It was the same in the fifties, before I went to the Mainland. Then it was the Korean War. The American embargo killed the Hong Kong manufacturing industry. I remember cases of unemployed workers jumping to their deaths because there was no work and they couldn't keep their families alive.

LEE Some sold their children.

CHEONG It was the same a few years ago when the States went into recession. Factories in Hong Kong received few orders, the workers had no work. And so no one could afford the instalment payments for things on hire purchase. People had all their things taken away, except their telephones. They needed the phones for the factories to notify them if there was any work.

WOON *[sighs]* Life here still depends entirely on other people.

CHEONG What makes us tick is that there are always people who never say die. *[Smiles at LEE]* Your neighbour Mr Kam for one. He never made anything much of his life. Then he learnt that people in China were allowed to wear Western suits. He took bags of old fashioned suits to sell in China every week, and made pots of money. In a year and a half, he could afford to just give away his old family home and move to somewhere really posh.

LEE *[jokingly to WOON and KWONG]* Perhaps you bought your suits from him! *[Though a little piqued, the two cannot help laughing.]* You see, we are what our circumstances make us. We are 'Hongkongers'. If Hong Kong had gone back to China earlier, and not been run

by the *gweilos**, we may not have been as prosperous,
and may have had to follow in China's footsteps to
modernize. Makes you ashamed, doesn't it? Look at
us—seeds of dragons, playing out for thirty years a
drama of our own making behind our closed doors.
Look what we've made of ourselves? Even if we rebuild
our economy, we won't get anywhere if we don't do
something to build up our people!

KWONG We're much more open now!

LEE *[gets carried away]* Yeah. Now, you have a new slogan:
'Leadership, not control.' But whose leadership? The
assumption is that only a handful of people know what
is right, right? The common folk are fools. So, how is
it different from control? *[Begins to get more thoughtful
and serious]* It's like saying to Hong Kong, 'Mind how
you go. If you can keep your stability and prosperity,
we'll let you go on with the game, otherwise don't
blame me for what may happen.' What do they take
us for? You bring up your son and then you say to
him, 'So, if you make lots of money, I'll love you.
But if you don't make a fortune, I'll have your guts!'
Call that love, I ask you? What kind of people can
you hope to bring up? *[Gets very worked up. They all
watch him in silence.]* Is that any different from the
colonials?

*[WOON and KWONG begin to feel a little uncomfortable.
LEE blinks, changes his tone, and becomes jovial.]*

Don't mind me. Nobody does. That's called freedom of
speech, get it? I'm my own man. I say what I like, as
long as I can square it with my conscience and it hurts
no one. Not like you. You have to go to meetings, ask
for guidelines, instructions before you know what
freedom you have, what freedom there is—

CHEONG *[realizes that the old man is not going to stop]* Let's go and
have dinner, Uncle.

LEE *[his train of thought interrupted, but cheerfully agrees]* Ah
yes. *[Points at CHEONG and says to WOON and KWONG]*
That's a 'Hongkonger' for you. When we can't work
out anything, or don't want to work out anything, we
go for a meal and all is well. *[To CHEONG]* Are we
going to Tsimshatsui East?

CHEONG Yes.

---

* *gweilo* is a Cantonese word meaning 'ghost man', applied to Westerners.

LEE Great! Wonderful! *[To* WOON *and* KWONG*]* That's a Japanese area, full of Japanese things!

CHEONG It's not a Japanese area—

LEE *[mock surprise]* Isn't it? *[Ironically]* I thought all things great were Japanese. Ha.

CHEONG Let's talk on the way.

LEE *[putting things away]* But, one day, we'll overtake them. We have lots of clever people in China. The Japs operate on the principle of expansion and cooperation. So they go from sole-ownership to partnership—you help me, and I help you. And the Chinese? We go from partnership to sole-ownership: yours becomes mine as well. Ha ha.

CHEONG Clear up when you come home.

LEE Take currency. The Japs conquered half the world, economically, and they only have one currency. But China excels! China has Renminbi, Foreign Exchange Coupons, and Special Economic Zone currency. You even accept the Hong Kong Dollar!

CHEONG They're waiting, Uncle—

LEE The Japs have no imagination. They eat steaks and drink sake. And they charge everybody the same, locals and foreigners whatever their colour. But China has a glorious variety in charges: friends of the nation, overseas Chinese, compatriots from Taiwan, compatriots from Hong Kong and Macau—all charged at different rates—

CHEONG We booked a table for—

LEE *[interrupting]* And the same goes for duty-free. Hong Kong and Macau compatriots are allowed two cartons of cigarettes and two bottles of liquor, overseas Chinese three cartons and four bottles, Taiwan compatriots four cartons and six bottles—

[LEE trips against a chair and stumbles. Everyone is alarmed. CHEONG dashes forward and helps him into a chair. The old man seems bewildered, looks around. On seeing him safely seated, everyone breathes a sigh of relief.]

[becomes quite thoughtful and sighs] Old age catching up with me. I am not going to be around to see what sort of a country China is going to be, nor Hong Kong in twelve years time.

    The first night I got to Canton from my home village, I heard a shriek at night, a whistle from an

English warship. I was still a kid then, and that was
when I first learned about battleships. When I came to
Hong Kong from Canton, my first contact with
'modern material civilization' was the sound of the bells
on trams. That was decades ago. So much has happened
in our country and the world since then.

I came to Hong Kong three times. The first time
was when the civil war broke out in Canton. My
relatives took me here for shelter. The second time I
sought refuge here from the Japs. The night they took
Hong Kong, I was with my uncle on the Peak. We
watched the city in dead silence. My uncle said, 'The
world is changing. Those who make money through the
Japs will emerge the winners.' Well, he's dead, and the
house is gone. The Brits have twelve more years—
strange! There must be some good people among
them—but in all these years I've never known any of
them! *[Pauses]* The third time I came to Hong Kong
was after the Communists had taken Canton. It's been
thirty-five years. And now, with '97 coming, our
leading families will again have to figure out how to
stay on top.

Hong Kong has been a trading port for over a
hundred years, and we've had almost a century of good
times. Luckier than most places in China. But I don't
seem to have got much from the luck of either Hong
Kong or China. I kept running between Canton and
Hong Kong to get away from the civil war, from the
Japs, and from the Communists. True, I made a living,
but I don't know where I belong. And no one has ever
asked me what I wanted so now I can only hope for
the best for China and Hong Kong. After all we still
have twelve more years to go! *[Looks up and sees*
CHEONG, *becomes more cheerful. Looks round for* KWONG]
Your uncle Kei Cheong has a great future ahead of
him. *[Stands up jovially]* He used to deal with South-
East Asia. Not doing badly. But beginning this year, he
got large orders from the States, from a chain-store, and
he invested all he had in the deal. By the end of the
year, well, we'll be talking not of millionaires but
billionaires. *[Gets up to go to dinner]*

Let's go to Tsimshatsui East. Splash out a little.
Your uncle can afford it. Then we can look at those
grand hotels. Just look around. *[Starts to go downstairs]*
The doors open automatically, or somebody in white

gloves will open them for you. Very grand. *[Stops abruptly and turns round as if to go back, and looks at those around him]* Ah, but if you want to go to the toilet, go now, because you will have to pay to use the toilets there. That, too, is modernization. See?

[They laugh and exit.]

S C E N E   T H R E E

[Morning. Three days later. In CHEONG's *office in Causeway Bay, a busy commercial district on Hong Kong Island.* WOON *is seated, waiting. The office is not large but tastefully decorated. The entrance obviously leads to a room offstage, an outer office for* CHEONG's *secretary and probably two or three clerks.* WOON *sits with his head bowed, looks up occasionally to glance around, and is resolved to wait for as long as it takes. Not long after the curtain rises,* CHEONG *pushes open the door and hurries in carrying a briefcase, an anxious look on his face.* WOON *sees him, stands up abruptly, startling* CHEONG.*]*

CHEONG Oh, morning.

WOON *[hesitates, a little apologetic]* Good morning, Kei Cheong.

CHEONG Didn't you go out with the tour group?

WOON The three of them did. I'd like to talk to you.

CHEONG *[puts down the briefcase, trying not to get exasperated]* I've told you I've got something urgent to deal with these couple of days. I'll keep you company once that's settled.

WOON I'm not asking you to keep me company, I only want to visit Mother's grave.

[The phone rings. CHEONG *answers the phone.]*

CHEONG Well? Can't find him? It's been three days. He can't have been absent from work for three days . . . not at home either. . . . Send someone to places he might go to. We've known him for years, it's not likely. . . . When did we see him last . . .? *[Waits. To* WOON*]* My assistant Lam Bunn has disappeared. Something has gone wrong with the shipment of shirts, and only he knows what has happened. *[Speaks into the phone again]* What? Last Saturday? Today is Wednesday. . . . Keep looking. Get Mr Ko for me. *[Hangs up and stares into space, obviously very worried]*

WOON Kei . . . Kei Cheong, just tell me where it is. In Cheungshawan? Happy Valley? Woohopshek? Which cemetery?

CHEONG [*as if he has not heard* WOON] I've put everything on this shipment. Now it is rejected, and the buyer in the States won't take delivery. I'm going to lose everything.

WOON I don't know a thing about business, but I know I shouldn't trouble you.

CHEONG Competition is deadly keen here. It's not easy surviving in business. In China the State looks after you: how could you understand!

WOON I understand that you've got a problem. Just tell me where and I won't bother you anymore.

CHEONG One shipment, and it ruins me.

WOON [*shouts*] Where is Mother's grave?

CHEONG [*starts, as if waking from a dream, then stands up, turns away from his brother, and remains like this a while*] She was not buried in Hong Kong. . . .

WOON But Uncle Lee said she never went to England—

[*The phone rings.* CHEONG *dashes to answer it.*]

CHEONG Well? Oh fine. [*Presses an extension switch on his phone*] Morning Mr Ko. Ho Kei Cheong here. . . . Yes, I know. The whole shipment was rejected. It wasn't late, but the American agent here said it didn't meet the specifications. What was that all about? [*Waits*] I know. Lam Bunn took care of all the orders we placed over all these years. . . . Yes, please read me the order. . . . Wait a minute, wait, what was the yarn count you said? . . . Just a sec . . . [*Checks against his files*] That's not what it says in my copy. It says the highest yarn count, best quality. . . . Impossible. For this American client, we always use the best yarn. They want the best, a low yarn count shows up right away as inferior. . . . What? Lam Bunn wanted a lower grade? But I paid for the best. . . . If you were paid for a lower grade, what happened to the difference? . . . [*It dawns on him. He sits down trying to keep calm.*] Yes, I understand. All right. Send me your copy. I know it wasn't you who cheated me. . . . it was my assistant, not you. . . . I'll make sure you get paid. . . . Yes . . . yes . . . [*Hangs up. He sits stunned, and then begins to shudder. He thinks for a while, then lifts the phone and dials a number.*] Stella, get me Mr Kam of Chup Lee Company. [*Puts down the phone and stares into space as* WOON *waits anxiously for his answer. He looks up, sees* WOON *watching him.*] I'm in deep trouble. I can't talk to you now.

WOON I'll go. Just tell me where, and I'll leave.

CHEONG I'll talk to you later.

WOON I know you are in trouble, and I shouldn't bother you, but why can't you just say where?

CHEONG I'll tell you later.

WOON You've been saying that for three days. Why can't you just tell me? *[CHEONG walks away.]* Are you still holding a grudge against me because I left Mother on her own? And you want to punish me now?

CHEONG My dear brother, I've got a disaster on my hands. The shipment is rejected and it's our fault. I'm a dead man.

WOON You blame me not only for abandoning her, but for not keeping in touch—

CHEONG If they won't take delivery, I won't get paid, the shipment will be returned, and I still have to pay the rent for the factory, pay the wages, the interest on the loan—

WOON Or is it out of revenge because I married May?

CHEONG *[turns away abruptly]* You have the nerve to mention that?

WOON *[stares at CHEONG's back and tries to reason with him]* You can blame me. I can take that. For thirty years I've been away and I did not keep in touch with Mother, it's true. I only learnt, when we met the other day, that she died in 1967. I know nothing of how she managed, or what she died of.

CHEONG You didn't care then. Why bother now?

WOON If you won't tell me, I can't force you. But please say where she's buried so I can take my family to pay our respects to her. I would feel better.

CHEONG Burn a couple of joss-sticks and some joss-paper, and that can make up for thirty years of neglect?

WOON *[deeply hurt. After a while]* Perhaps . . . Mother—being what she was—would not want to punish me like this?

[CHEONG slowly turns round to look at his brother. Lights fade.

Lights go up on the staircase and the upper level tenement where the HO *family lived in 1955.]*

S C E N E   F O U R

[About 5 pm one day in January 1955. Home of the HO *family in Shamshuipo. It is a room with a curtain in a doorway which leads into the corridor. The main door opens to the landing with the staircase, the other end of the corridor leads to a*

kitchen offstage. Through a high window at the top of the wooden partition on the upstage side of the room, the afternoon light shines into the room. Over the landing, hangs a naked light bulb. The staircase goes down to the pavement in the street at the front part of the stage. This part should be brighter.

When the lights go up, MOTHER *is sitting on a stool at the right side of the room, shredding yarn waste from pieces of scrap fabric by the light through the window. This room is where the* HO *family used to live in the 1950s. At this time,* WOON *is working in a textile mill and sleeps in the staff dormitory, so there is only one double-decker bunk in the room. In addition, there are a square table, a few chairs—one of them broken—and various odds and ends accumulated over the years.*

MOTHER *is only 42, but years of resentment and frustration have made her look older. She does not see the blessings she enjoys, but frets over what she does not have. She is quick to anger, quick to perceive what she considers unfair. Her face is etched with lines of self-pity. She has cold eyes, and a voice unconsciously sharp.*

WOON, *who is about 20, enters from stage right and goes home up the stairs. From his left hand dangle a piece of pork wrapped in old newspaper, some bean sprouts and some beancurds, also wrapped in old newspaper and wet through. In his right hand is a large parcel wrapped in cloth, with strands of scrap fabric hanging out of it. He also carries one or two other small parcels. He rings the bell at the top of the landing.* MOTHER *gets up to open the door.]*

WOON Mother.

MOTHER *[simultaneously. Grumbling]* Why are you so late?

WOON I had a long wait for the bus, and the market was crowded. *[Hands over the food to* MOTHER*]* I bought some pork, bean sprouts, and beancurd.

MOTHER *[goes into the kitchen]* Told you not to squander money, and you spend it on meat.

WOON *[puts down his various parcels]* Just a couple of times a month. It's pay day. You can do with something nice. *[Picks up* MOTHER*'s scrap fabric and takes a look]*

MOTHER *[from inside]* What does it matter what I eat? The important thing is to save some money so your brother can study abroad!

WOON There's more than a couple of pounds of yarn waste here, and that should fetch a few dollars. You must have worked very hard.

MOTHER *[comes into the room from the kitchen, not at all appreciative of her son's compliment]* That's why you shouldn't throw money away. *[Points at the broken chair]* That chair has come apart again. See if you can nail it together.

WOON What? Again? You should tell Kei Cheong not to rock on that chair, Mother.

MOTHER Is it such hard work putting a couple of nails in for your brother?

WOON No. But he should learn to do some of these things.

MOTHER He's sitting his School Certificate exam. What is more important?

[WOON *says no more. Pulls out some money from his pocket*]

WOON Pay day today.

[*He goes to repair the chair.* MOTHER *takes the money, counts it before putting it away.*]

MOTHER [*turns round to look at* WOON] Only ninety dollars?

WOON [*a little shame-faced*] Mm. I make one hundred a month. I have to pay for sleeping in the dorm, and a little for meals. This is all that's left.

MOTHER And you said you would save up for Kei Cheong! What's there to save?

WOON Mother, studying abroad is beyond the dreams of people like us.

MOTHER Why? If your father was not so irresponsible and hadn't died so young, perhaps the whole family could go abroad!

[*The two begin to raise their voices.*]

WOON He's been dead five years. Anyway, he got us this flat before he died. Now we get some rent from sub-letting the rooms. If we economize, Kei Cheong can go to university here. There's no problem.

MOTHER What? Study in Hong Kong? We agreed he should go abroad! I've got somebody interested in taking over the flat.

WOON Taking over the flat? Where would we live if anything should happen?

MOTHER When Kei Cheong graduates, he will take us abroad, and we'll never have anything to worry about.

WOON [*sighs. Keeps quiet for a while*] I've thought about it, Mother. It won't work.

MOTHER [*cuts him short*] Why not?

WOON I thought wages would be steadier in the mill, but with all the strikes there isn't any work. When there is, everything is in a mess. There's not much future at the mill. [*Plucks up his courage*] A lot of the workers have left for the Mainland.

MOTHER What? To turn Communist?

WOON Things are getting better on the Mainland. The land reform works, and the economy has improved. Life isn't as hard now.

MOTHER How would you know?

WOON I was in China with Dad during the war. I wasn't even ten, but I could tell it was bad. But it is better now.

MOTHER Better than Hong Kong?

WOON Given time. The Communists place great emphasis on industry and agriculture. Workers are treated well. They get to go to school!

MOTHER Use your head! Are you the stuff that scholars are made of?

WOON I could try. After junior middle school, I could only get that job as a shop assistant. Even now I'm no better. A factory hand does not have much of a future.

MOTHER You think only of yourself. What about your brother?

WOON Kei Cheong can study here. Universities abroad are not necessarily better. Dad was proud of his country. He was a patriot. He fought the Japs.

MOTHER That was the trouble! He went to fight the Japs, and after the war, he wanted to help rebuild the country, and he left me and Kei Cheong here in Hong Kong. And you want to follow in his footsteps!

WOON But Mother! He had a hard time too making a living in China. Do you think he wanted it that way?

MOTHER You *would* take his part! You *had* to follow him to China! You bummed around with him, never studied properly, and ended up a peasant, a failure, just like him!

WOON He had a hard time. I know. I was there. You can't blame him for what I've become. If it hadn't been for him, you wouldn't have got this place to live in.

MOTHER What good is this place? I have never had a day of ease and comfort since I married him. And he left me and Kei Cheong to fend for ourselves. Did he think buying me this shabby flat in Shamshuipo would make up for everything? Well?

WOON Forget it, Mother. You argued with him over that for long enough. He's dead and gone. Don't bring it up again.

MOTHER *[getting into a rage]* I didn't bring it up! You did!

WOON I didn't. I know you resent his leaving you behind, and I try to make it up to you, but there is so little that I can do. . . .

MOTHER Then why do you want to leave me and Kei Cheong behind? You know you can't do much, and all our hopes are on Kei Cheong, so we should help him to become somebody. You think only of yourself. How could you answer to your conscience if you left us behind?

WOON Mother. Not so loud—

MOTHER *[raises her voice]* What if I am loud! You're afraid people will hear? There's nothing this mother has to hide. It's the son who is unfilial. I have never given a thought for myself since I married your father. I worked so hard just so I could help to make something of your brother, so that we'd all—

WOON All right, all right, Mother. Forget it.

[He opens the door to go into the kitchen. MOTHER follows him.]

MOTHER *[offstage. In the kitchen]* How dare you even mention it! Your brother is so young, and me, a widow—

WOON *[offstage]* Mother, I will never talk about it again.

[WOON returns from kitchen to the room, closes the door behind him, and sits desolate in front of the broken chair.]

MOTHER *[crying and shouting in the kitchen]* You ask anybody, ask any of our neighbours . . . see who is in the wrong . . . you think your mother unfair . . . . You're the elder brother, and your father died young . . . of course you have to look after all of us . . . .

[CHEONG, at 18, and MAY, at 17, enter from stage right. Both are in school uniforms and each carries a pile of books. CHEONG is also carrying a bundle of yarn waste, and MAY a small papaya. Both look bright and pleasant. CHEONG begins to walk up the stairs and then sprints up. MAY looks up at him and follows, laughing. CHEONG drops all the things he is carrying on the landing, beckons to MAY, and dashes down himself. MAY laughingly asks 'What?'. CHEONG pushes her and gesticulates at the landing. She goes up and puts down her things. CHEONG then signals her to come down. MAY comes halfway down the staircase. The two stand face to face on the narrow staircase. CHEONG holds her arms, bends down to kiss her. MAY demures, looks around to see if they are alone. CHEONG looks too, and then kisses her again. MAY bows her head and hurries up the stairs. CHEONG follows. They both pick up their things on the landing. CHEONG leans over and kisses her on the cheek.

MAY *pushes him away, and rings the bell.* WOON *answers the door. The sight of the two happy young people cheers him up.]*

CHEONG Elder brother.

MAY Hello, Kei Woon.

WOON Mother is in the kitchen. *[Goes back into their room]*

CHEONG *[goes down the corridor, stops near the kitchen]* Ma! *[Returns to their room]*

MAY *[holding out the bundle of yarn waste]* Auntie. *[A little hesitantly]* I've finished shredding the yarn. *[Waits a moment, joins the brothers in the room. Picks up the scrap cloth bundle that* WOON *brought home]*

WOON *[watches as she picks up the bundle]* You'll have to sit the exams soon, May. Why don't you wait until the Christmas holidays before you help Mother with her work.

MAY It's all right. I can do this while I'm studying for the exams.

[CHEONG lays out the books and other things on the table for MAY *and himself to do their homework. He places a small radio on the table and switches it on. But the volume is so low only a hissing sound can be heard.]*

WOON May, look what I've made for you.

[WOON shyly presents her with a little wooden cradle. MAY *claps her hands in delight.]*

MAY A little cradle!

WOON I heard that you often go to a toyshop in Tsimshatsui to look at a little cradle. I didn't have ten dollars, so I made you this.

CHEONG And when I graduate from university abroad, I will be able to afford to buy you a real one!

WOON But you'll have to make the pillow and the mattress yourself.

MAY *[happily]* Thank you, Kei Woon.

[She rocks the cradle. CHEONG *holds out his hands,* MAY *looks at him, attempts to slap his hands,* CHEONG *pulls back his hands quickly, she misses. It is evident that the two often play this game. She misses three times.]*

CHEONG My turn!

[MAY holds out her hands, CHEONG *hits them swiftly.* MAY *laughs and holds out her hands again, and* CHEONG *hits them. The third time,* CHEONG *hits very hard, and the two are both startled.* MAY's *cheeks are flushed with pain, and she stares confusedly at* CHEONG.]*

WOON Hey, take it easy, Kei Cheong.

CHEONG *[simultaneously, rubbing* MAY's *hands]* Does it hurt?

*[*MAY *nods, looking at him.]*

MAY My turn.

[She misses three times. Then she holds out her hands again. CHEONG *strikes again with a loud smack.* CHEONG *rubs her hands again.]*

WOON Watch it, Kei Cheong.

*[*CHEONG *and* MAY *giggle.]*

CHEONG Work!

[The two settle down to their homework. CHEONG *reaches out to turn up the volume of the radio.]*

WOON I thought you said 'Work'.

CHEONG It's request time. Western pop songs.

MOTHER *[simultaneously from the kitchen]* Kei Woon!

*[*CHEONG *turns down the volume.]*

WOON *[goes out of the room]* Mother?

MOTHER We've run out of rice. Get a couple of catties.

WOON All right. *[Exits]*

*[*CHEONG *turns up the volume. The two work at the table, whispering together.* MAY *holds out her hands again.* CHEONG *does not hit them but holds them.]*

CHEONG Tell me, tell me true. When I've made some money after graduation, what would you like me to buy you first?

MAY I don't want you to buy me anything. I just want to be with you in England.

CHEONG That goes without saying. Maybe in three years, maybe two. I'll get you there.

MAY What if you forget?

CHEONG Forget you? I'm just afraid you won't wait that long.

MAY I will wait, till I grow old. I will sit on this chair and wait. If you don't take me there, I will grow old sitting here. Then, one day, when you come back, you will see an old lady, her hair all white, and you will say, 'Old lady, have you been sitting here long? Why, there's dust all over you, and cobwebs too!' *[The two laugh.]* Then I'll say, 'Yes. When I was young, I fell in love. My love told me to wait for him, and I wait for him still.'

CHEONG Impossible! *[Begins to rock the chair he is sitting on]* By then, we'd have become grandparents in England. Who knows, our grandchildren might even look like foreign devils.

MAY Don't rock the chair!

CHEONG *[abruptly stops rocking the chair, stands up]* By then you will have whatever you want. You can do everything with music in the background, like in the movies. When you cook, turn a switch and there will be fire. Turn on the tap, and there will be hot water, and cold. You'll go to the market in a limousine, and everything will be there for you to pick and choose. After dinner, you'll throw what you don't want into a gadget, push a button and it will vanish. I don't want you to work as hard as Ma does.

MAY And your mother?

CHEONG Oh, I will have hired somebody to look after her, got her a big house to live in, in the country, in England. Two storeys. The ground floor will all be hers. I'll teach all the ladies in the neighbourhood to play mahjong, so that they can play with her when they are free.

MAY She is going to miss you when you are away.

CHEONG *[pauses]* And will you?

[They look at each other, both feel forlorn. MAY raises her arms, and CHEONG comes over to embrace her. After a while, CHEONG notices that MAY is shivering.]

Hush . . . hush . . . I'll write to you everyday; I'll send you pretty clothes, and you can put them on and have photos taken and send them to me, and in my dreams I'll see you in the clothes I send you. *[MAY starts sobbing quietly.]* Don't cry. I like you better when you smile, than when you cry. *[MAY moves out of his arms to wipe her tears.]* You like blue, don't you? I like to see you in blue. I'll send you blue dresses, and hats, and shoes. . . . And a hair curler machine too. You stick your head in, press a button, and it will curl your hair in any style you like. *[MAY looks at him sceptically.]* It's true. That's what I heard. They have machines like that in England!

MAY But I won't have any money to buy you anything.

CHEONG *[shakes his head]* You don't have to buy anything. Knowing that you'll wait for me is enough.

MAY I'll wait for as long as you want me to.

CHEONG It won't be for long. Time will go quickly. Then, one day, you will receive an air ticket with a note: 'May, it is time for us to be reunited!'

[MAY stands up, her eyes glistening. CHEONG embraces her. After a while, he seems to hear something, turns round, turns up the volume of the radio. It is playing the song 'The Tennessee Waltz'. CHEONG dances with MAY. The two are not adept at dancing. They look down at the floor, keeping a distance so as not to tread on each other's toes.]

On your first night in England, I'll take you to the most luxurious restaurant. I'll hire musicians, like in the movie *Love in the Afternoon*, and they will follow us as we dance, and you'll be in an evening gown—

MAY A blue one?

CHEONG Yes. Blue.

MAY And we'll dance until everyone has left.

CHEONG But, before they leave, I'll introduce you: This charming lady, this fabulous beauty . . . is only a country girl I brought over from China.

[MAY stops dead, stares at him speechless. CHEONG laughs. MAY abruptly turns to go. CHEONG stops her just before she opens the door to leave.]

Don't be silly. I was teasing you! *[He kisses her hair. MAY turns round to push him away, but CHEONG holds her so tightly she can hardly breathe. From outside, MOTHER comes out of the kitchen to go into the room. She pushes the door but it won't open. CHEONG and MAY, startled, break free and return to their homework. MOTHER comes in.]*

MOTHER How can you work with the radio blaring? *[CHEONG turns down the volume.]* Will you stay for dinner, May?

MAY *[flustered]* N . . . no . . . thank you. My Dad is coming off the ship tonight. I've got to go home early. *[Finds MOTHER looking at her]* Oh . . . I bought a papaya for you. I'll get a knife. *[Goes to the kitchen]*

MOTHER What were you two doing just now?

CHEONG Nothing.

MOTHER You have the School Certificate exam coming. Don't get distracted from your work. *[Sees the cradle]* What's that?

CHEONG A cradle. Kei Woon made it for May.

MOTHER And him a grown man. Ridiculous!

[MAY returns with plate and knife. MOTHER watches her cut the papaya.]

A papaya like this costs at least a dollar. Don't buy any more.

MAY I remembered that you liked papayas.

MOTHER Don't cut this half. Give it to Kei Cheong.

MAY What about Kei Woon?

MOTHER I'll share my half with him.

MAY This piece is for him. *[Finishes arranging the papaya]* I've got to go. *[Goes to the kitchen to clean up.* CHEONG *packs her books for her, takes a look at the cradle, rocks it, and puts it together with her books.]*

MOTHER Kei Cheong, don't see her home. You'll waste a lot of time.

CHEONG I'll see her downstairs.

MOTHER Kei Cheong!

MAY *[at the door]* Goodbye Auntie. I'll bring the yarn waste as soon as I've finished.

[MAY and CHEONG go downstairs. On the way, CHEONG grabs MAY's arm and, seeing that they are alone, bows to kiss her. WOON comes back from his errand, looks up and sees them, hesitates, and moves away.]

CHEONG *[to MAY]* When your dad and mother are out, I'll come to your place again.

[MAY nods and bounces down the stairs. She does not see WOON. CHEONG goes back to the room upstairs.]

MOTHER Kei Cheong, I want to talk to you.

CHEONG I know, Ma. I can handle the School Certificate exam.

MOTHER I'm not talking about the exam, *[Pauses]* I'm talking about May.

CHEONG We're just studying together.

MOTHER You're going to England in a few months. You shouldn't get too involved with her.

CHEONG I'm going to send for her to join me.

MOTHER That day is a long way away. You can't plan that far ahead.

CHEONG She said she would wait for me.

MOTHER That's not the sort of thing a nice girl would say.

CHEONG I asked her to. I will marry her.

[WOON comes upstairs, opens the door, is about to enter when he hears the conversation and stops.]

MOTHER Marry her? Why would you marry a girl like that?

CHEONG I thought you liked her.

MOTHER I do. She's a good girl from a humble family. Her father is a merchant seaman—a good match for your brother.

CHEONG For my brother? What's he got to do with it?

MOTHER When you graduate in England, you will have your pick of girls.

CHEONG But I have picked May—

MOTHER As a graduate with a British degree, what good is a girl like May to you! You shouldn't commit yourself. You may regret it.

[WOON moves from the door, leans against the wall of the staircase, and listens to the row between his mother and his brother.]

CHEONG If I can't marry May just because I'm going to England, then I'd rather not go.

MOTHER *[stunned]* What? What is she that you should ruin your life for her? Is she worth it?

CHEONG You don't have to go to England to have a future! What if I can't make it at university? Perhaps I can stay here and start a business.

MOTHER Did she put you up to this?

CHEONG It has nothing to do with May. I've always wanted to start a business, just like Dad—

MOTHER *[furious]* Your Dad got nowhere! Do you want to be like him?

CHEONG Those were bad times. But now—

MOTHER But you've always said you'd go to university abroad!

CHEONG No, Mother. *You* have always said I would go to unversity abroad. I have not. I'm not all that wonderful as a scholar.

MOTHER If she has taught you to say all this, I forbid you to see her again.

CHEONG She taught me nothing! I can think for myself. If I can't keep up with my studies in England—

MOTHER She knows that if you go to university in England, she won't be good enough for you and so—

CHEONG She has never tried to dissuade me from going!

MOTHER If she encourages you to go against me, I won't let her into my house.

CHEONG It's got nothing to do with her!

MOTHER Do you hear? She's not to come here ever again! *[CHEONG turns to walk away from her.]* Where do you think you are going? *[CHEONG keeps going.]* Kei Cheong, come back here—

[CHEONG *dashes out.* MOTHER *rushes after him. When she gets to the staircase, she stops, seeing that* CHEONG *has gone out of sight. She is in a rage. She turns round and sees* WOON *leaning against the wall, looking down. Lights fade out.*]

SCENE FIVE

[*Set as in Act 1 Scene 3.* WOON *and* CHEONG *have changed part of their costumes so that they are dressed as they were in Act 1 Scene 3 and are confronting each other in* CHEONG's *office.*]

WOON I don't know what right you think you still have, after thirty years, to stand between Mother and me. She's not just *your* mother. She's *my* mother as well.

CHEONG Then where have you been these past twelve years?

WOON I *had* to leave.

CHEONG When I went abroad, I thought you would look after her. Oh, you made promises, and then you walked out ' on her!

WOON I meant to look after her so that you could carry on with your studies.

CHEONG I don't know what you meant to do. I just know that you let us down.

WOON [*loses his temper*] I let you down? I let you down? When I finished junior middle school, I went to work in a factory just so you could go on studying. The flat that Dad bought—I had a share in that too, but it was sold so that you could go abroad. I never got a cent out of that. Everybody thought that was the right thing to do, nobody ever thought to ask me whether it was fair. You were the one Mother loved. She gave you all the best things to eat, her nicest smile. If anybody is going to bear a grudge today, it's not you. It's me!

CHEONG That is why you married May. To spite me, to take revenge.

WOON [*flies into a rage. Dashes forward to seize* CHEONG] You have no right to talk about her like that! She's not a tool for revenge!

CHEONG [*pushes* WOON *away out of anger and fear*] May was mine! Mine! Mine since I first met her when I was six. We went to school together, every day. We did our homework together, we shared everything: our food and drink. Nobody came between us for over ten years.

Even the night I left, she promised to wait for me, all
her life, if need be. But when I got to England, I
didn't even get a letter from her. Then you married
her. [WOON *moves away.*] When I got to England, I
couldn't speak the language, I didn't know the way.
Every day I sat at home waiting for her letters. The
first one I got was from Mother. It said, 'Kei Cheong,
I want to tell you something. Your brother has married
May and taken her to China with him.' [*Pauses because
of the pain the memory evokes*] Why? Why did you? I've
wanted to ask you this all these years. I've thought
about it over and over again but I just don't know
why. Was it because Mother loved me more? Did you
hate me that much?

[CHEONG *waits for an answer.* WOON *says nothing. The
telephone rings. In the end* CHEONG, *deflated, picks up the
phone.*]

Yes? . . . Oh, put him through then . . . [*Rather flustered*]
Ah, Mr Kam . . . That's right, the shipment . . . No, no,
I know, it's our mistake . . . the yarn count *was* two
grades lower . . . much inferior, yes. . . . I understand . . .
anyone in the trade could tell at a glance. . . . No, no,
you can't pass it off as quality goods. . . . I'm willing
to give you a big discount. . . . The shipment is worth
millions, I'm taking a big loss. . . . Mr Kam, you've got
to help me out on this one. . . . I've mortgaged my flat
for this deal. . . . Say I beg them to take delivery. . . .
How long will that take? . . . have to wait two days?
. . . I understand, theirs is a chain store. Can I phone
them direct to discuss it? I can even fly out to the
States immediately. . . . Yes, yes . . . Thank you, I'll wait
for your reply. . . . Yes, yes . . . Thank you. [CHEONG
puts down the phone, too shaken even to cry. He looks up at
WOON.] I am going to be bankrupt. You don't have to
seek revenge. I've ruined myself!

WOON I never blamed you for anything. Never thought of
revenge. I have always known that May was yours. I
would not have married her if it wasn't for her sake.

CHEONG [*jumps up in hurt and anger*] For her sake? [*Contemptuously*]
What have you given her these thirty years? For her
sake indeed!

WOON I've pleaded and argued with you long enough, I've
said too much. I didn't come here to make you
understand. I only want to know where Mother is
buried.

CHEONG I won't tell you.

WOON Just tell me where and I'll go this minute. It doesn't matter if we never meet again.

CHEONG I have nothing to say. I'm busy. Please leave. Now.

WOON Why wasn't she buried in Hong Kong?

CHEONG Aren't you going to leave? What kind of a brother are you? I'm going bankrupt and you harass me with this?

WOON You may be going bankrupt, and I feel sorry for you. But unless you tell me where, I will not leave.

CHEONG You don't even know how to apply to the Immigration Department to extend your visa for a few days.

WOON I have my ways of staying. I will wait until you tell me.

CHEONG I will not tell you.

WOON Then I will stay.

CHEONG [in fury] Then stay!

[CHEONG turns round, opens the door, goes out and slams shut the door. WOON stands bewildered in the middle of the room. Lights black out.]

END OF ACT 1

INTERMISSION

ACT 2

SCENE ONE

[Morning. Three days later. CHEONG is speaking on the phone.]

CHEONG No, no. We *will* pay the factory hands. . . . If the
Americans won't take delivery, I will sell the shipment
at a discount here or in South-East Asia. Even if I
don't make a profit, I will pay the workers. . . . Give
me a couple of days. I'll settle the sum as soon as I've
sold the goods. . . . Yes, yes, of course. . . .
*[Puts down the phone, dazed and troubled. Then he stands
up, walks a few paces aimlessly, and goes to speak on the
phone.]* Stella, call Mr Kam; tell him that we must
leave the shipment in his factory for a few more days,
to give me time to find another buyer. . . . Of course
we'll move it as soon as possible, rent costs
money. . . . If he asks to speak to me tell him you can't
contact me, there's no point speaking to him
myself. . . . The bank loan? I don't know yet. . . . It
doesn't look likely, it's a large sum. . . . Yes, you go
ahead. *[Puts down the phone, anxious and desperate. Pauses.
Makes to pick up the phone again when it rings]*
Yes . . . Who? . . . *[Taken aback]* By herself? Is
she. . . . *[Hesitates]* Yes. Show her in.

*[The door opens. MAY comes in. She is dressed neatly in blue.
CHEONG at once notices it. She stands still. The two silently
acknowledge each other. Since CHEONG says nothing, she
looks around, and takes note of everything in the office.
CHEONG's eyes follow her. The phone rings, startling
CHEONG. MAY turns to look at him.]*

[picks up the phone and presses a button] Stella, note down
the calls for me. I'll return them later. *[Puts down the
phone. Waits]*

MAY The last time I saw your mother, she said if I loved
you, I should make a sacrifice to help you fulfill your
aspirations.

CHEONG You mean Mother had a hand in—

MAY *[gestures him not to interrupt]* I'm not blaming her.
[Pauses] I mean, at the time, I didn't know what your
'aspirations' meant. *[Looks around]* Now I know it
means an office like this, a picture on the wall, a phone
on the desk, a person to run errands when you press a
button—

CHEONG You can't judge by these—

MAY Your mother used to say you were the hope of the family. *[Looks at him]* Now I know what a university education and making money amount to.

CHEONG *[not knowing how to take this, sits down in confusion]* For five days since you arrived, I've been wondering whether you'd bring up the past, whether you would have the gall—

MAY I didn't know either, at first, whether it would make a difference. Or whether you would feel, as I did, that for thirty years I owed you an explanation.

CHEONG Now that you have to go in a couple of days, suddenly you want to clear things up. *[Hurtfully]* How do you know I want to hear any of it?

MAY I will say what I want to say whether you want to hear it or not.

CHEONG What if I've decided to forget all about it?

MAY *[shakes her head]* No, you have not.

CHEONG Oh? Are you so sure? Do you think you are still so important?

MAY Whether I'm important or not, you have not forgotten the past.

CHEONG Have you looked at yourself in the mirror lately? Do you think I would still carry a torch for someone like you?

MAY You do not carry a torch for me. You carry a grudge for losing me.

CHEONG You know about that?

MAY Kei Woon told me he had a row with you three days ago.

CHEONG Him!

MAY What happened between us has to be cleared up, or it will stand between you and your brother.

CHEONG So you've come on his behalf! He pestered me here for two days, and when he didn't get what he wanted, he sent you.

MAY He doesn't know I am here.

CHEONG *[in painful self-mockery]* And I thought you came because of me.

MAY I have come because of you.

CHEONG How stupid I have been! You've always stood between me and my brother, only I was too stupid to see that.

MAY What are you talking about?

CHEONG The toy cradle. Why did he give you that?

MAY The toy cradle?

CHEONG He knew you liked the toy cradle in the shop window. He knew I couldn't afford it, so he made one to please you.

MAY I was pleased.

CHEONG It was so crude. Bits of broken board. He never saw that toy cradle, and the lace canopy, the white muslin sheets—how fine it was.

MAY You have never understood him.

CHEONG Still taking his side? What has he ever given you? If you had waited for me here, would you have turned out like this?

MAY There is nothing wrong with what I am.

CHEONG How did he trick you into it?

MAY He didn't trick me.

CHEONG He was such a leftist. He talked about nothing but strikes and workers' benefits in the mill. And when he heard that workers were going to be the masters of the country, he told me he'd go back to help rebuild China as soon as I finished school. I've never heard you say a word about it. But as soon as my back was turned, he fooled you into going with him.

MAY He did it for my sake.

CHEONG [*viciously*] For your sake? And how did you pull through the last thirty years? You got there in 1955. Times couldn't have been good. Shing Kwong is thirty, so you must have been carrying him then. What did you do? You did your Big Leap Forward with your child in your arms? You were in your teens. How did you make a living? [*He has obviously stung her. She turns away.*] And the three years of famine. Did you have a good time? When you went hungry, did you stop to think that after seven or eight years in England, I would have sent for you, to a comfortable life there? Didn't you regret it? Didn't you want to come back? [MAY *cannot stop him, so she shakes her head and moves away.*] And the Cultural Revolution? Shing Kwong was, what, eleven? Was he a Red Guard chanting 'Don't want father, don't want mother—'?

MAY However bad you try to make it sound, our life was in fact harder. If you think we have betrayed you and deserve to be punished for it, perhaps you feel avenged now?

CHEONG Then why are you here?

MAY I thought you achieved all that you wanted in England. Only now do I know that you didn't, or else you wouldn't have come back here.

CHEONG What do you know anyway?

MAY That you were divorced from your English wife, and that your son doesn't use your surname—

CHEONG That's none of your business.

MAY That your present wife doesn't really need you, and would not have your children—

CHEONG [shamed into retaliation] And so you put on a blue outfit, doll yourself up, come behind your husband's back to see me, to prove for your satisfaction that I still care.

MAY I've come to tell you—

CHEONG Now how should we do this? Rush into a tearful embrace? Or go hand-in-hand to the cinema, or reminisce about how we did our homework together, or confess how for thirty years we have yearned for each other in our dreams . . .?

MAY Shing Kwong is your son. [They both stop. CHEONG stares at her stunned, wondering if he heard right.] Shing Kwong is your son. [Watching CHEONG standing there shuddering, her grief in all the long years surges in her heart.] Don't be like this. It hurts me to see you like this! [Begins to sob helplessly] If I hadn't told you, I know you would not have had any peace thinking of Kei Woon and me together. Now that I've told you, I don't know what it will do to you. I don't know if you want a son like Shing Kwong.

CHEONG Why didn't you tell me?

MAY [bows her head in silence. Pauses] I wanted to.

CHEONG [his voice choked with emotion] Then why didn't you?

MAY [sighs] If I had written you a letter, then the last thirty years would have been so different. . . .

CHEONG I would have done something, I wouldn't have left you to deal with it on your own.

MAY And Shing Kwong, our son, would have grown up differently.

CHEONG Then why didn't you tell me?

MAY [calms down] When I learnt that I was pregnant, I was terrified. Your mother had always been so good to me, so I went to see her—

[Lights dim. MAY exits, changes part of her costume, goes up the backstage stairs to the upper level into the HO family home.]

SCENE TWO

[Evening. Early summer, 1955. Only a dim light in the HO *home in Shamshuipo. In the half light,* MOTHER, *upon hearing* MAY's *news, prowls in a rage round the room like an animal in a cage, throwing what she can lay her hands on into the corners of the room. The light is so dim when the scene starts that* MOTHER *seems to be alone in the room, since it is too dark to make out* MAY *shivering in a corner.]*

MOTHER You wait until he is gone and you come up with this nonsense to hold him responsible! You think I'm a fool? If anything like that had happened, my son would have told me.

MAY He didn't know. I don't know what to do, that's why I've come to you.

MOTHER And you have the gall to talk to me! I told Kei Cheong long before he left not to get involved with you. I knew you would try to tie him down.

MAY But Auntie, it's not like that—we didn't know—

MOTHER I thought you were too young to be scheming, but I was wrong about you. You know he has a bright future, so you try shamelessly to hold on to him.

MAY It's not like that.

MOTHER To think that I watched you grow up, thought you a decent girl, allowed you to befriend my son, let you come here to work and to eat with us! Is this how you repay me?

MAY I'm sorry, Auntie. But we—

MOTHER Since my husband died five years ago, I've put all my hopes in Kei Cheong. We had this flat to sublet for an income, but we've had to sell it to send him abroad. I have to work pulling yarn waste, and Kei Woon gives me less than a hundred a month. *[Catches hold of* MAY*]* What do you want me to do? Tell Kei Cheong to give up everything and come back for you?

MAY *[shakes her head]* No, no, no. I just don't know what to do. . . .

MOTHER If Kei Cheong comes home like this, we will be poor all our lives. My hopes will be gone. What are you anyway? That you should ruin the future of my whole family.

MAY No, no, Auntie. I don't want—

MOTHER Tell her to go back to her parents.

WOON [sees that MAY is trying to run away] You know she can't go back. We've got to find some place. May, just hold on. . . .

[MOTHER stands firm at the top of the stairs.]

All right, then. I'll take her to China!

MOTHER What? [Thunderstruck] What did you say?

WOON I'll take her to the Mainland. Come on, May, come up and we'll talk things over. I'll take you to China.

MOTHER You're not coming up. The idea is absurd. She is carrying your brother's baby, and you take her to China? What kind of arrangement is that supposed to be?

WOON If there is no place for her here, I'll take her to China. If she's willing, I'll marry her and then go. . . .

MOTHER If you dare to do such a thing, don't you ever come back! Ever!

WOON [unable to take it anymore] How can you be so heartless?

MOTHER Dare you lecture me on how to behave? You are mad. What will you say to Kei Cheong?

WOON We can't drive May to desperation. . . .

MOTHER How can I face our friends and relatives?

WOON Tell them I got married and moved to the Mainland.

MOTHER I will never accept her as one of the family!

WOON When I've married her, you will have a daughter-in-law and you will have a grandchild.

MOTHER If you do that and bring shame to the family, I don't want to see you ever again!

WOON Ma—

MOTHER Go away! Don't ever come back!

WOON Mother, I don't want it this way. You give me no choice—

MOTHER Go! Go away! Now!

[Unable to change his mother's mind, WOON helps the tearful MAY down the stairs and exits. MOTHER stands alone at the top of the stairs. Lights dim.]

SCENE THREE

[Follows from Scene 1. CHEONG sits despondent in his office. MAY makes her way slowly into the scene.]

MAY [sees him shaking] Kei Cheong, don't be like this. [Attempts to console him] All the pain, the suffering are things of the past.

CHEONG I said some nasty things.

MAY You said them because you were in pain. *[Pauses. Laughs at herself]* You've said nothing for the five days I've been here. I really thought you'd forgotten about the past.

CHEONG How could I forget you! *[Looks at her tenderly]* You still look nice in blue. *[MAY blushes.]* But even if you didn't wear blue, I would remember.

MAY *[sighs]* It seems a lifetime away!

CHEONG I was in love with you and I thought there was nothing I could not achieve.

MAY We were young, we thought that life would bring happiness.

CHEONG And that right and wrong were absolutes.

MAY We thought one had to fight to survive, and fight fair.

CHEONG But life has not been so simple since the day I left you. *[Nods at MAY]* You haven't changed though. You still see so clearly, and you fight fair.

MAY After so much that one can't do anything about, I have learnt acceptance.

CHEONG Meeting you this time, and thinking about your thirty years on the Mainland, I was prepared to treat you with contempt. I was going to just ignore you. But seeing you reminded me of the better person that I had been: I had not betrayed anybody then, nor been betrayed; I had not become calculating and mercenary, I was capable of total commitment. That made me realize that you would always belong to the best part of my life; you would always be an important part of me.

[Pause]

MAY Shing Kwong . . . perhaps you find him ignorant and slow, but he is a nice person, he tries hard. And he takes care of us.

CHEONG I can see that.

MAY I know he's a bit of a country bumpkin, but we have done our best for your son.

CHEONG I know.

MAY We love him. Kei Woon especially. He will miss Shing Kwong. He is the only son we have.

CHEONG I know.

MAY But you will be able to give him a better chance than we'll ever be able to give him. We won't stand in his way, whatever he chooses to do.

CHEONG That's good.

CHEONG You don't mind?

CARMEN There are bound to be ups and downs in business. Besides, it's not my money. Why should I mind? When you came back from England hoping to make some money in business, you knew that there was a risk. You have to accept that. Oh dear, Shing Kwong will be here in a minute. I'd better hurry. *[Gets ready to go out]*

CHEONG Don't go. Sooner or later we'll all have to sit down and talk things over.

CARMEN Later rather than sooner. Who knows what may happen when a father claims his estranged son. I'd rather not get involved. *[She goes into the living room. CHEONG follows her.]*

CHEONG Where are you going?

CARMEN You worry about your problems. You needn't worry about me. I can amuse myself.

CHEONG You will be home soon?

CARMEN Look at you! You're all in a jitter. Pity I have no children, otherwise I might be able to teach you a few tricks to handle them!

CHEONG You don't have to teach me. Just come home soon.

CARMEN There are lots of scenes in old Cantonese movies in which estranged parents and children are reunited. *[Thinks about those scenes]* But in most cases nothing much happens after that and the movies come to an end.

CHEONG Are you saying my life is like an old Cantonese soap opera?

CARMEN Very similar! But they went in for eighteen-year estrangements, mostly. You outdid them with your thirty years.

CHEONG You're so Westernized. How do you know about Cantonese soap?

CARMEN You forget I buy films for the TV station! I'd better get a move on or I'll meet up with your precious child.

CHEONG Perhaps you should.

CARMEN Don't worry. You're not sure of yourself only because you've had a bit of bad luck. The fact is, even if you lose everything, you're still much better off than he is. Take it easy! *[Goes to open the door]* Remember, I don't mind helping out with his keep, but I won't live with him in the same flat. *[Muttering as she goes out]* His sister doesn't even know how to use the toilet, he's probably no better. *[Slams the door shut after her as she goes muttering out of the room]*

[CHEONG *stands by the door a while, looks around, switches on the hi-fi, potters about in the room, making unnecessary adjustments to the furnishings. Then he rushes into the bedroom and looks at himself in the mirror, goes into the living room, switches off the hi-fi and stands in the middle of the room. Then it occurs to him to prepare drinks. Just as he is about to get something ready the bell rings.* CHEONG *opens the door.* SHING KWONG *stands there with a polite but restrained smile.*]

KWONG [*respectfully*] Uncle.

CHEONG Come in, Shing Kwong, come in. [KWONG *comes in and stands in the middle of the living room.*] Sit down. Sit down. [KWONG *just stands and nods, waiting for* CHEONG *to sit first.*] What would you like to drink?

KWONG Oh. [*Looks at him*] Er . . . anything will do.

CHEONG Coca Cola?

[KWONG *nods excitedly.* CHEONG *goes out and soon returns carrying a tray with glasses, a bottle of Coca Cola and a beer.*]

Take a seat. [*Sits down and pours a drink.* KWONG *also sits down.*] Try some beer? [KWONG *smiles timidly and shakes his head.*] You've had dinner, haven't you?

KWONG Yes. [*Accepts the drink* CHEONG *passes him*] Thank you, Uncle. [*The two men sit drinking.* CHEONG *studies* KWONG.] Ma says you wanted to see me about something.

CHEONG [*nods, goes on studying* KWONG] Are you enjoying yourself here?

KWONG Yes. [*Sighs with relief, shaking his head*] Now I know there is a different world out here!

CHEONG You've only been here a few days. You can't have seen much.

KWONG I know. But quite enough to scare me.

CHEONG To scare you?

KWONG Hong Kong is so prosperous and so complicated. Everyone knows what they are doing, except me. I feel sort of inferior in everything, and not even as adventurous as my sister.

CHEONG [*smiles*] She's young and doesn't know what fear is, isn't that so?

KWONG She thinks if she is afraid it will show her up as a country bumpkin. That's the way it is now on the Mainland. Not like when I was young, always in fear.

was to build me a stool and write my name on it. The
next day I took the stool and my schoolbag to school.
After school I sat outside the park and helped the hot-
water seller tend the fire—ten fen a cup. I liked
drawing. When I saved up a few cents I would buy
pencil and paper—*[Apologetically]* But this was a long
time ago. You don't want to listen to—

CHEONG Oh no, no. I'd like to hear about—I'd like to hear
about your childhood days. . . . *[KWONG looks at him,
unable to pick up from where he broke off.]* I was in
England, so I knew very little of what was happening
in China. I'd like to know. *[Waits]* The famine in the
sixties, that was bad, wasn't it?

KWONG Bad? *[Shakes his head in resignation]* There was nothing
to eat. Sometimes we had rice, but nothing to go with
it. Dad was a cook in the canteen, and he sometimes
got special permission to bring home the dregs of the
cooking oil wrapped in an old newspaper. We ate that,
and a pinch of salt, with our rice. And that was a treat
we'd look forward to for days. . . . *[Stares into space]*
Those years, we ate up anything that was edible. When
I sold hot water at the park entrance, there wasn't a
bird to be heard.

[The two remain silent for a while.]

CHEONG *[encouraging him to go on]* You did well in school
though?

KWONG *[nods]* The teacher picked me as the first pupil to wear
the 'Red Scarf'.* Of course, anyone can do that now.
But, at the time, it was a rare honour. There was a big
ceremony. I can still sing that song. Do you want to
hear it?

> 'I love my red scarf,
> As I do my life.
> It's a part of the red flag
> Blood-stained in heroes' strife.'

CHEONG You like to sing as well as paint.

KWONG The music teacher liked me and made me conductor of
the choir. That was when China broke away from the
Soviet Union, so we sang rousing songs:

---

* The 'Red Scarves' were worn by members of the Chinese Young Pioneers, a nationwide organization of
primary school pupils who were chosen for their academic achievements as well as their commitment to
helping each other. These Young Pioneers were known as Little Red Guards during the Cultural Revolution.

'Mountain leads to mountains,
The sea flows into seas.
We travel along the highway,
The world's proletariat unite.'

I didn't know what the words meant but I managed
the rhythm well, so they called me 'The little
enthusiast'.

CHEONG What?

KWONG 'The little enthusiast'. To describe the way I conducted.
My teacher was 'The grand enthusiast', and I was the
mini version.

CHEONG [*smiles and nods*] You don't look it now.

KWONG But I was very self-conscious. I started school late, and
was a lot older than the other children. What's more I
was on a grant; that means I was a 'non-paying pupil'.
It was not very nice not to be able to afford the fees. I
remember one night, I was doing my homework by
lamplight, and Ma was so tired she couldn't even sit up
straight, yet she kept me company and said, 'Shing
Kwong, Ma and Dad will work harder so that one day
we can pay the fees.' Then one day, she told me that
we had got our permanent residence card, and we could
pay the fees. But the Cultural Revolution came and I
couldn't even go to school.

CHEONG That was when you were just over ten years old?

KWONG Yes. Primary school pupils had no part in the
Revolution. When school was suspended, I went to
read all the posters denouncing anti-revolutionary
activities and people. Not those at the factories, but in
the cinemas and art galleries. There were nice pictures.
I got to see whatever picture was criticized and
denounced.

CHEONG Wasn't that the time when the country was in chaos
and when the Revolution got everybody involved in
learning from one another?

KWONG Yes. It was called 'linking up'. All post-secondary
students could take free train rides, and wherever they
went, they were given free board and lodging, so they
travelled all over the country enjoying themselves, and
had a good time criticizing the intellectuals. The Red
Guards shouted slogans like 'Light the fire of the
Revolution' and 'Long Live the Reds!'

CHEONG And you went all over the place as well?

hand again and again as if voting in support] Everybody did the same thing. I said to myself, if, one day, I should see someone voting in opposition, if one single hand was raised, then there would be hope for China.

CHEONG *[smiles at* KWONG *in appreciation,* KWONG *becomes more at ease and smiles at* CHEONG*]* Have you got a girlfriend?

KWONG *[shakes his head]* In the past, my circumstances were too minimal for me to have a girlfriend. *[Smiles]* But things have changed since people found out that I have an uncle in Hong Kong.

CHEONG Oh, really?

KWONG I have become very popular.

CHEONG *[intrigued]* Is that so?

KWONG The yearning for freedom can lead the mind into fantasies. They think that I might go abroad, inherit a fortune, and so, in the minds of some girls, I've become something of a potential saviour. I get a lot of passionate letters.

CHEONG *[smiles]* What if your uncle goes bankrupt? What would they think?

KWONG If they saw this place of yours, they simply wouldn't believe it.

CHEONG Anyway, you must keep in mind that whatever I may or may not have, you must tell me if you need anything.

KWONG I will, Uncle. But we are doing fine, and it is a pity we can't help you, we don't know how to. . . .

[Someone is trying to open the door from the outside with a key.]

CHEONG Ah, your Aunt Carmen's here.

*[*KWONG *stands up, and turns round just in time to greet* CARMEN.*]*

CARMEN *[seeing that* KWONG *is about to greet her, holds out her hand to stop him]* Shing Kwong, *do not* call me 'Mother'.

[The two men are taken aback and do not know what to do. CARMEN *looks at one and then the other in turn and realizes she has said something she shouldn't have. She puts a hand over her mouth and turns to* CHEONG.*]*

How was I to know you hadn't told him the truth?

[All freeze. Lights out.]

SCENE FIVE

[Afternoon the next day. WOON is sitting opposite LEE in the old man's home. The two have obviously had a long conversation. When the lights go up, CHEONG enters stage right, and hurries upstairs. LEE and WOON are waiting and they look up occasionally. WOON looks as though he is on the point of tears or an outburst of anger, the pressure of all his long pent-up grievances having been revived. LEE is more solemn and restrained than in his last appearance. CHEONG stops at the door and won't go in. WOON glances at him and looks down, leaving his uncle to handle the situation.]

LEE *[to CHEONG]* You know your uncle never interferes in what goes on between you two, and I know that you have to deal with a crisis in your business. I'm sorry about that, and I know I shouldn't bother you with this. But Kei Woon is leaving tomorrow, and who knows when he'll ever be here again. How can you bear to let him leave like this?

[CHEONG heaves a sigh, leans on the doorway, and looks down at the ground.]

I know that your mother never made it to England, and I know that she is not buried here in Hong Kong. I think you should tell him the rest.

WOON Whatever it is, I will not bear a grudge against you.

CHEONG *[walks away in irritation and annoyance]* What right have you to bear any grudges?

LEE It is impossible to sort out the debts of love and gratitude with the wrongs done between the two of you. But isn't it enough that you should be reunited after thirty years? Do we have to let this thing drag on forever? You should be ashamed to call yourself a Hong Kong person.

[CHEONG and WOON are both puzzled by this comment. They look at him.]

Well, even China and Britain have sorted out their entanglements of a hundred years.

CHEONG Uncle, I have no time to discuss that.

LEE I'm just using that as an analogy. Are not the entanglements between China and Britain more complicated than what has happened between you brothers? But, if there is enough goodwill, everything can be settled without shedding a drop of blood.

CHEONG It's just talk and dreams. Who knows if it will work.

LEE At least both sides have peace and prosperity in mind. It doesn't matter whether the 'one country-two systems'* thing can work, or whether there will be any need for it, at least you see that they are willing to try: find a peaceful solution to save bloodshed and devastation. Don't think it's nothing. If you want a war, you can start one on the smallest pretext. Don't you see what is happening in Iran and Iraq? When there is a war, it brings down both countries. People have no food or shelter and they still carry on fighting. To be able to go to war and yet refrain from it, that's what one would call magnanimity. You should know that. After all, you are sort of half-British and half-Chinese.

CHEONG *[very impatient with his uncle]* Sorry, Uncle, I really am not in the mood to discuss that. *[Turns to go]*

LEE *[also growing impatient]* Who is talking about moods? I'm talking about decency and concern; I'm trying to reason with you.

CHEONG Another day, maybe.

WOON *[stands up]* I can't wait any longer.

LEE *[at the same time]* Kei Woon says he won't leave unless you tell him. Now, I'm the sponsor for his visit. It will get me into trouble with the Immigration people. Have a thought for me at least.

CHEONG *[turns to go]* It'll be all right, Uncle. He will leave. I'll give him an explanation in time.

LEE Why can't you talk about it? It's not as if you have mistreated your mother.

[CHEONG starts to go down the stairs. WOON rushes after him and catches hold of him on the stairs.]

WOON You've got to tell me today!

CHEONG *[at the same time]* Let go of me! Let go!

[The brothers struggle on the stairs and move down to the bottom of the staircase. LEE goes to the top of the stairs and calls to them.]

WOON I've even given you back my son. What more do you want?

CHEONG He was my son. Besides I didn't say I'd take him back.

* A political arrangement designed for Hong Kong to enable a peaceful transition of sovereignty from Britain to China in 1997. Hong Kong is to become a Special Administrative Region of China, with a high degree of autonomy and will retain its capitalist system and way of life.

WOON Then it must be because of May. You hate me for
marrying her.

CHEONG Let's not talk about that again!

WOON You know very well, even May is yours! *[CHEONG stops
fighting. WOON breaks down sobbing.]* Now I have
nothing left except Shing Yee. You could at least let
me go home in peace. True, I was young and rash. I
left and never turned back. It was heartless. But when I
was desperate in China, there was no turning back. As
time dragged on, it was too late for regrets. *[Pauses]*
Kei Cheong, tell me where Mother is buried, for her
sake if not for mine. She always loved you more than
me. That was because she thought me useless, like Dad
who let her down. I don't mind. She was my mother
and loved me as her son. But if I don't know where
she is, I will never have any peace.

[They let go of each other. CHEONG leans against the wall.]

CHEONG All my resentments against you, whether or not they
are justified, are excuses. I haven't told you where
Mother is buried because I can't bear to say it. *[WOON
and LEE look at him in surprise.]* In 1967, at the height
of the Cultural Revolution in China, the situation was
also very tense in Hong Kong. I got a letter somebody
wrote for Mother, which said she was very ill and if I
didn't come back to Hong Kong, I might not see her
again.

I had been away for twelve years. When I got to
the old home in Shamshuipo, I found the streets and
the staircase much narrower than I remembered. And I
was shocked at how dirty they were. Mother still lived
in the same room, where we all used to live and eat
and study together. It was so small, not even a hundred
square feet. But it never felt cramped before. You
taught me how to saw wood in that room, and it was
there that I made vows of love to May. *[Looks up at the
HO home upstairs]* That dingy little room once held all
my passion and joy. In it I was filled with hope and all
the possibilities of life. *[Goes up the staircase slowly,
stands outside the door, turns round to face LEE and WOON]*
Mother was lying in bed, dying. Her hair had turned
white, her face was haggard.

Poor woman! I remembered how when we were
young, she shredded yarns from scrap fabric, and put
the best morsels of food in our bowls. For twelve years,

she had asked a neighbour to write to me once a
month to say that she was well, that she could manage,
and that I was not to worry about her. All that just so
she would have that day, when I would return in glory
to stand before her.

[Lights dim. CHEONG *changes costume in the dark.* LEE
walks down the stairs slowly and exits.]

SCENE SIX

[Lights go up on the middle section of the upper level—the HO *family home in
1967. The naked bulb outside the door glows feebly.* MOTHER *is sitting in bed,
leaning against the headboard. She is very ill, her face pale and haggard.*
CHEONG *is about 30, and doesn't look very different from the last scene, but he is
very elegantly dressed. He paces the room, obviously ill at ease.]*

MOTHER *[smiles happily]* I knew I would see this day: see that
you have made your fortune and have come home to
take me abroad.

CHEONG Why did you tell me in your letters that you had
moved to the bigger room in the flat and that you had
been very comfortable all these years?

MOTHER But I am comfortable.

CHEONG Why didn't you tell me that you had been ill for so
long? You sent me a photo just a few months ago to
show me how well you looked. Why?

MOTHER I didn't want you to worry, so I sent you an old
photograph.

CHEONG I've been sending you money. Why do you live in a
place like this?

MOTHER I've saved up the money for a plane ticket, so I won't
be a burden to you when you take me abroad.

CHEONG But all that money all these years! That's more than
enough for a plane ticket!

MOTHER I sent money to China, to put advertisements in the
papers hoping to locate your brother.

CHEONG What? *[Astonished]* You used my money to look for
him?

MOTHER I've been looking for him for years.

CHEONG He was heartless. He abandoned you. You haven't
mentioned him for years, why look for him?

MOTHER I was heartless too. He did write at first—

CHEONG Mother, I don't understand this!

MOTHER *[sighs]* I don't know where to begin. . . .

CHEONG What things are you keeping from me?

MOTHER Even after I've gone with you to England, I will have to keep looking for him. If I should never see him again, and you brothers do meet, you must tell him that I tried to contact him for years.

CHEONG Ma, you can't come to England with me yet.

MOTHER I've saved up enough money for a plane ticket.

CHEONG You don't understand. You can't come, not yet.

MOTHER I'll be no trouble to you. I can cook for you, do your laundry, like I've always done. I don't eat much, you know that, and I can live a simple life.

CHEONG Mother, I can't take you there yet.

MOTHER I'll be good to my daughter-in-law, and my grandson.

CHEONG *[goes forward to hold his mother by the shoulders]* Listen Ma, I have not made my fortune. I had a tough time studying in England. I told you every year that I did well. Well, I lied. I managed to scrape through and I graduated, but I had no work permit, and no money to bring you to England. I didn't dare come home, so I signed up for some easy subjects and stayed on.

MOTHER You said you had a family?

CHEONG I got married six years ago and had a son, that's true. The happy family photos I sent you year after year do not tell the truth. I wasn't at all happy. I got divorced last year and I'm still involved in a lawsuit because of it. Half my salary goes towards the alimony, and I have to pay for my son's keep.

MOTHER But you wrote to say that you had not disappointed me . . . my hopes . . . that you had made it in the world?

CHEONG I said that to please you! This time, because you are ill, the Immigration people—er—gave me special permission to leave the country for a few days, but I must go back, and I can't take you with me. I can't afford to provide for you in England!

MOTHER Hong Kong is in a mess and everyone is scared. Those who can leave have left. I have a son in England. Why can't I go there?

CHEONG It's tough living there. Life as an immigrant isn't what you imagine it to be.

MOTHER *[reaches out a dry bony hand to clutch at* CHEONG*]* I have lived alone in this room for twelve years, waiting for the day when I could see you. All my life I have waited: waited for your father, and for you the last twelve years. I can't wait any longer. I've run out of time.

CHEONG Ma, perhaps we have been waiting for the wrong things!

MOTHER *[pulls at* CHEONG *with all her strength]* It's too late to say that! I don't care where you go, I will follow you, even to the ends of the earth! *[Hangs on to* CHEONG *for a long while]*

CHEONG *[yields at last out of desperation]* All right, Ma. *[Pulls away* MOTHER's *hand]* If you must come, I can't stop you. I'll try to get you there. *[Stands up and walks slowly to the top of the stairs]*

[Lights dim on this scene and go up on the next scene. CHEONG *changes back into his costume in the previous scene.]*

SCENE SEVEN

[Picks up from Scene 6. CHEONG *is standing at the top of the stairs, the naked bulb over his head.]*

CHEONG I scrounged around for money, begged and borrowed, and pulled all the connections I had to get permission to take her to England for treatment, then I took her on a stretcher to the plane. *[Pauses]* The plane was in the air for three hours and she died on it. *[Pauses]* There was a stopover in Bangkok, and a distant relative there got permission from the local government to bury her there in Thailand while I went on to England. *[Pauses]* To this day I still send money for them to take care of things. But I have never seen the grave. *[Walks slowly down the stairs]*

*[*WOON *dashes forward and hits* CHEONG. *As his fists rain on* CHEONG, *he breaks down and cries.* CHEONG *doesn't dare strike back, covers his head from the blows and kneels down on the ground.* WOON *loses control of himself and cannot stop hitting* CHEONG.]*

Kei Woon—

LEE *[calls out to the brothers in pain and desperation]* Kei Woon, that's enough. Stop it, Kei Woon! That's enough!

WOON *[at the same time]* For eighteen years you've left her by herself in Thailand! And she loved you so much! How could you? *[Hits him]* You could have brought her back here and given her a decent burial. How could you just dump her there and never even care to ask? *[Hits him again]* Have you ever given her a thought in the dead of night? *[Seizes him]* Is that why you donated that money to her home village to build a school, to ease your guilt? *[Hits him again. CHEONG struggles to his feet and begins to retaliate in a verbal barrage.]*

CHEONG It's because I resent her. Deep in my heart! She thought she loved me, and forced me to live the way she wanted. I struggled through half my life for her dreams, and it suffocated me. I resent her even today, she has made me lose May and my son. . . . *[Rushes to strike WOON]* And what sort of filial son are you? Where were you when she was alive? Did you hate her because she loved me more? And did you think about her in the dead of night, huh? Did it occur to you that for years she spent my hard-earned money trying to find you, hah? *[Lashes out at WOON]* All her lonely years, did it occur to you to write because she might have relented? When I took her on the plane, it was you she asked for with her dying breath! *[Seizes WOON]* Now you want to know where she is, just so you can prostrate yourself before her and ease your conscience?

[The brothers exchange blows. LEE shouts for them to stop but dares not go near them to part them. CHEONG is no match for WOON, he doubles up with pain, falls down on his knees, and bursts out crying.]

Mother!

[WOON is shaken by this. He stops and is about to kick CHEONG. He stops, bursts into tears and dashes away. Lights dim.]

SCENE EIGHT

[A room in the Miramar Hotel. The radio is playing the latest pop music, the television is on, but the sound is turned off. WOON, MAY, and YEE are packing. All three are moody, for different reasons. Only MAY seems to have acquired a kind of peace from having resolved something important.]

MAY *[to YEE, indulgently]* Oh look, your clothes alone have filled the suitcase. *[Picks up a dress]* Why don't you wear this on the train? You look nice in this. *[YEE comes over with only mild interest, and holds up the garment against her body to see the effect. MAY picks up another dress.]* Or this? Wear it with your grey shoes and you'll look like Miss Hong Kong. Your classmate Lee Yee Man has been to Hong Kong too, but she's not half as lucky as you.

YEE *[holds up various garments against her body, and then sits down dispirited]* Why is it so unfair, Ma?

[WOON and MAY are both startled. But, because the question brings up too many possibilities, WOON decides to play deaf.]

MAY *[calm and collected]* I don't know how to answer that. *[Thinks perhaps that is not the best answer]* Anyway, there isn't time to go into that now. . . .

YEE Everybody wants to get out of the country, to come to Hong Kong, why don't we even ask? Perhaps Uncle Kei Cheong and Aunt Carmen would apply for us to stay? And Great Uncle Lee? Perhaps he would help? Didn't you and Dad used to live here? Perhaps you could trace back and find the right papers. How do you know it's not possible if you don't even try? Uncle Kei Cheong's living room alone is bigger than our whole flat. They even carpet their bathroom. Why do we have to go home where life is so hard?

WOON *[abruptly, with unwonted gruffness]* If you can manage it then don't go home. I don't care if none of you comes home.

[YEE and MAY are both taken aback. YEE pouts, stamps her foot, and begins to cry.]

MAY *[looks sympathetically at WOON, then says to YEE]* You know that Dad loves you. We'll discuss this when we get home. *[Thinks for a moment, takes some money out of her handbag]* Didn't you say you liked that big bag in the shopping arcade downstairs? Why don't you go and see if it's still there and get it, mm? *[YEE looks at MAY and hesitates.]* It is a little expensive, but get it if you really like it. And you can use it as a school bag.

[YEE stands up, takes the money, wipes her tears, glances at her father. MAY gives YEE a nod, a signal for her to go.]

Don't take too long. Come back as soon as you've got it.

[YEE opens the door and goes out.]

WOON *[as soon as the door is shut, gloomily]* She'll have to learn sooner or later, there is no such thing as fairness in life.

MAY Later, then. *[Goes to switch off the television and the radio. Slowly]* Girls in Hong Kong her age get whatever they want, and nothing amazes them. Our Shing Yee is filled with amazement at so many new and beautiful things. Perhaps one day, she will pay a price for her curiosity. Our generation is hurt and scarred. It is just as well that the child can still dream and hope for the future.

At her age, I fell in love with Kei Cheong. We used to pay forty cents to go to the cinema after school. In those Hollywood movies, the streets of New York were spotlessly clean, and the ladies beautifully dressed. In the darkness of the cinema hall, I held Kei Cheong's hand, and it was like a hope to get to paradise. Kei Cheong was going to this paradise for sure. I thought I was going to share that chance, and offering him my heart and my self was a price to pay for that chance. At the end of that year, I married you, gave birth to Shing Kwong, and never dreamt again.

[WOON is shaking all over and cannot look up.]

I was only a simple, ordinary seventeen-year-old, weaving a harmless dream. It never occurred to me that I would have to carry such a heavy burden in life, and travel so far. *[To WOON]* Our generation has woken up from those dreams. But anyway, we have brought up two children. Shing Yee only wants a better future. And Shing Kwong. . . . Your sister-in-law is just a few years older than he is, but having grown up in Hong Kong, she is like somebody from another planet. Shing Kwong has only been around for thirty years, but he has grown up in the midst of turmoil in China, seen the horrors of deception, conflict, and betrayal among people. He came back after years of manual labour in the countryside, eager to make a fresh start, and didn't take any shortcuts. He chose to teach in the Art College to help the next generation. And he bears no grudge against the past. I admire his courage. Our lives have lost lustre, but at least our children have dreams for the future. We shouldn't be too hard on them.

WOON And you . . . *[With difficulty]* have you any regrets?

MAY *[pauses and then turns round slowly to look at* WOON*]* Regrets? *[She waits.* WOON *cannot speak for the many thoughts and feelings that he experiences at that intense moment.]* I regret telling Kei Cheong that Shing Kwong is his son.

WOON *[nods, and takes a deep breath]* Regret that you married me, regret going to China with me, regret that you did not leave me in the many years when you could have done that, and regret having Shing Yee, because after that you could not leave me even when you wanted to. *[Brushes away his streaming tears with his wrist, no longer bothering to hide his shame from his wife]* When I married you I thought it was for your good. I never thought that you would have to go through hell with me for thirty years. When I take you home today, it will still be to a grey worn city, to a dingy home. That's all that I can give you. But Kei Cheong—*[He breaks down.* MAY *comes over quietly, puts her arms around him.* WOON *does not dare hold her, or lean against her. Fearing for the loss of both his wife and his son, he sobs silently with anguish.]*

MAY *[pauses, when* WOON *calms down a little, she moves away quietly, and thinks and speaks softly]* I have been asking myself the same questions for thirty years. Now that I see him again, I know the Kei Cheong I loved and adored at seventeen does not exist any more. I panicked for a while, then I realized that was not the only love I had in my life. *[Pauses]* The years when you had to work in the countryside, and I stayed to look after the children, the first thought I had each day was of you, and the last thoughts of each day were of you. I worried that you might go cold or hungry, that your kind nature would be taken advantage of, that you could not cope with the rough work and the hard life. I prayed that you would come home, that I would have you by my side, and I reminded myself to keep well and strong, so that I could look after you when you came home. . . . *[Thinks]* What was all this if not love? *[Turns to look at her husband tenderly, her face breaking into a smile]* My life did take an unexpected turn and I found myself on a long hard road, but in the company of such a good kind man as you, I have no regrets.

WOON *[looks up in gratitude at* MAY. *After a while]* Can you bear to part from Shing Kwong?

MAY *[looks at* WOON *apologetically]* I know it wasn't fair to you, my telling Kei Cheong the truth without letting you know, especially when we had argued for so long over it. I knew you might be angry with me. But when I saw the deadlock between the two of you I felt that I had to do it.

WOON I am not angry with you. Besides, it's done. It hurts you more than it hurts me.

MAY I have never been magnanimous, nor brave. When I think that perhaps Shing Kwong may choose to stay with his father, I don't feel good. It's not fair to you.

WOON That was what I thought too, until I got here and went into Kei Cheong's flat. All such thoughts went out of my mind. What have I got to offer against all that?

MAY That was not what I meant. If Shing Kwong wants to stay here, to learn to make money, and a fortune for himself, it may not be the best thing for him. The important thing is that he should choose for himself. *[Wonders whether she should go on]* In any case, you should not repeat your mother's mistake. I remember how much she loved you both, and I think she was fond of me as well. Widowed before she was forty, she had to bring up both of you in a cubby-hole of a room. From what I remember, she never had a thought for herself. But she thought she knew what was good for us, and she tried to change all our lives. Look what happened! The love between brothers turned sour for thirty years. She had two sons but had no one by her side. She never knew her grandchildren. She was lonely alive, and lonely in death. But look at where we are now. Is that anything like what she wanted for us? And what control has she got over how we'll live our lives now?

WOON *[desolate]* If Kei Cheong does send Shing Kwong abroad to study, we'll never see him again . . . or perhaps, if we did, he would ask, 'How are you, Uncle?'

MAY *[consoles him]* I know you can't bear to part—

WOON *[nods with grim determination, and interrupts* MAY*]* For better or for worse, let him decide. *[Accepts the thought]* He has the right even to take the wrong road, and start all over again.

MAY Then your love for Shing Kwong counts for something.

[Husband and wife look at each other for a long while.]

WOON [*very tentatively, looking timidly at his wife*] And you?

MAY Me?

WOON What decision have you come to?

MAY [*puzzled*] Decision? [*She realizes what he means.*] After all that I've said—more than what I normally say in ten days—and you still don't know what I mean?

WOON [*smiles timidly*] But it is nice to hear you say it again— that you will not leave me.

[MAY *looks at her husband through her tears, and smiles.*]

SCENE NINE

[*The next morning.* CHEONG, *neatly dressed, stands waiting in his living-room. He walks to the window to look out, checks his watch, and then goes to stand in front of the sofa. The doorbell rings.* CHEONG *looks up in surprise, and looks at his watch again. He does not move. The doorbell rings again.* CHEONG *goes to answer the door, and sees* WOON *standing outside. He is puzzled.*]

CHEONG It's you? I thought Carmen had gone to pick you up at the hotel and take you to the railway station. [*Pauses*] I'll see you off at the railway station.

WOON [*nods*] I wanted to see you before I went.

CHEONG Oh. [*Pauses*] Oh, come in, come in. [WOON *enters.*] Please take a seat.

[CHEONG *stands there waiting.*]

WOON I hear that the American client won't take delivery and the local agent can only sell part of the shipment. The rest will have to be sold in street stalls by hawkers. You've lost quite a lot of money.

CHEONG [*nods*] All that I made in South-East Asia in the last few years.

WOON Our visit here cost over ten thousand dollars. . . .

CHEONG [*waves his hand impatiently*] That's nothing. [*Sees that* WOON *is silent, adds*] In fact, you needn't have come just to say that. Even if you were to pay me back the money, that small sum wouldn't help.

WOON I know that. [*Pauses*] I've come because I heard that your business is going to collapse.

CHEONG [*nods*] Yes, and you will see, before you go back to China, that in the end, I've failed to live up to Mother's expectations.

WOON You know that I will not—

CHEONG I don't think Mother ever understood what going abroad meant.

WOON She must have thought that just getting there would mean success. She never thought about how one lives from day to day.

CHEONG When people who grow up like us go abroad to study, we tend to shut ourselves in and not have anything to do with the foreigners. You feel so lonely and alienated. You're never at home. No sense of belonging.

WOON I thought you had turned into a foreigner.

CHEONG *[shakes his head]* In the years abroad, you send home good news, never the bad. You save and scrounge. But when you go to China from Hong Kong, you feel so grand, and you tend to boast about the good life out there. The fact is, if our country had done well, we would not have had to lie. Pathetic!

WOON Hong Kong has done well for herself in the last decade or so.

CHEONG *[nods]* Looking at it from the outside, you would have thought that the best thing about Hong Kong was its efficiency, its management, which make it a good place for making money. But the best thing about Hong Kong, in fact, is its rule by law, its freedoms, and the choice of lifestyles it offers. There is no threat of famine or unemployment, no threat that one's freedoms will be taken away, or one's dignity humiliated. Look at the way education has helped to improve the quality of its people, to raise their public spirit. One has actually got to live here to appreciate these things fully.

WOON And that is why people like you and Carmen have come all the way back here to set up home?

CHEONG But then, in the end, one still has to wait on other people's pleasure. I wait for orders from the Americans to make me rich. If the Americans don't think me good enough, I'm done for.

WOON But you can start all over again!

CHEONG *[nods]* Uncle was right. I am a Hongkonger through and through. However bad the setback, I will be patient, work hard, recover, and soon it'll be to the races and to the dances as usual, and I'll play mahjong and speculate on the stock market again!

WOON You are lucky to have the opportunities.

CHEONG *[shakes his head]* But that Hong Kong is changing now.

WOON You mean because of its return to China?

CHEONG I used to think that one could take care of one's own
life. But this reunion business affects everyone, and we
have all got to work at it together. And yet each one of
us will also have to decide what to do.

WOON Is it true that those who can leave have already left?

CHEONG Those with the qualifications and the opportunities are
at least setting up an escape route, even if it means
having to stay abroad for a couple of years to qualify
for citizenship. They come back when they have their
foreign passports.

WOON Oh?

CHEONG With a foreign passport, patriotism comes easier. Or
perhaps they come back because they have not
abandoned their roots. Or perhaps it sounds more
generous and is a lot safer to declare your patriotic
sentiments when you have a foreign passport.

WOON Not everybody can leave though?

CHEONG That is why, in the run-up to 1997, there will be
many more patriots among the Chinese who are stuck
in Hong Kong.

WOON Patriots?

CHEONG Yes. We go to China, hold our heads high among
friends and relatives there, but are scared as hell of
Communism. Back in Hong Kong, we queue up at the
bookies to bet on the ponies one moment, and shout
support for the 'Four Modernizations'* the next. That's
the form our patriotism takes!

WOON I never thought—

CHEONG [*laughs ironically at himself*] Odd, isn't it? I have been a
Chinese without a country all my life, in the end, my
life is still tied up with the destiny of my motherland!
They talk of autonomy! I don't know how they can
work that out. People of our generation have never had
any autonomy.

[WOON *sits down, shakes his head and says nothing.*]

CHEONG Look at me, brother. I am what you people call
'overseas Chinese'. Take a good look before you go
home. Apart from material prosperity, we don't have
much that you need envy.

WOON When I got here a few days ago, you told me that
since I was poor and ignorant, you would share what

---

* China's reform policy in 1977 which urged modernization in the fields of agriculture, industry, science and technology, and defence.

you had with me, as long as I didn't interfere with your life.

CHEONG I said that in anger and spite, please don't—

WOON I felt really bad. Even if you were richer and more successful, and you gave me a large part of your fortune, it would only make me feel indebted to you for life. That would only deepen the chasm between us.

CHEONG You would rather see me ruined?

WOON *[shakes his head]* Why would I want that? But what you said about our lives being tied to the destiny of our motherland is true. The roads we have travelled, whether we chose them or not, those are now part of our history. That is why I cannot blame Mother, or May, or you, for any part of the last thirty years of my life.

CHEONG I know that you did want to serve the country at the time.

WOON When I went back in '55, I had such hopes. I thought there would be a future for China, and for me too. To help build the country would liberate me from the endless drudgery of a miserable factory life.

CHEONG Nobody could have foreseen what happened there afterwards.

WOON The second year I was there, we were encouraged to speak our minds. I thought, 'Good. I can speak frankly for the sake of the country.' Then suddenly all the masks and the pretence came away, and I was taken from my wife and child to hard labour and re-education in the countryside.

CHEONG Why didn't you try to come back to Hong Kong?

WOON I was at a dead end. But how could I hope to turn back? Who knows what I would have found back in Hong Kong? What if Mother had been right, and you had returned successful from your studies and had taken Mother abroad for the good life? In which case, I would have done May a grievous wrong!

CHEONG You shouldn't have thought like that. Everybody knows you for your generosity and integrity.

WOON *[shakes his head]* Everybody thought I had integrity, but I lost that long ago. I suppose I just wanted an easy life. I went to meetings as I was told, I chanted slogans when I was told. When they went on an assault, I went half-way and then slipped home. *[Pauses]* Patriotism! It wasn't for the likes of me!

CHEONG *[pauses, feeling sorry for his brother]* That's all over and done with. . . .

WOON Living with lies, too scared to speak out, moving around in stealth. Sometimes I thought I was in a nightmare, and wondered why I could not wake up from it as it went on year after year.

CHEONG *[pauses]* But now . . .?

WOON I have woken up. But I'm past fifty now. And I find my daughter rejoicing just because she can buy a fake European brand watch.

[CHEONG understands his brother fully now, sighs and is silent.]

WOON The last thing I want is to see you ruined. But perhaps your broken dream may help you understand all the broken dreams we've had for the last thirty years. You here, we on the Mainland. We all lived through such a lot of hypocrisy, wrongs, and helpless acceptance. We let others down, and others let us down. We lost our respect for others and for ourselves, just to survive. We were riddled with inferiority, bigotry, stupidity, and the errors of the past. Today, the same feeling of inferiority, false pride, egoism, and bigotry are still with us as we face the days to come. We carry the same burden, the regrets of the irredeemable past. Perhaps only in sharing this inevitable destiny can we truly be brothers.

[The two brothers look at each other.]

CHEONG My brother! *[Walks towards WOON]*

WOON You know, you were right the other day, when you accused me of being jealous of the close bond between you and Mother. I didn't complain because I was also very stubborn. I thought that since she didn't love me, it wouldn't matter if I never went home to her. But looking back, I wonder whether I punished her, or whether it was the other way round.

CHEONG You were right about me too. I was jealous that you were always with Dad. I wanted to be like him, to go into business and make lots of money. I couldn't forgive Mother for not understanding that. I could have brought her home for a proper burial here, but the longer I left it, the less I wanted to bring up the matter. So I left her out there desolate all these years.

WOON *[pauses]* We are quite a pair!

[They look at each other, laugh through their tears and embrace.]

Poor Mother thought that her love could shield you from all that was tough in life.

CHEONG And when I came upon difficulties, I wasn't prepared because she wasn't there to help me. You've turned out to be stronger. For that, you should forgive her.

WOON *[shakes his head]* I need forgiveness too, from Mother, from May and from you.

CHEONG Yes. We are quite a pair. *[They smile at each other, and sigh.]* If Mother knew that she had a grandson like Shing Kwong, she would be pleased.

WOON *[hesitates]* A grandson like Shing Kwong might not be quite grand enough for her.

CHEONG Well, when she met Shing Kwong she'd think differently. After thirty years of trials and tribulations and he says, 'When everybody is trying to make a million, somebody has to think about things other than money'!

WOON Mother would be so surprised. How ever did she get such a rare creature for a grandson!

[They both laugh.]

CHEONG *[stands up]* That rare creature is our hope for the future. *[Looks at his watch]* Well, it's time, Brother. Let's go and pick him up.

[CHEONG and WOON link hands cheerfully, and exit arm in arm.]

THE END

WHERE LOVE ABIDES

A PLAY IN THREE ACTS

1986

By
RAYMOND K. W. TO

Translated by
Y. P. CHENG

ABOUT THE PLAYWRIGHT

RAYMOND K. W. TO (1946–) began his career in the theatre as a young boy, taking part in radio drama programmes. After completing his BA at the University of Hong Kong, and his Diploma of Education at the Chinese University of Hong Kong, he became a teacher and a pioneer in the promotion of drama in schools. In 1979, he was invited by the Hong Kong Repertory Theatre to collaborate with director Joanna Chan in the staging and adaptation of *Rickshaw Puller Camel Cheung*, a famous novel by Lao She. In the same year, his original play, *Ball*, was nominated as the 'Most Outstanding Work' of the Hong Kong Repertory Theatre's 'Original Script Project'. It marked the beginning of his freelance career in playwriting, which lasted until 1992 when he turned professional. Since 1993, he has been Playwright-in-Residence at the Hong Kong Repertory Theatre.

To is a prolific and versatile writer, adept at handling subjects related to all aspects of Hong Kong history, as well as subjects from classical Chinese literature and traditional Cantonese opera. He has produced works ranging from stage and radio plays to television drama and film scripts. His major stage plays include *Yesterday's Child* (1983), *I'm a Hongkonger* (1985), *Under the Banyan Tree* (1987), *Shatin Graffiti* (1988), *Boundless Movements* (1987), *A Gleam of Colour* (1988), *Tokyo Blues* (1990), *I Have a Date with Spring* (1992), *Where Love Abides* (1986), *Legend of a Mad Phoenix* (1993), and *Entrance from the P Side* (1984). The last four have also been adapted into film scripts by To. *I Have a Date with Spring* was a great success and received the 'Gold Award for Best Script' from the Hong Kong Film Association, as well as the 'Best Script Award' from the Hong Kong Scriptwriters Association in 1994.

But To's reputation as the leading playwright in Hong Kong preceded the success of this film. In 1989, he was named 'Playwright of the Year' by the Hong Kong Artists' Guild. In 1990, his play, *Tin Hau, Goddess of the Sea*, commissioned by the Hong Kong Academy for Performing Arts, premiered at the Istropolitana Festival in Czechoslovakia to enthusiastic reviews. In 1992, he received a grant to go to New York to study drama, and, in 1993, his *Strange Tales from a Chinese Studio, a Contemporary Version*—adapted from the famous Chinese novel *Strange Tales from a Chinese Studio*—won the 'Best Script Award' in the 'Second Annual Hong Kong Stage Plays Awards'.

ABOUT **THE PLAY**

Where Love Abides is a fictitious work inspired by the centenary celebrations of the Leung So Kee Umbrella Factory, which was established in Guangzhou during the late Qing Dynasty, and moved to Hong Kong at the time of the Japanese invasion. Raymond K.W. To consulted historical material supplied by those associated with the factory in order to research the play. Ironically, the centenary celebrations also marked the closing down of the factory, signalling the end of an era which nurtured small private enterprises of this kind.

Realistic in style and episodic in structure, *Where Love Abides* traces the saga of this small enterprise, and the family that ran it, through the significant stages in the hundred years of its operation. Not unlike Lao She's famous play, *Teahouse*, the story reflects a certain period in Hong Kong history and the way it affects the fortunes of the family and the firm. With a slightly smaller scope, and its focus trained more inwardly, this play commemorates nostalgically the family and management ethos of a bygone era. Many historians, sociologists, and successful Hong Kong businessmen would recognize this ethos: it is this that has enabled Hong Kong to grow and develop into the thriving centre of commerce, industry, and business that it is today.

Where Love Abides, first performed by the Hong Kong Repertory Theatre in Hong Kong in 1986, toured Guangzhou in 1987. The play received high acclaim from critics on the Mainland, many of whom ranked it with *Teahouse*. It is also considered by many Hong Kong drama critics to be To's best work to date.

—— **DRAMATIS** PERSONAE ——

THE LEUNG FAMILY:

LEUNG SO, founder of the So Kee Umbrella Factory in Canton
MADAM HO, wife of LEUNG SO
LEUNG TIN CHI, eldest son of LEUNG SO
LEUNG TIN YAU, second son of LEUNG SO
LEUNG MEI KIU, daughter of LEUNG SO, younger sister of TIN CHI
   and TIN YAU
CHAN YING, wife of TIN CHI
LEUNG CHEUNG WAH, son of TIN CHI and CHAN YING, third
   generation proprietor of the So Kee Umbrella Factory, also the
   narrator and the only member of the cast who addresses the
   audience directly
LEUNG CHEUNG WAH, as a young boy
SAU LING, wife of TIN YAU, a singer
LEUNG SIU LING, daughter of TIN YAU and SAU LING, as a girl, as a
   young woman, as a mature woman

THE FOKIS* IN THE SO KEE UMBRELLA
FACTORY:

AH KWAI, works in the factory in Canton, deeply in love with MEI
   KIU
AH CHOI, one of the younger *fokis* in the factory in Canton. Cheeky
   and garrulous, loves singing Cantonese operas
AH KAI, one of the younger *fokis* in the factory in Canton. Rather
   dull-witted and simple-minded but carefree
AH SHUN, one of the older *fokis* in the factory in Canton. Loyal to his
   masters. Was once a compulsive gambler
AH CHUEN, the oldest *foki* in the factory. Loyal to his masters
   (Except his wife and LEUNG SO, everyone addresses him as 'Uncle
   Chuen' to show respect for his age)
AUNTIE CHUEN, Ah Chuen's wife, kind-hearted and hard-working
   (The honorific 'auntie' is a customary term of endearment and
   respect, rather than an indication of family relationship)

---

* *Foki* is a transliteration. A *foki* is a long-term employee of a factory or company, rather like a family
retainer.

KIT TSAI, a young worker in the So Kee Factory in 1960s Hong
    Kong. Loves pop music
FAT TSAI, a young worker in the So Kee Factory in 1960s Hong
    Kong. Loves western movies

OTHERS

MING TSAI, a poor young man. Friendly with the *fokis* of the factory
    in Canton
NGAN HING, a businessman from Malaya. Courteous and urbane
PAK YING, a revolutionary
LI TSAI, a salesman of materials for manufacturing umbrellas

AGES OF THE CHARACTERS AS THEY APPEAR IN THE VARIOUS SCENES

Narrator (CHEUNG WAH)   57

	Prologue	1937	1950	1966
LEUNG SO	35–63	73	dead	—
MADAM HO	32–60	dead	—	—
TIN CHI	18	28	41	57
TIN YAU	16	26	39	dead
CHAN YING	17	27	40	56
MEI KIU	—	22	35	51
CHEUNG WAH (as a boy)	—	9	—	—
AH KWAI	17	27	40	56
AH CHOI	—	20	33	49
AH KAI	—	20	33	49
AH SHUN	—	33	46	62
AH CHUEN	40	50	dead	—
AUNTIE CHUEN	—	—	53	69
SAU LING	—	20	dead	—
SIU LING	—	—	8	24
MING TSAI	—	17	—	—
KIT TSAI	—	—	—	24
FAT TSAI	—	—	—	24
NGAN HING	—	40	—	—
PAK YING	—	26	—	—
LI TSAI	—	—	—	30

ACTS

Act One	Prologue
	So Kee Umbrella Factory in Canton, 1937
	Intermission
Act Two	Backyard of the branch of the So Kee Umbrella Factory at Rua das Estalagens in Macau, 1950
Act Three	The So Kee Umbrella Factory in Des Voeux Road, Central, Hong Kong, 1966

ACKNOWLEDGEMENTS

This is a fictitious story, inspiration for which came from the one hundred years of history of the So Kee Umbrella Factories in Canton and in Hong Kong. The playwright gratefully acknowledges the material provided by branches of the So Kee Umbrella Factories on Hong Kong Island and in Kowloon.

A special note of thanks to Mr Leung Chun Fat, General Manager and third-generation proprietor of the So Kee Umbrella factory in Hong Kong.

ACT *1*

At the centre of the stage is erected a large, sturdy, two-storeyed structure with a stairway in the centre leading to the upper storey. It is divided into four equal sections, two on top (Zone 1 on the left and Zone 2 on the right) and two below (Zone 3 on the left and Zone 4 on the right), providing four 'Performing Zones'. From the auditorium, this structure looks like a large four-paned-window that can be seen through. The space downstage from the structure makes two more acting zones (5 and 6). Props and sets could be brought in from the wings or lowered from the flies.

  The backdrop shows rolling clouds in a blue sky.
  Lights dim.

PROLOGUE

[The colour of the backdrop changes from light blue to greyish blue. Lights come up gradually in Zone 5. A man in his 50s, kind, relaxed, and cheerful, sits comfortably in a large swivel chair. He is LEUNG CHEUNG WAH. He speaks with the assurance of an experienced old man, but he does not look old. He slowly swivels his chair around to look at the sky, then swivels it around again to address the audience. There is a closed umbrella in his hand.]

CHEUNG WAH *[to the audience]* I'll tell you a story about umbrellas. It's a story about my family. A long story, that goes way back to my grandfather. He knew how to be 'human'. My father, too, was also 'human'. And naturally, I am 'human' as well. *[Waits for some response from the audience before proceeding, in a humorous tone]* We all know the word, but I'm afraid it can never be fully and adequately translated into another language. In our culture, knowing how to be 'human' means more than being kind, or humane, or tolerant of human foibles and weaknesses. It is the ultimate state that many of us strive to achieve, but it is more often experienced than defined. *[He smiles at the audience.]*

[Cantonese music is heard: the tune of 'Pattering Rain on Banana Trees' played on a yangqin—*a Chinese stringed instrument. The music is like the sound of raindrops. The sky turns greyish blue. Quite a change from the fine weather a moment ago. CHEUNG WAH opens his umbrella, walks downstage to face the audience, and stares into the distance, as if meditating.]*

Everyone wants a good life, a happy life, a successful life. *[He tilts the umbrella to make its round fabric surface*

face the audience.] Full and round. Like this umbrella. *[Pauses]* But life doesn't turn out that way. It's full of disappointments and frustrations. We know nothing of the will of heaven, what it has in store for us, but in the end we take it as it comes, and reconcile it with the will of man to attain that supreme state of peace and equanimity. That's what we mean by being human. *[He turns round to look at the rain.]* See what I mean? *[He moves to an appropriate position to introduce the action.]* The weather was fine a moment ago, and now it's pouring. Who would have expected it? Some people don't like the rain. They think it's a bad omen, and depressing. But one day, a hundred years ago, in the pouring rain, under a gloomy sky, my grandfather ran into good fortune. That's right, a hundred years ago, in the twelfth year of the reign of Emperor Guangxu of the Qing Dynasty. Grandad was a rag-and-bone man in Canton. He doubled as a tinker as well, mending pots and pans, and he bought scrap metal. There was a storm that day and he was squatting under a verandah to wait out the rain. Suddenly a *gweilo*∗ rushed by, flung down his umbrella and grabbed one of Grandad's frying pans to cover his head from the stones hurled at him by a mob of irate textile workers. Apparently he'd beaten one of them up. In the end the *gweilos* had to bring in muskets to stop the riot. Anyway, Grandad came into possession of this Western wonder, the Western umbrella. He was overjoyed. He wasn't going to have anything to do with boycotting all things Western. He shut up his stall, and took the umbrella home to explore its mysteries.

SCENE ONE

[Lights go up in Zone 1.

A middle-aged couple comes into view: LEUNG SO *and* MADAM HO. LEUNG SO *is sitting on the floor,* MADAM HO *is half-kneeling. The scene is a dilapidated hut, with a stack of hay here, some old pots and pans there.*

LEUNG SO *is in his 30s. He has a long pigtail and wears Qing-style tunic and trousers.* MADAM HO *wears her hair in a bun. She is drying* LEUNG SO *with a towel. Then, noticing that* LEUNG SO's *pigtail is still dripping, she wraps the towel round the pigtail and wrings it dry. A funny sight.]*

∗ *Gweilo is a Cantonese word meaning 'ghost man', applied to Westerners.*

LEUNG SO *[absorbed in the umbrella, opening and shutting it to see how it works]* So foreign umbrellas are just the same as our paper ones; the stem is straight like ours.

MADAM HO What a fool you are! Why didn't you open the umbrella in the rain?

LEUNG SO *[fiddling with the ring]* That's neat! Less than a quarter of an inch and it can support ribs nearly two feet long!

MADAM HO How many ribs are there?

LEUNG SO *[counting]* Two, four, six, eight, ten, twelve, fourteen, sixteen. Only sixteen ribs and they give such firm support.

MADAM HO And the fabric. Look at the fabric. It's better than a dozen layers of varnish on paper.

LEUNG SO *[trying to bend the rib]* How do they mount it? This metal is really strong.

MADAM HO *[touching the curved end of the handle]* This is different, too. The handle's shaped like a crook. Ours aren't.

LEUNG SO Hm, yes. It has a hook. But what is the hook for?

MADAM HO To hang up the umbrella like a bird cage? Then you could open it and put things inside!

LEUNG SO That doesn't make sense. I think it's to be used as a walking stick when it's not raining, for support.

MADAM HO *Gweilos* like to hit people, they could use it to grab your neck when they hit you.

LEUNG SO *[considers his wife naïve]* No. They could just stab you with this end. Why bother to hook your neck?

MADAM HO *[pensively]* We Cantonese rarely fight with umbrellas. The *gweilos* are rather crafty, I must say. So many uses for an umbrella. Really crafty!

LEUNG SO Hey, light me the lamp. *[MADAM HO looks puzzled.]* I want to see better how it's made so that I can repair foreign umbrellas as well. Tomorrow, I'll set up shop near the doors of the rich.

MADAM HO You think you're so smart you could do it just by looking at it, huh?

LEUNG SO And someday I'll open a shop to sell foreign umbrellas.

MADAM HO *[teasing him]* Dreams! Dreams! You've barely touched the umbrella and you're getting so carried away!

LEUNG SO I'll make Western umbrellas. That's it, that's what I'll do! They're useful when the sun is strong, and when it rains as well. Yes, I'm sure I'll make a fortune!

MADAM HO What if it neither rains nor shines? Who will buy them then?

LEUNG SO *[resentfully]* Come on! You've lived through more than
half of your life now. Have you had many days as good
as this one? *[MADAM HO pauses to think and agrees.]*
Don't you want to be the wife of a shop-owner?

MADAM HO *[heaves a long sigh, pensively]* Sure! And I want us to try
a few more times: I won't give up until I've brought
up a son or two.

*[LEUNG SO is stunned, a look of helplessness on his face.
MADAM HO quietly lights up an oil lamp, puts it in front
of LEUNG SO, and glances at him. LEUNG SO looks at the
lamp, then at MADAM HO, then at the umbrella, then at
MADAM HO again.*

*He takes a deep breath and blows out the lamp. Lights
out.]*

S C E N E   T W O

*[Lights go up in Zone 5. LEUNG CHEUNG WAH is standing there. The props are
set up in Zones 2, 3, and 4.]*

CHEUNG WAH *[facing the audience]* Grandma gave birth to five children
but they all died, either because they were born weak
or because of malnutrition. Grandad put it down to
fate. So he asked a *fungshui* man home. The man told
him to chop up the bed and burn it, then to rent a
few kerosene lamps and give a feast at the 'Four
Arches' for the neighbours. Grandad spent every cent
he had. And, believe it or not, things took a turn for
the better. Grandma gave birth to three children
though she was no longer young. They are: my dad,
my uncle, and my aunt. My dad, who was the sixth
child, now became the first to survive. Grandad was in
his forties then, and he called my father Tin Chi,
meaning 'heaven's gift'; my uncle was named Tin Yau,
meaning 'heaven's blessings'; and my aunt, the
youngest, was called Mei Kiu, meaning 'beautiful and
charming'. *[Reflects]* Mei Kiu? That's how it was
decades ago. Girls were nothing! Sons were destined for
better things and fortune, hence 'heaven's gift' and
'heaven's blessings'. But a daughter? Well, so long as
she was beautiful and charming enough to get herself a
husband, that was good enough. And so they were
given names that had something vaguely to do with

beauty, like flowers or the moon. *[Slight pause]* Grandad was really something. He sweated and toiled and finally started the So Kee Umbrella Factory at Hui Ai West Road, now known as Zhongshan Road, in Canton. What was more, he knew how to do business.

[Lights in Zone 5 fade out.]

SCENE THREE

[Lights go up in Zones 3 and 4 where a shop is set up. Inside the shop is hung a red shop sign, with the Chinese characters for 'So Kee Umbrella Factory' written in gold. LEUNG SO and MADAM HO look at the sign and smile with satisfaction. Then they busy themselves arranging the umbrellas.

Lights in Zone 2 are dim. One can just about see TIN CHI, father of CHEUNG WAH, sitting in front of some umbrella frames and a few bolts of blue fabric, keeping the books meticulously. TIN CHI is 18 years old, dressed in the early Republic style of Chinese jacket and trousers, and does not have a pigtail.

The following two scenes between LEUNG SO and MADAM HO, and TIN CHI and TIN YAU should be acted simultaneously, with the dialogue interlacing. In Zones 3 and 4, LEUNG SO is pasting on the wall a couplet written in black ink on two sheets of red paper. His voice is a little older than in the previous scene. He pastes one sheet first.]

MADAM HO *[reads aloud]* 'Waterproof fabric, colours will not fade'. H'm not bad, not bad at all! *[LEUNG SO pastes the second sheet. MADAM HO reads it]* 'Genuine steel frame, life-time guarantee from today'! *[Shocked]* What? Are you out of your mind?

LEUNG SO No.

MADAM HO Guaranteed for *life*? Someone buys an umbrella and you guarantee it for life?

LEUNG SO Sure! The *frame* is guaranteed for life. Not the fabric, of course. This is my unique way of doing business. It's unprecedented, you know.

MADAM HO Do you know what you're letting yourself in for?

LEUNG SO Look ahead. When people come to repair their umbrellas, we could become friends and what is a few coppers between friends? Word will spread, then everybody will know there's a So Kee Umbrella Factory in Canton which offers life-time guarantee for their umbrellas. More people will spread the word and even more people will come.

MADAM HO All right. All right. In no time even the Governor of
    Guangdong and Guangxi will know you, Leung So Big
    Shot!

LEUNG SO That goes without saying! What's more, when people
    come to repair their umbrellas, they won't go away
    empty-handed, will they? Repair one, buy one. That
    makes good business sense!

MADAM HO Well, well, you've got it all worked out, I must say!

LEUNG SO Help others and you help yourself! That's how I see it.

    *[The two laugh together. Lights in Zones 3 and 4 slowly go
    out.]*

    [In Zone 2, TIN YAU *is going lazily up to* TIN CHI. TIN
    YAU *is sixteen or seventeen.* TIN CHI *is not much older, but
    his expression is serious. He stares at his younger brother.]*

TIN YAU *[hesitantly]* Can't I go to the bathroom first?

TIN CHI No.

TIN YAU I can't wait!

TIN CHI That's just an excuse.

    *[*TIN YAU *has no choice but to come forward reluctantly.]*

TIN YAU *[pointing at a bolt of fabric]* Indanthrene.

TIN CHI Wrong! This is waterproof fabric. That one there is
    Indanthrene.

    *[*TIN YAU *grimaces.* TIN CHI *shows* TIN YAU *the
    Indanthrene.* TIN YAU *looks nonplussed.]*

TIN YAU Well?

    [trying his luck] Front, back, front, back, front, back,
    front . . . front?

TIN CHI Wrong! This is the back!

TIN YAU Oh, come on . . .

TIN CHI *[sternly]* Blockhead! *[He knocks his brother's head lightly
    with an umbrella frame.]*

SCENE FOUR

*[Lights up in Zones 3 and 4. The couplet pinned to the wall is faded now,
indicating the passage of time.*

    LEUNG SO *and* MADAM HO *enter. Both have aged a few years, and* MADAM
HO's *voice is weaker than in her last two appearances.]*

    LEUNG SO What are you thinking about?

    MADAM HO What else? About how business could be improved!

LEUNG SO Business can't improve much if it doesn't rain.

MADAM HO What I mean is, one doesn't buy an umbrella very often. And then our frames are made of steel and they last.

LEUNG SO In that case, we could sell something else.

MADAM HO Like what?

LEUNG SO Something people use everyday, just to balance it out?

MADAM HO That's a good idea. *[Ponders for a while]* Something people use everyday. . . . What about toothbrushes? People use them everyday!

LEUNG SO To make toothbrushes we need real bristle.

MADAM HO We can easily get that here.

LEUNG SO Making toothbrushes is not easy, though.

MADAM HO You learn as you go along.

LEUNG SO If one hair goes, then the whole row of bristle will go, too. We can't give the customers any guarantee.

MADAM HO Then we must make toothbrushes that last, toothbrushes of the best quality, that lose not a single hair.

LEUNG SO Right! So Kee toothbrushes, lose not a single hair.

[Lights out]

[In Zone 2, TIN CHI *is still drilling* TIN YAU. *On the table, other than the fabric and frames, there are some brass rings that hold the ribs to the stem.]*

TIN CHI *[picking up a ring]* How many ribs can this ring support?

TIN YAU *[looking at it]* Eighteen?

TIN CHI Wrong. Look at it more carefully.

TIN YAU Fourteen?

TIN CHI *[sighs]* Twelve! You're so dumb, how can you help in the shop?

TIN YAU *[piqued]* I don't want to learn, I don't want to learn! I'd rather spend the rest of my life making frames.

TIN CHI It's hard work making the frames. You have to have a lot of strength and it's not easy to make them straight.

TIN YAU *[immediately]* So what? It's better than having to memorize all that stuff. *[Walks away]*

TIN CHI Tin Yau! Tin Yau!

[Lights out in Zone 2]

SCENE FIVE

[In Zones 3 and 4, a sign is up: 'So Kee toothbrushes, lose not a single hair'.
MADAM HO *is at the counter, looking absorbed.]*

MADAM HO *[sighs]*

LEUNG SO What's wrong?

MADAM HO I'm still worried.

LEUNG SO What is it this time? The more you have, the more
you want.

MADAM HO Don't you also want a daughter-in-law?

LEUNG SO *[amazed]* Tin Chi is only eighteen!

MADAM HO You were eighteen when I married you!

LEUNG SO *[slight pause]* Do you have any nice girl in mind?

MADAM HO Mr Chan Sing of the fireworks factory at Gao Di Street
has a daughter.

LEUNG SO The gunpowder factory?

MADAM HO They make fireworks!

LEUNG SO It's gunpowder nevertheless. He prays for fine days and
I for rainy days. We could never mix.

MADAM HO I'm not asking your umbrella to marry his firecrackers.
It's his daughter that counts. *[LEUNG SO still hesitates.]*
Why don't you go and sound him out first. See how it
goes, all right?

SCENE SIX

[Lights out in Zones 3 and 4. CHEUNG WAH *enters and stands downstage, facing
the audience.]*

CHEUNG WAH *[to the audience]* Grandad and Grandma were successful
because they were willing to try anything. Grandma
chose three of our top-grade umbrellas. Made of the
purest steel and the hardest wood from Qingyuan, they
were called 'Lotus Canopy on Eighteen Ribs', and she
sent them as gifts to the girl's family at the fireworks
factory in Gao Di Street, together with the time and
date of Tin Chi's birth for a horoscope. Three days
later, the girl's family delivered to them a string of the
finest firecrackers, 328 red crackers in all, called 'Red
Lotus on a Golden Thread'. Happy and excited,
Grandad and Grandma gave the young couple's times
and dates of birth to an astrologer. And they were

found to match perfectly. Grandma was overjoyed. She followed the customs punctiliously, got the traditional wedding presents ready, and sent a matchmaker to the girl's family to propose on their behalf. Who would have thought that the girl would fly into a tantrum and refuse pointblank to agree to a pre-arranged marriage? Anyway, there was nothing the eager parents of the two families could do except look helplessly at each other. And Mr Chan Sing was deeply embarrassed, of course. Then, a few days later, my Grandad heard by chance that the girl intended to come and visit the So Kee Umbrella Factory herself!

[Lights go up gradually in Zones 3 and 4. TIN CHI *is already standing behind the counter.]*

In those days, only the young lad could go and look at the girl, not the other way round. How dare she be so audacious! Astounded by the news, Grandad and Grandma were at their wits' end. Grandad sent all the *fokis* away: they could go to the teahouse, to a folk-opera shed, take a walk, or whatever, so long as they were out of sight. Tin Chi was the only one who stayed and even he, usually so composed, was somewhat nervous. Every time someone walked by, he would wonder if that was the dauntless girl of the Chans.

SCENE SEVEN

[Sentimental Cantonese music—'Autumn Moon on a Still Lake'—gently is heard as background music. TIN CHI, *on tenterhooks, stands in the shop watching the passers-by. Eventually a lovely girl,* CHAN YING, *appears, her hair in two pigtails, and dressed in the early Republic style of the 1910s. She walks fearlessly to the front of the shop and stares at* TIN CHI. TIN CHI *looks away, embarrassed. There is a long silence.]*

     TIN CHI *[summoning up his courage and pointing at the umbrellas]*
     Please, please have a look, have a look at the umbrellas . . .

     *[*CHAN YING *realizes that she has been too forward. The two stand there, heads bowed, lost in embarrassment.]*

   CHAN YING *[whispering but to the point]* So you, you are Leung Tin Chi?

     TIN CHI *[not expecting* CHAN YING *to be so direct]* Yes!

CHAN YING And I'm the daughter of Chan Sing. *[TIN CHI nods his head.]* So you knew?

TIN CHI *[nodding again]* We were warned.

CHAN YING We've never met?

TIN CHI No.

CHAN YING *[a little annoyed]* So you haven't seen me before and yet you didn't object? *[TIN CHI, taken aback, just shakes his head.]* Why?

TIN CHI Perhaps it's the will of heaven.

CHAN YING *[annoyed]* And you think I would agree to it?

TIN CHI That's the will of heaven, too. If you don't, that means luck is not on my side.

> *[CHAN YING looks up, secretly pleased with the way TIN CHI expressed himself.]*

CHAN YING Do you believe in heaven's will then?

TIN CHI Sure! Heaven's will is unpredictable. Who can tell if it's going to rain or shine?

CHAN YING And you leave everything to the will of heaven?

TIN CHI *[immediately]* Not really. I make umbrellas, and an umbrella protects you from rain and from the scorching sun.

> *[TIN CHI looks at CHAN YING, she returns his gaze.]*

CHAN YING *[looks down, softly]* But you have to be sure you like the umbrella first.

TIN CHI Yes, you're right. I'm sorry. Tomorrow I'll send someone to your place to bring the umbrellas back.

> *[CHAN YING is a little anxious, seeing that TIN CHI has misunderstood her.]*

CHAN YING That's not what I meant! *[Turns to the umbrellas in the shop, takes one and toys with it to hide her embarrassment. After a long pause, speaks softly]* It's not easy to make umbrellas, is it?

TIN CHI *[taking courage]* You're right. The stem has to be straight, the ribs have to be hard and strong, and the fabric must be closely woven and soft. Then it can protect you from wind and rain.

CHAN YING That's also how one has to deal with life, I suppose?

TIN CHI Yes! Only those who don't mind hard work can make umbrellas. *[CHAN YING nods.]* Making firecrackers is not an easy job either, is it?

CHAN YING My father says things are getting worse. These days, gunpowder is used for fighting, and people don't care for firecrackers any more. Making umbrellas must be more satisfying than making firecrackers. It takes so much effort to make firecrackers and yet they're gone in a bang. Just the noise, nothing's left.

TIN CHI [*impulsively*] Then come and make umbrellas! They're guaranteed for life.

[*Both feel embarrassed again.*]

CHAN YING [*gathering herself all at once*] I have to go now. [*Turns and makes to leave*]

TIN CHI [*hurriedly*] Miss Chan . . .

[CHAN YING *stops, turns her head and looks at* TIN CHI. TIN CHI *blushes and doesn't know what to say, points awkwardly at the umbrellas in the shop instead.*]

Er . . . about those umbrellas we sent to your house . . .

CHAN YING [*blushes too, but more courageous than* TIN CHI] To tell the truth, the ones you sent over are the best . . .

[*She blushes, plays with her pigtails, then turns and leaves.* TIN CHI *stands there like a statue, his eyes following the steps of the girl.*]

SCENE EIGHT

CHEUNG WAH [*standing downstage and facing the audience*] Just a few words, and a look or two at each other, and there you are, husband and wife for life! One has to be really sharp before jumping into it. But then marriage is like a gamble, you never know whether you've won until the very end. Chan Ying went home and did some thinking. She knew that Tin Chi wouldn't make any move unless he'd been told to. The fool! So the next day she sent a servant with a letter to Tin Chi. There were only two lines in the letter: 'Know that someone waits for you each day? Let not wind or rain the good day delay.' Grandad was impressed. The girl was not only beautiful but well educated! Grandad even adapted the two lines for a sales jingle for his umbrellas: 'Know that some one waits for you each day? Let not wind or rain your return delay.' Then he hung it up in the shop. In those days, there were lots of travelling traders in Canton, from Hunan, Guangxi, or even from faraway places such as Tianjin, and they often came to the So

Kee Umbrella Factory to buy a few presents to take home. Naturally, the couplet touched a soft spot in their hearts. *[Pauses]* So, the first great event of the So Kee Umbrella Factory since its opening was the young couple's wedding. A wife for the young master and a daughter-in-law for the proprietor: a big event indeed! Everyone in the shop was busy preparing for the big day.

SCENE NINE

[Lights up in Zone 1. LEUNG SO sits at a desk piled high with invitation cards and lists of presents. He is keeping the accounts on an abacus, his face beaming with happiness. TIN YAU enters, looking bored, and glances at his father. He has none of the drive of a young man of 17. He stands beside his father and fiddles with the invitation cards. LEUNG SO, annoyed, raps the back of TIN YAU's hand.]

TIN YAU When will it be my turn?

[LEUNG SO, concentrating on his abacus, does not reply.]

[asks again] When is it my turn?

[LEUNG SO stops working and looks at his beloved son.]

LEUNG SO When will you grow up? Tell me!

TIN YAU Tin Chi is only two years older than I am!

LEUNG SO Ho, ho, ho! A world of a difference! He makes umbrellas, takes charge of the accounts, supervises the *fokis*. And you? You're a baby!

TIN YAU *[sitting beside his father and resting his head on the desk]* Well, anyone can do these things if he has to. Just as you have to walk if your horse collapses.

LEUNG SO True! And now the horse is over sixty years old and has one foot in the grave! You're only seventeen, and Mei Kiu is only twelve. If you don't grow up, how can I go with ease? *[Looks at his son sentimentally]*

TIN YAU You'll live to be a hundred! *[Grabs his father's arm]*

LEUNG SO Even if I live to be a hundred, I won't be able to see my great-grandchildren! *[Slight pause]* Where's Mei Kiu?

TIN YAU She's out by the pond catching dragonflies.

LEUNG SO And Tin Chi?

TIN YAU Up on the loft taking the inventory. Mother's in the shop making arrangements for the banquet. The *fokis* are chatting in the backyard, non-stop, about Yuan

Shikai, and then about Sun Yatsen, and then about the World War, and then about the workers in Shanghai bashing the Japs. Oh, how boring! Nothing suits me! *[Stretches himself]*

LEUNG SO Well then, think. *Think* what suits you! *[Looks at* TIN YAU *with reproof.* TIN YAU *pouts and covers his face with an invitation card.* LEUNG SO *looks lovingly at* TIN YAU.] The world is in a mess. No one knows what will happen tomorrow. I'm worried that when I'm gone, the two of you won't be able to carry on the business . . .

*[*TIN YAU *lets the invitation card sit on his face and is not at all worried.* LEUNG SO *removes the card.* TIN YAU *pretends to be asleep.* LEUNG SO *doesn't know what to do with him.]*

SCENE TEN

[Lights up in Zones 3 and 4. MADAM HO *and a young man* AH KWAI *are in the shop.* AH KWAI *is 18, handsome and smart.* MADAM HO *has in her hand a thick envelope full of cash. She hands it back to* AH KWAI.]

MADAM HO I can't accept it. It's too big a gift. Take it back to your mother and tell her I appreciate it all the same. Take it back.

AH KWAI She'll be angry with me if I do. She says you've been so kind to her, she owes it to you.

MADAM HO That's silly of her. Take it.

[Both try to force the envelope on to the other.]

AH KWAI Please don't. Last time you gave us a loan and didn't charge any interest . . .

MADAM HO Silly. It was capital for her to start the toothbrush business. In any case, she sends us the toothbrushes she makes, so she's been helping us. She mustn't be so silly. Go on, take it home!

AH KWAI And now you're willing to take me on . . .

MADAM HO Oh! That's a different matter. Take it now!

[While the two are pushing the envelope between each other, LEUNG SO *comes down the stairs.* AH KWAI *stands to attention as soon as he sees* LEUNG SO.]

AH KWAI *[bows]* Sir.

MADAM HO *[to* LEUNG SO, *indicating* AH KWAI] Ah Wong's son.

LEUNG SO *[looking at the boy, with approval]* So you're Ah Kwai?

AH KWAI Yes, sir. Thank you for taking me on.

LEUNG SO You must work hard if you want to make good umbrellas.

AH KWAI I will, sir.

LEUNG SO Um. *[Nods]* Follow your mother's example. The toothbrushes she sends us are the most sturdy ones we get.

[AH KWAI, still standing to attention, takes a deep breath to control his happiness. MADAM HO shows LEUNG SO the cash gift.]

MADAM HO *[whispering]* Look.

LEUNG SO Ah Kwai! *[AH KWAI stands to attention again.]* Take it and give it back to your mother. Tell her that everyone in your family must come to the banquet this evening and have a few drinks.

AH KWAI Er . . .

LEUNG SO What?

AH KWAI Yes, sir.

[Not daring to offend LEUNG SO, AH KWAI takes back the cash gift. MADAM HO is put out as well as amused at the respect her husband commands.

AH CHUEN, a foki of So Kee Umbrella Factory, enters at a brisk pace. He is 40 years old.]

AH CHUEN *[beaming with joy]* Sir, the Chans are sending the betrothal gifts.

[Cantonese music for a happy occasion is heard in the background. LEUNG SO and MADAM HO are getting a little nervous from excitement. The following lines are spoken almost simultaneously]

LEUNG SO Hurry! Send someone to stop them! Ask them to turn round and come in through the front gate. Yes, the front gate: it's more propitious.

AH KWAI *[smartly]* I will go, sir. *[Goes]*

LEUNG SO *[to AH CHUEN]* Ah Chuen, ask all the *fokis* to come out. Go to the loft to tell Tin Chi to wash his face and change his clothes. *[He goes.]*

AH CHUEN *[very excited, shouting as he goes]* Hey, they're coming, they're coming! Come and look!

LEUNG SO *[to MADAM HO]* The red packets, have you got them ready? *[calling AH CHUEN at a distance]* Get that string of firecrackers out!

MADAM HO *[shouting towards the direction of the staircase]* Tin Yau, Tin Yau, get your sister, hurry! *[Then shouting towards the other direction]* Tin Chi, Tin Chi!

[Lights out. People are setting up props for the next scene in various zones as if they were preparing for the happy occasion. Sound of firecrackers in the background. Musical interlude.]

SCENE ELEVEN

[A spotlight goes up on CHEUNG WAH *who is standing downstage at one side, facing the audience.]*

CHEUNG WAH Tin Chi is my father, and the dauntless girl of the Chan family is my mother. My name is Leung Cheung Wah. The story now takes us to the year 1937. The nation was at war and people in Canton were jittery. Every time some news arrived from Shanghai or Nanking people felt nervous and worried. Many had heard of the Manchukok in the north-east and believed it was just a matter of time before the Japanese attacked Canton. These troubled times left their marks on the common people. And the story of my family, this story of umbrellas, was likewise affected by the war.

[Pause. Lights up in Zones 3, 4, 5, and 6. MEI KIU *is twiddling with the umbrellas in the shop absent-mindedly, and all the time gazing towards the far end of the street. The shop looks a little run-down: the couplets on the wall are soiled and faded. But there are more umbrellas and the display is different.*

Zones 5 and 6 have become a workshop for umbrellas. There are frames and hand-operated machines on the floor. In the dim light, only AH CHUEN *and* AH SHUN *are working on the ribs.]*

In 1937, the twenty-sixth year of the Republic of China, the So Kee Umbrella Factory had already been in business for fifty years. Grandma had died, Grandad was in his seventies and couldn't walk very well. He rarely came to the shop. Because of the war and the recession, business had taken a turn for the worse. And now, I have to leave you for a while as I'm already eight years old, and I don't want to see my childhood self running around in the factory, making a nuisance

of himself. Besides, I've given you the background of
the story. See you later!

[Takes a few steps, then stops and turns.]

Oh, yes! *[Looks at* MEI KIU *at the shop]* That's my aunt,
Mei Kiu. She's getting more beautiful by the day, and
more intelligent. And my father, Tin Chi, is more and
more worried that she may have difficulties finding a
husband!

SCENE TWELVE

[Lights go up in the shop. MEI KIU *is still gazing into the street. A teenage boy,*
MING TSAI, *appears with a copy of the* Shanghai Special *newspaper in his hand,
and is gasping for breath. He knows everyone in the factory well and provides them
with the latest news about the war. He goes up to* MEI KIU.*]*

MING TSAI *[trying to give* MEI KIU *a fright]* Wah!

> *[*MEI KIU *starts, and raises her hand as if to hit* MING
> TSAI.*]*

> Look! *[Dodging neatly]* Special! Special! Important news!
> From Shanghai!

MEI KIU You liar! There haven't been any trains from Shanghai
for the last two days—Brother Tin Chi is so worried.
You and your news from Shanghai!

MING TSAI There may be no trains but there are aeroplanes. And
ships. I'm not kidding, this is really hot off the press.
Where there's money, there's a way.

MEI KIU *[snatching the newspaper from* MING TSAI*]* Did you steal it?

MING TSAI I picked it up, at Tai Sam Yuan. I was passing by and
had a peek inside. Wow! *[As if telling a story]* A
Shanghainese was there gulping down beef and then
chicken, and drinking like a fish, with one foot on a
suitcase that high . . . *[Illustrating with his hand]* Full of
gold, silver, and jewels, I bet. He left as soon as he
finished eating, and I followed him. He was trying to
find a taxi. Then he spat *[Gesturing]*, and the *Special*
fell into the gutter. *[At the word 'gutter'* MEI KIU *nearly
drops the newspaper.]*
I picked it up when he was not looking . . .

MEI KIU Good heavens! Enough! Enough! *[Covers her nose with
one hand, and pinches the paper with only two fingers and
holding it away from her.]* It stinks! Yuk!

MING TSAI That man is so dumb! He should have gone to Hong
        Kong, not come here.

MEI KIU What's so good about Hong Kong?

MING TSAI They say there's a bank in Hong Kong as high as the sky!

MEI KIU They say, too, that there's a place called Possession
        Point. And that it's a wicked place, full of drugs and
        prostitutes. Worse than the Upper and Lower Jiu Pu
        here in Canton!

        *[AH KWAI enters. He is 26 or 27 now and looks very
        mature. He sees MING TSAI.]*

MING TSAI Ah Kwai!

AH KWAI Ming Tsai!

MEI KIU *[to AH KWAI]* I'll show it to my sister-in-law.

AH KWAI Is the boss not back yet?

MEI KIU *[shakes her head]* He's still waiting at the train station
        for news. *[Exits]*

MING TSAI *[anxiously]* Mei Kiu!

MEI KIU *[turning round]* I know! You wait here. *[Exits]*

MING TSAI *[giggling at AH KWAI]* Mei Kiu is really nice, isn't she?

AH KWAI And what have you said to her just now?

MING TSAI I'll let you on a trick or two so you'll get some
        response from her. Ha, ha, ha . . .

        *[MING TSAI darts back, expecting AH KWAI to hit him.
        But AH KWAI seems surprised, then a little annoyed, and
        turns automatically to look at the other side of the street,
        saying nothing.]*

        [going up to AH KWAI again] I say, I was only joking.
        Don't be angry! *[Moves closer]* I say! *[He follows the
        direction of AH KWAI's eyes.]* What are you looking at?
        That rag-and-bone man? *[Looks again at where AH KWAI
        is gazing, silently]*
        Hell! He's not much older than me. Why doesn't he go
        and fight the Japs? Why be a rag-and-bone man?

AH KWAI *[teasing him]* Why don't you go? You're young, you
        have plenty of time to fight them!

        *[MING TSAI doesn't know what to say, but looks defiant. MEI
        KIU enters, carrying a brown paper bag with ten taels of rice.]*

MEI KIU *[giving it to MING TSAI]* Take it home. Be careful, there
        are snatchers in the street!

        *[MING TSAI is very grateful, takes the bag, bites his lip and
        runs, then turns back.]*

MING TSAI My father says some day when we have the money,
        we'll repay you. *[Dashes away like a rabbit]*

AH KWAI *[to* MEI KIU*]* What's in the *Shanghai Special?*

MEI KIU *[frowns]* The situation is really bad in Shanghai! A fleet
of Japanese warships is pounding Zhabei and
. . . . What's the name of the place? Oh, I can't
remember. Anyway, it's really serious and I'm worried
about Tin Yau.

AH KWAI Perhaps he's still in Changsha and couldn't get a train
ticket home. He doesn't get scared easily.

MEI KIU That's why Tin Chi is so worried!

SCENE THIRTEEN

[Lights dim in Zones 3 and 4, and go up in Zones 5 and 6. AH CHUEN *is
speaking. He is older than when he first appeared, about 50 years of age, while* AH
SHUN *is about 30.]*

AH CHUEN *[gesticulating as he speaks]* I started working here at
fifteen, and I was here when Miss Mei Kiu was born.
I'm not boasting, but I'm second to none in cutting
and mounting the fabric. I can't say, though, that I'm
good at making the ribs, I'm not as strong as you
young fellows. Time really flies. I've been here over
twenty years. You fellows have an easy time now, but
in those days, when business was good, we had to work
overtime practically every night. I met my Hakka wife
here. She was helping to make the toothbrushes. At
first, we just looked at each other, then we started
going to the Cantonese operas . . .

AH SHUN *[something is obviously troubling him and he tries to change
the subject]* I say, Ah Choi and Ah Kai are not back yet?

AH CHUEN *[engrossed in his happy memories]* I'm from Shunde, and I
never thought I would marry a Hakka woman. It's fate.
She works really hard, never wastes anything at home.
If she finds a patch of soil, she'll grow something there,
spring onions or . . .

AH SHUN Couldn't we talk about something else?

AH CHUEN *[taken aback]* Eh? All right! Let's not talk about my
wife. How about your wife? She hasn't come to visit
you for quite some time now!

*[*AH SHUN *stands up, not wanting to confide his troubles in
anyone, and turns and exits to the rear yard.]*

[surprised, murmurs to himself] Now what did I say?

[Lights dim, AH CHUEN *carries on working.]*

SCENE FOURTEEN

[*Lights up again in Zones 3 and 4. AH KWAI, a writing-brush in his hand, is writing on the wage-packets, one after another. He keeps watching MEI KIU as he writes. MEI KIU is dusting the counters but her eyes are on the youth at the corner of the street. AH KWAI, patience running out, goes up to MEI KIU, who gives a start and blushes.*]

MEI KIU [*looking at the distance*] He must be a god or something. Never seen him eat anything.

AH KWAI [*matter-of-factly*] He's no rag-and-bone man. More likely than not he's a revolutionar—

MEI KIU [*nervously interrupting*] Watch your words!

AH KWAI I think he must be here waiting for—

MEI KIU [*cutting in*] Don't be silly! [*Pauses, takes a breath*] It doesn't matter what he is, so long as he's a good man! [*Eyes turning tender*]

AH KWAI People like him don't care about their lives, [*Pauses*] and they don't care about women either.

MEI KIU [*angrily*] What are you talking about! [*Blushes and exits*]

[*AH KWAI is regretting what he said.*]

[*AH CHOI and AH KAI sneak in. They see AH KAI and sense trouble. But they have no choice except to come into the shop. AH CHOI is the younger, crafty and sly; AH KAI is not so smart and has a childish look. They laugh guiltily. AH KWAI flies into a temper upon seeing them.*]

AH KWAI Where on earth have you been?

AH KAI Wh . . . why is the back-door locked?

AH KWAI How dare you ask? You slipped out when you should have been working and now you want to sneak in from the back-door? I'll report you two to the boss.

AH KAI No, please!

AH CHOI Please, Ah Kwai, be kind.

AH KAI There were crowds and crowds and we couldn't make it back sooner!

AH KWAI What crowds?

AH CHOI There were demonstrations at Liuhua Bridge!

[*The two begin to speak one after the other, describing the situation vividly.*]

AH KAI Oh yes, there were workers and students, flags and banners. People were clamouring and shouting!

AH CHOI They were shouting 'Down with the Japanese
    imperialists! Down with Japanese invasion of China!'
    And they were marching towards the consular district.
    [Mimicking a marching demonstrator]

AH KAI They gave out handbills. *[Takes out a handbill from under
    his belt]* Look!

AH CHOI They said they're organizing a big demonstration in a
    day or two and there will be more than a hundred
    thousand people marching. More than a hundred
    thousand! Can you imagine? I've never seen anything
    like it.

    [AH KWAI looks at the handbill and frowns.]

AH KAI How dare the Japanese come here! There are so many of
    us Chinese, we can drown them just by spitting at them.

    [The two begin to argue.]

AH CHOI What do you know? They have aeroplanes and heavy guns!

AH KAI We will surge forward together and jam their gun barrels.

AH CHOI Yes, yes. But who will lead the charge? You?

    *[AH CHOI rushes to the back of AH KAI, holds him by the
    waist with both hands and pushes him forward as if AH
    KAI is a human cannonball.]*

    Ah Kai of So Kee Umbrella Factory is here! Charge!

AH KAI Hey . . . *[Turns round and struggles with AH CHOI]*

AH KWAI Be quiet, you two! *[Thinking aloud]* A march with
    more than a hundred thousand people? The two of you
    are not to go anywhere! Ah Kai, take out the shutter-
    planks, and put them over there. Be ready to board up
    the shop front any minute! Ah Choi! *[Gives him the
    handbill]* Show this to Mrs Tin Chi!

AH CHOI Yes.

AH KAI *[to AH CHOI, complaining in a whisper]* I brought home
    the handbill! Now you get the easy job and I have to
    carry the planks . . .

AH KWAI What are you going on about?

AH KAI Oh, nothing.

    [AH CHOI chuckles and waves the handbill to tease AH KAI.]

AH KWAI Mrs Tin Chi is reading the *Shanghai Special* to the boss.
    When the boss sees the handbill and asks about the
    situation at Liuhua Bridge, which of you can describe it
    better? Tell me!

AH KAI *[to AH CHOI, grudgingly]* It . . . it's better for Ah Choi
    to take it in.

AH CHOI *[raises his brows]* You can't do anything about it, can you? It's the fault of your mother—

AH KWAI Will you shut—

AH CHOI Okay, I'm going now! *[Goes like a bullet]*

> *[NGAN HING appears, dressed in a Hawaiian shirt. He walks to the front of the shop in an urbane manner. AH KAI is taking out a door plank, and AH KWAI is moving the umbrella display-stand inside the shop in Zone 3.]*

NGAN HING *[speaking to the two]* Excuse me. Is Ah Shun here please?

AH KAI *[remembering that he has been here before]* Oh, it's you. You were here yesterday!

NGAN HING I've been twice but he was out on both occasions and I've not been able to see him.

AH KWAI You are . . .?

NGAN HING My surname is Ngan, could you please let him know?

AH KWAI *[taking the ledger in and telling AH KAI]* Keep an eye on the shop. I'm going up to the loft. When the boss comes in, let me know at once. *[Speaks to NGAN HING]* Please wait a minute. *[Exits]*

> *[AH KAI looks NGAN HING up and down, senses that he must be quite wealthy or important, and becomes more respectful. NGAN HING feels a little uneasy.]*

AH KAI *[curiously]* I say, what is your relationship with Ah Shun?

NGAN HING *[hesitating]* Um, *[Thinks for a while]* we're relatives.

> *[AH KAI opens his eyes wide, amazed that AH SHUN should have such a respectable relative. He looks at NGAN HING again.]*

AH KAI *[inquisitively]* You've come from America?

NGAN HING No, from Malaya.

AH KAI *[getting bolder]* So you've made your fortune and come back?

> *[NGAN HING, not knowing how to reply, forces a smile.]*

SCENE FIFTEEN

[Lights up in Zones 5 and 6. AH CHUEN is working alone, snapping the ribs. AH KWAI enters.]

AH KWAI Where's Ah Shun?

> *[AH CHUEN, in a bad mood, gestures that AH SHUN is inside.]*
> *[shouting]* Ah Shun, Ah Shun . . .
> *[AH SHUN comes out, staring at AH KWAI.]*

There's someone by the name of Ngan out there looking for you. He said he'd been here several times but has not been able to see you. Go now, don't keep him waiting.

[AH SHUN hesitates, an embarrassed look on his face. AH KWAI makes to go, then ponders for a second.]

[turning and staring at AH SHUN*]* Were you really out the last few times he called? *[Goes in, wondering]*

[AH SHUN paces listlessly in front of AH CHUEN, *not knowing what to do.* AH CHUEN *stares at him.]*

AH CHUEN Stop it, will you?! You're making me dizzy!

AH SHUN Uncle Chuen, please, please help me out once again! Go and tell him I'm not here. Tell him I've quit my job.

AH CHUEN Yesterday you said you were out delivering goods and today you've quit?

AH SHUN Just tell him something! I don't want to see him.

AH CHUEN You can't avoid him forever, you must repay your gambling debts . . .

AH SHUN *[angrily]* I've stopped gambling. I've told you many times but none of you believes me.

AH CHUEN *[standing up]* I'll go and ask the old master to help you . . .

AH SHUN *[alarmed, pulling* AH CHUEN *back]* Don't! It's nothing. Trust me, please. Please!

[Pushes AH CHUEN *out step by step.* AH SHUN *sits restlessly on a stool, his head in his hands.*

AH CHUEN enters the shop. AH CHOI *also comes out from* TIN CHI's *room.]*

AH CHUEN *[towards* NGAN HING*]* So it's you?

[NGAN HING goes up to him politely.]

Ah Shun is again out delivering goods.

AH KAI *[surprised]* Delivering . . .?

[AH CHOI, being the smarter, kicks AH KAI.*]*

Ouch!

NGAN HING *[disappointed]* I shall wait for him here.

AH CHUEN He won't be back yet. You'll have to wait a long time.

[NGAN HING is not fully convinced, but has no choice.]

NGAN HING Well then, will you please tell him I'll be back first thing tomorrow morning, and that I really must see him? Thank you. Goodbye. Goodbye.

AH KAI Goodbye.

AH CHOI *[shouting]* Hey, what do you want to see him for?

NGAN HING Eh, I'll tell him personally. Thank you very much, and goodbye! *[Leaves in disappointment]*

AH CHUEN *[to* AH KAI*]* You and your big mouth!

AH KAI *[grimacing]* How would I know it was so complicated? But what's the matter with Ah Shun? That man is rich, and a relative. Why doesn't Ah Shun want to see him?

AH CHUEN Relative? He's more like a loan shark!

AH CHOI Loan shark? No, he was so polite!

AH KAI Come on, it's a relative all right, he said so himself. He said he came back from Malaya.

AH CHUEN No way, no way. It's all to do with his gambling, I tell you. So don't you gamble! Now he's in trouble and the loan shark's after him. What's he going to do? I ask you.

[AH KAI and AH CHOI are not quite sure what to believe. Lights in Zones 3 and 4 dim.]

SCENE SIXTEEN

[In the backyard, AH SHUN *is still sitting with his head buried in his hands, very depressed. A child enters. It's* CHEUNG WAH *at eight years old. An intelligent child, he has some coloured papers in his hands and a pinwheel. He runs round and round for the wind to set the pinwheel spinning. It doesn't work, so he purses his lips and blows at it. He is surprised to see* AH SHUN *in such a state and goes up to him.]*

CHEUNG WAH *[tapping* AH SHUN *with his small hand]* Uncle Ah Shun!

[AH SHUN looks up, sees the young master, and puts on a smile immediately.]

AH SHUN Young master!

CHEUNG WAH Are you not feeling well?

AH SHUN No, I'm fine. You are off school early?

CHEUNG WAH There's no school today.

AH SHUN How nice!

CHEUNG WAH Mr Lam says there will be no classes for a few days. He's taking part in the anti-Japanese campaign. Mr Lam also says that children can't go, but they can go home and ask Mummy and Daddy to give some money. If we get a big donation, then we're good children. I've told Grandad already.

AH SHUN What did the old master say?

CHEUNG WAH Grandad said he would donate something. But he has to wait until Daddy and Second Uncle come home. *[He takes a stool, puts it down at a suitable spot, kneels on the ground and starts folding paper toys on the stool.]* Uncle Shun, which is further away from here, Hong Kong or Macau?

AH SHUN Why do you ask?

CHEUNG WAH I heard Ma and Grandad say that we might go to Hong Kong, or perhaps Macau.

AH SHUN Your Mother's father has a fireworks factory in Macau. When you grow up you could go to Macau to visit him. *[Wondering aloud]* Which place is further away from here? *[Sighs]* Malaya is the furthest!

CHEUNG WAH Where is Malaya?

AH SHUN It's so far even the thunder god won't go there.

> *[Troubled by his thoughts, he picks up some paper and begins folding paper animals with* CHEUNG WAH.*]*

CHEUNG WAH *[looking at* AH SHUN *innocently]* Can you fold a pig's head?

AH SHUN *[continues to fold the paper, just to keep his mind occupied]* A pig's head? Nothing easier!

CHEUNG WAH *[tickled by what* AH SHUN *said]* Let's see who does it better.

> *[*CHAN YING *comes in to the backyard from her room, holding a wet towel. She is dressed as a young matron this time, and wears a bun at the back and no make-up. She frowns when she sees her son kneeling on the ground, his trousers dusty at the knees. She goes behind* CHEUNG WAH.*]*

CHAN YING Look at you! I told you to go back to your room to practise calligraphy and you slipped out to play!

AH SHUN Mrs Tin Chi.

CHAN YING You're keeping Uncle Shun from his work.

CHEUNG WAH Uncle Shun said he could play with me, didn't you, Uncle Shun?

CHAN YING You've just had a bath and now you've got yourself into such a mess again. *[Goes up and squats down to wipe* CHEUNG WAH's *hands and feet]* Get up! *[Wipes his knees]* You look a sight! Give me your hands!

AH SHUN Has old master gone to bed?

CHAN YING He's still got a headache.

AH SHUN Master Tin Yau should be all right in Changsha.

CHAN YING Tin Yau is so irresponsible! I'm really worried.

CHEUNG WAH Ma, are you worried that the Japs will lock up Second Uncle?

CHAN YING Do you want a spanking? Keep quiet when adults are talking!

[Noises from Zones 3 and 4. Lights go up.]

AH CHOI *[shouting]* The boss is back.

[TIN CHI enters, looking tense and tired. He is now twenty-nine, a self-possessed and steady character.]

AH CHUEN How are things, Master Tin Chi?

TIN CHI Shut up shop now. There won't be any business today. *[Goes into the backyard immediately]*

AH KAI *[shouting to the backyard]* The boss is back.

[AH CHOI and AH KAI shut up shop hurriedly. AH CHUEN goes into the backyard with TIN CHI. CHAN YING and AH SHUN look anxiously at TIN CHI as he enters.]

CHEUNG WAH *[calling]* Dad!

CHAN YING Cheung Wah, go back to your room and do your calligraphy, we have things to discuss. Be a good boy, go!

[CHEUNG WAH goes back to his room. MEI KIU and AH KWAI enter, everybody is looking at TIN CHI with concern.]

CHAN YING So, how are things?

[The backyard is now full of people. CHAN YING, noticing the sweat on TIN CHI's forehead, hands him the wet towel.]

TIN CHI *[wiping his forehead]* For the past two days, there have only been trains from Hengyang. The section between Changsha and Zhuzhou has been cut off because the Japanese might bomb it any time. *[Sighs]* If Tin Yau was smart, he should try to get to Hengyang first. If he doesn't, he'll be trapped in Changsha. That's my worry.

CHAN YING If he managed to collect the payments, at least he won't run short.

TIN CHI That's even worse! With chaos everywhere, people might attack him just for his money! He looks such an easy target. *[Sighs]*

CHAN YING I told you not to let him go! He's never been anywhere so far away all by himself. And he had a cold the day he left. But you said, let him see the world and have fun!

TIN CHI He begged me to let him go! How would I know that things would get so bad in just half a month?

MEI KIU May Buddha bless him! I just hope that Tin Yau hasn't gone on to Shanghai.

TIN CHI Shanghai?

MEI KIU He . . . he mentioned to me that he wanted to go to Shanghai to see more of the world.

TIN CHI Oh, he's so wayward and wilful! The more I think about it, the more worried I am!

AH KWAI Perhaps we can wait another day. If we don't see him tomorrow, I'll go to Hengyang.

AH CHUEN What's the point? There is no train beyond Hengyang!

AH KWAI So long as I get there, there'll be a way. I could spend a little more money and hire a car, follow the railway and go on to Zhuzhou, and then to Changsha.

TIN CHI I'll go. You stay and mind the shop.

CHAN YING It's best if I come with you.

TIN CHI No. You stay and look after Dad and Cheung Wah.

CHAN YING You're always in two minds about things. If I come along, there'll be no dithering.

AH KWAI Please don't argue. I've been collecting payments from Changsha all these years. I know the roads best and I know the most people. Come to think of it, I must bear part of the blame. I should have gone with Master Tin Yau! *[Troubled by the thought of the rag-and-bone man, he looks at* MEI KIU.*]* I'll pack tonight.

*[*AH CHOI *and* AH KAI *have shut up shop and now enter in a hurry.]*

AH CHOI There's a huge demonstration outside!

AH KAI With more than a hundred thousand people!

TIN CHI *[grimacing]* Shouting 'Down with the Japs' and all the time preparing to run away. I heard at the station that the universities are moving down to Hong Kong and Macau, the municipal government here may move to Baxiang any time, and there's looting in town already.

[All look stunned. CHAN YING *takes the* Shanghai Special *from her pocket and shows it to* TIN CHI, *who reads it at once.]*

[after quite a while] Once Beijing and Tianjin are gone, Shanghai surely can't hold out.

CHAN YING Your father says that as soon as Tin Yau is back, we should make a decision whether to stay here or leave.

TIN CHI *[mumbling]* So long as Tin Yau comes home safely, I don't even mind losing the business.

CHAN YING *[to* AH CHUEN *and* AH SHUN*]* Uncle Chuen, Ah Shun, go home now and make sure your wives are safe. There'll be no more work today.

AH CHUEN There's no hurry.

AH KAI *[teasing]* Go home, Uncle Chuen. Go home and see how your Hakka wife is doing. There is a war on!

AH CHUEN Hah, they won't come here.

AH CHOI *[even cheekier]* Right! Go home and hug her. *[Histrionically]* Don't be scared of the *gweilos*. Don't be scared of the Japs. Don't be——

AH CHUEN You brats! Shut your loud mouth! *[Chases the two, who laugh indulgently]*

[Everybody is laughing, except AH SHUN *who is rather unhappy, thinking of his wife.]*

MEI KIU Oh! *[A drop of rain falls on her face and she looks up.]* It's raining.

[Others can feel it too.]

AH KWAI Take the things inside! *[Directs everybody to move the frames, fabrics, etc.]*

[Sound of rain increases.]

MEI KIU *[to* CHAN YING*]* Let me do the cooking this evening.

CHAN YING Thanks.

TIN CHI *[to* CHAN YING*]* I'll go and see Dad.

CHAN YING Don't tell him everything.

TIN CHI I know.

[The two exit together, still talking. Sound of rain. The Cantonese tune of 'Lamentations of Two stars' is heard. Gradually lights and music fade.]

SCENE SIXTEEN

[A spotlight goes up on a youth, aged 25 or 26, squatting in a corner at stage left, a little distance downstage from Zones 3 and 4. He is PAK YING, *the rag-and-bone man. He huddles under the eaves to shelter from the rain. Beside him are some rusted iron buckets with some tools. He is a handsome young man, slender in build, and looks helpless and lonely. He looks up at the sky, stares at the rain, and gently wipes the rainwater from his brows.*

Not long after, MEI KIU *walks shyly up to* PAK YING, *an umbrella in one hand, a basket of food in the other.* PAK YING, *taken aback, stares at* MEI

KIU. MEI KIU *looks down and, feeling the rain pelting down on her, dodges under the eaves too. She mimes brushing off the raindrops, and puts down the umbrella. She hands the food from the basket to* PAK YING, *who is staring at her blankly, a faint smile on his face.* MEI KIU *hands him the food again,* PAK YING *does not accept.* MEI KIU *repeats gesture.* PAK YING *smiles lightly and shakes his head, even though he is really hungry.*]

MEI KIU Eat something. Or you will soon end up in heaven. Starving yourself like this!

[*After some hesitation,* PAK YING *takes the food and eats without further ado.* MEI KIU *grins at the way he devours the food.*]

PAK YING Thank you.

MEI KIU There's some more. [*Taps the basket*]

PAK YING [*shaking his head while eating*] When I've done a job or two tomorrow, I'll repay your kindness.

MEI KIU Really? [*A little unhappy that he is still putting on an act*]

PAK YING I'm sure there will be business tomorrow. [*Breaks into a grateful smile*]

MEI KIU Other rag-and-bone men set up shop in busy areas, and you pick this place.

[PAK YING *doesn't know what to say.*]

PAK YING I . . . I'm new here and I don't know the place.

MEI KIU You're lying. My grandfather used to be a rag-and-bone man.

PAK YING [*still playing innocent*] Then you could give me some tips so I don't have to go hungry.

MEI KIU I won't speak to you any more if you go on playing dumb with me. [*Feigning anger*]

PAK YING [*taken aback*] I'm sorry. I don't mean to offend you.

[PAK YING *is at a loss what to do, the bowl in his hand.* MEI KIU, *seeing him so lost, smiles and gestures to him to finish his food.* PAK YING *obeys at once.*]

MEI KIU [*mumbling, looking shy*] I understand. [*Pauses*] Relax. [*Another pause*] I'm not forcing you to tell me anything!

PAK YING What do you mean?

MEI KIU [*annoyed*] Forget it.

[PAK YING *takes a few more mouthfuls.*]

PAK YING [*softly*] What . . . what do you want to know?

MEI KIU Nothing.

[PAK YING *hurriedly finishes the last mouthful and returns the bowl gratefully to* MEI KIU.]

PAK YING That was really good. Thank you!

> [MEI KIU *stares at* PAK YING's *hands without taking the bowl from him.* PAK YING, *finding it a little odd, stares at* MEI KIU *too.* MEI KIU *becomes conscious of his gaze, blushes, and takes the bowl.*]

> [*looking at his own hands, smiling awkwardly*] A bit grubby, eh?

MEI KIU I just wanted to see if you were telling the truth.

PAK YING [*a little surprised, looks at his hands again*] Can you tell?

MEI KIU Dad says that when the Japs grab someone, they will first examine his hands. If there is a callus on the lower palm, the man is a soldier used to firing rifles and he'll be executed right away. If there is a callus on the upper palm, then the man is just a peasant and he'll be ordered to work as a coolie.

PAK YING [*smiling awkwardly and looking at* MEI KIU, *holding up his hands with the palms facing* MEI KIU] Am I to be executed or taken as a coolie?

> [MEI KIU's *heart beats faster, she gathers her courage and touches* PAK YING's *palms.*]

> [*Their eyes meet,* MEI KIU *coyly bows her head.*]

MEI KIU You lied!

> [PAK YING *looks puzzled.*]

> A rag-and-bone man wouldn't have hands as delicate as yours.

> [*Attraction grows between the two.* MEI KIU *suddenly realizes it is late. She puts the bowl back into the basket and makes to go.*]

PAK YING I say, wait a minute!

> [MEI KIU *turns round, waiting for him to speak.*]

> Nothing . . . nothing really. Please don't look in this direction all the time. Please.

MEI KIU You could set up shop further down the road.

PAK YING Then I wouldn't see you.

> [MEI KIU *feels a surge of sweetness, turns shyly and disappears into the dark.* PAK YING *looks at his palms, smiling faintly.*
>   *Music, 'Lamentations of Two Stars', is heard. Spotlight is turned off. The light at the front door of the So Kee Umbrella Factory fades out.*

MEI KIU *returns to the factory in the dark, holding the basket and an umbrella, still thinking of* PAK YING. *She opens the wooden door and enters closing the door.*

A little later, AH KWAI *appears at the factory's front door, holding up an umbrella in his hand. He has been following* MEI KIU *all the way. He stares expressionlessly at the door, feeling devastated.*

Music fades out. Lights go up in Zone 1. Only then does AH KWAI *push open the door and walk in.*

SCENE SEVENTEEN

[*Zone 1 is now the study of* TIN CHI. *He still looks worried as he watches* CHEUNG WAH *practise his calligraphy.*]

CHEUNG WAH [*suddenly looking up*] Dad, which is furthest away, Hong Kong or Macau?

TIN CHI They're more or less the same.

CHEUNG WAH I want to go to Macau to see Grandpa.

TIN CHI You have seen Grandpa! You were four when Grandpa moved to Macau.

CHEUNG WAH But I was a baby then. I don't remember. Dad, let's go to Macau.

TIN CHI What's wrong with going to Hong Kong instead? There are steam ships, trams, a race course, and skyscrapers in Hong Kong.

[*Suddenly he remembers something and takes out a stack of new Hong Kong dollar notes from his pocket, some $1 notes and some $10 notes.*]

[*giving one to* CHEUNG WAH] Now, have you seen this before?

CHEUNG WAH Wah! So colourful! How do they draw it?

TIN CHI [*laughing*] Silly boy. This is a $1 note, a new one. You can use it to buy toys or snacks when you are in Hong Kong.

[CHEUNG WAH *plays with the $1 note.* CHAN YING *enters and approaches him.*]

CHAN YING [*to her son*] Aren't you going to bed? [*Catching sight of the banknotes*] What are these?

TIN CHI So you haven't seen these before, have you? [*Hands them to* CHAN YING] They're brand new, the edges are razor sharp. Don't cut your hands.

CHAN YING Really? How beautiful! *[Smells the notes]* Who gave them to you?

TIN CHI No one *gave* them to me! I exchanged them! I asked a travelling trader from Hong Kong to change them for me. Look, these numbers come in order.

CHAN YING Do you have to spend them in that order?

TIN CHI No, of course not!

CHAN YING Then why are they in order? *[Takes the notes and examines them under the lamp]* So you really want to go to Hong Kong?

TIN CHI Dad supports the idea. Ah Kwai will stay and mind the shop here, and we'll go with Mei Kiu and Tin Yau. Hong Kong is under British rule, the Japs will give them some face. That's why there are so many banks there.

CHAN YING What about the *fokis*?

TIN CHI We'll probably just take Ah Choi with us, or none of them at all. We'll see what Ah Kwai says.

[CHAN YING wants to say something, but hesitates.]

We have to find somewhere safe.

CHAN YING *[sighs]* You . . . don't you know that Ah Kwai is in love with Mei Kiu?

TIN CHI Should we leave Mei Kiu here then?

CHAN YING But Mei Kiu doesn't love Ah Kwai.

TIN CHI That's the point. Mei Kiu has to go where her brothers go.

[By then, CHEUNG WAH has folded the $1 note into a pig's head.]

CHAN YING Oh you! You just don't know what love is!

CHEUNG WAH *[shows the pig's head]* Dad, look.

CHAN YING That's right. Your dad is a pig's head!

CHEUNG WAH Uncle Shun calls himself a pig's head too!

TIN CHI *[smiling]* Look at you! You've used such a beautiful banknote for your pig's head. I'll smack you! *[Frolicks with his son, CHEUNG WAH giggles.]*

CHAN YING You know, you can't just rein in or express your feelings whenever you like!

TIN CHI But if Mei Kiu doesn't love him, what can we do? What worries me now is, we may not be able to keep the business, and Dad's life's work and his trust in us will all come to nothing! I'm worried about Tin Yau, too.

[*At this, both sink into a melancholic mood.*

Lights at Zone 1 fade to a very dim light. The three of them remain in Zone 1, doing various things in the dim light.]

SCENE EIGHTEEN

[*Outside the factory gate,* AH CHUEN *appears. He has just come back, a lantern in one hand and an umbrella in the other. The rain has obviously stopped. He goes into the backyard through the shop, hangs up the lantern and goes upstairs. The lantern sheds a faint light in the backyard.*

Lights go up in Zone 2, now the fokis' *bedroom. There are two plain beds.* AH CHOI *is at the centre of the room performing excerpts from a Cantonese opera, with* AH KAI *and* AH SHUN *as his audience.* AH CHOI *has got into the swing of his acting. He holds out his arms, and then swings his body round with one foot raised, as if he were the male lead in the opera.*]

> AH CHOI [*sings the musical accompaniment*] 'Cang, cang, cang, cang— dukduk, cang.' [*Narrates*] 'Gui Ming Yeung turns round and mounts his horse.' [*Mimes the gesture of a general about to ride off*] 'The lady kneels, grabs hold of the whip and will not let go.' [*Sings in a falsetto voice of the female lead*] 'My lord!' [*Resumes the role of the general, narrates*] 'Gui Ming Yeung whips his horse.' [*Sings the musical accompaniment*] 'Dingdong dingdong ding'—[*Sings the general's part*] 'My men charge in battle, how can I think of love. *Dukduk cang, cang, cang, cang. Dingdong dingdong ding.* At this dire moment, I must my conscience follow. *Dingdong dingdong ding.* This debt of blood I'll claim, to cleanse the nation's sorrow. *Cha— cha cang.*'

> [AH KAI *and* AH SHUN *are entranced by his acting.* AH CHUEN *enters, impatiently.*]

> AH CHUEN Cang cang cang! Everybody is back, go down and lock up! We don't want to take any chances with the burglars!

> [*Takes the lock and the chain from* AH KAI's *bed and hands them to* AH CHOI, *who uses them as his props*]

> AH CHOI [*still singing*] 'Down I go to lock the gate, please wait.'
> AH KAI Hey, hurry up and finish the scene!
> AH CHOI [*with an operatic gesture*] The order will be obeyed, *cang cang cang.* . . .

[AH CHOI, *still singing, goes down the stairs. Then, still with the gait of an operatic actor, he proceeds to the backyard at Zones 5 and 6, holding the lock in his hands. At the same time, outside the So Kee Umbrella Factory,* TIN YAU *and* SAU LING *appear in silhouette, and enter the factory excitedly.*]

[*allegro*] 'Dingdong ding, dingdong ding, ding dong. Time for heroes to arise, save our country, save our pride. *Kwa—la la!*'

TIN YAU [*joining in*] '*Kwa—la la!*' Ha ha ha . . .

[AH CHOI *starts back a few steps and nearly falls on the ground.*]

AH CHOI [*frightened*] Wh . . . who's that?

TIN YAU [*excitedly*] Ah Choi, it's me, I'm back!

AH CHOI Master Tin Yau? Oh! Oh! It's Master Tin Yau! It's Master Tin Yau! [*Shouts*] Master Tin Yau is back! The Master is back, safe and sound!

[*His shouting creates a stir in the factory.* TIN CHI, CHAN YING, *and* CHEUNG WAH *come down from Zone 1,* AH KAI, AH CHUEN, *and* AH SHUN *from Zone 2. Noise everywhere.* AH KWAI *rushes out too.*]

AH KWAI Master Tin Yau!

TIN YAU Ah Kwai!

MEI KIU [*appearing from another direction*] Tin Yau!

TIN YAU Mei Kiu! [*Goes up and hugs his sister*]

MEI KIU We would have gone north to look for you if you hadn't come back!

THE FOKIS [*encircling* TIN YAU] Master Tin Yau!

TIN YAU Uncle Chuen, Ah Shun, Ah Kai!

TIN CHI [*annoyed, but overcome with relief and affection*] You threw us into quite a panic!

TIN YAU Tin Chi, my brother! My dear sister-in-law!

CHAN YING What happened to you?

CHEUNG WAH [*greeting* TIN YAU *delightedly*] Uncle!

TIN YAU [*lifting* CHEUNG WAH *up by the arms and swinging him round and round*] Cheung Wah! Ha ha!

CHEUNG WAH Uncle, Uncle, did the Japs get you?

TIN YAU Uncle was in Zhuzhou and nearly didn't make it back!

TIN CHI Zhuzhou? Why were you in Zhuzhou?

AH CHUEN I'll go tell the Old Master.

CHAN YING Don't let him get up, we are going in soon.

[*The following lines are spoken in quick succession, or overlapping.*]

TIN YAU After I'd collected the money in Changsha, I thought I should go to Shanghai to see the world.

MEI KIU I guessed as much!

TIN CHI Didn't you know Shanghai was in turmoil? People in Changsha should know! Didn't you see anything wrong then?

TIN YAU I only knew that when I got to Zhuzhou. Wow, it was total chaos—refugees everywhere.

[Only then does TIN YAU *remember the girl behind him. The girl has permed hair, carries a handbag, and wears a suit made in Shanghai, fashionable but not ostentatious. One can see that she has seen the world.]*

Oh! I'm so excited I forgot! *[Turns round and grins innocently at the girl. She looks at him and pouts.]*
[pulling her forward warmly] Come, come. My brother, my sister-in-law. This is my younger sister. And these are all our *fokis. [The girl smiles and nods to everybody. They all stare at her, as* TIN YAU *continues excitedly.]* This is Sau Ling . . . *[Looks round happily]* We met at Zhuzhou. And we're married!

[Everyone is shocked. TIN CHI *and the* fokis *are speechless.* CHAN YING *and* MEI KIU *look the girl up and down.]*

Sau Ling and I returned to Changsha from Zhuzhou. We walked all the way to Hengyang and then came down from Hengyang by train. Fortunately I had some money on me! *[Looks at* CHEUNG WAH*]* Be a good boy, come, this is your Aunt.

CHEUNG WAH *[addressing* SAU LING*]* Aunt!

SAU LING *[fondling* CHEUNG WAH'*s head]* Good boy. *[Bends down to speak to* CHEUNG WAH*]* What's your name?

CHEUNG WAH Cheung Wah.

SAU LING Cheung Wah, you're a good boy.

TIN YAU *[suddenly remembering his duty]* Come, let's go in and see Dad. Let's give him a surprise. *[Catches hold of* SAU LING'*s hand and makes to go]*

TIN CHI *[anxiously]* Tin Yau . . .

CHAN YING Tin Yau . . . er . . . your father is not feeling well, don't chat for too long.

TIN CHI You . . . you go in by yourself. As to your marriage, it's late now, tell him about it tomorrow. Give him a surprise when he gets up tomorrow!

TIN YAU All right, *[To* SAU LING*]* I'll go in and see my dad. *[To the rest]* It was pouring with rain. Look, I'm all wet!

[TIN YAU *goes in happily, leaving* SAU LING *to face the rest.* AH SHUN, AH KAI, *and* AH CHOI *stare at the girl from Shanghai. Everyone is quiet for a while.*]

SAU LING I'm sorry we've caused such a panic! Tin Yau has been telling me about you all. He asked me not to worry because his brother and sister-in-law are very kind to him. I can see that now I've met you. Tin Yau is so lucky! *[Sneezes]*

CHAN YING *[looking at* SAU LING*]* Oh, you're soaked through! *[To* MEI KIU*]* Go upstairs with her to change.

[SAU LING *sneezes again.*]

You must have caught a chill. Go upstairs and change. *[Ponders for a moment]* Make do with sleeping in the study tonight.

SAU LING *[to everyone]* I must be giving you all a lot of trouble. Oh, how nice it is to be able to have a good night's sleep. Good night. See you tomorrow.

[*The* fokis *respond.* AH KWAI *helps her with her luggage.*] Thank you so much.

[MEI KIU, AH KWAI, *and* SAU LING *go upstairs.* AH CHOI, AH KAI, *and* AH SHUN *are still gazing after her.* AH CHUEN *shouts at them, giving them quite a shock.*]

AH CHUEN Is this an opera, eh? The show is over! Good night! Go to bed!

[*The* fokis *go upstairs reluctantly, leaving* TIN CHI *there, still perplexed.* CHAN YING *approaches him, with* CHEUNG WAH *following her.*]

CHAN YING Are you all right?

TIN CHI *[looking lost]* What on earth has happened?

CHAN YING He's back, safe and sound. What more can you ask for?

TIN CHI *[still lost]* He left home all by himself and now he comes back with a wife! It's too sudden. I can't believe it! *[Sighs]*

[TIN YAU *dashes in happily.*]

TIN YAU *[looking around]* Sau Ling has gone to change?

TIN CHI I want to talk to you. *[To* CHAN YING*]* You and Cheung Wah go to bed.

CHAN YING Go, Cheung Wah, go to bed now. Be a good boy.

[CHEUNG WAH *says goodnight to* TIN YAU *and goes upstairs.*]

TIN CHI *[to* CHAN YING*]* You'd better go too.

CHAN YING I'll stay.

TIN YAU It's all right, Tin Chi just wants to grill me. We won't break into a fight.

CHAN YING *[to* TIN YAU*]* Change out of your wet clothes! *[Goes upstairs unwillingly]*

[The two brothers are now alone. TIN CHI *speaks at last.]*

TIN CHI How did you meet her? And where?

TIN YAU At Zhuzhou! She fled Shanghai and went there.

TIN CHI By herself?

TIN YAU Yes . . . er . . . no. . . . There were others too.

TIN CHI Her family?

TIN YAU They died ages ago. She was with her guardian, an acrobat. She sings and dances in his acrobatic troupe, you see. They had wanted to go to Sichuan. But the Japs opened fire on the refugees, and her guardian was wounded. He died when they arrived at Zhuzhou, and the troupe had to be disbanded. Then I met her. In the end, she decided not to go to Chongqing, but to come home with me. Tin Chi, we are destined for each other.

TIN CHI Has she told you all about her past?

TIN YAU Do you think I made it all up?

TIN CHI Didn't you know that there are hustlers everywhere in Shanghai?

TIN YAU *[laughs]* Have you met a lot of them? Does she look like one?

TIN CHI How many days have you known each other?

TIN YAU You and my sister-in-law married without having met each other at all! At least we've been together for the last three or four weeks and have had time to get to know each other.

TIN CHI *[takes a deep breath]* What does she see in you?

TIN YAU And what does my sister-in-law see in you . . .?

TIN CHI Stop arguing with me or I'll throttle you!

TIN YAU What if you do? We're married, and that's that. There is no turning back! *[*TIN CHI *again looks lost.]* My dear brother, I'm now twenty-seven and I've never done anything serious in my life. This is the first important decision I've ever made and I'll stand by it. Give me your blessing.

TIN CHI *[lost]* You tell me: how am I going to break it to Dad?

TIN YAU If you don't want to, let me tell him myself.

TIN CHI No, you're not going to tell him. I'll do it! *[Both are relieved.* TIN CHI *is reproachful and affectionate at once.]*

You were gone for nearly a month, I thought the Japs
had got you!

[TIN YAU *hugs his brother, very touched.*
Lights out.]

SCENE NINETEEN

[The sky lights up, birdsong in the background. A ray of daylight shines on the
backyard, now washed clean by the rain. Under the eaves stand two rows of
umbrella racks hung with umbrellas of different colours.

SAU LING *comes into the yard by herself and looks at the place, feeling*
refreshed. She takes a few deep breaths, smiles, and, seeing the umbrellas on the
rack, goes over there, picks one out of curiosity, puts it up, closes it, and then
feels the fabric.]

SAU LING *[speaking to herself]* Very well made indeed.

[CHEUNG WAH *and* LEUNG SO *enter, unnoticed by* SAU
LING. LEUNG SO *is now in his 70s. His hair and beard*
have turned white and he walks slowly, although he is still
very alert and in good health. Suddenly SAU LING *becomes*
aware of them behind her, turns around, and sees CHEUNG
WAH *standing there with an elderly man.]*

CHEUNG WAH Second Auntie! *[Goes up to her and lets her hug him]*

SAU LING Good morning, Cheung Wah. *[To* LEUNG SO*]* You,
you're . . . *[*LEUNG SO *comes forward.]* You are Tin Yau's
father, sir?

LEUNG SO Yes, and you're Sau Ling?

SAU LING *[shyly]* Tin Yau said you were in your seventies, but
you don't look it.

LEUNG SO *[laughs]* Ha! Very well put indeed.

[SAU LING *comes to her senses and gets a stool for* LEUNG
SO*.]*

SAU LING Sit down, Papa.

LEUNG SO Good, good. *[To* CHEUNG WAH*]* Go and ask Uncle
Chuen to make preparations. We'll come in and make
some offerings to the ancestors later. Do you know how
to tell him?

CHEUNG WAH Yes, I do. *[Goes away smartly]*

LEUNG SO *[looking at* SAU LING *again]* Tin Yau calls me 'Dad' and
you call me 'Papa', hm?

SAU LING *[hanging her head]* I lost both my parents when I was
very young and I've always wanted a papa.

LEUNG SO How old are you?

SAU LING Twenty.

LEUNG SO So you're even younger than my daughter! Tin Yau is seven years older than you.

SAU LING He doesn't look his age! He's still a child, and scatterbrained. *[Smiles]*

LEUNG SO Right. How right you are! Scatterbrained! That's the word. The boy is a scatterbrain. And you married him just like that? No second thoughts? What do you see in him?

SAU LING I don't know. At Zhuzhou, I saw him standing there alone in the railway station, looking so helpless. He did not have any baggage, just a couple of umbrella samples. I thought at first he was there selling umbrellas. *[LEUNG SO laughs heartily.]* So I went up and told him that people were too busy fleeing for their lives and no one would buy his umbrellas. I bought one though, feeling sorry for him. He gave me a silly grin. Then I realized I made a mistake.

[SAU LING is half kneeling and half sitting beside LEUNG SO, chatting casually with him as if he were her grandfather. LEUNG SO smiles but does not say anything. On the far side at the back, TIN CHI and CHAN YING appear. They stand there, listening but with no intention of disturbing them.]

I thought, he's still a boy, and all alone; he'll be an easy prey for swindlers. I've seen quite a bit of the world since I was young, and know how it is out there. So I kept him company and we went to Changsha together. He was really nice to me. No one has ever treated me like that. So I said to myself, I don't care if he is poor, I want to be with him for the rest of my life.

LEUNG SO And you two got married?

SAU LING *[nodding]* Yes. Only then did I find out he was far from being poor. But I got even more worried when I knew he was loaded with money. It really wasn't easy for us to make it home.

LEUNG SO *[nodding, and smoothing his beard]* I see.

SAU LING Papa, I come from a poor family. Do you mind?

LEUNG SO Mind? No! It's Tin Yau who is unworthy of you. This son of mine won't grow up, but he's got a pair of sharp eyes.

[TIN CHI and CHAN YING cannot keep quiet any longer.]

CHAN YING *[giggling]* Good morning, Dad!

LEUNG SO *[to* CHAN YING*]* Don't you agree? As the saying goes 'The mediocre enjoy many blessings'! This silly son of mine has always been lucky.

SAU LING *[to* TIN CHI *and* CHAN YING*]* Good morning.

CHAN YING Good morning.

TIN CHI Where is Tin Yau?

LEUNG SO He woke me up early in the morning and told me he had got married! Gave me quite a shock! But what can I do now that he's grown up. *[Pauses]* He said he would go out with Ah Kwai and Mei Kiu and bring something back for celebration. Oh well, whatever he says. If he's married, he's married. Anyway, that's what he's always wanted.

CHAN YING Dad, I hope your headache is better now.

LEUNG SO I'm in great spirits. Everything is fine now that Tin Yau is back. We'll have a big reunion dinner later. This is indeed a time for celebration!

CHAN YING I'll go and prepare the food now.

SAU LING Papa, I'll go too. I'd like to learn to cook.

LEUNG SO All right. You go.

TIN CHI *[going up to his father]* Dad, now that Tin Yau is married, we will have to change our plan.

LEUNG SO Whatever happens, you two will have to leave, even if you hate to. Staying in Canton is just not an option.

TIN CHI And you?

LEUNG SO Of course I'll stay. This is the shop I've built from scratch, I'll live or die with it!

TIN CHI Dad!

LEUNG SO My mind is made up. Tell Ah Shun to come in.

> *[*TIN CHI *goes in reluctantly. After a while,* AH SHUN *comes in, nervous, knowing that things don't bode well for him.]*

AH SHUN Old . . . Old Master.

LEUNG SO I've heard that you're in trouble lately, hounded by a creditor!

AH SHUN Wh . . . who said that?

LEUNG SO You can't hush things up, you should know that.

AH SHUN Old Master, I . . . I don't owe him money. He . . . he . . .

LEUNG SO Who's he?

AH SHUN Erm . . .

LEUNG SO You want to keep it even from me? *[Pauses]* There are only the two of us now. Tell me!

AH SHUN Old Master. I. . . . Oh, I'm a good-for-nothing! I pawned my wife!

LEUNG SO What? You pawned your wife? You pawned your wife?

AH SHUN To a man named Ngan Hing. He and his wife had returned from Malaya. His wife couldn't bear him any children. When he knew that I was deep in gambling debts, he settled them for me, bought me food, and made my home quite comfortable.

LEUNG SO I see. He wants you to be grateful and then repay in kind and give him a son. Pawn your wife? People used to do that, especially in places near Canton, but it was decades ago. You want to revive the custom now? And your wife agreed?

AH SHUN *[fuming]* That was the trouble. I wouldn't hear of it, but she was willing! And Ngan Hing, the old fox, sent his wife to work on her and the two women fixed everything behind my back. She told me she was going to visit her hometown. When she came back, she was already pregnant. Oh, the shame of it!

LEUNG SO But Ngan Hing is your benefactor, isn't he?

AH SHUN Now he's calling *me* his benefactor! The wretch bore him a son. Can you believe it? I've only got three daughters, and he got a son at the first shot. How can I swallow that?

LEUNG SO At least you've done him a good turn.

AH SHUN But he's like a thorn in my flesh, I can't stand him. I don't want to see him. But he insists on seeing me to thank me in person. He even offered to take me and my whole family to Malaya!

LEUNG SO Going to Malaya is not a bad idea.

AH SHUN Old Master, I've been with you more than ten years. You know how I feel. A loyal minister does not serve two emperors; a chaste woman would not have two husbands.

[Reminded of his wife]

LEUNG SO It seems to me that this Ngan Hing is a decent fellow. He doesn't forget the good deeds other people have done for him.

AH SHUN Then I . . .

LEUNG SO Do see him, you could become friends!

AH SHUN See him?

[TIN YAU, AH KWAI, *and* MEI KIU *come back in high spirits, carrying bags of goods.*]

LEUNG SO They're back. Let's leave it at that. Don't mention it again for the time being.

[AH KWAI *and* MEI KIU *leave some things in the shop, then bring the rest in.* TIN YAU *comes into the yard, very relaxed.*]

TIN YAU Dad, things are so expensive. Rice is now a thousand yuan a hundred catties. Looks like the war is almost here. And there were students demonstrating!

[AH SHUN *takes the goods from* TIN YAU *and goes inside.*]

LEUNG SO Ah Kwai!

AH KWAI Yes, Old Master.

LEUNG SO Starting from today, the So Kee Umbrella Factory will close for retail business. Close the shop.

AH KWAI Yes, Old Master.

LEUNG SO Tin Yau, help me go inside, I have something to tell you. Mei Kiu, take those things into the kitchen.

[TIN YAU *helps* LEUNG SO *in.* MEI KIU *goes into the kitchen.*]

SCENE TWENTY

[*In the yard, Zones 5 and 6,* AH KAI, AH CHOI, *and* AH SHUN *set up a large round table with twelve chairs. Then they lay the tablecloth and set out the wine cups.* AH CHUEN *puts out a small table for the offering, with candles and incense sticks burning. The following scene is played out as these preparations are being made. When the play returns to the backyard, everything is more or less ready.*

AH KWAI *goes into the shop. He has just taken off a couple of the planks used for the door shutter when he turns around and sees* PAK YING *stumbling up to the shop, his face pale.* AH KWAI *looks at* PAK YING, *feeling all at once a rush of jealousy, hatred, pride, and perhaps a touch of inferiority. He stands straight, facing* PAK YING.]

PAK YING [*outside the shop*] Please, could I see your miss?

AH KWAI [*matter-of-factly*] I know your type. You are not what you pretend to be.

[PAK YING *is stunned.*]

You may be destined for great things. You can pick things up and drop them as you feel like it: it's all the same with you. But our miss is not used to the winds and storms of life! Would you please leave her al—

MEI KIU *[appearing suddenly from the kitchen]* Ah Kwai! *[to* AH KWAI *as she comes into the shop]* Go in! Go in!

*[*AH KWAI *goes in, bitter and dejected, resentment written all over his face.* PAK YING *turns even paler upon hearing* AH KWAI's *words.* MEI KIU *is surprised and pleased to see her beloved.]*

Yes?

PAK YING Nothing, I . . . I just come to tell you that I'm leaving.

MEI KIU Leaving?

PAK YING Yes.

MEI KIU So, um, you've done your bit as a rag-and-bone man?

PAK YING *[after a moment of reflection]* I don't want to lie to you anymore. Yes, you're right. I'm not a rag-and-bone man. My . . . my mission here is accomplished, and I'm leaving for another one.

MEI KIU *[sadly]* Where?

PAK YING To Swatow. I'll write to you.

MEI KIU Promise?

PAK YING What's your name?

MEI KIU My name's Mei Kiu.

PAK YING My family name is Pak, and my name is Ying, as in *yingxiong*, 'hero'.

[He holds his head a little higher, heroically, at the mention of yingxiong. MEI KIU *nods.* PAK YING, *in fact, knows that he's going to die. He has many things to tell* MEI KIU, *but checks himself and only stares at her.]*

Mei Kiu, I'll go now. Goodbye.

MEI KIU I'll wait for you . . .

PAK YING Is it worth it?

*[*MEI KIU *nods, with tears in her eyes.]*

I'll be more than content so long as you remember there was once such a person. Goodbye.

MEI KIU *[calls]* Pak Ying . . .

[He's already gone, leaving MEI KIU *by herself, in a daze.]*

[It's getting more lively in the courtyard. AH CHOI, AH KAI, AH SHUN, *and* AH CHUEN *are all busy, talking and doing various things and* CHEUNG WAH *is also helping.* TIN CHI *looks at the round table, is suddenly overcome with sadness, and sits down disheartened.* CHAN YING *enters with a pot of wine, puts it on the table, and, surprised to find* TIN CHI *so dejected, approaches.]*

CHAN YING What's the matter?

TIN CHI *[looks up, his eyes tearful]* When we got married, we had
a gorgeous wedding, it's my brother's turn now and . . .
[Unable to continue]

CHAN YING Don't be silly, they're coming out any minute! Come
on! So long as Tin Yau is happy! H'm?

TIN CHI *[pulling himself together]* Hong Kong is a prosperous
place, it's a good idea to go there, don't you think?

*[MEI KIU has already come in and LEUNG SO is being
helped out by TIN YAU and SAU LING.]*

LEUNG SO Give thanks to the ancestors. Give thanks to the
ancestors!

AH CHUEN *[as the most senior]* Time now for the bride and the
groom to pay their respects to the ancestors. Sprinkle
the wine. That's right. Bow three times.

*[SAU LING and TIN YAU happily follow AH CHUEN's
instructions.]*

Till our hair turns white, never do you part. Good! The
bride will now offer a cup of tea to Old Master.

AH CHOI *[frolicking to brighten up the atmosphere]* Here comes the
bride! Please have a cup of tea, Old Master. *[Mimics a
tinkling musical interlude to accompany the walking movement
in Cantonese opera]* Ting, ting, ting, ting, ting-do-ting-do-
ting . . . *[All laugh.]*

LEUNG SO Come! *[Taking out some* laisee—*lucky red envelopes
containing money]* May fortune and prosperity be with
you. May you have a family that blooms and blossoms
like a large tree!

AH CHOI The bride now will offer a cup of tea to her brother-in-
law and sister-in-law. *Ting, ting, ting, ting, ting-do-ting-
do-ting . . .*

TIN YAU *[approaches TIN CHI]* Brother Tin Chi, dear Sister-in-law,
I'll be a responsible person, don't you worry.

[TIN CHI, deeply touched, cannot hold back his tears.]

CHAN YING *[bursts into tears, too]* Drink your tea, you fool! Don't
cry!

*[TIN CHI sips his tea, signals to CHAN YING, who hands
him a paper bag. TIN CHI gives it to TIN YAU.]*

TIN CHI May fortune be with you. May your marriage last a
hundred years, and never may you part.

*[TIN YAU opens the bag slowly and draws out the contents.
It is a wad of brand new Hong Kong dollars.]*

THE *FOKIS*. Wah! Banknotes! Hong Kong money!

TIN YAU *[to* TIN CHI*]* Why . . .?

TIN CHI You'll find it useful in Hong Kong.

SAU LING We can't take it. It's such a lot of money!

TIN YAU *[to* TIN CHI*]* I thought *you'd* be going down to Hong Kong?

TIN CHI We'll go to Macau, and the two of you to Hong Kong. Hong Kong is developing fast, and is more prosperous. Hong Kong is better, safer!

TIN YAU Why don't you go to Hong Kong too?

> *[The* fokis *are shocked and look at each other in bewilderment.]*

LEUNG SO *[standing up to speak]* The So Kee Umbrella Factory is to be divided into two branches. It's a good thing. And now that Tin Yau is married, this will come sooner rather than later. As we are all here together, we might as well work things out. Come, come, let's sit down and discuss it over dinner. Have some wine. Take your seats! Take your seats!

> *[Everyone sits, having asked others to sit first as a sign of respect.* LEUNG SO *sits at the head of the table,* TIN CHI *and his wife, and* TIN YAU *and his wife on either side of him.* MEI KIU *sits next to* TIN YAU, *and* CHEUNG WAH *next to his mother. On the other side of* CHEUNG WAH *is* AH KWAI, *then the other* fokis: AH CHUEN, AH SHUN, AH CHOI, *and* AH KAI. *They start pouring wine for one another.]*

Come . . . help yourselves. Help yourselves.

> *[They start to eat, though it is obvious the news has affected everyone. With different expressions on their faces, they all keep quiet as they eat, the silence being broken occasionally by* CHAN YING *helping* CHEUNG WAH *to some food.]*

[speaking at last] My plan is this. I'll stay behind and keep this old shop. Tin Chi will go to Macau where he has his parents-in-law to help him. Tin Yau will go to Hong Kong with Ah Kwai, and the two of them can open a shop there!

AH KWAI *[taken aback]* Old Master . . .

LEUNG SO Ah Kwai has been with us since he was a young lad. He's as dear to me as my own sons. He's done much for the factory. He will be co-managing the Hong Kong branch and I'm sure no one will say I'm unfair. But of course if you don't want to go, then I won't force it on you, Ah Kwai. The rest of you can decide whom you want to be with. It's all up to you. You don't have to make up your minds yet. Let me know in the next few days.

AH CHUEN My mind is set, Old Master. I've been with you for so long, I might as well stay with you for the rest of my life. Well, folks, I'm not leaving. I'll stay here. If the worst comes to the worst, I can ask my Hakka wife to come and help me serve Old Master. Master Tin Chi, Master Tin Yau, you don't have to worry.

AH SHUN I'm not leaving either. I'll stay with Old Master.

TIN CHI I can manage without a *foki*. Ah Kwai, Ah Choi, and Ah Kai can all go to Hong Kong with Tin Yau.

TIN YAU That's not fair to you!

[AH KWAI *is worried as no one has mentioned* MEI KIU.]

AH KWAI [*blurts out*] How about Miss Mei Kiu, then?

LEUNG SO Mei Kiu will go with Tin Chi. She can go to Hong Kong a little later.

SAU LING [*blaming herself*] Is it because of me that you're dividing up the business?

LEUNG SO No, it's the war. Things will be difficult here and we have to take the business to Hong Kong.

[*Suddenly a few explosions rock the house and everyone panics.* CHEUNG WAH *and* AH SHUN *take shelter under the table, the others cover their heads with their hands. Sound of further explosions and sirens.*]

AH CHUEN The war is here!

LEUNG SO Where are they bombing this time?

AH CHOI [*to* AH KAI] Let's go and find out.

AH KAI What?

AH CHOI Are you afraid?

AH KAI Who says I'm afraid?

AH CHOI Follow me then . . .

[*The two leave, and bump into* NGAN HING *inside the shop.* NGAN HING *has entered in a hurry.*]

NGAN HING How nice to see you! Where's Ah Shun? Is he inside?

AH KAI In the backyard.

[AH CHOI *and* AH KAI *pay no more attention to* NGAN HING *and run out.* NGAN HING *goes into the backyard and is surprised to find so many people there. The others also look amazed.*]

NGAN HING I beg your pardon. I'm looking for Ah Shun.

> [AH SHUN *is under the table and doesn't want to come out,
> seeing* NGAN HING *is here.*]

TIN YAU Oh, where is Ah Shun? Ah Shun!

LEUNG SO Ah Shun, come out!

> [AH SHUN *comes out reluctantly.*]

NGAN HING I've had great difficulties finding you, my dear . . . er
. . . brother . . . brother-in-er. . . . I have come here
especially to thank you.

AH CHUEN What? So you're really relatives?

AH SHUN [*looking very embarrassed*] Let's go out and talk! Let's go!
[*Pushes* NGAN HING *out, and looks at* LEUNG SO]

LEUNG SO Ah Shun, be polite!

AH SHUN Yes, Old Master.

LEUNG SO Come, let's finish the meal. What do we care if the
heavens should fall!

> [*Everyone in the backyard continues to eat.* AH SHUN *pulls*
> NGAN HING *out of the door.*]

AH SHUN What do you want?

NGAN HING Dear Brother-in-law, my heart would not be at ease
until I could thank you in person. The situation out
there is very bad. I'm boarding the boat very soon. You
can still consider whether you want to come to Malaya
with us!

AH SHUN No, I don't. You go!

NGAN HING Have you thought it over?

AH SHUN Yes. Go now. I don't want to see you!

NGAN HING Then . . . then I can't force you. Thank you, Brother-in-
law. Thank you for everything! Give my regards to all
members of your family. This is my address. Keep it.

> [AH SHUN *takes the card.*]

Goodbye! [*Leaves*]

AH SHUN By the way, [*Pauses*] what's the name of the boy?

NGAN HING To show my gratitude to you, I've named him Shun.
He's called Ngan Shun.

> [AH SHUN *is even more hurt.*] Goodbye, dear brother-in-
> law!

AH SHUN [*mumbling*] If only I could shun you forever!

> [NGAN HING *turns and walks smack into* AH KAI *and* AH
> CHOI *who are running in from outside.*]

AH KAI Ouch!

NGAN HING I'm sorry, I'm sorry. *[Turns and leaves]*

[AH SHUN angrily tears the card into pieces and throws them on the floor. AH SHUN, AH CHOI, and AH KAI hurry into the backyard.]

AH CHOI *[panting]* Listen! Listen! The Japs have bombed the Baiyun Airport. Someone said he saw six of their planes. Our forces have shot down two of them. Bravo!

AH CHUEN You idiot! The war is here. Bravo, you twit!

[Everyone reacts differently.]

LEUNG SO It's high time you left. You really should set off soon!

AH KAI There's more. Brother Ah Kwai, the rag-and-bone man on the other side of the street, he . . . do you know what he is?

[MEI KIU leaps to her feet as if she had an electric shock, looking tense and anxious.]

AH CHOI You stutterer! Let me tell the story. It all happened just a moment ago. Someone saw him carrying two grenades and dashing into the Asahi Shimbun office in the next street. The grenades exploded, blowing up the place. The Japs lost their intelligence agency, he lost his life. What a heroic death! A great man!

[MEI KIU is stunned. She dashes out as if she had lost her senses.]

TIN CHI Mei Kiu! Mei Kiu!

[AH KWAI runs after her without a word. Everyone looks puzzled and bewildered, only CHAN YING knows what the matter is.
Lights go dim in Zones 5 and 6.]

SCENE TWENTY-ONE

[Lights go up outside the shop. MEI KIU has already run out of the shop, but AH KWAI soon overtakes her and pulls her back. MEI KIU struggles fiercely. AH KWAI is even more fierce and will not let her go.]

MEI KIU *[unable to shake him off]* Let go of me. Let me go! Let me go . . .

AH KWAI *[exerting all his strength, and impassioned]* What's he to you? What's he to you to make you act like a fool? Forget yourself, forget your own safety?! *[MEI KIU is shocked.]* So you love revolutionaries? You love heroes?

All right, I'll pack ten grenades on me and blow up the Japs, bomb their aeroplanes, crash at their cannons, then perhaps you'd look at me!

[MEI KIU, feeling hurt, tries to slap AH KWAI in the face but AH KWAI reacts even faster and catches her hand. AH KWAI wants to hit back at MEI KIU but, having raised his hand, he tries hard to restrain himself. In the end, he grits his teeth, grabs MEI KIU by the shoulders, shakes her hard, and then pushes her away. MEI KIU stumbles back a few steps.]

[gasping, hurt, his low voice rising to feverish passion] I came to So Kee when I was seventeen. We grew up together. Twelve years, thinking of you day and night. Always concerned about you. But you never even looked at me! *[Points with his finger]* And him? He has only been here a few days! You don't even know who he is—whether he's a good man or just a cheat. Yet you care so much about him, you even brought him a bowl of rice! *[Getting more emotional]* Have you ever cared about me? If only you would look at me and say you loved me, I'd gladly bash my head against the wall and die right before you!

[AH KWAI is quite hysterical now, his voice choked with emotion, his eyes burning with tears. MEI KIU bursts into tears and runs back to the shop and upstairs. AH KWAI, as if just awaken from a bad dream, swallows his tears and strides into the backyard. CHAN YING goes up to him.]

CHAN YING How is she?

[Everyone is looking at AH KWAI.]

AH KWAI She's all right now. It must have been a shock for her. After a rest she'll be all right.

[AH KWAI returns to his seat, pours a generous cup of wine and knocks it back. The liquor burns his stomach, but his heart is dead. CHAN YING, after a moment's reflection, goes upstairs alone to see MEI KIU. AH KWAI pours another cup, a full cup.]

Old Master, I've made up my mind. Hong Kong it is. So long as Master Tin Yau likes it, nothing really matters.

TIN YAU *[pleased]* Ah Kwai, if you could give me a hand, what more could I ask? We'll stick together for better or for worse.

AH KWAI Come! *[Raises his cup]* Ah Choi, Ah Kai, you two come here!

[The two come to his side, all three holding their cups. AH KWAI *takes a ring from his pocket, and speaks to* TIN YAU.*]*

The three of us have nothing valuable to offer you on your wedding. Just a toast and a worthless ring. That's all we can offer. We wish you a happy married life and the best of luck! *[Knocks back his wine. Everyone is stunned: it is an expensive diamond ring.]*

AH KAI, AH SHUN Wow! A diamond ring! Wow!

TIN CHI Ah Kwai, have you gone out of your mind?

TIN YAU It's too expensive a present. Take it back!

AH KWAI I bought it a long time ago and I don't have any use for it now. Please take it!

SAU LING No, we can't accept it. You . . . you're all so kind. *[Moved to tears]*

TIN YAU Take it back, Kwai!

AH KWAI It's really nothing, just something to express . . .

[The two of them wrangle, making a lot of noise.

Lights come up in Zone 1, showing MEI KIU *in the embrace of* CHAN YING *and crying bitterly,* CHAN YING *is smoothing* MEI KIU's *hair, comforting her, in sorrow and in sympathy.*

In the backyard, TIN YAU *and* AH KWAI *are still arguing about accepting the ring and getting even noisier.*

Noise of gunfire coming from afar.

Cantonese music 'Lamentations of Two Stars' starts from the second bar, gradually becoming louder.

Lights fade and out.]

CURTAIN

ACT 2

Time: 1950
Place: Backyard of the So Kee Umbrella Factory at Rua das Estalagens, Macau

SCENE ONE

[The backyard is enclosed by a dilapidated brick wall, blocking out Zones 3 and 4. At the foot of the wall is a bamboo rack with some salted fish and shrimp paste laid out to dry. Stone tables and stools stand in the yard, and some umbrella frames and machines are lying on the ground. The thick foliage of a tree curtains off Zones 1 and 2, and there are two passageways, one leading to Zone 3, the shop, and the other to Zone 4, the living quarters. Offstage there is the sound of a young girl laughing.]

SIU LING *[offstage]* Penny if you catch me, a date if you don't.
Penny if you catch me . . .

> *[SIU LING runs on to stage, a lively girl of nine, laughing heartily and holding up a paper pinwheel sold at religious festivals for ritual offerings. A woman, AUNTIE CHUEN, chases after her, panting. AUNTIE CHUEN is the wife of AH CHUEN, also known as the Hakka woman. She speaks with a rough accent.]*

AUNTIE CHUEN Give it back to me. Give it back!

SIU LING Come and catch me!

AUNTIE CHUEN It is for the gods! You play with it and the House God will give you a tummy-ache. Give it back to me.

SIU LING Not unless you call me 'Your Majesty'!

AUNTIE CHUEN You've got a big head! All right, all right! You're the Queen! The Empress. The highest, the most powerful. . . .

> *[MEI KIU comes out of the living quarters. She is now in her 30s and still dressed in the simple clothes of an unmarried woman.]*

SIU LING Why don't you kneel before the Queen?

AUNTIE CHUEN *[lost for words]* Oh, you . . .

MEI KIU Siu Ling!

> *[Seeing her aunt, SIU LING immediately behaves herself.]*

Give it back to Auntie Chuen. Give it back!

> *[SIU LING hands AUNTIE CHUEN the pinwheel.]*

AUNTIE CHUEN *[taking the pinwheel and remembering that there is something else]* And the. . . .

MEI KIU Give it back!

SIU LING Nothing else, Auntie!

AUNTIE CHUEN And the pea-blower.

SIU LING It's mine!

AUNTIE CHUEN You hit me with the pea-blower, it hurt!

MEI KIU *[to* SIU LING*]* Give me the pea-blower.

SIU LING *[pouting]* No.

MEI KIU I want it, I want to play with it!

[SIU LING *gives it to* MEI KIU *reluctantly.]*

AUNTIE CHUEN *[shakes her head, and mumbles as she leaves]* Thoroughly spoilt by her uncle!

MEI KIU Siu Ling, can't you behave yourself? Remember what you promised me yesterday before I agreed to take you to the Camões Garden?

SIU LING You said you'd let me see Cousin Cheung Wah off, and you didn't!

MEI KIU But you'd have to take a big boat to go to Hong Kong first. Children are not allowed on to the pier. I didn't go either!

SIU LING Will Cousin Cheung Wah come back?

MEI KIU Of course! Cousin Cheung Wah is only going to England to study architecture. When he comes back, he'll build a lot of houses for us.

SIU LING Wonderful!

[AUNTIE CHUEN *comes out again to tend the salted fish and shrimp paste.]*

MEI KIU Auntie Chuen, please take the shrimp paste in. It stinks.

AUNTIE CHUEN It doesn't! It smells good, really good!

MEI KIU Come. *[Takes* SIU LING*'s hand]* Let's go and see if your papa is hungry.

[SIU LING *and* MEI KIU *go into the living quarters, leaving* AUNTIE CHUEN *on stage by herself. The voice of* AH CHOI *offstage is heard, calling for* AH SHUN.*]*

AH CHOI *[entering excitedly]* Ah Shun! Ah Shun! Ah—

[He sees AUNTIE CHUEN. *The two stare at each other.* AH CHOI *is now in his 30s, and looks his age.]*

[looking her up and down] *Auntie Chuen?

AUNTIE CHUEN *[also looking* AH CHOI *up and down]* You . . .?

AH CHOI Hakka woman? Hakka woman!

AUNTIE CHUEN Ah . . . Ah Choi?

AH CHOI Sure it is!

AUNTIE CHUEN The chatty one?

AH CHOI That's right! Ha . . . I still have dreams of playing Chinese dominos with Uncle Chuen, rest his soul.

AUNTIE CHUEN Are you married now, Ah Choi?

AH CHOI No, I'm such a loudmouth, no woman would have me. Ha, ha . . .

[AH SHUN *comes out of the living quarters, holding a large cardboard box full of old certificates and old photographs. He is now in his 40s, his hair a little grey on the sides. He is so astounded at seeing* AH CHOI *he forgets even to put down the box.*]

AH SHUN Ah Choi?

AH CHOI Ah Shun!

AH SHUN My goodness, it seems like a lifetime away! Oh my goodness! [*The two are overcome with excitement.*] How old are you now?

AH CHOI How old are you?

AH SHUN I'm forty-six, you should know!

AH CHOI Is that the truth?

AH SHUN Definitely no older than that! And you? Thirty-something?

AH CHOI Thirty-three, you should know, ha, ha . . .

AH SHUN [*sighing*] So it's been more than ten years. Hey, the three years and eight months you people had under the Japs in Hong Kong! Life must have been very hard then?

AH CHOI It was hell, but we survived. By the way, how's Master Tin Yau?

AH SHUN No better, no worse. Oh, yes. Master Tin Chi has gone to Hong Kong to see Cheung Wah off.

AH CHOI I know! I've just come back with them! It's a shame really, but I've never been here in Macau before in all my life. So I leapt at the opportunity to come with Master Tin Chi. [*Pauses, then hesitantly*] I say . . . you . . . um . . .

AH SHUN I what?

AH CHOI Have you really lost . . . ?

AH SHUN Yes, my whole family's gone. Of course it's true. All gone! [*Feeling a little sad*] The Japanese bombed Canton over 800 times. One of the bombs is bound to hit you. It's fate. Even the So Kee Umbrella Factory has been levelled. My wife and my three daughters. . . . Oh, forget it! Now I'm all by myself. No family, no nothing. [*Pauses*] By the way, how's Ah Kai?

AH CHOI He goes to Koshing for a cup of tea everyday, and to the Alhambra for a film show when he's got the time. He said that when you've been through hell, your fortune is bound to change for the better. In those days, we had to queue up overnight for a few miserable ounces of rice, and while we were queueing, we had to burn incense to keep the mosquitoes away, and sleep on a mat. When the Jap military policemen walked by, you had to get up and bow to their swords. Not only that, you had to jostle your way or leave empty-handed. And when you finally got your rations, then you had to worry about being robbed. Those who were big and strong fared even worse, for the Japs would grab them and send them off to Hainan for hard labour for the rest of their lives. In those days, you'd be lucky if you got some bean curd scraps and yam leaves for food. And if you tried to run away, like Master Tin Yau—

[Stops. Both think of TIN YAU *with a heavy heart.]*

AUNTIE CHUEN Enough, enough! Don't mention those bad days any more. Look, the moment I hang the pinwheel up, we have visitors! Our luck will take a turn for the better now.

AH CHOI Ah Kwai is here too. He's gone to the firecracker factory with Mrs Tin Chi and should be back soon. I'm here to help with the moving.

AUNTIE CHUEN So it's all set? They're going to move everything to Hong Kong?

AH CHOI That's what I've heard.

AH SHUN Yes, all set. Mrs Tin Chi told me to pack everything before she left: the account books, documents, and other age-old stuff. And Old Master's ashes. I brought it down from Canton with my own hands!

AH CHOI So you were the only two who made it from the factory in Canton?

AH SHUN Yes, we just refused to die.

*[*MEI KIU *comes out.* AH CHOI *is delighted to see her.]*

AH CHOI Miss Mei Kiu! *[Goes up to* MEI KIU*]*

MEI KIU Ah Choi! When did you arrive?

AH CHOI Just now. Master Tin Chi and the others are still at the firecracker factory.

MEI KIU Let me see if you have changed. *[*MEI KIU *gives* AH CHOI *a once-over, smiling.]*

AH CHOI I've grown old. But you're still so rosy-cheeked!

MEI KIU Don't flatter me. You were never one to tell the whole truth. Do you still sing Cantonese operas?

AH SHUN Yes, I've heard there are lots of operas in Hong Kong. They say there are often many operas on at the same time. Do you still sing your 'Cleanse the Nation's Sorrow'?

AH CHOI Nobody sings it now that peace is here. Now we have troupes like 'The Flowery Brocade', 'The New Voices', 'The Fortune Years', 'The Blue Skies'.

[*AH KWAI enters, sees* MEI KIU *and stops. He is now 39 but still looks handsome, with the additional charm of a middle-aged man. The cheeky* AH CHOI *has caught sight of* AH KWAI, *but pretends not to have seen him.* MEI KIU *notices* AH KWAI *as well, is taken aback, and embarrassed, her heart suddenly stirred by some strange feelings.*]

[*continuing*] These days, the popular opera songs are 'Fourteen Years in the Buddhist Temple', 'The Old Acquaintance at Rouge Lane'. These days, these days they sing [*Imitates a soprano voice*] 'Return . . . of the lovelorn . . . [*Turning to point at* AH KWAI] swallow. . . . Ah . . .' Oh, Ah Kwai! My goodness, I didn't know you were here.

AH SHUN Ah Kwai!

AH KWAI Ah Shun, Auntie Chuen.

AUNTIE CHUEN What a surprise! I haven't seen you for so long, Ah Kwai. We heard that you'd got a shop of your own. You're the boss now!

AH KWAI And you've never come down with Master Tin Chi to see me. Every time he came down I asked him to give you my regards.

AH CHOI [*tactfully*] I say, Ah Shun, let's go in to see Master Tin Yau.

AH SHUN Yes, yes. Hey, Hakka woman, come with us.

AUNTIE CHUEN [*still speaking to* AH KWAI] Business is not bad after the war, is it?

AH CHOI Hey, Auntie Chuen!

AUNTIE CHUEN Yes? Oh, go in? Go in?

[*AH CHOI winks.* AUNTIE CHUEN *gets the message and goes in. Only* AH KWAI *and* MEI KIU *are on stage.* MEI KIU *is in control of herself, fairly calm, but* AH KWAI *is letting his feelings show.*]

AH KWAI [*softly*] Mei Kiu!

MEI KIU [*forcing a smile*] Haven't seen you for a long time.

AH KWAI Yes, a long time.

MEI KIU Um, has Cheung Wah boarded the boat?

AH KWAI Yes. You should have come. The SS *Canton* was quite a ship. Cheung Wah was so happy.

MEI KIU I had to keep an eye on Siu Ling!

AH KWAI *[forcing a smile]* I learnt only just now that Cheung Wah is already twenty-one! Time really flies.

MEI KIU He's still such a scatterbrain. We all say he takes after his uncle. *[Smiles]*

AH KWAI So how are you?

[MEI KIU *does not say anything.*]

How have you been the last few years?

MEI KIU I don't go to the shop now. The chores at home are enough to keep me busy.

AH KWAI When you go to Hong Kong, you should really take a good rest. Oh yes, Master Tin Chi went to see the new house and liked it very much.

MEI KIU Is it large?

AH KWAI Land in Hong Kong is expensive, so it's not bad by Hong Kong standards. It's in Bonham Road, very close to the factory. Mrs Tin Chi finds it convenient. You'll love it when you see it.

MEI KIU I'm told your factory for umbrella frames is doing very well.

AH KWAI Not bad. Of course, I've just started, so it's bound to be hard work. But things should improve in time. In the future, I'll make the stems as well. Then the So Kee Umbrella Factory won't have to rely so heavily on outsiders for the material. *[Abruptly]* Mei Kiu!

[MEI KIU *is taken aback.*]

Do I look much older?

MEI KIU *[looking up]* Not at all. You still look the same.

AH KWAI Really?

MEI KIU *[nodding her head]* Really.

AH KWAI Oh good! Then I haven't changed a bit! My heart hasn't changed either, it's still the same . . . won't take no for an answer.

[He gazes at MEI KIU, *who looks down and turns away.* AH KWAI *realizes he has embarrassed her.*]

Hey . . . I. . . . Oh! I never know how to express myself! *[Embarrassed]*

[SIU LING *appears and shoots at* AH KWAI *with her pea-blower.*]

AH KWAI Ouch! *[Rubs the back of his neck]*

MEI KIU *[to* SIU LING*]* Siu Ling! You're so naughty! Come here!

SIU LING Why are there so many people today?

MEI KIU Say hello to Uncle Kwai.

SIU LING Uncle Kwai!

AH KWAI That's a good girl, Siu Ling! *[AH KWAI squats down and looks at* SIU LING*, his heart growing a little heavy.]* Which school do you go to?

SIU LING Hou Kong Primary School.

AH KWAI Uncle Kwai is here to take you to Hong Kong.

*[*SIU LING *looks at her aunt and* MEI KIU *nods.]*

SIU LING Is Papa going too?

AH KWAI Yes. Papa, Auntie Mei Kiu, Uncle and Aunt. All of you!

SIU LING Oh good!

*[*SIU LING *sees* TIN CHI *and* CHAN YING *at the outside of the gate.* TIN CHI *is now 41, a little over the hill.* CHAN YING *is 40 and dressed as a middle-aged woman.]*

[running towards them] Uncle, Auntie, are we going to Hong Kong?

TIN CHI Yes.

SIU LING Let's go and tell papa. Let's go, Uncle, let's go . . . *[She grabs* TIN CHI*'s hand and leads him towards the living quarters.]*

TIN CHI Hey, look, Uncle hasn't had time to catch his breath, hey—

*[*MEI KIU *and* CHAN YING *do not know what to do with the naughty girl.* TIN CHI *is dragged inside by* SIU LING.*]*

MEI KIU *[to* CHAN YING*]* Look at Siu Ling. She's thoroughly spoilt by Tin Chi. Such a tomboy!

AH KWAI *[smiles]* I'll go in and see Master Tin Yau. *[Exits]*

CHAN YING *[smiles]* Your brother is hopeless! He speaks harsh words, but his heart is so soft he lets everyone get away with murder. *[Pauses. Digressing deliberately]* That includes you.

MEI KIU Why me?

CHAN YING *[turning serious]* Mei Kiu, it's so rare to find someone who loves you your whole life.

MEI KIU Ugh! Spare me that!

CHAN YING No I won't. If you don't take the opportunity now, you'll regret it for the rest of your life.

MEI KIU So you're telling me I've been sponging on you?

CHAN YING *[immediately]* You can sponge on us all you like. But
        life isn't worth living if you're unhappy. Why run away
        from this chance of happiness?

        *[*MEI KIU *remains silent.]*

        Look at Tin Yau! He's in bad shape now, but it's been
        worth it for him. He took risks when he was young,
        and he found happiness. He's experienced great joy in
        his life. *[Pauses, presses a step further]* Mei Kiu, you can
        too!

MEI KIU *[sighs]* I'm past my prime.

CHAN YING So long as he cherishes you!

        *[At this moment, a group of people come out from the living
        quarters, and the atmosphere livens up at once.]*

TIN CHI Come, come and take some fresh air!

        *[*AH KWAI *and* TIN CHI *are pushing a wheelchair, in which
        sits* TIN YAU. *He is now 40 years old and paralysed from
        the neck down. Only his eyes, fingers, and mouth can move
        slightly. But he looks happy.* TIN CHI *pushes* TIN YAU *to a
        suitable spot, with* AH CHOI, AH SHUN, *and* AUNTIE
        CHUEN *following behind.* SIU LING *wriggles her way out
        from the crowd and helps to steady the wheelchair. All look
        jolly and cheerful.]*

        [to TIN YAU*]* Now, Tin Yau, take a good look at the
        place. We'll be leaving in a couple of days to go to
        Hong Kong.

        *[*TIN YAU *shows a little panic in his eyes.]*

CHAN YING *[moves forward]* Don't you worry! Hong Kong is a safe
        place now, unlike the past. It's very safe, Tin Yau!

TIN CHI The *fokis* have kept the shop going through the hard
        times. And after the war the British encouraged people
        to claim compensation from the Japs. Now business is
        picking up again.

CHAN YING Siu Ling can go to school in Hong Kong, and learn
        English.

SIU LING When I grow up, I'll take a steamship just like Cousin
        Cheung Wah.

        [All laugh.]

CHAN YING Cousin Cheung Wah is going to be an architect. What
        will you be?

SIU LING *[pondering]* Well . . . I won't tell you!

MEI KIU You're so naughty! You'll grow up to be a tomboy.

SIU LING No, I'll be a Queen, not a tomboy!

[All laugh.]

TIN CHI Siu Ling, look, your papa is laughing at you. Look! Ha, ha . . . Tin Yau is smiling! Tin Yau is smiling!

[TIN YAU is smiling in his eyes, TIN CHI is even happier. All laugh even as they feel sad for TIN YAU.]

CHAN YING Ah Shun, Auntie Chuen, you'd better pack your things. We'll go to Hong Kong in a few days.

AUNTIE CHUEN Well, I'm getting on now and no good for any heavy work. If I hang on to you, I'll just be a burden—

CHAN YING Hey—

MEI KIU *[cutting in with a remark aimed at teasing her sister-in-law]* You can sponge on them as much as you like. But if you don't grab the opportunity now, you'll regret it.

[MEI KIU and CHAN YING look at each other and exchange a mischievous smile, then both burst out laughing. CHAN YING looks at AH KWAI and laughs again. AH KWAI scratches his head. The others look on, baffled.]

TIN CHI Have you two gone crazy?

AUNTIE CHUEN What's going on? Are you laughing at me because I smell of shrimp paste?

[Another round of laughter. AUNTIE CHUEN walks away, a little annoyed, and takes the salted fish and shrimp paste in. AH SHUN brings the box up.]

AH SHUN *[to CHAN YING and MEI KIU]* What shall we do with this junk?

CHAN YING Make sure you don't lose any of those things! We'll take them to Hong Kong too!

TIN CHI What are they?

CHAN YING What are they? Old Master treated them as treasures before he died! *[Taking out a certificate of award]* Look, this is the award the So Kee Umbrella Factory won at the First Guangdong Provincial Show. And this one, the award at the Second Canton Show. This bronze medal is for his promotion of student umbrellas. And these few medals were given to him by the warlord Chan Jitang. They have all been kept from the days of the old shop!

AH KWAI I'll frame them when we go back. Ah Choi will look after them for the time being.

AH CHOI I will. Ah Shun, let's go to the shop and pack up. I don't even know those new *fokis* there.

[They exit.]

CHAN YING Oh, yes, Ah Kwai, come with me. I'll introduce our
fokis to you. Perhaps you can show them the ropes
when we get to Hong Kong? *[To* TIN CHI *and* TIN
YAU*]* Why don't you go inside? You could catch a cold
here!

TIN CHI It's all right. Let him stay for a bit longer. The breeze
is nice and cool. *[To* TIN YAU*]* Are you hungry?

MEI KIU He had some congee just now. See how happy he is
today. Siu Ling, come, let's go in and play. Let Papa
talk to Uncle.

CHAN YING Come, let's go.

[AH KWAI and CHAN YING *go into the shop, and* MEI
KIU *and* SIU LING *into the living quarters, leaving* TIN
CHI *and* TIN YAU *on stage.* TIN CHI *looks around. The
breeze is cool.* TIN CHI *then looks at* TIN YAU, *pulls the
blanket up a little and feels* TIN YAU's *hand to see if he is
cold.]*

TIN CHI Cheung Wah was thinking about you when he boarded
the boat. The silly boy said the moment he arrived in
England he'd go and examine the wheelchairs to see if
there were any new models. *[Pauses]* Wants to study
architecture, to be an architect! What can he do when
he comes back but build houses? Such a pity he can't
study umbrella-making. Otherwise he could take over
the factory. *[Sighs]* But now that we've let him go, we
mustn't expect to keep him in the shop. *[Pauses]*
Starting a business is difficult. Keeping one is even
more difficult. I can see it now. *[Pauses]* Dad held on
to the shop all his life. We've been keeping the shop
all our lives. But times are different for the new
generation. Cheung Wah will have no future if he
doesn't study more. And when Siu Ling grows up, I'll
send her to college, that's for sure, and let her study as
much as she likes!

*[Music comes in as background. It is 'The Wandering
Songstress,' played on the* yangqin. *The tempo is slow and
the melody sad.]*

Ah Kwai said Siu Ling was just like Sau Ling. An
exact copy!

[TIN YAU is reminded of SAU LING *and looks sad.* TIN CHI
turns melancholic too.]

Man proposes: god disposes. I've always put you before
everything and wanted the best for you. Who'd have

thought Hong Kong would be caught in the war!
[Pauses] But Hong Kong is different now. After the
liberation, lots of people from the Mainland fled to
Hong Kong, setting up factories and businesses. Hong
Kong is back to its fine old days, and people are
willing to buy more expensive umbrellas. *[Pauses]* You
know, there's a new type of plastic now. It's
transparent. Ah Kwai uses it as a cover for our top-
grade umbrellas. It really catches the eyes. Makes you
think the umbrella is wearing a transparent
mackintosh. I call it umbrella on an umbrella. They're
very popular and fetch quite a bit of profit.

[It begins to drizzle. TIN CHI *looks up and can feel it.]*

Ha. Start talking about umbrellas and it rains! Come,
let's go inside.

*[*TIN YAU *moves his fingers slightly, with expressions in his
mouth and eyes.* TIN CHI *reads* TIN YAU'*s mind.]*

What? You don't want to go inside yet? You want to
watch the rain? All right, we'll stay a while longer.
You and your funny ideas!

*[*MEI KIU *comes out.]*

MEI KIU It's raining! *[Makes to lend them a hand]*

TIN CHI No, he doesn't want to go in, he wants to watch the
rain. Can you get us an umbrella?

*[*MEI KIU *hurries in to get an umbrella. A row of umbrellas
is standing in the passageway, so she does not take long.* TIN
CHI *opens the umbrella and holds it over* TIN YAU. MEI KIU
*opens another umbrella and squats beside her brother. The
three gaze into the distance. 'The Wandering Songstress' can
still be heard in the background.]*

When we were young, we loved it when it rained. You
two would go out, catch tadpoles in the pond, or
dragonflies. But I was such a fool. I thought the shop
would only have customers when it rained.

MEI KIU *[laughing]* A fool indeed! And every time Tin Yau and
I were playing happily together, you would appear from
nowhere and summon us back. Such a wet blanket!

TIN CHI Cheeky brats! Remember how the two of you conspired
to give me a fright? You heard me coming out, and
you threw a piece of brick into the pond and then hid
yourselves somewhere. When I saw the ripples on the
pond and no trace of you anywhere, I really thought
you'd fallen in.

MEI KIU Ha ha! I do remember. I do remember. You were
shouting and screaming. *[To* TIN YAU*]* And we were
laughing our heads off, and just wouldn't come out
from hiding. Ha ha!

*[*TIN YAU *smiles in his eyes as tears stream down his cheeks.
'The Wandering Songstress' gets louder, eventually drowning
out their conversation.]*

TIN CHI Then I ran after you trying to hit you as you shouted
and screamed for help. I chased you all the way down
the street . . .

*[*MEI KIU *is laughing heartily. The foliage is lifted to reveal
the backdrop. The props on either side of the stage are
removed, leaving only a window against the rain. In front of
the window are* TIN CHI, TIN YAU *and* MEI KIU, *holding
umbrellas, gazing at the distance.*

Lights fade and out.

'The Wandering Songstress' continues.

The stagehands change the set in the dark.

Music leads into Act 3.]

CURTAIN

ACT 3

Time: 1966
Place: The So Kee Umbrella Factory at Des Voeux Road, Central, Hong Kong

Zone 1   *The study*
Zone 2   *The workshop*
Zone 3   *The retail shop, facing the backdrop*
Zones 4, 5 & 6   *The back of the factory, with a rosewood table, chairs, corner tables, as well as a western style desk, and a telephone, bills, and an abacus on the desk*

SCENE ONE

[Music, 'The wandering songstress', fades out.
A spotlight goes up on CHEUNG WAH as he appears downstage, facing the audience.]

CHEUNG WAH In 1950, the year after mainland China's liberation, my family closed down the business in Macau and in Canton, and concentrated on the business in Hong Kong. Hong Kong was very different from the horrors of wartime that Uncle Tin Yau remembered. But he left Hong Kong, and us, a few years later for the other world. *[Pauses]* In the 60s, Hong Kong industries moved into top gear: there was diversification, mechanization, and mass production. Factories sprang up everywhere, producing export-oriented products. We made great improvements to the quality of our umbrellas. But there was a problem. Family handicraft was no competition for machine-made goods. We persisted in keeping our prices stable, and we persisted in offering life-time guarantees and repairs, preferring a smaller volume of business to sacrificing quality for competitive pricing. The sudden boom in industry brought tension in labour relations. What with that and other political and social pressures from within and without, Hong Kong was heading for another crisis. *[Pauses]*
   In 1966, the So Kee Umbrella Family reached the ripe old respectable age of eighty. I was working in England then, after graduating from Cambridge, and learnt only from the media and letters from home about the labour disputes, the demonstrations against price increases, and the unrest in Hong Kong.

[Lights gradually go up. SIU LING is on the phone at the desk. She is now 23 and a university graduate. She looks intelligent and capable. Behind her in the retail shop are two fokis, *one old and one young, sitting facing the street and with their backs to the audience. The older* foki *is AH KAI, now aged 49. The younger one, recently employed and in his 20s, is KIT TSAI. He is listening to pop music, his body swinging.]*

Siu Ling has just graduated from university, with an economics degree. Papa is very pleased and wants to send her abroad for further studies. But, to everyone's surprise, Siu Ling insists on working in the shop.

[The Beatles' 'Hard day's night' fades up, with tram noise from outside.]

SIU LING *[on the phone, listening with her right ear, covering her left ear with her left hand]* The boss is out! Yes . . . yes! We sell top quality umbrellas, we use the best fabric, and our workmanship is superb. You're welcome to drop in and have a look. Yes, yes. All right. Thank you. *[SIU LING puts down the phone and resumes checking the accounts, but is irritated by the music. She shouts.]* Kit Tsai!

KIT TSAI *[turns his head]* Yes! *[Goes up to her]* What's the matter?

SIU LING Aren't you working?

KIT TSAI Ah Kai says he likes the music.

AH KAI *[turns around in protest]* I never said I liked it . . .

[AH KAI is now facing the audience, KIT TSAI reluctantly turns off the radio. Only the tram noise remains.]

What I said was, the news will be on in a minute, so I'll put up with your music. But you make me dizzy, rocking and shaking. That bloody song is just like someone wailing over the dead!

KIT TSAI *[to AH KAI]* You're old, and behind the times!

AH KAI It's all because of long-haired good-for-nothings like you that Hong Kong has become such a mess! When the cops grab people during the riots, they head straight for people like you. So don't you go near the Star Ferry Pier!

KIT TSAI *[teasing]* How malicious you are!

SIU LING Stop it. No one will come and buy anything if you keep bickering like this.

[KIT TSAI goes beside SIU LING while AH KAI exits with the radio.]

KIT TSAI Learning to do bookkeeping? *[Looks at* SIU LING*]*

*[*SIU LING *ignores him, looks at the account book.]*

How come a university graduate like you would work in this business?

SIU LING *[looking up]* Don't university graduates have to eat too?

KIT TSAI *[sighing]* There are not many who can go to university. If I had your education, I'd be able to fly away!

SIU LING Who does the bookkeeping normally?

KIT TSAI The boss himself. He's very good with the abacus.

SIU LING It must be very hard for Uncle.

KIT TSAI That's what he says. In the old days, you could do business on trust, but now you have to have contracts in black and white, and go to law firms to sign them. It's too much trouble.

*[*AUNTIE CHUEN *comes in with food from the market and a pinwheel in her hand. She is now 69, the oldest in the factory, and walks with a limp. She is looking for a suitable place to stick up the pinwheel.* KIT TSAI *and* SIU LING, *watching her movements, cannot help laughing.]*

AUNTIE CHUEN *[angry with* SIU LING*]* What's so funny? Today is the sixteenth day of the last moon, Mrs Tin Chi is joining the *fokis* for dinner. Special treat.

SIU LING I laugh because you're always so keen for a change of luck.

KIT TSAI Auntie Chuen wants better luck with her romance?

AUNTIE CHUEN You rascal. I'll rub your mouth with a piece of ginger! Teasing an old woman like me! I've just gone to pay my respects to the gods. May they bless us so there'll be no more wars in Hong Kong, no more riots, and everyone will live peacefully. What do you know, you scamp? *[Exits, limping]*

[At this moment, a SALESMAN *peeps in.]*

SIU LING *[to* KIT TSAI*]* Hey, shop!

*[*KIT TSAI *hurries out to the shop.]*

SALESMAN Is the boss in?

KIT TSAI He's out. What do you want him for?

SIU LING *[coming into the shop]* Who's there?

SALESMAN Oh, I want to show him some fabric samples. My name is Li. *[Hands her a namecard]*

SIU LING Please come in.

[The SALESMAN *goes into the back of the factory and takes out some samples from his briefcase.]*

SALESMAN These are the latest samples. See if you like them. This
is Italian fabric, this is nylon from Germany, and this
is cotton and synthetic material from Japan.

SIU LING Put these two back. I don't think we'd want anything
made in Japan!

SALESMAN Sure. And what kind of rings do you use, miss?

SIU LING Nylon rings and brass ones. Both from Britain.

SALESMAN Why don't you give this a try. Plastic. *[Takes out a
sample from his briefcase]*

SIU LING *[taking a cursory look]* Made in Japan as well?

SALESMAN It's very handy, and cheap!

SIU LING You like selling Japanese goods?

SALESMAN *[surprised]* Quite a lot of industrial materials come from
Japan these days!

SIU LING We in the So Kee Umbrella Factory never use material
from Japan.

SALESMAN Well then, I'll leave these two with you. I'll come back
tomorrow. So long!

SIU LING Thanks! Bye bye.

*[SIU LING takes the fabric samples to the desk and studies
them. KIT TSAI has taken in everything that has just
happened and now walks up to her.]*

KIT TSAI I never knew you hated the Japs so much!

[SIU LING does not answer.]

Did you have a hard time during the occupation? You
can't be that old!

SIU LING *[still studying the samples]* My grandad gave a lot of
money to the Nineteenth Army to fight the Japs!

KIT TSAI My dear miss, you weren't even born at that time. All
those national and family grudges—they exist only in
your imagination!

SIU LING Uncle had to run away from the Japs and flee to
Macau. He still gets mad when he talks about it.

KIT TSAI Wow, like those fancy stories on the radio!

SIU LING *[sharply]* Papa was tortured and crippled by the Japs.
The shock killed my mother. Do you call that a fancy
story?

*[KIT TSAI gapes in astonishment at SIU LING, realizing that
she is serious. SIU LING stares at him, and KIT TSAI shrinks
in embarrassment. Lights fade out.]*

SCENE TWO

[Lights go up at Zone 2, the workshop, where some fokis *are working.* AH SHUN *is now 62, the second oldest after* AUNTIE CHUEN. *Even* AH CHOI *is 49. And there is another new* foki, FAT TSAI, *who is in his 20s.*

The following dialogues could overlap, with AH SHUN *speaking to himself, and* AH CHOI *to* FAT TSAI.*]*

AH SHUN *[reminiscing]* The riots these days are nothing! Ten years ago, at Shek Kip Mei and Li Cheng Uk, heaps of people died during the riots. We had just recently come from Macau, and I saw the looting with my own eyes. Terrible.

AH CHOI *[mumbling]* Hm, I must go to see a foreign film someday!

FAT TSAI Yes, don't just go to the Cantonese Operas, try something else.

AH SHUN In Canton, we could run to Hong Kong to get away from the Japs. But Hong Kong is so small! Where can you run? Into the sea?

[Neither FAT TSAI *nor* AH CHOI *is really listening.]*

FAT TSAI *[to* AH CHOI*]* Hey, I know. Go and see *The Longest Day.* It's a good one, with lots of stars in it. It's a story about the landing at Normandy by the Allied forces in the Second World War.

AH CHOI Where is Normandy?

FAT TSAI I don't know. Anyway, they went there to fight the Germans!

AH SHUN *[still mumbling]* The family is gone. Everything is gone. I've been all alone for decades.

FAT TSAI Hey, have you seen *Stalag 17*?

AH CHOI *Stalag 17*? Sounds familiar. Another foreign film?

FAT TSAI Of course. I never go to Cantonese films. *Zombie Giving Birth to a Son*? Forget it! *Stalag 17* is great. It's about the prisoners-of-war, they dig a tunnel in secret, inch by inch, day after day . . .

AH SHUN Hey, Ah Choi, Fat Tsai, have you been listening to me?

[The two are taken aback.]

AH CHOI Huh? What? Of course we've been listening!

AH SHUN So what was I saying?

FAT TSAI You were talking about the war! We were talking about the war too! *[To* AH CHOI*]* They dig the tunnel, and then escape one by one. It's full of suspense, really breathtaking!

AH SHUN The young have no sympathy . . . none at all . . .

[*KIT TSAI comes upstairs in high spirits.*]

FAT TSAI [*scolding* KIT TSAI *the moment he sees him*] Where have you been? Shirker!

KIT TSAI Take it easy! I was minding shop downstairs. The boss is back. Pay time. Come down!

[*They go down one by one.*]

S C E N E   T H R E E

[*Lights go up in the downstairs zones.* TIN CHI *is wearing a pair of reading glasses, and holding some brown envelopes with the names of the* fokis *written on them. He is now 57, but still energetic and in good health.* SIU LING *looks on at one side. She does not consider this a good way of paying the* fokis. AH KAI *comes out from the kitchen too.*]

FOKIS [*coming down the stairs*] Pay time! Pay time!

TIN CHI Come. This is for Ah Shun. This for Fat Tsai, Ah Choi, Ah Kai . . .

[*All go up to collect their envelopes, and then check the money, all the time on guard against others' prying eyes.*]

And this . . .

KIT TSAI What about me? Where is mine?

TIN CHI Be patient! Here, this is yours!

KIT TSAI Ha. . . . Thank you! Thank you!

TIN CHI [*mumbling*] The others are not here yet, I'll keep them for the time being. [*Puts four brown envelopes back into the drawer*]

SIU LING [*could not keep her mouth shut any longer*] Uncle!

TIN CHI Yes?

SIU LING Why not pay them through the bank? Let everyone open an account there. It's so convenient, and safe. All the big companies do that!

TIN CHI I've thought of that. But it would't work.

SIU LING Why not?

TIN CHI They'd find it more troublesome.

AH KAI Right. You have to sign when you want to withdraw the money. I'm not used to writing.

KIT TSAI It's no trouble! Just scribble something and say it's your signature.

AH KAI Yes, so I just scribble something. Then, the next time I
　　go, they say my signatures don't match!

AH SHUN *[sighing]* I'm so old now and I have no children.
　　Heaven forbid, but I might go any time. Then all my
　　money would go to the bank! Put the money in the
　　bank? No!

　　[SIU LING looks exasperated.]

TIN CHI All right, all right. Everybody back to work.

　　*[Everyone exits, leaving only AH KAI at the shop, sitting
　　with his back to the audience.]*

　　Siu Ling, Your aunt Mei Kiu and uncle are coming to
　　dinner this evening.

SIU LING Just now, someone brought you some fabric samples.

TIN CHI I see.

SIU LING You're late today. Where have you been?

TIN CHI I went to pay the fire insurance premium, and the
　　electricity bill, and spent the better part of the
　　morning in the consulate with your uncle Ah Kwai.

SIU LING So auntie and uncle are really emigrating to Canada?

TIN CHI Yes. And so are you!

SIU LING *[shocked]* What?

TIN CHI I asked your uncle to apply for you too. You'll go for
　　an interview in a couple of days.

SIU LING I'm not leaving!

TIN CHI Why?

SIU LING I want to stay. To help you.

TIN CHI Help me? Help the factory?

SIU LING Yes. I want to shape it up.

TIN CHI It's easier said than done, Siu Ling. Take this
　　opportunity and go with your aunt. You could study
　　for a postgraduate degree if you wish, or you could
　　start your own career there!

　　[SIU LING remains quiet.]

　　[concerned] Do you have a boy friend?

SIU LING Oh, Uncle!

TIN CHI But why stay at the factory? Why would you want to
　　rot here after all your education?

SIU LING You think I can't help you?

TIN CHI The more you can help me, the more uneasy I'll be.
　　How can I face my dead brother?

SIU LING *[cheekily]* What do you have to do before you can face
　　him?

TIN CHI Well, either find you a good husband, or see to it
that you rise above the others. I must plan for your
future.

SIU LING *[cutting in]* You had plans for Papa, too, but things
ended in disaster all the same. Anyway, I don't want
you to plan . . .

*[SIU LING's tone was light-hearted, but still TIN CHI is
hurt. His face turns pale, and he slumps into a chair. SIU
LING did not expect TIN CHI to react so emotionally.]*

[gently] Uncle, Uncle!

TIN CHI *[dazed]* What did you say just now?

SIU LING Uncle, I didn't mean it.

TIN CHI Things ended in disaster?

SIU LING I didn't mean it.

*[The following lines overlap, and are spoken quickly, with
growing agitation to reach a climax. AH KAI, who is in the
shop, hears the noise and is now looking at them in
amazement.]*

TIN CHI You blame me—

SIU LING No I don't—

TIN CHI You've been blaming me all along—

SIU LING I've never ever thought like that—

TIN CHI I have! I've been carrying this burden for decades.

SIU LING I want to be with you! I told you again and again but
you just don't understand!

TIN CHI That's because I feel I didn't do right by Tin Yau!

*[Both have reached breaking point. They go quiet. SIU LING
looks at her uncle, with guilt, pity, regret, and amazement.
TIN CHI walks slowly away from her, dazed, depressed,
overcome with pain and guilt.]*

SIU LING Uncle!

TIN CHI I want to be alone for a while.

*[TIN CHI goes slowly up to the study. SIU LING wants to
help him, but TIN CHI waves her away. SIU LING sits
down, a blank look on her face. AH KAI does not know what
has happened. He goes up to SIU LING slowly.]*

AH KAI Siu Ling!

[SIU LING does not reply.]

What's the matter? Mm?

[SIU LING still says nothing, a blank look on her face.]

SCENE   FOUR

[Lights go up at Zone 1 upstairs. TIN CHI *sits down on an easy chair,
reminiscing. The following part takes place in Zone 1 and the back of the factory.*
CHAN YING *and* MEI KIU *enter the factory.* CHAN YING *is now 56 and*
MEI KIU *is 51. The two are dressed in the style of the 1960s.* MEI KIU *is
carrying bags of gifts. They talk as they walk in.]*

CHAN YING Buy a down quilt and take it with you. It'll keep you
warm. They say that in winter, the snow is several feet
deep. Cold!

MEI KIU I don't mind the cold. And Ah Kwai is only worried
that we may not be able to find a good school for the
child. *[Sees* SIU LING*]* Siu Ling!

[No response from SIU LING*]*

CHAN YING Siu Ling?

AH KAI *[addressing them]* Mrs Tin Chi, Miss Mei Kiu.

CHAN YING *[sensing something wrong]* What happened?

AH KAI I don't know. She was chatting with Master Tin Chi,
and then, suddenly things turned sour!

*[*CHAN YING *and* MEI KIU *look at each other.]*

CHAN YING Where's Tin Chi?

AH KAI He's gone upstairs.

*[*CHAN YING *hurries upstairs,* AH KAI *returns to the shop.*
CHAN YING *sees* TIN CHI *and goes up to him slowly.
Downstairs,* MEI KIU *also goes up to* SIU LING*. The
dialogues in the two zones interlace.]*

CHAN YING *[takes a deep breath, then humorously]* Well, well, the
news of the year! The palm is having a quarrel with
the back of the hand! What's the matter?

MEI KIU *[to* SIU LING*]* Is it about going to Canada?

SIU LING *[looking lost]* I made Uncle angry.

TIN CHI Siu Ling blamed me!

SIU LING I didn't know he'd be so angry! Stupid of me!

TIN CHI She was right, I've made a mess of everything all my
life.

SIU LING All I wanted to say was that I wished to stay with
him. I wanted him to know that all my life I treated
him like my own father!

TIN CHI I've been spoiling her since she was a baby, thinking
that could make up for everything.

SIU LING I wanted to repay him, help him!

TIN CHI You think I want to see her leave? But there are strikes, riots, and people are saying that the Communists are coming!

SIU LING I want to shape up the factory, to do what Papa was not able to do, just to make Uncle happy.

MEI KIU Silly girl. It's not easy!

CHAN YING You don't have to be so alarmed!

TIN CHI Everyone is planning an escape route. All those who can leave are leaving.

SIU LING Whatever Grandad and Uncle could do, I can do too!

TIN CHI She's just graduated from university, she would have a bright future elsewhere.

SIU LING So one must turn tail as soon as something happens? Not me! I want to face it, not run away from it.

CHAN YING Life is so unpredictable. You can't plan for everything. Things may look bad now, but they'll straighten out in the end. Hong Kong will be all right!

MEI KIU I have spent most of my life in the factory, I know what we're up against. We haven't got the capital to expand and we can't compete with the big factories. Uncle hangs on to the shop and won't close it just to keep your grandfather's memory alive.

CHAN YING You've been through so much in life, and you haven't learnt this lesson yet? Siu Ling knows her own mind!

MEI KIU Uncle isn't really after profits, don't you see? And look at Ah Shun and that lot. They're well into their sixties. Revamp the business? How? To begin with, you would have to replace the old *fokis* with a new bunch of people, and this goes against your uncle's principles!

CHAN YING Why not ask Cheung Wah to come back and lend you a hand?

TIN CHI Cheung Wah has his own career. Even if he came back, his heart wouldn't be in the shop.

MEI KIU, TIN CHI [*together*] There's no way out.

TIN CHI I'm just trying to keep the shop afloat so the old *fokis* will have somewhere to stay! [*Pauses*]

MEI KIU The shop will have to close sooner or later.

TIN CHI, MEI KIU [*together*] Anyway, let's keep the business going, for as long as we can.

CHAN YING [*pondering*] Ha! I sometimes wonder. If you should lose me one day, would you be so worried?

TIN CHI [*taken aback*] What are you talking about?

CHAN YING You've spoiled those you love—your brother, your sister, Cheung Wah, and Siu Ling. Have you ever spoiled me?

TIN CHI Go on! Shame on you! Jealous? At your age?

CHAN YING I have no shame, you knew that the first day you met me!

TIN CHI You don't think I've treated you well?

CHAN YING No, I don't. As I always say: I married a top-grade umbrella!

[TIN CHI *is astonished.* CHAN YING *continues mock-seriously.*]

My husband? The best in the world! He's got a good heart. Upright. Sturdy. Doesn't rust. Practical, and lasts. He keeps me from the rain and the heat of the sun. The only trouble is, he never opens his mouth to say anything tender!

[AH KAI *shouts from downstairs.*]

AH KAI Master Ah Kwai is here! Master Ah Kwai is here!

CHAN YING [*still teasing her husband*] Ah Kwai is different. He loves with a passion and hates with a passion. A man, one of the best . . . [*Goes downstairs, leaving* TIN CHI *there, flabbergasted.*]

[AH KWAI *comes into the shop. He is now 56, but looks younger. He is carrying two small bags of roast meat. The* fokis *come out to greet him.*]

AH SHUN Ah Kwai!

AH KWAI Ah Shun!

AH CHOI, AH KAI [*together*] Master Ah Kwai, when are you going to Canada?

AH KWAI Fairly soon. I got a letter from my partner over there urging me to go as soon as I can.

AH CHOI So all's well for you now!

AH KWAI Oh, I'm just doing it for my son. I'm in my fifties already, I don't expect a rosy future in Canada. [*Looks at* SIU LING] Siu Ling, you're quiet! [*Sees* AUNTIE CHUEN] Auntie Chuen!

AUNTIE CHUEN Master Ah Kwai.

AH KWAI Here, I've brought something. [*Hands her the roast meat*]

AUNTIE CHUEN Oh you shouldn't!

CHAN YING Since we are all here today, we'll have a celebration. Ah Kai, would you please go and buy a bottle of liquor? Kit Tsai, Fat Tsai, you two help lay the table.

AUNTIE CHUEN Come and help me burn the paper offering first.

KIT TSAI And what are your wishes this time?

AUNTIE CHUEN That Master Ah Kwai may meet kind and helpful people when he goes abroad!

[AUNTIE CHUEN, KIT TSAI, and FAT TSAI go inside. SIU LING, who has been watching them silently all this time, now goes upstairs without a word. TIN CHI turns around and sees SIU LING looking at him. His heart melts and the two look at each other. Finally, TIN CHI opens his arms. SIU LING runs over and rests her head on his lap. TIN CHI strokes her hair affectionately. It's still boisterous downstairs at the shop, a contrast to the scene upstairs.]

AH KWAI Hey, don't go out if you don't have to!

ALL Why?

AH KWAI The workers are staging a strike at the cotton mills and the cement factory. There are clashes with the police. Looks like a riot will break out anytime. So be careful!

MEI KIU *[to AH KWAI]* You'd better call home and tell our naughty boy not to go out!

CHAN YING Why didn't you bring him along?

AH KWAI He said he had to do his homework. He's got tests all the time and every night he studies into the night.

CHAN YING Siu Ling used to work very hard too.

MEI KIU That's exactly what I told him. Cousin Siu Ling went through all that and now it's his turn. Let's see if he can make it in Canada.

AH KWAI Wow, so many bags. What have you bought?

MEI KIU The sales are on and they offer lucky draws as well. Aren't these shirts lovely?

[As they chat, KIT TSAI, AH CHOI and FAT TSAI bring out the round table top. Everyone helps with laying the table for the meal. Lights fade. Back to Zone 1. TIN CHI is looking at SIU LING, a serene expression on his face.]

SIU LING Uncle!

TIN CHI Yes?

SIU LING I want to stay, I don't want to leave.

TIN CHI Aren't you worried there might be a war in Hong Kong?

SIU LING I have confidence in Hong Kong!

TIN CHI *[after a pause]* Let Uncle tell you a story.

SIU LING Great! You haven't told me any stories for a long time.

TIN CHI Once upon a time at the end of the Tang Dynasty,
Huang Chao led a rebellion which swept along the
coast in Zhejiang Province. He and his rebels killed
everyone in sight. There was a Hakka woman fleeing
from the turmoil with two children, and she ran into
Huang Chao himself. Huang Chao was surprised to see
her carrying the older child on her back, while the
younger child was stumbling along by her side, his
hand in hers. So he asked her why. She had no idea
who he was. She said that the older boy was her
nephew. His parents had both died, and if he were
killed as well, she wouldn't be able to face the dead. So
she carried him on her back. And the younger boy was
her own son.

[Music rises as background.]

*[getting a little sentimental, pauses for breath and then goes
on]* Huang Chao was deeply moved by the Hakka
woman. He spared her life, and even comforted her and
told her to go home and stick a pinwheel at her door.
Then he gave the order that his army should spare the
life of all those staying in houses with pinwheels on the
doors. Since then, the Hakkas have always bought
pinwheels at festival times, and stuck them on their
doors for good fortune. It's become a tradition now.

SIU LING I see. So I'm the child carried by the Hakka woman,
and you are the Hakka woman! *[Smiles]*

*[The two smile, with tears in their eyes. Music fades up.
Lights out.]*

SCENE FIVE

*[A spotlight goes up on CHEUNG WAH, who is standing downstage, facing the
audience.]*

CHEUNG WAH Siu Ling eventually gave in. She did not insist on
staying at the umbrella shop, and agreed to go out to
work, to serve society and help the needy. And she
found a good husband in the end. I came back to
Hong Kong in 1975, Papa was quite old by then.
Before he died, he told me over and over again to take
good care of the old *fokis* and keep the shop going
until an appropriate time. Papa had been a kind and
honest man all his life, and he had integrity. No matter

how life treated him, kindly or unkindly, he would
always face it with the same inner strength, ready to
overcome any difficulties. It's like some eternal law of
the universe, he never changed just because the outside
world has changed. *[A slight pause.]* There is good faith
in heaven and earth and the world is where love abides.
That's what papa believes in. That's what you can see
in the story of his life. *[CHEUNG WAH exits slowly.]*

S C E N E   S I X

[Lights go up in the shop. Everyone has gathered round the table, chatting.
TIN CHI *takes his seat.* CHAN YING, AH KWAI, MEI KIU, AH SHUN,
AH CHOI, AH KAI, KIT TSAI, *and* FAT TSAI *sit down one by one.* SIU LING
looks at the pinwheel which AUNTIE CHUEN *has stuck on the shop door, then
she looks at her uncle and smiles.* AUNTIE CHUEN *brings out the last dish
and, seeing* SIU LING *looking at the pinwheel, puts down the dish and looks at
her.]*

AUNTIE CHUEN *[to* SIU LING*]* Huh! You want to pinch my pinwheel
again? When you were a child, you always pinched the
things meant for the gods. If you do it again, I'll
smack you!

[SIU LING laughs, so does TIN CHI.]

CHAN YING Siu Ling, let's get started!

*[SIU LING walks to the table. The round table is now full.
People are urging each other to drink.]*

AH CHOI *[to* AH KWAI*]* Come, come. We the *fokis* will drink a
toast to you, wishing you all the best. Bottoms up!

AH KWAI Thank you, thank you! *[Downs his drink and fills his cup
again]*

MEI KIU *[glances at her husband reproachfully]* What a tippler!
I didn't know he had come to enjoy drinking so much!

TIN CHI Talking about drinking, Western liquors are no
comparison to the *Wujiapi* and *Meiguilu* of old! Yes,
liquors in the old days were much better!

AH SHUN Everything in the old days was better. Even the rice.

AH CHOI Exactly. Nowadays nothing is as good as it used to be.
Advertising is what counts now. Things that get
advertised the most will sell best.

TIN CHI That can't be helped. If you want to move with the
times, you have to pour money into advertising. It's
different from the days in Canton!

CHAN YING Look at you lot, the moment you get together you can't stop reminiscing.

TIN CHI In the old days, the So Kee Umbrella Factory never had to advertise! *[Sighs]* But when we came down to Hong Kong, we had to follow the tide. If you don't advertise, no one will know you.

AH KWAI Remember how much we spent to bid for a stall at the first Industrial Exhibition in Hong Kong?

AH CHOI Yes, yes. And we hired a group of young girls to compete for the title of Miss Industrial Exhibition!

KIT TSAI Wow, and you didn't snap one up for your wife? What a shame!

[All laugh.]

AH CHOI Your cheek is worse than mine when I was young!

AH KAI And then we advertised with commercials in cinemas!

FAT TSAI Big deal! I've seen it. I was only a toddler at the time. *[Imitates a woman's voice]* 'You can't go sunbathing without it, and you can't go picnicking without it. What is it? A So Kee umbrella. With a So Kee umbrella over your head, let it rain like mad.'

[All laugh.]

TIN CHI With such stiff competition, you have to make your brand name known, and you have to have new products every now and then, or people will forget you. In a word, you have to be smart and adaptable in Hong Kong, and you have to take things easy.

SIU LING Talk! Talk! Look! The food is getting cold and Auntie Chuen is getting cross!

KIT TSAI Auntie Chuen, I'm your loyal supporter.

AUNTIE CHUEN You rascal, just don't annoy me so often and I'll be grateful!

[KIT TSAI helps himself to big mouthfuls.]

CHAN YING Hey, careful you don't choke!

[All laugh.]

AH KAI *[to KIT TSAI]* When you walk, you're like a snail. When you mind shop, you take catnaps. But when you eat you are at your best!

KIT TSAI Give me a break. When a customer comes in, I'm wide awake.

AH KWAI How's business lately? Not too good?

AH CHOI No. The last year or two not many people have bought
our umbrellas. Don't people use umbrellas anymore?
Would they rather get drenched?

[All laugh.]

KIT TSAI People don't want to lug them around. Umbrellas are
so cumbersome.

AH KAI They're not! We are selling those folding umbrellas!
They're handy.

KIT TSAI But you look smarter in a raincoat! Yes, raincoats are
definitely in.

AH KAI What? A raincoat in summer? Smart? You'd sweat to
death! And it makes you look like a detective inspector.

[All laugh.]

AH SHUN That's right. Raincoats have got nothing to do with it,
nothing!

TIN CHI We are selling top quality umbrellas. So the market is
smaller!

FAT TSAI I think it's the unlicensed hawkers who screw up our
business. As soon as it rains, they come out in droves,
and the streets are swamped by cheap umbrellas.

KIT TSAI *[to AH KAI and AH SHUN]* Hey, you want business to
pick up? I have an idea. When it rains, we all take our
umbrellas and sell them in the street. Then we could
snatch some of the business back.

AH KAI Why not? You think I'm too old for that? I can still
walk and run!

AH SHUN Yes, let's do it together! See who chickens out first!
You'd better be as good as your word!

FAT TSAI 'Course I will! Let's go! Let's go! Get the cart! Off we
go! He who chickens out has four legs . . .

AH KAI . . . and a tail.

[All laugh.]

CHAN YING You're crazy!

[They continue talking and joking as CHEUNG WAH *enters
and walks downstage centre.]*

CHEUNG WAH *[facing the audience]* In 1986, the year of the centenary
of the Statue of Liberty in the United States, a very old
Chinese shop in Hong Kong also celebrated its one
hundredth birthday. And I, the proprietor, used the
occasion to announce the official retirement of the So
Kee Umbrella Factory from business. In the Chinese
tradition, a hundred is a very propitious number. It

represents perfection, fortune, and harmony. It indicates the passing away of an era, and the beginning of a new century. I followed my late father's instructions and continued to look after the old *fokis*. They all enjoyed quiet and comfortable lives in their old age, and had many happy memories as well. In their spare time, or after dinner, they would talk about the ups and downs in the fortune of the So Kee Umbrella Factory, chewing upon them like the most delicious morsels, remembering them with the fondest thoughts. *[Pauses]* Ladies and gentlemen, this story about umbrellas is at its close. The story about my family, though, goes on. Goodbye!

[Music, 'Pattering rain on the banana tree' fades up to maximum.

Lights fade.]

CURTAIN

THE END

AMERICAN HOUSE

A PLAY IN TWO ACTS

1990

By
ANTHONY CHAN

Translated by
KWOK HONG LOK

— ABOUT **THE PLAYWRIGHT** —

ANTHONY CHAN (1953–) was actively involved in the theatre when he was still in secondary school. In 1974, he emigrated to America and he received his BA in Theatre and Fine Arts from the University of Colorado at Denver in 1979. After graduation, he worked for several years as Art Director at the Denver Children's Museum before coming back to Hong Kong in 1982 to take up the post of Stage Manager with the Hong Kong Repertory Theatre. Four years later, he returned to the States for further studies and graduated with a MA in Theatre Studies from the University of Colorado. In 1989, he returned to teach at the Hong Kong Academy for Performing Arts and, since 1994, has been Head of Directing and Playwriting at the School of Drama at the Academy. He is also a director, a translator, and a set designer.

Chan has written and adapted over forty plays to date. They are widely performed in Hong Kong, by community as well as professional theatre companies. Of these, *Hong Kong Heartbeat* has been staged, as part of the 'Hong Kong Festival', in London in 1992 and in Toronto in 1993. Another play, *Nüwa Mends the Sky* toured Tarascon and Bordeaux in 1992.

In 1991, Chan was awarded 'Playwright of the Year' by the Hong Kong Artists' Guild. In 1992, *Nüwa Mends the Sky* won the First Prize in the Open Section of the 'Outstanding Original Scripts Competition' organized by the Council for Performing Arts in Hong Kong. In 1994, he received the 'Outstanding Achievements of the Decade' award from the Hong Kong Federation of Drama Society.

ABOUT THE PLAY

Set in Denver, Colorado, this play explores the experiences of a group of Chinese students living and studying in America. Realistic in style and autobiographical in subject, it examines the students' motives in coming to Denver, and what they hope for in their 'American dream'. Issues such as familial duty, isolation, race, and culture focus the priorities of these Hong Kong students, their aspirations, their hopes and fears, their evaluation of themselves, and their attitudes towards others. Their reactions to students from the Mainland and from Taiwan open up a further dimension in the relationship of the fraternity of overseas Chinese.

Written soon after the Tiananmen Incident of 1989, when the brain-drain problem had reached a crisis in Hong Kong, the play exposes some of the central concerns of the younger generation. The soul-searching of the students during their brief sojourn in their American house before the lease expires is a poignant reflection of the issues Hongkongers face before the expiry of the lease for the territory in 1997.

The play was first performed by the Shatin Theatre Company in 1991.

── **DRAMATIS** PERSONAE ──

YAN SIU YIN, ROSANNA, 22, majoring in Fine Arts

CHAN MAN BIU, BILL, nicknamed 'Joe Cool', 24, majoring in Urban
    Planning

CHU LAI SHAN, nicknamed 'Sha Sha', 23, female student, majoring
    in Hotel Management

WONG MING CHAU, 22, male student, majoring in Accountancy

KWAN WING HONG, 23, male student, majoring in Electrical
    Engineering

KWAN WING YIU, CASSIE, 21, sister of WING HONG, still hasn't
    chosen her major

LAU CHING NUEN, nicknamed 'Chief', 30, cousin of ROSANNA,
    tenant in charge of rent collecting for the house, majoring in
    Sociology for Ph.D. degree; minoring in Asian Studies

LOK CHI SHING, ERIC, 25, landed immigrant, majoring in
    Computer Science

WANG KUO-CH'AO, 30, Taiwanese majoring in Architecture,
    boyfriend of CHING NUEN

BRUCE LAMONT, about 28, American, owner and landlord of the
    house

LAN QIAN, just over 30, student from People's Republic of China

Time: The present

Place: Denver City, Colorado, USA

Act 1 starts at the end of summer when the new semester begins;
    finishes in early winter of the same year.

Act 2 starts in mid-winter and finishes the following year in June, at
    semester end.

SET

An old two-storey Victorian building. Chimney and ventilation pipes on steep roof. Trees nearby casting a shadow on the roof and the porch.

On one side of the house is a small porch with a rough plank fence. Two steps down the porch is the back garden with a small flower-bed. At the furthest end of the back garden is the back alley (the garden and alley could be a back cloth). At a corner on the porch are a stool, gardening tools, water hoses, newspapers, a snow shovel, and firewood.

From the porch a set of doors open into the living-room: a wooden door and a wire-mesh door. The living-room, not large, is cluttered. In the centre, thin foam mattresses of different sizes are piled on top of an old couch. In front of the couch stands a rattan coffee table piled high with Chinese and English magazines. On top of a wooden trunk is a small TV set with antenna covered with tinfoil for better reception. A VCR stands next to the TV, and a few chairs are scattered in the room. A short passageway from the living-room opens into the corridor (which leads to the front door at one end and to two bedrooms, the kitchen, and the bathroom at the other end). From the corridor a flight of stairs goes up to the rooms on the first floor and down to the basement with the laundry room and store room. These are not seen. Along the two walls of the passageway from the living-room are metal bookcases filled with textbooks, sports trophies, Chinese music cassette tapes, etc. On one side of the living-room are two desks on which are placed a computer, colourful files, ping-pong rackets, and books.

On the walls there are magazine cut-outs of photography masterpieces, road maps of America, old-fashioned calendars obtained from Chinese grocery stores, and a bamboo scroll with the words 'Don't forget you're on alien soil' in Chinese.

There is a window with open curtains. On the sill are a few plants; above, a copper Chinese wind-chime. Close by is a rack where two coats are hung. Below them a Chinese oil-paper umbrella leans against the foot of the rack.

ACT 1

SCENE ONE

[A snatch of an old song—'Olive Tree'—is heard playing softly. Gradually the tune changes from a melody played on an erhu—a Chinese stringed instrument—to a pop beat.

Lights go up on the porch and the flower-bed. It is a warm autumn evening. Everything is tinted yellow.

A lively and attractive young woman comes out to the porch from the house. She leans on the fence, and takes a deep breath. She is YAN SIU YIN, ROSANNA. She picks up a yellow leaf from the fence, studies it, holds it to her lips, gently blows it off, and watches it drift slowly to the ground.

Sound of 'Olive Tree' up again.

ROSANNA seems to be talking to the audience.]

ROSANNA The—United—States—of—America, five words, ten syllables which we Chinese, out of laziness perhaps, shorten to two, *Mei Guo*, the Beautiful Country. But are things really beautiful here? Is China, *Zhong Guo*, the Middle Kingdom, really in the middle of the universe? And is England, *Ying Guo*, the Clever Country, really clever? Is France, *Fa Guo*, the Prosperous Country, really rich? And is Korea, *Han Guo*, the Cold Country, really cold? Is Hong Kong, the Fragrant Harbour, really fragrant? Will it ever become fragrant? Everyone is waiting for the grand finale. And what will the ending be? Everyone says it depends on this generation, our generation of Hongkongers. On us? Why us? And on whom can we rely? On luck? Well, I am lucky. After all I, Rosanna Yan Siu Yin, have made it to America from Hong Kong; have left the seemingly fragrant place, for a seemingly beautiful world. It's been like watching a video fast forward. People rush by, cars rush by, I rush into the MTR, rush out of the MTR, wipe away the sweat, take the School Certificate Exam, hop into a taxi, hop out of the taxi, wipe away the sweat again, fill in a stack of application forms, and stand like a penguin at a long queue outside the American Consulate, watching the cars shoot down Garden Road, wondering where I should go. Then, I hop into a taxi again, hop out, get a physical check-up, go to the bank, turn up at a farewell party, sing at a karaoke bar in Tsimshatsui East all night long, rush to the airport, wipe away the sweat, wipe away the tears, eat airline food in a tray, watch heaps of baggage going

round and round on a carousel, get my passport
stamped, answer questions, change planes, go through
the gate, fasten the seat-belt. Strangers. More strangers.
I . . . I want to cry *[Yells]* 'Stop!' *[Pauses]* A moment
later, I'm here, softly blowing a leaf, and saying with a
touch of romance, 'Now settle down'. *[Pauses and looks
around]* Everything suddenly stops. It's unsettling.
Everything stops, leaving a sense of isolation. Yet,
things seem fresh, exciting. A new beginning. In
seventeen hours you go from one side of the globe to
the other. *[Sighs heavily]* I never thought the world
could be so small. This is Denver City in Colorado
State in the United States of America, a place I have
spoken of more than a thousand times and still find
strange. It's too quiet here. No, I should say it's too
noisy over there. Here it's so quiet you feel your voice
is floating in a vacuum, it's as if I'm listening to my
own voice for the first time in my life. Hello? *[Answers
herself]* Hello. How are you? *[Answers]* I'm fine, thanks.
[Asks herself] Don't you miss Hong Kong? *[Answers]* I
really don't know. *[Asks]* You talk to yourself, does that
mean you're lonely? *[Answers]* Lonely? I have no time
to be lonely. Don't jump to the conclusion that
everyone away from home is lonely. Especially when
you're staying in a big American house full of
Hongkongers, *[Indicates the house]* and you're in a new
country full of interesting things.

SCENE TWO

*[Lights go up in the living-room. A group of young people rush in, with WONG
MING CHAU in the lead holding up an electric rice cooker.]*

CHAU *[loudly]* Supper time!

> *[The following actions take place simultaneously and at a
> fast pace.*
>> KWAN WING HONG *follows* WONG MING CHAU *and
>> brings in a plate of steamed fish. He is holding the hot dish
>> with a dish cloth.]*

HONG Steamed fish with pickled vegetables! *[CHU LAI SHAN,
holding a pair of chopsticks, runs after HONG.]*

SHAN Yummy! I want a cheek of the fish!

HONG You've got a cheek! *[Dodging]* Go away!

[CHAN MAN BIU, BILL, comes in with the bowls and chopsticks, notices the computer is on.]

BILL *[runs over to the computer, puts down bowls and chopsticks]* How come Eric's mahjong programme is on? *[Taps the keyboard and calls out the names of mahjong tiles]* Waan Yak Sik. Needs a South tile.

CHAU *[puts down the rice cooker]* The table is still not set!

HONG Hurry up, it's hot! *[Paces about and finally puts the dish on the floor]*

[At this moment, KWAN WING YIU, CASSIE, enters from the porch door with a stack of mail in her hands. She's listening to her walkman, dancing, humming a song, and reading the mail.]

CASSIE Wo, wo . . . 'The hometown I dream about every night, millions of miles away. I'll stop wandering . . .' Wo! wo! *[Continues singing and dancing]*

HONG *[stops SHAN eating the fish on the floor]* Stop it! Can't you wait?

CHAU Whose turn is it to lay the table?

HONG Not me. *[Stops SHAN from getting at the fish]*

CHAU *[reading the chart on the wall]* It's Friday today . . . Whose turn is it?

BILL *[plays at the computer]* Got it! Score!

SHAN It's his turn. Joe Cool's turn on Fridays.

CHAU Joe Cool, your turn! *[Gets no response, goes to the kitchen]*

BILL *[ignores them]* I don't want this. Shit!

HONG *[seeing CASSIE dancing her way out of the room]* Cassie, can't you eat first and dance later?

CASSIE What? *[Takes off headphones]* What? Okay! *[Runs into the kitchen]*

SHAN *[jumps at BILL and tabs the keyboard at random]* Mahjong, mahjong, mahjong! Play to your heart's content then!

BILL *[pushes her away]* Lay off, you bitch!

SHAN You haven't set the table!

BILL Bitch! You screwed it up! It's jammed! *[Tapping the keyboard desperately]*

[LOK CHI SHING, ERIC, comes down from the first floor holding some books.]

SHAN *[tells on BILL]* Eric, Joe Cool's jammed your programme.

ERIC *[goes to the computer]* What have you done?

BILL She did it. I was going to hit three *fan* doubles.

SHAN You have your *fan* doubles, I'll have my fish doubles.
[Bends down again for more fish but HONG *stops her]*

*[*ERIC *presses 'Exit' on the keyboard, and argues with* BILL.
LAU CHING NUEN *comes in with two dishes of food.]*

NUEN *[seeing the confusion]* Hello!

[All four become quiet.]

Time to set the table.

SHAN *[points to* BILL*]* He only cares about setting the table for
mahjong.

[While SHAN *is speaking,* CASSIE *and* CHAU *move the
folding table and chairs stage centre.]*

NUEN Give us a hand, everybody! It's my cousin's first day
here, don't scare her away. Wing Hong, Ming Chau,
you set the table. Cassie, Sha Sha, you get the chairs.
Bill, you get the chopsticks. I'll take care of the food,
and Ming Chau will get the rice.

BILL Yes, Chief.

[Everybody laughs and helps to get things ready. CHAU
ladles out the rice.]

NUEN *[towards the basement]* Kuo-ch'ao, supper time!

SHAN Time for supper, future husband of our Chief tenant!

[Everybody laughs. Just then, WANG KUO-CH'AO *rushes up
from the basement. Everybody smiles at him. He notices this
and quickly helps at the table.]*

NUEN Shut your mouth . . . Hey, where's Rosanna?

CHAU In the back garden.

NUEN Oh? *[Goes to the back door and steps into the porch. Sees*
ROSANNA*]* Rosanna, what are you doing here?

ROSANNA Nothing. Just thinking.

NUEN It's time for supper.

ROSANNA It feels strange. Supper before it's dark.

NUEN Days are long in early autumn here. Sometimes it
doesn't get dark until about nine.

ROSANNA *[looks at her watch]* It's six in the morning in Hong
Kong. I still keep Hong Kong time on my watch.

NUEN Homesick so soon? Come and have supper. This is our
welcome treat for you.

ROSANNA It's so nice of you.

*[They walk into the living-room where everybody is holding
up their bowls to greet* ROSANNA.*]*

EVERYONE Rosanna, welcome to America!

ERIC Rosanna, welcome to the house!

EVERYONE Yeah!

NUEN Our chef Wong Ming Chau will tell us tonight's menu.

CHAU *[laughs]* Sweet and sour spareribs, steamed melon with dried scallops, braised chicken with black mushrooms, and—

SHAN And steamed fish. Let's tuck in!

[Everybody tucks into the fish. Some sit down and some take the food to eat on the couch.]

BILL *[to SHAN]* You're breaking the fish up into bits, bitch!

SHAN Shows how much respect I have for the fish. When I was in Hong Kong, you'd have to give me a thousand dollars before I would eat steamed fish!

CASSIE Why are you so keen now?

SHAN Because it's more tasty now that I don't get to eat it often.

HONG In the States my greatest enjoyment is eating Chinese food.

CH'AO *[in Mandarin, singing MING CHAU's praises]* Woman zuidade lequ jiushi chi Ming Chau zhude Zhongguo cai! *[Everybody agrees.]*

ERIC I suppose our taste in food never changes!

CASSIE When it comes to eating, Hong Kong is the best.

HONG Well, eat, eat, eat.

ROSANNA Did Ming Chau cook all this? It's really nice.

CHAU I didn't know anything about cooking back in Hong Kong, but here I have to know a bit of everything.

ERIC Don't be modest! You're a real chef!

CASSIE He's a chef in Peach Garden Restaurant.

CHAU No, no. *[To ROSANNA, a bit embarrassed]* I only work part-time as a kitchen helper.

NUEN He's the one who makes things work in the house.

BILL A good man. A real nice guy.

CHAU You go on like this and I'll ask you to help me wash the rice everyday.

BILL No thank you, sir!

[Everybody laughs.]

ERIC What's so funny about washing the rice?

[Nobody answers. ERIC is puzzled.]

NUEN Rosanna, you're lucky to have a meal like this on your arrival. Some of us had to eat bread every day when we first got here, not even instant noodles.

SHAN Of course you're lucky. You have your cousin to arrange this welcome party for you.

ROSANNA Thanks very much.

BILL Hey, how can you call this a welcome party and not offer people some wine? *[Runs to the bookcases and returns with a small bottle of brandy]* Look! Da Da!

[Everybody shows surprise.]

NUEN Bill, I made it very clear there is to be no smoking or drinking in this house.

BILL This is for the party. Just this once?

NUEN But we all agreed to follow the rules. So I hope—

BILL Rules are made by man. We can agree to make another rule today. You did claim to be democratic.

NUEN Well—

CH'AO *[in Mandarin, urging NUEN to give in just this once]* Suanle ba! Jiu yici. I'll get some glasses. *[Exits]*

NUEN Hey Kuo-ch'ao—*[Embarrassed by the situation, goes after CH'AO and exits]*

[They all express their views. ROSANNA is embarrassed.]

SHAN Take it easy Rosanna. Your cousin treats us like four-year-olds. It's not going to be easy for you. She'll act like a mother. You'll have to get used to it.

BILL *[to SHAN]* Of course she has to keep an eye on you. If she didn't, you might stay out all night.

SHAN It's none of your business where I sleep! Anyway it's better than going to the Labour Union to gamble at dominoes with those guys.

BILL I have face, so they play with me. Will they let you in?

SHAN What face? Why do you keep asking us for loans if you have so much face there?

BILL I never!

ERIC *[simultaneously]* Sha Sha, shut up and eat!

SHAN *[displeased]* Why? Isn't it the truth? And you turn on me! *[Angrily picks up her coat on the rack and makes to leave]*

ERIC Where are you going?

SHAN I hate you. I'm going for some ice-cream.

ERIC Finish your supper first.

SHAN I'm full. Drive me there.

ERIC I'm not finished yet! *[Ignores her]*

SHAN Eric! *[Turns to look at him, embarrassed]*

BILL *[with contempt]* Don't look at me. I won't lend you my Porsche.

SHAN I'll walk. *[Turns round and exits]*

HONG *[to ERIC]* Go after your sweetheart quick!

ERIC She's not sweet. She's crazy.

[ROSANNA observes everything. At this moment, CH'AO returns with some glasses, BILL pours the brandy. NUEN comes in holding a soft drink and some mail.]

NUEN How come the mail was left in the kitchen?

CASSIE Oh, I took it there. I'm . . . sorry.

HONG *[takes the mail, knocks CASSIE on the head with it]* You're hopeless.

NUEN The top one is for Ming Chau.

HONG *[sings casually]* 'A letter from home warms you to the bone.' *[Gives out the mail]*

CASSIE That's an old song, no one sings it anymore.

HONG I've been here all these years. My cultural identity is the same as when I left Hong Kong. I'm naturally old-fashioned.

ROSANNA I brought a number of music tapes with me. Shall I lend them to you guys?

CASSIE *[claps]* Sure, thanks.

NUEN *[to ROSANNA]* You better have this. *[Gives her the soft drink]*

HONG Joe Cool, the rest is all yours.

BILL *[takes the mail]* Shit. All bills. *[Troubled]* Shit. *[Throws away the mail]* Let's drink first. Cheers!

EVERYONE *[not quite sure if they should break their own rule]* Cheers!

[Lights dim.]

SCENE THREE

[ROSANNA emerges from the crowd. The others quietly remove rice-cooker and dishes. Spotlight on ROSANNA.]

ROSANNA So this is 'the big house'. Actually, it's just an old house on West Colfax Street. But it's near the college, and cheaper than the dorms, so many frugal Chinese students share the rent and live together. It's not as nice as the dorms of course, but to be able to stay with those who speak your language is not bad. My cousin says I am lucky to have friends throwing a welcome party for me as soon as I arrived. I count myself lucky to be a part of this group. They are all a bit weird, but fun. *[Pauses]* There are three floors in this house. The top floor is for the girls. The rooms on the ground floor are for the Kwans, brother and sister. The basement has four rooms for the boys. My cousin Lau Ching Nuen collects the rent and liaises with the landlord. That's why we call her 'Chief'. *[At this moment, NUEN comes in with a chair.]* This cousin of mine is real smart. She's done a master's and is finishing her doctorate this semester, and she gets more money from her grants and scholarships than she can spend. A clever woman indeed! If I make good use of my opportunity here in the States, I'll be as good as she is, I hope.

[Light change. ROSANNA goes back to the living-room.]

SCENE FOUR

[NUEN beckons ROSANNA to sit with her.]

NUEN Rosanna, let's talk about what courses you should take.
ROSANNA It's only my first day here. Do we have to do it now?
NUEN I promised my uncle. I gave him my word I'd look after you.
ROSANNA A fat lot he cares. I know, it's my mother who wants you to keep an eye on me and talk me into taking one of those popular subjects like Business or Computer Science to make sure I'll get a job that pays well. Dear cousin, I've been talked to about good jobs a thousand times. Not again, please!
NUEN I know why your mother is concerned.
ROSANNA Anyway, it's got nothing to do with Daddy. He doesn't care about me, or whether I'm in the States or in Hong Kong. But Mom nags at me all the time. One of the reasons I'm in the States is to get away from her. So please don't start nagging me.
NUEN But being in the States doesn't mean absolute freedom.
ROSANNA Here, there's the sky for whoever wishes to fly.
NUEN So you're no longer a bird in a cage, right?
ROSANNA Absolutely!
NUEN But Rosanna, I'm serious, I want to discuss your choice of subjects with you.

ROSANNA There's no need. My mind is made up, I'm taking fine
arts.

NUEN But what will you do afterwards?

ROSANNA Oh, not again! Please, Cousin Nuen, don't be Mom's
remote control! [Makes the gesture of pressing a remote
control button]

NUEN Rosanna, listen to me. Here in the States we are
making an investment with our youth. Don't bet
against the odds.

ROSANNA You're like my dad when he talks business.

NUEN All the years I've been here, I've seen lots of people
putting everything they've got into art, music, and all
that. When they graduate, they can't find a job. In
the end, they work in restaurants, banks, wasting
everything they've learned. Why bother to study fine
arts?

ROSANNA If fine arts is as useless as you say, how come the
universities still teach it?

NUEN Fine arts is not for us Chinese. You have to be very
good at English if you want to express yourself well.
Chinese students don't do well in fine arts.

ROSANNA In that case, what should Chinese students study? How
to make aeroplanes and weapons? Tanks? You know
what my marks were like in Hong Kong. Not high.
And that's because I'm not interested in Chinese,
English, or Math. I'm even less interested in learning
how to make tanks.

NUEN Rosanna, if you really want to study fine arts, do it as
a minor. Major in another subject.

ROSANNA Why don't we talk about something else? Let's talk
about our Chief's future husband.

NUEN Chinese students are good at science subjects like math.
There at least language is not a problem.

[WANG KUO-CH'AO enters, looking for something.]

ROSANNA Is he Taiwanese?

NUEN [ignores her] You could consider a design course. Better
job propects!

ROSANNA Do people go to university so that they'll get a good
job? Please, please, let's change the subject. How long
have you known him?

NUEN Known what?

ROSANNA I'm asking about you and him, your relationship.

NUEN What relationship?

ROSANNA *[giggles]* That's what I'm trying to find out.

NUEN *[displeased]* Oh, . . . well, there's nothing between us.
Don't listen to that lot. But, now that you mentioned
it, let me remind you that we're here to be students,
not to get mixed up with boys.

ROSANNA Oh, my God!

NUEN Please listen to me, Rosanna. You're young, and
impressionable. Someone treats you well, you fall for
him. You must try to be cool and concentrate on your
studies.

ROSANNA All right! All right! I swear I shan't waste my time on
anything not directly related to my studies. Otherwise,
may I be struck dead by a thunderbolt! How about
that for dramatic effect? *[Goes to the porch half angry,
half smiling]*

NUEN Rosanna—

[Light change.]

S C E N E   F I V E

*[Trees in the backyard cast shadows on the house. Sounds of autumn insects. WONG
MING CHAU appears from the alley holding a trash-can and sees ROSANNA
sitting on the porch idly.]*

CHAU Hi.

ROSANNA Hi.

CHAU How are things? Have you got used to living here?

ROSANNA I can't talk to you. If my cousin heard me talking to
you, I'd be struck dead by thunderbolts!

CHAU *[puzzled]* What?

ROSANNA *[laughs]* Don't mind me, I'm just joking. Do you leave
the garbage in the alley?

CHAU Oh yes. There's a big can there. They come round to
collect it every week.

ROSANNA *[looks in the direction of the alley]* Once a week? Won't it
pile up and attract rats?

CHAU We've never seen any rats. But sometimes bats come
for the fruit peel.

ROSANNA How horrible!

CHAU Ah, there are bats on the roofs of these old houses.

ROSANNA *[stands up and looks up]* Where? *[Looking around]*

CHAU They're just the size of sparrows, and they don't bite
people.

ROSANNA If you see any, show me! *[Looks ahead]* What's that?

CHAU *[laughs]* It's the moon.

ROSANNA *[surprised]* So large, and so yellow? *[Fascinated]*

CHAU It's not blocked by tall buildings like in Hong Kong.
In early evening, when it first rises, it's really large.
That's probably because America is at a more northerly
latitude than Hong Kong.

ROSANNA *[laughs at herself]* So that's why some people say the
moon is bigger in foreign countries.

CHAU It's autumn as well.

ROSANNA I like autumn. It's so beautiful.

CHAU When I first got here, I found it beautiful too. But
now nothing's new anymore. Come to think of it,
autumn is a pain. You have to sweep all those leaves in
the front and back. It tires you out and you no longer
care how beautiful the weather is.

ROSANNA Do you take care of the whole house?

CHAU Ah . . . Well, I do what I can.

ROSANNA I heard this little garden is your creation. You know
how to grow vegetables too, don't you?

CHAU I learned to after I got here. There's so much space
here, in front and at the back. Even if you just let the
grass grow, you'd still have to take care of it. I'm a lot
happier growing vegetables and things to eat.

ROSANNA *[laughs]* That's typically Hong Kong. Make the most of
what you plough in.

CHAU *[smiles]* Yes, perhaps. But it's so unfair. There's hardly
any standing space in Hong Kong whereas here you
could fit a few Hong Kongs into the land by the
highway.

ROSANNA That's probably why so many people want to come
here. *[Spreads her arms]* So much space!

CHAU Well, if you want more elbow room, this is the place
for you.

ROSANNA *[looking at the moon]* How nice it would be if they
could give some space to Hong Kong. There are so few
people here, but so many in Hong Kong.

CHAU *[smiles wanly]* That's the way things are. It's never
meant to be fair.

ROSANNA No. Even the moon is larger. *[They look at each other, smile,
and turn to the moon.]* Have you been here four years?

CHAU Who told you that?

ROSANNA My cousin mentioned all of you in her letters. I knew about you guys long before I got here.

CHAU *[laughs]* What else did she say about me?

ROSANNA She said you were a good son. You write home regularly.

CHAU Oh.

ROSANNA Do you miss your folks in Hong Kong?

CHAU We all do. All foreign students miss home. You will too.

ROSANNA I miss my friends more. But I'm not a good child like you. Even if I missed home, I don't think I'd have the patience to write.

CHAU Sometimes it's not a matter of patience. It's a responsibility. It's almost unfilial if you don't write. *[ROSANNA looks at CHAU.]*

ROSANNA Have you been living in this house for four years?

CHAU Yes, almost. When I first got here, there weren't as many Hong Kong students. I looked everywhere and ended up renting a place with an Indian family. I stayed there two months. There were so many things I couldn't get used to. For instance—*[Smiles wryly]*

ROSANNA *[sympathetically]* I know. *[Looks unhappy]*

CHAU Then I met Wang Kuo-ch'ao and moved in here. It's not a bad place. We're all Chinese. So there's that sense of security and of belonging.

ROSANNA Security? Well, I haven't yet got anything to compare it with.

CHAU Hmm, as the Chief says, you're lucky. You were taken care of as soon as you arrived.

ROSANNA Well, maybe I'm in heaven and don't know it! *[Looks at the living-room]* Heaven? In this house?

[Lights in the back garden slowly fade.]

SCENE SIX

[Lights go up in the living-room. The folding table is still there. KWAN WING HONG is busily sorting out all kinds of application forms and prospectuses which are spread out on the table. His sister, CASSIE, is sitting next to him reading an old entertainment magazine from Hong Kong.]

HONG *[reading]* Financial aid. Tuition deferment . . . Student Alliance? . . . Hey, Cassie, why did you bring all these home? None of these are for course enrolment. What exactly—hey, are you listening to me?

CASSIE Hm?

HONG Why are you always reading gossip magazines?

CASSIE *[righteously]* Because I want to be informed about Hong Kong. I don't want to be out of touch, like you!

HONG You call this being informed? 'Movie star Miss Lau taken to court by two men'? This is very important information, I suppose? *[Changing his tone]* Who's this Miss Lau anyway?

CASSIE See? Told you you were out of it. *[Goes back to reading the magazine]*

HONG Okay. Let's not talk about her. I told you to get the enrolment forms and you picked up a bunch of garbage.

CASSIE I didn't know which ones to get, so I brought everything for you.

HONG For me? Your Majesty, it's your enrolment we're talking about, not mine.

CASSIE You wouldn't get them for me.

HONG Oh really! I do practically all her assignments for her. And she says I don't help her!

CASSIE I didn't know where to find the forms.

HONG You could have asked.

CASSIE *[on point of tears]* You know very well my English is not good . . . and I didn't know the word 'enrolment'. So—

HONG And reading gossip magazines will help improve your English, I suppose. *[Snatches the magazine away]*

CASSIE This is the only thing I can read. *[Snatches back the magazine]*

HONG You've done a whole year of ESL English and still haven't got the confidence to talk to people?

CASSIE *[angrily]* All right, then. Help me one more time and I won't ever bother you again!

HONG What do you mean?

CASSIE Get me a plane ticket to Hong Kong.

HONG My God—

CASSIE I'm useless. I can't get anything done. Nothing I do is right. Why should I stay? Remember, I didn't want to come here, you wanted me to and then when I got here you told me that everything I did was wrong!

HONG *[softened]* All right, all right. Just don't yell! Oh, what a nuisance!

CASSIE *[deliberately raising her voice]* You are a nuisance!

*[CASSIE stares at HONG and pouts. HONG gives up.
ROSANNA comes in from outside, followed by CHAU.]*

HONG *[stacking the forms together, to CASSIE]* Okay. I'll help you. But please don't act like a shy tortoise anymore. Now that you are in the States, you should stick your head out from your shell, look around, and try everything. Don't just bury yourself in this so-called Hong Kong culture stuff. This is not what you've come here for. Come with me. I might have some enrolment forms left.

CASSIE *[obediently]* Okay.

[ROSANNA walks by and says hello to CASSIE and HONG. HONG throws the forms into the rubbish bin. CASSIE follows clutching the magazine to her chest. Before HONG goes into his bedroom, he turns around and snatches the magazine from CASSIE and throws it into the rubbish bin. CASSIE turns back and sneakily picks it up from the bin.]

CHAU *[looks at the two, smiles]* Wing Hong is really nice to his sister.

ROSANNA A shy tortoise? *[Chewing on the implication of this remark]*

[Lights dim. CHAU goes down to the basement.]

SCENE SEVEN

[Lights up.

CHU LAI SHAN *comes in angrily, holding a file in one hand and a can of Coca Cola in the other. ROSANNA is drawing a plate of fruit.]*

SHAN *[loudly]* Damn! Damn! Damn! *[Plumps down on the couch wiping her face]* I want to kill those guys! *[Drinks the Coke and then puts it down with a plonk]*

[ERIC enters, holding his car keys.]

ROSANNA Sha Sha, what happened?

SHAN Something shitty! This morning I went to the college to see this counsellor at nine. They said he wasn't in yet. So I went there again at ten, but was told I had to make an appointment first. Fair enough, I said, could I make an appointment to see him now? No, he couldn't see me until two o'clock. Two o'clock! Well, okay, I said. When I got there again it was five past two, I was five minutes late, and they said this guy had already gone to a board meeting or something. Board meeting his arse! Anyway, I went back at three, and was told it was not the time for my appointment! Holy Jesus! I refused to leave, of course, and sat outside his office. But at about four, they turned off the lights and told me this bloody counsellor's office closes at four. I swore and cursed, and yelled at the reception people. In the end, they called security and threw me out!

ERIC Luckily I happened to be there. If I hadn't been there to calm things down, she might have ended up in jail.

SHAN In the States, you have to act tougher than these foreign devils. They think we Chinese are meek and mild, and they bully us. We have to stand up against those shit-heads.

ROSANNA Yes, my two weeks here kind of confirm what I heard about things here. Compared with Hong Kong, everything is slower and less efficient. And the pace of life—it's so different from Hong Kong.

ERIC That's the USA for you, kid! Take it easy, hang loose!

SHAN *[looks sideways at* ERIC*]* Is that right? Will you hang loose too? How about a drive-in movie tonight? Will that be loose enough?

ERIC Not tonight! The Chinese Student Union wants to compile a name list of the new students. I have to go and give them a hand. *[Looks at* ROSANNA*]* Besides, I told Rosanna I'd teach her how to drive tonight. *[Smiles at* ROSANNA*]* Right?

SHAN *[jealously]* You can teach her to drive any time. It doesn't have to be tonight!

ROSANNA Yes, it doesn't have to be tonight.

ERIC But I've told you I have to do the name list.

SHAN Okay. Hang loose with your name list then. *[Struts into the kitchen in faked anger]*

ERIC Hey, are you painting something, Rosanna?

ROSANNA It's an assignment. *[Covers up the picture]* Don't look yet.

ERIC When will you paint me a portrait?

ROSANNA Our class is looking for a model. There's a notice. Would you be interested?

ERIC I would, on condition that I pose only for you.

ROSANNA I'll keep that in mind. Right now I'm doing still life.

ERIC Oh, by the way, where's the Chief?

ROSANNA She's not home yet.

ERIC I got a letter from the landlord this morning. He
wants to transfer ownership of the house to his son,
and the son wants to re-assess the value of this
property.

ROSANNA Oh, is he going to raise the rent?

ERIC It's okay if he just wants to raise the rent. I'm just
worried that he might want to pull it down to build
an apartment building.

ROSANNA But this old house is so nice. It would be a shame to
pull it down.

ERIC What do they know about the historical value of a
house? Anyway, we've been here for such a long time,
it would be a lot of trouble to move out. Besides we've
all got rather attached to the house. [Sits beside
ROSANNA]

ROSANNA To the house? Or to someone in it?

ERIC To someone in it? To whom in particular? I have lots
of attachments.

ROSANNA [smiles] I'm impressed. I hear that you immigrated here
a long time ago. Where are your folks?

ERIC Not in this state, they're in New Jersey. I moved here
by myself. [Reaches for the fruits on the plate]

ROSANNA Don't you touch my models.

ERIC Sorry, sorry. These are your models?

ROSANNA For my assignment. But tell me, why did you pick this
house?

ERIC It's convenient.

ROSANNA Is that the only reason?

ERIC Well, [Solemnly] you don't seem to know what a sad
case I am.

ROSANNA You? A sad case? You pay only one third the tuition
fee that we visa students pay, and that's a sad case?

ERIC Let me tell you something about myself. I came to the
States in my early teens and became an American
citizen. In the last few years I've begun to get
interested in my Chinese roots, and I wanted to show
others the fine qualities of the Chinese. So I chose to
live in places where Chinese students live. That way I'd
have more contact with Hong Kong culture. I've taken
courses in Chinese history and I've learned martial arts.
And I try to go to all the activities organized by the
Asian-American societies. I want to be one hundred per
cent Chinese.

ROSANNA In some ways you are more Chinese than most
Chinese.

ERIC I take that as a compliment. By the way, can you do
Chinese dances?

ROSANNA I learned some in primary school, but I've forgotten
them all.

ERIC It only takes a little practice to get them back. I think
it's the most beautiful thing in the world for Chinese
girls to do Chinese dances. Will you dance for the
Chinese Student Union show later in the year?

ROSANNA No, thanks.

ERIC But helping the Chinese Student Union is the same as
helping the Chinese.

[SHAN *comes in from the kitchen with another can of soft
drink.*]

ROSANNA [*simultaneously*] I can't dance.

ERIC Show me, and I'll judge for myself.

SHAN Show what? What's going on?

ERIC Hey, Rosanna can do Chinese dances.

SHAN I can too! [*Holds up the soft-drink can in a Cantonese opera
pose and gestures*] Like so, and so, and so—

ERIC [*ignoring her, to* ROSANNA] Let's go to the Student
Union after your driving lesson tonight, to give them a
hand.

ROSANNA I'd rather not.

ERIC It wouldn't hurt to get to know some of the guys in
the Student Union.

SHAN What about me? I've been helping them. Can't I come
along?

ERIC [*tetchily*] Okay, okay. Let's all go. [*Goes to the basement*]

SHAN [*following him*] Where're you going?

ERIC To take a shower, okay? And don't you dare break in.
[*Disappears into the basement*]

SHAN Hah! [*Turns round to look at* ROSANNA, *thinking*]

[ROSANNA *is packing up her painting materials.*]

[*goes up to* ROSANNA] Fast work.

ROSANNA Huh?

SHAN Didn't take you long to get invited to driving lessons
and to the Student Union.

ROSANNA I wasn't keen to go. But he—

SHAN It began like that for me too!

ERIC *[comes back up suddenly, to* ROSANNA*]* If you see the
   Chief, tell her I want a word with her. I've got the
   landlord's letter. *[Smiles at* ROSANNA*, then goes down to
   the basement again]*

SHAN *[bitterly]* Fast work indeed! Okay, Rosanna, let's get one
   thing clear. I'm very aggressive. What I want, I get.

ROSANNA *[feels the animosity]* So?

SHAN Eric is mine. Don't you get any ideas about him!

ROSANNA *[laughs]* Ha! *[Lost for words]* I . . . I . . . haven't!

SHAN Just to let you know in advance, to avoid
   embarrassment later, I might as well tell you I moved
   into this house to be near him. I've done lots of silly
   things for him—like going to protests and sit-ins with
   him over the June 4th Tiananmen Incident and helping
   the Student Union sell 'goddess of liberty' statuettes.
   In the end some god-damned yuppies came up and
   accused me of trying to make a packet selling
   souvenirs. I've put up with a lot of shit for Eric. Why?
   [Lies down] You tell me!

ROSANNA *[sarcastically]* All for love, of course.

SHAN Yes, more or less. Oh, he's beautiful!

ROSANNA He is? *[Intentionally]* I hadn't noticed.

SHAN I don't mean his looks. Yeah, he's not bad, but I'm
   referring to the fact that he's an American citizen, and
   can live and grow old in this Beautiful Country.

ROSANNA What does that mean?

SHAN Hey, are you sure you are from Hong Kong? Marrying
   an American citizen is the quickest way of getting a
   green card.

ROSANNA The 1997 phobia?

SHAN 1997 or not, I wouldn't want to go back. Hong Kong
   is such a dog-eat-dog world, people fight each other
   like crazy. I don't want to join the rat race again and
   fight. It's a lot better here.

ROSANNA Your folks are all in Hong Kong?

SHAN They are all waiting for me to get married. And when
   I've become an American citizen, I can help them come
   over.

ROSANNA Heavy responsibilities!

SHAN That's because I am the only one to make it here. *[Sits
   up]* Now that I've let you into my secret, don't you
   meddle with things you are not supposed to.

ROSANNA Me? Come on. *[Forces a smile]*

SHAN Okay. We're friends! [*Extends her little finger*] Friends!
ROSANNA [*they link their little fingers*] Friends.
　　　　[SHAN *smiles triumphantly.*
　　　　Lights dim.]

SCENE EIGHT

[*When the lights go up again,* BRUCE LAMONT, *the new owner of the house, is in the living-room examining the place, a displeased look on his face.* LAU CHING NUEN *and* WANG KUO-CH'AO *are carefully explaining things to him.* KWAN WING HONG *stands at the door watching them and* CASSIE KWAN *sits on the stairs looking down.* BILL CHAN *spreads himself out on the couch arrogantly.*]

BRUCE I can't believe what I see. Tell me again, how many people live here?

CH'AO Well . . . Nine.

BRUCE I believe we rented this house to just one family.

BILL [*coldly*] We are all one family.

BRUCE Sure! [*Starts to look around*]

BILL We are all brothers and sisters!

BRUCE And I am Uncle Sam! The electric wiring. I'm sure it's against fire regulations to have all these external outlets added on the wall. [*Points to the wiring*]

CH'AO The computer needs an outlet.

BRUCE But they are all over the house. You've sub-divided the rooms, added electric wiring, planted all those God-knows-what in the garden, which is supposed to be just a lawn. And you have nine people living here!

NUEN But it has always been this way. Your dad, Mr Lamont, knew about us.

BRUCE My dad is my dad. It's now my responsibility to look after this house, and I want to see things done properly. I'm not going to take the responsibility if a fire breaks out because of power overloading; I might get sued! [*Shakes his head*] I . . . I'll just have to leave this in my attorney's hands. Sorry. [*Exits*]

NUEN Mr Lamont! Hey—[*Runs after him, followed by* CH'AO]

BILL Fuck him! He's so high and mighty about things! The arsehole! 'The kitchen is so greasy. You shouldn't grow things in the garden, shouldn't add any wiring, shouldn't sub-divide the rooms.' Shit! Let him look at housing in Hong Kong, it would scare the hell out of him!

HONG *[comes into the living-room]* They don't think the same way we do.

BILL I'd say this was racial discrimination! He doesn't want Chinese tenants, that's why he wants to evict us. I don't care where I live, but I won't be kicked out by a racist. I'll fight him! He can take us to court but I'll call him a racist and see what he can do. Yeah, if he sued us, he'd be stuck with us for at least another six months or a year! Huh!

HONG It may not be discrimination.

BILL Even if it isn't, I'll say it is! Racial discrimination is a trump card.

[NUEN comes in looking very tense. CH'AO is trying to comfort her. They sit down in the living-room. CASSIE makes a gesture to tell those on the upper floor that BRUCE LAMONT has left. ROSANNA and SHAN also come down to the living-room. They have changed their clothes.]

SHAN Has the damned *gweilo* left?

ROSANNA *[nods her head]* What's going to happen now?

BILL If the worst comes to the worst, we go to court.

NUEN *[nervously]* No, we can't . . . I don't want to make trouble. If we can't go on living here, we can move.

BILL He's the one making trouble! *[Fiercely]* Are you scared of him?

SHAN Joe Cool, stop barking like a mad dog! *[Gestures to him to calm down]*

BILL You stop! You women are all chicken! Chief, you are a nice person and I shouldn't pick on you. But I was pissed off seeing you talk to the foreign devil all meek and mild. You were too soft. Why? What are you afraid of?

NUEN I . . . I can't argue with what he says, that's why.

SHAN *[faces BILL]* Why didn't you say something when he was here if you're so smart?

BILL I did! Chief, softies like you let the damned devils exploit us!

NUEN Me? I . . . I didn't. Oh, I don't know.

BILL Of course you do. You're a Ph.D. student, you're smarter than me. If you don't stand up for us, who will?

CH'AO *[tries to end the argument]* I think we should see if there's a way out of this.

HONG Yes, maybe we should invite him to come again. He's our age, I'm sure we can sort things out and make a better arrangement with him. The wiring, for example, we can re-do that.

CH'AO Where are Ming Chau and Eric? See what they say.

ROSANNA Ming Chau has been in the basement all day.

CASSIE He got a letter from Hong Kong today and he's been shutting himself in the basement. He didn't even go to class.

HONG Really? *[Looks in the direction of the basement]* I'll get him. *[Goes down]*

SHAN I know what Bruce Lamont is up to. He wants to raise the rent.

ROSANNA I thought we'd got at least another year before the lease ran out!

NUEN He's got every reason to say we've violated the lease by sub-dividing the rooms, and changing the wiring. He can use that as the reason to evict us. There's nothing we can do.

BILL In a word, discrimination!

CH'AO *[in Mandarin, to himself]* Man bu jiangli.

BILL *[deliberately provocative]* What did you say? I don't understand Mandarin!

CH'AO Okay, I'll speak English.

BILL To hell with you! We're all Chinese. You should learn Cantonese. Most of us here are Cantonese.

CH'AO The tragedy is we can't use Chinese here, even among Chinese.

[HONG and CHAU come in. CHAU looks dejected.]

ROSANNA *[worried]* Ming Chau . . . what's happened?

CHAU What? . . . Nothing . . . *[Softly]* My father's had a stroke. He's in hospital.

CASSIE Is he okay?

HONG Phone home and find out.

CHAU I have already. My mother wants me to go home at once.

CASSIE Go back to Hong Kong?

CHAU I . . . *[Dazed, facing everyone]* I won't go home! *[Runs downstairs hysterically]*

SHAN What's wrong with him?

[Everybody is shocked and doesn't know what to do. Light change.]

SCENE NINE

[ROSANNA *steps out from the group who are still talking about* CHAU. *Spotlight on* ROSANNA.]

ROSANNA I never thought it would be like this. Being in
America is not as neat, as free, or as cool as I
imagined. Just look at this house—four walls, a roof,
and a pack of problems inside. They're not my
problems, on the surface of it, but since I live here,
they all seem to have something to do with me. Is it
because we're all in the same boat? Or because we treat
each other as one family? Maybe, that's why no one
wants to move out. This house is our refuge. We hold
on to each other to survive. [Shrugs] This house is
comforting. When classes are over and you're back, you
feel as if you're in Hong Kong, in your own home.
You forget you're in America. But is that a good
thing? Is it better to have what Ming Chau calls 'a
sense of belonging' or is it better to come out of your
shell, which is what Wing Hong urges his sister to do?
A sense of belonging? Belonging to what? To the
'shell', I suppose. [Laughs] But then, these problems
have set me thinking too, about questions like why I
should be living in this house, why I should get so
involved with this group, why have I come to America
and what am I doing here? America is too quiet, too
aloof, it makes you think strange things—I never used
to have any questions and problems; now I can't get
away from them. Oh God!

[At this moment, MING CHAU, having put on a jacket,
quietly comes up the porch from the back garden. Lost in
thought, he looks at the flower-bed. The light makes the tree
cast a long shadow on the scene, dappling his body with
patches of dark.]

ROSANNA [looking at CHAU] With so many problems, I really
don't know which one to tackle first. One night, I
saw Ming Chau standing there in a daze. He's a
typical filial son. When I saw him there like that
I felt bad. I felt the weight of his burden on my
shoulders. Why shouldn't I? We live under the same
roof.

SCENE TEN

[Light change.
    ROSANNA *and* CHAU *are on the porch.]*

ROSANNA You're not going back to Hong Kong to see your
    father because of your exams?

CHAU I made arrangements six months ago to take the CPA
    exam next month. That's for the Advanced Diploma in
    Accounting. If I went home now, it would mean giving
    up the exam. I've worked so hard all these years for the
    diploma. All that will go down the drain if I go home
    now.

ROSANNA You could take the exam when you come back.

CHAU There are only two chances each year for the CPA. If I
    miss this one I'd have to wait half a year. But my
    student visa expires in less than six months.

ROSANNA Couldn't you get another visa?

CHAU Another visa for just one exam? Where do I get the
    money?

ROSANNA Isn't your father in business?

CHAU He runs a small grocery store.

ROSANNA Maybe you could find a job in Hong Kong, save some
    money, and come back.

CHAU It's easier said than done. What can I do without a
    diploma? How much can I save? It'll take years!

ROSANNA But, don't you want to see your father at all?

CHAU I don't want to do anything! He picked a very bad
    time to be ill. I can't afford to go home.

ROSANNA Parents are a pain sometimes. You are a good son—at
    least you write home regularly.

CHAU Good? If I were really good to my family, I wouldn't
    have left them behind in the first place!

ROSANNA To be frank, Ming Chau, I think you're just using your
    exam as an excuse not to go home.

CHAU *[looks at* ROSANNA] Why . . . why do you say that?

ROSANNA I can . . . I feel . . . I . . . I don't know! *[Shrugs
    reluctantly]*

    *[*CHAU *goes up to* ROSANNA. *They look at each other
    briefly. Then* ROSANNA *looks down and* CHAU *turns away.]*

CHAU It's absurd, isn't it? The truth is, I don't want to go
    back to see him . . . to watch him die.

ROSANNA What?

CHAU I used to hate my father. He's a male chauvinist, a rough man. He treated my mother like dirt, beat her up, and yelled at her. I hated him. He didn't care about us. Then, the day I left Hong Kong he came to the airport to see me off. And he actually cried. *[Painfully]* Tears streaming down his cheeks. The damn fool! I'd never seen him cry. When I had to go, he grabbed me by the arm, tight, but we could say nothing. Why? Why had I never realized that he could be so. . . . In that instant, I caught a glimpse of what I never dreamt existed *[Pauses]* The letter he sent me this time, he said he wanted me to go home, he wanted to talk to me, to see me. But what's the point? To watch him die? It was difficult enough the last time we parted, I don't want another goodbye, this time for good. I don't want to go home! I hate him. Why did he let me know that he cared about me when it was too late?

ROSANNA Maybe we Chinese are not very good at expressing our feelings. Ming Chau, I envy you. I envy you your father. I'd die for a father who'd grab hold of my arm like that and couldn't say a word.

CHAU *[mischievously]* He said he'd wait for me. If I don't go back, he might hang on longer! *[Smiles bitterly]*

ROSANNA Everything you said tells me you miss your father. You want to see him and he wants to see you. Why go on pretending you don't like each other?

CHAU I'm not pretending. I'm scared about seeing him die, is that good enough? I'm scared about lots of other things too. If I left the States, I'd lose everything I've got, do you know that?

ROSANNA What do you mean?

CHAU As soon as I'm home I'll become a grocer, the grocer in my father's shop, the shop that I hate more than anything! Back in Hong Kong, I did my homework behind piles of salted fish and dried oysters. So I stank of the smell of the shop, and people called me 'Shrimp-paste'. But my father used to tell me I wouldn't be what I was without the grocery shop. And now he wants me to inherit it and keep it going forever. Can't you see what that means? If I'd wanted to be a grocer, I wouldn't have bothered to come here for more schooling. If I have to spend my life with salted fish and dried oysters, I might as well forget all my plans, forget about me! No, I'm not going home. I'm not going home for as long as I live.

ROSANNA Some Chinese families have this problem.

CHAU That's why I'm staying in America.

ROSANNA But we can't run away from our problems by hiding in America! Can't you see that?

[MING CHAU *looks expressionlessly at* ROSANNA.
Distant sound of flute music fades up. It's an excerpt from 'Olive Tree'.
Lights dim.]

SCENE ELEVEN

[*Flute music fades as lights go up in the living-room, now bright with morning light.* NUEN *is asleep on the couch under a blanket.* CASSIE, *listening to a walkman and trying to sing along as she peers at the lyrics on the cassette tape wrapper, is watering the potted plants on the window sill.*]

CASSIE [*as if singing to the plants*]

'How are you my friends?
Have you got used to things?
Is winter too cold for you?'

[*At this moment,* SHAN *comes up from the basement in a nightdress. She is looking around for someone.*]

SHAN Cassie, have you seen Eric?

CASSIE [*takes the earphones off*] What?

SHAN Eric. Have you seen Eric?

CASSIE Oh, Eric. He's taken Rosanna out for a driving lesson.

SHAN What? So early! [*Displeased*] I'd better keep a closer watch. [*Seeing* NUEN] How come the Chief is sleeping here?

CASSIE [*shrugs*] She was sleeping here when I came in. She probably stayed up late reading and was too tired to go to bed.

SHAN [*shakes her head*] Reading! She has so many books! It will take her a lifetime to finish them. What's the point of working so hard?

[CH'AO *comes in with a pot of steaming hot food.*]

CH'AO Breakfast is coming. It's hot.

SHAN [*seeing* CH'AO, *loudly*] Oh God! A man! No man is to see me before I've put on my make-up! [*Runs upstairs*]

[CH'AO *is annoyed,* CASSIE *puts down the things in her hands and hurries to put some newspaper on the table.* CH'AO *puts down the pot.*]

CH'AO We've got congee and deep-fried bread sticks from the Vietnamese store.

CASSIE Really? *[Opens the pot to take a look]*

CH'AO *[goes towards the couch]* Wake up! Breakfast time!

NUEN *[waking up]* Oh! How come I'm here? *[Gets up quickly]*

CH'AO I don't know. You were sleeping here when I came in this morning.

NUEN I don't remember coming down! Is this your blanket?

CH'AO Yes, I thought you needed it.

NUEN How come I can't remember anything?

CH'AO *[with a forced smile]* What does it matter? Go and wash your face now, and have breakfast.

[NUEN gets up but is unsteady on her feet. The sound of a car is heard.]

[goes up to help her] Are you okay?

NUEN *[nursing her head]* I feel a bit dizzy.

CH'AO Go and wash your face and you'll feel better. *[Gently helping her. He watches her go upstairs. He is very worried. He turns around and goes to the basement stairway.]* Hey, breakfast is ready if you want some!

[CASSIE comes in from the kitchen with some bowls and deep-fried bread sticks and sets them on the table.]

[picks up a letter and shows it to CASSIE] Here's a letter for your brother. It's from MIT. *[Gives her the letter]*

CASSIE What is MIT?

CH'AO *[explains patiently]* MIT is the Massachusetts Institute of Technology.

CASSIE *[pouting her lips]* Forget it! I'll never understand. *[Goes away, leaving the letter behind]*

CH'AO *[shaking his head in disappointment. In Mandarin]* Zhenshi beiai.

[At this moment ROSANNA and ERIC come in from outside. They are in heavy jackets. ERIC says hello and goes to the computer.]

CASSIE *[goes up to ROSANNA]* Hi Rosanna! Did you enjoy your lesson?

ROSANNA Enjoy? I was scared to death! To make it worse, the instructor roared like a tiger!

[Everybody laughs.]

CH'AO *[glances at the first floor and pulls ROSANNA aside]* Rosanna, don't you think your cousin has been acting strangely?

ROSANNA Well, yes. . . . She seems . . . nervous. I wonder why.

CH'AO I've tried to get her to talk, but she didn't say anything. I hope you'll talk with her when you have a chance.

ROSANNA But I don't even know what started it. What should I say?

CH'AO I don't know either. I don't know whether she's worried about the house, or her chances of finding a job after graduation. But she seems really low, and she won't say what's troubling her. That's what worries me most!

ROSANNA I'm not sure if she'll tell me.

CH'AO Well, if neither of us can help her, then we'll just have to try to talk her into seeing the student counsellor.

ROSANNA Okay. I'll see if I can get anything out of her.

[HONG *takes out a typed sheet.*]

HONG [*to* CASSIE, *grudgingly*] Here, it's done!

CASSIE Wow, thanks a lot.

HONG Let me warn you! Next time I won't do your homework for you. I'll be damned if I do!

CASSIE We'll talk about it next time. [*Takes the sheet and turns to go*]

HONG What? Is that all you are going to do?

CASSIE What do you mean?

HONG Aren't you going to read it first? If you just hand it in without even glancing at it, how can you learn anything? Come with me, I'll explain the points.

CASSIE [*reluctantly*] Well, okay. [*Says as she goes*] Don't take too long, please!

[*The two go inside.*]

SCENE TWELVE

[SHAN *comes down from upstairs, having changed her clothes. She looks at* ERIC *and* ROSANNA.]

CH'AO Do you want some congee? There are also deep fried breadsticks.

ERIC Great! Thanks.

[SHAN *goes to where* ROSANNA *is.*]

SHAN [*provocatively*] Well? Have you got your driving licence yet?

ROSANNA What?

SHAN Why do you have to start your driving lesson so early in the morning on a Saturday if you are not in a hurry to get your licence? *[Sits down]* You know, it's easy to pass the driving test here. You put on a low-cut T-shirt, wear a bit more perfume, get into the driving seat, pull your skirt up tactfully, and you get your licence right away! But I don't think I need to tell you all this. You're so smart. You know how to work on men. You know everything already!

ROSANNA Sha Sha, please don't talk to me like this. I'm not used to this kind of insinuation. I've got enough problems! *[Walks to the window]*

SHAN All right. No insinuations. So why are you seducing my boyfriend?

ROSANNA We go out for my driving lessons, nothing else.

SHAN What's the difference?

ROSANNA I—

ERIC *[intervening, to SHAN]* What nonsense are you talking about?

SHAN *[to ERIC]* I don't want you to go out with her behind my back.

ERIC *[glancing at CH'AO and trying to be patient]* How many times do I have to tell you before you'll listen . . . *[Glances at CH'AO again; he takes the hint and goes into the kitchen]*

SHAN *[looking sidelong at CH'AO until he has left]* Eric, I love you. *[Points to ROSANNA]* That woman does not.

[ROSANNA turns to go upstairs. ERIC grabs her by the arm to stop her. She is surprised.]

ERIC Rosanna, stay here. Now that the three of us are here, let's get things clear.

ROSANNA *[frees herself from ERIC]* I've got nothing to say. *[Stays there]*

ERIC No, we must get things clear. Sha Sha, the way I behaved might have given you the wrong impression . . . I might have . . . misled you. But—

SHAN *[trying to avoid a confrontation]* Let's have some congee first. *[Moves away]*

ERIC Sha Sha, I'm not your boyfriend! I've never thought of marrying you! I've never loved you! Is that clear?

[SHA SHA is holding a bowl of congee and a spoon. Her hands tremble so much the spoon rattles against the bowl.]

[looks at ROSANNA*]* As to my love for Rosanna—
[Correcting himself at once] Well, there may or may not
be love between us, but it's got nothing to do with
you.

*[*ROSANNA *is amazed and stands there motionless.]*

SHAN *[suddenly turns around, laughing hysterically]* Ha ha! This
has got to be the ugliest declaration of love I have ever
seen. You trample on a woman and use her as a
stepping stone to get on to another. Perhaps other
women might let you have your way. Not me! Mr Lok
Chi Shing, I, Sha Sha, do not give up without a fight!
[Without any warning, she pours the congee on ERIC*, throws
the bowl to the floor and runs upstairs.* ERIC *and* ROSANNA
are stunned.]

ERIC Damn—

ROSANNA *[immediately]* Are you all right?

ERIC I'm okay. *[Looks at his soiled clothes]* I . . . *[Looks at*
ROSANNA *as if he has something to tell her]*

ROSANNA You go and change your clothes. I'll clean up.

ERIC Okay. *[About to leave, but turns round to see how*
ROSANNA *is reacting to his confession of love]*

*[*ROSANNA *is looking at him too but bows her head when
their eyes meet.* ERIC *forces a smile, and goes down to the
basement.]*

SCENE THIRTEEN

*[*ROSANNA *picks up some paper napkins to mop up the mess on the floor.*
NUEN *comes down from upstairs, a cardigan draped over her shoulders.]*

NUEN Did you spill some congee?

ROSANNA Yes.

*[*NUEN *sits down on the couch, still looking disturbed.]*

NUEN What happened to Sha Sha? She was in a huff when
she came upstairs.

ROSANNA Oh? She . . . she had an argument with Eric. *[Throws
napkins into rubbish bin]*

NUEN Over what?

ROSANNA Ask her yourself.

NUEN Was it because of you?

ROSANNA *[surprised, then with forced jocularity]* Then, I really
should be struck dead by lightning.

NUEN *[quickly]* Don't, Rosanna, don't get involved. Your only purpose in the States is your studies. I've said before it's not worth it, getting entangled in relationships, especially triangular ones.

ROSANNA Oh, come on!

NUEN At your age it's easy to be blinded by love. But that's not what you need now. The important thing is to get your BA and prepare for your future. Don't waste time fighting with another woman for a man!

ROSANNA I'm not!

NUEN Denying it doesn't mean you're not part of it.

ROSANNA I . . . *[Confused]* I don't know . . . I really don't know.

[At this moment, CH'AO *sticks his head out from the kitchen. When* ROSANNA *sees him, he nods to her and ducks back into the kitchen.* ROSANNA *becomes even more disturbed and confused.]*

NUEN You can't run away from it by saying 'I don't know'. We're responsible for our own actions even in the confusion of this world. We don't just shirk our responsibilities by saying 'I don't know'.

ROSANNA *[blurts out]* Well said. But what about yourself—

NUEN Me?

ROSANNA Yes, you! Did you take responsibility for your actions? Aren't you mixed up in emotional relationships? Don't criticize me and quietly cover up the same fault in yourself.

NUEN *[righteously]* I don't know what you're—

ROSANNA Why won't you admit your relationship with Wang Kuo-ch'ao?

NUEN What relationship?

ROSANNA You like him, and he likes you. It's as simple as that!

NUEN We are friends and classmates, that's all. There's nothing between us!

ROSANNA Come on, open your eyes, look at yourself more closely.

NUEN *[simultaneously]* Don't change the subject. I'm talking about—

ROSANNA He's very concerned about you. When he sees you acting strangely and not telling him why, he gets so worried.

NUEN What? I'm acting strangely?

ROSANNA Yes. You've changed. You're often lost in thought, as if you're worried about something. You. . . . Wang Kuo-ch'ao really cares about you. Talk to him and you'll

know what I mean. I'm very confused right now, I
want to be alone! *[Makes to go to the back garden but
changes her mind and stays there]* Cousin, I'm not the
kind to run away from responsibilities. I've been acting
that way because I'm not sure what my responsibilities
are. Please don't ask me any more questions, and please
don't be so protective. I don't understand why so many
things have to happen to me. I . . . right now, I just
want to move out, keep well away from this big house
and turn my back on everything. *[Rushes out to the porch]*

NUEN Rosanna—*[Follows her out]*

*[They stand facing each other thinking about their own
situation.]*

Rosanna, I didn't mean to—

ROSANNA Shall we leave it? I can't talk now, all right?

NUEN Okay. *[Turning to leave]* Don't stay too long. It's getting
cold and it might snow anytime. Don't catch cold.

ROSANNA Okay.

NUEN *[takes off her cardigan]* Take this.

ROSANNA *[feels she should not accept it and yet grateful for the concern,
mildly apologetic about what she had said]* What about
you?

NUEN I'm going in! *[Goes back into the living-room]*

SCENE FOURTEEN

*[CHAU comes up from the basement with a small parcel. NUEN is watching the
bamboo scroll with the words in Chinese 'Don't forget you're on alien soil'. She is
deep in thought.]*

CHAU *[to NUEN]* Where's Rosanna?

NUEN Eh? Rosanna? Outside.

CHAU Chief . . . I've decided to go back to Hong Kong.

NUEN Oh? Really . . . Good. That's good. . . . When will you
come back?

CHAU I . . . I don't know. *[Forces a smile]*

NUEN But . . . What made you change your mind?

*[ROSANNA looks into the living-room and sees CHAU.
CHAU looks at ROSANNA.]*

CHAU I don't know. I want to go home and see my father as
soon as possible.

[NUEN looks at ROSANNA and then at CHAU.]

NUEN When will you leave?

CHAU I managed to book a ticket this morning. I'm leaving the day after tomorrow in the morning.

NUEN So soon! We'll miss you.

CHAU I'll miss you guys too.

NUEN Do they know yet?

CHAU No . . . except for Rosanna.

NUEN Oh! Good. We'll give you a farewell dinner!

CHAU I'll cook.

NUEN Sure. And thanks for helping us all these years!

CHAU Thank you for taking care of us.

[ROSANNA *comes in and stands at the door.*]

NUEN Come back as soon as you can. [*Smiles and pats him on the shoulder*] Have some congee.

CHAU Okay. [*Gets a bowl*]

[NUEN *casts a glance at* ROSANNA, *and goes into the kitchen.*]

ROSANNA [*still standing at the door*] So you've got a ticket!

CHAU Yes, one-way.

ROSANNA I nearly got myself a one-way ticket too, and flew out of this house. But I've thought things through. I'm going to follow your example. I'll stay and not run away from my problems.

CHAU What do you mean?

ROSANNA I'll tell you later. . . . I'll write to you.

CHAU Promise?

ROSANNA Promise!

CHAU [*puts the bowl down and picks up the small parcel*] Hey, this is for you.

ROSANNA What is it? Can I open it now?

CHAU Sure.

[ROSANNA *opens it and finds a number of small souvenirs.*]

Old mementoes that have been with me for ages. Sometimes they seem useful and sometimes not. It's a shame to throw them out and too much trouble to keep them. So I thought I would give them to you. [*Points to a box*] I got this music box in Philadelphia. [ROSANNA *opens the music box and it plays 'Blowing in the Wind'.*]

[*points to the box*] There's an American flag on the lid, and the lyrics say, 'The answer is blowing in the wind!' It's ironic. I don't even know why I'm in the States, or what I've achieved . . .

ROSANNA That's my trouble too.

CHAU You still have a lot of time. Make good use of it. I hope you'll find your American trip meaningful.

ROSANNA Thanks.

CHAU We are hard to please. When I had to leave Hong Kong, I didn't want to. Now that I'm about to go back, I don't want to either. We are so mixed up.

[ERIC *comes up from the basement in a new change of clothes.*]

ROSANNA [*sees* ERIC, *and closes the music box. To* CHAU] You still haven't shown me the bats.

CHAU I wonder if there are bats in Hong Kong.

ERIC What bats are you talking about?

ROSANNA Ming Chau says there might be bats under the roof.

ERIC Is that right? I've never seen any. Well, [*To* ROSANNA] I'll go exploring with you. See if we can catch any bats.

CHAU [*to* ROSANNA] There might be bats in Hong Kong. If I find any, I'll take you to see them when you come back.

ROSANNA Do! [*Looks at the two men and smiles vaguely. To* ERIC] Ming Chau is going back—

[*The telephone rings.* ERIC *answers it.* ROSANNA *puts the souvenirs back into the parcel.* CHAU *looks at* ROSANNA.]

ERIC [*speaking on the phone*] Yes! . . . Just a minute. [*To* CHAU] It's for you. Your folks calling long distance.

CHAU Oh? [*Answers immediately. His expression suddenly becomes grave.*] Yes . . . I know . . . I'm coming back at once. [*Hangs up, looking dazed*]

ROSANNA What's happened?

CHAU I won't be seeing my father. I'm going back . . . for the funeral. [*Kneels on the floor and cries*]

[*Lights dim as cacophonous music fades up.*]

SCENE FIFTEEN

[ROSANNA *is on the porch, looking pale and confused.*]

ROSANNA What a mess! It's absurd! Is there someone playing games with our lives? How do we get into such messes? Why can't we get a hold on our lives? Why? [*Opens the music box and hears: 'The answer is blowing in*

the wind!'] Ming Chau changed his ticket and left
today. He didn't say another word to me. But I could
feel the resentment in his eyes. Family ties are not
peculiar to the Chinese, other races have family ties
too. Why do we carry them like burdens? Like an extra
shell on a tortoise's back? Why do we find it so hard
to show our feelings for our families? Or could it be
that we simply don't know how to express our feelings?
[*Closes the music box*] Since I moved into this house,
things seem to be getting more and more complicated.
Or was I too simple-minded before? What will become
of me? So many things have happened! And the
feelings they stirred up rush at me, bombarding me. I
feel I am changing. I feel as if, in this changing
process, I'm becoming three-dimensional. [*Cheers up*]
And the things that I see, the things that I think
about, are becoming three-dimensional, too. When I
become aware of this, I feel refreshed. Like new snow
in late autumn, so cool, so wonderful! [*Looks up*] Oh,
here comes the snow!

[*Reaches her hand out to touch the snow. The sound of
Christmas bells rises.* ROSANNA *dances in the snow. The
melody of the chiming bells sounds like a variation of 'Olive
Tree'.*

  Lights dim.]
END OF ACT ONE

  [*During the intermission, the residents of the house come
out to clear the living-room and the porch. The house looks
nice and tidy again.*]

ACT 2

SCENE ONE

[ROSANNA, *in a thick sweater, is sitting on the porch, resting, a snow shovel in her hand. She takes off her scarf and gloves, rubs her hands, and blows on to her palms for warmth. She talks to the audience. As she speaks, she puts on her gloves again.*]

ROSANNA This is not the first time I've seen snow. The first time was beautiful, like a miracle. But then, after I'd seen snow a few times, it lost it's wonder and it became just a dull fact, something inevitable. And now it means work for us all. Oh, shovelling snow is such a chore. [*Moves downstage*] When we Chinese say, 'he only clears the snow at his own doorstep', we mean that as a criticism of the man's selfishness. Here, it is the law. It is self-discipline. If you don't clear the snow at your own entrance and your part of the pavement, you get prosecuted. Ming Chau used to shovel snow for us. He volunteered. Now that he's gone, we take turns. The snow is frozen now in early spring. It's torture to have to clear snow at minus ten degrees. Luckily for me, everytime it's my turn, Eric offers to help—

[*At this moment,* ERIC *comes out with two cups of hot chocolate in his hands. He has on a thick overcoat, a scarf, and snowboots.*]

ERIC Hey, here's some hot chocolate to keep you warm. [*Sits on the doorstep*]

ROSANNA [*turns to smile at* ERIC, *then turns back to the audience*] He makes torture bearable. [*Goes over to* ERIC *and sits beside him. She puts the shovel down.*]

SCENE TWO

ERIC [*gives her a cup of hot chocolate*] I've cleared the front pavement.

ROSANNA Thanks.

ERIC This snow is a real pain. So many cars have stalled. They're blocking the streets.

ROSANNA I used to have fairy-tale ideas about snow. I thought there would be an endless expanse of the purest white everywhere and I thought it would be wonderful to be able to make snowmen, and dance, and roll on the

snow. I never expected it to be so much trouble.
[Parodying the romantic style] All these romantic ideas
about snow are no more than a beautiful dream!

ERIC *[laughs. In parody, too]* Reality is cruel!

ROSANNA *[laughs, but quickly becomes serious, and speaks as she goes
back into the house with* ERIC*]* The fact is, a lot of us did
come here because of those beautiful dreams. I'll tell
you mine, you'll be amused. I came here to study fine
arts because I thought I could live like those artists we
saw in movies. They were free and romantic, they spent
their time in cafés reading poetry, and when inspiration
struck, they did a painting. And they lived in studios
converted from barns. But after this first semester, I
realized it just wasn't like that. Studying fine arts is
reading a load of textbooks, huge piles of notes, stacks
of art history. On top of that, you have to study
Biology, Geography, English, Math—everything! And
in greater detail than in high school. So much for my
fantasy!

ERIC I've seen some of your paintings, they're good.

ROSANNA But I paint stupid objects, like apples, worn-out shoes,
and all that. And charcoal is so messy. My human
models are old women so fat and wrinkled they scare
all inspiration away.

ERIC *[parodying her]* Oh, art! All our romantic ideas about
art are no more than a beautiful dream!

ROSANNA *[laughs]* Like my fantasies about the snow. Hm, there's
such a wide gap between dreams and reality.

ERIC You can still change your major if you want to; you've
only done one semester.

ROSANNA What choices do I have?

ERIC Switch to Computer Science! My major.

ROSANNA I'd rather die.

ERIC It's an art too!

ROSANNA *[disbelieving]* You must be joking!

ERIC When I do a computer programme, I very often think
that every time I press a button on the keyboard, I'm
activating an electric current. It travels into the CPU at
a speed of eighteen thousand miles per second. The
electric current splits into two, then four, and soon into
a thousand, a million smaller currents. Like fireworks,
they knock against each other and cross each other's
paths. The whole process lasts less than a hundredth of
a second and the small currents are turned into sparks.

These tiny sparks form themselves into words, which enter my eyes at the speed of light. Then they go into my brain, and my brainwaves send electric currents to my hands. So when I press another button, another electric cycle begins. Every cycle is one second in time. To me, the cycle is full of mystery and beauty. From one electron, a cosmos comes into being. And the side-effects of every cycle will lead to new wisdom. All that is wonderful, and to me, art.

[As ERIC *talks,* ROSANNA *listens appreciatively.*]

ROSANNA If we put it like that, everything is art.

ERIC Indeed, life itself is art.

ROSANNA Shovelling snow is art.

ERIC To study art but to find it not sufficiently artistic, that's art too.

ROSANNA Once in a while, if we could slow down, and think about life a bit, then everything would be art.

ERIC What you just said is art.

ROSANNA What you just said is art too.

ERIC [*moves closer to her*] You are art too.

ROSANNA [*avoids him*] Your hair is a bunch of art.

ERIC [*ruffles his hair*] Really?

ROSANNA [*laughs*] Of course it is art if it gets washed in a bowl of congee!

ERIC [*laughs at himself*] Could be.

ROSANNA Has Sha Sha done that to you again?

ERIC She hasn't. But she's left a few scratches on my car.

ROSANNA [*scared but laughs*] Your car door? Was that done by Sha Sha?

ERIC I can't think of anybody else.

ROSANNA For a while, I thought she was going to move out.

ERIC She won't. For one thing, she couldn't find a place this cheap. Besides, if she moved out, it would be like admitting that she wanted to avoid us.

ROSANNA Avoid you, not us.

ERIC Your cousin and you. Both of you refuse to admit it.

ROSANNA What do you mean?

ERIC You both refuse to admit that you're in love! Hey, you forced me into saying this!

ROSANNA [*a little shy, but quickly becomes firm*] I'm not refusing to admit it, I just don't want to accept it.

ERIC [*anxiously*] Why?

ROSANNA It's happened too fast. I never thought it would happen like this.

ERIC Is it because you want to concentrate on your studies and don't want to get involved in other things?

ROSANNA That's my cousin.

ERIC And you?

ROSANNA I'm not sure. Sometimes I feel I'm looking for answers.

ERIC *[tenderly]* Well, we've got time.

ROSANNA Who knows?

[A moment of embarrassed silence.]

ROSANNA *[changes the subject]* Didn't the landlord say he'd come over again? Have we got everything in order?

ERIC He should be around in a day or two.

ROSANNA Do you think he'll give us another chance? We've done almost everything he mentioned in his letter. We've even torn down the partitions for Ming Chau's bedroom.

[At this moment, BILL walks in unsteadily from the back alley.]

ERIC In the end, he'll make all kinds of excuses to kick us out.

BILL Hello!

ROSANNA Hi, Joe Cool. Why did you come in through the back door?

BILL *[dejectedly]* What difference does it make? Whatever is the most convenient. *[Opens the door and goes inside]*

ERIC Where's your Porsche?

[BILL does not answer. He crosses the living-room and goes down to the basement.]

[after BILL has gone] Joe Cool's been quite strange over the last few weeks.

ROSANNA He comes in very late at night.

ERIC And he's got that strong kitchen smell on him—

ROSANNA He smells like Ming Chau used to. Is he working in a restaurant?

ERIC I've not heard him say anything about that. But he comes in late every day and goes straight to bed.

ROSANNA That's unusual—He seems to be hiding something from us.

ERIC He doesn't have to tell us, I suppose. We're not his family.

ROSANNA No. Maybe I'm nosy, but maybe it's all part of living in the same house. I want to know what happens to every one of us.

ERIC This house has a weird influence on you. *[Pulls faces]*

ROSANNA Do you think the landlord will really pull down the house and build an apartment building?

ERIC Who wouldn't? There's money in it!

ROSANNA True. But as my cousin says, if the worst comes to the worst, we can move out. Right now, I suddenly feel the house is just a brief stop on my way. Why cling to it? *[They both make a gesture of helplessness.]*
[Lights dim.]

SCENE THREE

[Lights go up in the living-room. SHAN *leads* BRUCE LAMONT *in from the front door.]*

SHAN Well, have a seat, Mr Lamont. Can I call you Bruce?

BRUCE Sure. *[Smiles in a friendly manner, then turns to inspect the house]*

SHAN Please have a seat and relax! *[Pulls him to the couch and makes him sit down]* Is it cold in here? I can turn up the heat.

BRUCE No, I'm fine.

SHAN Something to drink? That would warm us up a bit.

BRUCE Okay. Yes. Whatever . . . Things sure look different. Hey, but the extra wiring is still there.

SHAN *[gets* BILL's *brandy and glasses from the bookcase and gives* BRUCE *a glass]* How about this?

BRUCE *[amazed]* Wow . . . *[Laughs]* What's the big occasion?

SHAN Nothing . . . Oh! Because you are our honourable guest. *[Pours brandy]*

BRUCE I'm sure! Where's—

SHAN *[kneels on the couch and offers him the bottle]* You want to drink from the glass? Or from the bottle?

BRUCE The glass is fine! *[As if to himself]* I can't believe this! *[Smiles and drinks]* Cheers!

SHAN *[drinks from the bottle]* Well, we did everything you said in your letter. We cleaned up everything—the kitchen, the yard, the basement, everything!

BRUCE *[smiles]* Not everything!

SHAN *[pours more brandy for him]* Come on, be nice. *[Thinks for a second]* Well, I cleared up my room too. Would you like to take a look at . . . my bedroom . . . Come on! *[Pulls him]*

BRUCE I'll see your room in a bit.

SHAN Maybe you'll get a pleasant surprise.

BRUCE What 'pleasant surprise'?

SHAN That's for you to find out. *[Puts a hand on his chest]*

BRUCE *[pauses]* I . . . I think I'd better wait . . . *[Catches her hand and removes it gently]*

SHAN *[moves closer]* You haven't got much time. Don't waste it! *[Grabs his hand and won't let go]*

BRUCE *[confused, in a soft voice]* Why . . . all this?

SHAN *[moves even closer]* For you . . . our honourable guest. *[Puts his hand on her waist]*

[ROSANNA suddenly comes in from the back door. SHAN and BRUCE LAMONT break up immediately.]

BRUCE Hi!

ROSANNA Oh. . . . Hi!

[ERIC comes in next from the backdoor.]

ERIC Eh? It's our landlord. Hi, Mr Lamont! *[Takes off overcoat]*

BRUCE *[nods to him]* Hi!

ERIC I didn't expect you so early.

BRUCE Well, things have to be done one way or another. Plus I'm having a good time here!

[ROSANNA, ERIC, and SHAN look at each other. They all know what BRUCE LAMONT means.]

ROSANNA Excuse me. *[Goes to the stairs and shouts]* The landlord's here!

SHAN *[to BRUCE LAMONT]* Have another? *[Refills his glass]*

BRUCE Gee. . . . Thanks.

SHAN Cheers. *[Drinks from the bottle again]*

BRUCE Cheers.

[CH'AO, HONG, and CASSIE come into the living-room from upstairs and their own rooms. CASSIE, looking scared, stares at BRUCE LAMONT and hides behind HONG. ROSANNA joins them.]

BRUCE *[noticing the group behind him]* Oh! Is everybody here? *[Some say yes, and some say no.]*

HONG *[to CH'AO]* Where's the Chief?

CH'AO *[points upstairs]* She's coming down.

BRUCE Well, guys, I'm here today to confirm with you all that your lease will expire on . . . *[Gets a document from his jacket and reads]* on June first, this calendar year.

And I don't think I can renew this lease with you.
Sorry. *[Smiles]*

*[There's an uproar and the group starts discussing the
implications.]*

ERIC But you . . . you said in your letter that if we fixed up
the house you'd extend the lease with us!

[Everyone agrees. Just now, NUEN *drifts down from upstairs
like a phantom.]*

HONG Don't you want to look around first and see what we've
done?

SHAN And my room! Remember?

BRUCE Hey, hold your horses! I'm not here to argue with you,
or you, or you. I've decided I'm not going to rent this
house to a bunch of foreign students anymore!

CH'AO What's wrong with foreign students?

HONG We pay rent, don't we?

[Everybody looks agitated. BRUCE LAMONT *smiles blankly
at them.]*

ROSANNA Mr Lamont. If you had already made up your mind,
why did you make us clean up the house?

CASSIE Yeah!

BRUCE You are supposed to clean up the house and restore it
to its original condition before you move out!

ROSANNA *[to everyone]* So it's a trick. He makes us clean the
house, and then tells us he won't renew the lease and
he kicks us out!

[Another uproar]

CASSIE Chief, you talk to him!

NUEN Eh? . . . Er . . . *[Embarrassed at being forced to negotiate]*

CH'AO But you will let us stay here for another five months
until the lease runs out, right?

BRUCE That's right.

SHAN Is there anything we can do to change your mind?

BRUCE *[smiles]* You can try, but honestly I don't see that
there's a lot you can do!

ERIC You want to pull down this old house to build a new
apartment building!

BRUCE Nope! This lot isn't big enough, I've checked. But . . .
well, I don't know if I should tell you—

SHAN Tell us! Tell us!

BRUCE The city's Historic Buildings Society wants to designate
this entire street of old Victorian houses as a historical
landmark. And all the houses have to be preserved.

SHAN Wow! How many houses have you got here?

HONG What's that got to do with us?

BRUCE Nothing! And that's the heart of the matter. This historical landmark has nothing to do with you Chinese people. It belongs to us, the Americans!

ERIC I am an American too.

BRUCE You? *[Laughs]* I don't see any resemblance!

NUEN You're a racist!

BRUCE *[smiles confidently]* Don't make an issue out of it! A lease is a lease. I don't have to renew it with you, and you don't have to stay on.

CH'AO But isn't this still a residential neighbourhood?

BRUCE I'll rent it out to somebody else!

HONG And raise the rent!

BRUCE Definitely! It's our landmark! At least I can rent it out to someone with better taste!

SHAN I've got taste! *[Looks seductively at him]*

BRUCE *[ambiguously]* That I've got to see . . . *[To everyone]* Well, good day, gentlemen and ladies *[To SHAN]* And you, Suzie Wong! *[Makes to go]*

SHAN Hey, wait.

BRUCE Yes?

SHAN Can you give me a ride?

BRUCE Where to?

SHAN Wherever you're going. *[Follows him out without any hesitation]*

ROSANNA *[waits until they are gone]* Why did Sha Sha leave with that bully?

HONG That's her own business; leave her alone.

[They look at one another, upset.]

CH'AO *[in Mandarin]* Women shoupianle.

CASSIE What's that?

HONG *[translating]* We've been tricked!

ERIC *[angrily]* That shithead said I wasn't an American. I bet I could take him to court for saying that.

CASSIE We should have treated him to some Chinese Kung Fu.

ROSANNA If Joe Cool had been here, things might have turned nasty.

HONG We'd better put away the bottle. *[Puts the bottle back onto the bookcase]* If Joe Cool found out that Sha Sha gave his brandy to that foreign devil, he would kill her.

ROSANNA He might, he just might.

[Everybody is airing their views.]

NUEN *[suddenly speaks and everybody is surprised]* Could we cool down a bit?

[The noise stops and everybody, especially CH'AO, *looks at* NUEN.*]*

ERIC *[to* NUEN*]* I won't take it like this!

HONG Can we appeal?

NUEN *[immediately]* I don't know, I really don't. Why do you all ask me? I have no answers. I have no answers for anything! I'll move out if I have to. Please don't turn it into a fight. I have a bad headache. Don't ask me any more questions. *[Nurses her head]*

CH'AO *[comforts her at once. In Mandarin]* Suanle! Suanle! Meiwentile! It's okay. No problem.

*[*CH'AO *makes* NUEN *feel better, but everyone else is still at a loss what to do.]*

SCENE FOUR

[Lights grow dimmer, more meditative.]

ROSANNA *[comes forward, picks up the books lying on the television]* No problem. It's okay. We stay on in the house, we have 'No problem' with the landlord. We want to go on living here in peace and we say 'no problem'. But beneath the 'no problem' surface, our problems grow bigger and bigger. We all try hard to have the lease extended. Why? Is it because we really love staying in this house? Or is it because we are all as shy as a tortoise and would rather hide our heads inside our shells?

[Picks up a student handbook of the University of Texas at Austin, and walks into the kitchen with an uneasy mind.]

SCENE FIVE

[Lights grow stronger. BILL *enters. The living-room is empty. He searches a drawer and finds a parcel which he opens on the table. Inside the cloth bag in the parcel, there is a pistol. He covers the pistol with a towel. Then he picks up the telephone and dials a number.]*

BILL Hello. Is Jimmy Wong there? *[Looks at the pistol]* Jimmy. Bill here. Remember what we said last time? . . . Yes, I said I'd sell it. Yes, sell it to you.

[ROSANNA *comes in to put the student handbook back on the tea table. She's taken aback when she sees the pistol.*]

[*still on the phone*] Spare me the questions! If I let you buy it, it's yours. . . . You can say I'm tired of it. . . . No, there's no licence! Why else would it be so cheap? [*Notices* ROSANNA *and covers the pistol with the towel at once*] Bloody hell! I'll keep it if you don't want it. Tonight? I'm busy tonight. [*Hangs up and talks to* ROSANNA] How come you don't make any noise when you walk?

ROSANNA [*points to the pistol*] Where did you get that?

BILL [*looks round to make sure that nobody else is around, then boldly takes the pistol out*] Cool, isn't it? In the States, as long as you have the money, it's easy to get a gun.

ROSANNA Really?

BILL Of course. If that Lamont guy barges in again, I'll treat him to something real heavy. That's American law as I see it. Impressed?

ROSANNA Very.

BILL Life is short; come what may I'm going to enjoy it to the full. Here in the States, there's so much freedom. Take advantage of it, use it, get a kick out of it! Back in Hong Kong, you can't get a beauty like this. Here, you flash it around and they treat you with respect.

ROSANNA Then why do you want to sell it?

BILL Who told you that? I'm not selling it. [*Puts the pistol away immediately*]

ROSANNA You're not broke, are you?

BILL Like hell I am. No way!

ROSANNA They say you're working in the restaurant Ming Chau used to work in.

BILL Who told you that?

ROSANNA A college friend of mine.

BILL Really? No . . . I'm standing in for a friend a couple of days—he's ill.

ROSANNA I see.

BILL But don't spread it around. I don't want people to get the wrong idea and think I've come down in the world. It's no laughing matter, is that clear?

ROSANNA Yes, yes. I won't mention it.

BILL Good girl. You are okay. If it wasn't for Eric chasing after you all the time, I might take you out—I'd drive you around.

ROSANNA Someday, perhaps. *[Laughs]*

   BILL Don't tell the Chief.

      [The doorbell buzzes. ROSANNA makes to go and open it, but BILL stops her.]

      Don't let them know I have a gun, okay?

ROSANNA *[goes to the door]* Okay!

      [BILL quickly puts the parcel back into the drawer. ROSANNA shows a man in. He is LAN QIAN, a student from China. He is dressed plainly and conservatively, with a briefcase in his hand.]

      [shouting down the basement stairs] Eric, someone looking for you!

   ERIC Yeah! Coming!

      [LAN QIAN sees BILL and nods to him. BILL just stares at him and then turns away.]

   QIAN *[to BILL, in Mandarin]* Ah, *wo zai* urban development *de ketangshang jianguo nin.*

   BILL *[not listening, in an unfriendly tone]* We don't use Mandarin here!

      [Just then, ERIC runs up to the living-room from the basement.]

   ERIC *[to LAN QIAN, first in Mandarin]* Eh, *zheme zao jiulaile.* Let me introduce you. This is Rosanna. This is Bill. This is Lan Qian.

      [All smile politely. BILL leafs through a TV guide.]

      Have a seat. *[Gestures QIAN to sit down]* Lan Qian is from mainland China.

   BILL He looks it! They all look the same, the whole lot of them.

   ERIC Lan Qian is staying with us . . . for a short while. He can use Ming Chau's bed. I think that'll do—

   BILL Who says he can move in?

   ERIC He . . . he suddenly had to look for another place to stay. So this morning I told him he could come here.

   BILL Hey, how do we know whether we want him? Eric, did you ask us before you told him? *[Shouts at the stairs]* Hey, come on down you guys!

   QIAN *[in Mandarin]* You *shenme wenti ma?*

   ERIC No, no problem. It'll be—

      [CASSIE and SHAN come in from the kitchen. They are eating ice-cream.]

CASSIE What is it?

SHAN Is there a fire or something?

BILL Just a minute!

> [QIAN *bows to* CASSIE *and* SHAN. *They look at him curiously.* SHAN, *seeing* ERIC *and* ROSANNA *sitting together, goes up to them and plants herself between them.* CH'AO *and* NUEN *come downstairs from the first floor.*]

> [*to* CASSIE] Where's your brother?

CASSIE He's out mailing a letter for me.

BILL Okay. That means everyone's here. Now folks, Eric says he has invited this friend of his here to replace Ming Chau. Do we want him?

QIAN [*introduces himself in Mandarin*] Gewei, woshi Lan Qian—

CH'AO [*introduces himself*] Wo jiao Wang Kuo-Ch'ao.

QIAN [*in Mandarin asks* CHAO *if he is from mainland China*] Ni yeshi cong Zhongguo lai—

CH'AO [*replies in Mandarin*] Bu. Taiwan.

BILL Hey, no Mandarin in this house!

CASSIE Yeah.

BILL Now, do we want him or do we not?

NUEN Ming Chau . . . Ming Chau's bedroom has been knocked down.

BILL And we said we'd each chip in a bit more for the rent rather than have another person here.

SHAN How come Eric made the decision without consulting us?

BILL [*smiles to* SHAN] You're on my side, aren't you?

> [SHAN *puts on an affected smile.*]

ERIC Come on! We're just helping the Chinese Student Union to find a place for a newcomer! Lan Qian is looking for a place to stay because of some . . . some unforeseen problem. We're all Chinese, aren't we? Don't we want to help our fellow Chinese?

SHAN I don't know. He and his college friends from China are so cliquey and they don't treat us Hong Kong students as Chinese at all. What unforeseen problem does he have to make him want to share a place with a bunch of non-Chinese?!

ERIC He . . . [*To* QIAN] Do you mind if I tell them the truth?

QIAN [*to* ERIC *in Mandarin*] Rang wo ziji lai jiang haoma?

ERIC [*relieved*] Sure. He says he'll explain the situation himself.

QIAN [*in Mandarin*] Wo shi you Nanjing yixueyuan zhuanguolai—

BILL [*impatiently*] No Mandarin!

QIAN Okay, okay.

ERIC Let me tell them. After the June 4th Incident in Beijing, the Chinese Student Union petitioned the White House to allow Chinese graduates from the Mainland to extend their visas so that they wouldn't have to go home immediately. The petition was granted. But the Chinese students involved got a letter from the Chinese Embassy telling them not to extend their visas, but go home instead. There were a handful who didn't want to go home, and recently they've received threats on the phone. [*Everybody shows concern.*] They were warned on the phone that if they didn't leave the States at once, their lives would be at risk. They were told, too, that someone was following them, watching their every move—

SHAN [*disbelieving*] Is it so serious?

ERIC I don't know. Maybe someone is just doing it for a laugh. But Lan Qian thinks it's safer to find—

BILL [*cutting in*] A hiding place, right?

ERIC Yes, more or less.

QIAN I . . . I didn't really want to bother you. This is my last resort.

CH'AO Have you reported it to the police?

QIAN No, I haven't. We thought the police might not trust us. And we don't much like the police here anyway.

NUEN But moving in with us doesn't really help you solve your problem. They could track you down just as easily and make threatening phone calls.

ROSANNA [*to* ERIC] Does he know we've only got a few more months here?

ERIC I've told him.

BILL The Chief is right. If we let him move in, we might get into trouble ourselves.

NUEN I didn't mean that. But—

SHAN Don't forget their habits are very different from ours. What would we do if he brought his spitoon with him?

ERIC Don't try to stereotype people, please!

SHAN [*angrily*] I'll say what I want. You have no business stopping me!

QIAN *[embarrassed]* I, . . . I'm sorry. Please don't let me make things difficult for you. I'll go look for some other place. *[Turns to leave]*

ERIC No, we—

QIAN It's okay. I know I'm not welcome here. There's no point forcing yourselves to take me in. Even if you let me stay, I wouldn't feel comfortable. I think . . . *[Smiles]* I should go. Thank you. *[Leaves]*

CH'AO We could put this to a vote. *[Stops him]*

BILL *[to CH'AO]* Vote your arse! Let this Mainland guy go. Fuck!

QIAN *[at the door, to BILL]* I'll go, don't worry! But I don't understand why you Hong Kong people are so complacent. To be frank, very soon you'll find that we're all in the same boat. There's little to distinguish you as better off than I am. Very soon, you and I are going to be the same. Homeless. *[Looks at everyone and leaves]*

[ERIC follows him out, and CH'AO runs after them.]

BILL *[immediately]* To hell with him! These damn Mainland arseholes are the worst racists in the whole damn world! They never treat Hong Kong people as Chinese. Right? Sha Sha?

SHAN Go kill yourself!

[BILL, feeling like a fool, goes back to the basement.]

ROSANNA Why did we behave like that? We didn't want to help him, okay, but did we have to treat him like that?

SHAN You should talk to your Eric! You should ask him why he invited a total stranger to share the house with us. It's asking for trouble!

ROSANNA Didn't you guys tell me this story about June 4th? How in the heat of it all, you all went downtown to join the protests? All felt like warm-blooded citizens of China and thought it was your duty to support the Mainland students? And now, we have a Mainland student desperately needing our help; why are we so indifferent? We know deep down that these two things are one and the same. Why is it that we were so concerned about the Chinese ten thousand miles away and yet wouldn't do a thing for a Chinese student who has turned up at our door?

SHAN Talk! Talk! Why come to America if you're so eager to help them?

ROSANNA *[offended]* I . . . Well, the fact that I came here doesn't mean I won't go back to Hong Kong!

SHAN Really? If you really meant it, you wouldn't have to seduce Eric!

ROSANNA What? You don't know what you're saying!

SHAN In front of everybody, do you dare deny that you are after an American citizen because you want a passport?

ROSANNA I came to the States to better myself. My objective is different from yours.

SHAN Bullshit. Everyone can say that! *[Sarcastically]* Oh, I'm not going back to Hong Kong because I want to better myself!

CASSIE Sha Sha, be reasonable! *[ROSANNA is at a loss for words and runs upstairs.]*

SHAN Well, I was just telling her the truth.

NUEN Sha Sha, not everyone of us is like you.

SHAN Really? Chief, you're probably so confused by your blessed thesis that you don't see what's happening. Eric and Rosanna are madly in love!

NUEN I have noticed. That and so many other things have happened. . . . That's why I'm worried.

SHAN *[looking immensely proud of herself]* By the way, Chief, you don't have to worry about the house. I might be able to make Bruce Lamont extend the lease for two more years!

CASSIE Bravo! Sha Sha is going to wipe out the foreign devil!

SHAN *[smiles victoriously]* If you want the house to stay unchanged for fifty years, you shouldn't do it the hard way and fight it head on. The soft approach works better!

[CASSIE and NUEN stare at SHAN as she struts out complacently.
Music.
Lights dim.]

SCENE SIX

[Dusk. The scattered chirps and warblings of birds announce the arrival of spring. ROSANNA and ERIC are home. ROSANNA is holding a bouquet of flowers that ERIC has given her.]

ROSANNA *[stops on the porch]* That day when Sha Sha quarreled with me, I blurted out that I wanted to come to the

States to 'better myself'. *[Smiles wryly]* What a silly
thing to say. Sha Sha could have said it herself. When I
was back in my room, I sat there in a daze, amazed at
how foolish my remark was! But, like a thunderbolt, it
also made me realize that the crucial question was not
what I wanted to do in the States but what I wanted
to do after the States. Do you get my point? Now that
I've seen so many crises in the house, I'm beginning to
wonder why I'm here in the States at all!

ERIC How convenient! I walk my girlfriend home, and I'm
home too. Hey, Rosanna, wouldn't you say we're living
together?

ROSANNA Six million people in Hong Kong live on the same
island. Would you call that living together?

[ERIC tries to kiss ROSANNA, but she pushes him away.]

Don't do that, or I'll get struck by lightning! *[Pushes
the door open and goes in]*

ERIC What? *[Follows her in reluctantly and turns on the lights in
the living-room]*

ROSANNA *[continues to think aloud]* I'd never have thought that
what Sha Sha said would help me see things in such
sharp focus!

ERIC It's good to have her yell at you, isn't it? She should
do it more often! *[Loosens his tie]*

ROSANNA You're not listening. I said I wanted to know what I
should do after the States.

ERIC 'After the States'? What do you mean? You can stay
here.

ROSANNA But I'll have to leave one day.

ERIC Why?

ROSANNA I'll have to leave after graduation.

ERIC After graduation, visa students have ten thousand ways
of staying in the States. Get a job! Find a sponsor.
Marry an American!

ROSANNA *[hits him]* Oh, come on!

ERIC You've heard Sha Sha's theory. Over 60 per cent of the
students from Hong Kong now try to stay behind after
graduation. There are ways and means.

ROSANNA They might stay, but that doesn't mean I will.

ERIC You want to go home?

ROSANNA That's what troubles me most.

ERIC *[sits closer]* Isn't there something here that would keep
you?

ROSANNA *[looks at him knowingly]* Yes, certainly—*[Thinking]*

ERIC *[holds her hand]* Tell me.

ROSANNA Freedom . . . wild ducks on the lakes . . . the mountains, the lakes . . . the space, the air . . . the self-respect most Americans have . . . the big house . . . the back garden . . . you . . . the big moon in the sky . . . the flowers . . . *[Stands up and unwraps the bouquet]* Thanks.

ERIC Just a second. Tell me more about the third to last item.

ROSANNA What's that? *[Goes to the shelves to find a vase]*

ERIC Me!

ROSANNA If I go home after graduation, will you come with me?

ERIC Yeah! Sure! I haven't been back for over ten years. Yeah, I'd love to, I'll gorge myself on all the wonderful food, and get a new graphics card. They say computer software is much cheaper in Hong Kong.

ROSANNA I mean stay in Hong Kong for good.

ERIC For good? Why? Why would you want to live there again?

ROSANNA You're a democracy activist, and a Student Union executive. You said you wanted to find your Chinese roots. Have you ever thought about going back to do something?

ERIC You don't have to go to Hong Kong in order to promote democracy! Hong Kong can't compare with the States when it comes to freedom of expression. That's why many democracy fighters prefer to set up base here.

ROSANNA Don't you have any feelings for Hong Kong?

ERIC Yes, but I've been in the States for so many years, I'm attached to the States too. It's like the attachment I have for this house.

ROSANNA I see. But I've been in the States less than a year. My feelings for it have no roots. That's why I want to go home.

ERIC But what for?

ROSANNA It's like my feelings towards the house—there's no sense of belonging here. And I hate the tension between the Chinese and foreigners, and the tension among the Chinese themselves. Or perhaps *[Playfully]* I choose to go back because everyone else wants to stay!

ERIC That's blind rebellion! You're rebelling for the sake of rebelling!

ROSANNA Rebellion is not necessarily blind.

ERIC Just look at the size of Hong Kong! It's as small as a black bean and yet to you it's a pearl! You people from Hong Kong are parochial. Short-sighted frogs that dare not leap out of a drying well!

ROSANNA If we are short-sighted frogs, what are you? One moment you are Chinese; another moment you are American. I know what you are—you're a bat. A bat in the house. You are half bird and half mouse. No wonder Ming Chau said there were bats around the house!

ERIC Hey! What are we doing? Are we talking heart to heart or are we quarrelling?

ROSANNA Short-sighted frogs and bats don't mix. How can they talk?

ERIC [cheekily] At least they are both night prowlers. They are both most active after dark. [Tries to kiss her]

ROSANNA [picks up the vase] Please go away! [Goes into the kitchen to avoid him]

[ERIC is disheartened. He catches sight of HONG coming up from the basement stairs and going down again.]

ERIC [annoyed] What are you doing?

HONG Sorry Eric. I was going to use your computer to type a letter to MIT. I was—

ERIC Did they accept you?

HONG Yes, and I was given a scholarship too.

ERIC Bright kid! When did you know? I've never heard you say anything about it.

HONG Oh, I've known for quite a while. But I couldn't make up my mind. So—

ERIC You can't make up your mind about a scholarship at MIT? That's madness!

HONG No, I know it's the chance of a lifetime . . . but I . . . I'm worried about Cassie.

[ROSANNA is coming out from the kitchen holding the vase.]

If I'm not here, Cassie will have no one to take care of her.

ROSANNA [to HONG] Where are you going to? [Puts the vase down]

HONG I want to go to MIT for graduate school. They've given me a scholarship.

ROSANNA Wow! Congratulations!

HONG Rosanna, please keep this a secret and don't let Cassie
know. I still haven't quite made up my mind. I know
she couldn't cope if I went. So at first I thought I
should give it up—scholarship and all. I need to keep
an eye on her, you see!

ROSANNA Take her along if you're so worried. Don't throw away
the chance!

HONG How could she go to MIT?

ERIC Not MIT. You could find her a school nearby.

ROSANNA Do you think you're still living in the days of the
sentimental Cantonese films thirty years ago? Give up a
scholarship for your sister? Don't! You must take the
scholarship and go to MIT!

HONG I think so too! That's why I've finally decided to go
and leave Cassie here. I don't want her to think that
she can lean on me for the rest of her life. *[Smiles]*
Sometimes I really want to get away from her. *[Smiles]*
Stupid, isn't it? Like a soap opera! This morning, I
went to the Student Office to get her first term results
for her, I thought she hadn't collected them yet because
she didn't know where to go. But when I got the
results, I was shocked. Straight Fs, all five subjects! She
scored an F for Basic Algebra too, and that's a subject
every Chinese student gets an A in. She drives me up
the wall!

ROSANNA You've done everything you could for her.

HONG That's why it hurts.

ERIC *[irritated, looks at* ROSANNA*]* There are many things
that hurt!

HONG That's why I thought I shouldn't let her lean on me
any more! So long as I'm with her, she'll never pull her
socks up. What riled me even more was when I ran
into her in the Student Centre, she was reading a Hong
Kong gossip magazine. I told her off there and then.
But she said it wasn't her fault. The fault was with the
multiple choice questions. There were so many of them,
and so little time. She even blamed me for not taking
the exams for her! So it's all my fault! Huh! I might as
well go to classes for her!

ROSANNA She's gone too far, but—

HONG That's not the end of the story. After this row, Cassie
walked off like a shrivelled bitter melon and I felt
really bad. Then someone tapped me on my shoulder.
It was my professor. He had been watching us all the

time and had come over to console me. But he said, 'Having some problems with your wife?' 'My wife'? I told him I was talking to my sister. But my professor said he'd seen us together so often he thought we were husband and wife. My God, husband and wife! I quickly did a survey. I asked my professors in Electrical Engineering and they all thought Cassie was my wife. Holy Moses, do we look like a married couple?

ERIC *[coldly]* Yes, rather incestuous!

ROSANNA Don't be obscene!

HONG But this is really obscene. I made up my mind right away and decided to go to MIT. So I came back to type the letter.

ROSANNA You've been going on and on. But how do you think Cassie will take it?

HONG I just don't know. *[Lowers his head]* I don't have the heart to dump her here. . . . But I don't want her to follow me to MIT. I wouldn't have time for her anyway. *[Worried]*

ROSANNA Let her stay here. We should be able to help her.

HONG That's the problem. She's always hanging around with Sha Sha. I don't like it. *[To ROSANNA]* When I'm gone, could you keep an eye on her?

ROSANNA Me? That's not a very good idea, Wing Hong. If I helped her, I'd end up doing what you've been doing. If you want Cassie to be independent, you should let her look after herself.

ERIC You really are a different person from when you first got here.

ROSANNA Am I? *[Smiles, and turns to HONG]* Don't worry about Cassie. She'll be fine as long as she goes on living in the house.

HONG Yes, but unfortunately the lease is running out.

ERIC True, but we don't have to break up.

HONG Chief is graduating. Ming Chau has gone. And now it's my turn. How can we not part company?

ERIC Come on. Stop this nonsense! If you want to type your letter, do it. *[Switches on the computer]*

HONG I probably did something terrible to my parents in my previous life. That's why they sent me this sister to punish me forever!

[They laugh. HONG sits down and ERIC helps him with the format.]

SCENE SEVEN

[Light change.
   ROSANNA *comes forward.]*

ROSANNA It was like a thunderbolt again! What Eric said. Have I changed that much? I was certainly surprised that I could talk to Wing Hong the way my cousin talked to me—full of kind words and well-meaning advice. I don't think I knew what I was saying but it sounded convincing. The fact is, I've learned from everyone in the house. From Wing Hong and Cassie for example. They're so close, and love each other so much, and yet they can't grow up because they're so attached to each other. That sets me thinking about my relationships with those around me. How will they affect my growth and development? Wing Hong asked me to keep an eye on Cassie. He little knew that I needed to keep an eye on myself. Maybe I'm being selfish, but I'm beginning to think about my future plans. I'm rethinking my relationship with everyone in the house. *[Opens the music box* MING CHAU *gave her, listens for a while, shakes her head and smiles sadly]* All our troubles and worries—they are like spider's threads that bind us together, me and everyone else in the house. I'm the spider in the web. But I am the shy tortoise, too. And the frog at the bottom of a well. Right now, I don't think I like any of these creatures. *[Picks up a letter from the table]* I got this letter from Ming Chau the other day. *[Goes on to the porch and reads the letter]* Ming Chau thanked me for encouraging him to go home. Too late or too early he didn't know. But he was able to carry out the duties of an only son. After his father's funeral, he started to run the grocery store. His mother was overjoyed that he was willing to come home. He felt much better too because he had done what he should. He said he had gone back to a place that really needed him: *[Reads aloud]* 'I know we will meet again one day, perhaps in Hong Kong, or perhaps in the States. When we meet, what will the world be like? But it doesn't matter; whatever will be, will be. I'm happy to remember the past as it was.' *[Closes the music box and folds up the letter]* Ming Chau wants me to send him a photo of everybody in the house. He says he wants it for a memento. But he doesn't know things in the house have changed since he left. We're all different now. *[Reads the letter again]*

SCENE EIGHT

[Music. Evening lights go up in the living-room, where SHAN *is sitting on* BRUCE LAMONT's *lap, giggling.]*

SHAN *[patting her bottom]* Yak jill la!

BRUCE *[excited]* I like your 'Yak-jill-la'!

SHAN Yes, *yak jill la*!

BRUCE And what do you call that? *[Pointing at her breasts.]*

SHAN This? Oh, we call them '*Say gwei lo*' in Chinese.

BRUCE What?

SHAN *Say gwei lo*!

BRUCE *Say-gwei-lo*? I like your '*Say-gwei-lo*' too! '*Yak-jill-la*' and '*Say-gwei-lo*'. I must remember that.

*[*ROSANNA *comes out from the kitchen holding a potted plant. She tries not to look at them to avoid embarrassment.]*

SHAN Hello, Rosanna!

BRUCE Oh, hi, Rosanna! I like your '*Say-gwei-lo*' and '*Yak-jill-la*'. [Laughs]

[Flustered, ROSANNA *puts the potted plant back on the window sill.]*

She's shy. Well, I must go now. How do you say 'goodbye' in Cantonese again? *Ding . . .?*

SHAN *Ding nay gwor fight*!

BRUCE *Ding-nay-gwor-fight*! *[Blows her a kiss]*

SHAN *Ding nay* too!

*[*BRUCE *walks out, practising what Cantonese he thinks he has learnt.]*

BRUCE *Yak-jill-la, Say-gwei-lo, Ding-nay-gwor-fight*! *[Exits through the front door]*

SCENE NINE

*[*SHAN *doubles up with laughter when* BRUCE LAMONT *has left.]*

ROSANNA *[not amused]* What's so funny?

SHAN He said he wanted to learn Cantonese. So I taught him some really vulgar expressions, and he thought he was naming parts of the body. That'll teach him a lesson!

ROSANNA *[sharply]* You're so malicious!

SHAN Of course I am!

ROSANNA Isn't he your new 'American man'?

SHAN Yes! And he's got property too. He's a lot better off
than Eric!

ROSANNA You think he'll marry you?

SHAN I'm sure working on it! *[Still in an excited mood]* By the
way, you're really something. You got Eric in no time.
I knew it when I first saw you, I knew you were a
tough opponent! Eric loves girls like you: you're
Chinese enough for him! I'm sick and tired of people
like Eric who make such a fuss about his being a
Chinese. I throw up every time I see him! Since you
fancy him so much, you can have him. I don't want to
waste time fighting for one fish when there are so many
in this American pond!

ROSANNA Is that what you think?

SHAN It's a fact! I don't have to think anything.

ROSANNA Fine. *[Turns to go]* Good night!

SHAN Just a minute! What does that mean? I'm handing him
to you on a plate and you don't even say thank you?
I'm not used to being treated like this!

ROSANNA Okay, Sha Sha! I don't deny that there's something
between Eric and me. But I've never tried to take
anything away from you. How you see this is entirely
your own business. But I've got one thing to say to
you now. I don't care how you cheapen yourself, it's
none of my business. But if you want to fool around
with men, do it elsewhere, don't bring them home!

SHAN I like fooling around with men! I like cheapening
myself! So what? That's the American way of life. You
should get used to it if you're going to stay in
America, and stop being a prig!

ROSANNA I'm not as cheap as you are!

SHAN *[furious]* Me cheap? I bet you haven't got the guts! Or
maybe you haven't got what it takes! To get what I
want, I'll do things you may consider even cheaper!

ROSANNA No doubt you will! Ha, didn't you tell me Hong Kong
people scramble for everything and have no scruples at
all? Aren't you every bit as bad, and every bit as nasty?

SHAN Oh yes. I'm not like you, holier than thou! You're here
to better yourself? To study art? No, to study shit!
How much is art worth? Look at you! I know what
you'll do next. You'll find an excuse and marry a rich
man. Your art is your way of fooling the foreign devils.
You give me one good reason for studying art and I'll
kowtow to you!

ROSANNA I . . . I study art . . . to express myself!

SHAN Wow! Wonderful! I can say that too when I go to bed with a man—I can say I want to express myself too! Just tell me why your way of expression is perfume, and mine is shit! And come to think of it, the whole lot of you should thank me for what I've done!

ROSANNA Should we?

SHAN [proudly] I don't mind telling you. I'm more generous than you think. I don't always look after only myself! I've made Bruce Lamont promise to renew our lease, and not to raise the rent!

ROSANNA Oh! [Surprised]

SHAN Terrific, isn't it? But he wants to come next week and have another meeting with you guys, I mean all of us, to make sure everything is all right. So before we renew the lease, you'd better behave yourself and not foul things up for me!

ROSANNA [calmly] Really?

SHAN At the meeting he expects to see everyone. And I promised him everyone would be there. So tell them all to turn up and show our unity.

ROSANNA [almost speechless] You think this is a great achievement, don't you? [Runs upstairs to avoid further confrontation]

SHAN Eh, running away when you run out of words? You go and ask the foreign devil to renew the lease! You are the one to cheapen yourself! You pretend to be better than me! But you're a tortoise hiding your head in your shell! You are the one who's nasty and filthy, like Hong Kong people! You day-dream about studying art! You're studying shit! You bitch!

[From outside comes the noise of a door being opened and immediately shut. SHAN watches with surprise as BILL rushes in, his clothes all stained and covered in dirt. BILL runs to the drawer where the pistol is, snatches the parcel, turns round, and runs out again. SHAN is amazed.]

[trying to stop him] Bill, what are you doing?

BILL [pushes her away] None of your business! [Rushes out]

[SHAN is shocked. She paces up and down in the living-room. Lights dim. The sound of a car driving off.]

SCENE TEN

[Lights go up again in the living-room. It's late afternoon. NUEN is reading letters on the couch. After the second letter, her face shows anxiety. CASSIE is pacing back and forth in the passageway. After reading another letter, NUEN suddenly laughs, and the laughter grows louder and a bit hysterical. CASSIE gives a start and stands there looking at NUEN, not knowing what to do. The sound of a car arriving. CASSIE goes to the window and looks out.]

CASSIE They're back!

　　　[Shaken by the announcement, NUEN runs madly upstairs.]
　　　Chief? *[Extremely bewildered]*

　　　[HONG comes in hurriedly with a bunch of keys.]

HONG What's up, Cassie?

CASSIE Hm! *[Turns her back to HONG]*

HONG What's the matter now? *[Goes up to pacify her]*

　　　[CASSIE walks away angrily.]

　　　[ERIC, CH'AO, and ROSANNA come in, followed by BILL. Something serious has happened.]

CH'AO *[to BILL]* Wait, let's discuss this a bit. *[Tries to grasp BILL but BILL struggles free and runs down to the basement]* *[sighs]* Ai!

ERIC Let him go. Don't force him!

　　　[SHAN runs down from upstairs.]

SHAN *[to CH'AO, pointing to the basement]* How is he?

　　　[CH'AO shrugs his shoulders and cranes his neck to look down to the basement.]

ROSANNA *[to CASSIE]* Have you picked up today's mail?

CASSIE The Chief has. She read a few letters and ran upstairs as if she'd gone out of her mind.

ROSANNA Out of her mind?

CASSIE Yes. *[HONG goes up to her, but she walks away.]*

　　　[ROSANNA glances at the first floor, looking worried.]

ERIC *[to everyone]* What shall we do now?

ROSANNA What do you mean?

CH'AO *[comes over]* He doesn't want to tell us.

CASSIE *[to ROSANNA]* What happened to Joe Cool?

ROSANNA He's facing three charges. Er . . . Illegal possession of a firearm, er . . . wounding with malicious intent, and working without a permit.

CASSIE My God!

ERIC He'll have to appear in court next week.

SHAN Joe Cool is cool. He's worked in the restaurant for so many months without telling us!

ERIC You didn't want to know, that's all!

SHAN I wasn't talking to you! *[Walks away]*

CASSIE Did the chef really throw a bin of garbage on Joe Cool?

ROSANNA That's what he said. We don't know who started it.

SHAN I told you long ago he was heading for trouble. He wants to show off and pretends he's rich. Everybody knows it's not easy to run a Porsche. The insurance alone can ruin you! Anyway, I can't be bothered, I'd rather kill time my own way. I'll go and have a bite. Bye!

ROSANNA *[waits till SHAN has gone]* Joe Cool is such a bunch of contradictions. He hates the Americans, but he is just as brash!

ERIC So he ends up being the garbage in a garbage bin.

ROSANNA Don't talk so loud. He may hear us.

CASSIE Will he have to go to jail?

ROSANNA We don't know yet.

[A moment of silence. Everybody is worried.]

ERIC How much do we each owe you for the bail?

CH'AO We'll talk about that later.

[Another moment of silence. CH'AO goes upstairs.]

[HONG goes up to CASSIE again to try to talk to her.]

CASSIE Go away! I won't talk to you again as long as I live!

[Goes to the porch]

HONG *[seeking sympathy from friends]* What does that mean?

*[ERIC pats HONG on the shoulder. ROSANNA follows CASSIE out into the porch.
Lights fade in the living-room.]*

S C E N E   E L E V E N

[Lights go up on the porch.]

ROSANNA *[laughs]* The more I look at the two of you, the more convinced I am!

CASSIE *[surprised]* What? What do you mean?

ROSANNA I mean you and your brother!

CASSIE Who cares about him!

ROSANNA Yes, the more I look at the two of you, the more convinced I am that you're behaving just like a dating couple. You fall out with each other, make up, then fall out again.

CASSIE You must be joking! [Annoyed] Damn! That's what everybody says!

ROSANNA But it's true.

CASSIE Cut that out! Why do you all have to say that?

ROSANNA But the two of you do behave like that! We're not making it up!

CASSIE It's all his fault. He pampers me, he does everything for me. That's why I turned out like this! Now he says he has to leave, and I'm left high and dry!

ROSANNA It's true he wants to leave, but that's because he wants you to become more independent. Do you want him to stay with you all your life, as though he was married to you?

CASSIE [confused and agitated] Married to me? What are you talking about?

ROSANNA Did you know that he thought about turning down the scholarship in order to stay and take care of you?

CASSIE [surprised] What? He must be out of his mind!

ROSANNA Actually I'm very envious of the relationship you have with your brother. How I wish I could—

CASSIE My brother has always been like that. From the day my dad ran away, he's been playing my father. He makes all the decisions! He wants to manage my life! Since he gets such a kick out of it, I let him. [Pouts] It's he who wants to treat me like a three-year-old. I don't want him to! Don't you understand? He needs me, so I lean on him to make him happy!

ROSANNA That never occurred to me.

CASSIE Even if he drops me, you think he'll be happy? [Suppresses her tears] Can't you see I'm worried too! He'll know soon enough it's tough being alone, with no one around for him to boss. That'll kill him! If he's smart, he'd better get himself a wife, then I wouldn't have to . . . to worry about him. [Cries]

ROSANNA [at a loss what to do] You . . . you shouldn't cry if you . . . you don't want him to feel bad.

CASSIE I've only got this one brother. *[Wipes her tears away]* Huh! He cries more than I do. It's just that you haven't noticed. But every time he's cried, I can tell afterwards. He's weaker than I am!

ROSANNA *[surprised, and smiles]* What a revelation! Another thunderbolt!

S C E N E   T W E L V E

[Light change.

SHAN *is heard calling: 'Meeting time! Come on everybody, meeting time! Meeting time for all responsible tenants!' Lights go up in the living-room.* BRUCE LAMONT *is sitting on the couch.]*

SHAN Come down, everybody. Come on down! *[To* BRUCE LAMONT*]* You know, everybody is so pleased that you let us stay!

BRUCE They should all thank *you.*

SHAN *[coquettishly]* Really?

*[*CASSIE *comes in quietly.]*

SHAN Hey, Cassie, where's you brother?

CASSIE He's in his room. He says he's no longer part of the house.

SHAN Tell him to join us all the same!

CASSIE Okay. *[Turns to* HONG's *bedroom]* Hong! Come and join us!

[While she's calling, ERIC *and* CH'AO *come up from the basement.]*

SHAN Where's Bill?

CH'AO *[in Mandarin]* Bill *bu lai luo.*

SHAN I'll go find him! *[Runs down to the basement]* Hey, hiding away is not going to help!

*[*ERIC *and* CH'AO *come face to face with* BRUCE LAMONT *and feel a bit embarrassed.]*

ERIC Hi. . . . So it's you again!

BRUCE Hi! Don't use that tone with me!

ERIC We're glad you changed your mind. It'll make everything easier.

BRUCE I said don't use that tone with me! I'm doing you a favour, you know!

CH'AO Please don't argue with him!

BRUCE *[louder]* Why did you send that woman to me to beg me?

[ROSANNA and NUEN come down from the first floor.]

ERIC Who begged you?

BRUCE *[points to the basement]* You begged me! All of you! That's what she said! Ask her!

ERIC We never did!

CH'AO Okay, okay. Let's not argue. Let's wait till Sha Sha is here!

[The noise of a quarrel in the basement. BILL rushes up, followed by SHAN.]

BILL *[complains]* This woman's a real pain!

SHAN Of course I am!

BILL So what the hell is up? Why do I have to be here? Listen! I don't want to be bothered about this house. I'm getting deported! I don't care if you burn this place down!

SHAN I know you don't, but you've still got to sit here and listen!

BILL Talk to me in Hong Kong—I'm going back there!

SHAN Will you sit here please, for the last time? You don't have to say anything, okay?

BILL *Ding nay gwor fight!*

BRUCE *[keen to show off]* I know! It means 'goodbye'.

BILL He's crazy! *[Turns to leave]*

SHAN *[stops him]* Don't go!

BILL *[pushes her to the floor]* Fuck off! *[Runs down to the basement]*

SHAN Hey! *[Struggling to stand up]*

BRUCE Let him go! Gee! *[To SHAN]* What's going on? You told me they all wanted to stay here. That's why we're meeting today, right? Answer me now—how many of you really want to stay here and have your lease renewed?

[SHAN puts her hand up, and signals to the others to raise their hands.]

CASSIE I'm not sure.

SHAN Put your hand up! Put your hand up first if you want the lease renewed!

[CASSIE raises her hand. CH'AO watches NUEN and holds her hand. They do not put their hands up. HONG, on seeing CASSIE raise her hand, puts his hand up too.]

CASSIE *[to* HONG*]* Why are you putting your hand up? You
don't have to! You're leaving, aren't you! *[Pulls his hand
down]*

BRUCE Only two? Well, I am surprised! I'm wasting my time!

SHAN Well, I want to stay here!

BRUCE Forget it! *[Makes to go]*

SHAN *[refusing to admit defeat]* Then rent it to me! *[Looks at
the others angrily]*

BRUCE To you?

SHAN I can keep the house just as well as anybody else can.

BRUCE I don't see why I should! And honestly, I don't trust
you with the house!

SHAN Try me!

BRUCE I already did. *[Smiles]* Not so good!

SHAN *[slaps* BRUCE LAMONT *on the face]* You mother-fucker!
[Hits BRUCE LAMONT*]*

BRUCE Get off me!

*[*SHAN *grabs his jacket firmly.* BRUCE LAMONT *pushes her
away.* HONG *and* CH'AO *separate them.* SHAN *struggles
furiously and continues to kick and claw at* BRUCE
LAMONT.*]*

HONG *[holds* SHAN *tightly]* Calm down, will you?

BRUCE *[at the same time]* You bitch! Shit, I'm bleeding!

SHAN Bruce! I want to stay here! *[Howls]* I want to stay here!
[Even louder] I'm having your baby, you fool!

BRUCE *[surprised]* What? *[Pauses]* What do you take me for?
[Looks around] You guys are crazy, you know that? This
place is a zoo. You are a bunch of lunatics! *[To* SHAN*]*
What are you trying to pull? I . . . I can't believe you'd
stoop so low! *[To everyone]* I thought you'd at least stick
together, like the Japanese! But no, you Chinese are
just like loose sand.

NUEN That's enough! I . . . I—

BRUCE No wonder China is what it is! None of you really
knows what the others are doing! And please, don't
pull any crap on me, and get ready to move out of this
house. Or better still, move out of this country!
[Laughs]

SHAN *[collapses]* Ha, ha! . . . We had it coming! Ha, ha! . . .
We deserve to be kicked out!

*[*CASSIE *goes up to support her. The rest stand there in a daze.
Lights dim.]*

SCENE THIRTEEN

[ROSANNA walks into the spotlight.]

ROSANNA We're a zoo. We're like loose sand. We're not as smart
as the Japanese. We're a bunch of lunatics. That's why
China is what it is. We don't know and we don't care
about what others are doing. We've been kicked out.
We deserve it; we deserve to be told off. I could have
yelled back and told him what faults I see in the
Americans, but I didn't. Because we deserve a good
scolding. I didn't put up my hand to vote for the lease
because this house is no longer important to me.
I want to come out of my shell, bask in the sun, feel
the wind and the rain, and stand up to lightning and
thunderbolts! That way I can tell I'm alive; I can find a
meaning to my stay in America. I want to be a
responsible person, like Ming Chau. I want to live
independently, like Cassie, and find out for myself what
the American society is like. I don't want to be like
Eric, who is never sure if he's American or Chinese. I
don't want to be like Joe Cool either, who hates the
Americans but ends up hating himself. I hope I'll never
keep my studies separate from the living reality, which
is what my cousin is doing. I hope, too, I'll never
impose my values on others, which is what Wing Hong
has done to his sister. And I'm having more and more
sympathy for Sha Sha. Poor girl, she's really in a fix.
But then I suppose we all have the right to choose our
own way of life. I've even learnt a lot from the nasty
things she said about me. . . . I . . . I can see she has a
point.

BLACKOUT

SCENE FOURTEEN

*[Lights go up in living-room. It is early morning. NUEN comes in with some
cardboard boxes to pack the things on the bookshelves. ROSANNA goes to help
her.]*

ROSANNA You know, people laughed at me for majoring in Fine
Arts. They said I didn't know what I was doing—
NUEN I didn't mean to laugh at you!

ROSANNA Oh, I didn't mean you. Anyway, I've thought it over now. What would you think if I went on majoring in Fine Arts, and took Art Education for my minor? Would that be more sensible?

NUEN You want to be an art teacher?

ROSANNA Ming Chau and Sha Sha have both said we Chinese don't know how to express our feelings. So I thought maybe when I go back to Hong Kong, I could make myself useful by teaching young kids how to express themselves through art.

NUEN That is nicely put. *[Moves away to pack other things]*

ROSANNA But do you agree? *[Follows her]*

NUEN What difference does it make? Your mind is made up.

ROSANNA What's the matter, Cousin? You seem to be a different person these days!

NUEN People who study too much are likely to lose their sanity, you should know that!

ROSANNA I only asked for your opinion. You don't have to be angry with me!

NUEN Who am I to give you any opinions? *[Moves away]* Where's Eric? Ask him!

ROSANNA Come on! You're trying to change the subject this time. Why don't you open your eyes and look at yourself? When I first arrived, you told me that people my age were impressionable and would easily fall for anyone that treated them well. You are not much older than me, how come you're not impressionable? You know very well that Taiwanese guy is crazy about you. But you act as if there's nothing between the two of you, and you don't talk about it. Is it because you've been numbed by your studies? Or is it because you're scared? Why can't you face it?

NUEN Why, you're lecturing me! Rosanna, you've changed!

ROSANNA I certainly hope so.

NUEN I don't need your advice. I've taught myself a lesson, a painful lesson! Here I am, a fully fledged Ph.D. But where does that leave me? Earlier on, I sent out a big pile of job applications and was tense for weeks waiting for the replies. Now I've got them, and the answers are the same—I'm over-qualified! I used to think I needed higher qualifications to get a good job. Didn't expect things to turn out like this. Over-qualified, ha! You're right, the books have dulled my senses. I don't know what's happening in the big world, and I don't have the courage to find out.

ROSANNA Is it so hard to find a job in the States?

NUEN It's hard to find one in my field, not only in the States, but also in Hong Kong.

ROSANNA What are you going to do then?

NUEN Me? My best bet is to go for another Ph.D. and bury myself in my books. *[Laughs]* You don't approve? What else can I do? Well, I suppose I could go to Taiwan with Kuo-ch'ao!

ROSANNA *[delighted]* Would you really? So true love has triumphed!

NUEN *[climbs up a chair to remove the bamboo scroll with the message 'Don't forget you're on alien soil']* True love? Well, I don't know! *[Climbs down]*

ROSANNA Careful.

NUEN *[sighs]* I used to think that this flimsy thing we call 'love' was a luxury. Now it seems to me that when you're stuck and desperate for help, it could be mighty useful. *[Cleans the scroll with a napkin]*

ROSANNA Are you saying then that you've never been in love with Kuo-ch'ao?

NUEN I need him. Does that count as love? I have no youth, no future, what have I got left? So I say to myself: at least there's still a bit of 'love', and it's quite nice.

ROSANNA Yes, it's beautiful. When will you leave for Taiwan?

NUEN Not right away. I have to go to the graduation ceremony first. But I feel bad about asking you to come here, and now you can't stay in the house any longer.

ROSANNA I want to leave too. I mean I want to transfer to another university. If I'm going to take Art Education, I'll have to go elsewhere because it's not offered here. I'm thinking about the University of Texas at Austin. Their programme is just what I need. I'd like to go there for a change.

NUEN *[thinks for a while]* Not a bad choice. But if you want to transfer in the summer, you'll have to act fast.

ROSANNA I will.

[CASSIE and HONG run up from the basement. CASSIE has a piece of paper in her hand.]

CASSIE Chief, Chief, Joe Cool's gone!

[ROSANNA and NUEN are stunned.
Cacophonous music starts up as lights gradually fade.
They go down the basement.]

SCENE FIFTEEN

[Cacophonous music fades down. Lights go up. The summer sun fills the living-room.
CH'AO is taking ROSANNA's luggage to the living-room from upstairs. He walks into ERIC, who is carrying suitcases up from the basement. They do not say anything and just put the suitcases down in the corridor. ERIC then wraps up his computer with a piece of cloth. SHAN comes down from the first floor and smiles at ERIC, who ignores her. She picks up her things from the bookcases. HONG and CASSIE come up from the basement carrying a camera and a tripod. They look around and set up the camera. SHAN kneels on the floor and makes a phone call.]

SHAN Hello, Jerry? Are you coming to help me move my things out? . . . They'll give me a hand, but I like riding in your jeep . . . What time? . . . Okay. I'll wait for you! *[Hangs up and notices the camera]* Oh? Taking pictures?

HONG Family photo. Rosanna's leaving today. We're taking this picture as a souvenir.

SHAN Count me out!

HONG We're sending one to Ming Chau!

SHAN In that case, okay. Cassie, let's go and get ready.

CASSIE Okay.

SHAN *[says as she goes]* Hurry up with your packing. I pulled a trick on Jerry. He's coming over in his jeep to take us to the new apartment.

ERIC *[after SHAN has gone, to HONG]* Keep an eye on your sister.

HONG I'm so worried. She and Sha Sha have rented an apartment and they're talking about sub-letting it!

ERIC Is Sha Sha pregnant?

HONG How would I know!

ERIC Has she had an abortion, or was she just lying?

HONG Boy, you're nosy!

ERIC Well, just out of curiosity!

HONG Are you driving Rosanna to the airport or am I?

ERIC I will, of course!

[ROSANNA comes down from upstairs carrying a bag. NUEN comes down with her. CH'AO goes up to them.]

CH'AO Well, it's almost time. *[To ROSANNA]* You've been here almost a year now!

ROSANNA And now I shall go. *[Glances at ERIC]* It's like a cycle. Every time we go through it, there is a side-effect. We gain new wisdom.

HONG Well, Rosanna, that's very profound!

ROSANNA I was just quoting.

ERIC *[goes up to* ROSANNA*]* I'll come down to see you at Christmas for sure.

ROSANNA Don't just say it! I'll be waiting!

ERIC Austin and Denver are just thirteen hours by car. No problem at all, It'll be much harder going to Hong Kong from the States. That won't be just thirteen hours.

ROSANNA Seventeen hours by plane. It's not much longer! But, we'll see.

CH'AO Let's hurry up and take the picture. We should be leaving for the airport soon!

ROSANNA Is it time already?

NUEN Now you know time flies!

*[*CASSIE *and* SHAN *come back.* CASSIE *is heavily made up.]*

CASSIE Don't I look pretty?

HONG Wow, old lady, who are you looking for?

CASSIE Drop dead! *[Hits him]* You're not my father, and you're not my husband. Shut up! I've made myself up for tonight. Aren't I pretty?

ERIC I bet you'll give Ming Chau a fright!

*[*SHAN *finds something from the shelves. She goes over to* ROSANNA*.]*

SHAN Well, remember, if you want something, you have to go for it. And when you've got it, you don't forget to take it with you. *[Shows* ROSANNA *the music box]* Here! *[Gives it to her, and turns to* ERIC*]* Ming Chau gave it to her!

ROSANNA I hadn't forgotten it. I want to have it in my hands when we take the picture.

SHAN How very thoughtful! *[Goes away]*

HONG Come on folks. Get ready!

[Everyone goes to the couch to pose.]

CASSIE *[fighting for a seat]* I'll sit in the middle!

HONG Don't move! *[Focuses, and presses the button]*

CH'AO This picture will remind us that we once lived together in this big house!

*[*HONG *runs up and joins the crowd.]*
Ready! Smile!

[The flash goes off, the picture is taken.
Music.
Lights dim.]

THE END

CHRONICLE OF WOMEN
LIU SOLA IN CONCERT

1991

By
DANNY N. T. YUNG

Translated by
MARTHA P. Y. CHEUNG

— ABOUT **THE PLAYWRIGHT** —

DANNY N. T. YUNG (1943–) was born in Shanghai but moved to Hong Kong with his family at the age of five. He studied Architecture at the University of California, Berkeley, and Urban Design and Urban Planning at Columbia University. In 1979, he returned to Hong Kong and held his first one-man cartoon exhibition. On the day the exhibition opened, he presented his first structuralist theatre work, *Broken Record #1*. From late 1980 to early 1981, over a period of three months, he produced his first performance series, *Journey to the East* (in four parts) at the Hong Kong Arts Centre. In 1982, he went to San Francisco to co-produce Wayne Wang's feature film *Dim Sum*. In the same year, he and a few friends founded Zuni Icosahedron, an art collective, and he has been Artistic Director of Zuni since 1985.

Yung wrote the script for Zuni's first production, *Journey to the East—Part Five: Hong Kong–Taipei–Hong Kong*, which opened in Taipei for the 'First Asian Drama Festival' in 1982. Since 1982, he has co-ordinated, directed, and produced close to seventy stage productions, including the *One Hundred Years of Solitude* series, the *Chronicle of Women* series, the *Opium Wars* series, the *Journey to the East* series (*Parts 6 & 7*), the *Deep Structure of Chinese Culture* series, the *Two or Three . . .* series, and *The Book of Mountain and Ocean*. Many of his stage productions have provoked the Hong Kong and neighbouring governments to take a hardline policy on censorship, but they have also earned him the respect of many. Since 1984, he has been invited to give lectures and lead workshops in Tokyo, Shanghai, Beijing, Taipei, Singapore, London, Berlin, Brussels, Los Angeles, New York City, and Vancouver. Performance tours of his work with Zuni visited, among others, Taipei (1982, 1984, 1988), Japan (1989, 1992, 1995), London (1990), New York City (1990), Yellow Spring, Pennsylvania (1990), and Brussels (1994).

Yung is also a keen advocate of new art forms. His experimental films, video work, and installation works have been shown at festivals in Berlin, London, Rotterdam, Edinburgh, Tokyo, Los Angeles, and New York.

Since 1987, Yung has initiated a series of public forums on cultural policies on arts. In 1990, he organized the Cultural Policy Study Group that has since produced several influential reports, including *In Search of Cultural Policy, 1991*, and *In Search of Cultural Policy, 1993*. He has also founded two pressure groups to work on cultural policy issues. In 1993, he was appointed by the governor of Hong Kong to the 'Working Group' which in 1995 became the Hong Kong Arts Development Council, a statutory body. He has written extensively on arts, culture, and the media.

Chronicle of Women—Liu Sola in Concert is the fourth in Yung's *Chronicle of Women* series. It was first staged by Zuni in 1991.

ABOUT **THE PLAY**

The productions of Zuni Icosahedron have become almost synonymus with avant-garde theatre in Hong Kong. *Chronicle of Women—Liu Sola in Concert* is a fairly representative Zuni work. All the characteristic traits of a Zuni production are here: flouting of theatrical conventions, rejection of the conventional elements of a play—such as strong narrative and dialogue—and a style of composition more reminiscent of a piece of avant-garde music.

In place of the usual programme notes for theatre productions, Zuni's programme consisted of four line drawings, each showing five women in ancient robes in an incongruous modern setting. When the curtain went up, these same line drawings, among others, appeared in succession on a large screen through a slide projector. This suggested that the production's theme was the identity of women in contemporary society. And indeed it is, with issues such as popular stereotypes, roles and role models, and perceptions of gender issues at the focus. These issues are explored through a series of visual images and action sequences presented by the actresses on stage, and by the juxtapositioning of these images and actions with a host of elements such as props, sound, dance, and music, all of which are laden with cultural, political, and ideological associations. The music is a medley of Chinese folk music, Chinese propagandist songs, African dance music, and Western electronic music. It is played by Liu Sola, a mainland Chinese woman, well known as a singer, composer, and writer.

Much thought has been given to whether this play should be included in this anthology. Since there was no playscript it was not possible to translate and present this play in the same way as the others in this book. Thus an account in words is given of the interplay of the various elements in the performance. Where appropriate, footnotes are provided for cultural, contextual, and background information, but, as during the performance, the meaning remains open to interpretation. This script is based on performances given between 7 and 10 March 1991 at the Studio Theatre of the Hong Kong Cultural Centre.

DIRECTOR'S NOTE

What attracted me to the theatre was not the words. I am interested in the images evoked by words and the sounds of words, but loading the words with deep and profound moral significance is too heavy a responsibility for me. Chinese narrative literature is vulnerable to manipulation and tends too easily to turn into propaganda, or manifestos, or tools for didactic, moralistic, or educational purposes. Principles, principles, principles—one hears and reads about nothing else.

Maybe that is why many people have said that Zuni is exploring with body language, not verbal language. In *Chronicle of Women—Liu Sola in Concert*, however, I am also trying to explore with verbal language. In this play, words are first used in the slides. They are words to be 'read' by the audience. I borrowed a word often seen at the beginning of a literary work or a book—the word 'Foreword'—and used it at the beginning of the slides. I also borrowed the word 'postscript' and used it to end the slide sequence. In addition, I borrowed words often seen in slides used in the cinema or the theatre, for example, 'Don't forget your belongings'. When we toured Taiwan, we even used a slide with the words, 'Please encourage us with your applause'. It had a stunning impact on the audience. These words which are, as it were, 'appropriate to the occasion' often help me to observe and study the theatre from a new angle.

Equally stimulating is another group of words that are 'appropriate to the occasion'—descriptions of time, place, and characters, all of which are found at the beginning of traditional playscripts. These descriptions are often followed by a synopsis of the play, and then comes the dialogue. I borrowed this group of words, but tried to discover something about what really lies behind such a form of expression.

Apart from these written words, I have used only one passage of dialogue in this production. Originally, this dialogue was made up of a string of noises, and came in the last part of the play, between two interpreters sitting behind the chairs for the leaders. Through these noises, the audience became aware of their existence. But in the workshop sessions, I was persuaded to include a passage of dialogue I had intended only for workshop discussion, and it became the only passage of dialogue in the production. The argument was that without this passage of dialogue, the production would lack a 'central sustaining idea' and become too abstract. My feeling, however, is that the dialogue seems a little too 'concrete'. And yet I don't quite know how to make it 'just right'. It feels like a grain of sand in the eye, but so be it.

There is another line of dialogue that came from the workshop. One evening, one of the cast came to the workshop all dressed up. Everyone looked at her, surprised. She tossed her head and said in defiance, 'I'm going to a banquet this evening'. We were then discussing women's make-up, its history and its significance, and her answer stirred up a lot of interest in us. Suddenly, this line began to crop up on all sorts of occasions in this production. Soon, it settled into a recurrent soliloquy. The cast spoke the line on the phone, or mumbled it to themselves, or yelled it at the audience, as if in protest. . . .

Many of Zuni's productions function as a critique of the language of the theatre itself. *Chronicle of Women—Liu Sola in Concert* is no exception. The 'ending' comes twelve minutes after the beginning of the performance. Then the audience gets a full view of what happens backstage, or just before the performance begins. And then, without any hint to the audience, the performance begins again.

This backstage/pre-performance scene is played using improvisation. How it works depends on how relaxed the performers are, and how well each can draw from her backstage/pre-performance experiences and interact with the others. This scene lasts for five minutes and is completely devoid of drama. But I think that the more subdued and the more low-key the performance is, the more reverberative and dramatic the scene will become.

Zuni never relies on a script for its productions. Instead, we work within a framework of a script. Having established a framework, we then develop the content and the different forms of presentation at separate workshop sessions. When things are beginning to shape up, we meet to exchange views, make adjustments, look for new take-off points, or even restructure the overall framework. During the period of our performance, adjustments, modifications, and inspired changes are introduced even more frequently.

I should perhaps also provide some background information on Zuni's *Chronicle of Women* series. In 1983, a year after Zuni had been set up, I had a discussion with Zuni's members about feminism, about why women often made up the majority in the theatre, including theatre audience. As a result of that discussion, I decided to collaborate with the women members of Zuni on a production, taking the issue of gender as the topic. We then held a series of workshops from which the production evolved.

In this first version of *Chronicle of Women*, we took women, actresses, and Hong Kong as the central themes and attempted a balanced exploration of the relationship between women and men, between the actresses and the audience, and between Hong Kong and China–Britain. This exploration soon developed into a discussion of the relationship between women and humanity, between the actresses and the theatre, and between Hong Kong and the world. At the same time, we attempted to deconstruct the myths behind these discussions. Having done so, we then worked to reconstruct these myths again and to present them in a new rendition.

The production alarmed the Hong Kong government, though I think it was probably the subject matter and not the form that attracted their attention. Subsequently, the government put forward a proposed resolution for all local stage productions to be vetted by the Film and Entertainment Licensing Authority.

In most other places with a large Chinese community, the examination of playscripts may not be news at all. In Hong Kong, however, such a task had for years been designated as the responsibility of the administrative arm of the government. All of a sudden, the government was going to introduce legislation on this issue. Why?

Such a move by the government brought all of us in the performing arts circle together. The media too, was stunned by the implications which this piece of legislation would have for press freedom, and they played an important role in rallying support for us. Confronted with such strong and united opposition, the government withdrew the bill in 1985.

What happened motivated me to organize more workshops focusing on women. In 1984, when Zuni was invited to tour Taiwan, we attempted an all-male cast as well as a mixed cast for the production. Our Taipei run had a huge impact on the actors and actresses, and we had extremely stimulating discussions with the audience.

Time flew. It was 1989, and Zuni received an invitation from London to give five performances of *The Deep Structure of Chinese Culture*. An old friend, Liu Sola, appeared in the auditorium. When I saw her standing by herself at one corner in the theatre, I had a sudden urge to invite her to play a part in our next production of *Chronicle of Women*. This resulted in our 1991 production: *Chronicle of Women—Liu Sola in Concert*.

TITLE

Chronicle of Women is the English translation of the title of a well-known biographical work in classical Chinese literature. This work is about the life of one hundred and five famous as well as infamous women in ancient China, the famous ones being held as paragons of virtues providing positive role models for women while the infamous ones are meant to serve as warnings to women against transgression of behaviour.

LIU SOLA

Liu Sola was born in Beijing in 1955, the daughter of two highly influential members of the Communist Party. She writes fiction and lyrics, she composes music, and was one of the first generation of rock singers to emerge in China after the Cultural Revolution. In 1988 she went to England to pursue a career in music where she developed an interest in blending Chinese and Western music; she later worked with musicians in America on 'Chinese Blues'. As well as appearing in *Chronicle of Women—Liu Sola in Concert* she also composed the music, and was responsible for the sound effects on stage, as well as dubbing most of the background music for the performance. Criticism of her work on the Mainland—where one of her cassettes was banned—has made her a well-known controversial figure in Hong Kong. Her presence on stage would be charged with political and cultural significance.

THE SET

A huge slide screen hangs at the back of the stage. In front of the screen and directly facing the audience are four armchairs, each with a lace antimacassar. They are separated by low coffee tables with spittoons underneath.* Downstage, there are two tables. The one at stage left is covered with a white lace tablecloth, on top of which stand a gong and a pair of clapper sticks (castanet-like Chinese musical instruments). In front of the table there is a stool. Beside the table, a spittoon, inside which are placed two wireless microphones. A low table at stage right holds a television. The rest of the stage is bare.

---

* The armchairs, low coffee tables and spittoons, and the way they are positioned are obviously meant to evoke the picture thousands of viewers have seen on television or in the newspapers: the rooms in the Great Hall of the People in Beijing where Chinese political leaders meet their counterparts from other countries.

COSTUME

With the exception of Liu Sola, the women all wear cheongsams—a tight-fitting one-piece garment with a high collar, buttons or press studs running from the collar to the right side of the chest, and two side slits. Cheongsams usually end a little below the knees, but as formal evening wear, they sometimes reach the ankles. It is said that cheongsams can bring out the beauty of a woman's figure in a most elegant and graceful manner. Certainly a cheongsam imposes severe restrictions on a woman's movements, and this means that she has to sit, stand, and carry herself in a particular way. Such a mode of behaviour has become synonymous with good breeding, good manners, and social respectability. A few girls' schools in Hong Kong, such as the Golden Jubilee Secondary School mentioned in this play, still require their students to wear cheongsams as school uniforms. It is interesting to note, however, that prostitutes also wear cheongsams, but with high side slits. This type of cheongsam turns a woman into a sex object, for as soon as she starts to move about, one gets a full sideview of her legs. It also provides a lot of room for seductive and provocative posturing.

Liu Sola wears a raincoat over a skirt and a top that is cut like a cheongsam—with a high collar and buttons running from the collar to the right side of the chest and then in a straight line down to the seams.

─── **DRAMATIS** PERSONAE ───

LIU SOLA   Female, vocalist
ANTHONY WONG   Male, vocalist, wears a dark suit

Some twenty women (but at least thirteen) and at least four or five
men play the following parts. Performers may play more than one role
if they do not have to appear simultaneously in the same scenes. Unless
specified below, the women all wear blue or white cheongsams.

The parts are identified briefly as follows:

W O M E N

A	wears a raincoat over a purple cheongsam, sits in armchair at stage left
B	takes instructions from A, later kicks her
C	walks in slow motion, later carries a white kerchief
D	hides behind armchairs
E	talks with A, later appears with ANTHONY WONG
F	walks backwards
BB	with basketball
G, H, J, K	a foursome, stride across the stage, appear later in execution scene
L	with schoolbag
M	with sword, later carries a man on her back
N	with mobile phone
O, P	dance to African music, later wear red cheongsams and wrestle, then play the 'interpreters'
Q, R, S	trio, strike cover-girl poses

M E N

stage-hands

THE **PERFORMANCE**

SCENE ONE

The performance opens with a series of slides projected consecutively on to the screen.

SLIDE 1: Scenery of Hong Kong at night

SLIDE 2*

* Slides 2, 3, 4, and 5 also appear as line drawings in the programme notes and are likely to be the first images that greeted the audience. In terms of visual impact, of content, and of the interpretive possibilities they open up for the viewers, these four line drawings are an encapsulation of what Zuni Icosahedron attempted to do in this production of *Chronicle*.

SLIDE 3

SLIDE 4

SLIDE 5

SLIDE 6: Chinese character meaning 'woman' or 'women'

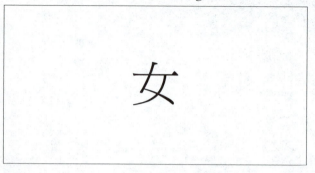

SLIDE 7: Chinese characters meaning 'a number of women'

SLIDE 8: Chinese characters meaning 'chronicle of women'

列
女
傳

SLIDE 9

> **Foreword**
> Have thought long and hard but still cannot think of what
> else there still is to say •

SLIDE 10

> **Foreword**
> Have thought long and hard but still cannot think of what
> else there still is to say • maybe it is
> a question of whom one is addressing •

SLIDE 11

> **Foreword**
> Have thought long and hard but still cannot think of what
> else there still is to say • maybe it is
> a question of whom one is addressing • maybe
> when understanding develops into responsibility •
> when ease of mind becomes pressure •
> when what is left of the content is just form •
> then

SLIDE 12

> **Foreword**
> Have thought long and hard but still cannot think of what
> else there still is to say • maybe it is
> a question of whom one is addressing • maybe
> when understanding develops into responsibility •
> when ease of mind becomes pressure •
> when what is left of the content is just form •
> then before the Foreword
> there is no more space •

SLIDE 13: Black-out slide

Lights go up. From the front row in the auditorium, eleven women, all in light blue cheongsams, rise from their seats. They stand there, hand in hand, their backs towards the audience. After a long pause, they begin to produce a string of sounds—'ah', 'ai', 'oh', 'hua', 'xie', 'xue'—that go up and down the scale, like someone practising vocal exercises. This is followed by a round of what sounds like giggles, like wailing. Then another round of vocal exercise. When they finish, the women remain standing. Lights dim.

SLIDE 14

	Act One
Place:	The Great Hall of the People
Time:	Several years later
Characters:	

The women sing again, producing the sound 'hua' a number of times. Then, another round of what sounds like giggles and laughter.

SLIDE 15

	Act Two
Place:	Cultural Centre, Studio Theatre
Time:	Several years ago
Characters:	

SLIDE 16*

	Act Three
Place:	Golden Jubilee Secondary School
Time:	Several years later
Characters:	

The women sigh.

SLIDE 17

	Act Four
Place:	In one's mind
Time:	Several years ago
Characters:	

The women sigh.

SLIDE 18

What is left • are bits and pieces of
memories • Ten years have passed • Finished •
It's finished • The story has finished •
Finished • The play is finished • The theatre
is finished • Ideals are finished • History is finished •
Finished • THE END •

Silence. Lights fade out. The women go on to the stage in the dark and stand in a row, their backs towards the audience. Silence.

---

* In the 1960s, students at Golden Jubilee Secondary School staged a demonstration in protest against the school management. This incident was remarkable as a sign of political awakening on the part of the young women.

SLIDE 19

> What is left • are bits and pieces
>
> Finished
>
> finished   finished
> Finished   finished
> finished   finished   finished
> Finished

SLIDE 20: Black-out slide

Silence.

SCENE TWO

Lights go up. The women turn to face the audience. The one in the middle steps forward, bows, steps back. Then they bow together. A long pause. They applaud together. The first from stage right steps forward and applauds the other performers, then returns to her place.

SLIDE 21

> The performance is over
> Please applaud
> the performance

The women applaud again. Anthony Wong enters from stage left, and joins the women in their applause. Liu Sola, with dark flowing hair falling down her back, enters from stage right, and joins the group in their applause. Bouquets of flowers are presented to Liu, Wong, and the woman in the middle. Meanwhile, slides 22 and 23 flash one after another on the screen.

SLIDE 22

> Don't forget
> Your belongings

SLIDE 23

> Applause
> Applause

Alternate performers from stage left step forward, bow, step back. The other performers repeat the routine. Meanwhile, slides 24, 25, 26 flash one after another on the screen.

SLIDE 24

> The war is over
> Applause for
> the performance

SLIDE 25

> The election is over
> Applause for
> the performance

SLIDE 26

> The movement is over
> Applause for
> the performance

Another round of applause, which turns rhythmical. The performers exit in two files.

SCENE THREE

SLIDE 27

> Don't forget
> your belongings

As slide 27 fades out, house lights go up. The back curtains are slowly drawn together. The audience is left to decide whether the performance is over.

SCENE FOUR

A phone rings offstage, nothing happens. After some time, the phone rings again. Nothing happens. The telephone rings at irregular intervals a few more times.

Several stagehands enter. One sweeps the floor with a broom. Another two take the TV set from stage right to stage left, while a third carries the table from stage left to a corner downstage at stage right. Then he takes the low table at stage right to where the TV is, and puts TV on it.

A, wearing a raincoat over a cheongsam, enters and sits slumped in the armchair at stage left. B, in a light blue cheongsam, enters from stage right, and steals her way towards A.

A gets up, moves downstage, and stands there watching B.

After a while, B shrugs her shoulders as if in irritation, or defiance.

A moves further downstage, still watching B.

B suddenly starts to dance, disco style, before the empty armchair.

A goes up to her, and mumbles some instruction or order. B obeys, goes behind the armchair and stands still.

A sits down in the armchair again.*

B exits stage left.

A man in a dark suit enters, stopping to look at the back of the TV set.

SCENE FIVE

C enters, walks in slow motion across the stage, exits.

D enters, steals up to the armchairs, and hides behind them. Now and then she crawls about on the floor behind the armchairs as in a game of hide-and-seek, or sticks her head up and moves it along the backs of the armchairs.

A, her chin resting on her palms, chats and laughs with the man. The man exits stage left.

E enters, carrying a bag. She runs up to A, puts the bag down, talks briefly with her, and exits. E re-enters, picks up a bag beside the armchair, dashes off stage left.

A looks as if she is asleep.

Liu Sola enters and sits crossed-legged on the floor downstage at stage right.

C enters from stage left, stops to look at A, walks resolutely, stops at centre stage to glance back at A, walks on, hesitates, then exits stage right.

F enters stage right, walking backwards.

D comes forward from behind the armchairs, skipping and jumping, and dances, disco style, at stage left. Then she sneaks behind the armchairs again.

BB enters, dribbling a basketball, and exits stage left. The sound of basketball bouncing on the floor continues to be heard for some time.

A quartet of women, G, H, J, K, file in from stage left. L, with a schoolbag slung over her shoulder, enters at the same time as K, her left hand in a gesture of salute. As she walks across the stage, she says, 'I'm going to a banquet this evening.' All five exit stage right.

D stands up, dances on the spot, ducks behind the armchairs again.

Liu Sola strikes the clapper sticks at intervals, each time to announce the entrance of more characters.

M enters from stage right holding up a sword in her right hand. As

* A sequence of actions suggestive of the mother–daughter and/or teacher–pupil relationship?

she crosses the stage, she asks, 'They're going to a banquet this evening?'

N enters from stage left with a mobile phone and speaks into it as she crosses the stage, 'They're going to a banquet this evening.'

G, H, J, K, enter single file from stage left, and ask, 'They're going to a banquet this evening?'

M, with the sword, stops before the TV, lowers her sword, pointing it at the floor, and says, 'They're going to a banquet this evening.'

The duo, O and P, enter, one from each wing. They go behind the armchairs, and stop where they meet face to face.

Liu strikes the clapper sticks, then the gong. The curtains are slowly drawn open. O and P turn round and slowly exit, following the movement of the curtains, as if they were drawing the curtains open.*

SCENE SIX

A stirs in her armchair and sits bolt upright, in a posture a woman in cheongsam does not normally adopt—back straight, legs wide apart, hands resting assertively on the armrests.†

D steals from behind the armchairs, crosses the stage, past A, stops just before the stage left exit, dances on the spot, then exits.

Lights fade out. A spotlight goes up on Liu downstage. Silence.

SLIDE 28

* An obvious hint that this scene functions like an overture: it introduces all the characters who will later re-appear, and many of the visual motifs of the play. The alert members of the audience will soon notice how these visual motifs recur, with a difference, and will realize that the play develops like a musical composition.

† Such an assertive posture runs counter to the submissive, decorous feminine behaviour normally associated with cheongsam. It implies an act of rebellion, of deliberate transgression and violation of established social codes and conventions of behaviour. Interestingly, such a posture is also reminiscent of that adopted by high ranking officials in ancient China, all of whom were men, the posture can therefore also be taken as a defiant assumption of patriarchal authority. The women assume this posture again and again in the course of the performance. The visual images thus created echo those seen in the line drawings and convey the theme of women's exploration of their identity.

SLIDES 29, 30, 31, 32, 33, 34: Close-ups of women's faces from various angles.*

SLIDE 35

> Act One
> Place: In the theatre

African music fades up, loud and strong.

SLIDE 36

> Act One
> Place: In the theatre
> Time: Around March 8, International Working
> Women's Day

SLIDE 37

> Act One
> Place: In the theatre
> Time: Around March 8, International Working
>   Women's Day
> Characters: Hong Kong

SLIDE 38

> Act One
> Place: In the theatre
> Time: Around March 8, International Working
>   Women's Day
> Characters: Hong Kong women

SLIDE 39

> Act One
> Place: In the theatre
> Time: Around March 8, International Working
>   Women's Day
> Characters: Hong Kong Women
> Question: How to find

* Slides 28–34 are strongly reminiscent of faces of women seen on Hong Kong calendars in the 1930s and 1940s.

SLIDE 40

<table>
<tr><td colspan="2" align="center">Act One</td></tr>
<tr><td>Place:</td><td>In the theatre</td></tr>
<tr><td>Time:</td><td>Around March 8, International Working Women's Day</td></tr>
<tr><td>Characters:</td><td>Hong Kong</td></tr>
<tr><td>Question:</td><td>How to find a voice</td></tr>
</table>

SLIDE 41

<table>
<tr><td colspan="2" align="center">Act One</td></tr>
<tr><td>Place:</td><td>In the theatre</td></tr>
<tr><td>Time:</td><td>Around March 8, International Working Women's Day</td></tr>
<tr><td>Characters:</td><td>Women at Golden Jubilee Secondary School, Hong Kong</td></tr>
<tr><td>Question:</td><td>How to find</td></tr>
</table>

SLIDE 42

<table>
<tr><td colspan="2" align="center">Act One</td></tr>
<tr><td>Place:</td><td>In the theatre</td></tr>
<tr><td>Time:</td><td>Around March 8, International Working Women's Day</td></tr>
<tr><td>Characters:</td><td>Women at Golden Jubilee Secondary School, Hong Kong</td></tr>
<tr><td>Question:</td><td>How to find new relations</td></tr>
</table>

SLIDE 43: The room as seen in Slides 2, 3, 4, 5, but without the women

As Slide 43 fades out, lights go up. African music is still heard. A is still sitting slumped in the armchair, as if asleep.

SCENE SEVEN

O and P enter, from stage left and stage right, and meet face to face behind the armchairs.

African music stops.

O and P turn round, go downstage, meet again at centre stage, and strike various poses, evocative at once of cover-girl poses in glossy fashion magazines, of models on catwalks, and contestants in beauty pageants.

African music fades up. O begins to dance to the music. P looks at her disapprovingly, but soon joins in dancing, first demurely then freely.

D steals in from stage left and hides behind the armchairs.

A stirs in her armchair, half removes her raincoat, revealing a purple cheongsam, and announces, 'I'm going to a banquet this evening.' She takes off the raincoat, and sits prim and proper in the armchair.

Q, R, S enter, stop at centre stage, turn to face the stage left exit, strike cover-girl poses, relax, turn to face the audience, then slowly exit stage right.

SCENE EIGHT

A rises from the armchair leaving the raincoat behind, and drifts downstage, her hands stretched out loosely before her.

African music fades out.

O and P stop dancing, and stand with their backs towards the audience.

A stops at centre stage, between O and P, as if in a daze, or deep in thought.

N enters, talking on a mobile telephone. She goes to sit in the armchair at stage left, drapes A's raincoat over her shoulders, curls her legs under her in a relaxed pose.

Liu Sola, now kneeling on the floor, begins to croon.

The trio downstage, O, A, and P, strike cover-girl poses.

Liu's voice begins to rise and she gives a solo performance that sounds like chanting, like groaning, like someone in lamentation, her voice at times dry and desolate, at times high, rich, and ringing.

A starts to move to the music, stretching, writhing, turning.

E enters from stage right and sits on an armchair with her legs apart, looking on.

O and P also start to writhe and wriggle. Then O rummages her schoolbag, takes out what looks like a giant toothpick, and puts it in A's mouth.

E exits.

O, A, and P begin to cover their mouths, ears, and eyes in turn.*

N in the armchair sits up, and speaks into her mobile phone, 'I'm going to a banquet this evening.'

The sound of basketball bouncing on the floor rises again, clashing with Liu Sola's lone voice, creating a powerful cacophony to accompany O, A, and P's next round of movements: they touch their breasts, place their hands over their crotches, then fondle their breasts.† Then A places her hands over the crotches of O and P. They freeze.

Sound of basketball stops. Liu's wailing grows louder. O and P shy away and exit. A begins slowly to dance.

The telephone rings.

N, in her armchair, is startled, puts on the raincoat, and paces the stage anxiously. She talks on her mobile phone, chattering gibberish, then sits in the nearest armchair.

The sound of chattering fades up.

Liu joins the chattering of gibberish, so does A, who is still dancing.

O and P enter, having changed into red cheongsams. They stand on either side of A, military fashion, arms akimbo, legs apart, their backs to the audience.

A suddenly collapses on the floor, still gibbering.

O and P lift her and carry her to the armchair at stage left, then exit. A continues to gibber. The sound of gibberish rises loud and piercing, like a recording played at the wrong speed.

B, in a white cheongsam, enters, orders A to shut up, and kicks her

---

* Suggestive of dumbness, deafness, and blindness? Also suggestive of the trio of monkeys: see no evil, hear no evil, and speak no evil?

† Suggestive of women's willingness to reduce themselves to sex objects? Or of how women have to force themselves to become dumb, deaf, and blind before they can do so? Or is it suggestive of women's deliberate defiance of the three 'no evil' teachings?

when she does not. A shuts up. B exits. Liu begins to croon again.

When Liu stops crooning, N rises from her armchair and speaks into her mobile phone, 'I think we should respect him a bit more; if he wants to play his own part, let him. Why force him to play someone else? That's too much!' Then she exits stage right.

SCENE NINE

Liu Sola, who has been kneeling on the floor, now leans forward, her forehead nearly touching the floor.

A man in a dark suit enters from stage right, goes behind Liu, stretches out his hand to touch her back, but looks up as if he has caught sight of something and stares straight ahead. Then he backs away and exits.

C enters from stage left, and moves towards Liu in slow motion, walking like a model on a catwalk with her hands swaying rhythmically by her side, a white kerchief in her right hand.

Liu straightens up. In a low, restrained voice, she begins to recite:

> In the days of Mao Zedong,
> How happy were our people!
> How beautiful was our country!*

C turns round, slowly crosses the stage again, and exits stage left.

Nine women enter from both wings, walking like models, three paces apart. Each is carrying a white kerchief.† While they walk around the stage, Liu Sola recites the lines again, first in a gentle lyrical voice two octaves higher, then dropping to a rich alto voice.

Meanwhile, the women begin to utter a string of sounds that swell like echoes, like reverberations of Liu's words. Amidst this chorus of echoes, Liu recites the lines again, in a loud firm oratorical voice.

There is a sudden burst of high screeching sounds against the chorus of echoes. Liu recites the lines again, in a slow, strong, chanting voice that surges high above the din.

The women continue to produce siren-like echoes and reverberations of Liu's words.

M enters from stage left, carrying a man on her back.§ She stops for a while before A in the armchair, then turns round to walk downstage and stops at the point furthest downstage.

---

* These lines are taken from 'The East is Red', a music and dance epic organized in 1964 by Premier Zhou Enlai to celebrate the fifteenth anniversary of the founding of the People's Republic of China.

† Introducing another visual motif?

§ A Chinese woman seldom carries a man on her back, let alone a Chinese woman in cheongsam. The action here is rich in ambiguities. It could be suggestive of women's strength, or of the burden women have to carry, or of the reversal of roles.

E enters from stage left with light tripping steps, and the women scatter, as if stricken with panic. Lights dim.

M, still carrying the man on her back, slowly steps backwards and stops before A.

C enters again, still carrying the white kerchief, and stops just before the table at stage right downstage, her face towards the stage right exit.

Liu gets up from the floor, goes to the table, sits down on the stool with her back facing the audience, rests her arms on the table and buries her head in her arms.

The nine women, who are dashing about the stage as if scrambling for shelter, suddenly squat down, protecting their heads with their hands, and then make a quick exit.

Lights become even dimmer.

A spotlight goes up on C standing before the table. She raises her hands high above her head, turns to face Liu, and then holds out the white kerchief with both hands, her head bowed.*

The nine women enter, and quickly gather round C to form a tableau. They stand in rows of three, one with her hand raised in clenched fist, as if in protest; one holding high her white kerchief, stretched taut, with both hands; one holding her kerchief high with one hand, and the rest holding their kerchiefs out before them with both hands.

A woman in the group begins to dab her eyes with the kerchief, then holds it out with both hands; then dabs her eyes again and holds out the kerchief again.

Another woman in the group starts to laugh. A loud, almost manic laughter fills the stage as the lights go out.†

* This could be taken as a gesture of supplication, or of someone presenting tributes or submitting evidence/documents at court in ancient times.

† The white kerchief is obviously symbolic. Whether it is meant to allude to the practice observed by many Chinese brides in the old days—producing bloodied sheets as proof of virginity immediately after the wedding night—is hard to establish, but this would no doubt be the educated guess of many among the Chinese audience. And the tableau, plus the laughter, will then be taken as an expression of women's attitudes towards this much cherished notion of virginity.

SCENE TEN

SLIDE 44: Another close-up of a woman's face

SLIDE 45: Yet another close-up of a woman's face

Sound of laughter continues to fill the stage.

SLIDE 46

	Act Two
Place:	In the Theatre
Time:	A little later
Characters:	The spectacular
Question:	How to start

Amidst the laughter, a few bars of African music fade up.

SLIDE 47

	Act Two
Place:	In the theatre
Time:	A little later
Characters:	The spectacular women
Question:	How to start new relations

As Slide 47 fades out, there rises, amidst the laughter, the sound of a man reciting, in a rich tenor voice, 'In the days of Mao Zedong'.

SLIDE 48

	Act Two
Place:	In the theatre
Time:	Around eight in the evening
Characters:	The happy
Question:	How to build up

Liu Sola utters a yell. Then as Slides 49 to 53 flash one after another on the screen, she gives another solo performance. She produces a string of 'ah' sounds in quick succession. This is followed by a sequence of sounds sung in a style that is reminiscent at times of a Peking Opera singer delivering the exclamatory note at the end of a line of lyrics, and at other times of a Peking Opera singer taking a note up and down the scale, sustaining it for a few bars.

SLIDE 49

```
                        Act Two
        Place:      In the theatre
        Time:       Around eight in the evening
        Characters: The happy audience
        Question:   How to build up new relations
```

SLIDE 50

```
                    Act Two
        Place:      In the theatre
        Time:       Yet a little later
        Characters: The performers
        Question:   Very very
```

SLIDE 51

```
                        Act Two
        Place:      In the theatre
        Time:       Fading into the past
        Characters: They filed past, one after another
        Question:   Everyone is looking
```

SLIDE 52

```
                        Act Two
        Place:      In the theatre
        Time:       Fading into the past
        Characters: The spectacular performers
        Question:   Very very
                    Very simple
```

SLIDE 53

```
                        Act Two
        Place:      In the theatre
        Time:       Fading into the past
        Characters: The spectacular performers
                    They filed past, one after another
        Question:   Very very very simple
                    Everyone is looking
                    for new relations
```

SLIDE 54

SLIDE 55

As Slide 55 fades out, lights go up on the armchairs, showing A in her seat.

Liu calls out what sounds like a series of military commands.

G, H, J, K enter, one after another, their arms raised, as if in surrender. They stand in a line downstage.

Lights go up downstage.

D enters stage left, steals behind the armchairs.

G, H, J, K, move in response to a series of commands from Liu, accompanied by the sound of the clapper sticks. Either singly or in pairs, they go through various motions: raise their hands, put them down, turn around, put their hands behind their backs, kneel down, stand up, turn around, kneel down again. Liu shouts out commands in increasingly rapid succession, clapping the clapper sticks and ending the sequence by striking the gong.

SCENE ELEVEN

G shouts an order, and all movements stop.

O and P enter, one from each wing, and go behind the armchairs.

Downstage, in the line of women, G shouts another order, and begins to march across the stage, followed by H, J, and K at four-pace intervals.

D, hiding behind the armchairs, steals to the armchair at stage right, straightens up, and stands facing the audience.

O and P move from behind the armchairs, and stand a little apart centre-stage.

Liu lets out a string of harsh noises like the barking of orders.

D sits in the armchair at stage right, back straight, legs wide apart, hands on the armrests.

A, sitting slumped in the armchair at stage left, stirs as if waking up, utters a shout, sits up, crosses one leg over the other, rests one foot on a spittoon, and watches O and P with interest.

SCENE TWELVE

O and P move closer to each other. O holds out her hand in a gesture of friendliness, while P bows politely. They turn round, standing back to back, then move a few steps away.

The sound of basketball bouncing on the floor is heard offstage.

D in the armchair at stage right also watches O and P with interest.

O and P turn to look at each other. O stretches out her hand to reach for P's hand, then suddenly yanks it, bringing P stumbling towards her.

Liu's voice suddenly goes up an octave or two, and she gives a vocal performance in a beautiful lilting voice, which lasts until the beginning of the next scene.

P returns to her position, does what O has done to her, scoring a tit-for-tat.

BB enters, bouncing a basketball, and crosses the stage from behind the armchairs. She stops at stage left, her back towards the audience.

O returns to her position. Then O and P each puts a foot forward, hitches up the lower part of her cheongsam, bends her knees a little, takes the other's hand in a firm grip, and the two begin a wrestle of strength.* O wins. They wrestle again, O again wins.

M enters, a sword in one hand, a scabbard in the other. She stands downstage, legs together, knees straight, with her sword in her outstretched hand, and her other hand held high up with the scabbard pointing skyward.

O and P wrestle again. P wins.

M lowers her sword and stands facing the audience.

BB with the basketball exits. O and P exit.

D in the armchair at stage right, now squatting on her heels like a child, breaks into enthusiastic applause. Lights dim.

SCENE THIRTEEN

SLIDE 56: close-up of a woman's face

The applause from D slows down and becomes rhythmical. Liu's voice goes yet higher.

SLIDE 57: close-up of a woman's face

* Another sequence of actions suggesting deliberate transgression of behaviour.

SLIDE 58

Act Three	
Place:	In the theatre
Time:	Around March 8, International Working Women's Day
Characters:	The authorities in Hong Kong, the players

The applause dies down. Rock music fades up. Liu's voice rises and falls melancholically.

SLIDE 59

Act Three	
Place:	In the theatre
Time:	Around March 8, International Working Women's Day
Characters:	The authorities in Hong Kong, the players
Question:	The spectators see the game best

Liu's vocal performance comes to an end. Rock music rises.

SLIDE 60

Act Three	
Place:	In the theatre
Time:	Around March 8, International Working Women's Day
Characters:	The authorities in Hong Kong, the players A few women
Question:	The spectators see the game best

Amidst the music, a man's voice recites the refrain, 'In the days of Mao Zedong'.

SLIDE 61

Act Three	
Place:	In the theatre
Time:	Around March 8, International Working Women's Day
Characters:	Identities as yet undecided
Question:	I have thought long and hard

SLIDE 62

```
                        Act Three
Place:      In the theatre
Time:       Around March 8, International Working
            Women's Day
Characters: Identities as yet undecided
            A few women
Question:   I have thought long and hard
            to no avail
```

The man's voice again rises in recitation.

SLIDE 63

```
                        Act Three
Place:      In the theatre
Time:       Around March 8, International Working
            Women's Day
Characters: Identities as yet undecided
            A few women
Question:   I have thought long and hard
            to no avail
            So I go and find
```

Rock music is mixed with the rousing music of Chinese revolutionary opera, and a phrase or two of squeaky notes played to the rhythm of the rock music. This is followed by the sound of gunfire, and a woman's voice declaiming, 'A businessman from imperialist America has opened fire.' Then, a man's voice rises, repeating the refrain, 'In the days of Mao Zedong'.

SLIDE 64

```
                        Act Three
Place:      In the theatre
Time:       Around March 8, International Working
            Women's Day
Characters: The authorities in Hong Kong, the players
            A few women
Question:   I have thought long and hard
            to no avail
            So I go and find
            Chairman
```

SLIDE 65

Act Three

Place: In the theatre
Time: Around March 8, International Working
            Women's Day
Characters: The authorities in Hong Kong, the players
            A few women
Question: I have thought long and hard
            to no avail
            So I go and find
            Chairman
            to build up a new relation

SLIDE 66

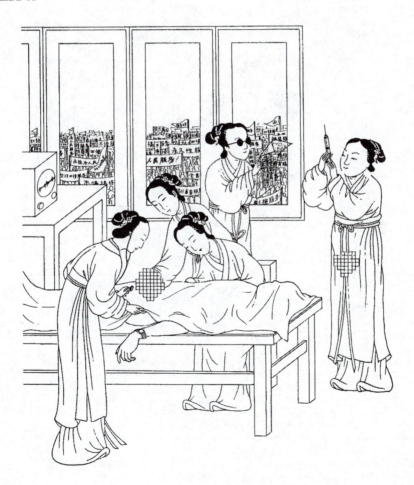

SLIDE 67

As Slides 64 to 67 flash one after another on to the screen, the same background music is played. At the end of each round of gunfire, a woman's voice is heard declaiming, 'A businessman from imperialist America has opened fire'.

As Slide 67 fades out, the man's voice rises, reciting the refrain.

SCENE FOURTEEN

Music fades out. Lights go up.

A is reclining sideways in the armchair at stage left, her back leaning against one armrest, her legs dangling on the other. D is sitting in the armchair at stage right, legs apart, hands on the armrests. Before them are G, H, J, and K, standing in a line facing the audience.

Lights dim downstage. G, H, J, and K, turn to face the armchairs. Then they raise their hands high above their heads, cover their faces with their hands, and hold their hands before them as if in supplication, their heads bowed.

A pause.

M, who has remained on stage all this time, stretches out her hand again, her sword pointing forward, and holds up her other hand, with the scabbard pointing skyward.

G, H, J, and K kneel down together.

Suddenly G, H, and K collapse on to the floor. J remains kneeling.

M returns her sword to the scabbard.

G, H, and K rise to a kneeling position, then all four collapse on to the floor.

Rock music fades up, mixed with rousing music of Chinese revolutionary opera and a phrase or two of squeaky notes played to the rhythm of the African music, the sequence being punctuated by the sound of gunfire. Then a man's voice rises in recitation,

> In the days of Mao Zedong,
> How happy were our people!
> How beautiful was our country!

A woman voice declaims, 'A businessman from imperialist America has opened fire!'

The sound sequence is repeated again and again. G, H, and K continue to replay the actions suggesting torture and execution. Then they rise to their feet and stand still.

G and K move downstage. H exits stage right.

J, who has been lying slumped in a heap on the floor, rises to her feet and replays the same sequence. Then she rises, goes to the armchair second from stage right, and sits down, legs apart, hands on the armrests, like A and D in the other two armchairs.

H enters, and takes the remaining armchair.

G and K exit. M with the sword exits.*

SCENE FIFTEEN

A tableau, with A, H, J, and D sitting in the armchairs, legs apart, hands on the armrests.

Background music and refrain continue as O and P enter, each carrying a stool. They go behind the armchairs, sit face to face on their stools, and begin to write in their notebooks.†

Music and refrain fade out.

H, J, and D each draws her feet together, rises from the armchair, and stands before the spittoon in front of her armchair. Then all three hitch up their cheongsams, sit on the spittoons, as if they were urinating into them.§ A pause.

H, J, and D get up from the spittoons, stand before the armchairs, hitch up their cheongsams, and sit down again, legs apart, hands on the armrests.

After a while, A, H, J, and D take up different postures and perform different actions.

A straightens out her cheongsam, and sits prim and proper with her hands resting on her knees. Then she begins to unbutton her cheongsam. Chinese bamboo flute music fades up.

H exchanges a few words with J, sits up prim and proper, lifts her right hand to touch her forehead, using the back of her left hand to support her right elbow, and holds this posture.

J draws her feet together, exchanges a few words with H, then with D, laughs, and again sits with her legs apart, her hands on the armrests.

H shifts to sit on the edge of the armchair. Her legs are parted provocatively, and one of her hands is stretched out in between her legs and holding the front flap of her cheongsam. Suddenly, she raises the front of her cheongsam and flashes at the audience, then sits prim and proper again.

---

* At the time of the performance in 1991, this scene, full of actions suggesting torture and execution, is almost certain to arouse strong emotions—emotions relating to memories of what happened in Tiananmen Square in Beijing in the summer of 1989, when the Chinese army opened fire on the students. The woman's refrain, apparently intended to convey an anti-imperialist sentiment, is therefore likely to stir in the audience a strong and painful sense of irony. The man's refrain, too, is likely to be taken as hinting at a bitterly ironic contrast between Mao's era and the post-Mao era.

† This is evocative of another picture thousands of viewers have seen on their television screens—Chinese leaders meeting their foreign counterparts/visitors in one of the rooms in the Great Hall of the People in Beijing, with the interpreters sitting behind them.

§ Yet another sequence suggesting deliberate transgression of behaviour?

D stands up, turns round, hitches up her cheongsam, climbs on to the armchair and squats down, her back towards the audience.

J, who left the stage while D was climbing on to the armchair, now returns to her seat, laughing, and sits with legs apart, hands on the armrests.

A, who has been unbuttoning her cheongsam, now flaps open the upper part of her cheongsam (also a flash?). Then she buttons up her cheongsam again.

H strikes various coquettish poses.

J breaks into a loud laughter, which becomes almost hysterical.

D, who has risen from her squatting position and is standing on the armchair with her back towards the audience, now begins to dance slowly.

Chinese bamboo flute music fades out.

The two women behind the armchairs, O and P, begin to talk.

O says, 'I think . . . (P utters 'H'm' in reply) maybe . . . ('H'm' from P) we . . . ('H'm' from P) should . . . ('H'm' from P) respect ourselves more; if we . . . (P lets out some meaningless noises) only want . . . (meaningless noises from P) to play other parts (noises from P), then by all means let's do that (noises from P), why force ourselves to play our own parts?' (noises from P).*

While O is speaking, A rises from her seat and turns her back towards the audience.

H begins to stroke various parts of her body provocatively, and then sways her limbs in a wild and expansive manner, as if she were dancing in her seat.†

J goes up to A, stands behind her, suddenly pulls off the cheongsam A has on, revealing another cheongsam underneath, and breaks into

* This exchange is a subtle dramatization of the identity crisis many Hong Kong people are facing because of the approach of 1997, when China will resume sovereignty over Hong Kong.

† It is not clear whether she is being seductive, thus indicating a willingness to comply with the patriarchal society's view of women as temptress, or being defiant, thus reinforcing the theme of deliberate transgression of behaviour and of women's refusal to play the role of a well-mannered, respectable lady. But the ambiguity is probably intended.

another round of laughter. Then J returns to her armchair, and sits with her legs apart, her hands on the armrests.

D, who has stopped dancing and turned to face the audience, now begins to dance again, at times with wild abandon and at times gently, as if in slow motion.

O and P begin to talk again. O says, 'My view is . . .'. P interjects with 'duk chang' in reply.* O continues, 'maybe we could . . . ('duk chang' from P) consider respecting men a bit more . . .'. P shouts out 'duk chang' and then repeats the word 'men' in a high-pitched, long drawn-out voice.

At this, J bursts into laughter, while P stops dancing, as if surprised by what O said.

O continues, 'if they only want to play men's parts, then we shouldn't force them to play human beings.' A short pause.

O again, 'I can't go to the banquet this evening'. A pause, followed by the sound of some high-pitched gibberish. Another pause.

O says, 'It's pathetic to have to be an interpreter.'

P replies, 'Damn right you are! From morning till night you do nothing except repeat other people's words.' Sound of high-pitched gibberish again.†

C enters from stage left, carrying a kerchief. The sound of gibberish fades out. C sits prim and proper in the armchair vacated by A, and covers her nose and mouth with the kerchief, as if sobbing.

H, J, and D all stop doing what they are doing and resume the posture of sitting with their legs wide apart, their hands resting on the armrests.

A man, Anthony Wong, enters from stage right. Behind him is E, her hands placed on Wong's waist, as if she is hiding behind him. They go up to C in the armchair. E emerges from behind Wong to stand beside him, then she bumps him with her hip. Wong staggers and steps sideways.

O and P begin to talk again. O says, 'I think . . . maybe . . . they could . . . consider respecting this place a bit more, if this place would rather be fucked . . .'

P yells, 'Hey, how the hell am I going to interpret that?'

E bumps Wong with her hip again. Wong staggers another step sideways. E positions herself in front of C, and then starts to dance. C wraps one corner of the kerchief round her fingers, then flicks her

---

* 'Duk chang' is the sound produced by the percussion instruments in Cantonese opera, its function is to punctuate phrases of the lyrics sung or recited by the singers.

† This last exchange would most probably be taken as an expression of the common problem of women through the ages: the lack of a voice, either because it has been suppressed—women are taught to be seen but not heard—or because they have been trained to say certain things. It could even be said that this is the situation highlighted by the women in this production, who are seen but whose voices are rarely heard.

kerchief sideways. After a while, she flicks the kerchief again.

O says, 'If this place would rather be . . . why bother to talk to her about independence and democra . . . autonomy, just let others you-know-what her as they like. After all, it's just like having another man.'

P answers, 'That's true, it's just like having another man.'*

While O and P are speaking, E stops dancing, goes behind the armchair where C is sitting, and stares at Wong.

C holds up the kerchief, stretched taut, with her hands, then ties a knot round her neck with the kerchief.

E goes behind Wong, and leans her head on his shoulders.

C uses part of the kerchief to cover first the lower half of her face, then her entire face.

E gives Wong a push from behind, sending him stumbling. She continues to lean on his shoulder and then pushes him until he stumbles to the table behind which Liu Sola is sitting.

C removes the kerchief from her neck, wraps it round her fist in a tight knot, and then suddenly holds up her hand as if in protest.

E turns round and stands with her back towards the audience.

Liu Sola utters what sounds like an order.

E begins to move backwards downstage. C exits stage left. A takes her seat again.

Liu picks up a wireless microphone from the spittoon, leans forward, and offers the microphone to Wong. When he does not take it, Liu makes some coaxing noises, and offers him the microphone again. She is about to withdraw her hand when Wong suddenly snatches the microphone from her.

African music fades up, mixed with heavy rock.

SCENE SIXTEEN

A tableau, with A, H, J, and D in the armchairs, legs apart, hands on the armrests.

Liu gets up from the stool, goes a few steps upstage and stands with her back towards the audience, another wireless microphone in her hand.

Wong holds up his microphone and chants a melody with some gentle vibrato.

Liu removes her raincoat and lets it drop on to the floor.

Wong, now singing in a voice like a cynical snigger, moves to the

---

* Many in the audience would no doubt understand this as a reference to Hong Kong's position as a colony—with Hong Kong as female, and 'others', possibly China, possibly Britain, as male. That is, the women are to be taken not simply as representatives of their sex, but also as representative of Hong Kong, and their behaviour thus registers not only a feminist protest but also a political protest.

right side of Liu, stops singing, and rests his head on her shoulder. A spotlight goes up on them.

Wong straightens up.

Liu, still standing with her back towards the audience, suddenly rips off her long dark flowing hair, revealing a clean shaven head.* She turns round, facing the audience, her microphone in her hands. Then she turns to face Wong, holds up her microphone with one hand, and stretches out the other hand. Wong, too, stretches out his hand. The two hands meet in a firm grasp, and a wrestle of strength begins as Liu and Wong sing in duet, with Liu chanting the sound 'ah' and Wong the sound 'er', at times in unison, at times separately; at times in harmony, at times ready to drown each other out, and every so often varying their pitches to convey the drama and tension of their struggle.

In the meantime, A, H, J, and D have risen from the armchairs and are now moving downstage, step by step. Then they exit.

Wong, now gaining the upper hand, flings Liu off, sending her stumbling towards centre stage. He sings to the music by himself, his voice choked with emotion, like someone sobbing. Then he goes behind Liu, and rests his head on her shoulder. Liu sings in a similar manner by herself. Wong pushes her from behind, sending her stumbling towards the armchair at stage left. Wong goes up beside her, and both sing in duet again, exploring the texture, timbre, and possibilities of voice to convey a range of conflicting emotions—attraction and revulsion, tenderness and harshness, elation and pain.

Liu goes behind the armchair at stage left and stands there.

Wong continues to sing, now and then letting out a few sighs like someone tormented with pain, or with desire.

The two interpreters, O and P, rise from their stools.

O climbs up the back of the armchair before her, turns a somersault, landing first on the seat and then on the floor. Then she crawls quickly downstage.

P climbs up the back of the armchair, turns a half somersault, lands on the seat, and sits with her legs wide apart, her hands on the armrests.

Liu, who has started to sing again, now hitches up her skirt and climbs up the back of the armchair. Then she sits there, each leg resting on an armrest.

O, who has crawled downstage, goes up to the armchair beside Liu, and sits with her legs wide apart, her hands on the armrests.

Liu begins to stroke her legs as she sings, both voice and movement now seductive as well as sensual, inviting and resisting at the same time.

---

* A statement about androgeny? If this play is about the relation between Hong Kong and others, particularly China (because of Liu Sola's Mainland background), then does Liu's androgenous appearance suggest that China is at once female and male, i.e. matriarchal and patriarchal, in her/his treatment of Hong Kong?

Wong goes up to the armchair and stands beside it, singing and groaning.

Liu lowers her feet from the armrests, stands up, puts her hands on Wong's shoulders and steps onto an armrest. She hitches up her skirt again and Wong holds her in his arms, while she twines her legs round his waist. Then she yells into the microphone, in a sharp, unrestrained voice bursting with raw emotions, like someone exploding with rage, or resentment, or bitterness.

Wong begins to carry Liu across the stage towards the stage right exit.

Liu continues to sing, her voice now tender, almost loving, but rising suddenly in pitch and in intensity of emotion as they make their exit.

Two women, A and D, enter, and sit down in the armchairs.

A tableau, with the four armchairs filled, and A, O, D, and P sitting upright, legs apart, hands on the armrests.

SLIDE 68: Female Cantonese opera singer, her back towards the audience.

Music continues. The sound of Liu's singing—submissive, unyielding, compliant, and protesting by turns, and interwoven with the man's sighing and groaning—continues to be heard until lights fade out.

After a while, A, O, D, and P rise from their armchairs, and walk slowly downstage. Lights fade out. They exit. Music continues.

SLIDE 69

Act Four
Place: How to find new relations

SLIDE 70

Act Four
Place: How to find new relations
Time: How to build up new relations

As Slide 70 flashes on the screen, Wong starts to chant, offstage, the same melody he chanted at the beginning of this scene.

SLIDE 71

Act Four	
Place:	How to find new relations
Time:	How to build up new relations
Characters:	How to break through new relations

Music continues.

SLIDE 72

	Act Four
Place:	How to find new relations
Time:	How to build up new relations
Characters:	How to break through new relations
Question:	How to create new relations

Music continues.

SLIDE 73

	Act Four
Place:	Outside the theatre
Time:	How to find
Characters:	In the theatre
Question:	How to find

Music continues.

SLIDE 74

	Act Four
Place:	Outside the theatre
Time:	How to find new relations
Characters:	In the theatre
Question:	How to find new relations

Music continues. The sound of Liu and Wong singing in duet fades up. But Liu's voice now sounds like love moans, turbulent, sensual, passionate; the same is true of Wong's sighing and groaning. The duet continues as Slides 75 to 83 flash one after another on to the screen, with the couple's voices growing more and more voluptuous, soaring towards a climax; growing more and more savage too, almost bestial, like two animals locked in a life-and-death struggle, panting, whining, gasping . . .

SLIDE 75

	Act Four
Find:	
Build up:	
Break through:	
Create:	

SLIDE 76

```
                  Act Four
Find:             How to find
Build up:         How to build up
Break through:    How to break through
Create:           How to create
```

SLIDE 77

```
                  Act Four
Find:             How to find new youths
Build up:         How to build up new youths
Break through:    How to break through new youths
Create:           How to create new youths
```

SLIDE 78

```
              Act Four
Place:
Time:
Characters:
Question:
```

SLIDE 79

```
              Act Four
Place:        find
Time:         build up
Characters:   break through
Question:     create
```

SLIDE 80

```
              Act Four
Place:        find new music
Time:         build up new music
Characters:   break through new music
Question:     create new music
```

A woman, H, enters in the dark and starts to dance by herself. Music and duet continue.

SLIDE 81

Act Four	
Place:	How to find new music
Time:	How to build up new music
Characters:	How to break through new music
Question:	How to create new music

SLIDE 82

Act Four

Theatre: How to break through new feelings

SLIDE 83

Act Four

Theatre: How to create new relations

Duet fades out. Music and dancing continues.

SLIDE 84

Act Four
Theatre: new women
Theatre: new Hong Kong
Theatre: new feelings
Theatre: new relations

As Slide 84 flashes on the screen, the sound of Wong chanting the theme melody fades up again. Liu soon joins in.

SLIDE 85

Act Four	
New Women:	new women
New Hong Kong:	new Hong Kong
New Feelings:	new feelings
New Relations:	new relations

SLIDE 86

```
                  Act Four
Find:              find
Build up:          build up
Break through:  break through
Create:            create
```

The sound of voluptuous passion, now indistinguishable from the sound of death throes, fades up, and soon fills the auditorium.

SLIDE 87

```
                Act Four
Relations:  How to find new
Music:      How to build up new
Youths:     How to break through new
            How to create new
```

SLIDE 88

```
                Act Four
Relations:   How to find new illusions
Music:       How to build up new illusions
Youths:      How to break through new illusions
Illusions:   How to create new illusions
```

Duet ends.

SLIDE 89

```
                     Foreword
Have thought long and hard but still cannot think of what
else there still is to say • maybe it is
a question of whom one is addressing •
```

Music continues, accompanied by heavy drum beats.

SLIDE 90

```
                     Foreword
Have thought long and hard but still cannot think of what
else there still is to say • maybe it is
a question of whom one is addressing • maybe
when responsibility develops into understanding
• when pressure becomes ease of mind •
when what is left of the form is just content •
then before the foreword there is no more
space
```

Duet fades up. Soon, the sighing and gasping give way to the sound of a man and a woman yelling and screaming and screeching at the tops of their voices, manic, nerve-wrecking, tortuous. This punishing cacophony is further amplified by the ear-splitting metallic shrieks of electronic music.*

SLIDE 91

> ### Postscript
> Have thought long and hard but still cannot think of what
> else there still is to say • maybe it is
> a question of whom one is addressing • maybe
> when responsibility develops into understanding
> • when pressure becomes ease of mind •
> when what is left of the form is just content •
> then after the postscript there is no more
> space

SLIDE 92

> ### Postscript
> Have thought long and hard but still cannot think of what
> else there still is to say • maybe it is
> a question of whom one is addressing • maybe
> when responsibility develops into understanding
> • when pressure becomes ease of mind •
> when what is left of the form is just content •
> then after the postscript there is no more
> space • just sounds

* Does the fact that Liu Sola is a woman and her partner in this scene a man invalidate the gendered reading of Hong Kong as female and China as male? Or should it be said that Liu's androgeny, the fact that the man is clearly the weaker, the more passive and more submissive party while Liu is the stronger, the more dominating and more assertive party—both in the vocal performance and in actions—allow the scene to be read as a comment on the man and woman relationship without invalidating the overall gendered reading of Hong Kong as female and China as male, albeit one who will not hesitate to cajole, coax, and seduce the female other into subservience? The man flings off Liu, yet goes up to her for comfort, pushes her off again, yet goes up to her again, and seems to be tormented with pain, with desire; and when she climbs on to him, he takes her, carries her off, and then engages in what sounds like an amorous act that grows increasingly erotic, more violent, more like a deadly fight between two animals. Is this not a dramatization of the fatal attraction China has for Hong Kong, and the deadly fight for survival in which Hong Kong is destined to be trapped? Whatever the conclusion, a Hong Kong audience would certainly read and interpret this scene, and the play as well, in the context of the politics and prevailing tension between China and Hong Kong.

SLIDE 93: Black-out slide

Music fades out. Duet stops. There is only the sound of the lone woman dancing in the dark.

After a few minutes, lights go up. All the performers have entered and are standing in a line facing the audience. Behind them, H is still dancing, spinning her body round and round, her arms flailing and fluttering. The performers bow to the audience, then exit in two rows. H is still dancing.

Lights dim, then fade out.

Lights go up again. H is still dancing. After a while, another woman, J, enters, goes up to H, holds her by the shoulders, and then slowly escorts her across the stage. They exit stage right.

SCENE SEVENTEEN

Chinese bamboo flute music fades up. Backstage crew enter and take the tables back to where they were placed at the beginning of the performance. Music fades out.

THE END

JAN 0 8 1998